Understanding Religion

RELATED TEXTS PUBLISHED BY ONEWORLD

Avatar and Incarnation, Geoffrey Parrinder, ISBN 1–85168–130–2
Believing – An Historical Perspective, Wilfred Cantwell Smith, ISBN 1–85168–166–3
Calendars of the World, Margo Westrheim, ISBN 1–85168–051–9
Concepts of God, Keith Ward, ISBN 1–85168–064–0
A Concise Encyclopedia of Christianity, Geoffrey Parrinder, ISBN 1–85168–174–4
A Concise Encyclopedia of Hinduism, Klaus K. Klostermaier, ISBN 1–85168–175–2
A Concise Encyclopedia of Judaism, Dan Cohn-Sherbok, ISBN 1–85168–176–0
Faith and Belief: The Difference Between Them, Wilfred Cantwell Smith, ISBN 1–85168–165–5
God and the Universe of Faiths, John Hick, ISBN 1–85168–071–3
God, Chance and Necessity, Keith Ward, ISBN 1–85168–116–7
God, Faith and the New Millennium, Keith Ward, ISBN 1–85168–155–8
In Defence of the Soul, Keith Ward, ISBN 1–85168–040–3
Life After Death, Farnáz Ma'sumián, ISBN 1–85168–074–8
Muslims and Christians Face to Face, Kate Zebiri, ISBN 1–85168–133–7
Patterns of Faith Around the World, Wilfred Cantwell Smith, ISBN 1–85168–164–7
Religious Truth for our Time, William Montgomery Watt, ISBN 1–85168–102–7
The Sense of God, John Bowker, ISBN 1–85168–093–4
Sexual Morality in the World's Religions, Geoffrey Parrinder, ISBN 1–85168–108–6
Ultimate Visions, edited by Martin Forward, ISBN 1–85168–100–0
A Wider Vision, Marcus Braybrooke, ISBN 1–85168–119–1

Understanding Religion

A Thematic Approach

Moojan Momen

ONEWORLD
OXFORD

A Oneworld Book

First published by Oneworld Publications as *The Phenomenon of Religion*, 1999
First published as *Understanding Religion*, 2009

A CIP record for this title is available
from the British Library

ISBN: 978–1–85168–599–8

Cover design by e-Digital Design
Typeset by Textype, Cambridge
Printed and bound in Great Britain
by TJ International Ltd, Padstow

Oneworld Publications
185 Banbury Road
Oxford OX2 7AR
England
www.oneworld-publications.com

For Wendi

Contents

List of Maps and Timelines

Notes and Acknowledgements

In this book, all dates are given as either BCE (Before the Common Era) or CE (Common Era) in place of BC and AD respectively. This usage has been adopted by many in the field of religious studies because it avoids the theological implications of the latter (AD: *Anno Domini* – in the year of our Lord), which believers in non-Christian religions may not find acceptable. For similar reasons, the terms 'primal religion' or 'tribal religion' have been used instead of 'primitive religion' with its pejorative implications. The titles of all sacred texts are italicized. On the question of the transliteration of the numerous religious terms and names used, this book takes the easy path by not using any diacriticals. I have taken the view that those who are experts in the field will know what diacriticals there should be and they would not mean anything to others anyway.

The author would like to thank the following for their help with this book: Dr Frank Whaley, Professor Ursula King, Dr Peter Smith, Dr Robert Stockman, Dr Peter Brooke, Stephen Lambden, Dr Saba Ayman-Nolley, Robert Parry, Gita Gandhi Kingdon, Dr William Collins, Sonja van Kerkhoff, Dr Todd Lawson, Dr Hooman Momen, Dr Rhett Diessner, Dr Paula Drewek, Dr Julie Badiee, Dr Wendi Momen, Dr Sedrhat Momen, Carmel Momen, Helen Coward, Judith Willson, and Kate Smith. The kindness and cooperation of the staff at Cambridge University Library should also be acknowledged.

The author would like to thank the following institutions and individuals for assistance and permission to reproduce the following pictures:

Italian Cultural Institute and Maria D'Angelo (pp. 33, 188a, 292, 319, 365, 407, 436, 467 bottom, 472 bottom right); Brazilian Embassy, London, Nelson Lafraia and Graca Fish (pp. 5, 93, 144, 175, 179, 392c, 400, 402); Turkish Tourist Office and Margaret Hopkins (pp. 26a, 39, 97, 167, 272 top left, 304b, 418, 461b, 467 middle, and picture of Selimiyye Mosque, Edirne, on p. 299); British Israel Public Affairs Centre and The Zionist Federation of Great Britain and Ireland (pp. 12, 136, 282c, 367, 372, 373, 433 bottom, 445, 494, 532, 536, and picture of orthodox Jew at the Wailing Wall, Jerusalem, on p. 85); Press Office, Cyprus High Commission, London, and Maria Phanti (pp. 14, 303, 427a); West Maryland College Slide Collection and Dr Julie Badiee (pp. 235, 241a); Nandan Gautam (p. 241b); Tourism

Authority of Thailand, London Office (pp. 40b, 130, 345a, 395, 397, 427b, 537); Baha'i World Centre, Haifa (pp. 15, 42, 232, 272 bottom left, 355, 421, 501, 517); Anjani and Mithlesh Singhal (pp. 22, 40a, 104 top, 477); Information Division, Taipei Representative Office in the United Kingdom (pp. 23, 36, 44, 45 top, 218); Israel Ministry of Tourism (New York Office: p. 15; London Office: p. 172 and picture of Russian Orthodox Church of Mary Magdalene on the Mount of Olives, Jerusalem, on p. 19); Ramin Habibi (pp. 107a, 390); Embassy of the Islamic Republic of Iran, London (pp. 377, 413, 420); Salvation Army, London (pp. 75 top, 486b); Saudi Information Office, London (pp. 279, 315c); Bhaktivedanta Book Trust (pp. 234, 469); International Society for Krishna Consciousness, Bhaktivedanta Manor, Watford, England, and Mr Bimal Krishna das (p. 502); Sherna Deamer (pp. 157a, 278b); Mr Shahrokh Vafadari (p. 272 bottom right); United States Baha'i National Office and Yael Wurmfeld (p. 349); Alliance of Religions and Conservation and Felice Kuin (p. 358); Baha'i International Community, New York (p. 358); Unification Church of Great Britain and Mr George Robertson (p. 512); Mongolian National Tourist Organization (Zhuulchin – pp. 104 bottom, 458); Arya Samaj, London and Prof. S. N. Bharadwaj (p. 383); Mr Holm Triesch (p. 215); Mr Vidya Raja (p. 515); Japanese Embassy, London (p. 45 bottom); Gafoor Jaffer (p. 261); Library of the Religious Society of Friends, London (p. 76); Ahmad Adab (p. 230); The High Commission of India, London (p. 8); Korean Embassy (p. 392b); Klaus K. Klostermaier (p. 225); Robert Harding Library (man meditating on the banks of the Ganges at Varanasi-Benares, front cover). The picture on p. 183 is of a statue of the Buddha in the Sarnath Museum, India. Also M. Mani for picture on p. 321 and P. Siroussi for picture on p. 371.

The author would also like to thank the following for their kind permission to reproduce the materials indicated:

Alliance of Religions and Conservation for text on pp. 359–61, mainly from Edwards and Palmer, *Holy Ground*; Dr John Lofland, Dr Norman Skonovd, and the Society for the Scientific Study of Religion for the table on p. 159; Dr Janet Goodwin, for quotation on pp. 232–3; Dr Peter Brooke for permission to use his unpublished translation of writings of Albert Gleizes quoted in the caption to the picture on p. 465.

Introduction

THE PHENOMENON OF RELIGION has pervaded the history of humanity from its earliest known beginnings to the present day. Few other aspects of human social activity have been so consistently and prominently present in every society in all parts of the world down the ages. Many of the earliest traces of human activity that archaeologists have unearthed relate to some form of religious activity. And in our time, just when many people were about to write it off as a fast-fading remnant of the past, about to be pushed into oblivion by the advances of science and technology, religion has staged something of a recovery. It is once more a prominent factor on the world stage.

The influence of religion has been very varied in world history. This has been both constructive and destructive. On the one hand some of the greatest civilizations of the world have been founded on the basis of a religious faith,[1] the Islamic Abbasid Empire or the Buddhist empire of Ashoka in India for example; on the other hand, some of the most prolonged and bloody conflicts in human history have stemmed from religious differences, the Crusades in the Middle East or the conflict between Hindus and Muslims in Indian history, for example. One of the features that is most striking when surveying the world of religion is the profusion of its differing and conflicting forms. A practice allowed and encouraged in one religion is forbidden in another; something that is considered impure and defiling by one religious system is pure according to another; a concept held to be true by one group is regarded as delusory or even the very source of error by another group. The concept in the Western religions that each human being has an eternal essence (a soul), for example, is considered a misguided delusion in Buddhism.

We must, therefore, ask ourselves: what is this phenomenon called religion? What is the source of the powerful grip it has on human beings? How can a religion be a source of inspiration and progress in one age and the origin of conflict and destruction in another? How are we to account for its many different and conflicting forms? Can we find any common themes and patterns in the history of religion? Indeed, are we dealing with just one thing or with a number of different phenomena that have all mistakenly been lumped together under the title of religion?

In addition, we may address ourselves to the problems that face religion in the modern world. These include the challenge of secularization and the seeming decline in the relevance of religion to everyday life. Are we seeing a terminal decline in religion or is it merely the downswing in a cyclical pattern? What is the cause of this decline? Is the recent resurgence of religious revivalism and fundamentalism in many countries the first sign of an upturn in the fortunes of religion, or merely part of its death throes, as some have asserted?

Religion is a phenomenon that has proved difficult to define. The minimal definition of a religious phenomenon would refer to a relationship between human beings and a transcendent reality (see p. 27). This relationship is the central experience of religion and is described in greater detail in chapter 4. But if religion remained at just this level, there could be no study of it (outside the realm of psychology, in any case), for it would be a purely personal experience. The study of religion becomes possible when a further factor is introduced: when this central experience finds some form of expression. The minimal level of this expression is language – when a mystic describes his or her experience, for example. Other expressions of religion include doctrinal formulations, stories and myths, rituals, religious hierarchies and administrative structures, popular religious forms, art, music, architecture and so on.

To achieve a fuller understanding of religion, however, we must also examine one more factor: the relationship between the observer and what is being observed. This last is a difficult and elusive task, which is, however, necessary. While one may have doubts as to whether one needs to take into consideration the interaction between the observer and the observed in an experiment with plants or animals in biology, the area of religion is a very different matter. Religion makes far-reaching claims about the ultimate concerns of humanity. It challenges the individual to make a leap of faith, to enter the religion's paradigm, and to see the world through this.[2] It is doubtful whether any observer who makes a deep study of a religion can be completely unaffected by such claims and truly neutral in his or her judgements. Indeed, the more an observer protests his or her impartiality, the more one suspects that some partiality is present beneath the surface.

The Study of Religion

It has been customary to describe and explain religions with reference to a limited number of religious manifestations: the written or spoken scripture, the ritual, the sacred place or object, and so on. But to describe these, no matter how precisely or perceptively, does not provide us with a comprehensive view of religion. This book has been born out of the conviction that religion, being a multi-faceted phenomenon, needs to be surveyed from a large number of viewpoints if light is to be shed on it.

The different methods for examining religion can be divided into two main groups. First, religion can be examined within its own terms: theology and metaphysics. These methods accept the religious viewpoint and seek to build up a systematic understanding of aspects of religion from within this framework. The phenomenology of religion seeks to perform much the same task but from a more objective viewpoint. Alternatively, religion may be examined analytically: sociology helps to explain the different social manifestations of religion; psychology can help to explain why people act in the way that they do in a religious context; anthropology also has important insights to contribute. These methods seek to explain the complexities of religion in terms of less complex interpretative frameworks. Thus they may be termed reductive. I shall return to a discussion of these two approaches in chapter 3 (pp. 77–82).

Other fields may also assist our understanding of religion. Philosophy can help to identify and clarify some of the issues to be studied. The philologist can shed light on what the texts of a religion meant to those who originally produced them. Historians of religion can describe the manner in which the religion's institutional form and even its self-perception has changed over the years. The problems arising in the field of the philosophy of science have many parallels with the questions facing the study of religion. There are also important contributions from such newly emerging fields as human ethology, cybernetics, semiotics and others.

Looking at religion from these various aspects does, of course, have its problems. Each discipline has its own set of theories, its own categories and frameworks, from which to view religion. This leads to a rather fragmented view; we are seeing religion from many different facets and this makes it difficult to gain an overall picture. The only alternative course would be to present religion from within a single theoretical framework. This would have the advantage that the result would be more coherent and cohesive. Several such possible overall theories are briefly described in chapter 3. Unfortunately, however, in the field of religious studies, we are still a long way from having a single theoretical perspective that illuminates all aspects of religion well. To have presented religion from just one theoretical viewpoint would, in my opinion, have given this book greater clarity at the expense of a much reduced level of understanding. Each of these theories tends to be particularly useful for considering one aspect of religion, but then has nothing to say (or nothing illuminating to say) about other aspects.

Those who have written about religion fall into several groups. The first division that can be recognized is between those who are broadly sympathetic to the subject of their study and those who are not. There have been many who have studied religion and religions whose writings betray a clear contempt for and lack of sympathy with their subject. Indeed, the whole area of the study of non-Christian religions in the West began as a basis for polemics and missionary education. I would categorize myself as being in the first group, those who are broadly sympathetic to religion.

I would hope, however, that this does not prevent me from describing some of the less savoury activities that go on in the name of religion.

Another division to be found between writers on religion is between those who feel that there are broad similarities between the different religions (and who therefore seek for points of convergence between them) and those who regard the various religions as being so utterly different that any search for similarities is illusory. It will become clear to the reader of this book that I am among the first group. Indeed the very structure of this book, which looks at specific topics across religions (rather than the more traditional layout of textbooks on religion, which considers each religion separately), predisposes to the search for broad common patterns. There are, of course, many stark differences between the religions of the world and it is hoped that this book does not seek to hide them; but there are also many similarities and parallels and these are even more interesting because of what they begin to tell us about the nature of religion itself (although, of course, the differences help to define what religion is not).

While reading this book, the reader should maintain an awareness of the fact that he or she is receiving the information it imparts at several removes from the phenomena themselves. In the first place, religious phenomena are experienced by believers, who interpret and describe these in terms of the conceptual categories available to them. This material is then analysed and interpreted by specialist scholars who read the relevant languages. These scholars, who are often from the West or some culture alien to the particular religion, may impose their own conceptual categories on the information. Finally, the reader is receiving this material as processed through and therefore interpreted by the mind of yet another intermediary – the present writer.[3] The reader cannot also, of course, escape the filtering effect of the preconceptions in her or his own mind.

Three Aspects of Religion

While many books on religion examine each of the major religions in turn, this book is structured around an examination of certain aspects of religion, looking at religious phenomena across the different religions. In this book, we shall explore in greater detail various aspects of the way in which religion is experienced (Part II), conceptualized (Part III) and the effects that it has on society (Part IV).

The Central Experience of Religion

Most religious people will report some religious experience that is at the core of their faith. The intensity of the experience may vary greatly from one individual to another. At one extreme there are the visions reported by saints of the appearance of heavenly figures or a deep trance state brought about by meditation. At the other extreme is the experience of comfort or joy that may come from singing a hymn or participating in a ritual. Most people will find it difficult to describe this experience, since it does not relate to the ordinary world of everyday experiences. They may use such words as 'joy', 'bliss' or 'ecstasy' in trying to describe it. The more creative person may resort to art or poetry to try to communicate this experience. Human beings have linked the strong feeling of certainty that comes from religious experience to the concept of salvation or liberation, and because of the importance that they attach to it, they have tried to systematize the pathways to this experience, calling them the pathways to salvation or liberation (see chapter 5).

PEOPLE IN AN ATTITUDE OF PRAYER: An open-air service, Brazil

Beyond the central experience described in general terms above, religion will take on different features according to the specific milieu in which it occurs. Each person experiencing the 'sacred' will then describe this experience to others in terms of the religious categories within their common culture. Those from a Western background will gain from the central experience of religion a consciousness of the 'presence' of a personal God. Those with an Eastern orientation will feel an intensification of their intuitive knowledge of Reality. These feelings form the basis of faith (see chapter 6). Religious experience is described and analysed in the chapters of Part II.

The Conceptual Aspect of Religion

When people try to communicate with others the religious experience that they have had, they must, of necessity, first create some mental concept of what has occurred and then try to convey this to others, usually in the form of words. This takes us on to the second central concern of religion, the formulation of a conceptual framework for talking about the central experience of religion. Theology and religious philosophy are attempts to formulate these feelings and to give them a propositional content, the beliefs and doctrines of a religion.

At the centre of this conceptual aspect of religion is the idea that there is some transcendent or immanent Ultimate Reality and that the most important activity for human beings is to establish and clarify their relationship with this reality. This Ultimate Reality itself is conceptualized in many different ways:

- In many primal or tribal religions there are considered to be many spiritual realities, spirits and gods, associated with particular holy places or with important aspects of social life such as the harvest or fertility. Usually such spirits and gods are transcendent to the world and are worshipped and appeased in communal or tribal ceremonies. However,

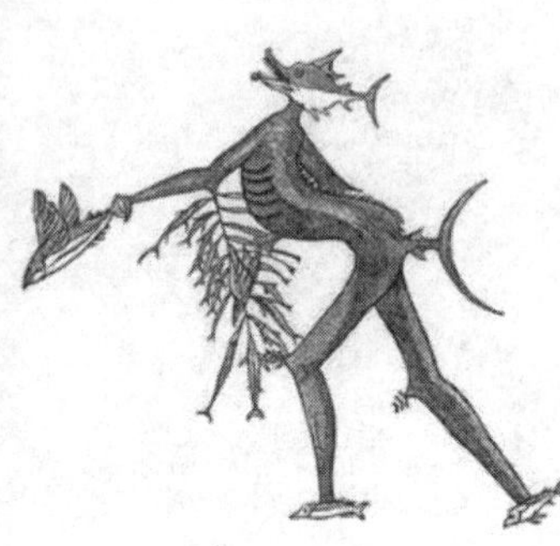

A Melanesian sea-god

certain individuals (shamans or witch doctors) are believed to be able, through special knowledge and magical means, to make the spirits or deities immanent within themselves. In this way, they become manifestations of the deity. However, many tribal religions also have the idea that behind the multiplicity of spirits and gods, there is a unity, an underlying Reality. This Reality may be identified with Nature itself, or with a power (*mana*), or with a supranatural entity (see pp. 46–7).

- The Western world developed towards the idea that there is only one deity. The God of Judaism, Christianity and Islam is conceptualized slightly differently in each of these religious traditions but it is nevertheless recognizably the same God.
- In the East, the evolution of religious thought came to the idea that what exists is an impersonal, noncontingent Reality (Brahman, Dharma, Nirvana, Shunyata, Tao).

These different ways of thinking of God or Ultimate Reality are further analysed in chapter 8. From this comes various other questions such as the nature of humanity's relationship with this physical world and with Ultimate Reality, questions about the nature of suffering and salvation or liberation. These are described briefly in chapter 2 and in greater detail in Part III.

The Social Effect of Religion

The third of the major aspects of religion is the drive to try to recreate the religious experience within institutional forms and to support it through institutional structures. But since the conceptualizations of the experience vary from one individual to another and from one society to another, the social mechanisms evolved also vary. Much of that to which we apply the word 'religion' is human beings trying to systematize in society the re-creation of this central religious experience.

Once the concepts and social structures of a religion are established in a traditional society, they become part of the taken-for-granted reality of the individuals in that society. All the individuals in that society are socialized into that religious world. The religious world and the social world become indistinguishable. It may then be that the central experience of religion arises more from an experience of group solidarity and social cohesiveness than from an individual experience. Of course, once a religion has become established in society and an important element within it, some may take part in religious activities from other motives such as power, economic gain or social enhancement (see chapter 16).

Most important in assessing the role of religion in a society is the fact that once a religion has become established at the core of a society, it becomes the basis for the ethos of the society and its social and moral values. This is the important role that religion has played in almost every society. Indeed, much of what is distinctive about societies such as those of Thailand, Kuwait or Greece is due to the mark made upon them by the values predominant in the Theravada Buddhism, Sunni Islam and Greek Orthodox Christianity respectively (see chapter 13).

There is some debate among those who study religion, however, about the relative importance and priority of these three aspects of religion that I have identified. If there is any underlying and unifying core to the concept of religion, which of these aspects is prior to and generates the others? Is the religious experience the primary motivating force that then generates social expressions of religion? Is the social role of religion its most important aspect, which then generates religious experiences (see the discussion of Durkheim's theories, pp. 53–5)? Do the conceptual aspects of religion, by creating certain expectations, determine the form and character of religious experience (see pp. 114–5)? (See also pp. 179–80.)

The interplay of these three aspects of religion forms a recurrent theme throughout the study of religion. The next three parts of this book are based upon these three aspects. Several of the chapters of the book, however, cover material that applies to more than one part. Chapter 5, for instance, on the pathways to salvation, also contains material relating to the social manifestations of religion that should more properly appear in Part IV; the second half of chapter 10, on the promise of a future saviour, contains much sociological material that would also be appropriate to Part IV, and chapter 14, on fundamentalism and liberalism, contains much material that relates to religious experience and so could be put in Part II.

The Religions of the World

The world contains a vast array of religions. Numerically the largest are Christianity, Islam, Hinduism and Buddhism. There are also a number of other well-established independent religions: Judaism, Zoroastrianism, Sikhism, Jainism and the Baha'i Faith. In addition, there are Chinese and Japanese religious systems, tribal or traditional religions and ancient or archaic religions, as well as many new religious movements. A map showing the distribution of world religions appears on p. 32. In the course of writing this book it soon became apparent that, to keep it to a reasonable size, examples for every statement could not be given from all the many religions of the world. Therefore a selection was made of six key religions. From the religions of the Abrahamic or monotheistic Western tradition, Judaism, Christianity and Islam were selected; from the Eastern, Indian line of religions, Hinduism and Buddhism; and as a representative of the new religious movements, the Baha'i Faith.[4] These will be the main religions referred to in the rest of this book. Occasional references will be made to the other religions, where relevant, when examples are being given of any particular phenomenon. Of course, the Baha'i Faith does not have the same historical depth as the other religions chosen and so while its conceptual aspects will be referred to frequently in Part III, there will be less to say about its social development in Part IV.

This selection of six religions will, I hope, be the most useful for two reasons. First, it will give sufficient variety and scope to be representative of much of the religious world. Second, it is five of these religions that are the most active in the field of propaganda and conversion (the exception being Judaism). This may mean that it is these religions that will grow (or at least maintain their numbers) as the years pass and the other religions that will suffer a relative decline in numbers. Thus, in looking at this selection, we are examining the religions that will probably be of greatest importance in the future.[5]

Since there is no other point in this book at which each of these religions is described in any systematic way, a brief description of them is given at this point for those who may be unfamiliar with one or more of them. In the accounts below, I describe mainly the official or orthodox religion, ignoring the fact that there are, in each religion, popular expressions of religion that are often contradictory to the official religion (a theme explored in chapter 15).

Hindu temples at Madurai, Tamil Nadu, India, named for Minakshi and Sundareshvara, local names for the Hindu god Shiva and his consort.

Hinduism

Hinduism is one of the oldest extant, textually based religions in the world. Its roots go back to a collection of scriptures called the *Vedas*, which are considered to have been divinely revealed to certain sages. These books, which are usually dated as being from about 1300 BCE, originated among the Aryan population of India. From these beginnings a complex and diverse religious tradition has evolved. Beyond originating in India and holding the *Vedas* to be sacred, there is little else that holds the wide diversity of groups that call themselves Hindu together. There is certainly no particular creed, doctrine or practice that is common to all Hindus. One strand in Hinduism is the ritualistic and legalistic religion which is officiated over by the Brahmins, the priestly caste. Another strand is the mystical and philosophical aspects of the Vedanta, based on the *Upanishads* and the philosophies of such writers as Shankara (788–820), Ramanuja (d. 1137), and Madhva

(d. c.1276). There is also the *bhakti* religion based on love and devotion to deities such as Shiva and Vishnu, and the latter's avatars (incarnations), Krishna and Rama. Pervading Hindu society is *jati*, the hereditary caste system. Most Hindus participate in worship both at home before a household altar and in the temple. For more detail on the political and religious history of Hinduism, see the timeline on p. 422.

Buddhism

The founder of Buddhism is variously called by his personal name, Siddhartha, or his family name, Gautama, or his clan name, Shakyamuni. His title, the Buddha (Enlightened One), refers to the fact that after a prolonged period of searching the Indian religious traditions, he achieved a state of enlightenment while sitting under a tree. During his lifetime (traditionally c.563–c.483 BCE, but more probably c.480–c.400 BCE), he wandered about north-east India with a band of disciple-monks. The Buddha avoided dogma and metaphysical speculation in his teaching and concentrated on the essentials for spiritual development. He thus set out the Middle Way, a pathway to enlightenment and Nirvana (extinction) avoiding the extremes of asceticism and self-indulgence. After the death of the Buddha, his religion spread throughout India and to neighbouring countries, although it had died out in most of India itself by the twelfth century. At present, one major branch of Buddhism is the Theravada Buddhists, who predominate in Sri Lanka, Burma, Thailand, Laos and Cambodia. These hold to the books of the Pali Canon. The main pathway for spiritual development is for men to become monks and then study, meditate and practise the path taught by the Buddha. The other main division of Buddhism, the Mahayana (which emerged between about the first century BCE and the first century CE), is very diverse. Many of the Mahayana sects have their own scriptures, some attributed to Gautama Buddha and some to other figures, such as the heavenly buddhas. In place of the Theravada ideal figure of the *arhat*, who achieves Nirvana, is the figure of the *bodhisattva*, who puts off reaching Nirvana in order to help others on the spiritual path. One strand of the Mahayana is Tibetan Buddhism, Tantric Buddhism or Vajrayana. This is an esoteric tradition which emphasizes symbolism (e.g. mandalas – symbolic cosmological maps) and sacraments such as initiation ceremonies, the chanting of mantras, and certain ritual gestures. Another strand of the Mahayana is the Ch'an (Meditation) school of China, better known under its Japanese name of Zen. This school believes that enlightenment comes suddenly, by direct and immediate insight for which one can prepare oneself by cultivating a mind that has no grasping feelings or thoughts. Quite different from this are the Amida or Pure Land sects that also originated in China and spread to Japan. These sects believe that through devotion to and faith in Amitabha or Amida Buddha, one can be born into his Western Sukhavati Paradise after death. Other important sects include the Hua-Yen, which is prominent

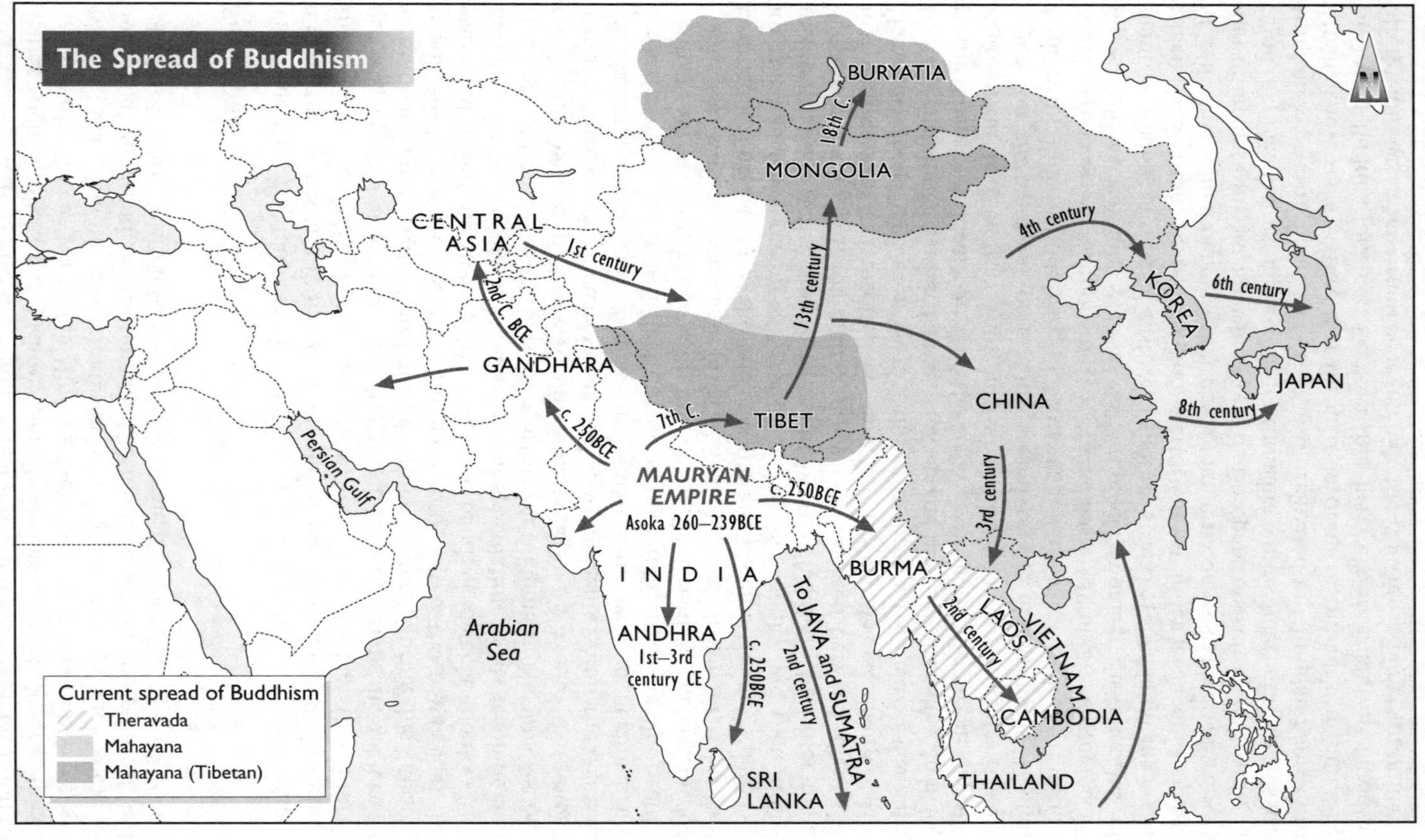
The Spread of Buddhism
BURYATIA
18th C.
MONGOLIA
CENTRAL ASIA
1st century
2nd C. BCE
13th century
4th century
KOREA
6th century
GANDHARA
JAPAN
CHINA
8th century
c. 250BCE
7th C.
TIBET
Persian Gulf
MAURYAN EMPIRE
Asoka 260–239BCE
c. 250BCE
3rd century
INDIA
BURMA
To JAVA and SUMATRA
2nd century
2nd century
LAOS
VIETNAM
Arabian Sea
ANDHRA
1st–3rd century CE
c. 250BCE
CAMBODIA
SRI LANKA
THAILAND
Current spread of Buddhism
Theravada
Mahayana
Mahayana (Tibetan)
N

Buddhism

c.480-400	Life of the Buddha
c.377	1st Buddhist Council, Rajagriha
c.300	2nd Buddhist Council, Vaishali – issues of discipline of the Sangha discussed
c.284	Buddhist Council, Patna – first signs of a split between the emerging Theravada and Mahayana
c.260	Ashoka embraces Buddhism
c.250	Buddhist Council, Patna – issues regarding certain heretical beliefs discussed
	Ashoka sends missions to north-east and south India, Sri Lanka and Burma
d.c.239	Ashoka
c.150	Menandar (Milinda), Bactrian-Greek king becomes Buddhist
c.150	Buddhism spreads to Central Asia
c.150-75	Development of Buddhist art at Sanchi, Amaravati and Bodhgaya
c.100BCE-100CE	Emergence of Mahayana Buddhism
80	Pali canon written down in Sri Lanka
c.0-200	Kushan empire (Buddhist) established in north-west India; Gandhara, important centre for Buddhist art
c.50	Buddhism spreads to China from Central Asia
c.150	Buddhism established in Cambodia
c.150-200	Mathura, important centre for Buddhist art
c.200	Nagarjuna, founder of Madhyamika school
c.250	Buddhism spreads to Vietnam
c.300-400	Buddhism spreads to Indonesia and Malay Peninsula; Prajnaparamita school emerges in China
c.300-600	Emergence of Tantric Buddhism
c.350	Buddhism spreads to Korea; Asangha, founder of Yogacara school
399	Fa-hsien, first Chinese pilgrim to India
c.400	Buddhaghosa, author of Visuddhimagga
d.416	Hui-Yuan, founder of Pure Land school (Amidism)
c.500-600	Buddhism spreads to Thailand and Japan in 538 CE
d.542	T'an-huan organizes Pure Land Buddhism school, China
d.543	Boddhidharma, first patriarch of Ch'an (Zen) Buddhism, China
594	Buddhism becomes state religion of Japan
d.597	Chih-i, founder of T'ien-t'ai school, China
c.630	Buddhism spreads to Tibet
d.712	Fa-tsang, principal figure of Hua-Yen school, China
779	Buddhism becomes state religion of Tibet
845	Repression of Buddhism in China
1044-77	Peak of Buddhism in Burma under King Anurudh
1065	Theravada Buddhism of Mahavihara monastery proclaimed as state religion of Sri Lanka
d.1097	Marpa, reformer of Tibetan Buddhism
c.1200	Disappearance of Buddhism in north India, Pakistan, Bangladesh and Central Asia
d.1212	Honen, principal figure of Pure Land Buddhism, Japan
c.1250	Tibetan Buddhism spreads to Mongolia
d.1282	Nichiren, founder of Nichiren school, Japan
1287	Mongol invasion of Burma – setback to Buddhism
c.1300	Theravada Buddhism of the Mahavihara monastery proclaimed as official religion of Burma
1505	Portuguese gain control of much of Sri Lanka
c.1600	Disappearance of Buddhism in South India, Indonesia (except Bali) and Malay Peninsula
1658	Dutch control much of Sri Lanka after defeating Portuguese
1815	British bring all of Sri Lanka under their control
1860-1900	Indo-China (Vietnam, Laos and Cambodia) comes under French rule
1875	Foundation of Theosophical Society (Hindu-Buddhist), New York
1886	Burma comes under British rule
1891	Foundation of Maha Bodhi Society by Dharmapala
c.1920	Communist attack on Buddhism in Mongolia
1947	Sri Lankan independence
1948	Burmese independence
1954-56	Sixth Buddhist Council commemorates 2500 years of Buddhism, Burma
1956	B.R. Ambedkar and followers convert to Buddhism, India

in Korea and believes in the complete and harmonious interpenetration of everything in the universe, and the T'ien-t'ai (Tendai in Japan) sect which is primarily intellectual, categorizing the Buddha's message into five periods and eight teachings. The important Japanese sect of Nichiren emerged from the Tendai. Further detail on the history of Buddhism is given in the timeline on p. 11. The map on p. 10 shows the spread of Buddhism.

JUDAISM: A Yemeni scribe at work restoring a Torah scroll (Sepher Torah). The Torah is written in a ritually prescribed manner, each word being said out loud before it is written, each letter separated from the next by a space, and without punctuation or accents. No mistakes are permissible.

Judaism

Judaism is the religion of the Jewish people and is another ancient, textually based religious tradition that is still extant. For Jews, the Torah is the revealed word of God. Of great importance also are the traditions, codifications and commentaries contained in the *Talmud*. Rabbinic Judaism is built upon the laws and rituals elaborated in the *Talmud*. Apart from legalism and ritualism, the other main strand in Judaism is mysticism. Jewish philosophy and mysticism flourished in the Middle Ages in Spain, Provence and the countries of the Islamic world, where the mystical tradition known as the Kabbala (or Cabbala) emerged. In central Europe, the mystical strand led to the Hasidic movement. The principal modern division, however, is between Orthodox Judaism, which holds to the traditional legalistic, ritualistic, rabbinic religion, and Reform Judaism, which seeks to modernize the religion. Conservative Judaism holds an intermediate position between these two. For more detail on Jewish history, see the timeline on p. 495.

Christianity

Jesus Christ was born to a Jewish family in about 4 BCE. He taught a religion of love and fellowship. As a result of his teaching and his life, Christianity arose and became the predominant religion of the Roman Empire after the Emperor Constantine's conversion in 312 CE. Christianity has gone on to become the largest and most widespread religion in the world. There are numerous strands to Christianity. The Eastern Orthodox Church and the other oriental churches (Armenian, Ethiopian, and so on) are centred on liturgy, mysticism and monasticism. Constantinople (Byzantium, now Istanbul), the prime patriarchate of the Orthodox Church, was the most important centre of Christianity throughout the Middle Ages. The Church in Rome had increasing disagreements with the Byzantine patriarchate, which culminated in the mutual exchange of anathemas (denunciations and excommunications) in 1054 and the sack of Constantinople by Western Crusaders in 1204. The Roman Catholic Church is also centred on liturgy

Christianity

c.4 Birth of Christ
30 Crucifixion of Christ
45-62 Missionary journeys of St Paul to the West, St Mark to Egypt and St Thomas to Iran and Iraq; scriptural epistles of St Paul
70 Destruction of Jerusalem, terminating its period as centre of the Christian world
c.85-c.150 Writings of the Apostolic Fathers (after c.150 the Church Fathers)

c.200 The bishops of Rome assert primacy over other bishops, leading to the papacy
c.250 Peak of Roman persecutions of Christianity
c.270 St Anthony becomes a hermit; beginnings of Christian eremitism
303 King of Armenia converted to Christianity
312 Conversion of Emperor Constantine
325 Council of Nicaea established the doctrine of the Trinity; defeat of Arianism
330 Constantine moves capital to Constantinople
d.430 St Augustine, greatest of the Latin Church Fathers and pre-eminent theologian
451 Council of Chalcedon, defeat of monophysitism and splitting off of the Coptic, Armenian, Syrian and Ethiopian Churc
c.500 St Benedict establishes first rules of a Christian monastic order; beginnings of the re-evangelization of Europe after the pagan conquests

635 Christianity taken to Xi'an, capital of China, by Persian missionary Alopen
638 Capture of Jerusalem by Muslim army

726 Byzantine Emperor Leo III prohibits use of images, begins period of iconoclasm in the Eastern Church (continued intermittently until 843)
800 Initiation of the Holy Roman Empire, Charlemagne crowned as first Emperor
826 Start of evangelization of Scandinavia
861 Start of evangelization of the Balkans (Bulgaria)
905 King Alfonso III begins Christian reconquest of Spain
954 Start of evangelization of Russia
975 Stephen I becomes first Christian king of Hungary
999 Millennialist mass movements sweep through Europe as the year 1000 approaches
1054 Rome and Constantinople exchange mutual excommunications (anathemas), final split between Eastern and Western Church
1095 First Crusade against Muslim occupiers of Jerusalem
1119 Founding of the first military religious order, Knights Templars

1204 Fourth Crusade sacks Constantinople
1231 Inquisition established by Pope Gregory IX
d.1274 St Thomas Aquinas, greatest of the Catholic scholastic philosophers
1309-1417 Period during which the Pope fled to Avignon and then, from 1378, there were rival claimants to the papacy

1453 Ottoman Turks capture Istanbul, greatly weakening Orthodox Christianity
1478 Establishment of Spanish Inquisition, at first against crypto-Jews and Muslims, later against Protestants
1492 Fall of Granada, last Muslim territory in Spain; expulsion of Jews from Spain
1517 Martin Luther publishes his 95 theses, the beginning of the Protestant Reformation
1534 Founding of Jesuits by Loyola; Henry VIII breaks with Rome, becomes head of Church of England
1541 Calvin returns to Geneva to set up a Protestant republic there
1545-63 Council of Trent called to reform the Catholic Church in order to counter the Reformation
1618-48 Thirty Years' War in Germany and elsewhere, mainly a religious war between Catholics and Protestants
1622 Founding of the Sacred Congregation for Propagation of the Faith, chief organ of Roman Catholic missionary effort
1633 Trial and condemnation of Galileo by the Inquisition
1698 Founding of the Society for Promoting Christian Knowledge, a British Protestant missionary organization
c.1750 Beginnings of the Enlightenment and of historico-critical scholarship of the Bible

1830 Establishment of Church of Jesus Christ Latter-Day Saints (Mormons)
1843-44 Height of millennialist movements in North America and Europe
1859 Publication of Charles Darwin's 'On the Origin of Species' – clash with the Church over biblical account of Creation
1910-15 Publication of 'The Fundamentals' in the USA, foundation documents of the Fundamentalist movement
1962-65 Second Vatican Council, leading to a more open attitude towards other religions by the Catholic Church
1965 Cancellation of the mutual excommunications (anathemas) of the Roman Catholic and Orthodox Churches

EASTERN ORTHODOX CHURCH: Icon of the Virgin Mary holding the child Jesus, in Panayia tou Araka (Our Lady of Araka), a twelfth-century Byzantine monastery in the Troodos Mountains of Cyprus.

and monasticism, but it is much more centralized and hierarchical in its organization. With the rise of Islam in the Middle East and the eventual fall of Constantinople in 1453, Rome gradually became more important than Constantinople as the centre of Christendom. The various Protestant churches that broke away from the Roman Catholic Church in the sixteenth century rejected, in the main, the traditions and hierarchy of that Church and proclaimed a *Bible*-based religion of faith and personal piety. The history of Christianity is represented in a timeline on p. 13.

Islam

Islam is the religion that arose as a result of the teachings of Muhammad (*c*.570–632 CE). He opposed the idolatry of the Arab tribes and also some of the doctrinal developments in Christianity. He taught a simple direct relationship with God through devotional acts and a way of life, emphasizing piety and justice. Within a few decades of the death of Muhammad, Islam had spread through the Middle East and North Africa. The Shi'a (Shi'is, Shi'ites) split away from the majority, who became known as Sunnis, over the question of the person and nature of the leadership of the community. The Shi'a believed that Muhammad had intended 'Ali to be the leader of Islam after him as the first of a series of hereditary Imams, and had intended a spiritual and political leadership. The Sunnis looked to a line of caliphs, who were mainly political leaders. The orthodox strand in

Islam has always been legalistic and most Muslims would identify being a Muslim with following the Holy Law, the Shari'a. This is based on the *Qur'an*, which Muslims believe is the word of God, and the Traditions (*Hadiths*), which record the sayings and actions of Muhammad. The other main strand in Islam is mysticism, Sufism. Individual mystics existed from the earliest days of Islam, but it was in the twelfth and thirteenth centuries CE that the great Sufi orders began to emerge. There has been a certain amount of tension between these two strands in Islam over the course of Islamic history. Classical Sunni political and social theory saw the Muslims as one community (*umma*) under the leadership of the caliph. The caliphate was, however, abolished in 1924 after the fall of the Turkish Ottoman Empire. Further details of the religious and political history of Islam is given in the timeline on p. 423 and in the map on p. 318.

The Baha'i Faith

During the nineteenth and twentieth centuries, a large number of new religious movements have arisen. Among these, the Baha'i Faith is one of the most interesting because of the way in which it has cut its links to its parent religion, Islam, and is increasingly being seen as an independent religious tradition. By studying the Baha'i Faith, therefore, we are able to examine more closely a process that other religions such as Christianity and Buddhism have undergone in their early history. Baha'is date the origin

Baha'i World Centre buildings on Mount Carmel, Haifa. The building with pillars and a small dome in the top is the Seat of the Universal House of Justice, the highest authority in the Baha'i Faith; below it and to the right is a building with pillars, the International Archives building; the domed building in the foreground is the shrine of the Bab.

of their religion to 1844 CE when a figure called the Bab (1819–50) began a religious movement in Iran. The followers of the Bab were severely persecuted and the movement was almost extinguished. From among the remnants of the Babi community in exile in Baghdad, Baha'u'llah (1817–92) came into prominence. He is the founder of the Baha'i Faith. In a series of private and public declarations in 1863–8, he put forward the claim to be not only the messianic figure foretold by the Bab but also the Promised One of all religions. His principal social teachings were of world peace and the unity of humankind. The whole corpus of Baha'u'llah's writings, which include laws, doctrinal works, mysticism, and ethical and social teachings, are considered scripture by Baha'is. The religion was brought to the West under the leadership of Baha'u'llah's son, 'Abdu'l-Baha (1844–1921) and to the rest of the world under the leadership of Shoghi Effendi (1897–1957), the grandson and successor of 'Abdu'l-Baha. The map on p. 500 shows the spread of the Baha'i Faith to 1950; the timeline on p. 329 highlights the major historical events.

Concept and Category

In writing this book, I have at all times been conscious of two conflicting pressures: the desire to describe the phenomena in detail and the necessity for clarity and conciseness. Religion, being a multi-faceted and complex human phenomenon, is constantly in a state of change, adapting itself to new social realities. In trying to reduce this complexity to the pages of a readable book, it has been necessary to simplify and organize the material in order to produce conceptual clarity. In particular, the task of comparing different religious phenomena and constructing typologies can lead to the danger of oversimplification. Religious phenomena do not exist in a small number of ideal types, but rather in a large variety of types, many of which overlap and interpenetrate. There is thus the danger of forcing the facts about a particular phenomenon to fit preconceived ideal types.

Some will consider the reduction of religious phenomena to two main types in chapter 2, for example, to be too schematic or a gross oversimplification. They may well regard it as highly problematic, in that there is considerable overlapping and interpenetration and there is, in fact, no such thing as a pure example of either ideal type. It is my hope that the reader will understand that the reduction of this and much other material in the book to simple dichotomies is intended only to increase clarity. For the purposes of a survey such as this, it is useful to describe phenomena in terms of the two extremes of the range. The reader will, I hope, bear in mind that in life, as distinct from textbooks, phenomena do not usually occur as discrete typical contrasting opposites but rather along a spectrum from one extreme to the other.

One of the founding fathers of this area of study, Max Weber, wrote, in particular, about the fact that we must at all times be ready to discard our typologies rather than allow them to dictate to us our understanding of the facts, a point recently restated by Jan Nattier:

> An ideal type (or typological category) is *not* the phenomenon itself, but is rather a conceptual yardstick against which a variety of phenomena can be measured. If we allow our typology to remain transparent – that is, if we allow the phenomena themselves to remain the primary focus, using the typology merely to act as a framework to illuminate their relative positions – then it can serve to amplify our vision of the people and ideas we wish to understand. If we do not, such categorization can actually detract from our understanding by leading to a premature pigeonholing of the subject matter.[6]

Without some degree of generalization and categorization, however, a book with the breadth of scope of this one could not be written. Readers will judge for themselves whether I have fallen into the trap described above by Nattier.

Some will also question my frequent statements about 'Christianity' or 'Hinduism' (or one of the other world religions). They will argue that each of these traditions is a vast network of smaller groups, some of which hold views that are directly contradictory to others. How then can general statements be made about 'Christianity' and 'Hinduism'? It should be clear to the reader that in using such designations, I am referring to the mainstream orthodox tradition in each religion. No doubt, each time that I make such a statement about one of the major religions, a counter-example could be found by searching the whole range of that religious tradition.

Finally, it is necessary to direct a few words to those who may feel, as a result of reading this book, that I have ignored the most important aspect of religion. These may think that I have failed to deal with the core of religion, the experience of the holy, the life of the spirit, and that this book deals only with the peripheral aspects. These may say that I have devalued and secularized religion and am guilty of positivism and reductionism. To such an accusation, my reply would be that nothing of what I have written should be interpreted as casting any doubt on the validity or reality of the central experience of religion. Nor does it disprove any putative transcendent source for religion. To be a participant in a religious movement is to recognize that it points to Something or Someone beyond itself. But while the participant is looking towards this transcendent (or immanent) Reality, we, as observers of religion, look only at the movement: what it says about the transcendent Reality as well as more mundane matters such as its organization. If we were to try to say something directly about the transcendent Reality, we would no longer be observers but participants. We would have strayed from the study of religion into theology or mysticism.

The central experience of religion is a purely personal and private experience of individuals. As such, it is difficult to make it a subject for objective analysis;[7] it can only be observed in the attempts that individuals make to interpret their religious experience (for instance, theology, mysticism or psychology: see chapters 4 and 7) and in the effects that it has on individuals and societies (see Part IV). Most religious persons would accept that, in whatever way they may ascribe perfection and infallibility to the source of their religion, the actual formulation and putting into effect of religion has been a human task over many centuries. As such, it is affected by all the usual factors that influence human behaviour and thus introduce the element of fallibility.[8] Any statements that might be made regarding this purely human secondary activity can in no way cast doubt on the central religious experience or its source at the primary level. My concern in this book has therefore been not so much with the question of what religion is, in any existential or essential sense, but rather with what can be observed of religion as a phenomenon of the human world. Of course, such observations may raise more fundamental questions regarding the essence of religion, but that is a matter for the believer, the theologian and the philosopher. Thus we can, as students of religion, observe the effects that the experience of religion has upon the individual and upon the world, but we cannot analyse what it is that has been experienced.

There remains a need for one final word of caution. As will be discussed in chapter 1, we all have a tendency to view religion from the perspective of the culture in which we were born and raised. And each culture 'sees' religion in a somewhat different way, as playing a different role in its social life. Each religion has, as it were, its own map by which it reads the cosmos. I would hope that one of the results of reading this book will be to sensitize the reader to such differences. The result should be that he or she will be prepared to put down his or her own map and to examine the map of other religions and cultures. But the reader should, of course, not assume that just by reading this book or other books like it, he or she has comprehended a religion. 'A map *is not* the territory.'[9] All that a map can do is to give one a representation of what the territory is like. It enables one to find one's way around, to know what sights to look for and what questions to ask. One cannot say that one knows what Papua New Guinea is like just because one has read guidebooks about it and looked at maps. So also one cannot say that, just because one has read about it, one comprehends what it is like to be a member of a religious community and to experience Ultimate Reality through that religion.

Further Reading

The following are introductory works on the main religions dealt with in this book: Hinduism: Flood, *Introduction to Hinduism*. Buddhism: Harvey, *Introduction to Buddhism*. Judaism: Cohn-Sherbok, *Short Introduction to Judaism*. Christianity: Gunton, *Cambridge Companion to Christian Doctrine*. Islam: Waines, *Introduction to Islam*. The Baha'i Faith: Momen, *Short Introduction to the Baha'i Faith*.

I
Understanding Religion

1

The Concept of Religion

Religion, as a human phenomenon, is founded on the basis of what is described as being the experience of the 'holy' or the 'sacred'. It can be seen to be very important to human beings in that the structure built upon its basis, the phenomenon of religion, has proved to be one of the most enduring and most important aspects of human life. Humankind has evolved a long way, socially and intellectually, over many thousands of years. Many social institutions and intellectual systems that were once central to human activity have now passed into obscurity. And yet religion, although it too has changed and evolved, still plays a central role in the world of humanity. As a result, some have gone as far as to consider this a key feature in describing human beings. They have even suggested that *Homo sapiens* be termed *Homo religiosus*.[1] This chapter examines the concept of religion and also some misconceptions about it. It looks at the question of the definition of religion and the characteristics of a religious person.

What is Religion?

The phenomenon of religion has had many varied expressions. One way in which this variation has manifested itself is in the central concern of different religions. Most people think that they know what they mean by the term 'religion'. In fact, however, in-built cultural biases predispose us to view religion in particular ways. Therefore, if we are to be successful in trying to understand religion, we must also achieve some degree of understanding of ourselves. Most people in the West, for example, will have a Christian background. This does not, of course, mean that they will necessarily be Christians. But it does mean that they will have been brought up in a culture that has certain preconceptions of what a religion should be, and these preconceptions are based on Christianity. A hypothetical example may perhaps clarify the extent to which we must come to an understanding of our own preconceptions and prejudices.

Jane, a young English woman, meets Gita, an Indian of the same age. Jane does not think of herself as a religious person – she never goes to church, for example. And yet, along with many other people of her age, she has a certain curiosity about religion in general. She sees that Gita's religion, Hinduism, clearly plays a very central role in her life. She therefore decides to find out more about this. One day, when she has some time to spare with Gita, she asks her: 'What do Hindus believe?' This may appear a very simple and innocuous question, and yet Gita may find it a very difficult question to answer. This is because the question itself has opened up a deep and fundamental divergence between the thinking of Jane and Gita about religion.

For Jane, with her background of a Western education based upon the premises of Protestant Christianity, religion is a system of beliefs. These are embodied in a creed to which a person may subscribe and thus become a member of that religion. Jane assumes that Gita, as a Hindu, subscribes to a set of Hindu beliefs, a Hindu creed. Jane wishes to know what these are – perhaps, she thinks, if she finds these beliefs acceptable, she will become a Hindu too.

In fact, however, Jane's thinking is based upon a series of assumptions that are not shared by Gita. Jane's thinking is based on a Christian view of what a religion is. Even though Christianity plays no prominent role in Jane's life, it has nevertheless shaped her thinking through its formative influence on her culture. For present-day Christians, a religion is a set of beliefs. Christians are asked to subscribe to one of the various creeds that have been produced in the course of Church history. If a Christian is asked what it means to be a Christian, he or she will, most likely, start by talking about his or her beliefs. Those who wish to become Christian priests spend three or four years at a theological college. This is an educational institution at which the main subject is theology, the study of beliefs about God and other Christian doctrines. They will also study Church history and the *Bible*, but these are as subsidiaries to the main study of Christian theology.

PUJA (WORSHIP): For Hindus, *puja* can be done at home or at the temple. It usually comprises the offering of flowers, candles, incense and a *bhajan* (hymn) or mantra (recitation) to a deity. Here the swinging of candles in front of the deity, *arati* (*arti*, *aarti*), is being performed in front of a home shrine in a kitchen in Britain.

Gita, however, does not think of religion in these terms at all. Even the idea that there is a Hindu religion is somewhat artificial, being a creation of foreigners who came to India.[2] The people of India certainly never originally had an idea of belonging to a religion called Hinduism. What the West called Hinduism and identified as being 'religious activity' (prayers, sacrifices and so on) was, for most Indians, a natural part of their daily activities, no more to be set apart than any other aspect of life, such as eating or washing. These 'religious activities' were not linked in the minds of Indians to any particular creed or set of beliefs. Apart from a very limited group of philosophers, most Hindus do not think of their 'religious activities' in terms of any belief system. These customary and traditional activities are an integral and natural part of family life, handed down through the generations of the family. They may be completely different from those of a neighbouring family. When Indians decide to devote themselves to religion, they do not go to a Hindu theological college to study. Depending on the aspect of the religion upon which they are focusing, they may seek out a guru (spiritual guide) who will teach them how to meditate and will disclose to them the reality within their own selves; the other main focus of religious education in India consists of the learning of scriptures, rituals and ceremonies.

A similar case can be made out for other religions. If Jane had met Fatima, a Muslim, and asked her: 'What do you believe?', a similar situation would have resulted. Islam is not a religion in which much attention is paid to beliefs. Its beliefs can be simply stated in a few sentences and are not the subject of much debate among Muslims. Islam is a religion that is centred around a Holy Law that lays down in great detail how one's life should be lived. All aspects of one's personal and social life are covered. This is the focus of the religion; this is what occupies the attention of the believers; this is the centre of debate. If one wants to become a religious professional in Islam, one does not go to a theological college and study theology. One goes to a *madrasa*, a religious college, where the main subject of study is the Holy Law, its foundations and the ways of applying it to everyday situations. This is what occupies the attentions of the students of the *madrasa* for as much as ten or fifteen years. Islamic theology is an optional subject dealt with in a short course of lectures.

With Chinese religion, matters become even more confusing for those whose concepts of religion are formed by the Christian West. There are several different religious traditions in China, the main ones being Confucianism, Taoism, Buddhism and Chinese folk religion. But if Jane were to ask Mei-Ling, a Chinese friend, about her religion, she would not find that Mei-Ling subscribes to any one of these traditions as someone from the West would. Mei-Ling uses elements of all four traditions in a mix that is probably unique to her family or village. Chinese religion revolves around public and family rituals and celebrations. Most of its practitioners have little concern for theology or the other aspects of religion that so concern those from the West.

CHINESE FESTIVAL: A dragon leads the festivities for the Chinese New Year. Picture taken in Taipei, Taiwan.

Therefore, when Jane asks Gita, Fatima or Mei-Ling: 'What do you believe?', this presents the respondent with something of a dilemma. It is not that Gita, Fatima and Mei-Ling have no beliefs, it is more a case that these are not the centre of their religious lives, and so the question puts them at a disadvantage. They try to answer it, of course, but in doing so, they have not in fact imparted what their religion means to them. This fact was put to use by Christian missionaries in the last century. When challenged to present their beliefs, those of other religions did not appear to produce anything that was as well thought out and systematic as Christian theology, thus 'proving' the superiority of Christianity.

In the twentieth century, the other religions have, under the influence of Christians and the challenge of Christian missionaries, sought to systematize their beliefs so that they can present themselves on a par with Christianity. This does not, however, alter the fact that this presentation is a departure from the traditional self-understanding of these other religions. Such presentations are not a natural product of these religions themselves but rather something imposed from the West in modern times. It is partly a response to and partly a defence against what has been termed 'Western cultural imperialism'. It represents an intellectualization that may well be sufficient for those who want to write tidy textbooks but must remain unsatisfactory to those who want to understand religion. Just to illustrate the complexities of the study of religion, however, it must be admitted that some aspects of these adaptations to the West are now part of the development of these religions and have become, so-to-speak, 'naturalized'; other aspects are, on the other hand, deeply resented and from time to time there is a movement from within the religion to expel them.[3]

A further example of the manner in which our preconceptions may predetermine and colour our views of religion can be drawn from the same hypothetical situation outlined above. Jane thinks to herself that if she likes what she hears of Hinduism she may become a Hindu herself. This may again appear to be a straightforward and unremarkable statement. After all, one of the major religious features of the present century is the manner in which all the major religious traditions have begun to compete with each other for converts. Even a religion such as Hinduism, which in former times was non-missionary (and many Hindus believed that you could not be a Hindu unless you were born into the system), is now actively competing in the world's religious marketplace. But this phenomenon represents yet another way in which the West has imposed its own ideas upon the rest of the world, and perhaps created a permanent change in the religious world.

The idea that religion is a matter of individual choice is one that has its origins in Islam but came to the fore in Protestant Christianity in the last few centuries. It is a comparatively new phenomenon even in the West. Six hundred years ago, the idea that individuals could change their religion independently of the society around them was as foreign to Europe as it now is to much of the rest of the world. For most of the rest of the world today, religion is not just a matter of personal choice. It is something that is decided by society as a whole. An individual is born into a religious community and stays in that community. The concept of a choice open to him or her does not even exist. Communities do occasionally change their religion; otherwise religions such as Islam and Buddhism could not have spread into new areas. This usually occurs, however, as a result of whole communities changing their religion, often at the instigation of a king or other ruling figure. Individual conversion has been a rarity in the past, except in a few other situations (the last centuries of the Roman Empire, for example). It is the individualism bred by Protestant Christianity that assumes that the individual is free to choose a religion to follow.

We must also be careful in our use of the word 'religion' for this is itself a culturally bound concept. Wilfred Cantwell Smith, one of the pioneers of the task of understanding religion, has pointed out that the very concept of 'a religion' is a result of a process of reification (the conversion of an abstract concept into a falsely concrete 'thing') carried out by the West.[4] Before this reification occurred, people were not conscious of belonging to a particular religion, nor that any part of their lives was the religious part.

The process of reification has gone, to a large extent, hand in hand with the secularization of society in the West. This has produced a state of affairs in which religion is viewed as a compartment in people's lives. The life of an individual may be likened to a room. As one surveys the room of one's life, one sees that part of the room is devoted to one's work; part to one's family; part to one's friends; part to one's hobby; and, in the West, one sees that a part is devoted to religion. But in most other cultures, and even in the West before reification and secularization, religion is more like the glasses with which the individual looks at the room of his or her life. It affects every aspect of everything in such a way that it is very difficult to separate the effects of religion from the part of the room that is being surveyed. For a person from the West, it is not easy to conceptualize how things were before the compartmentalizing effect of reification set in.

On the social level, we should also recognize that the tendency of the West to conceptualize religion as an aspect of humanity's social life, separate from government and culture, is again something that is alien to much of what would be called religion in other parts of the world. Most of the people of the world see their religion, culture and usually their political order as being one undivided whole. In one society, religion may provide the justification for the social order (for example the caste system in India); in another it may provide the legitimation of the political structure (for example the caliphate in Islam until the beginning of the twentieth century); and in most societies, culture and religion are almost indistinguishable.

The writings of Wilfred Cantwell Smith have alerted us to one further issue that complicates any attempt to understand religion. This is the fact that what may superficially appear to be equivalent phenomena in different religions may not, in fact, play equivalent roles functionally or spiritually. For example, Christ is the Word of God incarnate for Christians. For Muslims, the equivalent is not Muhammad but rather the *Qur'an*, which is the Word of God brought to earth (that is, incarnated). It is the person of

a

b

THE WORD OF GOD: a) This icon of Christ is called Christ Pantocrator (meaning 'Universal Sovereign'), from the Chora, or Kariye, Museum, previously St Saviour's Church. This building, originally located outside the walls of Istanbul, is rich in fourteenth-century mosaics and frescoes. b) With the Islamic prohibition on drawing images of humans and animals (as a safeguard against idolatry), the art of calligraphy, and of the illumination or embellishment of calligraphy, was greatly developed. This was taken to its highest form in the calligraphy of the *Qur'an*, the Word of God. This page shows the whole of the Sura of W'al-Layl (By the Night, Sura 92) and the conclusion of the previous sura as well as the title of the next. The calligraphy by Yaqut al-Musta'simi, Baghdad, 1282, is in the Rayhani style of calligraphy and the sura titles in Thuluth.

Christ and the book, the *Qur'an*, that are functionally and spiritually equivalent in the two religious traditions. They are each the locus for the appearance of the heavenly pre-existent Absolute[5] in an earthly form.[6] Calligraphy of the *Qur'an*, the most important of the Islamic arts, is the rendering of the image of the Word of God. It is therefore equivalent to the iconography of Eastern Christianity, which is also the rendering of the image of 'the Word made flesh'.[7]

DEFINITIONS OF RELIGION

Religion is thus a phenomenon that is difficult to define. Most of us would agree that we recognize it when we come across it but it is present in so many different forms that it is hard to pin down a definition. In this, religion is no different to many other human activities, for example art. Given that there are great variations among the different religious systems, can we find a core that is common to all of them? One approach would be to say that religion consists of three interdependent aspects (each of which forms the subject of the following three parts of this book):

- The first, at the individual level, is religious experience. It is what was described at the beginning of this chapter, as being the experience of the 'holy' or the 'sacred'. It is the personal, experiential aspect of religion.
- The second, at the conceptual level, is the universal idea that there is some Ultimate Reality, and that the most important activity for human beings is to establish and clarify their relationship with this Reality. This is the conceptual and doctrinal aspect of religion.
- The third, at the social level, is the fact that all religions are to a greater or lesser extent involved in creating social cohesion and the integration of the individual into society. All of them have created some form of social and institutional order. From this, the ethical and social aspect of religion is derived.

The various approaches to the definition of religion can be regarded as being associated with these three aspects of religion.

Substantive or Metaphysical Definitions

These are definitions of religion that attempt to use the concepts and words that religion itself uses about itself. They are attempts to describe religion in terms of the religious experience. Unfortunately, with the very wide range of metaphysical assumptions in religions, it is difficult to find a set of words upon which followers of all religions would agree, without lapsing into very vague and loose language. The best such definitions usually end up with words such as:

> Religion is that human activity that acknowledges the existence of another reality transcendent to or immanent within this physical world and that seeks to describe and put human beings into a correct relationship with that reality, in ways that may involve correct knowledge, beliefs and values, correct personal and social activity, correct ethics, correct law, or participation in correct social institutions.

Or, more simply:

> Religion is humanity's response to what it experiences as holy.

Symbolist Definitions

A symbolist definition of religion focuses on the role of religion in creating a symbolic universe which human beings perceive and respond to as reality. Such definitions look at religion in terms of its conceptual aspects. A typical definition would be:

> A religion is a system of symbols that creates a universal order that is so cohesive, coherent and compelling that it becomes 'reality' for the social group that adopts that religion.

Functional Definitions

Functional definitions concentrate on what religion does, rather than what it is. They conceptualize religion in terms of its social role and its response to human needs. Typical of such definitions would be:

> Religion is that which provides humanity with a worldview which unifies society, which provides a moral code, and within which human beings can orient their lives.

The problem with these functional definitions is that they raise the question of whether some ideologies, such as Marxism, which fulfil the criteria of the definition should therefore be regarded as religions, even though they are not usually thought of as religions.

Suffice it to say that the concept of religion used in this book is the more limited one that relates it to a concept of the supernatural or supra-human (or perhaps even supra-scientific), rather than the wider functional definition that would include such secular ideologies as Marxism and nationalism.[8] For a discussion of the way in which these latter 'pseudo-religious' ideologies have replaced religion in the modern world, see chapter 19 (pp. 480–1).

Religion also needs to be distinguished from magic. Probably the best distinction is to think of magic as providing immediate specific rewards (wealth, health, injury to enemies and so on) while religion deals with more general, ultimate questions (Who am I? Why am I here? How should I relate to others? What is going to happen when I die?). In so far as it does offer rewards, these are long term and more general, such as a happy life or heaven.[9] In practice, the two commonly coalesce and interpenetrate. (See chapter 15.)

The Religious Person or Society

An alternative way of trying to find a common core to religion is to examine what difference religion makes in the life of an individual or a society.

Those who are not religious often think of a religious person as being bigoted and inflexible. Many religious people would say that this is the very opposite of a truly religious person. The individual is by nature self-centred; everything is centred around advancing his or her own wealth, power, self-esteem and ease. Religious people would say that one major effect of the central experience of religion, and the faith that arises from it, is to cause people to become less self-centred; to free the individual from the tyranny of self; to cause him or her to be more selfless, more Other-centred or God-centred. Although few will attain it, the religious ideal is the individual who is freed from the need for the praise and approval of others (and can therefore think and judge matters independently), deems possessions and power to be ephemeral and valueless (and is therefore not swayed by base motives), and is more concerned with the common good than with self-advancement (see Table 1.1).

Table 1.1 Worldly Values Versus Religious Values

Throughout history, most religions have maintained that they hold to certain values which distinguish the religious person from the non-religious person. The non-religious person may be said to be self-centred, in that all of his or her concerns are centred upon the self. The religious person may, on the other hand, be said to be selfless, in that his or her concern is turned away from the self (indeed, the self may be considered to be delusory, as in Buddhism).

Worldly Values	Religious Values
Hold self-preservation as of supreme importance: loss of life is the ultimate loss.	Hold that self-preservation is of secondary importance to spiritual advancement: you may need to lose your life in order to find it.
Desire power over others; the individual may need to use others for his or her own ends.	Are concerned for the common good; relationships with others are determined by what will benefit them, especially spiritually.
Revel in self-glory.	Have true humility.
Are concerned about other people's opinions of them; crave admiration and popularity.	Try to be increasingly free of the necessity for the approval or praise of others.
Are rigid and self-opinionated.	Are flexible in thinking.

As with the individual, those who want to denigrate religion find no difficulty in listing societies in which religion has been a cause of hatred, conflict and destruction. A religious person would counter this by saying that a truly religious society is the foundation of a civilization in which there is religious tolerance, where new ideas can emerge and develop, and where there is an efflorescence of the arts and sciences. Examples of such societies include the Abbasid Empire centred on Baghdad, the Fatimids in

LION CAPITAL OF EMPEROR ASHOKA: This lion image was on the top of a column at Sarnath (Isipatana), built by the Emperor Ashoka at the place that the Buddha traditionally first preached. This image now appears on the Indian flag.

Egypt, and Muslim Spain, for Islam; the Byzantine Empire in the early Christian centuries; the Buddhist empire built by Ashoka in India and the Hindu Gupta empire in India.

FURTHER READING

On the subject of what the word 'religion' means in various cultures and has meant over history, see W.C. Smith, *The Meaning and End of Religion*. For a further consideration of the three aspects of religion described, see Otto, *The Idea of the Holy;* Eliade, *The Sacred and the Profane*; Durkheim, *Elementary Forms of the Religious Life*, especially chapter 1; Wach, *Comparative Study of Religions*, chapter 2.

2

Religion East and West – A General Survey

The basis for religion is the human conviction that there is a transcendent or absolute Reality that either lies beyond or underlies this physical world. As stated in the previous chapter, one definition of the phenomenon of religion is that it consists of the attempt by human beings both to describe this Ultimate Reality and to enter into a proper relationship with it. In this chapter, this process will be briefly surveyed, comparing the Western religions with those of the East. A fuller consideration of many of the topics in this chapter will be found in later chapters of this book. This chapter also briefly surveys Chinese and Japanese religion, as well as primal religions.

There is of course a very wide divergence of views within the fields of philosophy, metaphysics and theology. Even within a particular religion, there are greatly differing views, some of them even contradictory. To bring some order out of this kaleidoscope of views and theories, it is necessary to look for some common patterns. With regard to the major world religions that this book focuses on, it is useful to consider them as divided into two main groups. Initially, it will be helpful to call these the Western and Eastern groups of religions (although, as will become evident, these are not good names for these two groups). In this book I use the term 'Western religion' to refer to the mainstream orthodoxies of the Judaeo–Christian–Muslim group of religions. 'Eastern religion' refers to Buddhism, Taoism and Hinduism, especially of the Advaita Vedanta school. This division is useful in that these two groups of religions hold very differing and even contradictory views on the nature of the Ultimate Reality and of humanity's relationship to it.

The Nature of Ultimate Reality

One of the chief differences between Eastern and Western religions is their differing conceptualizations of Ultimate Reality. Both types of religion conceive of a reality that is greater than this physical universe but they differ radically in their descriptions of it. This initial difference then goes

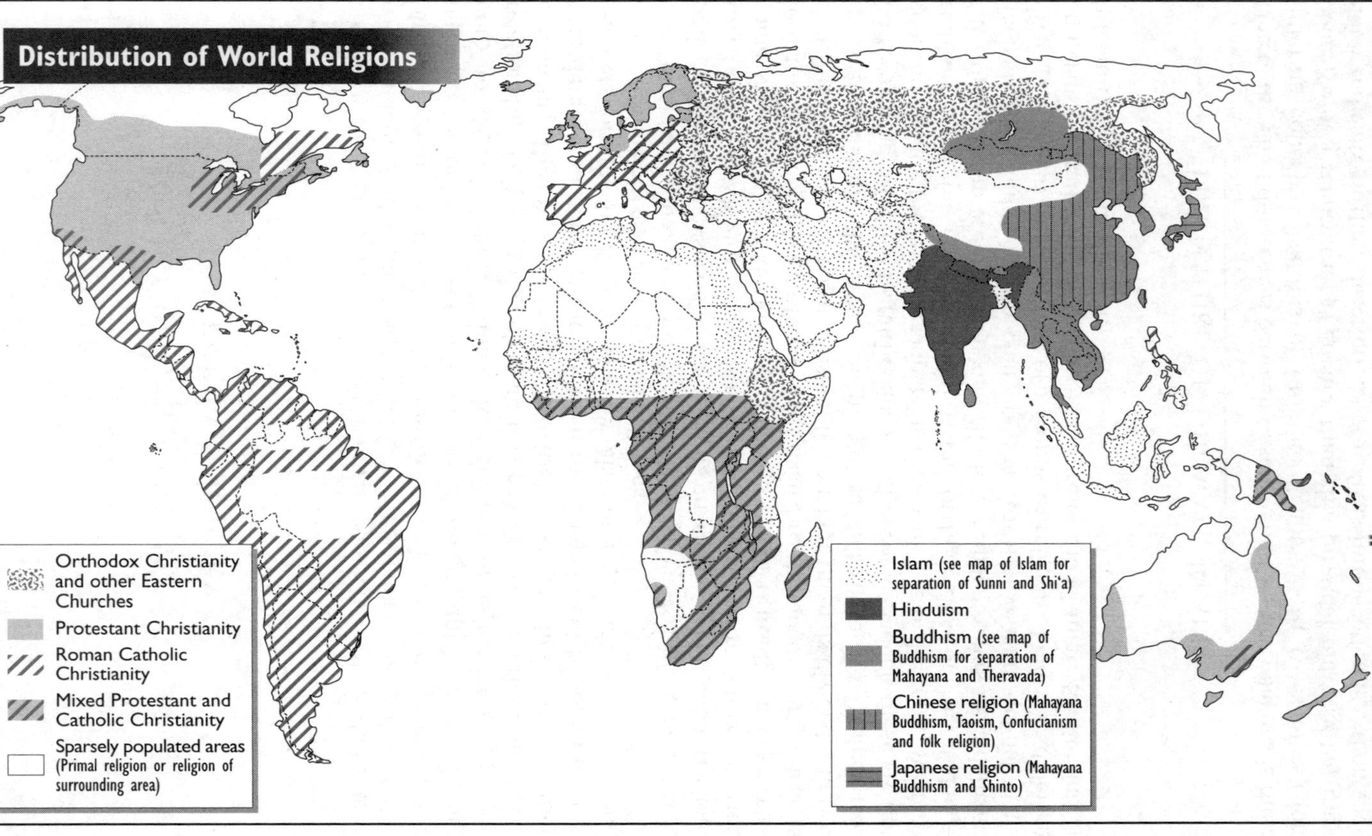

Distribution of World Religions
Orthodox Christianity and other Eastern Churches
Protestant Christianity
Roman Catholic Christianity
Mixed Protestant and Catholic Christianity
Sparsely populated areas (Primal religion or religion of surrounding area)
Islam (see map of Islam for separation of Sunni and Shi'a)
Hinduism
Buddhism (see map of Buddhism for separation of Mahayana and Theravada)
Chinese religion (Mahayana Buddhism, Taoism, Confucianism and folk religion)
Japanese religion (Mahayana Buddhism and Shinto)

on to cause dissimilarities in their accounts of the relationship of the individual to this highest reality. From these distinctions come other differences over such questions as evil, suffering, salvation, liberation and even matters such as time and space.

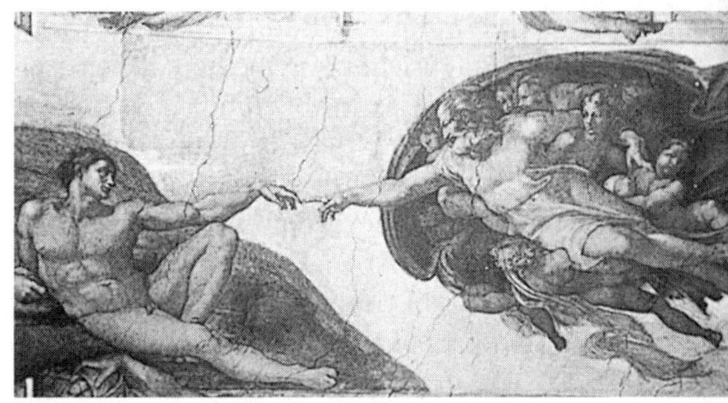

GOD AS CREATOR: This is the famous roof of the Sistine Chapel in the Vatican painted by Michelangelo between 1508 and 1512. This picture represents God creating Adam, from the biblical story of Genesis.

In the Western religions the transcendent reality is given the name of God and is thought of as a personal, omnipotent, omniscient Being. God as the Creator is usually conceived of as being wholly other than His creation. He is described in many ways, some of which are contrasting: wrathful and avenging, yet kind and beneficent.[1] God has a will and a purpose for human beings, which they must accept or face unpleasant consequences. But God is also benevolent and loving towards humanity, and in return He is the object of the worship and adoration of humanity. The world or the cosmos becomes, then, the arena for the interaction between God and humanity. Regarding the difference with the Eastern religions, the most important point is that in the Western religions those characteristics mentioned above, such as anger and kindness, all make God appear to have a personality, to act as a person. An impersonal entity would not have such characteristics.

In contrast, the Eastern religions, Buddhism, Taoism and Hinduism of the Advaita school, have no concept of God as a person; rather their concept is of Ultimate Reality as a process, a truth, or a state of being. This is usually stated as a concept of an Absolute Reality. The phrase 'Absolute Reality' implies that there is a single Reality in the cosmos; everything else that may appear real has only a relative or contingent reality or is illusory or non-existent. The Absolute is therefore both transcendent and immanent. It cannot be described in terms of the concepts of this phenomenal world. It is devoid of all empirical determinations. It is not an all-knowing Creator, for example.

The Absolute Reality is called Brahman in Hinduism. In Taoism, it is named the Tao. In Buddhism, the name of the Ultimate Reality varies depending on the context. In Mahayana Buddhism, the simple name Paramartha can be given to the Ultimate Reality; but the concept that all things are empty of substance or essence has led to the concept of Shunyata, the Void, as the underlying reality of the world. As such it is the Absolute Reality since nothing escapes it or is beyond it, even Nirvana, the ultimate goal for humans. The human inability to describe this reality is indicated by other names such as Tathata, Suchness or Thatness. The identity of the Buddha with this universal Ultimate Reality is indicated in the word Dharmakaya, the Dharma body of the Buddha.

In Theravada Buddhism, the Ultimate Reality is Nirvana or Dharma (Nibbana or Dhamma in the Pali texts of Theravada Buddhism). The former is described as 'unbecome, unborn, unoriginated, uncreated, unformed.'[2] Nirvana is both the Ultimate Reality and also describes the human being's state when identified with that Reality. Hinduism also uses the term Nirvana but more commonly the expression *sat-chit-ananda* (existence-consciousness-bliss) is used to describe the experiential aspect of the awareness of this state of identity. (See further details on the nature of the Ultimate Reality in chapter 8.)

The contrast between the concepts of Reality/God in the religions of East and West gives us another name by which we can describe these two systems. We can call the view held by many Eastern religions that there is only one fundamental reality in the world, 'monism'. And by contrast, we can call the Western view that God and humanity form two distinct and separate realities, 'dualism'[3]. Alternative names for the two systems would be 'absolutism' and 'theism' respectively. In the rest of this chapter, I shall use the designation 'theism' to refer to the Western religions and, to refer to the Eastern religions, I shall use the term 'monism' or sometimes 'non-theism' (to acknowledge the fact that some Buddhists maintain that their concept of Ultimate Reality is not that of an Absolute Reality, hence leading to monism[4]).

Concepts of Suffering and Evil

In the theistic religions, suffering is the result of sin. Sin is the breaking of the Holy Law, disobedience to God. God has clearly laid down His laws and injunctions in His Holy Book (whether this be the *Bible* or the *Qur'an*). Whoever acts in a contrary manner to these has sinned. Evil is thus the result of the rebellious will of human beings.

In the Eastern non-theistic religions, suffering is viewed quite differently. It is due to human ignorance (*avidya*) or delusion. The pressing immediacy of the physical world creates the illusion (*maya*) of its reality and importance. And so human beings become attached to the things of this world. This attachment to and desire for the things of this world are the source of suffering. (For further consideration of this subject, see chapter 9.)

The Path to Salvation

Salvation is the release from sin and suffering. Of course, since the theistic and non-theistic systems disagree on the cause of sin and suffering, they also disagree on the path towards salvation.

In the theistic systems, the source of sin is failure to obey the Will or Law of God as laid down in the Holy Book. Therefore, the path towards salvation must involve turning towards God and following the laws and ethics laid down in the Holy Book. The original sin was humankind's rebellious will, and so salvation is the bending of human will to the Will of God. The various groups within the theistic systems differ over what is the main element in the process of salvation. Some emphasize a person's own efforts to reform so as to live according to the Law. Others lay stress on the individual's faith and the grace of God. Most theistic systems combine elements of both faith in the grace of God and the individual's own works.[5]

In the non-theistic systems, the source of suffering and evil is human ignorance and the failure to perceive the real state of affairs. Therefore, the path to salvation involves the acquisition of knowledge or wisdom. This knowledge is not only the knowledge that one obtains from reading books, but intuitive and experiential knowledge arising from meditation, breathing exercises, contemplation and discipline of body and mind. It involves the realization that the immediacy and seeming reality of the physical world are illusions; the true reality is the monist truth that 'Thou art That' (in the Hindu *Upanishads*) or the Mahayana Buddhist concept that 'Samsara is Nirvana'.[6] The wisdom achieved by seeing through the illusion (*maya*) is called *jñana* in Hinduism and *prajña* in Buddhism.[7]

The Goal of Salvation

Both the theistic and non-theistic religions describe a heaven or paradise that is attainable after death. Here there is no sin or suffering. There is also a hell that is a place of suffering (see p. 234). But these states are treated in a markedly different manner in the two religious systems. In the Western religions, they are the final goal, the place where the individual remains for eternity. The state of being saved, the state of grace, is also achievable in this life although only exceptional people such as saints are in practice thought to achieve it.

In the Eastern religions, heaven and hell are temporary stopping points before there occurs a return to this world through reincarnation or rebirth. The ultimate objective is a less clearly defined goal. In Hinduism, the final goal is liberation (*moksha* or *mukti*). This state may be achieved in life, in which case it is called *jivanmukti*. Such a person is described as having achieved a state of existence-consciousness-bliss (*sat-chit-ananda*). For Buddhists, the final goal is the state of Nirvana (which means 'blown out'). This state is characterized by the extinction of all craving and desires, a complete detachment from the world. It is not, however, a state that can be described in any objective manner. All description of this state is void. (For a further consideration of salvation, see chapter 9.)

Ritual and Religious Practices

The differences between the theistic and non-theistic systems extend even to the matter of the most important ritual elements. For theists, the most important ritual elements are those that lay stress on the separation between human beings and God, the otherness of God, His remoteness and complete transcendence relative to human beings. These rituals include prayer to the Deity, sacraments that appease or turn attention to the Deity, and such activities as the singing of hymns that glorify and give praise to the Deity. In all, the effect is to emphasize the separateness of God from human beings. Even where the ritual involves a drawing closer to God (as in Holy Communion), it is still the drawing together of two unequal and separate realities.

In non-theistic religions, the emphasis is on ritual elements that produce an altered state of consciousness, such as a trance. These can be produced by actions such as the repetitive chanting of mantras or by deep meditation. The altered states of consciousness that result from such practices tend to make the individual feel that he or she is merged with the Absolute; thus they reinforce the monistic truth.[8] (For further discussion of altered states of consciousness and the implications of this for religion, see chapter 7.)

Chinese landscape painting: Taoism has been one of the major influences on Chinese art. Taoism teaches that human beings should seek to achieve harmony with the Tao (the Way). Chinese landscape painting seeks to reflect not the outer form of the scene but the inner harmony that unites landscape, human beings and the Tao in one.

Time and Creation

Even such concepts as time have different connotations in the theistic and non-theistic systems. In theistic systems, time is 'historical'. All events are placed in an orderly continuous flow of time. There is a creation event, which is the beginning of the world, and a final event, the end of the world. In between, time flows in a linear manner, interrupted on occasions by the irruption of the sacred world into this world, as occurs with the advent of a prophet. The non-theistic systems consider time as being cyclical. The world has no beginning, but rather has always existed in a series of great cosmic cycles of prosperity and disaster. (For a further consideration of this subject, see chapter 8.)

Theism and Monism

The theistic view is, as we have seen, that God is wholly other than His creation. There is, nevertheless, in most theistic systems some concept of the immanence of God within creation. In Christianity, this concept is enshrined both in the idea of the incarnation of God in a human form and the idea that the Holy Spirit is active in the world. But these ideas should not be confused with the monistic concept of the non-theistic religions. Despite being present and active in the world, God is nevertheless a separate and distinct reality that has chosen to descend into the physical world. In Christianity, God conceals His separateness from the human world by appearing and acting in the physical world. In the Eastern monistic religions, the physical world also has a concealing role, but this time it is giving the illusion of separateness that conceals the identity of the human being and Absolute Reality. In brief, the contrast may be said to be that in Christianity the physical world conceals the otherness of God from the human being; while in the Eastern monistic religions the physical world conceals the identity of the human being with Absolute Reality.

Table 2.1 Differences Between Eastern and Western Religious Thought

Western/Theistic	Eastern/Monistic
A Creator God who acts as a person.	A concept of the Ultimate Reality as undifferentiated and impersonal.
A human being is fundamentally different to and separate from God.	Either the human reality is identical to the Absolute Reality: Atman is Brahman (monism); or else, as in Buddhism, no statement can be made about the person who has achieved Nirvana.
Evil and suffering are due to sinning against the Law of God.	Evil and suffering are due to human ignorance and self-delusion.
The path to salvation depends either on good works and adherence to the Holy Law or is simply a matter of faith and the grace of God.	The path to salvation is through the acquisition of knowledge or wisdom, that is the ability to see things as they really are.
The purpose of salvation is to escape from the threat of hell to reach the goal of heaven or paradise.	The purpose of salvation is to escape from the suffering of this world and to achieve the state of blissfulness, Nirvana or *moksha*.
Most important ritual elements revolve around worship and sacraments.	Most important ritual elements revolve around meditation and achievement of altered states of consciousness.
Progressive 'historical' time with a beginning and an end.	Cyclical time with no beginning or end.

The Universality of Modes of Religious Thought

The points of difference between theism and non-theism are summarized in Table 2.1 (p. 37). I began this chapter by calling the theistic systems 'Western religion' and the non-theistic systems 'Eastern religion'. In fact, however, both types of religion occur in both East and West. The mainstream orthodoxies of Islam, Christianity and Judaism are clearly theistic in nature. They emphasize prayer to and worship of God. The holy life is considered to revolve around obedience to the Holy Law and expectation of the grace of God. Nevertheless, we find monism in the mystical elements of each of these religions. In Judaism, there are such works as the *Sefer Yesira* (third–sixth century CE) and the *Zohar* (Spain, thirteenth century CE)[9]. Taking many of their ideas from Neoplatonism, the authors of these two books write of the soul as an emanation from God that seeks to reunite itself with its source. In Christianity, particularly in the Middle Ages, such figures as Meister Eckhart (1260–1327), Henry Suso (c. 1295–1365), John of Ruysbroeck (1293–1381) and St John of the Cross (1542–91)[10] write of the perfect union of the soul with God as being the ultimate goal of the mystical path.

In Islam, many Sufi mystics are monistic in their conceptualization of the mystic path. In particular, there are those Sufis who follow the school of Ibn al-'Arabi (1164–1240). The concept of *wahdat al-wujud* (oneness of being) evolved by this school is clearly a monistic approach.[11] Similar concepts can be found among the Sufi poets. Jalal al-Din Rumi speaks of the

The Soul's Union with God

The Zohar
For all things are in him and he is in all things: he is both manifest and concealed. Manifest in order to uphold the whole, and concealed for he is found nowhere. (Quoted in Parrinder, *Mysticism in the World's Religions*, p. 117)

Meister Eckhart
If I am to know God directly, I must become completely He and He I: so that this He and this I become and are one I. (Quoted in Underhill, *Mysticism*, p. 420)

John of Ruysbroeck
But he who is united with God, and is enlightened in this truth, he is able to understand the truth by itself. For to comprehend and to understand God above all similitudes, such as He is in Himself, is to be God with God, without intermediary, and without any otherness that can become a hindrance or an intermediary. (*The Adornment of Spiritual Marriage*, III: 1, quoted in Happold, *Mysticism*, p. 259)

Jalal al-Din Rumi
Thou didst contrive this 'I' and 'we' in order that Thou mightst play the game of worship with Thyself. (*The Mathnavi of Jalalu'd din Rumi*, trans. Nicholson, vol. 2, p. 98)

illusion of otherness and of individuality arising from the interplay of the two aspects from which the Real may be viewed.

MONISM IN WESTERN RELIGIONS: This picture shows the tomb of Jalal al-Din Rumi, Konya, Turkey. Rumi was the greatest of the Islamic mystical poets who frequently alluded to the monist concept in his poetry. He is often referred to as Maulana (in Turkish, Mevlana) meaning 'our lord'. The use of calligraphy as ornamentation in Islam is particularly notable here.

And so, although mainstream religion in the West has been theistic, these Western religions have each evolved within themselves a stream of monistic thought. The three strands of mysticism in the West (from Islam, Christianity and Judaism) undoubtedly influenced each other to a large extent, particularly in places like Spain where they coexisted in the Middle Ages. It is very unlikely, however, that these monistic thinkers were influenced primarily by the Eastern religions. Most of the mystical writers that I have referred to above lived and wrote in the Middle Ages or earlier and, certainly, these Jewish and Christian mystics had little or no contact with the Eastern religions. However, if we want to trace a source of monistic inspiration for these mystical movements in the West, then it would seem that Hellenic thought, and in particular Neoplatonism, was a much greater influence.[12] Thus, these monistic patterns of thought appear to have been genuinely native expressions of religiosity rather than foreign imports. There have also been monistic philosophers in the West such as Parmenides and Spinoza.

Similarly, in the East there gradually evolved both theistic and monistic elements in the religion of India. The *Upanishads* are clearly monistic in character. The ultimate degree of wisdom that human beings can attain is the realization that the soul of the individual (Atman) is one with Ultimate Reality (Brahman). This wisdom is summed up in the statement: 'Thou art That' (*tat twam asi*)[13]. Based on such ideas, Shankara (*c.* eighth century CE) evolved his philosophical system called the Advaita (non-dualism). Taoism is also monistic in that the Tao is the all-pervading reality. Ultimate Reality for the Buddhist can be conceived in various ways according to different schools of thought in Buddhism (Dharma, Dharmakaya, Paramartha, Nirvana, Shunyata), but these are all non-theistic conceptions.

The religion of India has, on the other hand, also given rise to theistic modes of thought. The *bhakti* sects that worship various gods, in particular Shiva and Vishnu, are clearly theistic in their conceptualization. The followers of these sects pray to and worship these deities as well as offering

a

b

THEISM IN EASTERN RELIGIONS: a) *Bhakti*, the love of God in Hinduism, is expressed in various acts of devotion to particular deities. This picture is of a shrine set up in a home in Britain for the purpose of devotion to Rama. b) While the official religion in Theravada Buddhism is non-theistic, many of the practices resemble those of theism with the Buddha being effectively substituted for God. This picture is of monks sitting in worship before an image of the Buddha in the Wat Benchamabopitr (Marble Temple), Bangkok. The image of the Buddha is in the pose of *Bhumisparsha mudra*, calling the earth to witness.

---

gifts and sacrifices to appease and propitiate them. Hindu thought thus acknowledges both the monistic path, *jñana yoga* (the path of knowledge), and the theistic path, *bhakti yoga* (the path of worship and adoration). Sikhism is also theistic in that it is based on worship of God as the Sat Guru (True Preceptor). In India itself, the theism of the *bhakti* sects predominates numerically, but further east in Asia, it is the non-theism of Buddhism and Taoism that is the predominant religious expression. Yet even within the non-theistic world of Buddhism, we find elements of theism. Some of the Mahayana sects lean towards theism, with the concept of the Buddha as a source of grace who may be worshipped and prayed to as a saviour. This occurs, for example, in the Amida sects of Japanese Buddhism, although the Amida (Amitabha) Buddha is not a Creator God after the characteristic Western pattern. In Theravada Buddhism, the orthodox religion of the monks is non-theistic. But even here, much of the popular religion is theistic in its praying to and worshipping of Buddha and other deities (see chapter 11).

In summary then, theistic and monistic elements occur in both East and West. Although theism may predominate in the West and monism in the East, neither is exclusive in any area. It would appear that individual people in all parts of the world tend towards either theism or monism. The great religions of the world have been able to accommodate this by incorporating within themselves both elements in one way or another. Taking this further, we have the basis for a definition differentiating a religion from a sect. A religion must have the capability of satisfying the religious needs of a wide variety of types of mind, while a sect only appeals to a narrow range of religious outlooks. This idea is developed further in chapter 5 (pp. 138–9).

Mutual Attitudes of Theism and Monism

Another way of understanding and characterizing the theistic and monistic religions is to study the attitude of each towards manifestations of the other. Theists have always tended to look upon monism with profound disfavour. In the West, where theism predominates and has been the state-supported orthodoxy, theistic religious leaders have interpreted monism as the individual claiming to be God (this is in relation to the monistic concept that all reality is one and thus the human being and God have one reality). They have therefore considered monism to be blasphemy and heresy. They have persecuted and even killed those with monistic leanings. Meister Eckhart was condemned by the Pope for heresy, and other mystics such as Madame Guyon, Miguel de Molinos and Fenelon suffered at the hands of the Inquisition, some even meeting death. Similarly, Islam has persecuted Sufis down the ages. One of the early monistic martyrs in Islam was al-Hallaj (d. 922) whose famous dictum: 'I am the Truth/God (*ana'l-Haqq*)' is reputed to have been the cause of his execution;[14] while as recently as the nineteenth century, one of the leading religious figures in Iran prided himself on his title of *Sufi-kush* (Sufi-killer).[15]

The monistic religions, on the other hand, have a much more subtle attitude towards theists. For the most part they do not condemn theism as error. Rather they look upon theism as a 'lower' form of the truth, a stage through which the seeker after truth must pass before reaching the 'higher' monistic truth. Indeed, many non-theistic systems look upon theism as a system that is suitable for assuring morality among the masses, while only the monistic mode of religion leads to liberation.

Relativism

Apart from theism and monism, there is one further position that could be considered to stand between them. This approach can be called relativism. Briefly, it takes the position that the Ultimate Reality is unknowable, beyond human ability to conceptualize it. Knowledge (whether of the physical or metaphysical world) is always knowledge from a particular

Detail from the external ornamentation of the Baha'i House of Worship in Wilmette, near Chicago, USA (completed 1953), showing the incorporation into the design of the symbols of various religions. Among those that can be seen are a swastika (Hinduism), a Star of David (Judaism), a cross (Christianity), a star and crescent (Islam). This is a visual representation of the Baha'i teaching of the underlying unity of religion.

perspective and is therefore relative to that viewpoint. No statements of an absolute truth can be made. All concepts are merely perspectives on the truth, each being correct from its own viewpoint. This represents a cognitive relativism.

This mode of thinking arose in the Madhyamika school that was founded by Nagarjuna in India in about the second century CE. Although it is not now a major sect of Buddhism, it is of great importance because much of Mahayana Buddhism has its philosophical basis in the teachings of this school. This mode of thought also occurs in the Baha'i Faith as one way of explaining the unity underlying the diversity of religion in the world (for a lengthier exposition of both Madhyamika and Baha'i thought, see pp. 195–9).

Just as we have seen that elements of both theistic and non-theistic thought occur universally, so too can elements of relativistic thought be found among some writers in other religions. Apart from the thought of Nagarjuna in Buddhism described above, the concept of the 'God created in the faiths' of Ibn al-'Arabi, the Muslim mystic, has an implication of relativism in it. Ibn al-'Arabi proposed that each person has a certain aptitude and capacity for 'seeing' God and that God therefore appears to him or her in accordance with that capacity. On a wider scale, he saw the historical religions as the limited and particular ways of worshipping the Absolute.[16] There are also similarities between Baha'i relativism and the position put forward by the Christian scholar, John Hick. He asserts that the differences in the descriptions of the Absolute/God in the various religions are due to differing cultural influences and different modes of cognition (see also pp. 72–3).[17]

The relativistic perspective, of course, accepts both monism and theism. It also contains within it an explanation for the fact that, as described above, every world religion has both theistic and monistic expression. Relativism holds that the expressions of theism and monism are due to the varying types of mind perceiving reality in different ways. Therefore, clearly, if a religion is to have universal appeal and thus become a world religion, it must satisfy these varying types of mind by including both theistic and monistic elements.

With regard to the concepts discussed in the previous sections of this chapter, the relativistic Baha'i position accepts, as may be expected, aspects of both the theistic and non-theistic views of suffering, evil, and salvation. The salvation or liberation brought by the founders of the world religions is seen, from the Baha'i viewpoint, as having a twofold effect. It both liberates human beings from a state of ignorance at the personal level and leads humanity to a social salvation (peace and unity). The latter facilitates the striving of human beings for the former and vice versa.[18] Salvation or liberation is regarded more as a process than a defined state in which one either is or is not. The condition that occurs after death is not capable of being described. It can only be partially appreciated by the use of analogies, such as that of the world of the embryo in relation to our world (an analogy of our state of preparing ourselves for, but being ignorant of, what occurs after death: see p. 237).

In contrast to theistic and monistic religions, the Baha'i Faith has very few fixed rituals. This allows a great deal of flexibility to adopt religious practices that are in accordance with the preferences of the individual believer. Both prayer and meditation are daily personal obligations.

As regards concepts of time and space, the relativistic viewpoint is that both are matters which 'vary by reason of the divergences in men's thoughts and opinions.'[19] In the Baha'i view, cycles of progress and decline affect all aspects of human activity and religion is no exception. Overall, though, there is a general progress and development of human social life. When, therefore, a religion has gone into decline and its teachings no longer suit the present stage in human social development, a new religion arises. The Baha'i concept thus presents elements of both linear progression and cyclicality; one may therefore describe it as a spiral.

Chinese and Japanese Religion

Some special words must be said about Chinese and Japanese religion as these religious systems present some aspects that are not found elsewhere and require separate attention. In particular, we must note the syncretic nature of both systems. They have the ability to bring together elements from widely differing religious traditions and to synthesize these into an amalgam. This amalgam is itself not a single entity but differs in various parts of each country and even among different families living in the same region.

In China, there is a foundation of folk religion, which consists of several elements: various deities and legendary heroes who are venerated or worshipped, veneration and worship of ancestors, fortune-telling, magic and sorcery. Life-cycle rites (marking birth, puberty, marriage and death) as well as calendrical festivals play an important part in Chinese life. On this foundation, several 'higher', more philosophical elements are placed.

Taoism is said to have been founded by Lao-Tzu, a figure about whom very little is certain historically. He may have lived in about the third century BCE. Taoism states that the individual should live according to the underlying order of the universe (the Tao). Taoist teachings direct the individual to find his or her essential nature and comply with its impulses. In this way the individual is at one with the Tao and acquires a mystical power (*te*). In interaction with the folk religion, Taoism developed as a way of trying to achieve immortality or paranormal powers through alchemy, magical incantations or exercises. Taoism also incorporated a number of other systems of thought, such as the Yin-Yang, Five-Element school.

Confucius (c.551–479 BCE) taught a practical, ethical system. He claimed no religious source for his teaching, but merely said that he was restoring an ancient moral system that had fallen into decay. His teachings were centred on the virtues of kindness, faithfulness, uprightness, decorum, wisdom and altruism. Reverence for one's parents and duty and obedience to the state formed a major part of his teaching. Confucius also had much to say about the virtues of a good ruler and the way that society should be ordered.

Buddhism came gradually to China from about the first century CE onwards, although it was not until at least the fifth century that reliable translations and scholarly study were being carried out in China. Buddhism complemented existing Chinese thought by adding a religious dimension related to the explanation of suffering and the path to liberation. Buddhist thought also added to Chinese metaphysics. This, together with the

CHINESE RELIGION: A family praying and offering gifts to their ancestors at a home shrine, Taiwan

Boys participating in a ceremony to honour Confucius at a Chinese Temple in Taiwan

inevitable interaction with folk religion and Taoism, eventually led to a number of Chinese Buddhist developments. These include several schools which crossed to Japan and became prominent there also, including the Ch'an school, which in Japan became Zen and emphasized sudden enlightenment, and the Ching-t'u or Pure Land schools that venerate Amitabha (or Amida) Buddha.

Chinese religion consists of an amalgam of these different strands. Some may emphasize the philosophical elements, some the religious and some the magical. The same person may follow Confucian principles at home, celebrate Taoist festivals, and be buried according to Buddhist rites. An individual may discuss Buddhist philosophy but interact with others according to Confucian norms.

Japanese religion is similarly an amalgam of Japanese traditional religion (Shinto) and Buddhism, together with important additions from Christianity and Confucianism. Shinto is a highly complex phenomenon. It operates as a national religion for Japan, with the Emperor as the chief Shinto priest, as a community religion centred on Shinto shrines, and as a family or clan religion for Japanese families. To this picture, Confucian thought about individual and social morality was added from about the fifth century CE and the various Buddhist schools were introduced into Japan in

A SHINTO SHRINE: This is a typical entrance to a Japanese Shinto shrine. The pattern has become the symbol of Shinto.

stages, beginning in 538 or 552. Christianity arrived in 1549, although it was intensely persecuted during the sixteenth and seventeenth centuries. A typical family may use Shinto rituals to celebrate a birth and Buddhist rituals for a death. Many Japanese couples marry in a Christian church but do not consider themselves Christians.

With regard to the difference between monism and theism, Chinese and Japanese religion exhibit both types. Philosophical Taoism and many Buddhist sects are non-theistic in nature and most have some concept of an impersonal Absolute Reality, the Tao or Dharma. Much of Chinese and Japanese folk religion and such Buddhist sects as the Pure Land schools are, however, religions of love and worship, and are thus more akin to theistic religion. In Chinese temples, statues of various heavenly deities are worshipped and, similarly, *kami* (divinities or spirits) are worshipped in Japanese shrines. In Pure Land Buddhism, Amitabha (Amida) Buddha is raised to the status of a god and venerated.

One useful way of dividing Chinese and Japanese religion is to use the Japanese distinction between *jiriki* (self-power) and *tariki* (other power). *Jiriki* refers to those religions that encourage self-reliance. The individual must save himself or herself. The saying of the Buddha, 'Work out your own salvation' is much emphasized in these groups. Those who wish for salvation must, in the Buddhist tradition, leave their home life, become monks and practise the path of meditation and self-discipline in order to reach their goal. *Tariki* refers to the reliance on the grace of a power that is outside oneself in order to achieve salvation. The dependence on the grace of God among Japanese Christians or the dependence on the grace of Amitabha Buddha in the Pure Land sects of Buddhism are examples of this.

Primal Religions

Finally, in surveying the religions of the world, it is necessary to look briefly at the central concepts in primal religions. The wealth of variety of religious manifestations among primal peoples makes anything more than a few generalizations about this subject difficult, however.

In their conceptions of the supernatural, the primal religions can also be thought of as falling, in a more limited way, into the division of theism and monism described above. Primal religions can be considered to have two concepts of the supernatural that are like two poles of a continuum.

At one pole, which is analogous to the theistic religions described earlier, there are the personal concepts of supernatural power. These involve the concepts of deities such as are found in African religions, for example. These have the same characteristics as human beings (they can be pleased or angry; they can will some event to occur, etc.). There is also often a concept of a supreme deity (see also pp. 269–70). The characteristic religious activity here is that of propitiation of the gods by gifts and sacrifices.

At the other pole, which is analogous to the monistic religions, are the impersonal concepts of supernatural power. Examples of this include the concept of *mana* in Polynesian and Micronesian religion, *kami* in Japan, and similar concepts among Native Americans. These involve the belief in the existence of power that can be obtained, or a state that can be achieved, by a human being, which then enables that human being to have power over others or over nature. This type of power can be amassed and controlled by humans. It may even be bought and sold, lost, stolen or given to others. This impersonal concept of supernatural power often exists in religious systems that also have concepts of supernatural beings. The difference, however, lies in the fact that the power is not an inherent attribute of the supernatural beings. Their superiority to humans comes through their more abundant possession of, or their superior knowledge of how to use, this impersonal power. The characteristic religious activity in these religions is acquisition of the knowledge of how to obtain and use this power. In some societies, where the power is considered dangerous for ordinary human beings and can only be withstood by kings or priests, there is also an extensive system of taboos. Interestingly, this type of religious phenomenon, analogous to the monistic religions, remained unrecognized by Western anthropologists and observers for a long time, because of their theistic preconceptions of what a religion should be.[20]

Almost every conceivable object has at one time been considered sacred or invested with supernatural qualities by some group in the world, but the tendency is to select objects that are unusual in appearance. Holy words or symbols drawn on a piece of paper and worn around the neck or arm as an amulet, certain words said or chanted repeatedly as part of a ritual, or a particular form of art, song, or dance are also often considered sacred. Closely associated with the sense of some objects being sacred or supernatural is the sense that such objects are taboo. Events that are mysterious and transforming are also often associated with taboos: examples include death, childbirth, and menstruation.

SACRED OBJECTS: Representation of ancestral effigies used in ancestor worship. a) From the Bukundu tribe in Africa. b) From Irian Jaya. The wooden head is scooped out and the skull of the ancestor is dug up and inserted in this cavity – a graphic representation of the idea of a spirit dwelling within the effigy.

Religious practices in primal religions include magic, divination, prayer and various rituals for propitiating deities or spirits and expiating evil deeds. Propitiation is practised particularly where there is a wish to control natural phenomena such as the rain or wind. Practices such as offering the deities the first products of a seasonal crop, a hunt, or the first-born of domesticated animals are common. Historically, human sacrifice was the ultimate propitiation and was a widespread phenomenon. Rites of passage and rites of purification form a large part of the religious repertoire of many tribal and traditional peoples.

In primal religions, the religious specialist is most commonly of the type known variously as witch doctor, shaman or medicine man. These individuals are often picked out in childhood because of some unusual trait that they possess. They tend to be practitioners of magic and healers, and they often achieve altered states of consciousness in the performance of their religious functions. Many have visions and fall into trance states. The other type of religious specialist may be called a priest. These officiate over the rituals of a society or tribe. They tend to be the custodians of tribal lore and cosmology. Such individuals are usually given extensive training to fulfil their role.

Following the colonization of large parts of the world by the European powers mainly in the nineteenth century, religious movements began to arise among native peoples as expressions of their frustration and demoralization. A classic example of this type of movement is the phenomenon of cargo cults in Melanesia. Numerous such movements have arisen from about the middle of the nineteenth century onwards. They all share the common feature of a leader proclaiming the miraculous imminent arrival by air or sea of 'cargo', a shipment of the goods possessed by white people, which will be freely available to the followers of the movement. They usually also have a strong anti-colonial, xenophobic

RELIGIOUS SPECIALISTS: Representation of a tribal witch doctor (shaman or medicine man) from the Lower Congo performing a ritual. A poisonous drink (*kaske* or *kassa*, made from the bark of a tree) is given to the man accused of witchcraft. If he vomits it, he is innocent.

element to their teaching. (On the continuing influence of primal religions, see pp. 399–403, 506–8).

EXAMPLES OF PRACTICES IN PRIMAL RELIGIONS

DIVINATION AMONG THE CHIPPEWA OF THE MID-WEST OF THE UNITED STATES

A medicine man may be called on, day or night, to discover the cause and the cure of some internal disease. The sick man is placed on a mat outside the small wigwam in which the medicine man is exercising his powers. All during the ceremony someone on the outside beats the drum. It is absolutely necessary that the wigwam sway back and forth, for, without it, the procedure is ineffective. As soon as the tipi [wigwam] shakes – which indicates that the spirits are in the wigwam – the medicine man asks the persons on the outside who are interested in the sick man what they wish to know. The spirits on the inside answer. One can hear them talking but only the man in the wigwam usually understands the language, for only occasionally do the spirits speak Chippewa. The voices sound like those of a large crowd. It's these spirits that make the wigwam sway . . . Long ago the swaying was so violent that the wigwam touched the ground from side to side. If many spirits come into the wigwam, the medicine man comes out tired and weak. In the early days the medicine man performed ceremonies similar to the ones above to discover whether it was safe to break camp. (Lac Courte Orielle interpreter, quoted in Hilger, *Chippewa Child Life*, pp. 77–8)

INITIATION RITUAL AMONG THE HOPI OF THE SOUTH-WEST UNITED STATES

> The two Ho Katchinas take a position on the east and west side of a large sand mosaic, the Hahai-i at its southeast corner, the latter holding a supply of whips. The children tremble and some begin to cry and to scream. The Ho Katchinas keep up their grunting, howling, rattling, trampling and brandishing of their yucca whips. All at once someone places a candidate on the sand mosaic . . . and one of the Katchinas whips the little victim quite severely . . . When one child has been flogged another one is at once brought forward . . . Some of the children go through the process with set teeth and without flinching, others squirm, try to jump away and scream . . .

In the course of the ceremony the children are admonished to tell no one what they have seen and heard under threat of punishment . . . The children do not as yet know that the kachinas are men. This revelation is reserved for the last night of the Bean Dance, when the initiates see the kachina dancers perform without their masks. The initiation is then complete.

The initiation changes the status of the boy in several respects. His newly gained knowledge about the kachinas, together with the fact that he has passed through the ordeal which children dread, act to make him feel much less like a child and more like a man. Prior to initiaiton, he cannot enter the kivas [ceremonial buildings] as men do . . . After initiation, he can even work and sleep in the kiva. The girl's status seems to be changed less than is the boy's. At no time, even as a woman, do the privileges of the kiva belong to her. (Dennis, *The Hopi Child*, pp. 72–4; the first paragraph is quoted from H. R. Voth)

THE USE OF MAGIC TO CONTROL THE DANGERS OF NATURE AMONG THE LANGO OF CENTRAL AFRICA
The Lango of Central Africa always consult the omens before going on a journey. Should these predict danger from a lion, he moulds three clay figures. One represents a man lying dead and to this he gives the name of a personal enemy; the second represents his enemy's wife with her head shaved for mourning; the third is a lion which is in the act of devouring the man. He can now go on his journey happy in the thought that he has averted danger from himself. (Lewis, *Anthropology Made Easy*, p. 160)

THE MODERN WORLD

The modern world has produced much cross-fertilization of ideas and even of practices. Migrations from the Muslim countries, India, and East Asia to Europe and North America have resulted in the emergence there of large communities of people of religions other than Christianity. At the same time, Christianity has spread to every corner of the world through a well-organized and well-financed missionary effort. Primal religions, in particular, have come under increasing pressure as a result of this missionary activity, with many of their number being converted. Dialogue and inter-faith groups increase the extent to which cross-fertilization occurs.

Other, more subtle, cross-fertilizations have also occurred. Buddhism in South and South-East Asia was revived by Europeans who took an interest in that religion from the late nineteenth century onwards. The coming of the religions of the East, with their techniques of meditation, to Europe and North America has both sparked a revival of interest in the Christian mystical tradition and given strength to the fundamentalist backlash. Religions that migrate take on new forms in their new destinations. Christianity, although it went to India as a missionary religion, has there taken on many of the features of Hinduism. Buddhism in Europe has become detached from many of the traditional cultural practices of its homeland and is now very much more of an intellectual, philosophical movement.

Typical of the ethos of modernity, however, is the large number of syncretistic cults and new religious movements that have arisen. Cults in Japan, for example, will frequently combine elements of Buddhism, Shinto, Christianity, Confucianism and even Hinduism.

Further Reading

This chapter takes further the approach advocated by Zaehner in *The Concise Encyclopaedia of Living Faiths*, pp. xiv–xvii. For the differences between Western and Eastern religion, see also W. L. King, *Introduction to Religion*, pp. 187–218 and Copleston, *On the History of Philosophy*, pp. 66–79. Most of the concepts touched on briefly in this chapter are dealt with in more detail in the rest of the book, and suggested further reading for these topics can be found at the end of the relevant chapters. On Chinese religion, see Thompson, *Chinese Religion*. On Japanese religion, see Kitagawa, *On Understanding Japanese Religion*. On primal religion, see Norbeck, *Religion in Primitive Society*.

3

Theories of Religion

Almost every great philosopher and social scientist has had something to say about religion – about its origins, its social function or its structures. It is clearly impossible therefore to describe all of these theories. In this chapter, I shall concentrate on a small number of those whose writings focus on religion and whose ideas are influential today in the formation of ideas about religion. I shall not have space to deal with those who treat religion as a side issue to their main line of argument, as Marx does for example. Some of what follow are theories about religion itself while others are theoretical approaches to the study of religion. However, a theoretical approach to the study of religion will usually presuppose or imply a theory of the nature of religion. Therefore, the two are not clearly distinct and will be dealt with together in this chapter. Various typologies of religious groups that have been suggested are also examined in this chapter. Finally, we shall look at one aspect of the debate regarding the proper approach to religious studies.

As mentioned in the Introduction, it is useful to view religion from a multi-disciplinary approach. The different theories of religion that we shall be exploring in this chapter arise from these different disciplines. They therefore reflect, to an extent, the problem of the current fragmented approach to the study of religion. Not all of these theories are, however, rivals: some are looking at different aspects of religion from others, while some are looking at different types of religion from others. Thus, for example, anthropological theories of religion tend to relate to local tribal religions. They are often concerned with explaining phenomena such as totemism, since these are the types of manifestations of religion with which an anthropologist comes into contact. Such theories may or may not have any relevance to the major world religions. Similarly, there is no inherent reason why a sociological and a philosophical theory of religion should be mutually exclusive.

Sociological and Anthropological Theories

Religious studies is a relatively new academic field. Previously, and to a large extent still, much of the academic study of religion was undertaken under several different academic disciplines. Two disciplines that have been much concerned with observing and analysing religion from the nineteenth century onwards are sociology and anthropology. Several theories have emerged from these studies.

Functionalism

Functionalism is a theory that is bound up with the view that all phenomena in a system are interrelated. A change in one element of the system will, therefore, have consequences for all other elements in the system. Thus, according to this viewpoint, religion may be understood adequately by treating it in terms of its social function – its objective consequence for the social system of which it is part. Functionalism is thus based on an organic analogy – that every part of society plays some role in the social life of the community, in the same way that an organ plays a part in the life of an organism. The role of the scholar is to determine and describe the function that each part performs to enable the smooth and efficient operation of the whole.

The theory of functionalism was developed by Emile Durkheim (1858–1917) in explicit opposition to psychological theories that sought to explain religion in terms of factors relating to the individual. For Durkheim, religion was a social phenomenon and the explanation of it had to be sought at the social level. He considered that the critical social function of religion was to act as both a glue and a lubricant to the social process. It is a glue in the sense that it binds the individual firmly to the society. It is a lubricant in that, by providing legitimation and authority for the social structure and the moral order, it facilitates the smooth functioning of society.

Emile Durkheim (1858–1917), functionalism

In his principal book, *The Elementary Forms of the Religious Life* (1912), Durkheim wrote that the crucial factor in the social functioning of religion was its division of the world into the *sacred* and the *profane*. Religion deals with sacred things – 'things set apart and forbidden' (p. 47). Therefore, Durkheim considered ritual at least as important as beliefs in the social functioning of religion. Ritual emphasizes and reinforces the dependence of the individual on society. By thus creating a separate area of life with special properties and powers, religion establishes the authority with which to reinforce the moral dictates of society. In effect, religion acts as the mechanism for the imposition of the society's authority.

This leads us on to the most radical aspect of Durkheim's theories. Many anthropologists thought that humanity's sense of awe at the forces of nature was the origin of the concept of gods. Durkheim, however, asserted that the sense of something transcendent or supernatural arose out of our

DURKHEIM

The totem is before all a symbol, a material expression of something else. But of what? . . . It is evident that it expresses and symbolises two different sorts of things. In the first place, it is the outward and visible form of what we have called the totemic principle or god. But it is also the symbol of the determined society called the clan. It is its flag; it is the sign by which each clan distinguishes itself from the others, the visible mark of its personality, a mark borne by everything which is a part of the clan under any title whatsoever, men, beasts or things. So if it is at once the symbol of the god and of the society, is that not because the god and the society are only one? How could the emblem of the group have been able to become the figure of this quasi-divinity, if the group and the divinity were two distinct realities? The god of the clan, the totemic principle, can therefore be nothing else than the clan itself, personified and represented to the imagination under the visible form of the animal or vegetable which serves as totem. (Durkheim, *The Elementary Forms of the Religious Life*, p. 206)

experience of society – the fact that a social group has a living reality independent of the individuals that compose it. This reality may be experienced most intensively when the social group gathers to perform a ritual. Thus the idea of God or a god arose as a secondary phenomenon and is in effect the embodiment of the social entity. In other words, by worshipping God or a god, human beings are really worshipping (and hence reaffirming their commitment to) society (pp. 206, 226).

Although himself an atheist, Durkheim denied that he was trying to invalidate religion. Indeed, he considered that all religions 'are true in their own fashion; all answer, though in different ways, to the given conditions of human existence' (p. 3).

Later functionalists included the anthropologist, Bronislaw Malinowski (1884–1942). In his principal book, *Magic, Science and Religion and Other Essays* (1948), he wrote that social phenomena such as religion fulfil a function in relation to human psychological needs. In the case of religion, this function is to provide psychological safeguards against the fear of death and thus give human beings the feeling of mastery over their fate.

Another anthropologist, A. R. Radcliffe-Brown (1881–1955) concentrated on a social structural approach (not to be confused with structuralism: see the following section). In his book *Structure and Function in Primitive Society* (1952), he analysed the structural pattern of societies with regard to their overall cohesiveness and functioning. With particular reference to religion, he was interested in the contribution that it made to the formation and maintenance of social order.

Talcott Parsons (1902–78) rejected, in part, Durkheim's analysis of social structures. In works such as *Essays in Sociological Theory* (1944), Parsons described the main function of religion as being the creation of cultural values, beliefs and symbols. He considered that patterns of culture operate in varying degrees of independence from social structure and cannot be reduced to the latter, as Durkheim tends to. This approach developed into a major trend in anthropology, often called symbolist, associated with Mary Douglas and Victor Turner. According to this view, ritual action and religious belief are to be understood as forms of symbolic statement about the social order. They are expressive behaviour (rather than explanatory or intellectual activities).

Criticisms of the Functionalist Position. Functionalism has been criticized on several points. It has, for example, been pointed out that functionalists have difficulty coping with the phenomenon of secularization. If religion has a vital function in society, then why has society moved towards greater secularization? Some functionalists argue that the functions of religion survive the process of secularization. They merely transfer to such ideologies as nationalism and communism. This, however, brings us on to another weakness of functionalist theory in relation to religion. It has been argued that functionalism has confused two separate issues. Certainly the integrative aspects of religion are vital to society; but the question is whether what is indispensable is religion itself, or merely the function of religion (i.e. social cohesion).

Furthermore, functionalists tend to view society as homogeneous. There seems little recognition of the fact that almost all societies have divisions based on sex, class or ethnicity and that one section of society may use religion as a tool for the domination of other sections. Functionalists have also been criticized for being ahistorical (believing that the functioning of a society can be understood just by examining its present, without any need to refer to its past). Inherent in the approach of most functionalists is, moreover, a belief that conclusions reached from the study of primal societies can be transposed to developed societies. In other words, they assume that religion performs the same function in every society but that this function is more transparent in primal societies, and thus more accessible to investigation. This is, at the very least, a questionable assumption.

A number of further criticisms attach to Durkheim's work in particular. His division of the world into sacred and profane is breached in many social situations, such as illness, which often involves responses that have elements of both the sacred and profane. Durkheim also stressed the function of religion in general and ritual in particular as a means of integrating the individual in society. In some tribal groups such as Australian aborigines, however, clans meet together for ritual purposes but may live in separate communities with other clans. What then would be the point of reaffirming, through ritual, the group solidarity of a group that does not in fact live together as a social unit?

Structuralism

In publications such as *Structural Anthropology* (2 volumes, 1963, 1973) and *Introduction to a Science of Mythology* (4 volumes, 1969–81), Claude Lévi-Strauss (1908–) defined the outlines of structuralism. The structuralist approach to religion involves trying to establish the meaning of religious phenomena. 'Meaning' in this context, however, does not signify such simple explanatory sentences as: 'Bread and wine in the Christian Mass signify the body and blood of Christ.' Rather, the enterprise of the structuralist involves trying to locate a deeper meaning behind the conscious thoughts in the mind of the participant. Structuralism, then, denies that our immediate experience of the world is a valid starting point for investigations (that is, it rejects empiricism). Behind or beyond the visible interrelations of humanity lie structures that determine the form of what we observe. It is these structures that the structuralist is attempting to uncover. They are the structures of thought itself – in particular, the way in which language prefigures our processes of thinking. All social phenomena, including religion, are therefore considered to be manifestations of the innate structures of the human mind.

LÉVI-STRAUSS

The unconscious activity of the mind consists in imposing forms upon content, and if these forms are fundamentally the same for all minds – ancient and modern, primitive and civilized – it is necessary and sufficient to grasp the unconscious structure underlying each institution and each custom, in order to obtain a principle of interpretation valid for other institutions. (Lévi-Strauss, *Structural Anthropology*, quoted in Morris, *Anthropological Studies of Religion*, p. 268)

The structuralist is in opposition to the empiricist leanings of most functionalists. The latter consider that the starting point of all enquiries is the facts and that these can be apprehended in a relatively pure form. They are thus reliable and true representations of 'reality'. The structuralist casts doubt on these basic empirical assumptions. There are no such things as facts that can be taken as given. The mere apprehension of 'facts' involves the process of ordering and organizing them in accordance with the pre-set structures of the human mind. Thus, what is apprehended is not pure facts but interpretations.

To the structuralist, all rituals, religious laws and myths can be analysed in a way that reveals the workings of the mind or minds that have produced or are enacting them. For example, most traditional anthropological and sociological approaches to a religious symbol would involve an analysis of its cultural context or subjective meaning. The structuralist, however, will try to determine the meaning of a symbol from its position within a pattern of relationships. The patterns that

Table 3.1 Structural Analysis by Lévi-Strauss of Three Myths Regarding the Origins of Tobacco

Lévi-Strauss here undertakes the analysis of three myths from different South American tribes relating to the origin of the tobacco plant. He analyses these myths and demonstrates the structural similarities as follows (derived from The Raw and the Cooked, *pp. 99–104)*

TOBA-PILAGA MYTH AND TERENO MYTH	BORORO MYTH
A husband (affinal relationship)	A mother (blood relationship)
has a wife (jaguar).	has a son (snake).
She is destructive through the mouth	She is protective through the vagina
of her husband who has climbed a tree	of her son who has climbed a tree
looking for animals (birds)	looking for vegetable food (fruit)
that the wife ought not to eat (but does).	that the mother ought to eat (but does not).
Disjunction through the agency of the husband.	Disjunction through the agency of the mother.
Woman killed by affines (= children, in the case of patrilineal descent).	Son killed by relatives (= maternal uncles, in the case of matrilineal descent).

↘ Burning of the victim; origin of tobacco. ↙

structuralists find are usually based on paired oppositions of a fairly simple kind. Thus a phenomenon may be: animate/inanimate, male/female, human/inhuman, symmetrical/asymmetrical, and so on. Any cultural phenomenon can be placed at some point on such a matrix. The structuralist is thus looking at relationships among relationships.

These paired oppositions are partly the creation of our language. We think, for example, of day and night as a sharp discontinuity, precisely because our language encourages us to think thus. In fact, however, our experience tells us that there is continuity between the two; there is a period at dusk and dawn that is neither quite day nor quite night. The structuralist argues that because we think in terms of these bipolar discontinuities, this is reflected in the social world and culture that we build up as a result of our thought processes.

Claude Lévi-Strauss (1908–), structuralism

Some structuralists have indeed focused on this question of discontinuity as the key to understanding religion. They argue that religious phenomena often act as a threshold between two non-sacred, discontinuous states. By acting as the interface between these two states, religion helps to preserve the perceived discontinuity. Religious rites of passage are an obvious example of this phenomenon. They act to preserve perceived discontinuities: between childhood and adulthood, the single and married state, the married state and widowhood, and so on. Religious festivals may mark out the calendar into discontinuous units.

Criticisms of Structuralism. Structuralists have been criticized for the narrowness of their approach. By concentrating on the structure of the individual mind, the structuralist, in effect, denies the importance of society and of history.

There is some vagueness in the works of Lévi-Strauss as to the exact nature of the unconscious structures that he is attempting to uncover. Are they culturally specific classifications or socio-economic relationships masked by myth and symbolism? This leads on to a number of other questions. Can it really be that human culture is only a projection or transformation of innate structures in the human mind? Lévi-Strauss himself creates wide-ranging cross-cultural analyses which are based on such an assumption. However, many have raised doubts about such an exercise: surely geographical, climatic, economic and other factors must have some bearing on the structures and models in the human mind, and hence on culture.

It is difficult to see how such questions can ever be answered satisfactorily, and so the question is raised of the validity of the approach. A structuralist analysis can never be shown to be true in any objective sense. It remains a rather subjective viewpoint and structuralist interpretations are often criticized for being arbitrary. Some find that much of what is presented as a result of a structuralist analysis is no more than one would have thought intuitively anyway. However, others argue that even this is worthwhile as it provides a rational framework for intuition and common sense. Moreover, structuralist analyses occasionally throw up unexpected relationships that would not have been seen by other methods of analysis.

Historical/Interpretative Sociology

Both functionalism and structuralism are criticized for being ahistorical in their approach. Max Weber (1864–1920) initiated a different direction in the sociology of religion by concentrating on the historical process of the development of religion. He considered that religion had evolved through three stages.

The first stage, naturalistic religion, is concerned primarily with magic. The magician or shaman tries to control the powers of nature (such as rain, health and fertility) through magic. He is considered to be endowed with special powers that enable him to do this. The name that Weber gave to this state was 'charisma'.

In the second stage, animistic religion, ideas of gods and spirits develop. Religious activity is transformed from magic, which is a direct attempt to

Max Weber (1864–1920), sociology, history of religion

manipulate the forces of nature, into ritual, which is a symbolic activity. Two types of religious professionals arise during this phase: priests, who represent the rationalization and organization of religion, and prophets, who continue the charismatic mode by claiming the authority of personal revelation. The former hold office within a particular social order and are committed to maintaining the stability of that; the latter are agents of social discontinuity and change. In this second stage, two main groups emerge within religious communities. These differ in the way that they think of salvation: the first is a mystic–contemplative group that seeks to flee from the world and stresses a cessation of thought leading to a union with Absolute Reality; the second is a world-denying, ascetic group that rejects the world and therefore seeks to struggle with it and control it.

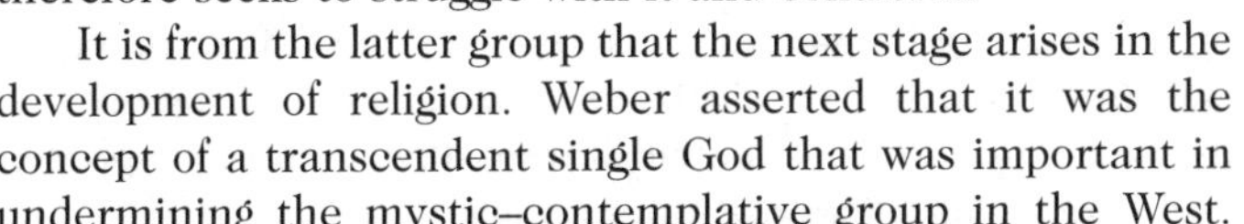

It is from the latter group that the next stage arises in the development of religion. Weber asserted that it was the concept of a transcendent single God that was important in undermining the mystic–contemplative group in the West. This was because any thought of union with such a God became blasphemous. This ascetic outlook came to the fore in the Protestantism that arose as a consequence of the Reformation. Previously, asceticism had been expressed through the monastic tradition. Now, the Protestant sects began to demand a world-denying ethic of everyone. In addition, the belief in predestination among Protestant sects was the final stage in the elimination of magic from religion. If God has already decided the fate of every human being, there is no point in trying to avert one's fate by magic. The elements of magic, sentiment and tradition in religion are supplanted by explicit, rational rules and systematic procedures. This takes the process of the rationalization of religion to a new and higher level. It establishes religion on the basis of what Weber called 'legal–rational authority'.

The most famous of Weber's works, *The Protestant Ethic and the Spirit of Capitalism* (1930), shows how the world-denying ethic induced by Protestantism led to the accumulation of capital among the wealthy (since money was not spent in indulging oneself). At the same time, the Protestant concept of a 'calling' (a task set for the individual by God) led to a workforce which did work for its own sake. The combination of these and other factors predisposed Protestant Europe to become the cradle of modern capitalism.

Thus, Weber saw the evolution of religion as a process of gradual rationalization. In animistic religions, life is filled with encounters with spirits or gods that inhabit every tree or rock or other natural phenomenon. Typically, the whole of life is immersed in rituals related to these spirits and gods, to such an extent that people do not consider that there is a separate religious element in their lives. Orgiastic or emotive rites have a powerful but temporary effect on individuals, but there is little effect on the individual's ethical behaviour. Rationalization leads to the progressive elimination of magical, ritual and charismatic elements at the centre of religion and their replacement by a situation in which the whole of an individual's life is lived within an ethical and rational framework determined by religion. The multitude of spirits and gods is reduced to a single God or a few gods or spiritual realities that stand apart from or above the little things in life with which the spirits of traditional religion are concerned. According to Weber's argument, animistic religion answers the great questions of life (What is the meaning of life? Why is there suffering?) in ways that are specific to an individual case: my child is ill because someone cast a bad spell upon her. Rationalized religion tends to answer these questions in general terms: evil and suffering occur because of the existence of the Devil or the yin side of the Tao. The religious part of life in rationalized religion is restricted to fewer specific occasions rather than imbuing the whole of life. Rationalization results in a demystification of life and a 'disenchantment' of the world. There is also a tendency in this process towards the adoption of a purely utilitarian, instrumental approach towards the natural world and towards other people.

Durkheim, as noted above, tended to see society as a homogeneous entity. Weber, on the other hand, laid a great deal of stress on what he considered to be the characteristic religious attitudes of different groupings within society. The peasantry, he maintained, for example, always inclined towards magic, while the lower-middle-classes preferred rational, ethical religion of the congregational type. Weber linked social deprivation with an increased susceptibility to the emergence of a world-changing prophet. He also considered that the various world religions were much influenced by those who were its main propagators. These 'primary carriers', as he called them, often set the ethos for much of the rest of the religion. For Islam, the 'primary carrier' was the world-conquering warrior; for Buddhism it was the mendicant wandering monk; for Christianity, it was the itinerant journeyman.

Weber commented on many other matters in his wide-ranging studies on religion (see, for example, the part of his uncompleted work *Wirtschaft und Gesellschaft* that has been translated under the title *The Sociology of Religion*). He noted a tendency for a popular religion to arise among the masses vis-à-vis the official religion. The popular religion usually focuses on magic and animism; the official religion emphasizes rational–legal norms. He was also much concerned with the question of theodicy, the way that religions explain the existence of suffering and evil in the world.

CRITICISMS OF HISTORICAL SOCIOLOGY. It is difficult to find evidence for Weber's division of the evolution of religion into 'ideal type' stages. There is no society in the world today in Weber's theoretical first stage of pre-animistic magic; nor is there any evidence that it has ever existed in any society. Even the most primitive tribal groups have developed notions

WEBER

Only ascetic Protestantism completely eliminated magic and the supernatural quest for salvation, of which the highest form was intellectualist, contemplative illumination. It alone created the religious motivation for seeking salvation primarily through immersion in one's worldly vocation (*Beruf*). This Protestant stress upon the methodically rationalized fulfillment of one's vocational responsibility was diametrically opposite to Hinduism's strongly traditionalistic concept of vocations. For the various popular religions of Asia, in contrast to ascetic Protestantism, the world remained a great enchanted garden, in which the practical way to orient oneself, or find security in this world or the next, was to revere or coerce the spirits and seek salvation through ritualistic, idolatrous, or sacramental procedures. No path led from the magical religiosity of the non-intellectual classes of Asia to a rational, methodical control of life. Nor did any path lead to that methodical control from the world-accommodation of Confucianism, from the world-rejection of Buddhism, from the world-conquest of Islam, or from the messianic expectations and economic pariah law of Judaism. (Weber, *The Sociology of Religion*, pp. 269–70)

about spirits and deities. Furthermore, most religions that are in Weber's theoretical second stage of religious evolution incorporate large elements of magic in their ritual and myths.

Weber's analysis of the rise of capitalism in Protestant societies has been much commented upon and criticized. Perhaps the most cogent criticism stems from the fact that we have witnessed the very successful adoption of capitalism by societies in East and South-East Asia. Yet these societies are also still very much attached to magical, traditional and mystical–contemplative forms of religion.

Weber was also somewhat arbitrary in his classification of religious phenomena. Since he was anxious to link the rise of capitalism to the Protestant West, he saw the order in a monastic society as being rational. But the high degree of order brought about by Confucian ethics or in Islamic society, he classified as traditional. Conversely, a large element of magic and traditionalism exists in Protestant ritual and religious history, if one cares to look for it.

Psychological Theories

The field of theoretical psychology that emerged at the end of the nineteenth century with the writings of Freud has historically always made the analysis and explanation of religion a central concern of its theories.

Sigmund Freud (1856–1939), analytical psychology

Analytical Freudian Psychology

Sigmund Freud (1856–1939) produced a very pessimistic view of religion in such works as *Totem and Taboo* (1913) and *The Future of an Illusion* (1928). He used his famous formulation of the Oedipus complex to trace the origins of religion. He postulated that, in the putative primitive society, the father, jealous of his growing sons, drove each of them away from the family as they reached a certain age. Then the sons banded together, returned, killed and ate the father (*Totem and Taboo*, pp. 141–5). They were filled with remorse (for they loved and admired their father also, remembering their need for his protection in their childhood) and guilt (because of their sexual desire for the mother). So the sons attempted to neutralize these emotions by substituting certain rites and moral edicts. Rites such as sacrifice and totemism commemorated the crime by ritually re-enacting it. Freud considered the Christian Eucharist, for example, to be such a commemoration. The institution of certain taboos against incest and endogamy that are found in almost every religion expresses the guilt felt at the patricide and the sexual desire for the mother. The guilt towards the slain father was further appeased by making the latter into a god, who is both loved and feared. The whole structure is then cloaked in the subconscious so as to hide its origins. It is given permanence through being endowed with an air of inviolable sanctity. This Oedipal complex, acting within the life-history of the individual, is responsible for the production of neuroses. Thus Freud drew a parallel between the processes that produce neuroses in the individual and the processes that produce religion in the social life of humanity.

The repressed wishes that lie in our unconscious find their way to the surface of consciousness eventually, according to Freud. But they emerge camouflaged as religious rituals and doctrines as well as religious wishes and actions. Because they are the products of repressed desires, their true source remains unapprehended by the religious person. The power and energy of religion, however, stems from the sheer pressure of repressed desires in the unconscious. Indeed, repressed desires become the main source of transcendent meaning in Freud's writings – almost a new metaphysics.

Freud also saw religion as a way of compensating for the sufferings and disappointments of life. However, Freud considered that there were other, more satisfactory, methods of compensation, such as art. He condemned religion as a compensatory mechanism, because it restricts choice and adaptation. Its technique is to depress the value of life and distort the picture of the real world, thus creating a delusional situation. Within this delusion, an individual may be spared a neurotic breakdown but at great cost to his or her mental and emotional development (see *Civilisation and*

FREUD

Its [religion's] technique consists in depressing the value of life and distorting the picture of the real world in a delusional manner – which presupposes an intimidation of the intelligence. At this price . . . religion succeeds in sparing many people an individual neurosis. But hardly anything else. (Freud in *Civilisation and its Discontents*, quoted in Morris, *Anthropological Studies of Religion*, p. 161)

its Discontents). Thus, Freud saw religion as a 'universal obsessional neurosis' (*The Future of an Illusion*, p. 39). Religion, Freud considered, is bad for humanity. It is a danger to society because it helps to perpetuate bad social institutions; it restricts critical thinking; and, by linking ethical norms to religious doctrines, it creates the dangerous likelihood that, when the doctrines are discredited, the ethical norms will be abandoned.

It hardly need be said that there is no evidence whatsoever for Freud's postulated course of Oedipal events in humanity's distant past. Indeed, anthropological evidence has been assembled to refute most of Freud's assertions. Nevertheless, this does not mean that we can ignore Freud. Freud's importance for the study of religion lies not so much with his theory of religion as with his uncovering of the realm of the unconscious and its mechanisms. Ever since the ideas of Freud became well known, students of humanity in general and of religion in particular have been left with the uneasy feeling that they are studying an illusion; that what we observe of human words and actions and what is recorded in the texts that we study are but shadows, distorted images, of the real causes of these phenomena lying in the unconscious. No longer can we be sure that such data as personal accounts of religious encounters, opinion polls, or religious art are exactly what they appear to be. All human activity now appears to be two-layered: an apparent, manifest, empirical content and a hidden, latent, psychological one.

Jungian Psychology

For a psychological theory that has a more positive approach to religion, we must turn to Carl Jung (1875–1961). To Freud's concepts of the conscious and unconscious mind, Jung, in works such as *Psychology and Religion* (1938) and 'Archetypes of the Collective Unconscious' (1934/1954) added a third concept: the collective unconscious. It is this last aspect of the mind that is, according to Jung, of particular importance for religion. Perhaps the best way of conceptualizing the collective unconscious is to draw a parallel with our human organs: for example, the arms, legs and kidneys. Just as any individual possesses these organs in a particular form that is the common inheritance of humanity as a whole, so there are psychological structures in the mind that are also part of this collective inheritance of humanity. This psychological inheritance acts as a primordial substratum

Carl Jung (1875–1961), analytical psychology

to our mental lives. It manifests itself in every instance of instinctual thought and behaviour and in the forms and categories that control these.

Within the collective unconscious, there exist a number of primordial archetypes or myths. These archetypes reflect the fundamental levels of human experience: examples include the wise old man, the earth mother, the mandala (magic circle), the hero, the divine child, and so on. From these archetypes in the collective unconscious there emerge all of the most powerful images and symbols that have motivated humanity, and in particular religious ones. This emergence may occur in dreams, myths, visions, religious symbolism and art. Freud saw these phenomena negatively, as the result of pathological, repressed, infantile sexual urges. Jung, however, regarded the unconscious motivation produced by these phenomena as a positive, healthy aspect of human life (although they also appear in pathological states such as neuroses). For Jung, this inner world of images and archetypes was just as real as the outer physical world. Indeed, in a sense it was more real since it casts its interpretations on the outer world. The outer world is only seen through the eyes of the inner world.

For Jung, religion could play a positive role in human life: 'Man positively needs general ideas and convictions that will give meaning to his life and enable him to find a place for himself in the universe.'[1] Religion thus acts as a form of therapy, explaining and reconciling human beings to the pains and suffering of the world.

CRITICISMS OF JUNGIAN THEORY. Some writers have stated that the whole of Jung's structure of archetypes in the collective unconscious is an unnecessary elaboration. After all, every human being goes through similar

JUNG'S CONCEPT OF THE COLLECTIVE UNCONSCIOUS

The collective unconscious contains the whole spiritual heritage of mankind's evolution, born anew in the brain structure of every individual. His conscious mind is an ephemeral phenomenon that accomplishes all provisional adaptations and orientations . . . The unconscious, on the other hand, is the source of the instinctual forces of the psyche and of the forms or categories that regulate them, namely the archetypes. All the most powerful ideas in history go back to archetypes. This is particularly true of religious ideas, but the central conceptions of science, philosophy and ethics are no exception to this rule . . . . For it is the function of consciousness not only to recognize and assimilate the external world through the gateway of the senses, but to translate into visible reality the world within us. ('The Structure of the Psyche', in *The Structure and Dynamics of the Psyche*, para 342, p. 158) experiences: being born, having a mother, viewing the natural cycle, living and dying under the sun and moon. It is not necessary to postulate a theory of archetypes in the collective unconscious to explain the universal existence of these images and symbols.

PHILOSOPHICAL AND HISTORICAL THEORIES

Philosophical approaches to the study of religion have ranged from those that attempt to pursue an objective study of the history of religion to those that are more empathic (that is, those that try to analyse religion in terms of its own categories and assumptions).

History of Religion

The exact methodology and limits of the academic discipline known as the 'history of religion' remain a matter of considerable discussion and disagreement. At its most fundamental level, it is the non-theological, non-normative commitment to the empirical task of uncovering the facts of religious history from the original sources. The basic historical methodology can be considered to consist of the following stages:

- examining the available data to establish the facts;
- induction from the facts to an explanatory or interpretative hypothesis;
- analysis of this hypothesis to explore its implications;
- checking the validity of these implications through assembling and examining further data.

In its wider meaning, the history of religion merges imperceptibly with the phenomenology of religion. Such writers as Mircea Eliade consider themselves as scholars in the field of the history of religion, despite their basically ahistorical method. Eliade's *Patterns in Comparative Religion* was, for example, originally published as *Traité d'histoire des religions (A Treatise on the History of Religions).*

CRITICISM OF THE METHODOLOGY OF HISTORY OF RELIGION. This methodology is so wide-ranging that it is difficult to find any criticism that would hold true of any more than a few of those engaged in the field. It is often criticized, at least in the way that some practise it, for being reductionist in its results and implications. Its empiricism is often linked to a methodological positivism (the concept that our study of religion should only concern itself with what is empirically observable) that has been much amended and criticized. One question that has been raised is whether we can regard the gathering of data as an uncontroversial, primary activity, following which hypotheses and theories can be built up. In fact, the collection of data is itself a theory-biased activity. In other words, each stage outlined above is largely predetermined by theoretical considerations.

One attempt to bypass this problem has been to adjust the principle of verifiability (that is, that to be meaningful, all statements must be empirically verified – or, at least, be capable of being verified) which is the usual criterion in positivism. As an alternative, Karl Popper (1902–94) suggested the principle of falsifiability (that statements are meaningful only if they are capable of being proved false).

Both verifiability and Popper's alternative, falsifiability, are, however, of limited usefulness in considering many religious phenomena. A statement such as: 'My sins are forgiven and I am saved', cannot be either verified or falsified. Therefore, according to 'scientific' methodology, it has no cognitive meaning. Yet few would doubt its intense meaningfulness to the person who makes it. By ruling such statements out of the arena of consideration, this approach leaves out large areas of the study of religion. An advocate of this method would respond that it is possible to study the impact of this statement historically and socially by this method.

The evaluation and interpretation of data is also not without problems. Religion deals with the human world and, as such, the data can often only be expressed in terms of probability rather than certainty. The evaluation of historical data involves interpretation and the construction of historical meaning. This, in turn, involves the use of evaluative criteria that are not deducible from the facts themselves. The nature of interpretation is such that seldom do two scholars agree to interpret the same facts in the same way. It is as though two scientists were trying to decide the length of a wall using differently calibrated rulers.

Phenomenology of Religion

The 'phenomenology of religion' is not so much a theory of religion as an approach to the study of religion. It is, however, based on the assumption that humanity's religious life is an entity in its own right and does not need to be reduced to sociological or psychological explanations. It is best understood as a 'neutral' description and an empathic attempt to get inside the experience itself. Unfortunately, the rather subjective nature of the method has led to the term being appropriated by many diverse approaches and, as a result, the term has lost much of its definition and meaning. This description will attempt to stay as close as possible to the original concepts of the philosophical phenomenology initiated by Edmund Husserl (1859–1938).

The phenomenological approach is in direct opposition to reductionism. It considers that the reduction of religious phenomena to social, psychological or other explanations is a false over-simplification. It is also formulated in opposition to those who want to describe some form of evolutionary scheme to religious history, for any such scheme must necessarily involve making value judgements. The best way of understanding such a complex phenomenon as religion is to try to get inside the religious experience itself in order to understand the intentionality of phenomena. By 'intentionality' is meant the concept that all consciousness is a consciousness of something. The phenomenologist tries to understand how the religious consciousness builds up the structure of religious phenomena.

One of the key methodological tools of the phenomenologist is 'bracketing' or the phenomenological *epoché*. The external world must be 'bracketed' or held in suspension. We must suspend our beliefs and judgements as to the truth, value or existence of particular religious phenomena. Instead, we should switch our attention to the experience itself as impartial observers. The second key aspect of the method is *einfühlung*, the obtaining of an empathic understanding of the religious position of others.

By using these two methodological tools, the investigator can gain insight into essential structures of the aspect of religion under study or of religion itself. These essential structures can be identified through what Husserl termed 'eidetic vision'. This means the intuitive apprehension of the *eidos* of a phenomenon. *Eidos* is a Greek term that Husserl took from Plato. It signifies the 'inner essence' or 'whatness' of things. 'Whatness' is that which answers the question 'what is X?' In other words, it signifies that which are the necessary and invariant features of a phenomenon. Husserl considered that the *eidos* of a phenomenon could be grasped through intuition and insight, not by experience or rational thought.

One particular method used by phenomenologists is to assemble a body of information about a particular phenomenon and then to search for its essential invariant core of meaning. The method involves discarding that which can be shown to be variable and thus not essential. Eventually, one is left with a core that cannot be removed or changed without changing the essence, 'whatness' or intentionality of the phenomenon. Husserl's original method involved a mental exercise, varying the factors in the mind. Most phenomenologists now use historical and comparative variation as the basis of their method.

To clarify this methodology, we can look at some examples of phenomenological interpretation. Perhaps one of the most important examples of this is the book *The Idea of the Holy* by Rudolf Otto (1869–1937). In this work, Otto tried to identify the essence of the religious experience, which he called the 'numinous'. He insisted on its irreducible nature, even going as far as to say to his readers that they could not conceptualize it through mere description; they needed to have experienced it themselves, to some extent. (See chapter 4.)

Rudolf Otto (1869–1937), phenomenology of religion

Another example of one who is usually considered to have followed this approach to the study of religion is Mircea Eliade (1907–86). His work will also be considered in chapter 11. With Eliade, phenomenology steps across the line from being just a methodological tool; it becomes the basis for a theory of religion. Eliade saw the essence of the religious experience as being not so much in the encounter with the 'numinous' as Otto did, but rather in religious symbols as the mediators between human beings and the sacred; they are the universal forms of religion. Through this mediator, humanity can transcend the finite world and chronological time, and experience the ultimate, meaningful, world of the sacred. The symbol is the revealer of a cosmic structure not discernible at the level of everyday experience. Eliade's books not only describe these symbols but help to show the way that they integrate disparate phenomena into a coherent system.

The concepts of phenomenology have evolved and altered at the hands of various scholars. Ninian Smart has developed the concept of *epoché* into what he terms 'methodological agnosticism'. By this he means that the investigator of religion should conduct his or her enquiries in such a way that they presuppose neither acceptance nor denial of the truth of an ultimate transcendent reality, God. Wilfred Cantwell Smith, on the other hand, has stressed the other main direction of phenomenology: the need to achieve empathy and understanding of what it is like to belong to a particular religious tradition; what it means to see the universe through those eyes.

CRITICISMS OF PHENOMENOLOGY. Probably the most frequent criticism of phenomenologists is that they are trying to introduce theological and other faith-based material under the guise of an academic study of religion. It is certainly true that many of the most prominent phenomenologists, such as Gerardus van der Leeuw (1890–1950), were also theologians. It is also true that this approach, based as it is on empathy and the viewpoint of the believer, is much more likely to find favour with those already committed to a religion. Indeed, some have gone as far as to say that commitment should be part of the phenomenological method. They assert that one needs to have some degree of religious commitment oneself to be capable of empathy towards the religious experiences of others. However, the majority would say that the phenomenological *epoché* requires the suspension of judgement: as to whether the religious experience is valid; as to whether the experience is of something real or illusory; and as to the status of the metaphysical assumptions entailed in the description.

Very few now accept the traditional phenomenological view that we can achieve complete freedom from presuppositions. Most modern phenomenologists try to reach a goal of identifying, clarifying and allowing for their own presuppositions. There is, in fact, an inherent contradiction between the two main methodological tools of phenomenology. The objectivity implied in the process of 'bracketing', *epoché*, contrasts with the subjectivity of *einfühlung* and 'eidetic vision'. Critics of phenomenology feel that this inherent contradiction means that the method is arbitrary; its findings cannot be subjected to either verification or falsification.

Most phenomenologists state that they pay due regard to history. However, their critics feel that the method is intrinsically ahistorical, in that it looks for universal structures that are independent of history. Phenomenology is also intrinsically against sociological or psychological explanations for religious phenomena.

Theological and Normative Theories

Although they are not strictly part of the academic study of religion, I shall briefly list the main types of such theories here, if only because these approaches are influential within religions themselves.

Justificatory or Polemical Theories

The origins of the study of religions can be traced back to theological or normative exercises to prove the superiority of one religion over others. There is, of course, an extensive history of polemical literature among the three Western religions, Judaism, Christianity and Islam, directed at each other, as well as between Hinduism and Buddhism. There exist books by Hindus describing other religions as defective or only partial expressions of the truths contained in Hinduism; similarly, Buddhist books exist which describe the truths in other religions as 'lower' forms of the truth of Buddhism. But these do not purport to be academic descriptions of the other religion. The use of purportedly academic studies as a tool for polemics is a modern phenomenon. In particular, Christian scholars and missionaries described other religions in book after book, comparing them unfavourably with Christianity. Other religions have been slow to follow in modern times but there are now some signs of this appearing.

Evolutionary Theories

Following the intellectual success of Darwin's theory of evolution, it became natural to look upon religious history as an evolutionary process. In this perspective, the primal tribal religions of the world were seen as surviving specimens, 'living fossils' or 'survivals' of the early stages of religious development. Out of this early phase the 'higher' religions evolved. A similar status was accorded to the folklore and mythology of Europe. Such writers as Edward B. Tylor (1832–1917) took evolutionary ideas for granted as the basis for their views on humanity's religious development. Several Christian writers also found it useful to use an evolutionary schema as a polemical instrument to prove that Christianity was the most highly evolved religion, although in the case of Christian theologians such ideas pre-dated Darwin, for they are foreshadowed in the writings of Hegel and Schleiermacher.

In the academic study of religion, however, evolutionist ideas died out in the years following World War I. They gradually became discredited as it was realized that they were, in fact, based on presumptions of the cultural and religious superiority of the Christian West and were therefore normative in nature. Evolutionary theories were also discredited by works such as those by Andrew Lang[2] and Wilhelm Schmidt.[3] These pointed out that the evidence may equally suggest that the earliest notion among primitive peoples was that of a single High God and that this later 'degenerated' into polytheism, thus destroying the idea that primal religions were necessarily 'survivals'.

There is, however, one evolutionary theory that sets out to be non-normative in nature. This theory is put forward by Robert Bellah (*Beyond Belief*, pp. 20–45). He states that his theory is one of religion becoming more complex as it evolves. He is quite categorical in asserting, however, that 'Neither religious man nor the structure of man's ultimate religious situation evolves, then, but rather religion as symbol system' (p. 21). He considers that primitive humanity is as fully religious as humanity at any stage of human existence on this planet. What has evolved and differentiated is religious symbolization and its relationship to human existence and society. The capacity for symbolization gives human beings the ability to transcend and dominate their environment. Religious symbolization, at each stage of human development, images both humanity's view of the ultimate conditions of its existence and its view of itself. As humanity has evolved an increasingly complex social structure, religious symbolization has also developed in interaction with this. Bellah describes five stages of evolution.

Australian Aboriginal paintings of the 'Dreaming' usually show human or animal ancestral figures (totems).

1. PRIMITIVE RELIGION. This religious form has only one clear example, Australian Aboriginal religion, although elements of it occur among other hunter–gatherer societies. Australian Aboriginal religion involves a mythical world called 'the Dreaming'. This is inhabited by human and animal ancestral figures who have great powers but are not gods – they do not control the world, nor are they worshipped. The mythical world is closely related to this world, such that every person and thing in this world has its counterpart in that mythical world. The two worlds interpenetrate in such an intimate way that they may be considered as one. Religious action is not concerned with worship. It is concerned with maintaining the social and cosmic

harmony of that cosmos and obtaining specific benefits – rain, harvest, children, health. The whole religious world is a 'given', fixed, with almost no element of choice or will. There is, moreover, no sense of salvation in this religious system. Any notion of a life continuing after death is vague and unstructured. There is also no religious organization at this level. Religious roles are fused with other roles and ceremonies are handed down within clans. The social implications of primitive religion are very limited. There is limited possibility for any change emerging from the religious world.

2. ARCHAIC RELIGION. In Bellah's scheme, this refers to the religious systems of Africa and the Pacific as well as the ancient religions of Egypt, the Middle East, India and China. This type of religion emerged once human beings began to develop agriculture and to trade. The mythical beings in the religious symbol system have evolved here to become more objectified. They are now definitely recognizable as gods who control aspects of the world and who must be worshipped and appeased. There is still essentially one cosmos, with different gods dominating different parts of it. Religious action here takes the form of religious veneration and worship, typified by sacrifice. Religious organization is, at this level, still merged with other social functions and relatively non-differentiated. Socially, there may be a division into a religiously superior class, which may have priestly functions, and an inferior class. Political power is usually merged with religious power. The social implications at this level are much the same as for primitive religion. The traditional social structure is considered to be grounded in the divine order of the cosmos, and so there is little or no impetus to change.

3. HISTORIC RELIGION. The next stage in Bellah's scheme is the emergence of historic religions from about the year 800 BCE – what has been called by the philosopher Karl Jaspers the 'axial age'. This stage evolved once people began to live in cities and great empires emerged. It includes Buddhism, Taoism, Vedantic Hinduism and, later, Christianity and Islam. At the level of religious symbolization, the most important factor is the emergence of a religious cosmos that is superior in value to, and different from, this world. This leads to a decline in the value given to this empirical world and the emergence of world-rejecting doctrines of salvation. Religious action is now directed towards the achievement of salvation. This in turn creates a definite sense of the self of the individual, a self that is deeper than the empirical self, a self that is capable of understanding and participating in the deeper structure of the universe revealed by the religious symbol of a transcendent world. Religious organization in the historic religions reflects both the social complexity of the societies that had emerged at this time and the complexity of the religious symbolization. Society now has a four-class structure, with one class holding political and military power, a religious élite, an urban lower-status group of merchants and skilled artisans, and the peasantry.

4. EARLY MODERN RELIGION. Bellah identifies this stage of the evolution of religion with the emergence of Protestant Christianity. The religious symbolization removed much of the mythological baggage associated with the previous stages and concentrated on a direct relationship with the deity. The main difference with the historic religions is the fact that salvation is now available in this world and in a direct form that is not mediated through the religious classes. Special devotional and ritual practices no longer have a place. Religious action now involves the whole of one's daily life in a daily struggle to perfect oneself. The empirical world thus regains its importance as the theatre in which the human struggle takes place and God's plan is realized. The implications for religious organization are to remove the need for a religious class. Human beings are still divided into those who are saved and those who are not, but the former are no longer a qualitative élite. Some implications of this development were spelled out by Weber in his theory about the rise of capitalism.
5. MODERN RELIGION. The modern religious world, at least as far as the West is concerned, has seen the complete collapse of the traditional religious symbol system. Belief in a single coherent vision of a spiritual world has all but disappeared. Philosophers such as Kant asserted the futility of basing human action on metaphysical foundations. An infinitely complex religious world has emerged, with almost every individual creating his or her own system of spiritual symbolization. There is a widespread acceptance among all religious people of the need for a personal interpretation of religion, a personal search for meaning and standards. The inevitable result of this is a loss of authority among religious organizations and the loss of the strong sense of voluntary submission to orthodoxy and religious groups that was a feature of early modern religion.

Relativistic Theories

With the emergence of relativistic thought in many other spheres of intellectual life, there have emerged several relativistic models of the relationship between religions. One of those who advocated such a view was Ernst Troeltsch. He came to the conclusion that all religions (and he eventually included Christianity among them) were relative manifestations of the universal Absolute.[4] Another relativist was Arnold Toynbee. He considered that each religion was true for (that is, suited to) a particular type of personality.[5]

One contemporary model is that of John Hick. He draws upon the Kantian distinction between *noumenon*, the thing in itself, and *phenomenon*, the thing as it is experienced and known. God, or Absolute Reality, as *noumenon*, is beyond description and even beyond knowledge in any comprehensive sense. Therefore, as far as religious experience is concerned, we are dealing with *phenomenon*. However, *phenomenon*, our experience of the Absolute, is inescapably coloured by our different individual experiences and cultural contexts. This is the reason for the wide-ranging, differing descriptions in the world's religions.[6]

It was also noted, in chapter 2, that the Baha'i position on metaphysics, and therefore on the question of the differing religions, is also based on relativism. The Baha'i concept is very similar to Hick's view, with the exception that the Baha'i concept also contains the idea that religion is evolving. This evolutionary idea is not, however, similar to those described above, in that the evolutionary process is not considered to be at work at the level of metaphysics or theology, or in the fundamentals of ethics. So the Baha'i Faith does not make judgements about the relative worth of different religious traditions at these levels; its evolutionary concepts are at the social level. At this level, the Baha'i Faith considers that the social teachings of religions have evolved in accordance with humanity's social evolution. As humanity has evolved and become more complex socially, so successive religions have brought social laws and teachings that solve the problems created by this increasing complexity. In this analysis, each religion conveys an eternal spiritual truth, which is right for all time, and social teachings that are appropriate for the time in which the religion appeared.

Another model that has been much advocated in recent years is what is generally called the perennial philosophy or *philosophia perennis*. This approach to religion, whose leading advocates in recent years have included Frithjof Schuon and A. K. Coomaraswamy, considers that it is the extension of a traditional school that has been associated with most religions from primordial times. It differentiates between the exoteric or outward forms of a religion and the esoteric truths that these outward forms manifest. While the exoteric aspects of the religions of the world may be widely diverse and even contradictory, the esoteric point to a single Absolute. The cosmos consists of a series of hierarchical levels through which the One (the Absolute) becomes the many (phenomena) and also through which the individual can ascend to the truth. The path to the Absolute does not involve neglecting the exoteric. To reach this Absolute, one needs to immerse oneself fully in both the exoteric and esoteric aspects of one of the religious traditions.[7]

Typologies of Religion

A typology of religious groups tries to divide them into different categories. Typological theories are not in themselves theories of religion but they necessarily presuppose a theoretical structure. They make assumptions about what aspects of religion are fundamental and are thus the basis on which categorization occurs.

One of the best-known typologies is that delineated by Ernst Troeltsch (1865–1923) in his book *The Social Teaching of the Christian Church*

(1912, trans. 1931). He expanded a distinction that had been implied in the work of Weber, between a 'church' and a 'sect'.

Troeltsch saw the history of Christianity as a struggle between two conflicting tendencies: compromise with and acceptance of the world, and rejection of the world. A church, which manifests the former tendency, aims to include in its membership the whole of a society, which often corresponds to ethnic or geographical borders. Children are recognized as members by virtue of birth within that society. A church considers that it is the sole means of grace and that salvation can only be attained through its dogmas and its hierarchy of priesthood. It is a conservative organization, strongly supportive of the established social order and usually of the state.

A sect, on the other hand, emphasizes voluntary membership of the group through conversion. Membership frequently involves convincing the group that the applicant has a specific qualification such as knowledge of the sect's doctrines or a particular experience. Children, therefore, are frequently required to become members of their own accord when they reach a particular age. The emphasis in sects is not on rituals and dogmas. There is usually no sense in which grace is the exclusive property of the sect, to be mediated through the priestly hierarchy. Instead the emphasis is on ethics and morality. Sects are often exclusive both in attitude and social structure, rejecting the rest of the world. Because of these features, sects usually develop in one of two ways. They either become revolutionary, seeking to change the existing order radically, or they withdraw into small communities where they can live according to their ideals and from where they can criticize the rest of the world.

H. Richard Niebuhr (1894–1962), in his book *The Social Sources of Denominationalism* (1929), tried to make Troeltsch's picture more dynamic by examining the way in which a sect moves towards becoming a church. He suggested that the sect gradually modifies its original rejectionist ideals so as to adapt to social realities. This idea was developed and the notion grew of an intermediate category of the 'denomination' as a partially routinized and accommodated sect. However, the distinction between church and denomination has never been clear and there is a marked tendency to use these two terms interchangeably. J. Milton Yinger, on the other hand, in his book *Religion, Society and the Individual* (1957), described those sects that refused to accommodate themselves to the world, and indeed reinforced their opposition to it. These he called the 'established sects' (for example the Amish, Hutterites, and the Jehovah's Witnesses). Yinger also suggested subdividing sects into three categories: world-accepting, world-transforming, and world-rejecting. This categorization is not very different from that of Bryan Wilson (see 'An Analysis of Sect Development', 1959):

1. Conversionist sects. These are mainly concerned with evangelism, thereby hoping to change the world. Examples include most

CONVERSIONIST SECTS: This picture shows the Salvation Army, an evangelical Christian organization, playing in a shopping centre in Britain.

fundamentalist groups such as the Salvation Army and the Elim Foursquare Gospel.

2. ADVENTIST OR REVOLUTIONIST SECTS. These focus on prophesying the imminent overturn of the existing social order; they emphasize that we are living in the 'times of the end'. Jehovah's Witnesses are an example of a sect of this type.
3. INTROVERSIONIST OR PIETIST SECTS. These turn away from the world and focus in on the community of believers; this is the only place where the high ideals of the group can be realized. Examples include Old Order Amish and the Hutterites.
4. GNOSTIC (MANIPULATIONIST) SECTS. These believe that they possess a special teaching through which worldly goals such as success or health can be achieved. Christian Science is an example of such a sect.

INTROVERSIONIST OR PIETIST SECTS: The Mennonites or Anabaptists are a group of radical Protestant Christians who form close-knit isolated communities based on New Testament models. Sub-groups (such as the Amish and Hutterites) have migrated to Russia, the USA and Canada to escape persecution. This picture is of a member of a community that emigrated from Canada and Russia to Paraguay from 1926 onwards. It shows some typical features of the Mennonite rejection of the modern world: a rural agricultural community, wearing traditional clothes and using traditional farming methods.

REFORMIST SECTS: Some religious groups become concerned with social action and reform. The picture shows Elizabeth Fry (1780–1845) of the Society of Friends (Quakers) visiting women prisoners in Newgate prison, London, in 1823, and reading to them from the *Bible*. She brought about major reforms in the way that women prisoners were treated and the influence of her reforms was felt worldwide.

To these four, Wilson later added another three categories (see 'A Typology of Sects', 1963):

5. THAUMATURGICAL SECTS. These are groups that insist that it is possible for human beings to experience the direct effects of the supernatural, for example spiritualist churches. They often use this contact with the supernatural to achieve worldly goals such as curing illness. They are thus similar in many ways to the sects in category 4 above (which Wilson renamed in this classification 'manipulationist') except that they are less universalist and more personal.

6. REFORMIST SECTS. Revolutionary sects (see category 2 above) often adapt to the world in the course of their development by becoming concerned with reforming the world through good deeds and social action. Examples of such a sect include the Society of Friends (Quakers).

7. UTOPIAN SECTS. These try to reconstruct their world on a communitarian basis. They withdraw from the world and set up communities in which they can practise their ideals. They are, however, different from the introversionist sects, in that they do not see the creation of communities as a defence against the outside world. Rather, they see the creation of their communities as a positive step, as the way that the world should be organized. Examples include the Oneida Community.

Troeltsch, as well as describing his division between church and sect, also described a third type of religious response which he called mysticism. This consisted of a purely personal religion with minimal social form. This group is now more commonly subsumed under the name 'cults'. These are usually characterized as groups that have a positive attitude towards the secular world. They often offer their teachings as a way of achieving success, health or happiness in the world. These goals may be gained through a special knowledge or through particular techniques of interpersonal relationships. They have little social structure (although they may be focused on a charismatic leader) and poorly defined membership criteria. They are basically the same as Wilson's category 4 above. Such groups are exemplified by Scientology and Christian Science. Roy Wallis has suggested that one key difference between sects and cults is the fact that the sect is epistemologically authoritarian (its members must subscribe to an authoritative set of beliefs); while cults are epistemologically individualist (the members can choose what they like of the teachings of the cult).[8] A different typology is that proposed by Robert Bellah as an evolutionary scheme (see pp. 70–72).

The major criticism of all these typologies has been and continues to be that they were primarily evolved with Christian churches and sects in mind. They are therefore of limited usefulness when applied to religions that organize themselves differently and have other priorities. The definitions of sect, denomination and religion given in chapter 5 are an attempt to break out of this limited perspective.

The general description of other religions and the creation of typologies was taken to an advanced level by Muslim scholars such as Shahristani and al-Biruni in the Middle Ages. This development in the Islamic world has been little noted by historians of the development of religious studies.

Approaches to the Study of Religion

There have been many issues in the methodology of the study of religion and it is not possible to consider all of them in a book such as this. I shall, however, consider one major issue that has been the subject, directly or indirectly, of much debate.

We can broadly divide the theories of religion discussed in the first part of this chapter into two main groups. This division is somewhat confused by the fact that these groups have been given several different names. On the one hand, there are the reductive, empiricist, analytical, determinist or positivist approaches and, on the other, the synthetic, integrative, relativistic or holistic approaches. Some scholars have preferred to use the terms 'etic' ('outside', referring to interpretative categories that a scholar might impose on a religion) and 'emic' ('inside', meaning the understandings and categories of a religious tradition that the adherents themselves recognize).

The Reductive/Empiricist Paradigm (Analytical/Determinist/Positivist/Etic)

The guiding principle of this approach to the study of religion is to try to analyse the phenomenon of religion. Analysis involves trying to break down a phenomenon into its component parts. With regard to religious phenomena, the goal is to analyse these in terms of factors derived from such disciplines as sociology, economics, psychology and anthropology. This approach regards religious phenomena as being *nothing but* particular instances of the workings of the objects of inquiry of these other disciplines – 'nothing but' being the key words. This approach considers that an analysis reducing religious phenomena to sociological (or psychological or anthropological) mechanisms of lower levels of complexity gives a complete explanation with no loss of comprehensiveness. In other words, that religion is *nothing but* the working out of these lower-level mechanisms. It can be completely understood thus, with no residue of data that need further, higher-level explanation (such as new laws that emerge only at the level of religious phenomena).

The background of this approach comes from classical scientific method, which seeks to analyse complex phenomena by looking for explanations at a lower, more basic level. The conceptual model is of phenomena as being like a giant mechanism. So the best way of finding out how the mechanism works is to take it to pieces and find how each part functions. Ideally, then, all human phenomena would be explained by analysis or reduction to biological phenomena (for example, war can be explained by animal territoriality and Darwinian survival of the fittest); all biological phenomena would be analysed down to chemical phenomena (for example, genetics can be explained by the molecular biology of DNA; animal behaviour by the action of hormones and chemical transmitters); then all chemical phenomena would be analysed down to physics (for example, chemical reactions can be explained in terms of the stability of electron orbits around atoms). By a parallel process, the complex phenomenon of religion can be analysed down to the more fundamental level of sociology or psychology.

We can view the same approach from the opposite direction as maintaining that the lower-level phenomena determine the higher-level, hence the name 'determinism'. The implication of determinism, if carried to its logical conclusion, is that since everything at the higher level is determined by what occurs at the lower, all human action is determined. Indeed, if we had sufficient data, it could be predicted. Because the cosmic machine is in motion, everything in the future is already determined and has been from the beginning of time, a working out of processes that have already been set in motion. One of the philosophical consequences of a strict application of this approach is to assert that human free will is a delusion.

Closely linked to the analytical approach to phenomena is the other aspect of the 'scientific approach', empiricism or logical positivism. This is based on the idea that the correct manner in which to proceed is to obtain and assess the facts first; then to evolve by induction from these a hypothesis that can be put to the test.

The Synthetic/Relativistic Paradigm (Holistic/Emic)

The alternative viewpoint considers that complex phenomena cannot necessarily be analysed down to simpler phenomena, at least not completely. Complex phenomena have properties that arise at that level of complexity and cannot be predicted from lower levels of complexity. In other words, the very fact that several phenomena from a lower level of complexity have combined to produce a more complex phenomenon leads to the emergence of new properties that are not properties of, or even predictable from, the lower-level features. A simple example is the fact that the combination of hydrogen and oxygen yields a substance, water, the properties of which are not in any way derived from or predictable from the properties of hydrogen and oxygen individually. Thus, no matter how far we may progress in understanding the behaviour of atoms and subatomic particles, this will not lead to any greater understanding in the field of, for example, animal behaviour, let alone human behaviour. These higher levels of complexity require their own levels of explanation. While analysis to lower levels of causative explanation may often be useful and even illuminating, these lower levels never in practice fully explain all the features of the higher level of complexity.

A key aspect of this line of thinking is the idea that the higher-level phenomena act so as to constrain the lower-level phenomena towards certain pathways of action. In other words, the direction of causation is downwards, from the higher level to the lower. This does not mean that the higher level phenomena cause the lower-level phenomena to break the laws that operate at that lower-level. The activities of a cat, for example, can never cause the atoms of which it is composed to break the laws of physics. It only means that where the lower-level phenomena have different possibilities of action, the higher level (that is the system as a whole) constrains this choice in one particular direction. This is sometimes called the holistic view, as it envisages the system-as-a-whole as being the key operant. This viewpoint is in direct contrast to the determinist viewpoint, which sees the direction of causation as being from the lower levels to the higher ones, so that what happens at the lower levels determines what happens at the higher ones.

For scholars who adopt this approach, the key to the study of religion lies in understanding the phenomenon of religion in itself, at its own level, and not by reduction to lower levels. The goal must be to understand the religion or the religious phenomenon in its own terms (at its own level of complexity), to understand how human beings come to believe as they do and why they act as they do.

Closely linked to this is relativism. This viewpoint opposes the empiricist vision that conceptualizes religious data as 'given', facts that are seen and agreed upon by all. Relativism stresses that the data can only be seen relative to a particular observer and that the observer has his or her own viewpoint. So there are no independent or absolute data, only people holding particular views and seeing the world in a particular way.

Also opposed to reductionism are such scholars as Clifford Geertz who champion an interpretive approach to cultural anthropology. For such scholars, grand theories of religion are not helpful. All knowledge of human culture is 'local knowledge'. Each culture should be examined in depth with regard to its particular worldview and ethos (religion being a fusion of the worldview and ethos in each culture). The study of culture can only be done in relation to specific cultures, or at most in a comparison between two cultures, not in search of general laws but as an interpretive exercise in search of meaning. Some have seen this as the abandonment of a scientific approach, in that one is no longer seeking to discover general laws that have predictive ability. Geertz maintains, however, that his approach is scientific in that it involves a body of knowledge systematically acquired through the critical weighing of observations and involving the proposing of theories regarding the meaning of events and their testing with evidence from further observations.

The Debate

The debate between these two approaches has been intense and multi-faceted. On the one hand, those favouring the analytical approach claim for themselves the title 'scientific'. They maintain that the empirical approach that they advocate is the scientific approach to religion and therefore the only truly academic study of religion. Their position was forcefully put forward, for example, by R. J. Zwi Werblowsky at the 1960 Marburg Conference of the International Association for the History of Religions and in papers that he published at about this time.[9] Werblowsky was particularly concerned to separate the academic study of religion from theology and all normative positions. True academic scholars should eliminate their personal religious beliefs from all aspects of their scholarly work. The academic study of religion should adhere to the standards of scientific and historical research. It should be rigorously defended from the attentions of 'dilettantes, theologians and idealists'.[10]

The contrary viewpoint is exemplified by the writings of Wilfred Cantwell Smith who considers that there is no such thing as a neutral academic statement that can be examined in isolation from the scholar who makes it. Every statement is a personal statement; it is made from a particular point of view (and thus potentially reveals as much about the author as about the subject of the statement).[11] Smith also objects to the concept of 'religion', which he claims is only a reification, imposed upon the data by empiricists. He prefers to think in terms of the religious faith of individuals (that is the religious experience relative to the individual) and the ongoing religious tradition.[12]

Those who support the holistic view point out that the analytical/empiricist view of scientific method is itself outdated. It belongs to the classical Newtonian paradigm, which is no longer fully accepted by the scientific community. The Newtonian paradigm is only strictly applicable to regular bodies of intermediate size in closed systems, acting in a smooth, regular manner. The way that Newtonian methods are applied to most real situations (which in practice rarely meet these criteria) is to approximate these to regular systems. This works in optics or engineering, but the more complex a system becomes, the less accurate these approximations become. By the time we are dealing with biological and human phenomena, Newtonian methods have become almost useless.[13]

New scientific approaches to complexity and irregularity are being pioneered but these are as yet only in the early stages of development. The important point is that the reductionist, analytical model is no longer seen as appropriate in these studies.[14] Similarly, the empiricist view can be criticized, as it assumes that pure facts can be obtained. Relativity theory, however, leads to the conclusion that there are no such things as pure facts. All data are dependent on the methods used to obtain them. In the field of religious studies this would mean that the data that we collect and study are determined by our theoretical framework. In other words, our data, far from being the seed from which to derive our theories, as the empiricist tradition would dictate, are themselves theory-dependent.

The empiricists would argue against the holistic view by saying that it leads to meaninglessness. Once one allows for the introduction of high-level phenomena and for high-level laws to be operating, one can no longer examine phenomena in any systematic, 'scientific' way. This is because the whole of scientific thought is based upon the idea that a hypothesis is an explanation of a phenomenon that occurs; it explains at a lower, simpler level the occurrence of a phenomenon. Such a hypothesis should lead to a prediction of further phenomena. Therefore, it should be possible to verify the hypothesis by seeing whether the prediction is accurate or not. All of this depends, however, on the principle of determinism – that the lower-level phenomena determine the observations one makes of the higher-level phenomena. Once one allows that, at the higher level, new laws may begin to operate, then the principle of determinism can no longer apply. Any discrepancies from the predictions of the hypothesis could be due to the operation of new laws. The scientific principle of verifiability breaks down. Since, according to logical empiricism, verifiability is the main criterion for cognitive meaning (that is, only statements that are verifiable, or at least potentially falsifiable, are meaningful), the holistic approach results in cognitive meaninglessness.

The debate will no doubt continue, resurfacing in various guises, for many years to come. In practice, both approaches yield useful and illuminating results. The present writer's inclination is to view both approaches as complementary. In other words, religion is a complex phenomenon for which new laws emerge at the phenomenon's own level of complexity. These new laws constrain events at the lower level; the phenomenon of religion cannot, therefore, be fully explained by lower-level hypotheses from other fields such as sociology, psychology, or economics. These higher-level laws, however, only constrain the lower-level laws, they do not break them. An understanding of the lower-level laws is also of value, therefore. The analogy would be that biology is a complex field with its own laws that constrain the occurrence of lower-level phenomena such as biochemical reactions. For example, of the hundreds of ways that a long protein molecule could fold, it is constrained to fold in the only way that would make it have the desired biological activity. However, the laws of biology do not contravene chemical laws. It is, therefore, legitimate and useful for our overall understanding of biological processes to investigate the manner in which the lower-level laws of chemistry affect the biological world.

The Goal of the Study of Religion

Finally, it is necessary to say a brief word about an issue that is in some ways a reflection of the above debate. A tension exists within religious studies between two points of view. The first, the academic goal, considers that the study of religion should aim solely at achieving greater knowledge and understanding, comparable, for example, to the study of geology or chemistry. The second looks to some further benefit from this study, which may be in terms either of drawing the peoples of different religions together in dialogue (the dialogical goal) or of achieving greater understanding of humanity's position in the universe and thus helping to solve humanity's current problems (the soteriological goal).

On the surface, there is no dispute. Those engaged in research in academic departments of religious studies would usually assert that they are pursuing the academic goal. But in analysing the writings of some of the most respected and influential figures in the field, one frequently finds statements that indicate a dialogical or soteriological goal underlying the work. Only a few examples of this tendency can be cited here: Mircea Eliade saw his theories of the sacralization of time and space as a way for human beings to escape the terror and alienation of the modern world;[15] Wilfred Cantwell Smith sees his work on religion as contributing to 'our understanding of man' and so helping us to 'think clearly and to live faithfully, in the new world in which we find ourselves';[16] Peter Berger wrote his book *The Heretical Imperative* in order to show a way out of 'the impasse of contemporary Christian thought'.[17]

Religion is a very challenging area of study, which makes claims relating to all aspects of life. One can speculate that it is really not possible to study such a phenomenon completely dispassionately. Either consciously or subconsciously, all scholars must bring their own preconceptions and biases to this study. One can perhaps make the same statement about scholars in religious studies as E. H. Carr made in his Trevelyan lectures regarding historians: 'Study the historian before you study [his] facts . . . When you read a work of history, always listen out for the buzzing [of bees in the bonnet]. If you detect none, either you are tone deaf or your historian is a dull dog.'[18]

Bronislaw Malinowski (1884–1942), anthropologist (functionalism)

Talcott Parsons (1902–1978), anthropologist (functionalism)

Mircea Eliade (1907–1986), phenomenology, history of religion

FURTHER READING

For a historical overview of the development of the study of religion, see Sharpe, *Comparative Religion*. For a detailed description and assessment of different approaches to the study of religion, see Waardenburg, *Classical Approaches to the Study of Religion* and Whaling, *Contemporary Approaches to the Study of Religion* and *The World's Religious Traditions*. Another useful book is Morris, *Anthropological Studies of Religion*.

II

The Religious Experience and its Expression

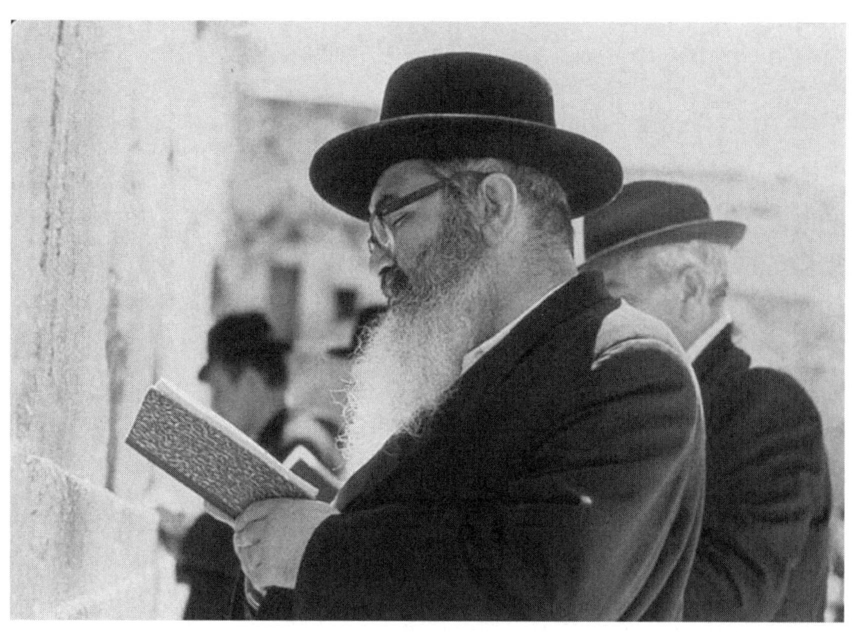

4

The Religious Experience

No two persons' experience is exactly the same and so it is difficult to find words with which all would agree. Any description of religious experience or attempt to analyse it is, therefore, bound to be unsatisfactory, at least in some respect, for all who read it. At the heart of this problem is the question of whether religious experience is in a class of its own (*sui generis*) or whether it is merely a particular interpretation of sensations that all people experience at some time. The former approach to religious experience would maintain that since it is *sui generis*, it can only be described in its own terms. The latter would try to analyse religious experience in terms of psychology, social psychology, neurophysiology and so on. In this chapter I shall start by taking the first approach, attempting to give a description of religious experience as a phenomenon in its own terms. I shall then proceed to the second approach, looking at the social psychology perspective on religious experience and religious conversion and answering the question: what are the social influences on religious experience? The material regarding the first approach is complemented by the description of faith, belief and conversion in chapter 6 (especially the section on conversion); the material about the second approach is complemented by the experimental psychology and neurophysiology work relating to religious experience described in chapter 7.

Describing the Central Experience of Religion

The central experience of religion, the experience of the sacred, is intensely private and personal. It is not easy to communicate the content of this experience to others, although the circumstances in which it occurs may be described. For some it occurs in the midst of prayer, or in the process of contemplation or meditation; for some it may be achieved through the performance of rituals, or through the chanting of verses and mantras or the singing of hymns, or even in a moment of complete silence; for others it is the reading of a passage of scripture or experiencing a work of religious art or drama that creates the necessary conditions. For many, it is experienced within a religious community or in a particular place, or there may not be one specific set of circumstances that triggers this experience; rather, it occurs at various times in the religious life of the individual.

Three features apply to the phenomenon of religious experience:

1. UNIVERSALITY. Numerous surveys have consistently shown that even in the highly secularized societies of North America and Europe, a large proportion of the population have had what they describe as religious experiences. The proportion approaches one hundred per cent in traditional societies.
2. DIVERSITY. Religious experience is unique for each individual. Religions may attempt to impose a uniformity of doctrine or of action upon their followers, but each person's religious experiences, when taken as a whole, will be different to those of another person.
3. IMPORTANCE. Religious experience is almost invariably very important to the individual to whom it occurs, in a way that other experiences usually are not. A religious experience can result in change in the way that individuals think about themselves, a complete alteration of lifestyle, or a reorganization of the individual's conceptual world.

One author who has made a very penetrating and influential study of the sacred or holy and the individual's response to this is Rudolf Otto. To describe the human experience of the holy, he uses the Latin phrase: *mysterium tremendum et fascinans*. *Mysterium* indicates that the holy is something ultimately mysterious and unknowable; it emphasizes its 'otherness'. *Tremendum* indicates its overpowering nature and the sense of awe that it induces. *Fascinans* indicates that it draws one to it in spite of oneself and in spite of the awe or dread that it invokes.[1]

Otto distinguishes this deeper, less rational meaning of 'holy' from what he considers to be a later overlay of meaning that makes the word 'holy' merely equivalent to 'good'. In order to emphasize this difference, Otto proposes the use of the word 'numen' and the adjective 'numinous' to specify this more profound sense of the word 'holy'. Regarding this meaning of 'holy',[2] Otto says that 'there is no religion in which it does not live as the real innermost core, and without it, no religion would be worthy of the name'.[3]

Otto's work has been criticized as being too influenced by and oriented towards Christianity. There is certainly some truth in this. However, Otto's basic description can be adjusted to make it more universally applicable. No one can, however, give a description of the experience of the holy that will be satisfactory to all who have experienced it. Among its features that are generally agreed upon are the following:

1. It is a very intense, energizing experience. It feels important and demands respect and attention.

2. It is a liberating experience, in that it seems to free one from the demands of the physical world (but, in some, it may induce a sense of dependence on an 'other reality').
3. It brings peace, joy, exultation, even exhilaration, although this can, on occasions, be mingled with awe and even dread. Some may even report the feeling of being possessed by a spiritual power.
4. It seems to give one a feeling of having achieved insight or knowledge, although it is often difficult to specify the content of this knowledge (it is ineffable, incapable of being adequately expressed in words). It is often described as 'confirming', in the sense of giving one the assurance that one's faith is true.
5. Time may appear to stop and space may seem to become distorted. It may seem that the experience occurs 'outside' time and space.
6. Many would say that for an experience to be truly religious, it should involve the whole person, lead to some element of personal transformation and result in some outward manifestation of the change in terms of action. Some may report a feeling of having been summoned to a mission through this experience.

FEATURES OF RELIGIOUS EXPERIENCE

AN INTENSE, ENERGIZING EXPERIENCE

My body became immovably rooted; breath was drawn out of my lungs as if by some huge magnet. Soul and mind instantly lost their physical bondage and streamed out of my lungs like a fluid piercing light from my every pore. The flesh was as though dead, yet in my intense awareness I knew that never before had I been fully alive. My sense of identity was no longer narrowly confined to a body, but embraced the circumambient atoms . . .

An oceanic joy broke upon calm endless shores of my soul. The Spirit of God, I realised, is exhaustless bliss; His body is countless tissues of light. A swelling glory within me began to envelop towns, continents, the earth, solar and stellar systems, tenuous nebulae, and floating universes. The entire cosmos, gently luminous, like a city seen afar at night, glimmered within the infinitude of my being. (Yogi Paramhansa Yogananda, *Autobiography of a Yogi*, quoted in Cohen and Phipps, *The Common Experience*, pp. 103–4)

A LIBERATING EXPERIENCE

O Son of Worldliness! Pleasant is the realm of being, wert thou to attain thereto; glorious is the domain of eternity, shouldst thou pass beyond the world of mortality; sweet is the holy ecstasy if thou drinkest of the mystic chalice from the hands of the celestial Youth. Shouldst thou attain this station, thou wouldst be freed from destruction and death, from toil and sin. (Baha'u'llah, *Hidden Words*, Persian 70)

PEACE, JOY, EXULTATION

The soul of man is his friend when by the Spirit he has conquered his soul . . . When his soul is in peace he is in peace, and then his soul is in God. In cold or in heat, in pleasure or in pain, in glory or in disgrace, he is ever in Him . . .

The Yogi who, lord of his mind, ever prays in this harmony of soul, attains the peace of Nirvana, the peace supreme that is in me . . .

Thus joy supreme comes to the Yogi whose heart is still, whose passions are peace, who is pure from sin, who is one with Brahman, with God. (*Bhagavad Gita* 6:6–7, 15, 27)

But when the soul is naughted and transformed, then of herself she neither works nor speaks nor wills, nor feels nor hears nor understands . . . And in all things it is God Who rules and guides her, without the mediation of any creatures. And the state of this soul is then a feeling of such utter peace and tranquillity that it seems to her that her heart, and her bodily being, and all both within and without is immersed in an ocean of utmost peace; from when she shall never come forth for anything that can befall her in this life. And she stays unmovable, imperturbable, impassible. So much so, that it seems to her in her human and her spiritual nature, both within and without, she can feel no other thing than sweetest peace. And she is so full of peace that though she press her flesh, her nerves, her bones, no other thing comes forth from them than peace. Thus she says all day for joy such rhymes as these . . . (St Catherine of Genoa, quoted in Underhill, *Mysticism*, p. 441)

INSIGHT OR KNOWLEDGE, COMBINED WITH INEFFABILITY

One day, being in orison, it was granted me to perceive in one instant how all things are seen and contained in God. I did not perceive them in their proper form, and nevertheless the view I had of them was of a sovereign clearness, and has remained vividly impressed upon my soul. It is one of the most signal of all the graces which the Lord has granted me . . . The view was so subtile and delicate that the understanding cannot grasp it. (St Theresa of Avila, quoted in James, *The Varieties of Religious Experience*, p. 411)

We receive this mystical knowledge of God clothed in none of the kinds of images, in none of the sensible representations, which our mind makes use of in other circumstances. Accordingly, in this knowledge, since the senses and imagination are not employed, we get neither form nor impression, nor can we give any account or furnish any likeness, although the mysterious and sweet tasting wisdom comes home so clearly to the inmost parts of our soul . . . The soul then feels it is placed in a vast and profound solitude . . . There, in this abyss of wisdom, the soul grows by what it drinks in from the wellsprings of the comprehension of love . . . and recognizes, however, sublime and learned may be the terms we employ, how utterly vile, insignificant, and improper they are, when we seek to discourse of divine things by their means. (St John of the Cross, quoted in James, *The Varieties of Religious Experience*, p. 407)

TIME MAY APPEAR TO STOP AND SPACE MAY SEEM TO BECOME DISTORTED

The overture to Weber's opera *Oberon* was announced [on the radio], and I listened in pleasant anticipation . . . After a minute or so I suddenly became aware of an alteration in my perception. The music became blurred and indistinct, and at the same time the bedroom was bathed in a light of iridescent radiance so that its outlines and furniture could no longer be delineated . . .

I was no longer in the universe at all, but in the realm of eternal life which is neither past nor future but only the ever-lasting present. I had been lifted to a height above all measurable heights. I was able, in this situation, to perceive the entire created world, for I was outside it. I 'saw' and 'heard' with the 'eyes' and 'ears' of the soul which also 'felt' the loving impact of the supreme power that embraced and raised me . . .

I was no longer a separate isolated unit. Although I had not lost my identity – indeed, for the first time in my life I had really experienced the identity of a whole person – I was in union with all creation and my identity was added to it, giving of its essence to the created whole . . .

The silent music of eternity gave way to the strains of the *Oberon* overture. I could establish, through my knowledge of the music, that the entire episode had lasted about three minutes. (An experience of Martin Israel, a South African Jew, quoted in Cohen and Phipps, *The Common Experience*, pp. 149–50)

PERSONAL TRANSFORMATION

My previous outlook has been entirely changed on account of the new possession. I find no life now in worldly life. A new possession of the soul has taken place. The former outlook has changed. My life has been filled with divine joy. The tongue has partaken of a new sweetness, God's name is fixed in my mouth, and my mind has become tranquil. (Tukurama, a seventeenth-century poet and saint of Maharashtra in India, quoted in Ranade, *Mysticism in India*, p. 304)

It was as though my mind broke bounds and went on expanding until it merged with the universe. Mind and universe became *one within the other*. Time ceased to exist. It was all one thing and in a state of infinity. It was as if, willy-nilly, I became directly exposed to an entity within myself and nature at large. I seemed to be seeing with another sight in another world . . .

> Although my 'cosmic experience' was irrational in terms of our accustomed view of the world, I am not satisfied that it was simply an illusion, or delusion. It affected me in a very real way, reoriented my outlook and enriched and enlarged my consciousness in many ways. But it did pose a riddle – the kind of riddle one cannot attempt to solve without becoming keenly aware of the ultimate mystery of creation. In this sense, I would call my experience 'religious'. (The experience of an atheist, quoted in Cohen and Phipps, *The Common Experience*, pp. 173–4)

I have attempted to formulate these descriptions so as to include all levels of religious experience. Many of these descriptions have been attributed to mysticism and states of deep meditation, but I would maintain that it is more useful to see the mystical and meditative experience as being at one extreme of a continuum of religious experience and activity. At the other end of this spectrum are the mundane tasks of the religious life, such as arranging the flowers in the church or sweeping out the Hindu temple. As one goes from one extreme to the other, the intensity and frequency of the experience may change, but all the above features may occur at any point of the continuum.[4]

The experience of the holy is the core of religion and its initiating and driving force. But this does not mean to say that the experience is equally intense for all (clearly, it is probable that a religious experience felt while singing a hymn will be of a different magnitude to the experience of a vision or trance). It does not even mean that everyone who participates in religious activity does so because of such a personal experience. Nevertheless, it remains true that, for most of those who participate in religious activity, their involvement is validated and reinforced by some degree of personal or group experience of the holy or sacred (although more humble people may, in verbalizing their faith, seek to transfer its validation onto the experiences of a priest, saint, guru or other religious leader).

Types of Religious Experience

Although I have given here a generic description of religious experience, it is possible to break this down into several types of religious experience that each have their own particular characteristics. Religious experience may be classified into four types according to the way that the experience is described and by the result of the experience.[5]

The Regenerative Experience

This is the experience to which most people refer when they speak of a religious experience. It is the experience of coming into contact with a

RELIGIOUS REVIVALISM: Christian evangelicals believe that it is necessary to have the experience of being 'born again' in order to achieve salvation. In this picture, taken in Brazil, Protestant evangelicals are baptizing someone who may have already considered herself a Christian, but has now been 'born again' in faith.

reality that we recognize as greater than us and capable of transforming us. It can be subdivided into several forms:

1. CONVERSION EXPERIENCE. For many people, the experience takes the form of a conversion, leading them to align themselves to a religious movement to which they have not previously been aligned, because they experience the truth of that movement.

2. CONFIRMING EXPERIENCE. For others, the experience regenerates their faith within a religious movement to which they already belong; the 'born-again' experience in Christianity and religious revivalism in Islam are two common examples.

3. COMMISSIONING EXPERIENCE. This experience may be in the form of a 'call', a divine commission to carry out some action or take up a new way of life.

William James gives several examples of regenerative religious experience. He quotes, for example, the account of a young man whose father was a minister but who had turned his back on religion and spent his days drinking heavily. Bouts of drinking would be followed by periods of remorse for wasting his life and a determination to give up drinking. Then, one day, during one of his periods of sobriety, he began reading a book sent to him by a friend who sought his opinion on its literary quality.

> I took the book to my bedroom . . . intending to give it a thorough study, and then write her what I thought of it. It was here that God met me face to face, and I shall never forget the meeting. 'He that hath the Son hath life eternal, he that hath not the Son hath not life.' I had read this scores of times before, but this made all the difference. I was now in God's presence and my attention was absolutely 'soldered' on to this verse, and I was not allowed to proceed with the book till I had fairly considered what these words really involved. Only then was I allowed to proceed, feeling all the while that there was another being in my bedroom, though not seen by me. The stillness was very marvellous, and I felt supremely happy. It was most unquestionably shown me, in one second of time, that I had never touched the Eternal: and that if I died then, I must inevitably be lost. I was undone. I knew it as well as I now know I am saved. The Spirit of God showed it me in ineffable love; there was no terror in it.[6]

The account goes on to relate the young man's eventual abstention from alcohol and other sins. Not all conversion experiences are that dramatic but many are as profound. The person concerned feels that his or her life is now filled with meaning and has a worthy purpose and direction that it lacked before. The individual's moral life is transformed. Another account relates the experience of a convert to Islam:

> In the blessed pages of the Holy Qur'an I found solution to all my problems, satisfaction to all my needs, explication for all my doubts. Allah attracted me to His light with irresistible strength, and I gladly yielded to Him. Everything seemed clear now, everything made sense to me, and I began to understand myself, the Universe and Allah . . . My whole world was shattered in one instant; all concepts had to be revised.[7]

The Charismatic Experience

This experience makes those involved feel that a gift has been bestowed upon them. This gift may include a feeling of being in a 'wider life than that of this world's selfish interests', a sense of being in continuity with the powers of the universe, and a sense of elation and joy as the sense of self and attachment to this world is abandoned. There is inner equilibrium and calm. It has been described as the experience of saintliness.[8]

Typically this 'gift' gives its recipient the ability to heal, drive out evil spirits, speak in tongues, and perform other miracles and wonders. The receipt of this 'gift' is often marked by trance or ecstasy. The following is a description of a scene in an African independent church for women that mixes African traditional religion with Christianity:

> The air is heavily charged with emotion. Women stand up and speak out their troubles, sometimes wailing or screaming, sometimes in frenzied whispers. Their bodies tremble. Their eyes are tight closed or fixed

> heavenwards. Talk is of miracles, of the sick and the dead . . . until one will start shaking violently in preparation for the moment when 'she is taken by the Spirit' and begins to speak. The other women listen intently, in close participation, and while the speaker slowly works herself up to a high pitch of emotion, the feelings of the listeners find in her a channel through which they pour themselves out, and by so doing generate again renewed tension in the individual who acts as a focus of, and outlet for, the collective mood.[9]

Such experiences are found among the Jewish prophets, many Christian saints, members of Christian charismatic movements, *walis*, shaykhs and *pirs* in some Islamic Sufi orders, Hindu gurus and *sadhus*, and shamans and ecstatics in primal religions. Such individuals are often credited, in traditional and ancient societies at least, with grace, purity, wisdom, and the power of prophecy. People would often turn to them in times of personal or social crisis.

The Mystical Experience

This experience is characterized by James as being ineffable (impossible to describe in words), noetic (giving insight and knowledge that feels authoritative), transient (it cannot be sustained for long) and passive

THE EXPERIENCE OF SAINTLINESS

Mulla Sadiq was a prominent Babi and later a Baha'i. On one occasion, he was arrested for his faith, led through the streets of Shiraz and then lashed in public.

An eye-witness . . . related to me the following: 'I was present when Mulla Sadiq was being scourged. I watched his persecutors each in turn apply the lash to his bleeding shoulders, and continue the strokes until he became exhausted. No one believed that Mulla Sadiq, so advanced in age and so frail in body, could possibly survive fifty such savage strokes. We marvelled at his fortitude when we found that, although the number of the strokes of the scourge he had received had already exceeded nine hundred, his face still retained its original serenity and calm. A smile was upon his face, as he held his hand before his mouth. He seemed utterly indifferent to the blows that were being showered upon him. When he was being expelled from the city, I succeeded in approaching him, and asked him why he held his hand before his mouth . . . He emphatically replied: "The first seven strokes were severely painful; to the rest I seemed to have grown indifferent. I was wondering whether the strokes that followed were being actually applied to my own body. A feeling of joyous exultation had invaded my soul. I was trying to repress my feelings and to restrain my laughter. I can now realise how the almighty Deliverer is able, in the twinkling of an eye, to turn pain into ease, and sorrow into gladness."' (Nabil, *The Dawn-Breakers*, pp. 147–8)

HINDU HOLY MAN: In this nineteenth-century Indian picture drawn for the prince of Mandi, a king and merchant who have suffered misfortune visit the hermit-saint Medhas for his blessing.

(although certain steps may be taken to induce the experience, it then takes over and possesses the person).[10]

A wide range of experiences can be included in this category. At its simplest level is the sudden illumination with which one understands a religious truth in a text that one has read previously without 'seeing' this truth in it. A deeper level comes from flashes of intense experience:

> On my way back, suddenly, without warning, I felt I was in Heaven – an inward state of peace and joy and assurance indescribably intense, accompanied with a sense of being bathed in a warm glow of light, as though the external condition had brought about the internal effect – a feeling of having passed beyond the body, though the scene around me stood out more clearly and as if nearer to me than before, by reason of the illumination in the midst of which I seemed to be placed. This deep emotion lasted, though with decreasing strength, until I reached home, and for some time after, only gradually passing away.[11]

Although all agree that to describe fully the advanced mystic state is impossible, the Muslim theologian and mystic al-Ghazali tried to outline it:

> With this first stage of the 'way' there begin the revelations and visions. The mystics in their waking state now behold angels and the spirits of the

> prophets; they hear these speaking to them and are instructed by them. Later, a higher state is reached; instead of beholding forms and figures, they come to stages in the 'way' which it is hard to describe in language; if a man attempts to express these, his words inevitably contain what is erroneous . . . He who has attained the mystic 'state' need do no more than say: Of the things I do not remember, what was, was; Think it good; do not ask an account of it (Ibn al-Mu'tazz).[12]

Al-Ghazali's last remark refers to the fact that many mystics have asserted that in the highest mystic state, they become one with Ultimate Reality. In the words of Meister Eckhart: 'God must be very I, I very God, so consummately one that this he and this I are one *is*.'[13] Statements asserting an identity with God (for a Western mystic or with Absolute Reality – Brahman, Nirvana, or Tao – for an Eastern mystic), were unacceptable to an orthodox Muslim theologian such as al-Ghazali. Having experienced the state, he did not, however, doubt its authenticity, merely the interpretation put upon it by many mystics. He considered the experience to be beyond description, beyond any analysis.

Islamic artists, prohibited from drawing human images, tried to depict their religious experience through abstract patterns. This picture shows tilework from the Sultan Ahmet Mosque, Istanbul.

The Paranormal Experience

A wide range of paranormal experiences have been reported. Some of these have no particular religious connection in the West: for example telepathy, psychokinesis and clairvoyance. Some may consider that the difference between clairvoyance and the power of prophecy (which is considered a religious 'gift') is merely a question of the setting in which it occurs. Clairvoyance, however, tends to be giving an individual specific information, usually about worldly matters. Prophecy tends more to be a general warning and is usually about religious matters. Some holy men are credited with being able to read the minds or souls of others. Again, this differs from telepathy in that the content of the former tends to be spiritual affairs, the latter worldly matters. In the West, this sort of paranormal activity is frowned upon by the religiously orthodox. In the Hindu and Buddhist traditions, however, paranormal activities are often regarded as evidence that a holy man has reached a high spiritual station.

Some of these experiences have, however, even in the West, been taken as evidence for the reality of the spiritual world and hence for the truth of religious claims. These include contacts with the dead through mediums and, more recently, near-death experiences. If accepted as true, the contact of mediums with those who are dead would powerfully confirm religious teachings about life after death. The following oral account of a 'being of light' encountered in a near-death experience may appear to some to confirm popular Western religious expectations about what will happen after death:

> It did seem that it [the being of light] was a little dim at first, but then it was this huge beam. It was just a tremendous amount of light . . . it was just too much light. And it gave off heat to me; I felt a warm sensation. It was a bright yellowish white – more white. It was tremendously bright; I just can't describe it. It seemed to cover everything, yet it didn't prevent me from seeing everything around me . . . From the moment the light spoke to me, I felt really good – secure and loved. The love which came from it is just unimaginable, indescribable.[14]

The Religious Crisis

Very often the precursor to an intense religious experience, such as those described above, is a religious crisis. In our lives, we build up cognitive structures that enable us to interpret and deal with our experiences, to make sense of our perceptions (for more on this, see pp. 167–9). A religious crisis is usually a period of existential doubt; a questioning of one's cognitive structures; a loss of confidence in one's interpretation of the world. The previous answers to existential questions (Who am I? Why am I here? What will happen after death?) no longer seem adequate or convincing. Interestingly, although many such crises are precipitated by a stressful situation such as ill-health, bereavement or financial problems, many report that their existential crisis occurs at a time when all other needs are satisfied. There are three possible outcomes to such a crisis.

1. A resolution within current cognitive structures. The person in crisis may eventually be able to resolve the crisis within his or her existing cognitive structures. This may be done by delving more deeply into the scriptures of one's religion and finding an answer there. Alternatively, discussion with one's fellow-believers may result in a solution being found. This may then be reported as a confirming religious experience.
2. A creative response, change to a new cognitive structure. The inner struggle may reach the point at which the existing cognitive structures dissolve. Since our cognitive structures define reality for us, some report it as a dissolution of reality. At this point, the religious person often reports a sense of surrendering the self (giving up one's existing cognitive structures, which define one's self). Following this surrender, a new vision may emerge, a new way of looking at the questions, a new self, a new cognitive structure, the basis for a new reality. This may be reported as a confirming or conversion experience, but will usually be more intense than the first outcome.

3. A PATHOLOGICAL RESPONSE, COGNITIVE DISSONANCE. Some may react to the threatened breakup of their reality by retreating into denial of the problems that caused the crisis. In effect, they build up a fantasy world in which they create a reality that accords with their cognitive structures. This type of process is usually unstable and eventually breaks down, as such a response negatively affects the way that such people function in society. The process can usually only be stabilized by indivduals either retreating from society or finding social support for this pathological response. In Hitler's Germany, for example, it was possible for people who considered that they held high ethical standards to stand by and do nothing when Jews were attacked. The internal inconsistencies in their mental processes received a large degree of external social support. A combination of social isolation and social support occurs in some fundamentalist groups or new religious movements. In these groups, beliefs that are at variance with the conceptual universe of society can be kept up by restricting interaction with the outside world. Tightly knit communities are established, so that almost all of the social interactions of the believer are with others of the group.

A Psychological Model of the Stages of Religious Experience

The descriptions of religious experience given above have caused some to propose psychological models for religious experience. It has been suggested, for example, that the stages of religious experience are similar to the stages that have been described for creativity. One description of the creative process involves four stages:

1. PREPARATION. A problem arises that baffles the individual because it cannot be accommodated within the existing structures, giving rise to an intense, frustrating struggle with the problem.
2. INCUBATION. The struggle ends with the individual giving up and either going off to some form of relaxation or turning their attention to other matters.
3. ILLUMINATION. While attention is not on the problem, it seems as though the mind is able to reorganize the problem at the subconscious level, so that a new and often unexpected insight appears.
4. VERIFICATION. The new concept must be tried out, elaborated and compared with existing concepts to see if it is really able to solve the problem that was causing bafflement in the first stage.[15]

These stages may have a physiological base, in that ceasing to think about the problem may allow it to be transferred from the dominant to the non-dominant hemisphere, which is probably responsible for the maintenance of cognitive structures. This then allows a reorganization of the cognitive structures leading to a new insight into the problem (see also p. 178)

It is postulated that religious experience follows a similar sequence. The first stage is that of the religious existential crisis, described above. This corresponds to the stage of preparation in the creative process. The struggles of the first stage of the religious experience end in a point of despair and hopelessness, which some religious writers have referred to as the 'dark night of the soul' while others call it the stage of self-surrender. At this stage, the individual acknowledges his or her inability to resolve the problem or crisis and 'lets go', allowing the old ways of thinking to dissolve. This corresponds to the stage of incubation in the creative process. Out of the despair of this situation a new vision emerges, a new truth is revealed, often suddenly and unexpectedly, transforming everything in that person's previous life. This is what has been described above as the religious experience itself, and corresponds to the stage of illumination in the creative process. Lastly, as mentioned above, most would say that a true religious experience must have some consequent beneficial effect in the way that one lives one's life. This corresponds to the stage of verification in the creative process.[16]

A religious experience may therefore be thought of as a cognitive restructuring that occurs to deal with an existential problem or crisis. It must be noted, however, that not every religious experience results in a cognitive restructuring that enables one to deal better with a wider range of people and experiences. Just as not everyone who goes through the stages of the creative process comes out with a solution that can be confirmed as being better than the existing solutions, in the same way, some religious experiences can lead to a decrease in one's repertoire of adaptive responses to life. Religious experiences can lead to a flight from the real world into fantasy, excessive emotional dependance on a religious leader or group, or an increased rigidity in one's conceptualizations, through an excessive attachment to dogma.

One can therefore construct psychological criteria for the evaluation of a religious experience (although it may be difficult to assess whether these criteria have been met). One can ask whether, after the experience, a person is better able to deal with his or her social and physical environment; whether the actions of that person are consistent with the values and teachings that he or she espouses; and whether that person can be shown to have a greater sense of direction and well-being.

Mediators of Religious Experience

A religious experience occurs whenever a person believes that the sacred has appeared. A hierophany (the appearance of the sacred) can be mediated through a number of different objects or activities. Many of these mediators have symbolic or mythic significance. This issue is discussed at greater length in chapter 11. A few mediators and aspects of this subject that are not covered there are given here.

Scripture, Recital and Chanting

One of the most important aspects of the major world religions is their scriptures. For many the sacred is embodied in scripture. For the Western religions, scripture is considered to be revelatory. This can be understood in two interlinked senses: scripture reveals the will of God; and scripture reveals to human beings what the world is really like. For Muslims, for example, the *Qur'an* is the revealed Word of God. The earthly *Qur'an* is a replica of the Mother Book, an uncreated heavenly entity that is co-eternal with God.[17] It is stated to be inimitable. Hindus similarly believe that the *Vedas* exist eternally. At the beginning of each cosmic cycle they are revealed to certain sages to serve as a guidance for humanity for that cycle.

The language of most scriptures is different from ordinary, everyday speech. Most of what we say and write attempts to convey a straightforward unambiguous message. Scripture is sometimes like that, but its most important task is to try to describe that which cannot be described. The reality to which it is refers transcends our worldly reality. Since our language is confined to words that describe our experiences in this world, scripture cannot use language in a straightforward manner. The statements that it makes are not intended to convey information in the same way as a cookery book. It does not envisage that all readers will read it in the same way. In trying to convey its message, scripture uses various devices. It uses images, metaphors and parables. These have the advantage that they can be understood at many different levels, according to the state of mind and capacity of the reader. They contain multiple layers of meaning, evoking in different people divergent responses. Some may take what is written literally, some may take it symbolically, allegorically or metaphorically.

In þe bigynnyng was þe word & þe word was
at god · & god was þe word/ þis was in þe bigy̅
nyng at god/ alle þingis weren maad bi him:
and wiþouten him was maad noþing/ þat þing
þat was maad in him was lif · and þe lif was
þe lizt of men/ and þe lizt schyneþ in derknessis · and
derknessis comprehendiden not it/

LANGUAGE OF SCRIPTURE: Beginning of St John's Gospel in the version by John Wycliffe (c.1330–84), a forerunner of the Protestant Reformation, who initiated the first translation of the *Bible* into English

In the *New Testament*, for example, Jesus is recorded as restoring sight to the blind (*John* 9:6–7). Some may read that literally as a physical miracle. Others may look to the words that Jesus said to the man: 'For judgement I am come into this world, that they which see not might see; and that they which see might be made blind' (*John* 9:39) and decide that the real meaning is a metaphorical restoration of the man's spiritual sight so that he could recognize the true nature of Christ. Alternatively, a non-logical juxtaposition of words or a paradox challenges the mind to

a

c

b

RELIGIOUS METAPHORS: The Tree of Life. a) Christ as the Vine. This is an iconic representation of the verse "I am the vine, you are the branches" (*John* 15:5). Jesus is in the centre, with his arms in a gesture of conferring blessings. The disciples are the branches. God and the Holy Spirit (in the form of a dove) are above Jesus. Icon in the Museum of Icons, Venice, by Victor, 1674. b) The Buddha Amitayus as Tree of Life. On the left side of this view of a pillar at Sanchi (first century CE) is an aniconic representation of the Buddha, with feet (*padaka*) at the bottom, marked with the wheel (*chakra*), and a tree as a body consisting of superimposed lotus palmettes with fruits and garlands of pearls to the side; another wheel forms the head, crowned by a trident (*trishula*). c) In the Baha'i Faith, Baha'u'llah often refers to himself in his writings as the Sadrat al-Muntaha (the Tree beyond which there is no passing), the tree being both guide on the spiritual journey and a limit. In this calligraphy by the Baha'i artist Mishkin Qalam, there is also reference to the metaphor of Baha'u'llah as a bird of paradise singing the divine melody.

break through its conventional reality to the transcendent reality towards which scripture is pointing.

> And he [Jesus] said unto another, Follow me. But he said, Lord, suffer me first to go and bury my father. Jesus said unto him, Let the dead bury their dead: but go thou and preach the kingdom of God.[18]

In this passage there is a metaphor contrasting the spiritual life offered by Christ and the death suffered by refusing his message; there is also a contrast between the significant sacred activity of spreading the gospel and profane family obligations. These ideas are forced upon the mind by the non-logical paradoxical picture of the dead being instructed to carry out an action.

This creative function of trying to propel people into a new vision and hence into a new life by the use of words is also found in the Zen Buddhist *koan*. The *koan* is a question or problem that tries to force the student to view reality in a new way, thus leading to enlightenment. A famous example is: 'What should you do if you meet the Buddha coming along the road?' While the conventional mind may come up with an answer such as 'Follow him', one Zen answer is 'Kill him'. The shock to the mind caused by the answer is meant as a trigger for thoughts about the necessity for self-reliance.

Scripture is thus like poetry. It seeks to be evocative and even emotive, rather than descriptive or rational. It is trying to convey a picture or an ethos. It is trying to evoke in the reader a certain response. Ultimately, it is trying to get its readers to transform themselves. It seeks to create a new reality within its reader or hearer. In summary, then, scripture performs the dual functions described above for the creative process: first, it breaks down a persons's existing conventional reality; second, it creates a new alternative reality. Religious art and poetry can act in a similar way as mediators of religious experience.

Scripture, in most religions, is also the writing down of the sacred stories that were, for many centuries, handed down from one generation to the next

EVOKING GOD: DESCRIBING THE INDESCRIBABLE

In this verse, an attempt is made to describe the indescribable using imagery and non-logical language ('light upon light') to evoke a certain mental picture:

God is the Light of the heavens and the earth. The similitude of His light is as a niche wherein is a lamp. The lamp is in a glass. The glass is as it were a shining star. [This lamp is] kindled from a blessed tree, an olive neither of the East nor of the West, whose oil would almost glow forth [of itself] though no fire touched it. It is light upon light. God guideth unto His light whom He will. And God speaketh to mankind in allegories, for God is the knower of all things. (*Qur'an* 24:35)

THE COMMUNAL EXPERIENCE OF THE SCRIPTURES: Recitation of the Hindu epic, the *Ramayana*, the story of Rama, in a home setting in Britain

orally. In this way, scripture parallels the oral traditions of tribal and traditional cultures. This aspect of scripture usually preserves the myths that explain for the believer how things came to be the way they are. (On this aspect of scripture, see pp. 286–95, 332–7.)

Although some people may use the scriptures privately, the majority of people experience the scriptures communally. The recital of scripture, said in an attitude of sincerity and devotion, whether privately or communally, will often result in a religious experience. Many scriptures are, however, written in a language beyond the understanding of their audience. In such cases, it is not the reading and understanding of the scripture that creates the religious experience, but the hearing of the recital or chanting of it and the atmosphere evoked by this. The scriptures are often in a form that makes them suitable for chanting in order to evoke an atmosphere. This chanting is carried out in accordance with a specific tradition. In the Jewish synagogue, the office of cantor was created for the person who carries out the liturgical chanting. The *Bible* may be chanted by Christians according to the Gregorian, Armenian, Greek, Russian or other traditions. In Islam, much of the *Qur'an* is in the form of rhymed prose, which is especially evocative when chanted. Among Baha'is in the Middle East, the scripture is usually chanted rather than read, although this is a practice that has not spread much to other Baha'i communities. In Hinduism, the chanting of mantras is considered to bestow special powers. In Buddhist monasteries, the scriptures are chanted at regular intervals during the day (a practice called *paritta* in Theravada Buddhism). Hearing such chanting within the atmosphere evoked by a holy place such as a church or temple is itself a religious experience for many believers.

THE USE OF MUSIC IN A RITUAL CONTEXT: Buddhist monks blow conch shells and beat a drum accompanying a ritual recital of the scriptures. Gandantegchinlen Monastery, Mongolia.

Ritual

Human beings organize a great deal of their social interactions into formal customary patterns. On meeting someone for the first time in the West, for example, one goes through a formal set of exchanges of words and a handshake. Ritual is the set of formal customary practices related to religion. For the followers of a religion, however, ritual is, like scripture, a hierophany: it is the appearance of the sacred. Through the performance of the ritual, the sacred is evoked. The ritual may include reading or chanting from scripture, hymns, certain actions, certain sounds (such as gongs, cymbals and bells), certain smells (such as incense), religious symbols and music, all contributing towards the evocation of the sacred.

Ritual is probably the most common source of religious experience for the majority of people. Indeed for many people, ritual is religion. For many Indians, Japanese Shintoists and tribal peoples, religion consists almost exclusively of various rituals (such as rites of passage and daily or seasonal rituals). Although these rituals may imply certain beliefs, these tend to be the interpretation of scholars and are not usually in the consciousness of ordinary people when they participate in a ritual.

Ritual may be regarded as an important part of the knowledge that a believer has about her or his religion. While cognitive knowledge may give the individual the facts about a religion, ritual gives knowledge of the 'feel' or 'milieu' of the religion; it conveys non-cognitive, affective information (what some may call holistic knowledge). The simple fact that one kneels before an icon of the Virgin Mary in some sects of Christianity conveys a great deal more information about the religion than hours of preaching or instruction would do. Attitudes towards oneself, other people, and towards Ultimate Reality, are all conveyed more directly and powerfully through ritual than by any other means. Most importantly, ritual can itself be the source of the central experience of religion. Whether the ritual is that of an incense-filled church where the priest is changing the bread and wine into the body and blood of Christ, or the techniques of meditation that lead to an altered state of consciousness, the result can be a direct experience of the sacred. To new converts, therefore, the learning of ritual is just as important as the learning of facts about their new religion. Indeed, I pose the question in chapter 7 (p. 180) whether it is the ritual elements in the religion that predispose those of that religion towards their theology and metaphysics or whether it is the theology and metaphysics that is primary and the ritual that merely supports it. Ritual also reinforces the communal religious experience, the feeling of group solidarity and unity and the sense of belonging to something that is greater than the individuals who comprise it (see Durkheim's views on this, pp. 53–4).

There are numerous forms of ritual: rites of purification, regeneration, thanksgiving, self-denial, penance and propitiation. It is difficult at times to differentiate religious ritual from magic. Both imply a supra-natural process. Rituals are often rites of passage (that is, related to the life-cycle: birth, puberty, marriage, death), rites related to the calendar (weekly rituals, spring, harvest, winter and New Year rituals), or the formal re-enactment of a sacred story or event. This aspect of ritual is discussed further in chapter 11.

Prayer, Fasting and Other Austerities

Prayer and fasting are to be found in some form in most religions. They are ways in which people prepare themselves for religious experience. Prayer

DAILY PRAYER: Some Sikh families have a room dedicated to prayer where their scripture, the *Adi Granth*, is kept. Prayers are said there daily.

acts by creating the circumstances in which the believer is able to focus, in a complete and concentrated way, on the sacred. Prayer may be said in penitence, imploring forgiveness of the Deity for something one has done wrong; in propitiation, to try to regain the favour of the Deity when one has offended it; in thanksgiving for some bounty received; in petition for some bounty; or simply in praise of a Deity. Some would consider that prayer should be discussed under the heading of rituals. In traditional societies, prayers are often said as part of a ritual attempt to influence, or gain power over, natural events. In the major world religions, apart from the prayer that is ritual and formal, there is also prayer that is performed privately and spontaneously. It is then no longer a ritual.

The various positions adopted during the Muslim daily ritual prayer (*salat*). The left-hand half shows the standing positions (*qiyam*) and the bending position (*ruku'*). On the right are the sitting positions (*jalsa*) and the prostration (*sajda*). The numbers indicate the order in which the positions are adopted, some positions being taken more than once.

In Islam, for example, there is the obligatory ritual prayer (*salat*) to be said five times a day, preferably congregationally, in the mosque. This is said in obedience to the command of God in the *Qur'an*. There is also private prayer, invoking and supplicating God (*du'a*) or in private conversation with God (*munajat*). Christians say public congregational prayers in church services and private prayers at home. Prayer is also to be found in the Eastern religions. Although Theravada Buddhism does not have the concept of a deity, sections of the scripture are chanted (*paritta*) in a manner that is functionally identical to the saying of communal prayers in Western religions.[19]

Fasting is also to be found in most religions. It may be a symbolic expression of a desire for purity and self-denial in order to be fit to experience the presence of the deity. Alternatively, fasting can be done in penance and expiation for wrongdoing. Some traditions have also regarded it as a means to spiritual regeneration.

In Western Christianity, fasting is rapidly disappearing as a form of religious activity. It is still practised in Catholicism to a limited extent, but much more in the Eastern churches. Jews fast on particular days, especially Yom Kippur, the Day of Atonement. The Muslim fast is from dawn to dusk during the month of Ramadan. Baha'is fast from sunrise to sunset during the nineteen days of the last month of their calendar. Most Hindus observe fasts, although these differ among the various branches of the religion. Fasting is also part of many traditional religions. Native Americans fast in order to become worthy of being possessed by a spirit or as part of a vision quest.

Apart from, or as part of, fasting, other austerities are often practised in religions. These signify self-denial, a readiness to be detached from the physical world in order to be worthy of entering the spiritual realm, a

a

b

Self-flagellation is an extreme expression of penitence and repentance. It is often an expression of grief at the suffering and martyrdom of a central figure in the religion and an acknowledgement of humanity's common responsibility for this event. a) A Shi'i Muslim Muharram ceremony, Karachi, 1982. These ceremonies take place in Iran and Pakistan to commemorate the martyrdom of the Imam Husayn. b) Self-flagellation was also common in medieval Christianity and has survived in a few places to the present day. This picture of flagellants was taken in the 1960s in San Vicente de la Sonsierra, Spain, during Holy Week.

preparation for religious experience. Austerities include abstaining from sexual intercourse, which is part of the Islamic and some Jewish fasts, and wearing harsh, simple clothing, which is part of the Islamic pilgrimage. More severe austerities are usually confined to monks or ascetics. Self-flagellation is, however, performed by ordinary people at the Muharram commemorations in Shi'i Islam. Severe self-denial of food, to the point of starvation, together with self-inflicted pain (mortification of the flesh) can be found in both Hindu and Christian tradition. It is also part of some primal religious traditions, such as the vision quest of Native Americans. Such austerities can lead to a trance-like state by inducing altered states of consciousness and psychic phenomena. Severe austerities are specifically forbidden by the founders of Buddhism and the Baha'i Faith.

Meditation and Altered States of Consciousness

The process of meditation appears to work by stopping the normal flow of thought, thus allowing the individual to open himself or herself to concepts and ideas that would not have emerged otherwise. Some techniques of meditation and other activities prescribed by some religions can also bring about an altered state of consciousness.

There are many different techniques of meditation in the world's religions. In Hinduism, which has perhaps developed these techniques more than any other religious tradition, there are a range of practices: controlling bodily functions, especially breathing (*pranayama*); concentrating on visual images (*mandalas*); repetitive chanting of a word or phrase (mantras); or a simple repetitive bodily movement (*mudra*). In Theravada Buddhism, the technique involves focusing the attention on some object or concept. Zen Buddhist techniques include contemplating a *koan* (see p. 103) or becoming aware of, but not distracted by, thought, sensations or one's breathing. In Islam, Sufi techniques have involved repetitive chanting and, in one Sufi order, a whirling dance. Christian meditation techniques can involve long prayer vigils, contemplation of the Cross, or repetition of simple prayers. Meditation is a daily activity for Baha'is, but no particular technique is advocated.

Altered states of consciousness can be brought about by some of these techniques, especially repetitive chanting, rhythmic dancing, and hyperventilation (over-breathing, rapid shallow breathing). This altered state of consciousness is then interpreted by the participant as a religious experience. Some religious groups (such as Rastafarians and the Native American Church) have used drugs to achieve altered states of consciousness. (The scientific background to altered states of consciousness is considered in chapter 7.)

The Performance of the Religious Professional

The religious professional may himself (or, less commonly, herself) be a mediator of religious experience. This can be in the form of a rousing and stirring oration, for example the preaching of a Christian evangelical preacher, or through a more dramatic performance, as occurs with shamans and other similar religious professionals. The religious experience comes as a result of the highly charged, emotional atmosphere that is created. In such conditions, some participants may have charismatic religious experiences and exhibit features typical of that, such as ecstatic trance and speaking in tongues.

It has been suggested that the charismatic religious experience mediated through a preacher or shaman occurs through the participant hyperventilating, the experience being the result of an altered state of consciousness induced by this. Certainly, a trance-like state can be induced by hyperventilation which is not dissimilar to the trance-like state brought on by repetitive chanting in certain mystical groups.

Unity and Fellowship

Although many in the West think of religious experience as a private, individual affair, in the rest of the world religious experience usually occurs communally. A communal religious experience may be said to occur whenever the community feels that the 'sacred' has appeared. This can occur communally through ritual, as described above, but it can also occur

NATURE AS MEDIATOR OF THE RELIGIOUS EXPERIENCE IN TAOISM: 'Having embraced Tao the sage responds harmoniously to things. Having purified his mind, the worthy man enjoys forms. Landscapes exist in material substance and soar into the realm of the spirit . . . Mountains and rivers in their form pay homage to Tao, and the man of humanity delights in them.' (Tsung Ping, quoted in Parrinder, *Mysticism in the World's Religions*, p. 71)

in any meeting of the body of the believers. Among the effects of religion is the strong sense of unity and fellowship among the members of a religious community. This can itself be a significant religious experience. Religion, by creating a bond between members of the community, acts to knit the community together. It provides a higher focus of loyalty, under which petty disputes and antagonisms can be set aside. For Durkheim, this was the primary function of religion and the source of the religious experience (see pp. 53–4).

Nature

Many people, from all religious traditions, have found the contemplation of nature a mediator of religious experience. This can be found, for example, in English poets such as Blake and Wordsworth, in the Hindu *Upanishads*, in Japanese Buddhism, in many native African and American religious traditions and in Taoism.

Dreams and Visions

Dreams and visions have played an important role in the religious experience of humanity. Visions are part of the religious experience itself, but dreams can be considered mediators of a religious experience. There are two main ways that dreams mediate religious experiences. The first is the veridical dream, the dream that later comes true. In the religious context, these are usually dreams that provide some form of guidance that shapes the person's life.

A VERIDICAL DREAM

Again I had an unusual dream. In this dream I felt oppressed by the crowded city. I walked for blocks until I came to an open meadow . . . I looked up and saw a man coming across the meadow. He walked with such dignity and grace that I knew he was a man of God. He wore a white turban and long robes of black and white. A snow-white beard framed his face. His eyes were crystal blue like an early morning sky.

He stood before me and I asked him a question. 'Why isn't man as beautiful as the flowers?' He looked away for a moment and I saw a sadness in his eyes that told me he had seen men do worse things than I could ever imagine. Then he looked at me and said, 'Because a man does not live in the Will of God as much as a flower does.'

Seven years passed and there was still nothing to lead me to the wise man of God. Perhaps it had, after all, been only a dream . . .

One of the booths at the Fair caught my attention. It had in bold letters: 'BAHA'I . . .' I had never heard of the Baha'i Faith and had no idea what it could be . . . One of the pamphlets caught my eye. On it was a drawing of an elderly bearded man. A white turban crowned his head. I stared in amazement.

Could this be the man whom I had been seeking for so long? The pamphlet said the man's name was 'Abdu'l-Baha . . .

As I walked into the Baha'i home, the first thing that caught my eye was a portrait of 'Abdu'l-Baha . . . His eyes were a clear blue . . . Mr Stephens showed me some photographs of 'Abdu'l-Baha. One of them was taken in 1912 when he was in Chicago. In this picture he was slender and wore a long black robe exactly like the wise man I had dreamed about. (Terralin Carroll, quoted in Gottlieb, *Once to Every Man and Nation*, pp. 38–41)

A second way in which dreams and visions are important is when they provide a vision about the fate of humanity in general. Dreams and visions of this sort include much of the apocalyptic literature in the world's religions. One of the best-known of these is the *Book of Revelation*, also called the *Apocalypse of St John,* in the *Bible*.

AN APOCALYPTIC VISION

I John . . . was in the isle that is called Patmos . . . I was in the Spirit on the Lord's day, and heard behind me a great voice, as of a trumpet, Saying, I am Alpha and Omega, the first and the last: and, What thou seest, write in a book, and send [it] unto the seven churches . . . And I turned to see the voice that spake with me. And being turned, I saw seven golden candlesticks; And in the midst of the seven candlesticks [one] like unto the Son of man, clothed with a garment down to the foot, and girt about the paps with a golden girdle.

And I John saw the holy city, new Jerusalem, coming down from God out of heaven, prepared as a bride adorned for her husband. And I heard a great voice out of heaven saying, Behold, the tabernacle of God [is] with men, and he will dwell with them, and they shall be his people, and God himself shall be with them, [and be] their God.

And I John saw these things, and heard [them] . . . And he saith unto me, Seal not the sayings of the prophecy of this book: for the time is at hand . . . I Jesus have sent mine angel to testify unto you these things in the churches. I am the root and the offspring of David, [and] the bright and morning star. (*Book of Revelation* 1:9–13; 21:1–3; 22:8–10, 16)

In Mahayana Buddhism, instructions are given for the stages of meditation required to construct a vision of the Western Paradise (Sukhavati) of Amitabha Buddha. This vision leads the believer in stages to Nirvana[20] (see p. 112).

Dreams and visions also play an important part in many primal religions and also in most forms of popular religion. Among Native Americans of North America, dreams and visions (often while in a state of trance) are a common feature (see p. 113). In some tribes these are restricted to the shaman, in other tribes they are open to all.

The Buddha Teaches how to Gain a Vision of the Western Paradise (Sukhavati)

Thou shouldst sit down properly, looking in the western direction, and prepare thy thought for a close meditation on the sun; cause thy mind to be firmly fixed (on it) . . . and gaze upon it (more particularly) when it is about to set and looks like a suspended drum.

After thou hast thus seen the sun, let (that image) remain clear and fixed, whether thine eyes be shut or open; – such is the perception of the sun, which is the First Meditation.

Next thou shouldst form the perception of water; gaze on the water clear and pure, and let (this image) also remain clear and fixed (afterwards); never allow thy thought to be scattered and lost. When thou hast thus seen the water thou shouldst form the perception of ice. As thou seest the ice shining and transparent, thou shouldst imagine the appearance of lapis lazuli.

After that has been done, thou wilt see the ground consisting of lapis lazuli . . . Beneath this ground of lapis lazuli there will be seen a golden banner with the seven jewels, diamonds and the rest, supporting the ground . . . Every side of the eight quarters consists of a hundred jewels . . .

Each jewel has rays of five hundred colours which look like flowers or like the moon and stars. Lodged high up in the open sky these rays form a tower of rays . . . Both sides of the tower have each a hundred millions of flowery banners furnished and decked with numberless musical instruments . . . – such is the perception of the water, which is the Second Meditation.

When this perception has been formed, thou shouldst meditate on its (constituents) one by one and make (the images) as clear as possible, so that they may never be scattered and lost, whether thine eyes be shut or open. Except only during the time of thy sleep, thou shouldst always keep this in thy mind. One who has reached this (stage of) perception is said to have dimly seen the land of Highest Happiness (Sukhavati).

One who has obtained the Samadhi (the state of supernatural calm) is able to see the land (of the Buddha country) clearly and distinctly . . . – such is the perception of the land and it is the Third Meditation.

Thou shouldst remember, O Ananda, the Buddha words of mine, and repeat this law for attaining to the perception of the land (of the Buddha country) for the sake of the great mass of the people hereafter who may wish to be delivered from their sufferings. If any one meditates on the land (of that Buddha country), his sins (which bind him to) births and deaths during eighty millions of *kalpas* [aeons] shall be expiated; after the abandonment of his (present) body, he will assuredly be born in the pure land in the following life. The practice of this kind of meditation is called the right meditation. If it be of another kind it is called 'heretical meditation.' [The Buddha goes on in this *sutra* to give another thirteen meditations] (*Amitayur-Dhyana-Sutra*, in Cowell et al., *Buddhist Mahayana Texts*, pp. 169–172)

LAME DEER'S VISION QUEST

I was all alone on the hilltop. I sat there in the vision pit, a hole dug into the hill, my arms hugging my knees as I watched old man Chest, the medicine man who had brought me there, disappear far down in the valley . . .

Now I was all by myself, left on the hilltop for four days and nights without food or water until he came back for me . . . I was sixteen then, still had my boy's name and, let me tell you, I was scared. I was shivering and not only from the cold. The nearest human being was many miles away, and four days and nights is a long, long time . . .

Night was coming on. I was still lightheaded and dizzy from my first sweat bath in which I had purified myself before going up the hill . . .

Sounds came to me through the darkness: the cries of the wind, the whisper of the trees, the voices of nature, animal sounds, the hooting of an owl. Suddenly I felt an overwhelming presence. Down there with me in my cramped hole was a big bird. The pit was only as wide as myself, and I was a skinny boy, but that huge bird was flying around me as if he had the whole sky to himself . . . This feeling was so overwhelming that it was just too much for me. I trembled and my bones turned to ice . . .

Slowly I perceived that a voice was trying to tell me something. It was a bird cry, but I tell you, I began to understand some of it . . . All at once I was way up there with the birds . . . A voice said, '. . . We are the fowl people, the winged ones, the eagles and the owls . . . and you shall be our brother . . . You are going to understand us whenever you come to seek a vision here on this hill. You will learn about herbs and roots, and you will heal people. You will ask them for nothing in return. A man's life is short. Make yours a worthy one.'

I had lost all sense of time. I did not know whether it was day or night. I was asleep, yet wide awake. Then I saw a shape before me. It rose from the darkness and the swirling fog which penetrated my earth hole. I saw that this was my great-grandfather, Tahca Ushte, Lame Deer . . . I could see the blood dripping from [his] chest where a white soldier had shot him. I understood that my great-grandfather wished me to take his name. This made me glad beyond words.

I didn't know how long I had been up there on that hill – one minute or a lifetime. I felt a hand on my shoulder gently shaking me. It was old man Chest, who had come for me. He told me that I had been in the vision pit four days and four nights . . . He would interpret my visions for me. He told me that the vision pit had changed me in a way that I would not be able to understand at that time. He told me also that I was no longer a boy, that I was a man now. I was Lame Deer. (Halifax, *Shamanic Voices*, pp. 71–5)

The Social Influence on Religious Experience

The Western Paradise of Amitabha Buddha: 'Passing from here through hundreds of thousands of millions of Buddhalands to the West, there is a world called Ultimate Bliss (Sukhavati). In this land a Buddha called Amitabha right now teaches the Dhamma, . . . All living beings of this country endure none of the sufferings, but enjoy every bliss.' (From the *Amitabha Sutra*)

Most people who have a religious experience at any level assume that it is a pure experience coming to them from outside themselves – in other words, its form and content originate in some other reality and are unaffected by the particulars of the person to whom it occurs. This has been described as an 'irruption' of the sacred world into the profane (see chapter 11). On closer examination, however, this cannot entirely be the case. We shall look at some reasons for this.

The first point worth noting is that religious experiences tend to conform closely to cultural and religious expectations. Village girls in Portugal have visions of the Virgin Mary – not of the Indian goddess Kali. Native Americans on their vision quest see visions of North American animals not of African ones. Thus it would appear that religious experiences, no matter how intense and all-consuming, are subject to constraint by the cultural and religious norms of the person to whom they occur. Another way of looking at this is to say that there can be no such thing as a pure experience. An experience always happens to a person, and that person already has an interpretative framework through which he or she views the world. Thus, experience and interpretation always combine and interpenetrate.

The most basic interpretative framework is language. We do not have an experience and then find the words to describe it. Our language prefigures our experience of the world. A Canadian Inuit has many different words that are equivalent to the single word 'snow' in the English language. Arab Bedouins have many different words for the single word 'camel' in the English language. This means that when native English speakers look at snow they see just one thing, whereas an Inuit sees many different types of snow. Similarly, when native English speakers look at camels, they see just one type of animal; an Arab Bedouin will see many different types of camel. Thus, it is language that enables us to have experiences, or at least to have the richness of experience that we have. Therefore, the description of a person's religious experience is confined within the language and conceptual world of that person.

All human beings are constrained in the range of their possible experiences by the culture and society in which they live and were brought up. We may think that we are free to choose whatever religious style of life we like, but in fact we are very unlikely to choose some and very likely to choose others, because of our background. This background to our lives, which plays such a large part in determining our actions and experiences, can be divided into two aspects. The first is our history: what we were taught in our family and school, our childhood experiences and our culture. The second is our current environment: our social role, our current group of family and friends. Both of these factors play a large part in the way that we experience the world. If we have a religious experience, we are very likely to interpret it in a way that conforms to the norms of our culture and upbringing and makes sense to our family and friends. If a person has an intense religious experience, they are likely to attribute it to a meeting with God or Christ if they are from a Christian background, which emphasizes a close personal relationship with God or Christ. If they are from a certain Hindu background they may describe it as encountering the Divine Self (Atman).

Using surveys and interviews, researchers have been able to document the effects of social factors on religious activity and experience. Most of this work has been done in the United States and so the results that can be presented here are from that country only and may not apply elsewhere. The following social factors have been reported[21]:

1. SEX. Women are more likely than men to attend religious services (a ratio of 55:45), to pray daily (64:38), and to report having mystical experiences (44:36). Women are also more likely to experiment religiously than men. As one moves from the traditional orthodox churches to the new religious movements, the proportion of women members increases. This is one finding that is likely to be different in other parts of the world. In traditional societies, it is usually young men who have the greatest freedom to change. Thus it is they who are more likely to be able to break away from traditional religious structures and join new religious movements.

2. RACE. Black people are more likely than white to attend religious services, feel strongly about religious beliefs and report religious experiences.

3. SOCIO-ECONOMIC STATUS. Members of the upper and middle classes are more likely to attend religious services regularly but are less likely to report religious experiences, than members of lower classes. Members of lower classes are more likely to join religious groups that involve emotional, spontaneous, physically active, fundamentalist religious expression; middle- and upper class people prefer religion that is verbal, intellectual, reflective, liberal and organized.

4. EDUCATION. Education is strongly correlated with socio-economic status and thus parallels what has been stated in point 3. Increasing

educational attainment correlates positively with attendance at religious services, but negatively with reporting religious experiences.

5. SIZE OF COMMUNITY. Those living in small towns and in rural areas are more likely to attend religious services and are more likely to report religious or mystical experiences than those living in cities.
6. PARENT'S RELIGION: Not surprisingly, given the important role of parents in their children's upbringing and socialization, there is a strong correlation between a person's religion and their parents' religion.

Using such information, we can go a long way towards predicting the religious experiences that a person will probably have, given his or her cultural background. We can predict that an African-American working-class woman raised in the American South will have a close personal relationship with God, with whom she will talk daily in prayer. Her religious experiences will occur from about the age of eleven throughout most of her life. We can predict that her most intense religious experiences will occur at tent revival meetings held in her town. They will be of an emotional nature (not visions or auditory experiences). At the peak of one of these revival meetings, she may feel that she has lost control and been taken over by the Spirit of God. She will believe that Jesus has saved her and that she will go to heaven when she dies. On a day-to-day basis, she will be closely involved in her local Pentecostal church and will derive much satisfaction and comfort from that.

Of course, this picture is a generalization. There are always exceptional individuals. The woman may, for example, show a high degree of academic ability. If she succeeds in breaking through the social influences that would constrain her to follow her mother's occupation and lifestyle, and if she wins a scholarship to a university, then we can make a new prediction about her. By obtaining an education, she will probably move into the middle classes. She will probably move from her Pentecostal church to a less emotive church such as a Methodist or suitable Baptist congregation and she may have fewer and less intense religious experiences than before she went to university.

FURTHER READING

Some of the earliest books in this field are still the best (although they tend to be heavily oriented towards Christianity): Otto, *The Idea of the Holy*, and James, *The Varieties of Religious Experience*. See also Stace, *Mysticism and Philosophy*; Cohen and Phipps, *The Common Experience*. For social influences on religious experience (social psychology), see Batson and Ventis, *The Religious Experience*, especially chapters 1–3.

5

Pathways to Religious Experience

In chapter 4 we noted that the central experience of religion is exhilarating and desirable; it commands respect and attention. It is not surprising, therefore, that human beings have sought to recreate and channel this experience in predictable and well-regulated ways by setting up formal, communal pathways to it. (On the historical evolution of this impetus, see chapter 12.)

On a more cynical note, one could say that the central experience of religion, although potentially very powerful, remains useless to individuals who seek power unless its very personal and private nature is given expression in some way. It is only by creating some form of social expression, some performative dimension, that religion can become a source of social power, that a professional religious class that instructs and educates people in one particular pathway can come into being, and that the potential power of religion can be harnessed by government or by those who seek power (see chapter 16).

People from widely differing religious cultures have described the central experience of religion itself in very similar terms (see chapter 4). Human cultures and personality types, however, vary greatly. It is not surprising, therefore, that the formal, communal pathways to recreating the religious experience, the performative dimension of religion, exhibit an enormous variety.

In this chapter I shall survey the various pathways that attempt to recreate the central experience of religion in a systematic way in society. These then are the principal forms in which religiosity expresses itself in society. Since the religious experience gives one the feeling of salvation or liberation, these pathways to religious experience may be called pathways to salvation or liberation.

Ritualism

This pathway to salvation is that of worship. It is the path of theism *par excellence*. On this path the believer concentrates her or his efforts on the correct performance of often very elaborate ritual. Participation in a

Figure 5.1 Social Expressions of the Central Experience of Religion: The Pathways to Salvation or Liberation

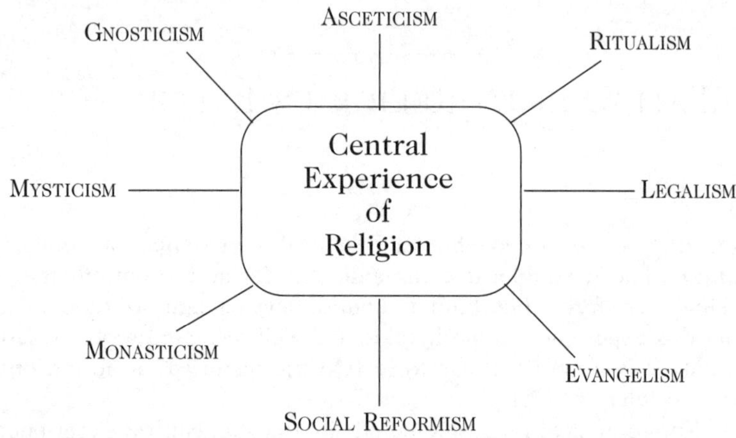

correctly performed ritual will atone for the sins of the believer and will in some way appease the Deity. Salvation then flows from the grace and beneficence of the Deity.

Very often, it is not just the form of the proceedings that must be correct but also the person carrying out the ritual. For it is in this type of religious proceedings that the priest plays a vital role. The priest must be correctly initiated into his priesthood; he (for it is almost always a man) must be of the correct lineage spiritually. For example, Roman Catholicism attaches great importance to the ordination of its priests and bishops in the Apostolic Succession (the spiritual lineage from St Peter). The priest may even have to be of the correct lineage physically: in many forms of Hinduism, only Brahmin descent entitles a person to priestly function; in ancient Israel, the descendants of Levi were the priestly tribe; and in Zoroastrianism, the priesthood is maintained among particular families. Only the priest can carry out the ritual correctly because only the priest can convert the mere form of the ritual into a vehicle for salvation; only the priest is empowered to turn the bread and wine into the body and blood of Christ. A comparison may be drawn between this mysterious power of the priest and the magical power of the shaman or witch doctor in primal religions.

Brahmin priests performing ablutions to purify themselves for a ritual. The three white horizontal lines mark them as being followers of Shiva.

Ritualism is usually based on theistic assumptions (see pp. 31–7) of the otherness of a God or god to whom praise and glorification are due. In turn, the processes of ritualism reinforce that theism by emphasizing the majesty and utter incomparability of the Deity. Such an exalted deity usually requires some form of saviour figure who will intercede on behalf of the believer. This saviour/intercessor is usually the prophet of the religion, such as Christ or Zoroaster. Lesser degrees of mediation are, however, often performed by saints or other figures such as the Virgin Mary in Catholicism or the Imams in Shi'i Islam.

An important aspect of ritual is the need for purity in order to participate in the ritual. Weber has pointed to an important distinction between these traditions. In those traditions in which the participant is only expected to be ritually pure (in other words, there is some mechanistic route to purification) the ritual has an emotive but temporary effect on the mass of the people. It has little effect on their lives. In those traditions where the person is also expected to be ethically purified in order to gain benefit from the ritual, there is a greater influence over the daily life of the individual. Weber stated that the effect is greater if the ethical purification comes as a result of striving to live a pure life (as in puritanical forms of Protestant Christianity) rather than confession of sins (as in Catholic Christianity).[1]

On this path, human beings achieve salvation partly through the grace of the Deity and partly through their own individual efforts and works. Usually these works include some meritorious ritual act that involves an element of expiation or penance for sins, and also the performance of good deeds. Judaism has its Day of Atonement (Yom Kippur) during which Jews undertake fasting and other rituals. Penance has in the past even taken extreme forms such as self-flagellation. This may still be seen today in Shi'i Islam, where there is ritual mourning and self-flagellation over the martyrdom of the Imam and humanity's failure to turn to the source of true guidance.[2]

Before the daily prayer, all Muslims must be in a state of ritual purity (*tahara*). In order to achieve this they perform ritual ablutions (*wudu'*).

The Goddess Kali is the wife and *shakti* (primal energy) of the god Shiva. She represents dissolution and destruction, but as she especially destroys evil and ignorance, she is also beneficent to her worshippers, blesses those who seek knowledge and maintains the world order. She is usually represented in a four-armed form with a sword in one hand, a decapitated head (of a demon) in another, the upper right arm making a gesture of fearlessness, while the lower right arm confers blessings. She wears a girdle of severed arms and a necklace of human skulls. She dances on the chest of Shiva.

Ritualism is by no means confined to the theistic religions. It is also to be found, for example, in most forms of Buddhism and Hinduism. Its appearance, however, usually accompanies the emergence of an attitude of devotion and worship.[3] In the case of Buddhism, the object of adoration is often the Buddha himself.

The typical religious attitude on this path is that of piety, love and devotion. There is both love and often some degree of awe or fear of the Deity or figure that is the object of the ritual or worship. In the object of devotion, whether it be the Western God or the Hindu deity Kali, there is a loving aspect which is beneficent and gracious. There is also a fearful aspect to the Deity, who can be wrathful, vengeful and destructive. The typical religious experience of this path is of the regenerative type, confirming and commissioning (see pp. 92–4).

Legalism

This path to salvation is characterized by the belief that the will of a deity has been revealed in the form of a Holy Law. This law determines most of one's actions in daily life. One achieves salvation by living one's life according to it. Ritualism and legalism are sometimes closely connected and difficult to differentiate. The holy laws are often obeyed as a way of maintaining the ritual purity of the individual or community, thus enabling the rituals to be effective. One can think of the difference between ritualism and legalism in terms of the intention or motivating factor behind an action: in legalism, an action, such as a prayer, is carried out because the Holy Law states that such a prayer should be said in particular circumstances; in ritualism, a prayer is said in order to achieve some spiritual, supra-mundane change.

The two major Western examples of this form of the social expression of religion are Judaism and Islam. In Judaism, the development of rabbinical law in the *Mishnah* and Halakhah has created a set of laws that lay down the details of most aspects of social life. The same situation occurs in Islam. The Shari'a (Holy Law) developed out of the *Qur'an* and the oral tradition (the *Hadith*) of the words and deeds of Muhammad. It defines

Table 5.1 Religious Experience and the Pathways of Salvation

PATHWAY	FOUND MAINLY IN	RELIGIOUS ATTITUDE	SOURCE OF RELIGIOUS EXPERIENCE	TYPE OF RELIGIOUS EXPERIENCE
Ritualism	Theism	Piety, devotion	Ritual, scripture, community	Regenerative, confirming or comissioning
Legalism	Theism	Discipline and self-control	Ritual, scripture, community	Regenerative, confirming or commissioning
Evangelism	Theism	Puritanical; love, devotion	Scripture, preaching	Charismatic
Social reformism	Theism	Outward-looking: service, love and charity towards all	Fellowship	Regenerative, commissioning
Asceticism	Theism Monism	Detachment	Scriptures, prayer, fasting and other austerities	Mystical or charismatic
Monasticism	Theism Monism	Inward-turning detachment	Scripture, prayer, fasting and other austerities, community	Mystical or regenerative, confirming
Gnosticism	Monism	Disciple: search for truth, obedience Spiritual master: detached love	Scriptures	Mystical or regenerative, confirming
Mysticism	Monism	Turning inwards, seeking direct experience, expansive love	Altered states of consciousness	Mystical

NOTE: See chapters 1 and 8 for theism and monism. See chapter 4 for the different types of religious experience.

most aspects of personal life and social intercourse. This extends from personal matters such as cleanliness, prayer and fasting, to legal matters such as marriage and inheritance, and even to commercial matters such as the terms of trade.

Legalism is also to be found in Brahminical Hinduism. The whole of the caste system is a legalistic framework concerned with maintaining the proper functioning of society. The rules laid down in books such as the

LEGALISM: RULINGS ON FORBIDDEN DEGREES OF MARRIAGE

HINDUISM

A (damsel) who is neither a Sapinda [related within three generations] on the mother's side, nor belongs to the same family on the father's side . . .

He who has approached the daugher of his father's sister, (who is almost equal to) a sister, (the daugher) of his mother's sister, or of his mother's full brother, shall perform a lunar penance. A wise man should not take as his wife any of these three; they must not be wedded because they are (Sapinda-) relatives, he who marries (one of them), sinks low. (*Laws of Manu* 3:5, 9:172–3)

JUDAISM

None of you shall approach any one near of kin to him to uncover nakedness. I am the Lord. You shall not uncover the nakedness of your father, which is the nakedness of your mother; she is your mother, you shall not uncover her nakedness. You shall not uncover the nakedness of your father's wife; it is your father's nakedness. You shall not uncover the nakedness of your sister, the daughter of your father or daughter of your mother, whether born at home or born abroad. You shall not uncover the nakedness of your son's daughter, or of your daughter's daughter, for their nakedness is your own nakedness. You shall not uncover the nakedness of your father's wife's daughter, begotten by your father, since she is your sister. You shall not uncover the nakedness of your father's sister; she is your father's near kinswoman. You shall not uncover the nakedness of your mother's sister, for she is your mother's near kinswoman. You shall not uncover the nakedness of your father's brother, that is, you shall not approach his wife; she is your aunt. You shall not uncover the nakedness of your daughter-in-law; she is your son's wife, you shall not uncover her nakedness. You shall not uncover the nakedness of your brother's wife; she is your brother's nakedness. (*Leviticus* 18:6–16)

ISLAM

Do not marry women whom your father had married, unless it is already a thing that has occurred. Truly it was a shameful and hateful practice and an evil custom. And it is forbidden to you to marry your mothers, daughters, sisters, aunts whether maternal or paternal, brother's daughters, sister's daughters, foster-mothers who have suckled you, foster-sisters, your wives' mothers, your step-daughters who are in your care and are from your wives whom you have been into – but if they are from wives whom you have not entered, then there is no sin in it. (*Qur'an* 4:22–3).

Laws of Manu are considered to keep the whole of society in a state of ritual purity.

Legalism is, therefore, the result of two main impulses in religion. The first is a concern to maintain ritual purity in society. This ensures that the rituals of the religion can be performed in the manner decreed and so be pleasing to the Deity. The second, which is in a sense a correlate of the first, is to maintain the ethics and morals of the society, and thus to maintain the order and correct functioning of the society. The legal system acts as a formalization and codification of ethical and moral imperatives.

In this path of salvation, the religious professional is not, as with ritualism, one who has a mysterious power to transform the ritual act into a path for salvation; rather he (for it is almost always a man) is the man of learning who knows the Holy Law. Only such a person can guide the believer in the snakes-and-ladders world of its injunctions and prohibitions. He is able to relate the Holy Law to the situations of everyday living. The method by which this system operates is very similar in Judaism and Islam. In both, the laity ask questions of the learned (the rabbis or ulema) and receive written responses. These responses are based on the authority of scripture, the oral tradition, and certain principles of jurisprudence such as analogical reasoning. This method allows the limited code of laws to be interpreted so as to cover the wide range of human situations.[4]

The religious attitude on this path is one of discipline and self-control. The believer must control his or her life so as to stay within the limits of the Law. One's religious life may be likened to keeping a bank account. Every time that one does something according to the Holy Law, one's account is credited and every time that one does something against the Law, the account is debited. Some actions are neutral in their effect. At the end of one's life, if one's heavenly bank account is in credit; one goes to heaven; if one's account is in deficit, one goes to hell.

Legalism is usually linked to some extent with ritualism. The Holy Law prescribes rituals that must be performed according to the Law. Religious experience on the legalistic pathways usually arises, therefore, out of the ritual that is performed – often in the saying of a prayer. In Islam, for example, the congregational prayer is said according to a precise ritual outlined in the Holy Law. It is often said communally, in the mosque. Hence, the sense of the sacred is evoked not just by the correct performance of the ritual but also by the fellowship of the believers gathered for the occasion. The religious experience on this pathway tends to be of the regenerative type, confirming or commissioning (see pp. 92–4).

Evangelism

In this group the emphasis is on the grace and beneficence of the Deity. Salvation is then usually a matter of faith that this grace will be extended to all who seek it with love and devotion. These groups will tend to emphasize a personal relationship with the Deity. This pathway is also, therefore, predominantly a pathway of theistic religion.

The task of the religious professional in these groups is to make the personal relationship between the Deity and the believer seem real. This is usually achieved through an appeal to the emotions. The religious professional among these groups is, therefore, usually a skilled orator who can raise the

EVANGELISM

In India, Islam came into close contact with the Indian bhakti *tradition. The results of this interaction can be seen in the following Sindhi poem by Shah 'Abd al-Latif of Bhit (1689–1752):*

My Prince will give me protection
– therefore my trust is in God,
The beloved will prostrate, will lament and cry
– therefore my trust is in God,
Muhammad, the pure and innocent, will intercede there for his people
– therefore my trust is in God,
When the trumpet sounds, the eyes all will be opened
– therefore my trust is in God,
The pious will gather, and Muhammad, full of glory
– therefore my trust is in God,
Will proceed for every soul to the door of the Benefactor
– therefore my trust is in God,
And the Lord will honour him, forgive us all our sins
– therefore my trust is in God.

(Annemarie Schimmel, 'The Veneration of the Prophet Muhammad', pp. 135–6)

EXPERIENCING THE GRACE OF THE DEITY: Representation of an African shaman ("witch doctor") in an ecstatic trance driving out evil spirits, Congo

emotions of his audience. In the course of an evangelical religious event, it may be claimed that miracles (thaumaturgy), ecstatic trances, speaking in tongues (glossolalia), exorcism, healing and other extraordinary events have occurred. In traditional religions, the shaman performs a similar function, healing, discerning evil spirits and driving them out, and inducing trances.

Although evangelism is a term normally used only in connection with Christianity, I have been compelled to use it here in connection with other religions for lack of a suitable alternative. A possible alternative would be the Hindu term *bhakti* (love and devotion), which emphasizes other aspects of this pathway from those associated with the term 'evangelism'. The term *bhakti* is, however, also closely linked to one particular religion.

This pathway is, of course, exemplified by the 'salvation by faith' of Protestant Christianity. It is particularly found in the more radical Protestant sects, such as the Pentecostalists, and among the many evangelical movements in modern Protestantism, such as Billy Graham's Evangelistic Association. In such groups, salvation is only achieved through the grace of God and by faith in Christ, not through any human action or merit.

This approach is also a feature of many Hindu *bhakti* sects.[5] In particular, the sects devoted to Shiva often stress the grace and beneficence of their deity. Some even consider that this grace can deliver the devotee from the inexorable workings of karma (the law of cause and effect). This parallels the belief of the radical Christian Protestant sects that their personal relationship with God can cancel the effects of sin and therefore lead to salvation. A further example can be found in the Pure Land Buddhism of Japan and China; faith in the grace of Amitabha (Amida) Buddha is the key to enlightenment and liberation. Through devotion to and faith in Amitabha Buddha one can be reborn in the Pure Land of the West, and thus achieve Nirvana. According to Honen, the main exponent of Japanese Pure Land Buddhism, merely calling on the name of Amitabha Buddha (a practice called *nembutsu*) is sufficient to ensure rebirth in his Western Paradise.[6] It has already been pointed out that the religious ceremonies of many traditional societies, especially those that involve a shaman-like figure, have many of the features of this pathway.

The perception of these groups is of a world in which God intervenes personally and directly. The most important of these divine interventions will be the coming of a messianic figure that will signal the end of the world. Thus evangelism has close links with millennialism[7] (see chapter 10). Other divine interventions include miracles, healing and the other signs described above.

The religious attitude of this group usually involves a 'puritanical' approach to the world. It is expected that one's life be lived according to a strict moral code. The world is divided into the 'saved' and the 'unsaved'. Believers try to spend as much time as possible with the 'saved'. Their main interactions with the 'unsaved' involve proselytism. Another aspect of the religious attitude of these groups is triumphalism, the belief that their religion will triumph in the end over all others. These are also features of fundamentalism (dealt with in greater detail in chapter 14), with which evangelism is closely linked. The source of religious experience on this pathway is scripture and preaching (or perhaps more accurately, the performance of the religious professional). The main religious experience of this pathway to salvation is often of the charismatic type (see pp. 94–5) that is brought on by the preaching of the evangelist. Signs of this include ecstatic trance, speaking in tongues, and the other phenomena described above. There may also be regenerative religious experiences of the conversion type (see pp. 92–4).

Social Reformism

Many have felt the central experience of religion most powerfully in the context of the spiritual upliftment of a community united in love and devotion. These feel that the best way of recreating this experience is to create an ideal community that would be conducive to it. This impulse has, historically, had two main directions. The first approach has been to try to isolate a small group from the rest of the world and create a small island of perfection in the midst of a sea of imperfection. This is the path of monasticism and is dealt with below. The second approach, called here, for want of a better term, social reformism, has taken the opposite path. It goes out into the world and seeks to transform it into an ideal society. This pathway has historically been mainly that of the theistic religions.

This path of working towards the setting up of the perfect society has recurred in various forms throughout the years. Sometimes these groups with their vision of a perfect society have tended to be revolutionary, aiming to overthrow the established order and substitute for it their own vision of society. In Jewish history there have been several groups such as the Zealots, whose aim was to overthrow Roman domination and set up the ideal community. The Muslim armies, as they swept across the Middle East and North Africa in the seventh century CE, had before them the vision of a perfect society. Many of the civil wars and sectarian uprisings that were such a feature of early Islam were also due to this impulse. Groups such as the Shi'a and the Kharijiyya were disillusioned with the societies created under the Umayyad and Abbasid caliphs and wanted to substitute their own vision of society. This vision often included goals of egalitarianism and social justice.

Liberal Christians in Victorian Britain were also aiming to change society. They felt that it was the responsibility of Christians, both individually and collectively, to work towards improving the lot of their fellow human beings. To this end they set up and supported many societies with such aims as temperance, the abolition of slavery, missionary medical work, rehabilitating prostitutes and helping the poor.

Social reformism in the Baha'i Faith: The Vocational Institute for the Education of Rural Women, Indore, India is a Baha'i community project promoting education and self sufficiency in tribal and rural women.

Many of the new religious movements also see themselves as engaged in the task of revitalizing and reforming society. The Baha'i Faith emphasizes service to the community, playing particular attention to the promotion of

SOCIAL REFORMISM IN RELIGION

SIKHISM

. . . every Sikh acts and prays for the universal brotherhood: the Sikh prayer seeks *sarbat da bhala* (welfare of all) . . .

Sikhism is quite clear as to what kind of service should be rendered and to whom. Material, physical service like providing rest and relaxation to others or reading out the scriptures for others to get spiritual solace is by far superior to the countless sacrifical fires and performances of ceremonies or mere meditation and worldly knowledge . . . Sikhism also lays down injunctions against offering food or money to the so-called twice-born, rather it is the poor and the needy who should be helped. Guru Gobind Singh makes quite an unequivocal statement in this regard: True service is the service of these (ordinary) people. I am not inclined to serve the high-caste; charity will bear fruit in this and the other world only if given to such needy people. (Singh, *Sikh Theology of Liberation*, pp. 124, 127–8)

THE BAHA'I FAITH

The fourth principle or teaching of Baha'u'llah is the readjustment and equalization of the economic standards of mankind. This deals with the question of human livelihood. It is evident that under present systems and conditions of government the poor are subject to the greatest need and distress while others more fortunate live in luxury and plenty far beyond their actual necessities. This inequality of portion and privilege is one of the deep and vital problems of human society. That there is need of an equalization and apportionment by which all may possess the comforts and privileges of life is evident. The remedy must be legislative readjustment of conditions. The rich too must be merciful to the poor, contributing from willing hearts to their needs without being forced or compelled to do so. The composure of the world will be assured by the establishment of this principle in the religious life of mankind. ('Abdu'l-Baha, *Promulgation of Universal Peace*, pp. 107–8)

CHRISTIANITY

Theology must come from the poor . . . The Church needs the poor's reflection. They know death on an intimate level no intellectual can know . . . The starting point of liberation theology is commitment to the poor, the 'non-person'. Its ideas come from the victim . . . Commitment to the poor is the very place for spiritual experience. In commitment to the poor . . . one encounters God. [Gutierrez] acknowledged that God is not the main subject in liberation theology, but added, 'We're working on it.' . . . Liberation theology is not optimistic. It speaks often of sin and sin situations. 'We are not sure of another society, but we are sure the present society is not possible and we must change it.' (Report of address of Gustavo Gutierrez at a meeting of the Catholic Theological Association, 7–10 June 1978, in Schall, *Liberation Theology in Latin America*, pp. 36–7)

JUDAISM

A Jewish theology of liberation recognizes that the world has changed and that by simply applying pre-Holocaust and Holocaust categories to the contemporary world we close our eyes and ears to the pain and possibility of the present. By carrying our own history we bequeath insight to contemporary struggles. If we are overwhelmed, though, by history and seek to overwhelm others, our memory becomes a wedge of anger and insularity, a blunt instrument rather than a delicately nurtured memory . . . Those who sought a return to Egypt were refusing the risk of the wilderness, certainly an understandable position. Yet freedom lay elsewhere, beyond the known, and new patterns of life and worship were to be developed in the pain and struggle of liberation. (Ellis, *Toward a Jewish Theology of Liberation*, p. 121)

education, agriculture and health in those areas of the world where large communities of poor Baha'is exist. An Office of Social and Economic Development has been set up at the Baha'i World Centre.[8]

If, however, a religious group decides to migrate to a new land in order to set up the ideal society, then we are dealing with a somewhat different phenomenon. These groups are usually more closely linked with social isolationism and pietism than social reformism. They are probably better considered as a type of monasticism (see pp. 131–2).

In recent years, social reformism has been revived in the Christian world, particularly in South America. Here, the promoters of 'liberation theology' call for the Church to be more active in the field of social action. Their aim is to bring about, in the near future, a society in which there is political, economic and cultural freedom, this being a sign and anticipation of the liberation to be achieved in the Kingdom of God on earth promised in the *Bible*. Those who have pursued this path have often become closely associated with Marxist philosophy and developed links with socialist revolutionary groups dedicated to the overthrow of the totalitarian regimes in Latin America. A similar process has also occurred in the Muslim world, where groups have arisen trying to make Islam a more socially active force. The desire to set up the perfect Islamic society came to the surface most strongly in Iran where it was the basis of the 1979 Revolution. This was preceded by several decades of vigorous debate. Writers such as 'Ali Shari'ati sought to evolve a new formulation of Islam based on communalism and social action. As in the Christian world, some of the groups dedicated to the task of bringing out the social egalitarianism inherent in Islam set up a dialogue with Marxism.[9]

Religious movements aimed at social reform have also arisen among the Eastern religions in modern times. Some Buddhist monasteries have developed programmes aimed at benefiting the ill and deprived, while in Hinduism there exists the Sarvodaya movement (see pp. 501–2).

The religious attitude in this pathway is an outward-looking one that expresses itself in service and shows love and charity towards all, in particular the poor and disadvantaged. The source of religious experience on this pathway is the feeling of unity and fellowship with others who are imbued with similar ideals. Some may have a commissioning type of regenerative religious experience (see pp. 92–4) on this pathway.

Asceticism

Some of those who see the world as the source of evil and corruption have considered that the best means of achieving salvation is to isolate oneself as far as possible from the world. This is often linked to disciplining the body severely, to reduce its dependence on the physical world. The world and its pressing concerns are the source of evil; it is the pressure of worldly cares and the temptations of the flesh that prevent human beings from achieving salvation. Therefore, the best way of achieving salvation is to live away from contact with other human beings. This is the solution of the hermit or ascetic. This pathway is common to both theistic and monistic religion.

Christianity has, in the past, had a strong ascetic tradition. It has tended to consider the world as the domain of the Devil; the human presence in it is the result of the curse of Adam. Asceticism also occupies a central position in Hinduism. The latter considers the world as an illusion obscuring Reality and thus preventing human beings from achieving liberation. The ascetic ideal is represented by the *sannyasin*, who is at the fourth and culminating stage in a human being's social progression. In this stage, a man who has led a full and fruitful life as a householder gives up all of this. He retires to a life of seclusion in which he can read the scriptures and meditate, free of the concerns of the world. He then undertakes a life of wandering, devoid of earthly possessions and free of all social bonds and obligations, even the obligations of religious rites and ceremonies. Even more committed to the ascetic ideal is Jainism. In this, the main path to liberation is the separation of *jiva* (sentience or the soul) from *ajiva* (non-sentient matter). This is a process that can best be promoted by the renunciation of all things physical.

Jain Ascetic: There are two main sects in Jainism – the Shvetambara (white-clad), who dress in white, and the Digambara (space-clad), who take the doctrine of the renunciation of all physical things even further and are naked. Here a Digambara *sadhu* offers prayers while standing in the holy water of the Ram Kund (Godavari River) during a Kumbha-Mela festival (a gathering of *sadhus*).

The ascetic aims to discipline the physical needs of the body as much as possible so as to regulate the appetites, cravings and passions of the flesh. This disciplining of the body aims to cut the individual away from all that is extraneous to spiritual development. In the Hindu tradition, this is manifested in its mildest

ASCETICISM IN BUDDHISM: A line of statues of the Buddha in a gallery at Wat Benchamabopitr, Bangkok. In the statue nearest to the camera, the Buddha can be seen with ribs showing through the chest wall. This represents the Buddha during the severe fast that he undertook to try to achieve enlightenment. Later the Buddha taught the 'Middle Way' which prescribes avoiding both undue austerities and undue attachment to material things.

form in the *brahmacarya* doctrine preached by Mahatma Gandhi: self-control and abstinence from all evil desires and passions. Its more extreme form, *tapasya*, involves the severe self-discipline of the body.[10] Mortification of the flesh is also an honoured part of Christian tradition in both the Catholic and Orthodox churches. Some have even taken it as far as such practices as self-flagellation or the austerities of St Simeon Stylites who sat at the top of a pillar for thirty years without descending. Asceticism, or at any rate its extremes, are disapproved of in Buddhism and the Baha'i Faith.

The religious attitude of those who follow this pathway is one of detachment from the world. They put themselves outside the social world in which other human beings participate; they become outside observers. The main source of religious experience in this pathway is the reading of the scriptures, prayer, fasting, and the other austerities that the ascetic undertakes. The ascetic may have any of the types of religious experience, but typically the mystical or charismatic (see pp. 94–7).

MONASTICISM

Similar to ascetics in their vision of the world, are those who turn to monastic communities. Here again the world is seen as the greatest obstacle to spiritual progress and, therefore, the aim is to isolate the individual from the concerns and temptations of the physical world. But rather than an individual becoming a hermit or ascetic, a community is set up in which the outside world is shut out as much as possible. The monastic community provides the opportunity to concentrate on the religious life for those who see no way of doing this in the outside world. In some monastic communities, austerities and disciplining of the body are practised. There is also a concern with the building up of an ideal community in these groups (see the discussion of social reformism, p. 128). This pathway is to be found in both theistic and monistic religions.

As with asceticism, Christianity has found monasticism in accord with its view of the world. The monastic orders (both male and female) flourished in Europe during the Middle Ages, forming the backbone of Roman Catholicism during this period. Monasticism has also been very important in the Orthodox and Oriental churches. The walls of the monastery enabled the monks to block out the concerns, passions and impurity of the secular world. In addition, the monastery provided the ideal circumstances in which learning and ritual traditions could be taught and transmitted from one generation to the next. Buddhism, forbidden by its founder from embracing the ascetic ideal of Hinduism but sharing with the latter its view of the physical world as an illusion hindering human spiritual progress, has also turned to the monastic ideal. In Theravada or Southern Buddhism (in Sri Lanka, Burma, Thailand and Cambodia), most males spend some part of their lives in the monastery. Monasteries also play a central role in many forms of Mahayana Buddhism, especially Tibetan Buddhism. In India, there are many Hindu monasteries but monasticism is particularly important among the Jains. Although Muhammad forbade monasticism, one finds elements of the monastic ideal in the Sufi retreats called *takiyyas* or *khanigahs*.[11] Monasticism is also forbidden in the Baha'i Faith, but there are spiritual retreats in the form of summer schools which temporarily perform the same function.

MONASTICISM: The Great Lavra is first in the hierarchy of monasteries on Mt Athos in Greece and is dedicated to the Dormition of Athanasius, who with the help of his spiritual protégé, the emperor Nikephoros II Phokas, founded in 963 the first lavra (small group of hermits with a common superior and a central house of prayer) on Mount Athos and introduced the rule for cenobitic (monastic) life. The monastery is famed for its library and fifteenth-century frescoes.

We may consider as a subgroup of monasticism those sectarian groups of Protestantism that decided to separate themselves from the rest of society. These tried to set up an ideal society away from the wicked ways of the world. Such groups emphasize personal piety and the ethical and moral obligations of the individual. In Christianity, many religious groups who left Europe to settle North America in the seventeenth and eighteenth centuries had before them the vision of creating a perfect society in their new homeland. Within North America, there are many such groups: for example, the Old Order Amish and the Hutterites in the United States.[12] German and Dutch Mennonites moved to southern Russia in the eighteenth and early nineteenth century and a group called the Templers of southern Germany moved to Palestine in the nineteenth century.[13] We may also include, as a subgroup of monasticism, several new religious movements that segregate their followers in small self-contained communities which have minimal contact with the outside world. ISKCON (International Society for Krishna Consciousness, Hare Krishnas) and the Children of God are examples of this.[14]

We have noted (see p. 128) the close link between monasticism and social reformism. The balance between isolationism and social reformism has varied over the years in most monastic communities. Many monastic communities have moved away from the aim of isolating themselves from the world. These are now active socially in the world and are thus tending towards social reformism. Monastic orders in Christendom, Sufi orders in Islam and Buddhist monasteries have increasingly undertaken educational, medical and other social roles in the modern world. These then cease to be of the monastic pathway as defined here.

The religious attitude in monasticism is towards an inward-turning detachment from the world. The source of religious experience is reading from the scripture, prayer, fasting and sometimes some austerities. There may, in some monastic communities, be a religious experience from the sense of community and fellowship. The main types of religious experience on this pathway are the mystical or the confirming type of regenerative experience (see pp. 92–4, 95–7).

GNOSTICISM

The principal idea of the gnostic movements is that the central religious experience is linked to a special knowledge to which only a select few have access. The knowledge usually takes the form of an inner (esoteric) understanding of either the scriptures or the rituals of the religion. This inner understanding, which can only be achieved through the path set out by the group, leads to enlightenment and hence liberation.

Most gnostic groups are not concerned with proselytism. They consider that only a small number of people are capable (or have reached the stage) of appreciating the gnostic truth. Their smallness of numbers does not, in any way, invalidate their claim for them, indeed it underlines it.

Gnosticism usually has some form of religious hierarchy in which the esoteric knowledge that leads to enlightenment is handed down through the

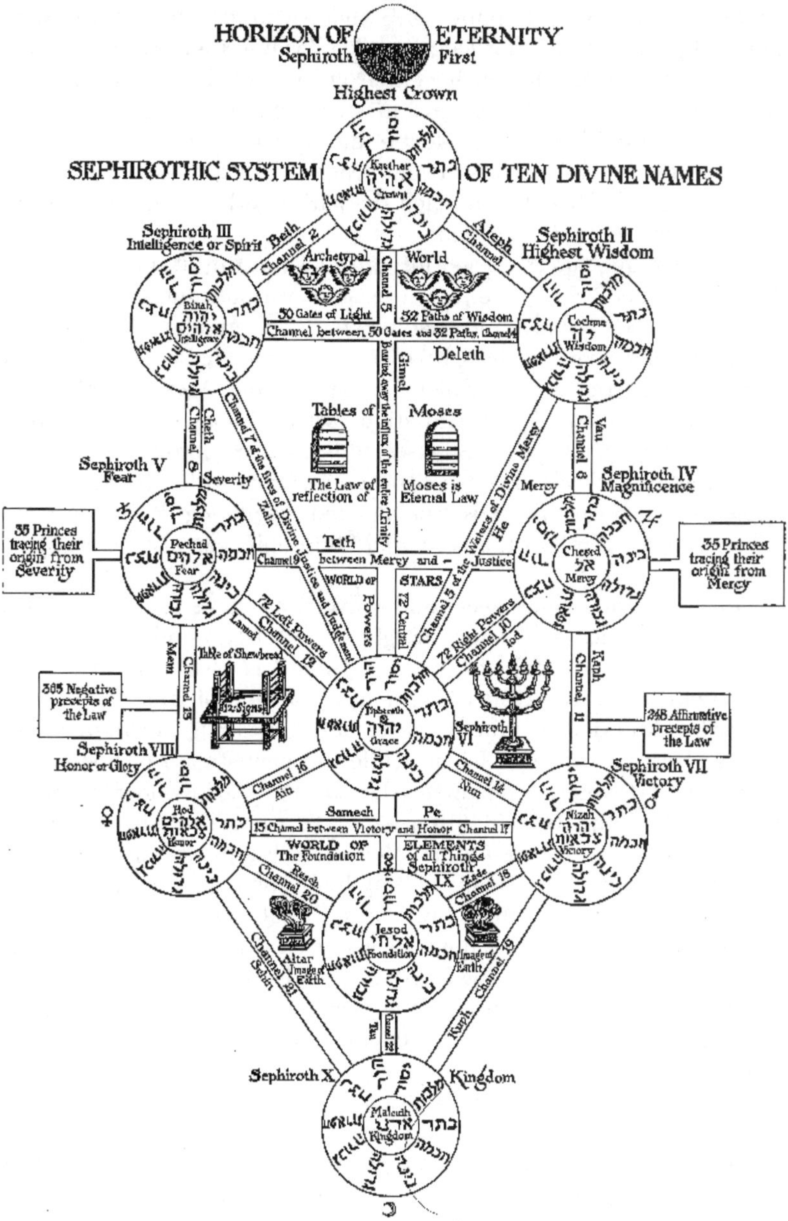

THE KABBALIST MOTIF OF THE SEPHIROTH TREE: This motif is often also referred to as the Tree of Life. The ten Sephiroth, the ten circles in the picture, are the primary emanations from the unknowable Godhead (En-Sof or Ein-Sof, 'without end'). The seven lower Sephiroth are based on 1 Chronicles 29:11. Much Kabbalist literature is concerned with delineating the associations and relationships between the Sephiroth. This depiction of the tree is a Christianized one, drawn from a Latin original published by Athanasius Kircher, a German Jesuit scholar, in his *Oedipus Aegyptiacus*, vol. 2, part 1, Rome, 1653, p. 289.

generations from master to pupil. Only those who have been through the system and have had the knowledge handed down to them in the approved manner can appreciate it and benefit from it fully. The knowledge can, usually, only be learned on a personal master-to-pupil basis. In other words, it cannot be learned from books. Most traditions allow that some eventually become masters of their own spiritual progress. An even smaller number reach the stage of being able to teach the path to others and thus become spiritual masters in their own right.

Gnosticism appears in varied forms in all the world's major religious traditions. In Judaism there have existed various gnostic groupings: historically, the Essenes and Kabbalists, and, among contemporary movements, Hasidism. In the Christian West, gnostic sects such as the Cathars were particularly prevalent in the Middle Ages, but they still exist today, for example in Christian Science. One of the features of this tendency in the West is its eclectic nature. Consequently, many gnostic groups in the West have little connection with Christianity, for example New Thought, the Rosicrucians and Scientology.[15] The approach that has become known as the Perennial Philosophy can also be classed as gnostic.[16]

Among Muslims, many sects and movements have exhibited gnostic features. The mystical philosophy taught in Shi'i Islam under the name of *irfan* (spiritual knowledge) or *hikmat* (wisdom) is a strongly intellectual gnostic tradition. Another Shi'i tradition, the medieval Isma'ilis, believed that they had knowledge of the inner (esoteric) meaning (the *batin*) of the *Qur'an* and of the rituals of Islam, while the mainstream orthodoxy had only the outer (exoteric) meaning (the *zahir*). Those who reached the higher stages of the Isma'ili initiation were introduced to yet deeper meanings (the *batin* of the *batin*). Most Sufi groups are also to a large extent based on an inner teaching. Only by becoming an initiate (*murid*) of the order and being taught by the spiritual master, the shaykh or *murshid*, can this inner teaching be acquired. There are several other gnostic groups in the Middle East such as the Mandeans.

However, the gnostic approach emerges from being a minority interest and becomes the mainstream of the religion as one passes from the Western religions to the East. In Hinduism, the guru is able to guide his followers to self-realization and eventually to *sat-chit-ananda* (existence-consciousness-bliss) and *moksha* (liberation). In Buddhism, there is a close connection between monasticism and gnosticism. Most forms of Buddhism centre, as described above, on monastic communities; within the Buddhist monastery, however, there is often a spiritual master–pupil relationship, within which the individual monks develop. In particular this is true of Tibetan Buddhism. The role of the spiritual teacher (the lama) and the passing on of esoteric teachings are central to this religious system.

The principal religious attitude on this pathway involves a search for truth. This search is principally intellectual, a struggle to understand; some would say that it is also élitist. Part of the religious attitude must also be

GNOSTICISM

THE MANDEANS OF IRAQ

The 'saving truth' (kusta) is praised in an old acrostic psalm, which is recited, for example, at wedding ceremonies.

In the name of the Great Life,
the sublime light be glorified.
Come in kindness, kusta . . .
You are the path of the perfect,
the way which leads up to the Place of Light.
You are eternal life,
who went forth and settled in a true heart.
Woe to him who is not attentive to you, my lord . . .
You are the armour of the perfect,
the truth (*Srara*), in which is no error.
You are wise and pleasant,
you teach wisdom and praise to all who love your name . . .
The dead heard you and lived
the sick heard you and became well.
You grant forgiveness to the elect and perfect,
in whose hearts kusta has settled.

(Foerster, *Gnosis*, vol. 2, pp. 136–7, 234–5)

WRITINGS OF THE FOLLOWERS OF BASILIDES (SECOND-CENTURY CHRISTIAN GNOSTIC OF ALEXANDRIA)

So whoever learns these things and becomes acquainted with all the angels and the causes of their existence – such a person becomes invisible and incomprehensible to all angels and authorities . . . And few people can know these things – only one in a thousand, and two in ten thousand . . .

One is wholly forbidden to reveal their mysteries; rather, one must keep them secret in silence. (Quoted in Layton, *The Gnostic Scriptures*, p. 425)

that of obedience to one's spiritual master, particularly in the early stages of the path. The attitude of the spiritual master to others is one of compassion but detachment. The main source of religious experience is the scriptures; it occurs when there is an intellectual enlightenment regarding the true meaning of the scripture. The gnostic pathway is closely linked to mysticism. Many gnostic pathways use the experiential dimension of mysticism, including meditation or chanting, which helps to achieve altered states of consciousness.

MYSTICISM

The term 'mysticism' is used to describe a wide variety of religious phenomena. For lack of a more suitable word, I shall use it to refer to those groups that consider that the central religious experience can best be recreated through achieving altered states of consciousness. Such states can be reached in two different ways. The first is the path of increased psychological arousal achieved, for example, by rhythmical chanting or dancing. This culminates in mystical ecstasy (in Sufism, the state of *wajd* or *hal*).[17] The second is the path of decreased mental activity leading to a deep state of meditation (in Yoga, this is called *samadhi)*. Both paths lead finally to a trance state. This state is considered to lead the believer to see Reality and, therefore, it leads to liberation. A common technique used in mysticism to achieve an altered state of consciousness is the ritual repetitive chanting of a name or a short formula. This practice can be found across the religious world. It is known as *hesychasm* in Eastern Orthodox Christianity, *dhikr* in Sufism, *japa* (the reciting of mantras) in Hinduism, and *nembutsu* in Japanese Pure Land Buddhism.[18]

This type of religious experience, which can be found in both Eastern and Western religions, is usually closely linked to gnosticism. This is because the method of achieving the trance state can only usually be taught by a spiritual master, who acts as a guide on the mystic path. In the Christian West mysticism is a fringe activity of a small minority but in the Islamic world, the Sufi orders play a much more important role. As we proceed further East, the importance of this approach increases greatly and it occupies a central place in Hinduism and Buddhism. The various systems of meditation are a central concern in these Eastern religions.

RITUAL REPETITIVE CHANTING: Members of a Sufi order chanting (*dhikr*)

There is one important difference between the mysticism of the West and of the East. The trance-like state achieved by Western mystics is often described as filled with vivid visions and auditions. Examples of this include the visions of Christ, Mary, angels and so on reported by such figures as St Theresa and St John of the Cross.[19] The trance-like state of the Eastern mystic, however, is usually a formless, visionless experience. This difference perhaps takes us back to the orientation of these respective religions. Western religion is predominantly devotional in nature, and so the product of the trance-like state is a vision of either the object of devotion or something closely associated with it. Eastern religion is predominantly oriented towards achieving an abstract notion – insight. The trance-like state therefore tends to be empty and formless. The main method of achieving altered states of consciousness is also different in the two forms of mysticism. It is achieved by increasing levels of mental arousal through chanting and similar activity in the Western religions, and decreasing levels through meditation in the Eastern religions. This may also have a bearing on the content of the trance. (See chapter 7 for a further consideration of this theme.)

A nineteenth-century depiction of the prophet Ezekiel's vision of God's glory. Four angels emerge from a storm and above them is the Lord seated upon His throne. (*Ezekiel* ch. 1–3).

The religious attitude on this pathway is one that tends to be turned inwards, trying to obtain a direct personal experience of the sacred. Once it is felt that this has been attained, then there is usually a feeling of love and compassion, not just towards other individual human beings, but more expansively, towards the whole cosmos. The main source of religious experience on this pathway is in the achievement of altered states of consciousness by such methods as chanting and meditation. The religious experience on this pathway is of the mystical type described in chapter 4 (see pp. 95–7).

The Evolution of the Pathways

Of course, religions take time to evolve this variety of religious expressions. From the initial small group of disciples gathered together after the death of the founder of the religion, there is a gradual growth and development of the religion during which these pathways emerge. Different religions have manifested them at different stages in their evolution. This depends to some extent on the teachings of the founder, and to some extent also on the spiritual culture of the environment. The Buddha gave instructions to his disciples to form a monastic community; this pathway therefore developed early in Buddhism. Buddhism arose in an environment in which the guru–disciple relationship was well established: the Buddha had modelled himself on this pattern in his relationship with his disciples and therefore the gnostic pathway also arose early in the history of Buddhism.

In Christianity, monastic orders took some 500 years to emerge (although some proto-monastic communities, the cenobites, had existed for about 250 years). Muhammad forbade monasticism and therefore this pathway evolved late and only to a very limited extent in Islam. The mystical pathway in Islam probably did not arise until Muslims had been in contact with Indian religions and learned the techniques of achieving altered states of consciousness from them. The Sufi orders, therefore, took some 500 years to emerge in Islam.

A newer religion such as the Baha'i Faith has not yet, in its 150-year history, had time to develop these social paths of religious expression to anything more than a rudimentary extent. The potential is nevertheless present within the teachings and structures of the religion to satisfy those who would incline towards legalism, reformism, mysticism, or any other of the pathways. The most important distinctive feature of the Baha'i Faith in this regard, however, is the absence of a class of religious professionals to act as priests, men of learning or spiritual guides. The only individuals who have a degree of personal prominence in the religion, the Counsellors and Auxiliary Board members, have only limited terms of office and no authority. This restricts their ability to build up any degree of personal leadership or religious professionalism.

I am not, of course, in this book trying to answer any such questions as: which of these social expressions of religion is the most valid? Such a question is, on reflection, pointless. Individuals or societies choose particular forms of religious expression because these forms seem to bring them closest to the central religious experience. Thus it seems that particular forms of religious expression evolve to suit particular types of individuals and societies. One can think of this as the way that the vast array of human types and cultures express the central experience of religion. The only sensible answer would therefore appear to be that each form of religious expression is the most valid for those follow it and find it to be satisfactory.

A Classification of Religious Groups

We have seen in this chapter that the various pathways to religious experience, the performative aspects of religion, overlap to some extent. Any one religious group may exhibit one or more of these pathways to salvation. These expressions appeal to different human beings based on differences in personality and culture. This leads us to a possible way of classifying religious groups that is different in basis to the classifications given in chapter 3 (pp. 73–7).

Some religious groups only exhibit one of these methods of social expression (or possibly two interlinked methods). Therefore their appeal will be to only a narrow range of psychological types from among the general population. We may name these groups 'sects' or 'cults'. Pentecostalist churches, for example, predominantly exhibit evangelism. Sufi orders in Islam chiefly exhibit mysticism and gnosticism. In general, the word 'sect' applies to those groups that are more tightly organized and where beliefs are more narrowly defined (that is, they are epistemologically authoritarian); the word 'cult' to the more loosely organized groups where there is not such a strict insistence on adherence to particular beliefs (see also p. 77).

On the other hand, any religion that would claim to be a 'world religion' should include all the different forms of religious expression and thus, potentially, be able to appeal to all types of people. Any of the major religious traditions, such as Christianity, Islam, Hinduism or Buddhism, are able to do this and can thus appeal to all types of individuals.

Of course, many religious groups exist that are intermediate between the two extremes depicted above. An approach incorporating more than one, but not all, social expressions can be found in intermediate groupings that we might call 'churches' or 'denominations'. As an example of this from the West, we may cite the Church of England, which incorporates ritualism, evangelism, reformism and even a limited degree of monasticism and mysticism. From the East, we could cite Tibetan Buddhism. This combines gnosticism, ritualism, monasticism and mysticism. Because these groupings incorporate several different approaches, they appeal to a wider cross-section of the population. They are often, as in the two examples cited, national religions, or as in the case of Sikhism, the religion of a particular people. This category would also include most of those groups that have usually been called denominations, such as the Baptist and Congregationalist churches in America.

As discussed in chapter 2 (p. 41), this way of defining religious groups can be extended from the social expression of religion to the conceptual level also. As well as catering for all types of social religious expression, a world religion must also appeal to all types of individuals at the conceptual level, by its ability to encompass both the theistic and monistic viewpoints. A sect will usually only appeal either to the theistic or to the monistic viewpoint.

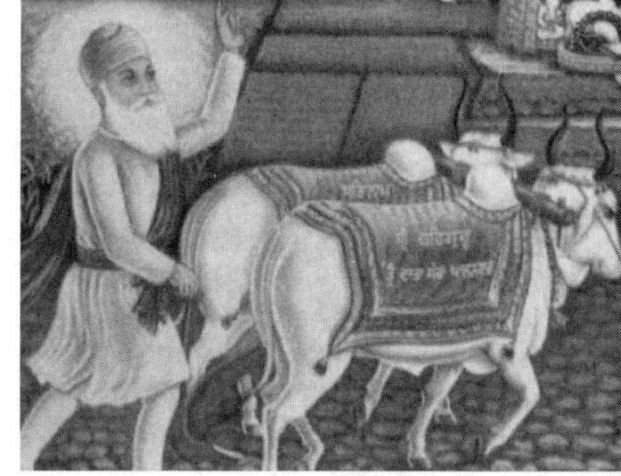

SIKHISM: Guru Nanak (1469–1539), after many years of travelling, settled in Kartarpur where he farmed and preached, gathering around himself a group of followers. Many of his hymns are included in the *Adi Granth*. He is considered the first of the ten guru-founders of Sikhism.

Further Reading

Information on each of these different pathways of social expression of religion must be sought in books that deal with them individually. On ritualism, see Grimes, *Beginnings in Ritual Studies*. There are no adequate studies of legalism, but see Falk, *Law and Religion*, esp. pp. 9–24, and M. M. J. Fischer, *Iran*, pp. 32–103. The best accounts of evangelism are to be found in books on millenarianism and fundamentalism: see Marsden, *Fundamentalism and American Culture*; Sandeen, *The Roots of Fundamentalism* and Caplan, *Studies in Religious Fundamentalism* (see also the suggested further reading for chapter 14). On social reformism, see Gutierrez, *A Theology of Liberation*. On asceticism, see Anson, *The Call of the Desert* and Shiraishi, *Asceticism in Buddhism and Brahmannism*. On monasticism, see Panikkar, *Blessed Simplicity*, and Lawrence, *Medieval Monasticism*. On gnosticism, see B. Walker, *Gnosticism*. On mysticism, see Woods, *Understanding Mysticism*, and Underhill, *Mysticism*. See chapter 3, pp. 73–7, for various other typologies of religious groups.

6

Faith, Belief and Conversion

In chapter 4, we examined the central religious experience that is the originating impulse of religion. Closely connected with and arising from this is religious faith, which keeps religion going. In this chapter, we shall look at the nature of faith and belief, examining how it arises in individuals as they grow up and how faith can change (conversion) or renew itself.

The Nature of Faith and Belief

Many philosophers and theologians have tried to define religious faith. Clearly, there is no agreed formula that adequately describes all aspects of this phenomenon. One useful distinction that can be made is between two concepts that have been variously described as 'immediate and intuitive' faith and 'intellectual' faith;[1] 'faith in' and 'faith that';[2] 'belief in' and 'belief that';[3] or holding to a 'personal' and 'impersonal' truth.[4] Even in Buddhism, which is sometimes considered to be a religion that does not involve faith, these concepts exist.[5] To clarify this matter, I shall define here the first part of each of the above pairs, which I shall call 'faith-in'. Faith-in is immediate and intuitive; it is pre-propositional in the sense that it does not depend on doctrinal formulas and propositions. It can be described as a disposition to believe in something (or someone or some event), or as having a particular, committed worldview. It is personal in the sense that it must be located in the heart of the individual believer. The second of the above pairs, which I shall call 'belief-that', is what results when an attempt is made to formulate a content to faith-in. At a simple level, this may just be a credal formula; at its most complex it can be a multi-volume work of systematic theology. Belief-that is intellectual; it relates to a proposition or doctrine; it indicates a disposition to believe that a proposition is true; it is impersonal in the sense that it is independent of the person making it. Faith-in is represented by statements such as: 'I have faith in (or believe in) God'; while belief-that would be represented by: 'I believe that (or have faith that) God is three persons in one.'[6] The first is only meaningful when taken in relation to the person who makes it; it is not a freestanding proposition. The second has a meaning independent of its author.

Having made this preliminary distinction, we can now try to extract some of the meaning from within the concept of religious faith. In the following analysis, each aspect of faith will be examined with regard to faith-in and belief-that.

Faith-in and Belief-that:

Trust

Faith-in: Faith-in involves an element of trusting in the object of one's faith; it involves the feeling that the object of one's faith is in some way greater than oneself and is able to lead one to greater fulfilment and happiness; that one can trust it to act in a beneficent way.

Belief-that: Trust expresses itself in doctrinal formulas that speak of the Deity as the Beneficent. This aspect of belief is found in Japanese Amitabha (Amida) Buddhism, where doctrine holds that calling on the name of Amitabha Buddha with faith will lead to the believer's rebirth in Amitabha Buddha's Western Paradise.

Dependence or Reliance

Faith-in: The factor of trust leads naturally to the feeling of dependence on the object of faith; a feeling that one can, with confidence, rely on the object of one's faith.

Belief-that: Dependence is expressed in such doctrinal formulas as determinism (that all of one's circumstances and actions are already predetermined by God), which is to be found in Protestant Christianity and Ash'ari theology in Sunni Islam; there is a less extreme form in the Sufi idea of *tawakkul* (reliance upon God) and *rida* (contentment with the will of God).

Faithfulness

Faith-in: Part of the faith-in relationship involves a sense of loyalty and faithfulness towards one's object of faith, together with confidence that this is reciprocated.

Belief-that: Most religions have a doctrinal formula that emphasizes the need for faithfulness and loyalty. This is often translated into doctrines of faithfulness and loyalty to the institutions of the religion and to the religious community. Laws relating to marriage and the bringing up of children often emphasize the need for this loyalty to the religion.

Love

Faith-in: Faith-in involves a great sense of love towards the object of one's faith and a feeling of being in turn loved.

Belief-that: Love is often emphasized in credal formulas that refer to the mutual love between God and humanity.

Obedience

Faith-in: One aspect of faith-in is the willingness to obey the instructions of the object of one's faith.

Belief-that: This aspect of a belief is expressed in the religious requirement to carry out the details of ritual law or spiritual discipline. Any deviation from the laws and rules of the religion need repentance and expiation. This aspect of a belief is also usually extended to obedience to the institutions of the religion.

Sacrifice

Faith-in: One aspect of faith is the feeling that one would be willing to sacrifice for the object of one's faith. There is also often the idea that the sacrifice is mutual, that the object of one's faith has already sacrificed for one.

Belief-that: This aspect of belief may be expressed at the simplest level in sacrifices of one's property and wealth to the object of one's faith; it may also be expressed as a state of detachment from material things. From the other perspective, the object of one's faith is considered to have sacrificed also – in the doctrine of atonement through the sacrifice of Jesus in Christianity, for instance. A similar doctrine can be found in relation to the martyrdom of the Imam Husayn in Shi'i Islam.[7]

Certitude and Meaning

Faith-in: Faith-in is accompanied by a feeling of certainty concerning the promises made in the scriptures, together with the disappearance of the feeling of doubt and meaninglessness.

Belief-that: Belief-that formulations of this aspect of faith include St Anselm's maxim *credo ut intelligam* – I believe in order to understand. The various creeds, doctrines and dogmas express the certainties of the religion.

Consequences

Faith-in: The consequence of faith-in should be seen in the life of the individual. Faith-in leads to a focus and direction for one's life. It acts as an absolute standard for one's conduct.

Belief-that: The consequences of faith are expressed doctrinally as being born again, enlightenment, transformation, the work of the Holy Spirit.

Thus we can see that religious experience produces a certain disposition in the individual – faith-in. If the believer tries to express this faith-in, he or she can only do so in terms of concepts that are available to him or her – this immediately then enters the realm of belief-that. We may say that faith-in is analysed by theologians and religious philosophers and put into doctrinal formulas that seek to express it – and so becomes belief-that. However, the formulation and expression must always be a secondary matter. Indeed it may even be somewhat incidental. Wilfred Cantwell Smith has noted that:

> From time to time one meets a person the winning quality of whose living is an immediate embodiment of his faith in so spontaneous yet compelling a way that one at once recognises the incomparability and finality of human character. When we do meet such a person, we realise how secondary, if not actually irrelevant, are other religious expressions. It matters little if that person's faith may be related perhaps to a systematic verbal statement that to us is curious or alien, to a form of worship that to us is remote, and so on.[8]

Statue of Madonna and Child in a Roman Catholic church in Brazil

Faith and Superstition

D. Z. Phillips has given as an example of faith a woman who brings her baby before a statue of the Virgin Mary and asks her to bless it. A non-believing philosopher would describe such an action as sheer superstition and magic. An experiment could be set up and would almost certainly show that there is no demonstrable difference in the lives of those who have received such a blessing and those who have not. Religious faith is, however, a much more complex matter than this. If it could be shown that the mother's intention in her action was only to secure the material prosperity of her child then it would be true to call it superstition. But then it would not strictly speaking be a religious action either. The Virgin Mary would here be merely a means to an end that is intelligible without reference to her. The religious aspect is therefore somewhat incidental: if the mother's only intention were her child's future material prosperity and if it could be shown to her that this could be obtained in some other way, then that way would be adopted. In such circumstances, homage to the Virgin Mary is incidental to the main aim and the mother's action is the equivalent of using a lucky charm or magic spell.[9]

Magic and religion are not easily separable entities. Most religions have incorporated at least some magical elements, if not into the orthodox religion, then at least into the popular religion (see chapter 15). Indeed, if we consider the miracles said to have been performed by the founder of the religion as magic, then almost all religions have what may be called magic even in their orthodox elements. Most religious people do, however, recognize a difference between religion and magic (see p. 28). In most examples of religious faith, although there may be some of this superstitious, quasi-magical element, there is also more. In the example of the action of the mother bringing her baby before a statue of the Virgin

Mary, we may analyse several processes that may be going on consciously or subconsciously in the mother quite apart from any magical or superstitious thoughts:

1. She may be expressing her trust in the Virgin Mary and her confidence that Mary will protect and watch over her child.
2. She may be wishing to express her dependence and reliance on the beneficence of the Divine.
3. She may be wishing to express her veneration of the Virgin Mary.
4. She may be identifying her own situation with that of the Virgin Mary and her care of the infant Jesus. She may thus be seeking to identify her situation with its sacred archetype (see chapter 11).
5. She may be wishing to express her faithfulness to the Virgin Mary and to the Church by bringing to it her most valued possession.
6. There may even be a sense of sacrifice in her wish to consecrate the life of her baby to the service of the Church.
7. She may be seeking to establish that the birth of her baby is not an anonymous, trivial event in a vast universe but that the life that she has given birth to has significance and importance.

Acquisition of Religious Belief and Behaviour

In terms of the numbers of people involved, the most important pathway to acquiring religious faith and beliefs is the learning that goes on in childhood. This is a different phenomenon from the conversion experience in adulthood (see pp. 151–3). Children go through phases in their acquisition of attitudes, beliefs and behaviour.

Kelman's Stages of Attitude Development

Herbert Kelman has given a general description of the ways that a person can appropriate new attitudes. His description can be applied to a wide range of attitudes, beliefs and behaviours, including religious ones.[10] More particularly, Kelman's description can be applied to the progressive stages in a child's acquisition of religious attitudes, beliefs and behaviours. We can thus outline three phases.

1. Compliance. Initially, a child learns certain religious beliefs and behaviour through a mixture of reward and punishment. Any belief, behaviour or attitude that is continually reinforced by appropriate rewards or punishments tends to become established within a child, even if there is no real understanding of them. Such influences can be very powerful and are often effective even in adult life. Teenagers, for example, can express certain attitudes and behaviour with which they

do not really agree, in order to fit in with their friends and appear sophisticated and 'adult'. Social pressure can induce adults to express attitudes and behaviour which they know in their heart to be wrong (racial and religious prejudice, for example). Most religious people would agree, however, that true religious behaviour should not be based upon such considerations. Compliance only results in a particular effect as long as the reinforcement continues. It does not, therefore, represent a self-perpetuating, permanent change within the individual.

2. IDENTIFICATION. This way of acquiring beliefs, attitudes, and behaviour involves taking someone whom one admires and trying to be like that person as much as possible. It no longer depends on rewards to perpetuate it. Children will often talk about, and even think about, religion in the same way as their parents, or as some admired person. There is always a danger of the admired person being shown to be seriously flawed, thus causing a crisis in the individual. In older children and adults, the identification will often be with a central figure in the religion such as Jesus, Mary, Muhammad, or the Buddha.
3. INTERNALIZATION. While identification involves conforming, in order to think and act like an admired person, internalization involves a process of transforming oneself so that new ways of thinking and acting become a part of one's personality and being. These new ways are thus valued for themselves and can exist independently of what others may say or do and independently of whether an admired person says or does them. Most religious people would say that a person's religion is not true religion until it exists at this level within the individual.

Fowler's Stages of Faith Development

Some have gone further and attempted to describe the whole of an individual's religious development. Drawing on Piaget's work on cognitive development, Kohlberg's on moral development (see pp. 341–2) and Erik Erikson's on psycho-social development,[11] James Fowler has produced an analysis of individual faith development. Fowler regards faith as the human way of finding meaning and pattern in one's life. Following a structured interview, scores are assigned for seven aspects of faith development:

- form of logic
- perspective taking
- form of moral judgement
- bounds of social awareness
- locus of authority
- form of world coherence
- symbolic function.

From this, people are assigned to one of six stages of faith development that are considered to evolve out of the basic pre-stage of undifferentiated faith that is characteristic of the first two years of life.

1. INTUITIVE–PROJECTIVE FAITH. This is characteristic of ages 3–7. The child's faith is fantasy-filled and imitative of parents and other significant adults. There are the beginnings of awareness of self-identity, death and sex, and of the taboos related to each.

2. MYTHIC–LITERAL FAITH. This corresponds to Piaget's stage of concrete operations (ages 7–11). It is when the child appropriates the stories, beliefs, and practices of his or her faith community. Whereas, previously, perception of experience had been episodic and unstructured, there is now a logical construction of experience involving order and meaning. Narratives and myth become important ways of understanding experience. Interpretation is, however, concrete and literal rather than abstract and symbolic.

As children grow, they first learn the stories, then the beliefs and practices of their religion. Here a group of children in Iran in the early twentieth century attend a school where they are taught the *Qur'an*.

3. SYNTHETIC–CONVENTIONAL FAITH. At this stage, which is considered to emerge around adolescence, a much greater diversity of life experiences emerges and the individual begins to define an identity for him- or herself (the identity crisis) and to establish a life narrative. It is at this stage that deeply-held values and beliefs are established often by identifying with and internalizing those of authority figures and role models: a personal ideology evolves.

4. INDIVIDUATIVE–REFLECTIVE FAITH. This stage, which may occur in young adulthood, involves the integration of the various roles and patterns that the adolescent has acquired. The individual moves away from reliance on identifying with authority figures and role models and consciously develops and assumes responsibility for his or her own commitments, lifestyles, beliefs, and attitudes. In relation to faith, this involves a realization of the fact that one's own view is only one of many possible worldviews and a rejection of literal interpretations of narratives and myths learned in childhood. The strength of this style of faith is its capacity for critical reflection; its danger is an over-reliance on critical, analytical thought.

5. CONJUNCTIVE FAITH. This stage, which may emerge in mid-life, involves a sensitivity to patterns of interrelatedness. Efforts are made to accept and unify apparent opposites. There is a re-examination of the symbols

and myths of the faith community and the development of an appreciation of these as a source of non-logical insight. The dangers of this stage are the development of passivity, complacency and cynical withdrawal.

6. UNIVERSALIZING FAITH. Rarely, individuals may reach the stage which involves an awareness of an ultimate environment that is inclusive of all being. These individuals incarnate the spirit of an inclusive and fulfilled human community. They not only free themselves from the social, political, economic and ideological shackles that bind humanity but they create this possibility for others. Theirs is a universal, affirming, transcendent viewpoint. Because of this, they are often regarded by social institutions, including those of their religion, as being subversive.[12]

The surveys that have been done to assess Fowler's stages have shown that there is a definite movement through stages 1 and 2 and into 3 in the first two decades of life (probably due to cognitive maturation, as described by Piaget). The evidence beyond this gets somewhat weaker, with roughly equal numbers past the age of 20 being assigned to stages 3 and 4, while 5 is uncommon and stage 6 is rare. The evidence may equally suggest that what Fowler calls 'stages of development' are, in adult life, different *styles* of faith. Stage 3 corresponds to an orthodox adherence to traditional religious beliefs; stage 4 is a style involving critical analysis and self-reliance for interpretation, and stage 5 involves symbolic and paradoxical interpretation of religious concepts. Thus it may be that, as will be discussed in chapter 13 for Kohlberg's staging (see pp. 341–2), Fowler has taken the different styles of faith that exist in the world and given these a hierarchical value based on his own liberal Protestant Christian background.

THE LANGUAGE OF FAITH

One philosopher who directed a great deal of attention towards trying to identify the nature of religious faith was Ludwig Wittgenstein (1889–1951). He asserted that religion is a unique 'universe of discourse' or 'language-game'. An atheist may present evidence against the existence of God and a believer may present evidence for it. Wittgenstein argued, however, that they are not contradicting one another, nor are they in disagreement with one another. They are not engaged in the same language-game; they are speaking by different rules about different things: hence it is not surprising that they are unable to agree.

Wittgenstein's view is effectively a relativistic stance. Runzo has taken it further and developed the idea of differing conceptual schemata that portray differing realities to those who possess them.[13] Since all concepts

Ludwig Wittgenstein (1889–1951), philosophy

arise from within one conceptual scheme or another, there is no neutral position from which one language-game may be judged against another. In this view, it becomes illogical and irrelevant to criticize statements made within one language-game (or worldview or conceptual schema) from the viewpoint of another.

Since a religious faith is a particular worldview, it is a self-contained, internally coherent conceptual schema. Thus, a judgement as to whether a particular religious statement is correct or not will depend on whether the judgement is being made from within the religious worldview or from outside it. If we accept that religious and non-religious statements are different language-games, then it follows that no one from outside a religious language-game can ever easily refute a statement made from within it. Indeed, if we accept that all judgements have to be made from within one conceptual schema or another, it would seem that intellect and reasoning (which must always operate within a particular worldview and therefore favour that view) can rarely provide compelling reasons for us to choose one worldview over another.

William James argued that, in practice, human beings choose a particular conception of the world on the basis of faith and only then do they look for arguments to support the conclusions that they have reached.[14] The work of several writers from fields other than religion seems to support James's view by describing parallel processes in other fields of human activity.

Thomas Kuhn has advanced the view that science progresses through a series of what he calls 'paradigm shifts'. Each scientific paradigm, within which science works for a considerable period of time before it is replaced by another paradigm, shares many characteristics with the worldviews of the different religions. Each is based primarily on faith; each regards the other paradigms (other religious worldviews) as myths. Thus, for example, modern science regards such theories as the phlogiston theory and the theory of humours as myths, finding it strange that former generations of scientists believed them. And yet the evidence seems to suggest that these former theories were neither less scientific nor more the product of human idiosyncrasy than those current today. If these former theories were myths, then it would appear that they were myths produced by the same sorts of methods and held for the same sorts of reasons as modern scientific theories. If, on the other hand, they are to be called science, then we must acknowledge that science has included bodies of belief that are completely incompatible with the ones we hold today. Kuhn, indeed, states that the move from one scientific paradigm, which has a massive body of writing and research behind it, to a new paradigm, which has as yet tackled only a fraction of the area with which science is concerned, must be a decision that is 'made on faith'. If we are to be realistic, then we must acknowledge that in several hundred years time, the scientists of the future will look upon our present firmly held scientific beliefs with the same sort of incredulous condescension with which we look upon the theories of the past.[15] This conceptual gap between scientists today and those of the past is not very different from the conceptual gap between those within one religious worldview and those in another (or between those within a religious worldview and those in an atheistic one). The main difference is that the scientific conceptual gap is a sequential, historical one while the religious gap is usually a contemporaneous one.

Hayden White has argued that historical truth is established rhetorically. The disparate explanations of a historical episode by various historians are based on different meta-historical presuppositions about the nature of the historical field. There is no point in discussing whether one nineteenth-century European historian, such as de Tocqueville, is more correct than another, such as Burckhardt; or whether one interpretation of history, such as Marx's, is more correct than another, such as Nietzsche's. Their status as historians or as philosophers of history does not depend on the correctness of their data or the strength of their reasoning and logic. It is difficult to refute them with data or alternative explanations. Their influence is the result of the consistency, coherence and illuminative power of their visions of history (the viewpoints that they create within their body of work). This in turn depends on the pre-conceptual, poetic, rhetorical persuasiveness of their models.[16] Religious worldviews operate in very much the same way. They cannot easily be proven by any external logic. They appeal by the persuasiveness of their internal coherence and the illuminative power of their vision of humanity's place in the cosmos.

We can see from these two examples that the idea that each religion forms an internally coherent system that is not susceptible to disproof from outside is not unique to religion – it also obtains in science and in history. It would appear that human beings have to live within one worldview or another. Which one they choose may largely be due to birth, culture or the accidents of life, but their basis for choosing must ultimately depend on a leap of faith. Once having chosen and securely established themselves with a worldview, however, human beings are able to produce very good reasons as to why this choice is logical, reasonable and compelling. Their reasons, however, originating as they do from within this worldview, will not necessarily be logical, reasonable and compelling to those within another worldview (unless the two worldviews already share a large common area). It will not always be apparent to believers that the reasons that they adduce to support their beliefs are only true from within their conceptual universe. This is because all of us tend to treat our conceptual universe as the only real universe (that is, as reality itself). We therefore consider to be self-evident truths and basic premises what are in fact only truths within our conceptual universe (see, for example, the discussion about the nature of religion itself, as viewed from different religious traditions, pp. 21–4).

Different worldviews, language-games or conceptual schemas are not usually, of course, totally incommensurable and isolated from each other. Worldviews are social constructs and so will be similar to other worldviews constructed by that society or by similar societies. Even completely differing societies will have a small area of common experience that can form the basis of some degree of overlap in their worldviews. We are, after all, strongly influenced by certain biological factors that apply in whatever society we grow up. Each worldview, therefore, will have a number of adjacent worldviews with which it shares many concepts and an additional number of more distant worldviews with which the degree of overlap is less.

Conversion, Reform and Renewal

If, as I have indicated, reasons given from within one worldview are not convincing to those operating within the realities of another worldview, how does it come about that conversions from one religion to another occur; how does it come about that people do switch from one worldview to another?

The phenomenon of change of religious worldview occurs whenever an individual or a whole social group converts from one religion to another, when a reform or renewal movement occurs within a religion, or even when a religion itself changes in response to outside influences. Again, the parallel insights of other disciplines can be of help here.

Thomas Kuhn has, for example, outlined what happens when a scientific revolution occurs, when the scientific community shifts from one explanatory paradigm to another. The first necessity is for there to be some source of dissatisfaction with the old paradigm. A number of troublesome questions must have arisen to which the old paradigm was unable to provide adequate answers. The word 'troublesome' is an important element here, because there will always be some observations that do not fit in comfortably with any paradigm but these can be explained away or even ignored as long as they are marginal. The old Ptolemaic astronomy would have continued to predominate (and any untoward observations would have been explained away by such theories as epicycles), if the failure of observations to fit the theory had not begun to have serious consequences for navigation and calendar calculations.

The second requirement for a scientific revolution is the presence of an alternative theory. The decision to jettison one theory is always simultaneous with the decision to accept another. By and large, existing paradigms are not overturned because they fail to fit the observations. They are overturned because they give a worse fit than the new paradigm.

When a new paradigm is advanced and is seen to be successful in dealing with the troublesome questions that the old paradigm was unable to resolve, that is not the end of the revolution but merely the beginning. For the proposers of the new paradigm will usually meet stiff resistance at first from the establishment. The latter are people who have invested a lifetime of work in the old paradigm. The new paradigm means a complete reappraisal of that work, even its possible jettisoning. There will be an additional resistance from the fact that the old paradigm is firmly embedded in the educational system that prepares and licenses the student for professional practice. This process results in the old paradigm having a deep and subtle hold on the minds of all educated persons in that society.

Those who adopt the new paradigm, particularly in its earliest stages, must often do so on the slenderest of grounds. All they will have is the knowledge that the old paradigm has failed in a few instances and the new paradigm works in those instances. They must have faith that the new paradigm will eventually be able to replace the whole of the vast area that has been covered by the old paradigm so successfully for so long. But until all that work is done, the move to the new paradigm must involve a large element of faith.[17]

This rather lengthy description of Kuhn's explanation of scientific revolutions is justified by its close parallel to religious revolutions. When a religious revolution occurs, whether this be in an individual conversion, the mass conversion of a society or a religious reform, many of the same features arise. The first necessity is for a sense of dissatisfaction with the old religion. There must be important, 'troublesome' questions that the old religion is either unable to resolve or over which it cannot agree. Twentieth century society has, for example, made a great deal of religion's old concerns irrelevant while the new concerns (equality of men and women, global poverty, environmental issues, and so on) are either inadequately addressed in the established religions or there is disagreement over them.

An alternative religious viewpoint must be available which addresses these issues (or at least some of them) coherently and in an illuminating manner. The increasingly pluralistic nature of our society makes this availability of alternative religious worldviews truer today than in almost any past age.[18] One important point to note is that there must be some degree of overlap between the old religious worldview and the new one. If there were no area of overlap, it would be impossible for the new even to talk to the old. A modern European is extremely unlikely to understand, let alone adopt, the religious worldview of a Papuan head-hunter, but there is a considerable overlap between the Christian-based European worldview and those of communism, Islam or the Baha'i Faith.

Those who represent the old worldview, in particular the priests or religious professionals of the established religion, will put up resistance to the new viewpoint.[19] Among other measures, they will adapt the old worldview so as to make it more compatible with the new questions that have arisen (in parallel, for example, to the theory of epicycles that sought to make the old Ptolemaic system fit new astronomical observations).

Those who adopt the new religious worldview are, in effect, making a leap of faith. The change from one worldview to another cannot be solely justified on rational grounds, for each worldview is wholly consistent and coherent within itself. Moreover, the new worldview, if it is one of the new religions (rather than another of the established world religions), will not have the depth of systematic theology or breadth of social involvement that the old religion has.

These parallels give us a model for the way that religious change occurs, whether in an individual or in a society. Once the shift to the new worldview has occurred, everything is different. Everything that appeared established and comfortable has to be looked at again from the new viewpoint. All previous relationships have to be worked out anew. Some of this reappraisal may result in little change, while other aspects will be radically altered.

The Social Psychology of Conversion and Religious Commitment

There are, however, factors in religious conversions that are not found in the analogy with scientific paradigm shifts. Conversions have been presented above as though they were purely intellectual decisions, but they are frequently, especially in the case of individual conversions, a result of social and emotional factors.

Psychologists and social psychologists have studied the phenomenon of religious conversion and the subsequent process of commitment to a new religion extensively (although mainly concentrating on the phenomenon in the West). There are a number of general factors that psychologists have found motivate all human actions. These include:

- the desire to experience pleasure and avoid pain
- the need for a conceptual system
- the desire to enhance self-esteem
- the need to establish and maintain relationships
- the desire for power
- the yearning for transcendence.

All of these may apply in the case of religious conversion. Psychologists have also identified a number of benefits that can accrue from an action such as a religious conversion. In general terms these can be stated to be the acquiring of:

- a system of meaning (cognitive)
- emotional gratification (affective)
- techniques for living (volitional)
- leadership and power.

More specifically, in the process of religious conversion and commitment to a new religion, a number of social and psychological factors have been noted in research.[20]

MARGINALITY. Individuals who are at the margins of society (in terms of being connected to the sources of power or being involved in the culture) are more likely to convert to a new religion that is presented to them.

SOCIAL OR CULTURAL CRISIS. Individuals from cultures and societies that are in crisis are more likely to convert than those from stable cultures and societies. A cultural crisis is one where the established worldview, the conceptual world of a people, is under the threat of being substantially undermined: for example, a traditional indigenous culture confronted with modernity. A social crisis is one that affects the ordering of society. The perceived breakdown of law and order in modern urban environments may, for example, be contributing to the modern quest for new forms of spirituality. The crisis shows up the deficiencies in a culture or society, thus stimulating the search for alternatives. In a social crisis, it will be those who are affected most by the crisis, usually the poorest and least powerful elements in the society, who will be most open to conversion. In a cultural crisis, it may well be the most talented and creative members of the community who convert, since it is they who see the crisis and the advantages of conversion most clearly. Social and cultural crises often, of course, coexist, since the one may well lead to the other. In general, the closer the new religion is in its general cosmology and worldview to a person's culture, the more likely it is that that person will be attracted to the new religion. A high degree of cultural and conceptual dissonance will inhibit conversion.

INDIVIDUAL CRISIS. Just as social and cultural crises serve to highlight the breakdown of the old order and lead to a search for a new basis for society, so an individual crisis may destroy the old framework of a person's life and open up the possibility of a new worldview. Apart from the usual personal crises in health, finances or family that individuals may experience, mystical experiences, intellectual doubts, leadership crises in their present religion, or dissatisfaction with life can all lead to individual crises that leave a person open to conversion. In the case of conversion to the new religious movements, there is evidence that important positive contributory factors are the strong communal spirit of these movements and the sense of commitment to a useful cause (both of which may be felt by the convert to be lacking in his or her other social interactions; see p. 512). Of course, both with individual crises and social and cultural crises, the new religion must offer some new vision or a means of interpreting the current situation that offers a better resolution of its problems than the existing religion.

INDIVIDUAL BACKGROUND. Research has shown that those who do convert to a new religion have a much greater likelihood of having had a long history of emotional problems in childhood, adolescence and in the period immediately before conversion (often resulting in problems in making relationships), when compared to those who remain within a religion.[21]

KINSHIP AND FRIENDSHIP NETWORKS. Religious conversion is much more likely to occur within networks of families and friends. The conversion of a friend or relative whom one knows to be trustworthy opens one up to the possibility of converting oneself, especially if one observes a change for the better in that individual. The formation of a strong bond between the believer and the potential convert is an important factor in the conversion process. This facilitates the movement from a superficial enquiry to a deeper attraction. A close personal relationship helps the potential convert to feel accepted; it increases self-esteem and enables the potential convert to overcome conflicts and uncertainties that may block the path to conversion. Of course, those who have experienced emotional and social deprivation in their earlier years will be more attracted to the new religion by the formation of a close personal relationship with a member of the religion. It should be noted that just as frequently, kinship and friendship networks may be a constraint upon conversion. If the family and friends of a potential convert are strongly against the potential conversion, this may be a decisive factor in his or her withdrawal from the process.

CHARISMATIC ATTRACTION. Many converts report that what initially attracted them to a religious movement was the charisma of the leader of the group. The perceived power, energy, and authoritative exposition of the leader can be an important catalyst that opens a person up to the possibility of change.

ENCAPSULATION. I noted above that human beings are constrained in their choices by their background, their culture, family, friends, social roles and so on. All of these may act to inhibit a person from changing religion. From such considerations, we can appreciate the significance of the action of those new religious movements such as ISKCON (Hare Krishnas) and the Unification Church (Moonies) that move potential converts away from their homes and surround them with a new environment. In this way, they are creating the circumstances that enable the potential convert to break away from his or her social roles, social norms and the constraints of family and friends. In this encapsulated environment, strong personal relationships can be built up with the potential convert to bind him or her to the community; rituals can be taught that help the newcomer to integrate into the community; teaching can be given that creates for the potential convert a vision of a new interpretative framework that gives guidance and meaning to her or his life and new social roles can be presented. If the person does convert, the commitment of the new convert is thus more firmly established by the creation of new social roles, social norms and a new environment of 'family' and friends.

Encapsulation may be of different kinds and degrees. Physical encapsulation may be achieved by removing a person from all contact with his or her normal daily life. This would usually be achieved by going to a remote location or a physically surrounded building such as a retreat. Social encapsulation means restricting the access of the potential convert to all normal social interactions. This may be achieved in some groups by filling up all free time with group activities. Christian missionaries usually insist on indigenous converts changing their names to Christian names and frequently even changing their style of dress, thus making the conversion public and, often, isolating the convert socially. Ideological encapsulation means the creation of a state of mind that resists consideration of alternative religious options. This may be achieved by teaching that the group's doctrines are the only pure and redeeming path and that the outside world is irredeemably evil and corrupt. By preparing the convert for arguments that may be used against his or her conversion by friends and relatives, the convert is 'inoculated' against the creation of doubt.

These encapsulation strategies are used by many religious groups (and, indeed, to some degree, by anyone who seeks to convince someone else of anything). They only become objectionable when they become overbearing and coercive. Many of the objections that have been raised against new religious movements concern their real or imagined excessive use of these strategies (see pp. 512–5).

After Conversion

The process of conversion is often sealed by a ritual, such as the Christian baptism or confirmation. This serves to give public testimony of the event that has occurred in the convert's life; it sets the boundary between the new and the old and it serves to burn the convert's bridges, thus making it less likely that the convert will return to his or her previous allegiance.

Religious literature is full of accounts of conversion (see pp. 94 and 160–1). A certain degree of caution is needed when reading these. They are often full of assertions that the convert's life has been radically and irreversibly changed by the conversion experience. Often this statement is corroborated by the assertion of friends of the convert that he or she has changed greatly.

The first note of caution lies in the fact that, however enthusiastic the convert may be, a considerable proportion of converts do leave the religion again. Inevitably, after a time, the initial euphoria of the conversion experience wears off and a 'post-conversion depression' may set in. Unless the new religion has some inbuilt mechanisms for renewing enthusiasm and maintaining commitment, the likelihood of a person drifting away again is high. Some writers have likened this to the process of falling into

Conversion Rituals

In some religious traditions, requirements to modify one's clothing, diet, or other patterns of common daily behaviour can serve this same function of reinforcing the rejection of old patterns and behaviours and the incorporation of new behaviours into one's life. At the heart of conversion ritual is the difficult combination of saying no and saying yes. Conversion implies that a person is 'turning away from' the past and 'turning to' a new future. Ritual witnessed by others can be powerful in advertising the new condition of the person or persons who are converting. One of the most dramatic conversions in the twentieth century took place on 14 October 1956. An estimated five hundred thousand people gathered near Nagpur in the western Indian state of Maharashtra. Led by B. R. Ambedkar, hundreds of thousands of Mahars renounced their Hindu faith and embraced Buddhism. Dressed in white robes, the people followed Ambedkar in reciting the Buddhist oaths administered by Chandramani Mahasthavir, the oldest and most revered Buddhist monk in India. The massive gathering of people, the white robes, and the recitation of oaths were simple but powerfully effective rituals in transforming the Mahars from being Untouchables to being Buddhists. (Rambo, *Understanding Religious Conversion*, pp. 127–8)

a

b

Faith and conversion bring about a spiritual cleansing, one universal symbol of which is the use of water in ritual cleansing. a) Christians being baptized in the holiest river of Christianity, the River Jordan. b) Hindus bathing in the holiest river of Hinduism, the Ganges, at Varanasi (Benares).

and out of love. Some may fall out of love and gradually drift away, while with others something may trigger conflict and acrimony.

The second note of caution relates to the degree of change that has occurred. Although it is conventional to think of a conversion as being a complete rejection of the past and a turning to a new way of life, in fact there is rarely such a complete change. Human beings cannot change their structure of reality so rapidly and completely as a religious conversion would theoretically require them to do. Inevitably, each convert brings into the new religion something of his or her previous religion. All converts view their new religion to some extent through the viewpoint of the old. This remnant of the old will sometimes decrease and disappear but sometimes it remains and is even passed on to subsequent generations. Examples of this abound in all religions. The Emperor Constantine converted to Christianity and did much to establish that religion in the West. He appears, however, to have retained a great deal of attachment to his previous belief in the cult of the Sol Invictus. St Augustine is the greatest of the Western Church Fathers. He converted to Christianity in 387, and yet his writings betray the continuing influence of his previous belief in Manichaeism. In the present day, it is possible to study, for example, the manner in which Western Baha'is recast the Baha'i teachings and give them a distinctive Western 'Christian' or 'New Age' ethos when the Baha'i Faith passed from a Middle Eastern environment to the West at the beginning of the twentieth century.[22] We can also see the continuing influence of traditional African religion among the converts to Christianity and Islam in Africa (see pp. 506–7). Perhaps more remarkable is the persistence of African religious practices among the descendants of African slaves in South America despite unopposed indoctrination by the Roman Catholic Church for several hundred years (see pp. 399–403, 507–8). Indeed, most of what is called in chapter 15 'popular religion' is, in fact, the remnants of religious beliefs pre-dating the established religion of each area.

Motifs of Religious Conversion

The experience of religious conversion is reported differently by different individuals. This experience is partly moulded by the expectations of what conversion will be like; for example, if one is black and lives in the American South, one expects religious conversion to occur suddenly and emotively in a revivalist setting. John Lofland and Norman Skonovd ('Conversion Motifs') have described six patterns or motifs of religious conversion (see Table 6.1).

1. Intellectual. This involves an intensive study of a religion, using books, lectures, television, the Internet and other media that involve little interpersonal contact. Social pressure is usually avoided and belief precedes participation in the community.

2. MYSTICAL. The prototype of this is the 'Road to Damascus' experience. It occurs suddenly and dramatically and may be associated with dreams or visions.
3. EXPERIMENTAL. This involves an active exploration of different religious options with the potential convert assessing whether a religion 'works' and what benefit it brings. This motif is gradually worked through over a long period of time and participation in the community precedes belief.
4. AFFECTIONAL. This involves the creation of a direct, personal bond with members of the religious group over a period of time, thus giving the potential convert the experience of being loved and nurtured.
5. REVIVALIST. This is the type of conversion that occurs in a revivalist meeting. It uses crowd conformity and a high degree of emotional arousal to achieve the conversion.
6. COERCIVE. This is the type of conversion that involves brainwashing, coercive persuasion and thought programming. Although many new religious movements are accused of using this method, it is, in fact, probably rare (see pp. 512–15) and is often reversed if the coercive pressures are removed.

INTELLECTUAL MOTIF: Dr Bhimrao Ramji Ambedkar (1893–1956) was a Hindu of Untouchable birth who rose to become India's law minister in 1947. Despairing of the effects of the caste system, he led several hundred thousand fellow Untouchables in a mass conversion to Buddhism in 1956.

Table 6.1 Conversion Motifs

CONVERSION MOTIFS	DEGREE OF SOCIAL PRESSURE	TEMPORAL DURATION	LEVEL OF AFFECTIVE AROUSAL	AFFECTIVE CONTENT	BELIEF-PARTICIPATION SEQUENCE
INTELLECTUAL	Low or none	Medium	Medium	Illumination	Belief – participation
MYSTICAL	None or little	Short	High	Awe, fear, love	Belief – participation
EXPERIMENTAL	Low	Long	Low	Curiosity	Participation – belief
AFFECTIONAL	Medium	Long	Medium	Affection	Participation – belief
REVIVALIST	High	Short	High	Love (and fear)	Participation – belief
COERCIVE	High	Long [or short]	High	Fear (and love)	Participation – belief

SOURCE: Based on John Lofland and Norman Skonovd, 'Conversion Motifs', p. 375.

Four Conversion Motifs

Intellectual

Looking at Ambedkar's actions, speeches and writings [in the process of his conversion to Buddhism] . . . one can draw up a list of 'necessities' which any religion hoping to draw the Mahars [Ambedkar's caste] should possess . . . No current religion met all these demands. One by one, Ambedkar rejected the possibilities. Even before the 1936 caste meeting he told reporters: 'I shall not take the responsibility of starting a new sect. There are some difficulties in the way of our accepting Buddhism. We shall consider the question of joining the Sikh religion.' Sikhism came closest to meeting the Mahar needs. But, although Ambedkar went to Amritsar to visit Sikh leaders, he seems to have abandoned the possibility of conversion to Sikhism. (E. Zelliot, 'The Psychological Dimension of the Buddhist Movement in India', in Oddie, *Religion in South Asia*, pp. 192, 197–8)

Experimental

I learned quite a bit that day, but wasn't ready to make a commitment. So my brother gave me his prayer book and encouraged me to try some of the Baha'i prayers. Underhanded? Maybe, but it worked.

I left, and began saying a few prayers each day. Slowly, I became a happier person, better able to deal with life. After a while, other things took priority and I stopped saying the prayers. I noticed that the quality of life went down. I thought it rather strange that it happened right when I quit saying those prayers. So I got the old prayer book and started up again. The quality of life went back up. I was not as apt to lose my temper, and could be more tactful, with less stress to myself. Two weeks went by and I quit saying the prayers again, this time on purpose, to see if there was any correlation. Of course there was, but I wasn't convinced until I'd run the experiment three more times. I decided I'd better give in. (Gottlieb, *Once to Every Man and Nation*, pp. 54–5)

Affectional

Their personal contact with Muslim friends or acquaintances whose opinions or behaviours are valued played a role in their conversion. Emily recollected how she was impressed by the Muslim family that she knew: '. . . At that time I was seeing this Muslim family and I was watching and listening to what they said and what they did. I was trying to see how they were different. They were very sincere in their faith and they were friendly in this materialistic and selfish society. That really helped towards my reversion.' (Kose, *Conversion to Islam*, p. 101)

Coercive

Owing to the unbearable oppression of the village authorities not only myself but all my kinsfolk have become Christians. In former times when a theft occurred, whoever might be the thief, the village authorities used to arrest us and put us in prison for some days. But since we have become Christians we are free from such troubles. no one is bold enough to touch us without the permission of our pastor. Besides that we are now worshipping the true God. (Oddie, 'Christian Conversion among Non-Brahmins in Andhra Pradesh', in Oddie, *Religion in South Asia*, p. 115)

Because Lofland and Skonovd are considering people from North America, they fail to mention one further form of conversion that commonly occurs in poorer countries, when pressure is applied to those in the poorest sections of the population and those with the lowest status. This pressure may be in the form of financial inducements or in the promise of a higher social status. It may be considered as a form of coercive conversion in Lofland and Skonovd's scheme.

The Conversion of Whole Societies

As I note elsewhere (see pp. 24–5), the phenomenon of individuals converting from one religion to another is a particular feature of the modern world. The concept of conversion as a choice for the individual is itself a product of the individualism of modernity and is rarely found in previous societies (one other major period in which there does appear to have been a large degree of choice for individuals is the latter centuries of the Roman Empire). In general, the religion of a traditional society is a matter that is decided by the society as a whole. Thus any change in religion also tends to be a matter for social rather than individual concern.

One way in which whole societies have been converted is as a result of imperialism and coercion. This coercion has sometimes been a matter of brute force: 'convert or die', as for example happened to Jews and Muslims in Spain under the Inquisition in the sixteenth century. It has, however, sometimes been a matter of psychological, social or financial pressure. In classical Muslim societies, for example, non-Muslims had to pay a poll tax which they could avoid by the simple expedient of conversion. In Tonga and other Pacific islands, conversion to Mormonism is the only realistic way for poorer islanders to obtain for their children a university education and all the social advantages that entails.

In most traditional societies religion tends to be a communal rather than an individual concern. This picture shows a Muslim religious gathering at Oyo, Nigeria, in the early twentieth century.

There have been a few studies of the process involved when a whole society changes religion. One situation that has been studied is

CONVERSION UNDER IMPERIALISM

The two societies of Barolong and Basotho along the Caledon Valley, generally got along with the missionary sects among them. The chiefly class specifically admired their secular usefulness and was determined to keep them close. If that was achieved at the cost of a bearable sacrifice, they were prepared to pay the price. But, when it came to converting people, missionaries aimed a blow at their traditions, and little differentiated between Christianity . . . and Westernization, which represented a conflicting cosmic view. Throughout the nineteenth century the two missionary sects failed to realize or did not care that they could evangelize despite, or even through, their adherents' traditions. In short, missionaries were unmistakeably imperialistic in their view. [Rather] than have their traditions and hence their identity destroyed the Barong and Basotho rebelled against the imperialism. Like various communities under slavery, they even feigned complete lack of understanding of simple *dicta* about Christianity, which led the missionary to think that they were either stupid or inherently depraved. So the Barolong and Basotho engaged [in a] passive resistance, more against the missionaries, than against Christianity. (Machobane, *Christianisation and the African Response*, p. 32)

the Islamicization of an African tribe (the movement from the traditional African tribal religion to an Islamic way of life). The process results in a radical alteration in the cosmology, social relations and even eating habits of the tribe. All this change cannot occur at once; it is a process that may take several generations to complete. Moreover, the change occurs piecemeal, with some matters being accepted more rapidly than others.

At first, a Muslim injunction such as avoiding nudity is adopted by some for reasons of social prestige; it then becomes a matter of respectability to be clothed; finally it becomes a matter of public decency, such that failing to be clothed becomes a matter of shame. The crucial shift that occurs is when the individuals in the tribe cease to think in terms of 'to be a good Muslim one should not eat pork' and instead think 'to be a good person one does not eat pork'. In other words, the injunction ceases to be merely a religious injunction (and thus only a matter for religious merit or demerit) and becomes a question of tribal morality (with the full force of customary social sanctions against anyone who breaks the injunction). The fact that the eating of pork is wrong is then no longer a question of individual choice: it has become part of the way that the world is, the symbolic cultural universe of the tribe. The tribesman would then no more think of eating pork than a European would think of eating cockroaches.[23]

Another study, on the conversion of tribal peoples to Islam in eastern Bengal, has described a number of stages in the process whereby the deities, symbols and concepts of the former religion were replaced by those of Islam.

1. INCLUSION. First, the Deity, symbols and concepts of the new religion are included alongside those of the existing religion. The new is seen as a more effective way of achieving spiritual or supernatural power.
2. IDENTIFICATION. The Deity, symbols and ideas of the new religion are identified as being the same as those of the old religion. The God of Islam is identified with the high god of the tribal religion.
3. DISPLACEMENT. The Deity, symbols and ideas of the new religion displace those of the new religion.[24]

THE RELIGIOUS LIFE

As well as the different pathways to salvation, the different ways of recreating the religious experience communally (outlined in chapter 5), there are different ways for the individual to be religious, different modes of the religious life. Psychologists who have looked at this have described several modes of religious life, although it must be noted that almost all studies have been done on North American Christians. One categorization that is very influential distinguishes between extrinsic and intrinsic ways of being religious. Persons with an extrinsic religion tend to use their religion for their own ends. Religion is thus instrumental (for some other purpose) and utilitarian. Thus, for example, such persons may use religion to provide security, solace, or self-advancement. Persons with an intrinsic religion, by contrast, have their religion as an end in itself. They attempt to internalize the beliefs and prescriptions of their religion. Other considerations are subordinated to religious beliefs and living the religious life.[25] In summary, the 'extrinsically motivated individual *uses* his religion, whereas the intrinsically motivated *lives* his'.[26]

To this, a third mode of religious life has been added by some psychologists, the *quest mode*. This is characterized by persons who are open-ended and questioning in their approach to religion. They resist clear-cut tidy answers to the existential questions that trouble human beings. While acknowledging the importance of religion and of a transcendent religious dimension to a person's life, such persons feel that they do not know, nor can they ever know, the final definitive truth about such matters.[27]

When these modes were first described, they were considered developmentally; it was thought that people moved through these modes as stages in their religious development. Thus, when originally describing these modes, Allport called extrinsic religion 'immature religion' and intrinsic religion 'mature religion'. It would appear more satisfactory, however, to regard these as independent modes of religious life.

Table 6.2 Psychological Comparison of Different Modes of Religious Life

	EXTRINSIC	INTRINSIC	QUEST
LIBERTY OR BONDAGE			
Religion experienced as freedom or bondage	Bondage	Freedom	Neutral
Willingness to bind oneself to religious beliefs	Unwilling	Willing	Unwilling
MENTAL HEALTH			
Fear of death, death anxiety	No effect or increased	Decreased	No effect
Mental illness	More likely	Less likely	No clear effect
Appropriate social behaviour	Less likely	More likely	No data
Freedom from worry and guilt	Decreased	Increased (but decreased for guilt)	No clear effect (possibly decreased)
Personal competence and control	Decreased	Increased	No clear effect (possibly increased)
Open-mindedness and flexibility	Decreased	No effect	Increased
FREEDOM FROM PREJUDICE			
Prejudice proscribed by religion, assessed overtly	Increased	Decreased	Decreased
Prejudice not proscribed by religion	No effect	Increased	Decreased
Prejudice, assessed covertly	Increased	Increased	Decreased
CONCERN FOR OTHERS			
Help in response to low-cost requests	Decreased	Increased	Increased
Help that is responsive to need	Decreased	Decreased	Increased

Various studies have been done assessing these three ways of being religious against both individual factors, such as mental health, and social factors, such as freedom from prejudice. The results of this research are complex and some of them are contrary to what one might expect. Extrinsic religion performed poorly in all areas. Individuals with extrinsic religion have poorer results on mental health, are more prejudiced, and are less likely to help others. Taking the mental health of the individual as one's criterion, intrinsic religion scores best of the three types in the various factors that have been examined. If one examines what most religions consider to be good relationships with others, however, one finds that individuals with intrinsic religion perform well only in circumstances where they are promoting a positive self-image. When measured by more subtle, covert techniques, they are also prejudiced, they only help others when there is minimal inconvenience to themselves and their help in such circumstances is likely to be only poorly related to the needs of the other person. In other words, it was found that their actions were motivated more by a desire to present themselves as good, caring people than by a concern for others. Individuals with the quest type of religion were found to be less prejudiced than others, even when this was measured covertly. They were not particularly more motivated to be helpful than the other groups but when they did help, their assistance was more closely related to the needs of the person being helped.

Further Reading

Many books have been written on the subject of this chapter. Most, however, have been written from a theological perspective rather than from the more neutral viewpoint of religious studies. Among the more important works from the religious studies perspective are: on faith in the Western religions, W. C. Smith, *Faith and Belief* and *The Meaning and End of Religion*; on faith in Mahayana Buddhism, Park, *Buddhist Faith and Sudden Enlightenment*. See also Rouner, *Knowing Religiously*; Runzo and Ihara, *Religious Experience and Religious Belief* and the article by Jaroslav Pelikan on 'Faith' in Eliade, *Encyclopedia of Religion*. On the development of religious belief and faith, see Batson, Schoenrade and Ventis, *Religion and the Individual*, chapter 3, and Fowler, *Stages of Faith*. On religious conversion, see Rambo, *Understanding Religious Conversion*. On modes of the religious life, see Batson, Schoenrade and Ventis, *Religion and the Individual*, Part 3.

7

Towards a Scientific Understanding of Religious Experience

Chapter 4 examined the various ways of describing religious experience and undertook some preliminary analysis of this. In chapter 2, I attempted to define the distinguishing features of two contrasting types of religion. These I called theistic and monistic (non-theistic) religion. Each side of this dichotomy has claimed that it holds the truth and that the other side either is misinterpreting reality or holds to a 'lower' form of the truth. This chapter will examine work in experimental psychology and neurophysiology that sheds light on the nature of the religious experience and on this question of the interpretation of reality in theistic and monistic ways.

Much of the scientific research presented in this chapter relates to states of deep meditation and trance. However, the results of these investigations have a much wider significance than may at first be apparent. First, altered states of consciousness as a result of religious activities are not as uncommon as one may think. One survey of 487 cultures and societies found that 90 per cent of these had one or more institutionalized, culturally patterned form of altered state of consciousness, usually within a religious context.[1] Second, we can think of deep meditation and trance as situated at one end of a continuum of religious experience. Thus statements made about this state may apply in lesser degrees to less intense forms of religious experience.

This chapter begins by looking at some findings and experimental models from experimental psychology and neurophysiology. The reader is asked to bear with a number of pages of material that do not at first appear to have any relationship to the study of religion. It is hoped that the relationships will become clear later in the chapter. Before proceeding, though, the reader may find it useful to review some of the main characteristics of the central religious experience (see pp. 88–92).

We shall start with a passage which describes the religious experience of one individual.

> Suddenly, at church, or in company, or when I was reading, and always, I think, when my muscles were at rest, I felt the approach of the mood.

> Irresistibly it took possession of my mind and will, lasted what seemed an eternity, and disappeared in a series of rapid sensations which resembled the awakening from anaesthetic influence. One reason why I disliked this kind of trance was that I could not describe it to myself. I cannot even now find words to render it intelligible. It consisted in a gradual but swiftly progressive obliteration of space, time, sensation, and the multitudinous factors which seem to qualify what we are pleased to call our Self. In proportion as these conditions of ordinary consciousness were subtracted, the sense of an underlying or essential consciousness acquired intensity. At last nothing remained but a pure, absolute, abstract Self. The universe became without form and void of content. But Self persisted, formidable in its vivid keenness.[2]

The interiors of many religious buildings are designed to elevate the human spirit and evoke a religious experience. This picture shows the interior of the Selimiyye Mosque, Edirne, Turkey.

This passage, by the noted literary historian James A. Symonds, mentions several of the factors of religious experience to which we shall return in this chapter:

- his inability to explain or describe it (despite the fact that he was a writer by profession)
- changes in time and space
- a dissolution of the personal self into an absolute, abstract Self
- the vividness of the experience.

Scientific studies have shed some light on some aspects of such phenomena.

Piaget and the Perceptual Development of Children

In the 1920s, Jean Piaget, the Swiss psychologist, published several books and papers which, although much refined by later work, remain the basis of scientific thought about the perceptual development of children. This work helps us understand how our sense of self develops and therefore what happens when this sense of self dissolves, as many have described it doing in their religious experiences. Using observations and extrapolating from his findings in older children, Piaget tried to define the perceptual world of the newborn baby. He concluded that a newborn baby has no perception of itself as being a separate entity from its environment. 'A baby has no consciousness of self . . . There is a total continuity between internal and external experience.'[3] As the baby grows and begins to manipulate its environment, it learns by experimentation that the hand is part of 'me' and the cot is 'not-me'.

Gradually, the child imposes schemata upon the external world (recognizing certain patterns of sensory stimuli as specific things experienced before). After a while, these schemata become automatic and subconscious and do not have to be thought through each time. However, even as late as the time during which the child is learning to speak, it does not distinguish between 'thoughts' and 'things'. The thought 'chair' is considered to be an inherent part of a chair. It is only increasing age that brings about the complete subject–object detachment of adult thought. In this latter stage, incoming stimuli are processed rapidly through pre-existing schemata, which become subconscious. These schemata are thought to lie in the subcortical zones of the brain. These areas analyse the incoming stimuli and integrate them into the meaning patterns built up during childhood. This information is then presented, already imbued with meaning (that is, interpreted), to the cortical areas of conscious thought.[4]

Although much more information can be processed as a result of this adult adaptation, each individual unit of stimulus must necessarily have less impact. This is another way of saying that childhood sensory experiences are more vivid. To give an example, if an adult picks up a book, he or she usually looks at the title. The visual information regarding the size, shape and colour of his or her own hand that goes forward to pick up the book will be suppressed. It will barely register in conscious thought, as it will be automatically processed in the subcortical zones and filtered out. Even the shape and colour of the book may not have any great impact on conscious thought as the adult concentrates attention on the title of the book. If the book is put into the hand of an infant, however, all the sensory information relating to hand and book arrives in the brain making equal demands for attention. The infant may therefore pause to gaze intently at its own hand. The changeover from the infantile pattern to the adult pattern is a gradual process. There are several intermediate stages in childhood.

In adults, incoming stimuli are compared with the schemata in the subcortical areas. If the stimuli are recognized as being of a similar pattern to one of the schemata held in the subcortical areas, then the related memories and associations are automatically switched on. All this happens at the subconscious level. It only becomes conscious if the person turns his or her attention to these particular incoming stimuli, or if the incoming stimuli are completely different to the patterns (schemata) held in the subcortical areas. In the infant, however, the schemata at the subcortical level are as yet undeveloped. The incoming stimuli are therefore not 'recognized' and go through to the conscious level unprocessed. There is no separation of cortical and subcortical function; both are within the consciousness of an infant, whereas only the cortex is in the conscious domain of an adult in normal states. In the adult, it is the cortex that is responsible for the conscious perception of the stimuli that have come into the subcortex and been analysed subconsciously by it.

It can be noted, in passing, that Bellah has proposed a scheme for the historical evolution of religion (see pp. 70–2) that has parallels with Piaget's scheme for the development of the individual. Bellah proposes that primitive or archaic religion is characterized by world acceptance, since this was the only possible response to a 'reality that invades the self to such an extent that the symbolizations of self and world are only very partially separate'.[5] The emergence of the historic religions is characterized by world rejection, enabling the human mind to stand back from its encompassing environment and become conscious of itself as a distinct entity capable of salvation.[6]

Meditation and Brain Function

Some forms of meditation, in particular Zazen (a form of meditation in Japanese Zen Buddhism), have been shown to produce a state that has similarities to the way that Piaget postulates that the infant brain functions. When a person is in Zazen meditation, alpha brain waves appear in the electroencephalogram (EEG). These are similar to what occurs as a person goes from a state of wakefulness into drowsiness. When a person who is going into a state of drowsiness (and is exhibiting alpha waves on the EEG) is subjected to a regular clicking noise, at first the noise causes a disturbance in the EEG. After a while, however, the brain appears to become habituated so that no further disturbance in the EEG occurs. The clicking noise can also interrupt the brain's alpha waves seen when the subject is meditating, but this time no habituation occurs.[7] On Piaget's model we can postulate that in the person going from wakefulness to drowsiness, the clicking noise at first intrudes into the consciousness. But as soon as it has been processed, interpreted and integrated into the brain's schemata as not being of any consequence, it fades from consciousness. It no longer disturbs the brain waves. This is the adult pattern of perception. In Zazen, however, no such integration occurs and the sensory perception of sound continues to impinge on the consciousness. Each click is treated as new information that has never been heard before. The subject reports apprehending the sound as pure perception. 'Each stimulus is accepted as stimulus itself and treated as such.'[8] This corresponds to what has been described above as the infant's mode of perception.

Not all meditation results in the state described in the preceding paragraph. As a Zen meditator increases in skill, a state is reached in which a clicking sound is no longer apprehended at all. It produces no change in the EEG.[9] A similar state is found in deep meditation (*samadhi*) among yogis.[10] A yoga master in deep meditation shows no interruption in his EEG pattern despite flashing lights, sounding gongs, or the touch of a hot test tube.[11]

State-Dependent Learning and State-Bound Knowledge

A second area of research is of interest with regard to the reports of the inability of the subject to describe his or her religious experiences. The more intense an experience, the less the subject is able to put it into words. This research into the phenomenon of state-dependent learning and state-bound knowledge (or meaning) also helps to explain the way that rituals and religious symbols function at the psychological level. Religious experience often involves a state of altered consciousness. Experimentally, in order to investigate this phenomenon, it has been found useful to use drugs to achieve states of altered consciousness.[12]

In brief, it can be stated that any task or memorization learned at one level of consciousness is best remembered at the same level, rather than at other levels. It is not, however, just memory that is affected by varying levels of arousal. As we move away from the level of consciousness associated with our ordinary, everyday routine, the distinction between subject and object becomes blurred. Most of our rational processes, such as Aristotelian logic, depend upon discounting any interaction between the observer and the observed. These processes are therefore only applicable at the level of arousal of daily routine. Our system of logic and even the meaning of words begin to break down once we leave this level. Thus, as Fischer has stated: 'Meaning is "meaningful" only at that level of arousal at which it was experienced', and so 'every experience has its state-bound meaning'.[13]

What is experienced in states of altered consciousness is, first, not so well remembered once the individual returns to normal levels of arousal. Second, even what is remembered can only be poorly expressed in terms of a vocabulary that is firmly bound to the normal level of arousal. In recounting these experiences, recourse can often only be made to metaphor, symbols, art, poetry or music.

Religious Symbols

After a particularly disturbing experience, most people find that for a long time afterwards, seeing or experiencing something that reminds them of the episode leads to a sudden flashback. It raises them to a high level of arousal again. Take, for example, having an accident at a crossroads with a red car. For a long time afterwards, a driver will experience unpleasant symptoms of arousal whenever he or she comes to a similar crossroads or

The Use of Metaphors and Images to Portray Mystical Experience

What can I say about the stations of those who have attained union except that they are infinite, while the stations of the travelers have a limit? The limit of the travelers is union. But what could be the limit of those in union? – that is, that union which cannot be marred by separation. No ripe grape ever again becomes green, and no mature fruit ever again becomes raw. (Jalal al-Din Rumi, quoted in Chittick, *The Sufi Path of Love*, p. 247)

When the wise knows that it is through the great and omnipresent spirit in us that we are conscious in waking or in dreaming, then he goes beyond sorrow.

When he knows the Atman, the Self, the inner life, who enjoys like a bee the sweetness of the flowers of the senses, the lord of what was and what will be, then he goes beyond fear: This in truth is That . . .

As the water raining on a mountain-ridge runs down the rocks on all sides, so the man who only sees variety of things runs after them on all sides.

But as pure water becomes one and the same, so becomes, O Nachiketas, the soul of the sage who knows. (*Katha Upanishad*, part 4, in *The Upanishads*, pp. 62–3)

The duality that so long existed between the Self and the world, now ceased to exist. The mind became immediately composed. Internally there was a feeling of joy. On the outside, the strength of the limbs faded away . . . Drops of sweat crept over his body, as drops of water creep on the moon-stone when it is touched by the rays of the moon. As an unblown lotus swings to and fro on account of the bee which is enclosed within its petals, similarly the body of the devotee began to shake on account of the feelings of internal bliss. As particles of camphor drop down when the womb of the camphor-plant is full-blown, similarly, tears of joy trickled down from his eyes. As the sea experiences tide after tide when the moon has arisen, similarly his mind experienced surge after surge of emotion from time to time. Thus all the eight . . . emotions began to compete in the mind of the mystic and he sat on the throne of divine joy. (Jñaneshvara, quoted in Ranade, *Mysticism in India*, pp. 125–6)

sees a similar red car. This gives us an insight into the role of a religious symbol (see also pp. 278–9). The central experience of religion is undoubtedly one that leads to a certain level of arousal. The symbol is an aspect of that experience. When encountered again in the course of our everyday life, the symbol can transport us immediately to that level of arousal where we can again partake of the experience. In the case of the red car, the experience recalled is unpleasant, while in the case of the religious symbol, the experience recalled is pleasant and attractive. Thus a Christian, for example, may have a profound emotional experience in reflecting upon, or seeing an artistic or dramatic representation of, the

RELIGIOUS SYMBOLS: In modern times, each religion has adopted a symbol that has become the hallmark of that religion. In some cases, such as the cross for Christianity and the Star of David for Judaism, the symbol has had long-standing associations and its adoption has been natural and uncontroversial. In other cases the adoption is more questionable. Islam, for example, cannot be said to have had a symbol. Its armies, when fighting religious wars, usually fought under banners with quotations from the *Qur'an* on them. The star and crescent was more properly the emblem of the Ottoman Empire, but has been adopted by Muslims for lack of a suitable alternative. Similarly, the Hindu symbol comprises the Sanskrit letters for the holy sound 'Om'. It is the sound that is considered holy rather than the letters. There are numerous other holy symbols in Hinduism such as the swastika and *padma* (lotus).

Christian pilgrims at Easter re-enact the last journey of Jesus by carrying crosses past the 'Stations of the Cross' in Jerusalem.

sacrifice and sufferings of Christ when he was crucified. The symbol of the cross brings these feelings back.

It is not only an object or sign that may act in this way as a religious symbol. Elements of a religious ritual can have the same effect: a particular smell (as with incense), or a sound (as with a bell or the voice of the muezzin), or the words of a prayer. Any of these can take the believer immediately to that level of emotional arousal at which the religious experience is relived.

Fischer and a Map of Mental States

What has been presented thus far is relatively uncontroversial and is accepted by most workers in this field. Some of Roland Fischer's work, however, has been subjected to criticism, chiefly that it is oversimplified.[14] Since it does, however, lead to several valuable insights, it is here briefly presented.

Roland Fischer has collected data both from his own work and the work of others to describe the neurophysiological changes that occur in a variety of states of altered consciousness. These include meditation and trance states associated in particular with the Eastern religions. He has described two ways in which consciousness can be altered. He names these two the *ergotropic* pathway, signifying increasing arousal culminating at the extreme in mystical ecstasy, and the *trophotropic* pathway of decreasing arousal culminating in deep trance. These two pathways can be demonstrated to be different. For example, the pattern of the brain waves on the electroencephalogram (EEG) shows increasingly higher frequency discharges on the ergotropic and increasingly lower frequency discharges on the trophotropic pathway. Other measurable differences have also been shown to occur.[15] Some of the features of these two pathways can be seen in Figure 7.1 (p. 174), which is adapted from Fischer.

However, these two pathways should not be considered as opposites, for they are in fact paths that proceed in parallel. At the extreme end of the two pathways lie mystical ecstasy and deep trance, respectively. But, in fact, these two states are not very far from each other. They are inter-convertible, in that a person in a state of hyper-aroused ecstasy can go directly into a state of trance without retracing his or her steps along the ergotropic pathway. This frequently observed phenomenon is called *abreaction* in some studies and *rebound phenomenon* in others. Movement in the opposite direction is also to be found, in that a state of trance is frequently followed by a state of ecstasy. This link between the ergotropic and trophotropic pathways is not just confined to their end-points. Experimental data suggest that each level of hyper-arousal is linked to a corresponding level of hypo-arousal. Thus, for example, it was found that a series of numbers memorized at one level of hyper-arousal is best remembered at either the same level of hyper-arousal or the equivalent

Figure 7.1 Pathways to Altered States of Consciousness

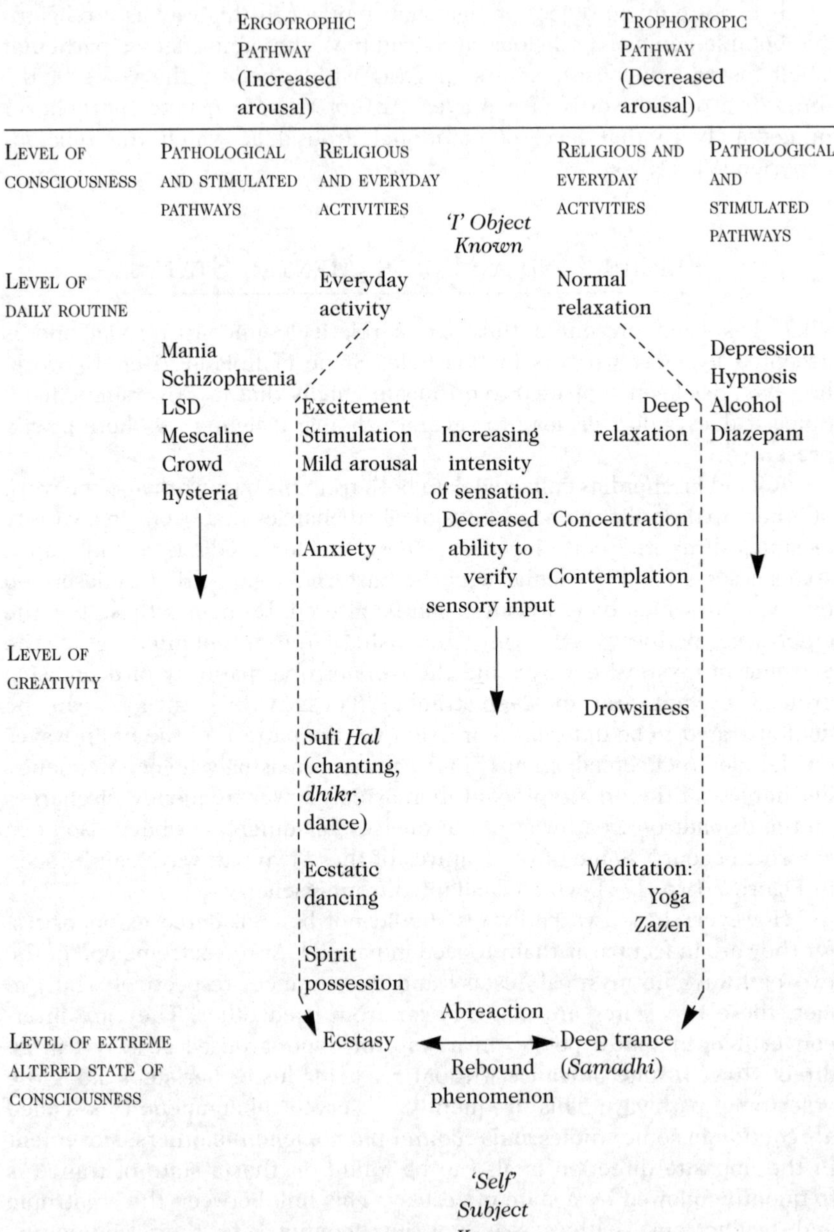

SOURCE: Based on R. Fischer, 'A Cartography of Ecstatic and Meditative States'

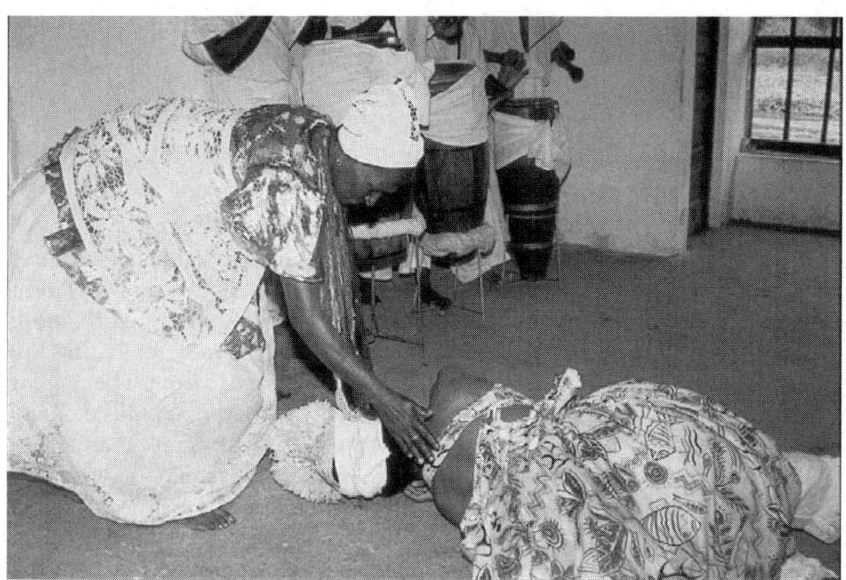

A woman in a trance state on the floor during a ritual of Candomblé, Brazil

level of hypo-arousal. But it is not so well remembered at other levels of either hyper- or hypo-arousal.

What has been found experimentally is that, as a person goes along either pathway, several subjective and objective phenomena are consistently reproduced. These apply whether the stimulus for proceeding along these pathways is natural, pathological or artificially induced by drugs. In our routine activities, we maintain a high level of motor activity, which continuously acts to verify the perceptions of our sensory input.[16] As we go into states of altered consciousness, hyper- or hypo-arousal, we are less able to perform voluntary motor activity. And so we become increasingly unable to verify sensations. With increasing levels of either hyper- or hypo-arousal, moreover, the EEG shows decreasing variability. This is reflected subjectively in a loss of the ability to interpret sensations.[17] Thus, as states of hyper- or hypo-arousal are induced, there occurs 'an intensification of inner sensations, accompanied by a loss in the ability to verify them through voluntary activity'.[18] The overall effect of this is a marked diminution in our interpretative repertoire.

At the level of daily routine, there is a sharp subject–object definition. Individuals are able to view themselves and their actions in an objective manner. One of the effects, as we travel along these two pathways away from our everyday level of consciousness, is that we begin to lose this distinction. The boundary between the observer and the observed becomes more and more blurred. Other boundaries also break down. The link with the chronological time of the physical world is broken and time can appear to speed up or slow down depending on certain personality parameters.[19] A person who is in a high state of hyper- or hypo-arousal becomes, as noted previously, increasingly impervious to external stimuli.

The Neurophysiological Basis of Religious Experience

It would be wrong to think that we are here dealing only with the extremes of experience, such as trance states and mystical ecstasy. These phenomena are more marked in these extreme states and, therefore, more easily measured experimentally. But they are, in fact, phenomena that are frequently experienced in everyday life in less extreme forms. They occur whenever anything happens to change our level of emotional arousal. Many commonly heard expressions bear witness to the fact that these phenomena, in less intense form, are part of our everyday experience: 'How time flies when you're having fun!' or 'Every moment of the ordeal seemed like an hour' (time passing more quickly or slowly at a raised level of arousal); 'I can't remember what happened last night but it must have been good!', or 'If you haven't experienced it, you cannot know' (state-bound memory and knowledge); 'He was so wrapped in thought that he did not hear me' (decreased awareness of external stimuli). And of course, if these phenomena are a common part of everyday life, they are very much more a part of all forms of religious life, which is usually charged with emotion and may therefore be considered to be at a different level of consciousness to our daily routine.

What light do these findings in neurophysiological and psychological research shed upon religious experience? We have already noted in chapter 2 (p. 36) that the Eastern religions place a great deal of emphasis on meditation or repetitive chanting, activities which lead to altered states of consciousness. This alteration in the state of consciousness produces a state similar to that described by Piaget for the infant (an integration of cortical and subcortical activity). Deikman called this state 'deautomatization'[20] because there is a deactivation of those automatic schemata (in the subcortex) which organize and interpret incoming stimuli. Meditation transfers the attention from abstract thought activity (cognition) to perceptions. 'The active intellectual mode is replaced by a receptive perceptual mode.'[21]

Experiences of Trance or Mystical Ecstasy

Many writers from Eastern traditions, as well as from those Western traditions that encourage the achievement of trance states, have tried to describe their experiences (see pp. 94–7 and 166–7 for examples of this). We find that many of their descriptions match what we would expect from the scientific findings of Piaget, Fischer and others.

1. Those who enter states of trance or ecstasy report the experience of a monist state (i.e. when the 'me' and 'not-me' division in the world breaks down and they experience an intense sense of unity with Reality). Trance or deep meditation produces a state that appears to correspond in many respects to the 'infantile state' (Piaget), the 'state of hyper- or hypo-arousal' (Fischer), or 'deautomatization' (Deikman). These states result, as described above, in a breakdown of subject–object differentiation. The self and the world around become merged. A monistic state is experienced.

2. They report the phenomenon of the differing passage of time. Those who have an intense religious experience often claim that time stood still or passed very slowly during this.[22] This, again, was found by Fischer to be a phenomenon associated with altered states of consciousness, hyper- or hypo-arousal.

3. They report that their intense religious experience is ineffable (its reality cannot be communicated by words). It can only be understood by another who has also experienced the state. This phenomenon can, as described above, be explained on the basis of state-bound knowledge and meaning. The experiences of a person at extremes of hyper- and hypo-arousal only have meaning in those states. The experiences cannot easily be communicated once the person has returned to the level of everyday life.

4. They report unusual perceptions: perceptions of infinite energy, dazzling light and so on.[23] In states of altered consciousness, controlled analytical thought is absent. The subject's attitude is one of receptivity to stimuli. There is heightened attention to sensory pathways. All sensations are therefore experienced more vividly. It may also be that psychic phenomena (such as tension, conflict or repression) will be perceived by being translated via the relatively unstructured sensations of light, colour or movement.[24]

5. They report a feeling of reality associated with the mystical experience. Those who have had intense religious experiences often assert that they do not need external evidence for their reality, because of the intense 'feeling of reality' experienced during the state. In fact, however, this intense 'feeling of reality' has no connection with an objective judgement of reality. It may, for example, be experienced in dreams. On the other hand, objective reality may on occasion be deprived of the 'feeling of reality'. This occurs, for example, in the brief feelings of depersonalization (where one feels as though one's self is unreal) or derealization (where one feels as though the world around is unreal) that most of us experience from time to time (often associated with *déjà vu* and other similar phenomena). During the early childhood stages of individual development, the 'feeling of reality' becomes fused with the objects of the outside world. In states of altered consciousness, however,

the process of deautomatization breaks this link. The 'feeling of reality' can then become linked to the feelings and ideas that enter awareness during this state. The stimuli and images of the inner world become thus endowed with the 'feeling of reality'.

An additional reason for this 'feeling of reality' results from the process of deautomatization. Due to this, stimuli are no longer systematized and selected before being presented to conscious thought. Therefore all stimuli present themselves equally strongly to the consciousness, which is only able to focus on one unselectively. That one stimulus therefore has none of its features attenuated by subcortical processing. It also has the 'feeling of reality' attached to it and so it appears with a vividness unlike anything that is experienced in ordinary life.

6. Lastly, it should not surprise us if the mystic describes his or her world as being outside the bounds of reason or not attainable by intellect and analysis.[25] This is to be expected because, as we have noted, in moving away from the level of everyday experience, we are moving away from the realm in which Aristotelian logic and intellectual analysis function.

Sperry and Split-Brain Experiments

Another area of research that is illuminating with regard to religious experience involves the results of split-brain experiments. There are a small number of people in whom the brain has been vertically split into left and right halves (either due to an accident or for therapeutic reasons). When such people have been tested, it is found that one half of the brain (usually the left) is the active, verbal half. It is this half that directs intellectual and analytical activity; it is usually called the dominant hemisphere. The other half of the brain is receptive and concerned with spatial and other non-verbal information, as well as intuitive or integrative (gestalt) experiences.[26]

These considerations can also lead us to examine the differences between the mystical states achieved in the religions of East and West. In the West, activities associated with the 'dominant' hemisphere (activity, verbal, analytical and rational thought) are highly prized. Religion also reflects this tendency. The type of mystical state most often achieved in the West is active, hyper-arousal mystical ecstasy. This can be seen among Christian mystics like St Theresa, in Christian ecstatic/revivalist groups, and among many Sufis through *dhikr*, repetitive chanting. In the East, the emphasis is on hypo-arousal techniques such as meditation culminating in trance. This corresponds to the fact that receptivity and intuitive thought are generally more highly prized in the East; this in turn corresponds with the activity of the 'non-dominant' hemisphere of the brain.[27]

We noted in chapter 2 that within the predominantly theistic religious tradition of the West there are nevertheless groups or individuals, such as

Dance as a means of achieving a trance state in Afro-American religion, Brazil

Meister Eckhart, who came to monistic conclusions without any knowledge of the Eastern traditions. Similarly, within the Eastern traditions, many subscribe to a theistic view of metaphysics: the followers of the Hindu *bhakti* cults and Japanese Pure Land Buddhists for example. This should not surprise us, given the above analysis, for all human beings possess two halves of the brain and thus are capable of both types of experience. Which type of experience predominates in a given society must depend to a large extent, one suspects, on upbringing and other cultural influences, but it is always possible for the other type of experience to break through this social conditioning in a particular individual.

Types of Religious Experience

If we now leave aside the specific area of mysticism and turn to the more general areas of religion, we find ourselves with three sets of interrelated facts:

- most Eastern religions have a monistic metaphysics
- the Eastern religions encourage meditation and other activities that result in an altered state of consciousness
- altered states of consciousness result in a monistic mode of seeing reality.

These findings leave us in a quandary of the chicken-and-egg variety. Do Eastern religions meditate because it helps them to perceive reality as they consider it really is; that is, in monistic mode? Or do they see reality in monistic mode because they meditate? Similarly, do Western religions emphasize such acts as prayer and ritual worship because they help the believer to see the reality of the theistic mode? Or do they tend to see reality in a theistic way because of the activities of prayer and ritual worship? In other words, is the pattern of religious activity established because it helps to reinforce the metaphysical standpoint of the religion? Or did the metaphysical standpoint of the religion arise because of the predominant pattern of religious activity and the viewpoint towards which that activity predisposed the individual in that society?[28]

There is an alternative response to this quandary, that of relativism (see pp. 41–3 and 195–9). This regards all metaphysical standpoints as being relative to the viewpoint of the believer. The viewpoint of the believer can then be regarded as dependent, to a greater or lesser extent, on various factors such as personality type and upbringing. With regard to the material presented in this chapter, one could say that the viewpoint of the believer may also be dependent on the type of religious activity which he or she predominantly undertakes.

Cautionary Notes

It is perhaps necessary to interpose some words of explanation. Some religious people may dislike the fact that the results of research often obtained using drugs or resulting from highly abnormal situations such as the split brain should be applied to religious experience. But it should be realized that these scientific findings have nothing to say about the validity of the religious experience itself. All that they do is to shed some light on the different ways that this experience manifests itself. Fischer's work on state-bound knowledge, for example, shows that the aroused state of mind produced by religious experience is also produced by several other mechanisms (including the use of drugs), all of which produce certain common features (time passing differently, state-bound knowledge, and so on). It is therefore reasonable to assume that these features are due to the common result of the different mechanisms (the aroused state of the mind) rather than the mechanism of arousal itself (mysticism, drugs and so on). In other words, if trance-like states produce several common features no matter whether they are induced by religious mysticism or drugs, then one can assume that these features are a general property of the neurophysiological state induced in the brain, rather than the specific property of the religious experience or drugs themselves. This observation casts no aspersions on the veracity of the religious experience. It merely indicates that these phenomena probably cannot be used as proof of the truth of religious experiences. It should be noted in passing, however, that several religions have used or still do use mind-altering drugs in their rituals, thus attaining states of altered consciousness. Examples include soma in Hinduism, haoma in Zoroastrianism, kava in Polynesian religion, peyote and various other plant substances in Native American religion and cannabis in Rastafarianism.[29]

A second cautionary note regards the fact that what has been described above may tempt some into value judgements. They may argue that living life in an adult mode (with respect to Piaget) and at the everyday level of consciousness (with respect to Fischer) would appear to be the more desirable state of affairs. This would seem to favour the Western religions that encourage this, rather than the Eastern religions that promote altered states of consciousness, which lead to an infantile mode of perception. Indeed, superficially, it may appear that humankind's greatest triumphs have come from the world of science, where modes of logical thought predominate. This would, however, be a premature conclusion. For even in the field of science, the writings of Kuhn[30] have demonstrated that the greatest advances do not come merely from perseverance in the application of logical thought to the sum of what is known. That only produces sterile logical progression within the same framework. The major advances in science involve jumps to a new framework, 'paradigm shifts' as Kuhn calls them, that come from a spark of inspiration welling up from the subconscious. For this to occur, the individual needs to be operating somewhere between the two extremes of everyday consciousness (where no sparks of inspiration come), on the one hand, and extreme hyper- or hypo-arousal (where what is understood cannot be communicated), on the other. This medial position between the two extremes seems to be the position of humankind's maximal creativity – the source of all of the greatest philosophy, art, science and religious thought.

Further Reading

Sources for this chapter include Deikman, 'Deautomatization and the Mystic Experience', R. Fischer, 'A Cartography of Ecstatic and Meditative States' and Lewis, *Ecstatic Religion*. Many of the sources used for this chapter are compiled in Woods, *Understanding Mysticism*. The book is primarily about mysticism, but, by treating mysticism as merely the extreme end of the range of religious experiences, it can provide information about other forms of religious experience. Another useful compilation of articles is Tart, *Altered States of Consciousness*.

II

Conceptual Aspects of Religion

8

The Nature of Reality

RELIGION HAS ALWAYS BEEN CONCERNED with explaining the nature of reality. The anthropologist Edward B. Tylor (1832–1917) propounded the theory that religion came into being in humanity's early history as a way of explaining the world. Primitive human beings, Tylor argued, were disquieted by, and therefore needed to explain, such phenomena as death and dreams. Why would close relatives who had died still sometimes be felt to be present? Why would they still appear in dreams? This led people to believe in a spirit that occupies the body during life but continues to exist after death. This belief in spirits was then extended to nature: such things as mountains and trees were thus considered to have spirits. This helped to explain such violent natural phenomena as lightning, storms or volcanoes. Tylor called this belief in spirits 'animism'. A parallel development is fetishism, which involves the belief that a particular object or person has special powers, usually because it has been possessed by a spirit.

FETISHISM: Representation of the worship of a fetish, Congo

Religion's explanations of the nature of reality have changed and developed considerable complexity since prehistoric times. This chapter examines the views propounded by the different religious systems concerning the nature of reality. The first area to be considered is the nature of what is beyond, or transcendent to, our physical world (the existence of a spiritual world, questions regarding the Ultimate Reality, the spiritual nature of the human being and so on). This is an area of enquiry that may be described as metaphysics, although the word is here being used in a restricted religious sense, rather than in the more general philosophical usage that is concerned with the whole of reality. The second area to be considered concerns the origins and end of this physical world (cosmogony and eschatology). The third area to be considered is the question of knowledge itself (epistemology). What can be known of reality? How can reality be known? Much of this chapter is a more detailed exposition of some of the themes outlined in chapter 2.

The Nature of Ultimate Reality

As described in chapter 2, the major religious systems of the world appear to be divided into two main groups over the question of the nature of Ultimate Reality. Those that we can call the theistic religions hold that there is an Ultimate Reality whose nature is completely beyond and transcendent to this physical world. The other group, which may be called the monistic religions, believes that this physical world, or at least human beings, are inherently part of, or identical to, the Ultimate Reality. There is then a third group that holds that metaphysical questions are ultimately not cognizable; we can only view them from a limited viewpoint and thus gain a relative knowledge of the truth.

The Nature of Ultimate Reality in Theistic Religions

Judaism

Praise the Lord! . . . The Lord is high above all nations, and his glory above the heavens! Who is like the Lord our God, who is seated on high, who looks far down upon the heavens and the earth? (*Psalms* 113:1, 4–6)

Christianity

And when they heard it, they lifted their voices together to God and said, 'Sovereign Lord, who didst make the heaven and the earth and the sea and everything in them . . .'(*Acts of The Apostles*, 4:24)

We give thanks to thee, Lord God Almighty, who art and who wast, that thou hast taken thy great power and begun to reign. (*Book of Revelation*, 11:17)

Islam

He is God, beside Whom there is no other god, the King, the Holy, the bringer of peace and security, the Protector, the Almighty, the All-Subduing, the Supreme. Praise be to God above what they associate with Him. He is God, the Creator, the Maker, the Fashioner. To Him belong the Most Beautiful Names. All that is in the heavens and on earth praise Him. He is the Almighty, the All-Wise. (*Qur'an* 59:23–4)

Sikhism

There is one Supreme Being, the Eternal Reality. He is Creator, without fear and devoid of enmity. He is immortal, never incarnated, self-existent, known by grace through the Guru. (Opening words of Guru Nanak's *Japji*, quoted in McLeod, *Textual Sources for the Study of Sikhism*, p. 86)

Theism

The theistic religions believe in the existence of a supreme being, God, in the universe. Recognizably the same God is found in the *Qur'an*, the *New Testament* and the *Hebrew Bible*. If we take some of the key attributes and actions of God, we can find parallel passages in each of these scriptures.

The scriptures of all three religions are emphatic with regard to the unity of God. There is but one God and idolatry and polytheism are among the greatest of sins.

THE UNITY OF GOD

HEBREW BIBLE
Hear, O Israel: The Lord our God is one Lord. (*Deuteronomy* 6:4)

Thus says the Lord, the King of Israel, and his Redeemer the Lord of hosts; I am the first and I am the last; and beside me there is no God. (*Isaiah* 44:6)

NEW TESTAMENT
One of the scribes came up and . . . asked him, 'Which commandment is the first of all?' Jesus answered, 'The first is, "Hear, O Israel: The Lord our God, the Lord is one."' (*Mark* 12:29)

We know that 'an idol has no real existence' and that 'there is no other God but one.' For although there may be so-called gods in heaven or on earth – as indeed there are many 'gods' and many 'lords' – yet for us there is one God, the Father, from whom are all things and through whom we exist. (*I Corinthians* 8:46)

QUR'AN
There is no god but He: that is the witness of God, of His angels and of those endowed with knowledge . . . There is no god but He, the Mighty, the Wise. (3:18)

God hath said: Choose not two gods. There is only one God. So fear Me, and only Me. (16:51)

God is regarded as the creator of this phenomenal world.

GOD THE CREATOR

HEBREW BIBLE
In the beginning God created the heavens and the earth. The earth was without form and void, and darkness was upon the face of the deep; and the Spirit of God was moving over the face of the waters. And God said, 'Let there be light'; and there was light . . . And God said, 'Let there be a firmament in the midst of the waters' . . . And it was so . . . And God said, 'Let the waters under the heaven be gathered together into one place, and let the dry land appear.' And it was so. (*Genesis* 1:19)

NEW TESTAMENT
And the four living creatures . . . day and night they never cease to sing, 'Holy, holy, holy, is the Lord God Almighty, who was, and is, and is to come!' And . . . the four and twenty

elders fall down before him who is seated on the throne, and worship him who lives for ever and ever; they cast their crowns before the throne, singing, 'Worthy art thou, our Lord and God, to receive glory and honour and power, for thou didst create all things, and by thy will they existed and were created'. (*Book of Revelation* 4:8–11)

QUR'AN

Verily, your Lord is God Who created the heavens and the earth in six days, then He mounted the Throne. He causeth the night to cover the day, pursuing it swiftly. And He hath made the sun, the moon and the stars subservient to His command. Do not creation and command belong to Him? (7:54)

Praise be to God, the Creator of the heavens and the earth . . . He adds to creation what He wills; for God has power over all things. (35:1)

a

b

a) GOD THE CREATOR: Representation of God creating the Sun, from the ceiling of the Sistine Chapel by Michelangelo Buonarotti (1475–1564). b) GOD THE ALL-POWERFUL: Calligraphic expression of the power of God in Islam. The writing in the centre says 'God is most great'. Around it is text from sura 112 of the *Qur'an*, 'Say: He is God, the One, God the Eternal. He gives not birth nor is He born.'

In the following scriptures, God is declared to be all-powerful, to be able to do as He wishes.

GOD THE ALL-POWERFUL

HEBREW BIBLE
Say to God, 'How terrible are thy deeds! So great is thy power that thy enemies cringe before thee. All the earth worships thee; they sing to thee; sing praises to thy name. Selah. Come and see what God has done: he is terrible in his deeds among men. He turned the sea into dry land; men passed through the river on foot. There did we rejoice in him, who rules by his might for ever.' (*Psalms* 66:3–7)

NEW TESTAMENT
Let every person be subject unto the governing authorities. For there is no authority except from God, and those that exist have been instituted by God. (*Romans* 13:1)

QUR'AN
Say: 'O God, Lord of Power! Thou giveth Power to whom Thou pleaseth and Thou removeth power from whom Thou pleaseth. Thou exalteth whom thou pleaseth and thou bringeth low whom Thou pleaseth. In Thy hand is all good. Verily thou hast power over all things.' (3:26)

Another of the attributes of God that is common to all three of these scriptures is the fact that He knows all things.

GOD THE ALL-KNOWING

HEBREW BIBLE
Whence then comes wisdom? And where is the place of understanding? . . . God understands the way of it, and he knows its place. For he looks to the ends of the earth, and sees everything under the heavens. (*Job* 28:20–4)

NEW TESTAMENT
For God is greater than our hearts, and he knows everything. (*I John* 3:20)

QUR'AN
God knoweth whatsoever is in the heavens and whatsoever is on the earth, and, verily, God is the Knower of all things. (5:97)

PROOFS OF GOD'S EXISTENCE. Because God is a supranatural reality – not immediately apparent to the senses – a great deal of effort has gone into proving His existence in Western religion. The commonest lines of argument used by religious philosophers in the West have included the following.

1. The Common Consent Argument attempts to prove the existence of God by appeal to the fact that the belief in some form of God has been held in all cultures and ages. Not surprisingly, this argument is considered somewhat weak. First, the universality of belief in God may be questioned in relation both to all cultures (it is doubtful whether Theravada Buddhism can be said to entail a belief in God, for example)

and to all ages (the modern world has seen a marked decline in the belief in God). Second, other widely held beliefs (such as the idea that the sun goes around the earth) have been shown to be false.

2. The Cosmological Argument has been expressed in a number of different ways. What these different ways have in common is that they all proceed from the observable facts of the universe and argue towards God as the entity lying behind these observable facts. For example, a simple form of the argument runs somewhat along the following lines: it is an observable fact that every motion in the universe has a mover, every effect has a cause; since the universe itself exists and is in motion, there must be some Prime Mover, some Primary Cause – this is God. In this line of argument, it is necessary to stress the radical difference between God and the rest of creation. God as First Cause does not, in turn, have a cause; God, as Prime Mover, is not moved. This, in turn, sets up other radical differences: God is eternal, everything in creation is ephemeral; God is self-sufficient, everything in creation is dependent; God is unchanging, everything in creation changes.

   Can the cosmological argument succeed in taking us from the observed, the world, to the unobservable, God? Critics of this line of argument would say that this drawing of a line between God and the rest of creation is purely arbitrary. Why should there be an entity that is the First Cause? Why could there not be an infinite regression of causes?

3. The Teleological Argument or the Argument from Design is an extension of the Cosmological Argument and is based on an analogy between the universe and a machine. A simple form of this argument would state that if we found a watch on the ground (and we had never before seen a watch), we would be forced to postulate that such a well-ordered entity could not have come into existence by chance; it must be the product of a mind. Our universe is also well-ordered; therefore it is probable that a Cosmic Mind is the source of this order. This Cosmic Mind, this Grand Designer, is God. The universe as a whole has a purpose towards which it is moving. God is the originator and sustainer of this purpose.

   Criticism of this argument questions whether in fact the universe is like a machine. A watch has a purpose that we can identify and each part of the watch can be seen to forward that purpose. But we are not in a position to identify the purpose of the universe nor to observe how its parts serve that purpose. Moreover, even if these objections could be satisfied, we are not in a position to observe the entire universe. There may be parts of the universe in which chaos reigns. There is also the problem of the existence of evil, which would appear to cast doubt on whether the world was created by a morally perfect being (on the question of theodicy, see chapter 9).

4. The Ontological Argument takes various forms, all *a priori* arguments seeking to prove that God must necessarily exist. Thus, rather than arguing from our experience or from observable phenomena, this line of

> argument seeks to demonstrate from formal reasoning that God exists, because to postulate that He does not exist would lead to contradiction or illogicality. One form of this argument, advanced by St Anselm and Descartes, starts from the fact that our concept of God is of a supremely perfect being, than which nothing more perfect is possible. Since existence is an attribute of perfection, it follows that God must necessarily have this attribute – otherwise He would not be that entity 'than which nothing more perfect is possible'. There is an inherent illogicality in the idea that that being 'than which nothing more perfect is possible' could have been more perfect (by having the attribute of existence). Therefore our concept of God forces us to the conclusion that He necessarily exists.
>
> Those who have criticized this argument have pointed out that existence is not the same sort of attribute of perfection as wisdom or beneficence and to treat it as such is fallacious. Moreover, the same line of argument could be used to prove the existence of things that we know do not exist – for example, an island than which none greater is possible.

It may be logically satisfactory to develop these lines of argument but to use them as proof of the existence of God implies a complete identity between the real world and these conceptual worlds – an identity that few would automatically grant. Thus, whatever proofs the medieval world may have found satisfactory, the modern world has found that there is no longer one purely rational proof or combination of proofs of the existence of God that carries universal conviction.

One reaction to this failure has been the fundamentalists' counter-offensive. The latter have insisted that there can be no human proofs of God since human beings can only know what God chooses to reveal of Himself, and that most particularly in the scripture. Our religion is only true religion, they assert, if it is based on faith, not on reason and human intellect. This reaction can be found historically in the Protestant 'dialectical theology' of such figures as Karl Barth, produced in reaction to the Catholic 'natural theology' of Aquinas and Anselm; and also in the Ash'ari reaction to the rationalist theology of the Mu'tazila in medieval Islam.

Monism

The idea that this phenomenal world, or at least the human reality, is identical to the Ultimate Reality in some way can be found in many religions. It stands most clearly identified in the Advaita Vedanta. It can also be seen to some extent in Buddhism, where everything in our physical or mental world is conditioned and impermanent, leaving Nirvana or Shunyata (Voidness) as the only permanent, unconditioned reality. In Taoism, the Tao is the Absolute Reality. It is the dynamic but impersonal process through which and within which everything else comes into existence.

The Nature of Ultimate Reality in Monistic Religions

HINDUISM

'Place this salt in water and come to me tomorrow morning.'
Svetaketu did as he was commanded, and in the morning his father said to him: 'Bring me the salt you put into the water last night.'
Svetaketu looked into the water, but could not find it, for it had dissolved.
His father then said: 'Taste the water . . . How is it?'
'It is salt.'
'Look for the salt again and come to me.'
The son did so, saying: 'I cannot see the salt. I only see the water.'
His father then said: 'In the same way, O my son, you cannot see the Spirit. But in truth he is here. The invisible and subtle essence is the Spirit of the whole universe. That is Reality. That is Truth. Thou Art That.' (*Chandogaya Upanishad* 6:13, in *The Upanishads*, pp. 117–8)

Even by the mind this truth must be seen: there are not many but only One. Who sees variety and not the Unity wanders on from death to death. Behold then as One the infinite and eternal One. (*Brihad Aranyaka Upanishad* 4:4:19–20, in *The Upanishads*, p. 141)

THERAVADA BUDDHISM

Depending on the oil and the wick does the light of the lamp burn; it is neither in the one nor in the other, nor anything in itself; phenomena are likewise nothing in themselves. All things are unreal; they are deceptions; Nibbana [Nirvana] is the only truth. (*Majjhima Nikaya* 3, Dialogue 140, para. 245, quoted in Murti, *The Central Philosophy of Buddhism*, p. 50)

MAHAYANA BUDDHISM

Since dharma-nature is round and interpenetrating
It is without any sign of duality . . .
In One is All
In Many is One
One is identical to All
Many is identical to One . . .
Samsara and *Nirvana*
Are always harmonised together.
Particular-phenomena (*shih*) and Universal-principle (*li*)
Are completely merged without distinction.
(The 'Ocean Seal' of Uisang, the first patriarch of Korean Hwaom (Hua-Yen) Buddhism, quoted in Odin, *Process Metaphysics and Hua-Yen Buddhism*, pp. xix–xx)

TAOISM

The 'way' [tao] which can be designated by the word 'way' ['tao'] is not the real Way [Tao] . . . In its state of eternal Non-Being [i.e. its unmanifest state] one would see the mysterious reality of the Way [Tao]. In its state of eternal Being one would see the determinations of the Way [Tao] . . . These two are ultimately one and the same. But once externalized, they assume different names (i.e. Being and Non-Being) . . . The

> Tao in its absolute reality has no 'name' . . . It is (comparable to) uncarved wood . . . only when it is cut out are there 'names'. (*Tao Te Ching* I:1–2, 4; 32:1, quoted in Izutsu, *Sufism and Taoism*, pp. 382, 384, 392–3. Material in square brackets is added.)

This concept of the nature of the Ultimate Reality can be called monistic since it considers that there is only one reality. This reality is called the Absolute Reality because it is unconditioned (there are no conditions that give rise to it). Monism also differs from theism in that it considers the Ultimate Reality as an impersonal reality, void of any attributes. This reality does not act in the world and cannot be said to possess those personal features that are typical of theism, such as being pleased with certain human beings and angry with others.

In the Hinduism of Advaita Vedanta, the ultimate truth is the realization that behind the veil (*maya*) concealing us from the truth, reality is one. The Absolute Reality is named Brahman. But since Brahman is the reality underlying the cosmos, it is also the reality of all things.

> Exalted in songs has been Brahman. In him are God and the world and the soul, and he is the imperishable supporter of all. When the seers of Brahman see him in all creation, they find peace in Brahman and are free from all sorrows.[1]

In Taoism, the Tao is the primordial and ultimate reality. The Tao itself is beyond description or understanding. The opening words of the Taoist scripture, the *Tao Te Ching*, state

> The Tao that can be spoken of is not the eternal Tao
> The name that can be named is not the eternal Name
>
> The Tao is like a well: used but never used up.
> It is like the eternal void: filled with infinite possibilities.[2]

The Tao can only be known through its opposites, just as beauty can only be known by seeing ugliness, and longness is defined by shortness.[3]

In Buddhism, the word for 'unconditioned' is *asamskrita*. Those entities that are *asamskrita* do not arise, subsist, change or pass away. Different schools of Buddhism consider different entities to be *asamskrita*.[4] Theravada Buddhism considers Nirvana, the state of liberation towards which the Buddhist strives, to be *asamskrita*. The Buddha refused to describe the nature of Nirvana itself. He said that it was not an annihilation, but one could not even say whether a person who passed to Nirvana continued to exist or not. Such a person was beyond description (for a further discussion of Nirvana, see p. 240). The following passage from the *Udana*, a Theravada scripture, describes the unconditioned nature of Nirvana.

> There is, monks, an unborn, unoriginated, uncreated, unformed. If, monks, there were no unborn, unoriginated, uncreated, unformed, there would be no escape from the born, originated, created, formed. But as, monks, there is this unborn, unoriginated, uncreated, unformed, therefore escape from the born, originated, formed, is possible.[5]

The Mahayana schools have many ways in which Absolute Reality is described. The Dharmakaya is that aspect of the Buddha which is at one with Absolute Reality. It denotes the unity of the Buddha with everything that exists, and is thus a monism. The all-encompassing nature of the Dharmakaya is emphasized in the following quotation from the writings of Vasubandhu, an outstanding early Indian Mahayana scholar:

> Just as there are no material forms outside space, so there are no beings outside the Dharmakaya.[6]

Most Mahayana schools, however, recognize a higher level of Absolute Reality, the Absolute of Absolutes (if such a contradiction in terms can be accepted), Shunyata, the void or emptiness. Shunyata is the true reality behind all phenomena and all mental states. Shunyata can be considered to be the logical extension of the principle, found in Theravada Buddhism, of *pratitya-samutpada* (Pali: *patichcha-samuppada*), the interdependent, mutually-conditioned causal nexus (for one formulation of the chain, see below). According to this concept, all things in this cosmos originate out of a mutually self-sustaining causal chain – each link in the chain arises because of the other links. Nothing in this chain has an independent self-sustaining origin. The analogy is drawn, in the Theravada scriptures, with a bunch of sticks, each leaning on the other; take away one stick and the

THE CHAIN OF MUTUALLY DEPENDENT ORIGINATION (*PRATITYA-SAMUTPADA*) IN BUDDHISM

This formulation is found in many Buddhist scriptures and writings, with minor variants.

1. As a result of ignorance (*avidya*), mental formations (volitions, karma-formations, *samskara*) arise.
2. From mental formations, consciousness (*vijaña*) arises.
3. From consciousness, mental and physical names and forms (*namarupa*) arise.
4. From mental and physical names and forms, the six sensory faculties (the five senses plus the mind, *shadayatana*) arise.
5. From the six sensory faculties, contact with the world (*sparsha*) arises.
6. From contact, sensation and feeling (*vedana*) arise.
7. From sensation and feeling, craving (*trishna*) arises.
8. From craving, clinging to existence (*upadana*) arises.
9. From clinging, becoming (*bhava*) arises.
10. From becoming, birth (*jati*) arises.
11. From birth, old age, death, grief, suffering, distress and

lamentation arise. Such is the uprising of suffering. (See, for example, *Samyutta Nikaya* 22:90, in *The Book of Kindred Sayings*, vol. 2, pp. 1–2; *Digha Nikaya* 2:55–71, in Rhys Davids, *Dialogues of the Buddha*, vol. 2, pp. 50–70; *Vinaya-pitaka* 1:1, in Conze, *Buddhist Texts*, pp. 66–7)

whole structure collapses. From this and other lines of argument that were common to both Theravada and Mahayana Buddhism, Mahayana scholars built up the concept of Shunyata. They argued that if everything is impermanent (*anicca*), devoid of essence (*anatta*) and arises out of other impermanent mutually dependent entities, then the reality at the heart of the cosmos is emptiness. The concept of Shunyata means that nothing that leads to multiplicity (all concepts, ideas, names, designations and so on) is applicable to the true nature of the world.

This doctrine of emptiness, Shunyata, is not simply nihilism (that nothing exists), but rather an assertion that things are nothing but their appearance. This then takes the Mahayana Buddhist on in his or her meditation, to the proposition that one should not attach oneself to these things of the world, but rather, having comprehended this truth through wisdom (*prajña*), direct oneself towards Nirvana.

The concept of emptiness also extends to Nirvana, however. Nirvana, since it is unconditioned and unoriginated, is also Shunyata, devoid of all substance. Inasmuch as one directs oneself to the true reality behind the world, Shunyata, then this phenomenal world (Samsara) and Nirvana are one. This is summed up in the Mahayana formula that 'Samsara (this phenomenal world) is Nirvana'; they are not two separate realities, but rather the field of Shunyata seen by spiritual ignorance (in the case of Samsara) or by true knowledge (in the case of Nirvana).[7]

The Mahayana conclusion, therefore, is that there is nothing real associated with this impermanent world. There is only one permanent Absolute Reality. This is given different names according to the context in which it is being discussed: Nirvana, Shunyata, Dharmakaya, and Tathata (Suchness).

The question of whether Buddhism is a monism that can be fitted into this scheme in the way indicated here remains a matter of debate and ultimately a matter of opinion. There are some Buddhist scholars who would say that Buddhism should not be considered a monism. There are, however, at least some Buddhist scholars who would appear to agree with this analysis.[8]

Relativism

While theism and monism may appear to be contradictory and mutually irreconcilable, the path of relativism, as briefly described in chapter 2,

Relativistic Views of the Nature of Ultimate Reality

Madhyamika Buddhism

[Buddha has proclaimed] the monistic Principle of Relativity, the principle that nothing in the Universe can disappear, nor can anything new arise, nothing has an end, nothing is eternal, nothing is itself, nor is there anything differentiated in itself, there is no motion, neither towards us, nor away from us – everything is relative.

The subject matter, the central idea of the treatise [Nagarjuna's book] is the monistic principle of Relativity characterised by these eight negative characteristics . . . The aim of the treatise is indicated in the same salutation. It is Final Deliverance, Nirvana, which is characterised as the bliss of Quiescence of every Plurality. (Chandrakirti, *Prasannapada*, a commentary on Nagarjuna's *Madhyamika Karika*, quoted in Stcherbatsky, *The Conception of Buddhist Nirvana*, p. 123; cf. Candrakirti, *Lucid Exposition of the Middle Way*, p. 35. Stcherbatsky is here translating *pratitya-samyutpada* as 'Principle of Relativity'. This would appear to be justified by Chandrakirti's own explanation of the term as: *pratitya*, 'dependent' or 'relative', *samyutpada*, 'arising' or 'becoming manifest'. *Lucid Exposition*, p. 33)

Islam: Sufism

Thus a man who sticks to the belief of his particular religion believes in a god according to what he has subjectively posited in his mind. God in all particular religions . . . is dependent upon the subjective act of positing . . . on the part of believers. Thus a man of this kind sees (in the form of God) only his own self and what he has posited in his mind. (Ibn al-'Arabi, *Fusus al-Hikam*, quoted in Izutsu, *Sufism and Taoism*, p. 254)

Baha'i Faith

It is clear to thy eminence that all the variations which the wayfarer in the stages of his journey beholdeth in the realms of being, proceed from his own vision. We shall give an example of this, that its meaning may become fully clear: consider the visible sun; although it shineth with one radiance upon all things, and at the behest of the King of Manifestation bestoweth light on all creation, yet in each place it becometh manifest and sheddeth its bounty according to the potentialities of that place. For instance, in a mirror it reflecteth its own disc and shape, and this is due to the sensitivity of the mirror; in a crystal it maketh fire to appear, and in other things it showeth only the effect of its shining, but not its full disc. (Baha'u'llah, *The Seven Valleys*, pp. 18–21)

takes the approach that all human knowledge is necessarily relative. Human beings can, therefore, never have an absolute knowledge of the Ultimate Reality. All that we can achieve is a limited contingent knowledge from a particular viewpoint.

The Madhyamika school was founded by Nagarjuna in India at about the end of the second century CE. Its teachings form the philosophical basis of much of Mahayana Buddhism. According to this school, all categories and doctrines are illusory; no absolute knowledge of any reality, let alone the Ultimate Reality, is attainable. All conceptualizations and views are relative and subjective only. Nagarjuna's method was to remove all notions and conceptualizations of the truth. Truth or the Real is to be reached not by creating a new viewpoint but by rigidly excluding all viewpoints, as they overlay and thus hide the truth from us. Truth or the Real can only be known by uncovering it, by the removal of the opacity of ideas. This is not nihilism, which is itself a viewpoint, but a rejection of all viewpoints.

> The Madhyamika method is to *de*conceptualise the mind and to disburden it of all notions, empirical as well as *a priori* . . . The method is negative. Universality and certitude are reached not by the summation of particular points of view, but by rigidly excluding them; for, a view is always particular. [The Madhyamika method] is the abolition of all restrictions which conceptual patterns necessarily impose . . . The implication of the Madhyamika method is that the real is overlaid with the overgrowth of our notions and views.[9]

Nagarjuna, the second-century Buddhist monk who founded the Madhyamika school. This is a traditional Tibetan block print.

Thus, in the Madhyamika system, Shunyata, the voidness or emptiness of all things (substance, causality, motion, concepts, etc.), is not itself another concept or dogma. It does not claim to be an object of knowledge, but rather an attitude to knowing.

> Emptiness, then, is an adjectival quality of 'dharmas', not a substance which composes them. It is neither a thing nor is it nothingness; rather it refers to reality as incapable of ultimately being pinned down in concepts.[10]

The apprehension of this truth of Shunyata is gained through *prajña*, which is unitive (or non-dual) knowledge or wisdom. It consists of the negation of all doctrinal views and categories (Shunyata: hence this school is sometimes called the Shunyatavada, the teaching of emptiness or void). This is a knowledge freed from conceptual distinctions and from the illusions caused by *avidya* (ignorance).

The Madhyamika system may thus be characterized as epistemic or cognitive relativism, that is, reality as it appears to the intellect empirically or through rational thought is subjective and therefore only relatively true. There are many other features of the Madhyamika school (its concept of liberation, its concept of time, and so on) which would tend to align it with the Eastern, non-theistic religions.

The approach of the Baha'i Faith is also that of relativism, but in this case the religion comes from a background of the theistic Western religions. The Baha'i scriptures contain statements that tend towards both monistic and theistic metaphysics. This dichotomy is resolved through a relativism found in the writings of Baha'u'llah, and based on the following line of reasoning.

An absolute knowledge of the metaphysical structure of the cosmos is, Baha'u'llah states, impossible for human beings to achieve because of the finite nature of the human mind.

> So perfect and comprehensive is His creation that no mind or heart, however keen or pure, can ever grasp the nature of the most insignificant of His creatures; much less fathom the mystery of Him Who is the Day Star of Truth, Who is the invisible and unknowable Essence.[11]

Therefore, no absolute knowledge of the cosmos is available to human beings. All descriptions, all schemata, all attempts to portray the metaphysical basis of the universe, are necessarily limited by the point of view of the particular person making them. They are relative truths only.

> All that the sages and mystics have said or written have never exceeded, nor can they ever hope to exceed, *the limitations to which man's finite mind hath been strictly subjected*. To whatever heights the mind of the most exalted of men may soar, however great the depths which the detached and understanding heart can penetrate, such mind and heart *can never transcend that which is the creature of their own thoughts*. The meditations of the profoundest thinker, the devotions of the holiest of saints, the highest expressions of praise from either human pen or tongue, are but *a reflection of that which hath been created within themselves*.[12]

This Baha'i symbol is called the 'Greatest Name' because the letters of which it is formed, 'BHA', form the word 'Baha' (glory), which is considered the Greatest Name of God. The three levels of the symbol represent God, the Manifestation of God (the prophet) and humanity. There are many other symbolisms associated with this form.

Thus the Baha'i position regarding the different metaphysical systems is that they differ not because they are in disagreement about what they are referring to (the metaphysical structure of the universe), but rather because they are each looking at the same structure from different viewpoints. They have each constructed a metaphysics from their own perspective. The source of the differences is not in what is being observed but in the fact that each observer has a particular psycho-social background that pre-determines the way that she or he looks at these matters. 'The differences among the religions of the world are due to the varying types of minds.'[13]

Indeed, in the Baha'i writings, it is asserted that no matter how hard human beings strive in their efforts to gain knowledge of the Absolute, the only ultimate success is to achieve a better knowledge of their own selves (or rather of the Absolute as manifested within themselves), not of the Absolute itself. This is likened to a compass: no matter how far the compass travels, it is only going around the point at its centre. According to Baha'i belief, this is also the meaning of those passages in the scriptures of various religions that enjoin humankind to praise God and to strive to know God.[14]

It should be emphasized that the Baha'i concept of relativism only extends to metaphysics. In other areas, such as morality, Baha'u'llah gave definite teachings which all Baha'is are expected to follow. There is no relativizing of ethics or of religious law.

Transcendent Worlds and Beings

Most religions have the concept that between the Ultimate Reality, whether the theistic God or monistic Absolute Reality, and the world that we inhabit, there are intermediate worlds and beings that inhabit them. These worlds are pictured as either paradises or hells and the beings that inhabit them as gods, spirits, angels, or devils. These worlds and human beings' relationship to them are described further in chapter 9.

The Founders of the World Religions as Intermediaries

As stated above, there are intermediate worlds between the Ultimate Reality and this physical world. One figure that plays an important role as an intermediary between the Ultimate Reality, the transcendent worlds, and our physical world is that of the founder of each of the world religions. In the cosmology of most of the world religions, the founder plays a role that places him between the Ultimate Reality and this physical world. He is usually conceptualized as being more than just an ordinary human being.

In most forms of Christianity, Jesus Christ is considered to be part of the Godhead, the third person of the Trinity. At the Council of Nicaea in 325, Christ was stated to be 'of one substance (Greek: *homoousios*) with the Father'. The debate about the exact nature of Christ was not concluded, however, with this council, and theologians have continued to debate up to the present day about the nature of Christ. All schools of thought in Christianity, however, agree in giving Christ a supra-human status.

In Islam, we come closer to conceptualizing the founder, Muhammad, as merely a human being. In part, the *Qur'an* portrays this as a reaction to the excessive

THE UNIVERSAL ORDER IN ZOROASTRIANISM: Fravahi (representing the Holy Spirit) sits above; the King is seated on his throne in the centre, and his subject bears his throne beneath him. From a bas-relief at Persepolis, Iran.

a

b

THE SPIRITUAL STATION OF THE FOUNDERS OF WORLD RELIGIONS: a) In the traditional art of the Russian Orthodox Church, the Trinity is identified with the three angels who visited Abraham (*Genesis* 18:1–16). This icon shows Abraham and Sarah serving the three angels, who are, from left to right, the Father, the Son, and the Holy Spirit. b) In Shi'i representations of Muhammad such as this Turkish picture, his face is blank to indicate that it is not possible to represent it adequately and his head is surrounded by flames alluding to descriptions of the Muhammadan Light, the primordial light from which Muhammad and the Imams were formed.

deification of Christ in Christianity. In the *Qur'an*, Muhammad is made to proclaim: 'I am but a man like yourselves . . .' (18:110). Despite this declaration, some schools of Islam project Muhammad into a higher station. In Shi'i mystical philosophy, the reality of Muhammad is described as a light that was the first thing that God created before He created the rest of creation. The first Shi'i Imam, 'Ali, is reported to have said: 'God is one; He was alone in His singleness and so He spoke one word and it became a light and He created from that light Muhammad.'[15]

In the Baha'i scriptures, the founders of the world religions are called Manifestations of God. This is because they are considered to be manifestations of all of the names and attributes of God. They are not however, incarnations of God. The analogy that is found in the Baha'i writings is that of a mirror. The Manifestations of God are like a mirror that perfectly reflects the attributes of God. These figures, therefore, have the authority of God.

> The door of the knowledge of the Ancient Being hath ever been, and will continue for ever to be, closed in the face of men . . . As a token of His mercy, however, and as a proof of His loving-kindness, He hath manifested unto men the Day Stars of His divine guidance . . . and hath ordained the knowledge of these sanctified Beings to be identical with the knowledge of His own Self. Whoso recognizeth them hath recognized God . . . Every one of them is the Way of God that connecteth this world with the realms above.[16]

In Hinduism, one finds the concept of the avatar. Figures such as Krishna and Rama are considered to be avatars, incarnations of the deity Vishnu. In the *Bhagavad Gita*, Vishnu, speaking as Krishna, says: 'The foolish deride me when I am clad in a human body; they know not My supreme nature, that I am the great Lord of all being.'[17]

RAMA, INCARNATION OF THE DEITY: Rama with Sita (his wife), Lakshmana (his half-brother), and Hanuman (the monkey god) with whose help he defeated the demon Ravana.

In Buddhism and Taoism, the author of the major scriptures of the religion is regarded not so much as an intermediary between the transcendent world and this world but as the discoverer of a pathway or of an ancient truth. The Buddha is seen as having achieved his enlightenment as a result of his own efforts. Yet even in Theravada Buddhism, where there is a great emphasis on the fact that all human beings are capable of achieving what the Buddha achieved (enlightenment and Nirvana), there are nevertheless hints in the scriptures that the Buddha is not like other humans.

> Since a Tathagata [that is, a Buddha], even when present, is unknowable, it is inept to say of him – the Uttermost Person, the Supernal Person, the Attainer of the Supernal; that after dying the Tathagata is, or is not, or both is and is not, or neither is nor is not.[18]

> Whoever, Sariputta, knowing that it is so of me, seeing that it is so, should speak thus: 'There are no suprahuman states, no excellent cognition and insight . . . in the recluse Gautama; the recluse Gautama teaches Dhamma [Dharma] on a system of his own devising beaten out by reasoning and based on investigation' – if he does not retract that speech, Sariputta, if he does not cast out that view, he is verily consigned to Niraya Hell for this sin.[19]

DEVOTION TO THE BUDDHA: A woman kneels in front of a roadside shrine to the Buddha, Bangkok.

Quite apart from these hints in the scriptures, the extraordinary devotion paid to statues of the Buddha in Theravada temples amply demonstrates that, whatever the theoretical position may be, Buddhists themselves give the Buddha a far higher station than is accorded to any other human being. Popular religious practice in the countries practising Theravada Buddhism makes the Buddha, in fact, an intermediary between this world and higher realms, able to grant wishes and requests.

In Mahayana Buddhism, this tendency to elevate the station of the Buddha is taken much further. The number of buddhas in Mahayana Buddhism is greatly increased. Hundreds of buddhas are named and they are said to be as many as the grains of sand in the Ganges. They are all, however, in their inner reality one, for the same spiritual reality is active in all of them. This reality is called the Dharmakaya. The buddha-reality is stated to have three bodies, the Trikaya. The first is the earthly body, Nirmanakaya, which is what appears to humanity. It is through this body that the Buddha is able to fulfil

THE MEANINGS OF THE WORD 'DHARMA'

The Sanskrit word 'Dharma' ('Dhamma' in Pali) has several meanings in Hinduism and Buddhism that can cause confusion if they are not differentiated. The basic meaning of the word is 'carrying, holding or supporting', therefore that which holds or supports things, the natural state of things. If things are in their natural state, they are true to themselves.

1. The cosmic law (Hinduism and Buddhism).

   Dharma can mean the cosmic law, the order of the universe, the world norm.
2. The truth, specifically religious truth (Hinduism and Buddhism).

   Dharma means the truth. It is often used with the secondary derived meaning of 'religious truth', that is, the specific doctrines of Hinduism and Buddhism, the doctrines that lead to liberation. Thus Hindus call their religion *sanatana-dharma* (eternal dharma) and Buddhists call theirs *buddha-dharma*.
3. Norms of behaviour, ethical rules, the moral order (Hinduism and Buddhism).

   Dharma can also mean being true to oneself as a human being, being the way that human beings should be; hence it comes to mean righteousness, duty, virtue, law, morality. The Dharma is for Hindus the basis of human morality; more specifically, for each individual, it is fulfilling the duties of one's caste. Similarly, in Buddhism, Dharma refers to the norms of behaviour and rules for ethical conduct. For Theravada Buddhist monks and nuns, this is set out in the part of the scriptures called the *Vinaya-pitaka*.
4. A phenomenon, a thing, a factor of being (Buddhism).

   Any existing phenomenon can be called a dharma. Thus for example, it may be said that *rupa* (body or form) is a conditioned dharma, while Nirvana is an unconditioned dharma. This meaning may include mental constructs, ideas.

his vow to guide all beings to liberation. The second body, the Sambhogakaya, is the heavenly body, in which the buddhas enjoy the truth that they embody. Each Buddha occupies a buddha-field, a pure land or paradise. The third body is the Dharmakaya, the transcendent reality which is the true body of the Buddha. At this level the Buddha is the essence of the universe, at one with all things. This level also represents the cosmic law, the universal order, the Dharma. The Dharmakaya is therefore unconditioned, timeless, free of duality, free of characteristics, hence identical to Shunyata and Nirvana.

If we now take these Mahayana concepts and consider what they mean regarding the nature of the historical Siddhartha Buddha, we find it has great implications for the conceptualization of that figure. While the biographies of the Buddha speak of his having achieved enlightenment while sitting under the Bo tree, in the Mahayana cosmology the buddhas have all, in their Dharmakaya, been enlightened from the beginning of time. According to some Mahayana schools, the very appearance of Siddhartha Buddha upon the earth, his Nirmanakaya, was an illusion created by his Sambhogakaya, in order to guide human beings. Since it was just an illusory body, there was nothing present to pass into Nirvana at his death.[20]

Revelation and Enlightenment

Corresponding to the difference between the Western, theistic religions and the Eastern monistic religions in the ways they view their founders is the difference in their view of their scriptures. For a theistic religion, scripture is considered to be the word of God or the will of God revealed to the world through the mediation of the founder/prophet of the religion. In Islam, Muhammad and the other prophets are thus regarded as passive transmitters of the scriptures. The word ‘revelation’ conveys a sense of uncovering to humanity something that has always existed. This, again, is brought out most strongly in Islam, where the *Qur’an* is considered to have a pre-existent heavenly archetype of which the earthly *Qur’an* is merely a copy. The function of Muhammad was therefore to uncover, or reveal, the text of the heavenly Qur’an.

The process of revelation in the theistic religions is seen as having four major aspects:

- the origin of the message (God)
- the transmitter of the message (the prophet)
- the recipients of the message (humanity)
- the message itself (the scriptures).

There are various elaborations of this basic pattern in the different religions. In Christianity, Christ is both the transmitter and is himself part of the message. He is the Word made flesh.[21] In Islam, the Angel Gabriel, through whom Muhammad receives the scripture, shares in the role of transmitter.

There is, in the theistic religions, also a more general sense of the word 'revelation'. This can mean any divine self-disclosure. Thus visions and intimations experienced by saints may be considered to be revelations in this sense. Indeed, the whole of the natural world is revelatory of God to some extent (see below).

THE BUDDHA AS A SOURCE OF LIGHT: This is an aniconic representation of the Buddha as a pillar of fire. A throne can be seen upon which the pillar is set. Flames emerge from either side of the pillar. In front and on either side followers are engaged in devotion and worship of the Buddha. Amaravati, second-century CE.

In Buddhism, by contrast, the words of the Buddha that are contained in the various Buddhist scriptures are not considered to be transmitted by the Buddha from some transcendent source. They are the result of the Buddha's own wisdom and insight, the enlightenment that he achieved through his own efforts.

Hinduism has, perhaps, an intermediate position between Buddhism and the theistic religions in this context. Part of its scriptures can be said to be revealed. These are the *Vedas* and the *Upanishads*, which are termed *shruti* (heard) scriptures. These are held to have been direct, divine revelation to the *rishis* (seers) of ancient times. The remaining Hindu scriptures, called *smriti* (remembered), are ascribed to tradition and are thus the work of human sages and scholars.

HUMAN NATURE

The subject of the nature of the human being is one that has received extensive coverage in the religions of the world. There are, moreover, profound differences between the religions on this subject. All that can be attempted here is a brief overview.

The nature of the human being in classical orthodox Christian theology is closely tied up with the doctrine of original sin. This doctrine holds that ever since Adam and Eve committed their sin in the Garden of Eden, humanity has had an innately sinful nature which is transmitted from one generation to the next. As a consequence, human beings are inherently in a state of alienation and estrangement from God.

In Islam, by contrast, there is a much more positive attitude towards human nature. Adam's sin is not considered to be transmitted through the generations. According to the *Qur'an*, God created man, 'breathed His spirit into him', and made him superior to other creatures, such that even the angels were commanded to bow down before him.[22] Human beings are God's vicegerents (*khalifa*) on earth.[23] They have, however, an innate propensity to certain evil traits such as lust and greed, but they are commanded by God to oppose these tendencies within themselves, and the reward for success is paradise.[24]

In the Baha'i Faith, human beings are considered to have a dual nature. They have a spiritual nature, which is their true identity. While they are in this world, it is their task to perfect their spiritual attributes to the greatest possible extent. Human beings also have an animal nature that functions to satisfy their physical needs and if they allow this side of themselves to become dominant over their spiritual nature, then they commit evil deeds. Through spiritual discipline and education (such as the teachings brought by the founders and prophets of the world religions), human beings can control their animal aspect and realize their true spiritual identity.[25]

For all religious systems that believe in an Absolute Reality, human beings have a relative or contingent reality only. Indeed, the apparent reality of the physical world, is, in fact, illusory. The real is the Absolute Reality which is masked by this physical world. If human beings could see things as they really are, they would see that there is only one Reality which 'is'. Everything else (including our human notion of having an identity separate from the Absolute) has but an illusory or relative reality. In Mahayana Buddhism, the reality of the human being is identical to the Absolute Reality, Shunyata. In Advaita Vedanta, this truth becomes real for human beings when they come to understand that the Atman (inner reality within each person) is identical to the Brahman (the Absolute Reality). In the words of the *Upanishads*, '*Tat tvam asi*', 'Thou [Atman] art That [Brahman]' (see p. 192).

> Brahman is all and Atman is Brahman. Atman, the Self, has four conditions . . . The fourth condition is Atman in his own pure state: the awakened life of supreme consciousness . . . He is Atman, the Spirit himself, that cannot be seen or touched, that is above all distinction, beyond thought and ineffable. In the union with him is the supreme proof of his reality. He is the end of evolution and non-duality. He is peace and love.[26]

In Theravada Buddhism, human beings are composites (*skandhas*) of bodily form, sensation, perception, mental formations and consciousness. All of these are impermanent (*anitya*) and have no essence (*anatman*). They all lead to craving (*trishna*) and hence to suffering (*duhkha*). For Mahayana Buddhists, enlightenment is to see the emptiness (Shunyata) at the centre of all these *skandhas*.

In Confucian thought, human beings are essentially good but in need of guidance and education in order to show their inherent goodness. This inherent goodness is most fully demonstrated when cultivated human beings participate in and thus improve the social and political order.

The Physical World

The views of the various religions about the physical world follow approximately their views about the nature of the human being; they range from viewing the world as the abode of evil, as unreal and illusory, to seeing it in a positive light as a place for human spiritual education and training.

In Christian theology, God is the creator of the world, but He has put it under the rule of Satan. The phrase 'prince of this world' in the following verse of the *Gospel of St John* is interpreted as referring to Satan: 'Hereafter I will not talk much with you: for the prince of this world cometh, and hath nothing in me.'[27] Because of such considerations, the Christian tradition has generally had a negative attitude towards the world, which has, in turn, strengthened the tendency towards asceticism and monasticism.

Satan

The Devil is a creature of God, the chief of the fallen angels, but he most of the time acts as if he had far greater power. He is lord of this world, chief of a vast multitude of powers spiritual and physical, angelic and human, that are arrayed against the Kingdom of God. Satan is not only the Lord's chief opponent; he has under his generalship *all* opposition to the Lord. Anyone who does not follow the Lord is under the control of Satan . . . As Christ commands the armies of light, Satan commands those of darkness. The cosmos is torn between light and darkness, good and evil, spirit and matter, soul and body, the new eon and the old, the Lord and Satan. The Lord is the creator of all things and the guarantor of their goodness, but Satan and his kingdom have corrupted this world . . . In the end, Satan and his powers will be defeated, cast down, and perhaps annihilated, and Christ's other world, the kingdom of goodness, of light, of spirit, will be forever established. (Russell, *The Devil*, pp. 147–8)

Islam has a more positive attitude towards the world, believing that it is God's creation and that He is in command of everything that happens. He is sovereign over the earth[28] and has created it for 'just ends'.[29]

The Baha'i Faith also has a positive attitude towards the world. In Baha'i belief, God has created the world as a training ground for humanity, the place where human beings can perfect their divine attributes. Humanity is, however, neglectful of God's providence.

> Out of the wastes of nothingness, with the clay of My command I made thee to appear, and have ordained for thy training every atom in existence. And My purpose in all this was that thou mightest attain My everlasting dominion and become worthy of My invisible bestowals. And yet heedless thou didst remain . . . thou didst neglect all My bounties and occupied thyself with thine idle imaginings.[30]

In the Eastern religions, there is also a negative attitude towards the world, because it is considered an illusion that veils us from progress along the path to liberation. The illusory nature of this world is summed up in the concept of *maya* in Hinduism and similar concepts in Buddhism, such as *parikalpita*. This physical universe presses upon us because of the immediacy of our contact with it. It ties us to it by the innumerable threads of our daily concerns, enmeshing us in a social and psychological network of systems that order reality for us. By continually reinforcing the apparent objectivity of the outside world, it strengthens our subjectivity. It reinforces our feeling of being a separate, existent reality.

This world cannot, however, be the Real because it is a place of impermanence, continuously changing; everything in it is ephemeral and evanescent (the concept of *anicca* or *anitya* in Buddhism). Therefore our attachment to this world and the consequent strengthening of our egos lead us to false knowledge (*avidya*). This false knowledge in turn engenders false concepts: duality and difference. In this way, we are caught up in the law of karma, which states that what we do in this world has consequences that must be worked out either in this life or in a future one. This leads to the cycle of rebirth, from which there is no escape except through right knowledge or wisdom (*jñana* in Hinduism; *prajña* in Mahayana Buddhism). *The Dhammapada*, a Buddhist scripture, summarizes it as follows: 'When a man considers this world as a bubble of froth, and as the illusion of an appearance, then the king of death has no power over him.[31] Having stressed that this world is illusory, however, Eastern religions do accept that everything, including this world, is part of the Absolute Reality. It is therefore possible to come to right knowledge through this world. Thus, in Vedanta Hinduism, *maya* both conceals and reveals the Absolute; in Mahayana Buddhism, this contingent world (Samsara) is the Absolute Reality (Nirvana).[32]

As a consequence, each of these religious systems has a concept of Reality and Appearance, the Absolute as hidden and revealed. In Hinduism, there are the two concepts of Nirguna-Brahman (the Absolute in its aspect of being devoid of qualities, beyond conceptual thought) and Saguna-Brahman (the Absolute with qualities, as it appears in the world);[33] in Mahayana Buddhism, the Absolute Truth (*paramartha-satya*) is named Shunyata (the Void or Emptiness, that which is devoid of all concepts, all predicates, all relationships), while the contingent world is only *samvriti-satya* (apparent or conventional truth).

Time, the Origins and the End of the World

As far back as we are able to go in trying to reconstruct the history of human thought, human beings have asked and most religions have tried to answer the questions of how this universe came into being (cosmogony) and how it will end (eschatology). Most of the primal religious systems that

Cosmic egg: *Prana* (literally 'breath') is described in the *Athara-Veda*, a Hindu scripture, as the cosmogonic principle, the lord of the Universe. In the *Upanishads*, the formless creator is stated to enter the body right down to the tips of the nails and assumes the name and function of Prana. Prana is here shown standing upon the cosmogonic egg.

anthropologists have described include some story of the origin of the world. Often, there is an act of destruction or sacrifice that results in the genesis of the world. In many creation myths, the world emerges from a cosmic egg. Such myths have been found in places as far apart as India, Finland, Central America and Polynesia. In some instances, the world is created by the action of a supreme God. In the Polynesian myth, Io summoned creation into being in much the same way as does the God of the *Hebrew Bible*. In other myths, the world emerges from the womb of a goddess. The cosmogonic myth is also closely related to myths and rituals associated with the fertility of the land and of women.[34]

The Hinduism of Advaita Vedanta is, as we have described above, a monistic system. The following passage from the *Taittiriya Upanishad* describes how the cosmos comes into being from Atman-Brahman, the Absolute Reality:

> From Atman-Brahman in the beginning came space. From space came air. From air, fire. From fire, water. From water came solid earth. From earth came living plants. From plants food and seed; and from seed and food came a living being, man.[35]

From the Tao all other things come into being. The following passage is from the Taoist scripture, the *Tao Te Ching*. Very similar passages occur in the *I-Ching* and in Neo-Confucian texts (the traditional interpretations are in parentheses):

> The Tao begets one; (*t'ai-i,* the Greatest One, or *t'ai-chi*, the Supreme Ultimate)
> The one begets two; (*yin* and *yang*)
> The two begets three; (three heavenly beings in charge of heaven, earth and water)
> The three begets the myriad creatures.[36]

Time in the monistic systems is cyclical. These cycles take the world through periods of alternating prosperity and disaster. There is often no beginning and no end postulated to this process; the world evolves to a peak of prosperity and good fortune and then declines again from this state. The advent of avatars and buddhas usually signals the onset of a period of decline or the start of a golden age. These cycles may last thousands and even millions of years. Even if there is complete destruction at the end of a cycle, this leads into a further cycle with the eventual re-emergence of the world.

The Western religions have in common a story of God's creation of the world. The world, therefore, had a beginning when it was created. This represents the beginning of time, which is then viewed as being like a river, flowing inevitably and irreversibly downhill. This flow of time is seen as the working out of God's purpose for humanity. The theistic religions are keen to record the history of the evolving relationship between God and humanity, since this is what gives meaning to humanity's presence on the planet. At the end of this flow of time, there is a cataclysmic event, the end of the world, the Day of Judgement.[37] Between these two, there are a number of crucial events in the course of the flow of time. The most important of these is the appearance of the prophet-founder of each religion.

The appearance of a Christ or a Muhammad marks a turning-point. Time flows on, in one sense, after this event, since humankind continues to head towards the final event. But in another sense, time seems to stand still. Before this event, humanity's relationship with God was evolving, but afterwards it is fixed, from the appearance of the founder forwards to the end of time. It really makes no difference now when a human being enters the world, as this state of affairs remains the same until the end of time.

I-CHING, THE BOOK OF CHANGES: The symbol of Yin and Yang (male/female, light/dark, heaven/earth, etc.) forms the centre of this diagram. Around it are the eight trigrams formed from varying combinations of broken and unbroken lines. The top trigram (three unbroken lines, *ch'ien*) represents the male (*yang*), the bottom trigram (three broken lines, *k'un*) represents the female (*yin*). The central circle appears more commonly in contrasting black and white (see p. 172).

Christians, for example, see time as having been linear and historical before Christ, with the history of God's relationship to humanity evolving through a succession of major and minor prophets portrayed in the *Old Testament* – what is called salvation history in Christian theology. But once Christ comes into the world, sacred history stops; the relationship between God and humanity is now fixed and constant, back to Christ and forwards to the Day of Judgement, with no further evolution. The Revelation of Christ has established it for all time. 'There is no other name under heaven given among men by which we must be saved.'[38] The Christian *Bible* takes sacred history up to the first generation after Christ; then in the final book, *Revelation*, it refers forwards to the Day of Judgement. There is nothing between these two points in time because, in effect, sacred history has been frozen; God's relationship with humanity is no longer evolving.

The same state of affairs exists in Islam. Here the *Qur'an* clearly portrays an evolving relationship between God and humanity through the medium of a series of prophets. Muhammad himself is portrayed as another prophet in this series who is sent 'after a break in the succession of prophets'.[39] But the doctrine that Muhammad is the 'Seal of the Prophets'[40] again freezes the flow of time. The *Qur'an* thus becomes the final revelation from God and the relationship between God and humankind ceases to evolve any further until the Day of Judgement.

Thus the theistic religions have a twofold relationship to time after the appearance of their founders. On the one hand, there is a ceaseless flow of time towards the inevitable Day of Judgement. But on the other hand, the spiritual evolution of the world has reached a peak beyond which there is no further progress to be made. God has spoken for the last time, the relationship between God and human beings is now established. There is no longer any concept of forward evolution in the spiritual development of humanity. There is, of course, some degree of change (the traditions of a religion are constantly evolving), but this represents only the working-out of a relationship that is fixed. Indeed if anything, it is considered that there has been a deterioration in society since the coming of the religion's prophet-founder. The social goal of the religious community is often conceptualized as travelling backwards in time in order to try to recreate some ideal primitive religious community. For many Christians, the ideal is often portrayed as being the early circle of apostles and disciples[41] while the Islamic ideal is the community in Medina with Muhammad as its head (see pp. 323–4). And so not only is the spiritual evolution of humankind perceived to be frozen in time, but human social evolution is considered to be deteriorating from this primal ideal.

Baha'u'llah refers to the two conflicting views on the question of the beginning of time and creation; the view of philosophers that the world is eternal, has always existed and always will exist, and the view of theologians that the world was created at one point in time and will end at a set time in the future. He says that 'this is a matter on which conceptions vary by reason of the divergences in men's thoughts and opinions'.[42]

> As to thy question whether the physical world is subject to any limitations, know thou that the comprehension of this matter *dependeth upon the observer himself*. In one sense, it is limited; in another, it is exalted beyond all limitations.[43]

In the Baha'i view of time, cycles of advance and decline affect all human affairs. Religion is no exception: each religion ascends to a golden age when it becomes the foundation of a civilization. It then declines into a winter of rigid formalism and spiritual bankruptcy. However, underlying this cyclic concept, there is also an element of linear historical time. Humanity is seen to be progressing and evolving socially. Each religion takes humanity a further step forwards in spiritual and social evolution, which is not completely lost even when the religion eventually goes into decline. This process does not cease with the coming of Baha'u'llah, as a further figure is expected in the future to continue the process. The Baha'i concept of time may perhaps therefore be best described as a spiral, rather than as linear or cyclical.

Epistemology

The question of what we can know and how we can know (epistemology) is one that has exercised many theologians and philosophers. What are the foundations of knowledge? The religious person sees the whole of life in a religious mode. His or her faith is thus an interpretative medium for all experience and, hence, knowledge. A philosopher may try to build up from first principles a systematic picture of what we can know and how we can know; for example, the well-known enterprise of Descartes, starting with the statement 'I think, therefore I am'. A religious person tends to treat the scriptures or dogmas of her or his religion as foundational knowledge.

The major difference regarding epistemology falls again between the theistic and non-theistic religions. For the theistic religions, truth is revealed by God and is to be found in the scriptures. The major branches of knowledge, therefore, are related to interpretation and understanding the texts (hermeneutics). There is, however, a tradition in most theistic religions that also maintains that truth can be derived from reasoning. It is usually considered, however, that knowledge that is derived from reasoning is, in fact, identical to knowledge derived from the scriptures, because both ultimately derive from God. In theistic religions, there is also a tradition, influenced by Neoplatonism, that refuses to describe God in any way. For theologians and philosophers, apophatic theology maintains that the knowledge of Ultimate Reality (God) is not obtainable by human beings. The *via negativa* of the mystics arrives at a point where the only way of characterizing Ultimate Reality is through negation and such words as 'unknowing', 'darkness' and 'emptiness'.

For non-theistic religions, truth is discovered or uncovered. It lies potentially in the world, but is concealed (by *maya*, illusion). Acquiring knowledge involves discovering this truth. In most non-theistic religions, this discovery of truth is experiential. It involves certain activities such as meditation, which lead to the uncovering of the truth inherent in all things. The knowledge that is obtained through this path is not, however, the discursive knowledge that is implied in the term 'epistemology'. It is a holistic, non-dual knowledge that, in most traditions, cannot be reduced to words. The English word 'wisdom' conveys better, perhaps, the meaning of this type of knowledge. 'The Tao that can be spoken of is not the eternal Tao.'[44] It is, therefore, similar to the apophatic theology mentioned above.

There is thus, in both theistic and the non-theistic religions, a tradition that holds that while discursive, analytical, conceptual knowledge is of some value, it can only take human beings a part of the way on their spiritual path. To go further, one must rely on an inner, intuitive knowledge or wisdom that cannot be described in words. It can only be achieved by following the different spiritual paths of each religion, such as prayer, meditation and fasting.

In summary, theism, non-theism and relativism are similar in expressing a polarity regarding epistemology. At one pole is the Ultimate Reality. No discursive knowledge is available regarding this area of religion and, according to relativism, any statements that are made are relative to the viewpoint of the observer. At the other pole are matters concerning the world and humanity. Here, for the Western religions, the scriptures are the standard by which all knowledge should be judged, while for the Eastern religions, the scriptures are the guide for progress along the path to knowledge and wisdom.

Further Reading

The subjects covered in this chapter are usually discussed in books on the theology and philosophy of religion in each of the various religions. A good compilation from a Christian perspective can be found in Rowe and Wainwright, *Philosophy of Religion*. See also Smart, *The Philosophy of Religion* and *Reason and Faiths*; Copleston, *Religion and the One* and Ward, *Concepts of God*.

9

Suffering, Sacrifice and Salvation

One of the central concerns of religion is to give meaning and purpose to human life. In particular, religion seeks to give meaning to one area of human life that perhaps most appears to demand it: the phenomenon of random and seemingly undeserved human suffering. The Buddha even made the question of suffering the starting point of his religious teaching. One of the aims of religion is to deal with the problems of humanity's psychic and spiritual life. One of its main roles is therefore to provide a means of understanding, and escaping or relieving the suffering that comes inescapably to human beings in this life. The first part of this process – understanding the origin and role of evil and suffering in the world – will be dealt with in the first part of this chapter. In the second part of this chapter we shall consider the related issue of sacrifice. In the third part, we shall look at the ways that religion gives to human beings of escaping from evil and suffering – the process of salvation or liberation.

Evil, Sin and Suffering

Suffering is part of everyone's life to a greater or lesser extent. Physical suffering (illness, injury, hunger, old age) and mental suffering (despair, loneliness, frustration) are part of everyone's experience and, even if one tries to, one is not always able to avoid being the cause of suffering to others.

Western theologians and philosophers refer to that which results in suffering as evil. In discussing the question of evil and suffering, it is useful to differentiate between moral evil (that which is intentionally caused by human beings) and natural evil (that which is caused by natural phenomena such as earthquakes or floods, or by human beings unintentionally). Both types of evil have been a particular problem for those Western religions that believe in a loving and all-powerful God. For these religions, the problem can be formulated thus:

1. If God is loving then He presumably wants to prevent evil and suffering;
2. if God is all-powerful, He presumably can prevent evil and suffering;
3. and so if a loving and all-powerful God exists, why then does evil and suffering exist in the world?

This is the issue referred to in Christian theology as the problem of theodicy. Using this reasoning, the presence of evil and suffering in the world has even been argued by some philosophers from Epicurus (341–270 BCE) to David Hume (1711–76 CE) to cast doubt on the existence of God. Other more modern writers such as Freud and Marx sought to show that religion's explanations of the presence of evil and suffering were based on delusions.[1]

Because the question of the cause and role of suffering and evil has been such a central concern for religions, it has been an area of much philosophical and theological elaboration, resulting in a variety of answers to the question of why suffering exists. Consequently, there is a mass of theory and speculation in the writings of the various religions on this issue. The following is an attempt to create some degree of order out of this morass of complicated theories and intricate elaborations. As with all simplifications, some may consider it an oversimplification. Nevertheless, it outlines some of the main ways in which religious thinkers have sought to explain suffering and evil:

1. Cause and effect. Evil and suffering are the consequences of human actions.
2. Ignorance. Suffering results from human failure to see things as they really are.
3. Evil being (or beings). Evil and suffering are the result of the actions of an evil being: Satan, the Devil, Iblis; or there is an inherent tendency in creation opposing God.
4. Evil is inherent in human beings. The doctrine of original sin.
5. Result of human free will. Since human beings have been given free will, it is inevitable that they will sometimes do evil otherwise they could not be said to have free will.
6. Denial of genuine evil. There are only differing degrees of good, and evil only appears to be evil relative to the higher degrees of good that exist.
7. Best of all possible worlds. The world that exists contains the greatest amount of good and the smallest amount of evil that it is possible for God to have created.
8. Mechanism for spiritual growth. The suffering that individuals experience in the world is part of their spiritual education.
9. Action of God or of gods. All suffering and evil is determined and decreed by God (or one of the gods).

It should be pointed out that any one of these explanations does not necessarily rule out the other. The main orthodoxies of almost all of the major religions have used several of the positions outlined here.

1. *Cause and Effect*

Whatever suffering falls to a person is the result of past actions by that person. The law of karma in Hinduism and Buddhism is a law of cause and effect. Every event that occurs is caused by previous events. If suffering occurs in the life of a person, then this has been caused by evil deeds done by that person in the past. With the concept of reincarnation or rebirth, 'the past' includes past lives. The Buddha taught that:

> Evil in the future life is the fruit of bodily offence. Evil is the fruit of offence by word, by thought, in the future life. If I offend in deed, in word, in thought, should not I, when the body breaks up, after death be reborn in the Waste, the Way of Woe, the Downfall, the Purgatory?[2]

THE WHEEL OF LIFE, A REPRESENTATION OF THE LAW OF KARMA: The outermost circle shows the twelve links in the chain of causation. The next circle shows the six realms of rebirth referred to in the Tibetan Book of the Dead: gods (at the top), titans, human realm, animal world, spirits, and hell (at the bottom). At the centre are images of the forces that keep the wheel turning: desire, ignorance, hatred. The whole wheel is in the grip of the demonic god of time. Tibetan Buddhist T'anka.

A notion of cause and effect is also to be found in the *Bible* and *Qur'an*. Here evil and suffering are often stated to fall upon people because of what they, or even what their ancestors, have done.[3] The wrath of God is said to fall upon them because they have transgressed the law of God or disobeyed God.[4]

2. *Ignorance*

In the Advaita school of Hinduism it is taught that suffering arises from a failure to see things as they really are (*avidya*, wrong knowledge or ignorance).[5] This physical world possesses an illusion of reality, *maya*. Because of this, the world takes on a spurious importance that distracts from and thus hides true Reality. Thus the Real is concealed and human beings are distracted from seeking it. Instead they seek the things of the world and are led into greed and passion. Suffering is the result of this state of affairs.

This concept of ignorance as the underlying cause of suffering is further developed by the Buddha. The classical analysis by the Buddha is given in the Four Noble Truths (*ariya-satya*).[6]

THE FOUR NOBLE TRUTHS

1. All aspects of our worldly life lead to suffering (*duhkha*) – birth, sickness, decay, death. Even pleasurable experiences are involved in the concept of *duhkha* since they are evanescent and therefore ultimately unsatisfying.
2. The root cause of this suffering is the craving for sensory pleasure, the attachment to the things of this world.
3. The way to the cessation of suffering is the stopping of craving, the liberation from this attachment, achievement of the state that is called Nirvana (Nibbana).
4. The path leading to the cessation of suffering is the Noble Eightfold Path.

The ultimate cause of suffering is ignorance of the path taught by the Buddha. The remedy is wisdom and knowledge (knowledge here means a deeper existential comprehension rather than a superficial knowing) of the path – 'right view', which is the first part of the Noble Eightfold Path.[7]

THE NOBLE EIGHTFOLD PATH

1. Right view. A view based on understanding the Four Noble Truths and such doctrines as *anatta* (see p.238).
2. Right resolve. Resolution to renounce the world and to act with beneficence towards all sentient beings.
3. Right speech. Speaking truthfully and kindly, avoiding slander and gossip.
4. Right conduct. Conducting oneself according to moral principles (*shila*).
5. Right livelihood. Adopting a livelihood that does not harm oneself or others.
6. Right effort. Striving to achieve noble qualities and avoid ignoble ones.
7. Right mindfulness. Self-awareness, compassion, equanimity; avoidance of unwholesome thoughts and feelings.
8. Right concentration. Concentration of the mind culminating in absorption (*dhyana*) and wisdom (*prajña*).

The Buddha taught that everything that arises or comes into being in this world – including physical things, emotional states or mental concepts – is all ultimately *duhkha*, suffering. Suffering itself arises as a result of craving. This craving is in turn caused by sensation and thus one builds up into a chain of causation that is in fact circular, the Wheel of Life (or Wheel of Becoming). Through ignorance of the nature of this chain, human beings are bound to the Wheel of Life, which goes on turning. The entire chain rests upon ignorance, and so this is often seen as the firstlink in the chain. This leads to the concept of *pratitya-samutpada*, co-dependent or mutually dependent origination (see p. 194) – so called because each link in the chain arises because of the other links.

In the religions of the West, a similar attribution of suffering to ignorance is to be found in a number of gnostic and esoteric schools. In gnostic cosmology, the world has a 'light' side that is nearer to God and a 'dark' side that is remote from God. In physical terms, this 'dark' side is matter, the physical world, the human body; in psychological terms, it is ignorance and forgetfulness. The darkness can be transformed into light through the acquisition of knowledge or wisdom (gnosis).[8]

AZTEC DEITY: Teoyaomiqui, the goddess of death

3. *Evil Being (or Beings)*

In the theistic religions, there is a belief that evil is in the world due to the actions of an evil being who opposes God. This concept, which is often called dualism (but should be distinguished from the dualism described in chapter 2 as an alternative name to theism), finds its clearest expression in Zoroastrianism. Here the evil principle, Ahriman (Angra-Mainu), struggles against the good, Ahura-Mazda. It is probable that many Judaeo-Christian–Muslim concepts of the Devil, Satan or Iblis can be traced back to Zoroastrianism.

ZOROASTRIAN COSMOLOGY

A revolution in the history of concepts occurred in Iran . . . with the teachings of the prophet Zarathustra, who laid the basis for the first thoroughly dualist religion. Zarathustra's revelation was that evil is not a manifestation of the divine at all; rather it proceeds from a wholly separate principle . . . The dualism of Zoroastrianism or of Manicheism is overt; that of Judaism and Christianity is much more covert, but it exists, and it exists at least in large part owing to Iranian influence . . .

In the beginning there were two spirits, Ohrmazd and Ahriman, and they were separated by the void. Ohrmazd is good, light, and unlimited in time (eternal), though limited in space by the void and by Ahriman, who lies on the other side of the void . . .

In the beginning, Ohrmazd knows of the existence of Ahriman, but Ahriman, in his dark ignorance on the other side of the void, knows Ohrmazd not. But in the course of the first three thousand years, Ahriman discerns across the void a point of light and, seeing that light, covets it, longs for it, lusts for it, and determines to possess it. Ohrmazd now creates the good things, and Ahriman creates evil things, such as scorpions and toads. In his envy and lust, Ahriman attacks the work of Ohrmazd with his weapons of darkness, concupiscence, and disorder. (Russell, *The Devil*, pp. 98–9, 107, 108–9)

THE CHINESE FESTIVAL OF GHOSTS: During the seventh lunar month (usually sometime in August), it is believed that all the souls suffering in the underworld are freed and permitted to roam about the earth. The climax of the Ghost Festival is on the fourteenth and fifteenth of the month, when lanterns are set afloat upon the water to signal to the water spirits the preparation of a great feast. This picture, taken in Taiwan, shows the Lang Yang dancers during the Lantern Festival in Taipei.

In most examples of this type of theodicy, it is believed that the role of the anti-God is limited by God's omnipotence and that, at the end of time, God will defeat the forces of evil. It may be said that this set of beliefs solves the problem of theodicy by maintaining that God has voluntarily but temporarily suspended His omnipotence. This allows the Devil to cause suffering and evil in the world until the Last Judgement. In the popular religion of many parts of the world there is a belief in evil or malevolent beings or spirits that cause suffering.

Evil spirits, or spirits that have become angry and need to be propitiated if they are not to cause suffering, play a prominent role in many other religions, including Hinduism, Buddhism, Chinese and Japanese religion, and especially in the primal religions. One of the commonest forms of belief is that when people die, their souls become malevolent spirits who roam the earth trying to harm human beings. Most religions have at least some rituals, invocations or incantations for warding off such spirits.

4. *Evil is Inherent in Human Beings*

The idea of a fall from grace is the traditional (Augustinian or Calvinist) Christian view of suffering and evil. In the Garden of Eden, human beings had the possibility of not sinning and therefore not suffering. But Adam and Eve did sin (as a result of their free will) and were consequently exiled from the Garden of Eden to this world. Here the possibility of not sinning is no longer present. In Christian belief, we are all Adam and Eve's children, therefore in a state in which our nature is inherently flawed and thus tends towards evil.

This position can also, by extension, account for natural evil. For it was not only Adam and Eve who fell, but also Satan, an angel who disobeyed God. The distortion of Satan's nature in disobeying God, is now reflected in the world in the form of natural disasters, according to some beliefs.[9] This view thus develops to become closely related to a belief that evil is caused by an evil being.

The idea that human beings have an inherent tendency towards the morally wrong can also be formulated in ways that do not involve the idea of a fall from grace. In the Baha'i scriptures, for example, human nature is seen as having two aspects: an animal side and a spiritual side. It is the former that draws humans towards evil if it is not balanced by the latter.[10]

Ghosts and Evil Spirits

Hinduism

Let Agni the killer of demons unite with this prayer and expel from here the one whose name is evil, who lies with disease upon your embryo, your womb.

The one whose name is evil, who lies with disease upon your embryo, your womb, the flesh-eater – Agni has driven him away with prayer.

The one who kills the embryo as it settles, as it rests, as it stirs, who wishes to kill it when it is born – we will drive him away from here.

The one who spreads apart your two thighs, who dies between the married pair, who licks the inside of your womb – we will drive him away from here.

The one who by changing into your brother, or your husband, or your lover with you, who wishes to kill your offspring – we will drive him away from here.

The one who bewitches you with sleep or darkness and lies with you – we will drive him away from here. (Incantation for defending the unborn child from evil spirits, *Rig Veda* 10:162, p. 192)

Chinese Religion

Ghosts are the souls of people who died in the wrong way or at the wrong time . . .

Most souls avoid the worst horrors of the underworld. The living save them by hiring priests who know how to bribe the appropriate underworld officials. The socially marginal ghosts, however, have no one to perform these rituals, and thus never make it through the complexities of the underworld. Often buried without ceremony, they must undergo lengthy punishment from which funeral ritual has released more fortunate souls. Unworshipped, they have neither food to eat nor money to spend. Many thus remain in the world of the living to take what they can . . .

Ghosts are thus dangerous because they are the souls of people who fall into the interstices of the system of social categories . . .

The first type of answer to why people worship ghosts was to ask for a peaceful life (*kiu pieng an*). *Pieng an* is a frequently-stated goal of religious worship. Literally 'smooth and peaceful', it means freedom from all types of misfortune. The second category covered a wider range of answers, but all carried some implication that the worshipper was doing an act of kindness for the ghosts. (Weller, *Unities and Diversities in Chinese Religion*, pp. 60–63)

Inuit

Eskimos [Inuit] believe that ghosts are harmful and relentlessly malicious as long as they remain in the memory of the living. On death, the corpse is not removed from the igloo by way of the door; this would make it too easy for the lingering ghost to re-enter. Rather, a hole is chopped in the back, later to be refilled after removal of the body. This baffles the ghost. Then, in case the ghost does find the entrance, knives are set in the snow floor of the doorway for three nights after burial. Such booby traps discourage ghosts. (Hoebel and Weaver, *Anthropology and the Human Experience*, pp. 562–3)

A variation on this concept that evil is inherent is expressed in many Middle Eastern creation myths, and by several philosophers from Plato (in the *Timaeus*) onwards. This view presents God as a fashioner creating order out of a pre-existent chaos. Since God is working with pre-existent materials, He can only constrain or persuade the creation towards the perfect order that He wants to bring about. But there is an element in everything that resists God's constraining and it is this inherent resistance to God that is the source of evil. This idea also represents a way in which God's power is limited. The concept has been taken up as a system of theodicy by the Process Philosophy of the school of Alfred Whitehead and Charles Hartshorne.[11]

5. *Result of Human Free Will*

Also part of the traditional Christian view of the presence of moral evil in the world is the concept that God gave human beings free will when He created them. Since free will entails the ability to do both good and evil, it follows that some human beings will incline towards evil. Moral evils are thus the result of humankind's exercise of this free will. This line of reasoning involves God's voluntary cession of part of His power as He allows humanity dominion over part of the world. The Mu'tazila in Islam also held that human beings have free will.

This view appears to leave open the question of why God would have chosen to create humankind and the universe, knowing that this would result in much evil and suffering. This is usually answered by the assertion that, in the long run, the good resulting from God's creation will outweigh the bad. The 'long run' here means primarily that we must take eschatology (what happens when human beings are judged after death or on the Day of Judgement) into account in our final summing up of the amount of good and evil in the world.

6. *Denial of Genuine Evil*

This view can be traced back to the Neoplatonic philosopher Plotinus. It consists of two principal assertions: that the universe as a whole is perfect and good; and that the perfection of being requires that every level of existence must come into being (the principle of plenitude). Since there are different levels of being, there must also be different levels of goodness. Some things will be at a lower level of goodness (and so will be less good) compared to other things. But since the existence of these less good entities is required for existence as a whole to be perfect, these are part of the greater good. There is thus no genuine evil in the world – if by genuine evil, we mean that without which the world would be better.

This view was taken over by St Augustine and St Thomas Aquinas and became one of the main planks of the traditional Christian theodicy. The main argument advanced by these philosophers was that nothing is created evil by nature, humanity's moral evil is only evil by will. Furthermore, evil is allowed to exist in the universe only in order that there may be a greater good. If this amount of evil were not permitted by God, then a much greater amount of good would also be absent.[12]

7. *Best of All Possible Worlds*

Closely associated with the previous view is that put forward in the Christian world by Gottfried Leibniz (1646–1716). He asserted that there were many universes that God could have created. Since God is good, the universe that He has created must necessarily be the best of all possible worlds. Evil exists because, although individual things in isolation could be created without evil, when brought together in a composite, a certain amount of evil becomes necessary; what is evil for one individual is good for another. Leibniz also accepted the fact that human free will (see (5) above) results in some moral evil.

In brief, then, this view holds that of all the worlds that God could possibly have created, the net amount of good in this world is the greatest that it is possible to obtain. This view was centuries earlier put forward by Plato in the *Timaeus*. More modern proponents of this view tend to merge it with the Irenaean position (see (8) below).

In Islam, this position has held a prominent position since it was advocated in the eleventh century by the eminent Muslim scholar, Abu Hamid al-Ghazali (1058–1111). He held that there is nothing possible that is more wonderful than what is at this precise instant. This view had the corollary that whatever exists or happens does so by divine decree; nothing exists or happens by necessity, but only by the divine will (see (9) below). This position was opposed, however, by many Muslim scholars. They considered that this view undermined God's omnipotence by implying that God was not capable of creating anything more perfect than this world.[13]

While al-Ghazali emphasized God's abilities as a creator, the Mu'tazili position (which was prominent in Islam up to the eleventh century CE) went further. It placed a moral obligation upon God to create the best possible world. The Mu'tazila went as far as to assert the perfect rightness of every individual thing, no matter how ugly or lowly it might be. (Al-Ghazali's position was that some things are not good and have no intrinsic worth but that they are necessary so that this most wonderful world can exist; they act in a way as a ransom for the more perfect.) The Mu'tazila themselves faded into history; their positions were, however, adopted and continue to the present day in Twelver Shi'i theology.[14]

8. *Mechanism for Spiritual Growth*

The idea of suffering as a test from God may be found in both the *New Testament*[15] and the *Qur'an*[16] together with the concept of suffering as a punishment from God (see (1) above). This is sometimes called the

EVIL AND SUFFERING

HINDUISM

Indra created this ignorance (*avidya*) for the destruction of Asuras (devils).

By this [ignorance], men declare that the inauspicious is auspicious, that the auspicious is inauspicious. They say that there should be attention paid to a *dharma* which is destructive of the Vedas and of other scriptures (*shastras*). (*Maitri Upanishad* 7.9, in *The Thirteen Principle Upanishads*, p. 456)

Into blind darkness enter those who follow ignorance. Joyless are those worlds, covered with blind darkness. To these worlds, after death, go those who have not knowledge, that are not awakened. (*Brihad Aranyaka Upanishad* 4.4.10–11, in *The Thirteen Principle Upanishads*, p. 142)

BUDDHISM

This is the Noble Truth as to suffering: Birth is painful, old age is painful, disease and death are painful . . . Association with the uncongenial is painful; separation from loved ones is painful; not getting what one wants is painful. In fact every part of us, existing, as we do, because we grasp hold of life – is subject to suffering.

But as to the noble Truth as to the cause of suffering: it is ignorant craving which leads to rebirth and is associated with desire-attachment; seeking after pleasure everywhere, the craving for happiness in this life or in a future life. (The first two of the Four Noble Truths preached by the Buddha and accepted by all Buddhists as the foundation of Buddhism, quoted in Allen, *The Buddha's Philosophy*, p. 32)

BAHA'I FAITH

The mind and spirit of man advance when he is tried by suffering. The more the ground is ploughed the better the seed will grow, the better the harvest will be. Just as the plough furrows the earth deeply, purifying it of weeds and thistles, so suffering and tribulation free man from the petty affairs of this worldly life until he arrives at a state of complete detachment . . . Man is, so to speak, unripe: the heat of the fire of suffering will mature him. ('Abdu'l-Baha, *Paris Talks,* p. 178)

CHRISTIANITY

Whosoever committeth sin transgresseth also the law: for sin is the transgression of the law. (*1 John* 3:4 AV)

JUDAISM

They shall therefore keep mine ordinance, lest they bear sin for it, and die therefore, if they profane it. (*Leviticus* 22:9 AV)

ISLAM

Muhammad is reported to have said: 'All my people will enter paradise except those who refuse.' On being asked who refused, he replied: 'He who obeys me will enter Paradise and he who disobeys me has refused.' (Tradition from Bukhari, in al-Baghawi, *Mishkat al-Masabih*, vol. 1, p. 39) instrumental theory of suffering – the theory is that suffering is an instrument of God's purpose for humankind.

A further development of this view, in association with the concept of 'the best possible of all worlds' (see (7) above), leads to the position that sees suffering as a mechanism for spiritual growth. Suffering, if accepted and responded to positively, becomes a means of moral and spiritual education. Suffering and difficulties can be seen as tests of faith, obstacles to be overcome, opportunities for sacrifice, detachment and spiritual growth.

There are many aspects to this idea. Suffering, it suggests, helps human beings to realize the illusory importance of the material world and thus to detach themselves from this and turn towards the spiritual world. Moreover, it is felt that the occurrence of suffering enables human beings to show their best attributes of compassion and love. Indeed, if there were no suffering, there would be no point to many moral qualities – what would be the point of prohibiting stealing if no one suffered as a result of theft? For suffering to give rise to spiritual growth, it is necessary for there to be an element of mystery about the exact reason for the suffering. For example, if every instance of suffering could be seen to be caused by the individual's own past actions or as part of the process of moral education, there would be less impetus for human compassion towards the sufferer. A personal or general catastrophe can also, from this viewpoint, be an opportunity for a new start, the first event in a chain leading to a much better situation – if human beings take up the challenge of the catastrophe. Moral and natural evils can thus be an important source of humanity's spiritual and social education. If seen in their long-term perspective, they are not evils at all.

This view has been credited to the early Christian writer Irenaeus, but it is more completely identified with Friedrich Schleiermacher (1768–1834) and the modern theologian John Hick.[17] It is also one of the ways in which the question of suffering is tackled in the Baha'i Faith. In the Baha'i scriptures, it is asserted that the whole of creation is for the training of human beings so that they come to know and worship God.[18] Therefore, in this view, it is not so much a question of whether God has created the best possible world or not, but rather what He has created the world for. If the purpose of creation is the spiritual development of human beings, the presence of some of the suffering in the world can be seen as part of the process of spiritual growth. An episode of suffering can also be seen as a test that allows the individual to assess how much spiritual progress he or she has made. If, for example, our love is not put to the test, how can we know how strong it is? Suffering is thus both the instrument for growth and at the same time the yardstick by which to measure how much growth has occurred.

9. *Actions of God or of Gods*

In Hinduism, natural evils are seen as parts of the actions of Hindu deities. Most of the Hindu deities have a positive and negative side to them. Shiva,

Holocaust Theology: Three Modes of Response

Reaction Against God

Why, but why should I bless Him? In every fiber I rebelled. Because He Had thousands of children burned in His pits? Because He kept six crematories working night and day, on Sundays and feast days? Because in his great might He had created Auschwitz, Birkenau, Buna, and so many factories of death? (Elie Wiesel, quoted in Ellis, *Toward a Jewish Theology of Liberation*, p. 13)

Determination to Survive

They had condemned us to die in our own filth, to drown in mud, in our own excrement. They wished to abase us, to destroy our human dignity, to efface every vestige of humanity . . . From the instant when I grasped the motivating principle . . . it was as if I had been awakened from a dream . . . I felt under orders to live . . . And if I did die in Auschwitz, it would be as a human being. I would hold on to my dignity. (Pelagia Lewinska, quoted in Cohn-Sherbok, *Holocaust Theology*, pp. 49–50)

Search for Meaning

The Holocaust cannot be used for triumphalism . . . Its moral challenge must also be applied to Jews. Those Jews who feel no guilt for the Holocaust are also tempted to moral apathy. Religious Jews who use the Holocaust to morally impugn every other religious group but their own are the ones who are tempted thereby into indifference at the Holocaust of others . . . Neither faith nor morality can function without serious twisting of perspective, even to the point of becoming demonic, unless they are illuminated by the fires of Auschwitz and Treblinka. (Ellis, *Toward a Jewish Theology of Liberation*, pp. 21–2)

for example, is a loving god, full of grace, especially towards his devotees, but there is also a dark aspect to his character – he is the destroyer. The dance of Shiva simultaneously creates and destroys the world. Thus events such as natural catastrophes as well as personal misfortunes, are seen as acts of the gods.

This view is also to be found in orthodox Islam and traditional Christianity where there is a marked tendency towards determinism (often in association with (7) above). This means that all events are predetermined by God and are thus God's will. In the majority Ash'ari position in Sunni Islam, God was held to be responsible for the creation of every action. However, the Ash'aris rejected extreme determinism by maintaining that, when God has created an action, the individual human being acts to 'acquire' it. Even the terms good and evil have, according to the Ash'aris, no intrinsic content that can be discovered by the intellect. They are defined primarily in relation to the will of God. Whatever God does (including therefore natural disasters) is right and just. Moral good and evil are defined by God's will as manifested in the Holy Law (the Shari'a). Whatever is commanded in that is good, whatever is forbidden is evil.

The extreme version of this view is represented in Protestant Christianity by Luther and Calvin and among Muslims by the more extreme of the Ash'ariyya as well as the Jabriyya. Such groups see all events, both natural and moral evil, as determined by God. According to this view, God is fully responsible for everything that occurs. Every event is to be accepted as the will of God, without question.

ACTS OF THE GODS: Nataraja, 'King of the Dance' is a classical depiction of Shiva. His dance simultaneously destroys and creates, maintains, embodies and liberates. This is the vigorous, masculine dance called *tandava* to differentiate it from *lasya*, the delicate feminine dance. Beneath his feet he crushes the demon Mujalaka, symbolizing ignorance.

SACRIFICE AND DETACHMENT

The concept of sacrifice occupies a prominent place in the religions of the world. In the oldest religions, the concept was one of offering up something valuable to the Deity as a symbol of the fact that ultimately everything belonged to Him and as a token of obedience to Him. An important part of the earliest religious literature that we have, including the *Hebrew Bible* and the *Vedas*, consists of instructions about and hymns for the ritual associated with the sacrifice. The paradigmatic example of this aspect of sacrifice (the giving up of something valuable in obedience to the Deity) in the Western religions is Abraham's willingness to sacrifice his only son[19] on the command of God.

> Thus spoke the Lord of Creation when he made both man and sacrifice: 'By sacrifice thou shalt multiply and obtain all thy desires. By sacrifice shalt thou honour the gods and the gods will then love thee. And thus in harmony with them shalt thou attain the supreme good. For pleased with thy sacrifice, the gods will grant to thee the joy of all thy desires. Only a thief would enjoy their gifts and not offer them in sacrifice . . .' (*Bhagavad Gita*)[20]

Sacrifice also enables human beings to enter into the functioning of the cosmos:

> Food is the life of all beings, and all food comes from rain above. Sacrifice brings the rain from heaven, and sacrifice is sacred action. Sacred action is described in the Vedas and these come from the Eternal, and therefore is the Eternal ever present in a sacrifice. Thus was the Wheel of the Law set in motion, and that man lives indeed in vain who in a sinful life of pleasures helps not in its revolutions. (*Bhagavad Gita*)[21]

In the non-theistic primal religions (see p. 47), sacrifice is also important. 'Every endeavour is made to secure the favour of the spirits so that *mana*

The paradigmatic example of sacrifice – the giving up of something valuable in obedience to the Deity – in the Western religions is Abraham's willingness to sacrifice his only son (Isaac in the Jewish-Christian tradition; Ishmael in the Muslim tradition) on the command of God. This picture is a traditional Christian representation of that story.

Offerings at a Tibetan Buddhist shrine in a library at Ulan Bator, Mongolia

[power] will always be available. Sacrifices are the commonest method of winning approval.'[22] Sacrifice thus became both an expression of homage to a higher or more powerful Being (or beings) and an expression of thanksgiving. One of the commonest expressions of this, for example during a time of trouble or danger, involves the sacrifice of something to the Deity (a propitiatory offering). Alternatively, a vow may be made such that, if the danger is averted, a sacrifice will be made later (a votive offering). A sacrifice may also be made as part of a supplication for an anticipated favour from the Deity. Such expressions of sacrifice exist to the present day in popular religion: for example, the sacrifice of an animal on behalf of a sick African tribesman or the gifts offered to spirits for prosperity in Thailand.

However, with the passage of time, the emphasis in many religious communities gradually shifted to a more metaphorical form. The sacrifice that was now made was of the self (its desires, will or views), rather than of one's possessions, for the sake of a higher object – this higher object being conceived of either as God's pleasure or as one's own spiritual progress (or both simultaneously). The *Bhagavad Gita* expresses the change of emphasis: 'There are Yogis whose sacrifice is an offering to the gods; but others offer as a sacrifice their own soul in the fire of God.'[23] The transaction involved is often conceptualized as one in which something ephemeral is given up for something that is of permanent value. Obviously, the religious person believes that what is given up now is worth less than what is gained ultimately.

The corollary of these 'higher' notions of sacrifice is 'detachment' or 'self-surrender'. Sacrifice involves detachment of the self from its desire and craving for the things of this world. This spiritual purgation, the death of the self-centred life, is deemed to be an essential prerequisite for spiritual progress. Such concepts occupy a central position in the major religions of the world and there is much literature on the subject. In this literature, the individual human being is described as being grasping and self-centred by nature. As such, there is an innate fear and doubt regarding the claim of religion that it is better to become detached from this grasping and self-centredness. In particular, religions ask that a person gives up the control that we feel we must have over our lives; this control must be given up either to the religious leader (a guru or shaykh, for example) or to the spirit of the religious teaching, allowing it to enter into the individual's heart and being. There is often a conflict within the individual between the desire for the perceived benefits of the spiritual life and the fear of giving up control. Ultimately, the conflict must be resolved, often by taking a 'leap of faith' and committing oneself to the new path. This is experienced as a liberation, relief or breakthrough.

This process of detachment became the central plank of the Buddha's teaching. The third of the Four Noble Truths is that:

> This is the noble Truth as to the end of suffering: it is the putting an end to ignorant craving, giving up that desire-attachment, abandoning that pleasure-seeking and craving for life or for the cessation of life.[24]

In the *Bhagavad Gita*, we read:

> When a man dwells on the pleasures of sense, attraction for them arises in him . . . But the soul that moves in the world of senses and yet keeps the senses in harmony, free of attraction and aversion, finds rest in quietness . . . The man who therefore in recollection withdraws his senses from the pleasures of sense, his is a serene wisdom . . . For the man who forsakes all desires and abandons all pride of possession and of self reaches the goal of peace supreme.[25]

The same insight is to be found in the writings of the Christian mystics such as St John of the Cross:

> In order to arrive at having pleasure at everything
> Desire pleasure in nothing.
> In order to arrive at possessing everything,
> Desire to possess nothing . . .
> When the mind dwells upon anything,
> Thou art ceasing to cast thyself upon the All.
> For, in order to pass from the all to the All,
> Thou hast to deny thyself wholly in all.[26]

It is found in the writings of Muslim mystics such as Farid al-Din 'Attar:

> Until your heart
> Is free of ownership you cannot start.
> Since we must leave this prison and its pains
> Detach yourself from all that it contains;[27]

Detachment From the Things of this World

Christianity

And a ruler asked him, 'Good Teacher, what shall I do to inherit eternal life?' . . . Jesus . . . said to him, 'One thing you still lack. Sell all that you have and distribute to the poor, and you will have treasure in heaven; and come, follow me.' But when he heard this, he became sad, for he was very rich. Jesus looking at him said, 'How hard it is for those who have riches to enter into the kingdom of God! For it is easier for a camel to go through the eye of a needle than for a rich man to enter into the kingdom of God.' (*Luke* 18:18, 22–5)

Islam

Woe unto every back-biting slanderer, who hath gathered up wealth and counteth it. He reckoneth that his wealth will make him immortal. Nay, he shall surely be thrown into the crushing torment. (*Qur'an* 104:1–4)

Baha'i Faith

O Son of Being! Busy not thyself with this world, for with fire We test the gold, and with gold We test Our servants.

O Son of Man! Thou dost wish for gold and I desire thy freedom from it. Thou thinkest thyself rich in its possession, and I recognize thy wealth in thy sanctity therefrom. By My life! This is My knowledge, and that is thy fancy; how can My way accord with thine? (Baha'u'llah, *Hidden Words*, Arabic, 55–6)

Taoism

Fame or integrity: which is more important?
Money or happiness: which is more valuable?
Success or failure: which is more destructive?

If you look to others for fulfillment, you will never truly be fulfilled.
If your happiness depends on money, you will never be happy with yourself.

Be content with what you have; rejoice in the way things are.
When you realize there is nothing lacking, the whole world belongs to you.

(*Tao Te Ching* 44)

Buddhism

Wealth destroys the fool who seeks not the Beyond. Because of greed for wealth the fool destroys himself as if he were his own enemy. (*Dhammapada* 355)

and in the writings of Baha'u'llah:

> They that tread the path of faith, they that thirst for the wine of certitude, must cleanse themselves of all that is earthly – their ears from idle talk, their minds from vain imaginings, their hearts from worldly affections, their eyes from that which perisheth.[28]

The end of this path, the loss or absence of selfhood, is expressed somewhat differently in the various religions. In the Western religious traditions, it is thought of as a state to be achieved or a goal to be realized. In the Eastern religions, it is thought of as a discovery of the real state of affairs. In Theravada Buddhism, for example, the absence of any reality to the concept of self (*anatta*), is a central doctrine. In Mahayana Buddhism, this is associated with the idea of Emptiness (Shunyata) as the reality underlying the cosmos.

Another aspect of the idea of sacrifice is found in the concept that the sacrifice made by the individual should be not be just for his or her personal spiritual progress; rather it must be for the advantage of humanity as a whole. This idea is to be found in Mahayana Buddhism. Here, the preoccupation with the attainment of Nirvana for the individual, which is the *arhat* ideal in Theravada Buddhism, is displaced in importance. It is replaced by the *bodhisattva* ideal. In this, the one who is close to Nirvana puts off final attainment to that goal in order to help others to achieve it. Similarly, in the *Bhagavad Gita* we read: 'Even as the unwise work selfishly in the bondage of selfish works, let the wise man work unselfishly for the good of all the world.'[29]

In Christianity, the spiritual life has always been seen as linked to compassion for fellow human beings:

> And therefore the most inward man lives his life in these two ways; namely, in work and in rest . . . And he dwells in God, and yet goes forth towards all creatures in universal love, in virtue, in justice (Blessed John of Ruysbroeck).[30]

In the writings of Baha'u'llah, the same concept occurs in many places:

> That one is indeed a man who, today, dedicateth himself to the service of the entire human race. The Great Being saith: Blessed and happy is he that ariseth to promote the best interests of the peoples and kindreds of the earth.[31]

This theme is further expressed in the concept of individual suffering as the source of salvation for all. This is expressed, for example, in the *Book of Isaiah*, where the figure of the suffering servant represents all the Israelites who had suffered in exile in Babylon:

> Surely he has borne our griefs, and carried our sorrows; yet we esteemed him stricken, smitten of God, and afflicted. But he was wounded for our transgressions, he was bruised for our iniquities; upon him was the chastisement that made us whole; and with his stripes we are healed.[32]

The theme of sacrifice as being expiatory also appears in the Baha'i writings. Baha'u'llah stated that he had 'consented to be bound with chains that mankind may be released from its bondage, and hath accepted to be made a prisoner within this most mighty Stronghold that the whole world may attain unto true liberty.'[33]

Martyrdom

The ultimate in sacrifice is martyrdom, in which a person sacrifices his or her own life itself for the religion. This theme is particularly important in Christianity and Shi'i Islam. In these religions, the killing of a major religious figure in the religion (Jesus Christ and the Imam Husayn respectively) becomes the sacrifice that redeems the sins of humankind. The suffering of these major figures gives them the right to intercede with God on behalf of those who follow them and have faith in them. This intercession is thought of as occurring particularly on the Day of Judgement.

In Christianity, Christ is regarded as having suffered crucifixion in order to save all humankind. Starting from the concept that all human beings are tainted by original sin (see p. 218) or that all humans do sin[34] and that God's justice demands that a penalty be paid, the doctrine of substitutionary atonement states that Christ consented to die on the cross as a ransom for human sin, thus ensuring salvation for all those who believe in Christ.[35]

> Indeed, under the law almost everything is purified with blood, and without the shedding of blood there is no forgiveness of sins . . . For Christ

The Martyrdom of the Imam Husayn: This picture, taken in Shiraz, Iran, shows a painting on a large banner depicting various scenes from the life of the Imam Husayn, the third Imam of Shi'i Islam. The scenes include the Imam slaying an enemy (centre); the Imam with his dying sons (top left and top centre); and some of the scenes that occurred after the martyrdom of the Imam when his head and the captured women of the holy family were brought before the Umayyad authorities.

> has entered, not into a sanctuary made with hands . . . but into heaven itself, now to appear in the presence of God on our behalf . . . But as it is, he has appeared once for all at the end of the age to put away sin by the sacrifice of himself . . . so Christ, having been offered once to bear the sins of many, will appear a second time.[36]

Although there are traditions in Sunni Islam concerning the merits of one who is martyred in the course of holy war (jihad),[37] it is in Shi'i Islam that the theme of sacrifice and redemption becomes a major factor in the religion. The martyrdom of the Imam Husayn at Karbala is considered redemptory or expiatory; the Imam allowed himself to be killed in order to purge the Muslim world of its sins.[38] The Shi'a regard all twelve of their Imams (the twelve leaders of the religion after the Prophet Muhammad) as having been martyred by their enemies.[39] Thus martyrdom has become part of the ethos of the religion. It is commemorated throughout the year on the anniversaries of the deaths of the Imams, through recitals, passion plays and mourning processions. It also plays a major role in the literature and art of the Shi'i world.

In Baha'i history, the supreme act of martyrdom was that of the Bab, the forerunner of Baha'u'llah. Baha'u'llah stated that all the great sacrifices in religious history, Abraham's intended sacrifice of his son, Jesus' crucifixion, and the martyrdoms of Husayn and the Bab occurred 'as a ransom for the sins and iniquities of all the peoples of the earth.'[40]

The theme of sacrifice and martyrdom stands uncomfortably in today's secular, hedonistic world. Most of the mainstream orthodoxies, in the Christian world at least, appear embarrassed by it and do their best to minimize its place in the religion. However, it appears to be a resilient theme and continually re-emerges unexpectedly, especially among the young. In the Iranian Revolution of 1979, youths were prepared to die in order to ensure the success of Islam, while in the following years, young Baha'is were prepared to face torture and death in Iran's prisons rather than recant their faith. In some new religious movements, such as the Unification Church, there is a strong emphasis on self-sacrifice and arduous work to advance the cause.[41] Perhaps its appeals to youth lies in the commitment, intensity and idealism that it demands, which contrasts with their bland, cocooned existence.

Concepts of Liberation and Salvation Before and After Death

In considering what differing religions have to say about salvation or liberation from the sufferings of this world, we must bear in mind that we are looking at three different issues:

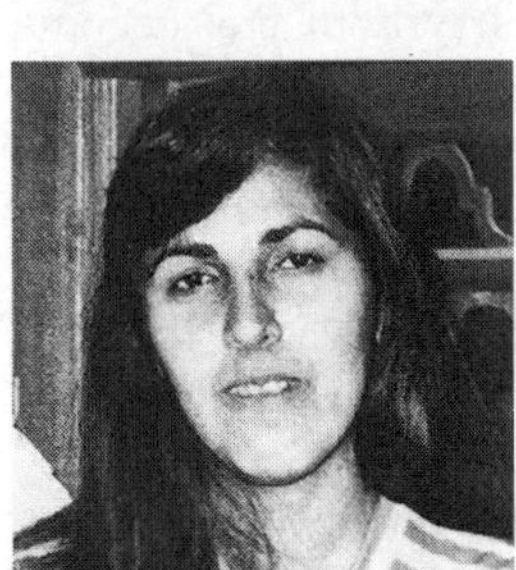

BAHA'I WOMEN MARTYRS OF SHIRAZ, IRAN: These seven young women were arrested for engaging in Baha'i communal activies such as teaching children. After being given a chance to save their lives by recanting their faith, they were executed on 18 June 1983.

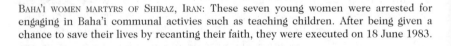

JAPANESE RITUAL SUICIDE (*SEPPUKO*, *HARA-KIRI*)

One day in 1868, nineteen boys committed ritual suicide on Iimoriyama, a hill on the edge of Wakamatsu City, the capital of their lord's domain. The boys were members of the Byakkotai (White Tiger Brigade), a corps of young samurai in the service of the Aizu daimyo. They were sixteen and seventeen years of age by Japanese count – meaning that in Western terms, some may have been as young as fourteen.

Engaged in a last-ditch effort to defend their domain, the boys intended to follow their lord to his death when they saw smoke in the distance and mistakenly identified it as a fire destroying Tsurugajou, the daimyo's castle. The war was lost and the castle was eventually destroyed, but the daimyo himself lived well into old age.

The Byakkotai suicide captured the imagination of the people of Aizu, and the ninteen boys – plus a twentieth who remained alive to tell their story – are celebrated as heroic exemplars of bushido, the samurai code that enjoyed loyalty and absolute sacrifice for one's lord.

Bushido was codified by the samurai intellectual Yamaga Sokou, a native of Aizu who had moved to Edo as a child. The code took principles of loyalty and obedience to superiors from Confucian ethics, and combined them with a Zen-based stoicism in the face of death . . .

Educated at the Nisshinkan, the Confucian school of the Aizu domain, the Byakkotai youths had learned well the principles of bushido. One can view their mass suicide as the pinnacle of samurai loyalty. One can also view it as a tragic example – similar in some ways to the Children's Crusade of medieval Europe – of how war wastes the lives of the young. (Janet Goodwin, 'Bushido and the Byakkotai' on Internet site: http://cs.ucla.edu/~jan/ah/byakkotai.html)

- escape from suffering while still alive in this world
- escape from suffering after death
- millennial escape from suffering at the end of time or end of the cycle.

The first of these is dealt with wholly in this chapter. The second is treated partly in this chapter and partly in chapter 10. The third is treated wholly in chapter 10. The communal actions that enable salvation to be achieved, the pathways to salvation, are discussed in chapter 5.

All the major religions appear to agree that it is possible, while still alive in this world, to achieve a state in which the ills of the world no longer affect one – usually in the sense of no longer causing one suffering. This state of salvation or liberation while still in this world is usually strongly linked with what occurs after death, which is, however, an area in which religions vary greatly. The major religions that we are looking at in this book all agree that there is something beyond this life, but the similarity ends there. Probably no area in religious studies offers more intractable problems for those who look for an underlying unity in the religions of the world.

Some aspects of what occurs after death are described similarly in all religions. Christianity, Islam, Hinduism and Buddhism all have descriptions of places of delight after death, which are variously called paradise or heaven. Here there is no suffering, grief or evil. The following description, which is taken from a Mahayana Buddhist source, could apply to any of the other religions:

> And that world system, Sukhavati [the Western Paradise of Amitabha Buddha], Ananda, emits many fragrant odours, it is rich in a great variety of flowers and fruits, adorned with jewel trees, which are frequented by flocks of various birds with sweet voices, which the Tathagata's miraculous powers have conjured up. And these jewel trees, Ananda, have various colours . . . Such jewel trees, and clusters of banana trees and rows of palm

> trees, all made of precious things, grow everywhere in this Buddha-field . . . And many kinds of rivers flow along in this world system . . . And all these rivers flow along calmly, their water is fragrant with manifold agreeable odours . . . And everyone hears the pleasant sound he wishes to hear.[42]

Opposite to heaven is hell and, again, the descriptions of this are very similar in the different religions. The following is from the Theravada Buddhist scriptures but is not very different from medieval Christian or Muslim descriptions of hell:

> To begin with, the wardens of hell subject the sinner to the fivefold trussing. They drive redhot iron stakes first through one hand, then through the other, and then through his two feet and his chest. After that they carry him along to be trimmed with hatchets. Then, head downwards, they trim him with razors. Then they harness him to a chariot, and make him pull it to and fro across a fiery expanse blazing with fire . . . The flames leap and surge right across, and fill it throughout.[43]

There are, however, major differences between the viewpoints of the Eastern and Western religions. Perhaps the most obvious fundamental difference is between those religions, predominantly of the East, that believe in reincarnation or rebirth (the belief that we return to this world

A modern Hindu depiction of the process of reincarnation. People enter death, here represented as a river, and emerge from the other side either as other people or as animals.

after death), and those religions, predominantly of the West, that believe in some form of other-worldly future existence. Therefore, the heaven (or hell) of the Western religions is eternal while that of the Eastern religions is a temporary abode which is then left for a further rebirth in this world. For the Buddhist and Hindu, the eventual goal is beyond heaven; it is described as Nirvana ('Nibbana' in Pali) in Buddhism and the state of union with Brahman, *sat-chit-ananda* (existence-consciousness-bliss) in Advaita Hinduism. These terms and the differences between the religions are described in greater detail below.

There is also a difference in emphasis. The Western, theistic religions emphasize salvation after death and their teachings concentrate on what the individual must do to achieve this. Salvation in this world receives comparatively less attention, except among mystics. In the Eastern, non-theistic religions, the emphasis is on liberation in this world, which will ensure salvation after death. Therefore it is easier to consider beliefs in salvation after death and in this world together, for theistic, relativistic and non-theistic religions.

Theistic Religion

WHAT OCCURS AFTER DEATH? The goal of salvation after death in the theistic religions is variously named heaven, paradise, or the garden of delights. This is conceptualized as a realm wherein there is contentment without any more suffering. It is attained after death by one who has achieved salvation during this life. For those who have not achieved salvation, there is the infernal world, hell. The description of hell is the exact opposite of heaven: torment and suffering. These two states are usually described as permanent, in the sense that once a person enters one or the other, this will endure for ever. In Roman Catholicism and among some groups of Muslims, there is, however, a concept of purgatory or *barzakh*, where those who have narrowly failed to be admitted to heaven suffer torment to punish them for their sins. They are then admitted to heaven. The goal of human beings during this life, then, is to achieve the state of salvation so that they will, after death, go to heaven rather than hell.

PURGATORY: Dante's vision of Purgatory is a mountain that must be ascended with great effort and suffering. This painting, by the fifteenth-century artist Domenico di Michelini, shows Dante at the foot of Purgatory. From the Church of Santa Maria del Fiore, Florence.

> The paradise promised to the righteous is as a place beneath which rivers flow, and the fruits thereof are eternal, as is its shade. This is the

> recompense of the God-fearing, while the recompense of the unbelievers is hell-fire. (*Qur'an*)[44]

The greatest differences in the Western religions have, often, not been between the different religions but rather between those in the same religion who take the words of their scriptures to represent a literal physical truth and those who consider that the descriptions should be taken metaphorically and spiritually. There are thus several different versions of the Christian view of the sequence of events after death: some emphasize that after death there is an other-worldly, spiritual, eternal life in heaven or hell (according to one's merits); others emphasize that after death, one lies in the tomb until the day of resurrection, when one will be raised up as a physical body and then given either eternal earthly life or destruction, according to one's merit or according to God's decree.

The Islamic views are similar to those of Christianity. In the *Qur'an* there are many descriptions of both heaven and hell, as well as a promise of resurrection. These have been taken literally and physically, or symbolically and spiritually by different groups of Muslims over the years.

SALVATION IN THIS WORLD. Many of those who follow theistic religions also recognize a state in which a person who has achieved salvation can be 'in heaven' or partaking of the 'Kingdom of God' while still on earth: 'For behold the Kingdom of God is within you' (St Luke).[45] The concept of this state has been taken in various ways by the different groups in Christianity. The evangelicals' confidence of being saved through the grace of God is clearly very different to the Unitive Life of the mystics:

> Those mystics . . . often see in the Unitive Life a foretaste of the Beatific Vision: an entrance here and now into that absolute life within the Divine Being, which shall be lived by all perfect spirits when they have cast off the limitations of the flesh and re-entered the eternal order for which they were made. For them, in fact, the deified man has run ahead of history: and attained a form of consciousness which other men will only know when earthly life is past.[46]

In Islam, an equivalent of this theme of salvation while still on earth is found in the Sufi concepts of the state of *fana* (obliteration of the self in God, the journey to God) and the subsequent state of *baqa* (continuance of the journey in God). Islamic mystics and philosophers are divided into two schools. One school, which can be considered to be aligned to theism, maintains that the states of *fana*, *baqa* and the union with God represent an ethical annihilation of the egoistical self, a submergence of the individual's will in the will of God. The monistic school, on the other hand, regards these states as being existential such that the self is annihilated completely in God. In Islamic mysticism, the state of *walaya* (usually translated as 'sainthood', the highest mystical state) can be considered as the equivalent of the state of salvation while still on earth.

Relativistic Religion

With regard to salvation, the Baha'i writings do not differentiate greatly between this life and what comes after. Salvation is not so much a state as a process that the individual is engaged upon continually. In this world, the Baha'i point of view is that the highest state of salvation cannot be gained solely through the individual's own efforts. Salvation is best gained through a combination of individual spiritual endeavour (prayer, fasting, meditation and the acquisition of spiritual qualities) and efforts to help others in society. Indeed the purpose of religion itself is said to be both the salvation of the individual and social salvation for humanity as a whole. A third element is also necessary to achieve salvation, and this is the grace of God.

The Baha'i view of salvation after death is that the classic pictures of heaven and hell are merely metaphors for the condition of a person after death. Baha'u'llah reaffirmed the reality of a salvation after death but the religion holds that there is no way of knowing what this condition is like. Human beings can only accept the words of the founders of the world religions. Their knowledge, however, can only be framed in the words of human beings and within the cosmology of their societies. This results in word-pictures that may appear contradictory, a conflict which is, however, a result of differences in linguistic and cosmological predeterminants rather than necessarily in what is being described.

An analogy that is often used in the Baha'i writings (because there can be no direct description) is that of the embryo in the womb, developing various organs such as arms or eyes which do not really benefit it there. Once the baby is born, it can use and appreciate what it has developed. If it has not developed these, it suffers greatly. Baha'is believe that the human being in this world is charged by the founders of the world religions to develop certain characteristics in preparation for what occurs after death, although humans can have no more idea of exactly how this will work than an embryo has of the workings of this world. For Baha'is, the meaning of hell is that, if we do not try to put these teachings into effect, we will suffer after death; conversely, if we live our lives according to these teachings, the result is heaven.

Another concept in the Baha'i writings, which is, in some ways, a bridge between Western ideas of an other-worldly existence after death and Eastern ideas of reincarnation, is the concept of return. Although individuals do not, according to the Baha'i teachings, return to the world after death, their personality types do return. Thus the coming of each of the major founders of a religion is, in this sense, the return of the founder of the previous religion; his followers are the return of the followers of the previous founder; his opponents, the return of the opponents of the previous founder. In this way, the whole cosmic struggle between the founder and his opponents is replayed in each religious cycle. There is

Table 9.1 Words Used for Salvation in This Life and After

	This Life	After Death
Hinduism	*jivanmukti*	Brahman–Nirvana
	moksha, sat-chit-ananda	
Buddhism	Nirvana (*sopadhishesha-nirvana*)	*Parinirvana* (*nirupadhishesha-nirvana*)
Christianity	state of grace, salvation	heaven, salvation
Islam	Sufism: *walaya*, 'sainthood'	heaven
Baha'i Faith	certitude, heaven, paradise, God's favour	

some similarity between this view and the Buddhist concept that what returns to this world is not the Atman or soul of the individual but the collection of *skandhas* (see below).

Non-Theistic Religion

The *chakra* (wheel), symbol of *samsara*, the Hindu symbol of the cycle of birth, death and rebirth

What occurs after death? Hinduism holds that human beings possess an inner reality called Atman. This inner reality is eternal. After the end of a lifetime, the Atman, after perhaps spending some time in one of the Hindu heavens or hells (according to its merit), returns to this world and is reincarnated in a different body. This cycle of death and rebirth continues infinitely in the cycle of Samsara unless *moksha* (release or liberation from this cycle) is achieved.

The Buddhist view appears superficially similar to the Hindu, in that it also speaks of rebirth. There is, however, one important difference because of the Buddhist doctrine of *anatman* (Pali: *anatta*). This doctrine states that an individual has no eternal, independent, essential self called Atman or soul. That which people have attached themselves to and call a self is nothing but a collection of *skandhas* (*khandhas*, aggregates that constitute the person: the body, sensation, perception, mental tendencies, consciousness).

Liberation in this world. In the Advaita Vedanta of Hinduism, the person who has attained liberation (*moksha* or *mukti*) is, while still alive, called *jivanmukti*. In Buddhism a distinction is made between the state of Nirvana, which can be achieved while still on earth (*sopadhishesha-nirvana*), and Parinirvana (or *nirupadhishesha-nirvana*), which can be achieved only after death.

The Buddhist View of Rebirth

If there is no eternal soul, what is it that passes on from one life to the next in the process of rebirth? This difficult question was explained by the great Buddhist monk Nagasena to King Milinda thus:

The king asked: 'When someone is reborn, Venerable Nagasena, is he the same as the one who just died, or is he another?'

The Elder [Nagasena] replied: 'He is neither the same nor another.'

'Give me an illustration.'

'What do you think, great king: when you were a tiny infant, newly born and quite soft, were you then the same as the one who is now grown up?'

'No, that infant was one, I, now grown up, am another.'

'If that is so, then, great king, you have had no mother, no father, no teaching, and no schooling! Do we then take it that there is one mother for the embryo in the first stage, another for the second stage, another for the third, another for the fourth, another for the baby, another for the grown-up man? Is the schoolboy one person, and the one who has finished school another? Does one commit a crime, but the hands and feet of another are cut off?'

'Certainly not! But what would you say Reverend Sir, to all that?'

The Elder replied: 'I was neither the tiny infant, newly born and quite soft, nor am I now the grown-up man; but all these are comprised in one unit depending on this very body.'

'Give me a simile!'

'If a man were to light a lamp, could it give light throughout the whole night?

'Yes, it could.'

'Is now the flame which burns in the first watch of the night the same as the one which burns in the second?'

'It is not the same.' . . .

'Do we then take it that there is one lamp in the first part of the night and another in the second?'

'No, it is because of just that one lamp that the light shines throughout the night.'

'Even so must we understand the collation of a series of successive dharmas. At rebirth, one dharma arises while another stops; but the two processes take place almost simultaneously (i.e. they are continuous). Therefore the first act of consciousness in the new existence is neither the same as the last act of consciousness in the previous existence nor is it another.' (*Milindapañha*, in Conze, *Buddhist Scriptures*, pp. 149–50.)

In Vedantist Hinduism, suffering arises, as has been mentioned above, from ignorance (*avidya*) and illusion (*maya*). Once knowledge (*vidya*) of this state of affairs is attained, wisdom (*jñana*) is achieved, and the state of liberation (*moksha*) can be attained. *Moksha* occurs when *avidya*

Nagasena, a Buddhist monk who, according to tradition, lived in the first century CE and whose discourse with the Greek-Bactrian king Milinda (Menander) resulted in the well-known text, the *Milindapañha*. A Tibetan Buddhist block print.

(ignorance) vanishes and the state of identification with the Real is 'realized' (that is, made into a conscious reality). The qualities of Brahman, the Absolute, which are revealed in the state of *moksha* are described as *sat-chit-ananda* (existence-consciousness-bliss).

In Buddhism, the state of liberation in this life is called Nirvana (Nibbana). Those in this state:

> do not take delight in the senses and their objects, are not impressed by them, are not attached to them, and in consequence their craving ceases; the cessation of craving leads successively to that of grasping, of becoming, of birth, of old age and death, of grief, lamentation, pain, sadness, and despair – that is to say to the cessation of all this mass of ill. It is thus that cessation is Nirvana.[47]

Nirvana is not a state of annihilation, as is often thought, but rather a state in which all desire and craving has been 'blown out' (the literal meaning of 'Nirvana'). The state of a person who has achieved Nirvana cannot, however, be described, for the realm of Nirvana is *avyakata* – ineffable or inexpressible. One can no more say anything about this state than one can say anything about the direction in which the flame of a candle goes when it is blown out. It can only be described in negative terms, by stating what it is not.

We have seen above how the whole mass of *duhkha*, suffering, arises through a process of *pratitya-samutpada*, co-dependent origination (see p. 194). All the elements in the chain of the arising of *duhkha* support each other. This then suggests how the whole chain can be collapsed, summarized in the Buddha's saying: 'That arising, this comes into being; that ceasing to be, this ceases to be.'[48] In this way the whole chain described on p. 194 can be broken. 'From the stopping of ignorance is the stopping of karma-formations; from the stopping of karma-formations is the stopping of consciousness . . .'[49] If the chain can be broken, it ceases to be. The person who has succeeded in collapsing this illusory chain, who has escaped from craving and ignorance, is said to have reached Nirvana.

There is, however, as mentioned above, a concept in Mahayana Buddhism of a higher ideal while still on earth than just the achievement of Nirvana; that of the *bodhisattva*, who voluntarily puts off achieving Nirvana to help others along the path. In other words, the highest state is one where one's thoughts are turned away from one's own salvation and towards the salvation of others.

a

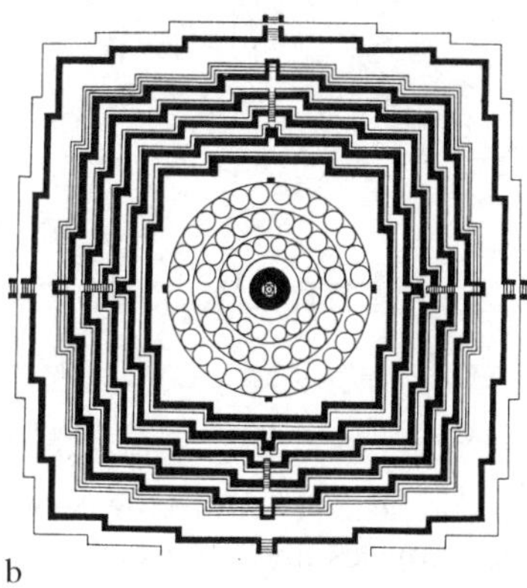

b

JOURNEY TO NIRVANA: a) A ninth-century stone mandala in Borobdur, Java. Its layout (b) represents levels of existence: 'The traveler enters through a door and begins to circle the monument, understanding that the journey through the monument is a replica of the journey through life. Carved reliefs along the walls illustrate the lower levels of existence, in which one is unaware of one's spiritual nature and tied only to the physical realm. Fittingly, while on this level, the traveler can only see directly ahead, the view upward and outward is blocked by high walls . . . At this point the squared path turns to that of a circle. As the visitor ascends, the way becomes freed from closed, tunnel-like passageways and one's vision now expands to see outwards to the landscape . . . and upwards to . . . sky. At the summit of the monument, there are sculptures of hundreds of hidden Buddhas. Finally, at the apex of the monument, the journey culminates in a central image, the Vairocana Buddha, the Supreme Buddha.' (Badiee, *An Earthly Paradise*, pp. 65–9)

FURTHER READING

For a general account of suffering in the world religions, see Bowker, *Problems of Suffering in the Religions of the World*. For a general account of Christian theodicy, see Hick, *Evil and the God of Love*, and S. T. Davis, *Encountering Evil*. On theodicy in Process Theology, see Griffin, *God, Power and Evil*. On Islamic theodicy, see Ormsby, *Theodicy in Islamic Thought*. On the Buddhist view of suffering, see Pruett, *The Meaning and End of Suffering*. On salvation, see Brandon, *The Saviour God*.

10

The Promise of a Future Saviour

THE RELIGIONS OF THE WORLD ARE VERY DIFFERENT in terms of their metaphysics and philosophy, cultural background, and the circumstances of their evolution over time. Despite these differences, it is a very striking fact that almost all of the major religions have remarkably similar accounts of a future promised Golden Age and the advent of a saviour. The texts in each religion describe the degraded condition of the world before his coming, his arrival and victory over opposition, and the Golden Age that he will inaugurate. These accounts all resemble each other remarkably. Indeed, they are so similar that, as will be shown in this chapter, many of the eschatological texts of one religion could even be transferred to another without occasioning much feeling of being out of place. For the sake of completeness the second half of this chapter will examine some of the social consequences of the promise of a saviour, although such matters more properly belong in Part IV of this book.

It would be useful at this stage to review several terms. The doctrine of the future advent of a Golden Age is variously named millennialism, millenarianism and chiliasm. The expectation of a saviour who will usher in this Golden Age (or may come at the culmination of the Golden Age) is termed messianism. Eschatology refers to the study both of what occurs after death and of what will occur at the end of time or the end of the age. Soteriology is the study of pathways to and doctrines of salvation (whether referring to salvation in this world – with the coming of the millennium – or after death). Some aspects of soteriology and eschatology are dealt with in chapter 9.

Descriptions of the Coming of the World Saviour

All the scriptures of the major religions appear to give the promise of a world saviour who is to come. For the Western religions, his coming would signal the end of the world. The Eastern religions consider that his coming signals the end of an era (see Table 10.1).

Table 10.1 Comparative Eschatology

	NAME	WILL END	WILL USHER IN
HINDUISM	Kalki Avatar	Kali Yuga (The Age of Decay)	Krita (Golden) Age
TAOISM	Hou Sheng (Coming Sage)	Evil	T'ai P'ing (Great Peace)
BUDDHISM	Maitreya Buddha	Period of the disappearance of all signs of true religion	Revival of religion; reappearance of *arhats*
ZOROASTRIANISM	Hushidar Bahram Varjavand Saoshyant	Period of Ahriman's reign on earth	Frashkart (rehabilitation of the world)
JUDAISM	Messiah	Persecution, humiliation and dispersion of Israel	Re-establishment and recognition of Israel's place in the world
CHRISTIANITY	Return of Christ	Period of Satan's rule over the earth	Kingdom of God on earth
ISLAM	Mahdi (For Shi'is: Hidden Imam Mahdi) and return of Christ	Period of injustice	Establishment of justice and the rule of God's law
BAHA'I FAITH	Future Manifestation	Present dispensation	New divine teachings

The Condition of the World Prior to the Advent of the Saviour

The scriptures of the different religions are unanimous in describing the degraded state of the world prior to the coming of the saviour. The physical state of the world will have decayed or become unstable, with numerous natural catastrophes. Droughts and failures of crops are frequently mentioned, as well as earthquakes, fires and astronomical phenomena such as the sun being darkened. More emphasis is placed, however, in these prophecies on the deterioration of the moral and spiritual state of humanity. Public and private morality will have fallen to a point where everything that is regarded as abominable occurs: there will be dishonesty and theft; greed and covetousness will rule people's lives, sexual immorality and perversity will become commonplace and the government will be in the hands of persons who abuse it. In particular, the social structures that maintain the stability of society, such as filial piety and the caste system (in Hinduism), are predicted to become destabilized. Interestingly, some of the features of modern society which we regard as improvements are predicted

The Four Horsemen of the Apocalypse, a frequent image in depictions of the Day of Judgement (based on *Revelation* 9:14–19). Albrecht Dürer, *Apocalypse*, Nuremberg, 1498.

in these prophecies as signs of the degraded state of humanity; for example, a greater equality between the classes or castes in society and a greater social role for women.

Not surprisingly, numerous religious groups throughout history have looked at their own age and wondered whether the problems and disturbances that afflict them may not be signs of the age of the promised saviour. Such speculation has been particularly rife at times of unprecedented disasters (such as the Black Death in Europe) or at significant dates (such as the end of a millennium).

The main difference between the Western religions and the Eastern religions relates to their concepts of time. In the Eastern religions, the pattern of the world is cyclical and therefore both the evil state of the world before the saviour's coming and the Golden Age afterwards are an inherent unalterable part of this cyclical pattern. In the Western religions, however, the emphasis is on the fact that it is the advent of the saviour that causes the end of the period of darkness and the beginning of the Golden Age.

THE CONDITION OF THE WORLD PRIOR TO THE ADVENT OF THE SAVIOUR

HINDUISM

In the Kali age . . . people will be greedy, take to wicked behaviour, will be merciless, indulge in hostilities without any cause, unfortunate, extremely covetous for wealth and women . . .

When deceit, falsehood, lethargy, sleepiness, violence, despondency, grief, delusion, fear, poverty prevail, that is the Kali Age . . . mortal beings become dull-witted, unlucky, voracious, destitute of wealth yet voluptuous, and women, wanton and unchaste. Countries will be ravaged by robbers and miscreants; the Vedas will be condemned by heretics; kings will exploit the subjects, and twice-borns like Brahmanas will be given to the gratification of their sexual desires and other appetites . . . Petty-minded people will conduct business transactions and merchants will be fraudulent.

In the Kali age, men will abandon their parents, brothers, friends, and relatives and establish their friendliness on a sexual basis. People will have their minds weighed down with constant anxiety and fear, due to devastating famines and heavy taxation. (*Bhagavata Purana* 12:3:24–5, 30–2, 35, 37, 39)

THERAVADA BUDDHISM

Among such humans, the ten moral courses of conduct will disappear, the ten immoral courses of action will flourish excessively; there will be no word for moral among such humans – far less any moral agent. Among such humans, brethren, they who lack filial and religious piety, and show no respect for the head of the clan – it is they to whom homage and praise will be given, just as today praise and homage are given to the filial-minded, to the pious and to them who respect the heads of their clans . . . The world will fall into promiscuity, like goats and sheep, fowls and swine, dogs and jackals . . . Among such humans, brethren, keen mutual enmity will become the rule, keen ill-will, keen animosity, passionate thoughts even of killing, in a mother towards her child, in a child towards its mother, in a father towards his child and a child towards its father, in brother to brother, in brother to sister, in sister to brother. (The Buddha's address in the *Cakkavatti-Sihanada Suttana*, *Digha Nikaya* 3:70–2, in Rhys Davids, *Dialogues of the Buddha*, vol. 3, pp. 70–1)

MAHAYANA BUDDHISM

And in that latter terminal age, when the Buddha-dharma is extinguished, when woesome teachings are on the ascendant, in a time such as this disasters will increasingly arise. In that future age in Jambudvipa (the southern continent on which humans live), a generation of sentient beings who are unfortunate and lacking in wisdom will increasingly engage in woesome acts . . . The winds and rains will not revolve [in their proper seasonal order], and woesome stars will cause transmutations. Contention and battle among devas, humans and asuras will increasingly arise. (Scripture T. 1185A, quoted in Birnbaum, *Studies on the Mysteries of Manjusri*, p. 13)

ZOROASTRIANISM

And at that time, O Zaratust the Spitaman! all men will become deceivers, great friends will become of different parties, and respect, affection, hope, and regard for the soul will depart from the world; and the affection of father will depart from the son; and that of the brother from his brother; the son-in-law will become a beggar from his father-in-law, and the mother will be parted and estranged from the daughter . . . the earth of Spendarmad is more barren, and fuller of highwaymen; and the crop will not yield the seed . . . and vegetation, trees and shrubs will diminish . . . And men are born smaller, and their skill and strength are less; they become more deceitful and more given to vile practices . . . gifts are few among their deeds, and duties and good works proceed but little from their hands . . . They recount largely about duties and good works, and pursue wickedness and the road to hell; and through the iniquity, cajolery, and craving of wrath and avarice they rush to hell . . . and the helpless and ignoble will come to the foremost place and advancement. (*Bahman Yast* 2:30, 31, 32, 33, 35, 39, in West, *Pahlavi Texts*, part 1, pp. 203–4, 205)

JUDAISM

And the people will oppress one another, every man his fellow and every man his neighbour; the youth will be insolent to the elder, and the base fellow to the honourable. For Jerusalem has stumbled, and Judah has fallen. (*Isaiah* 3:1, 5, 8)

CHRISTIANITY

Tell us, when will this be and what will be the sign of your coming, and of the close of the age? And Jesus answered and said unto them: . . . And you will hear of wars and rumours of wars . . . For nation will rise against nation, and kingdom against kingdom, and there will be famines and earthquakes in various places . . . And then many will fall away, and betray one another, and hate one another . . . And because wickedness is multiplied, most men's love will grow cold . . . For then there will be great tribulation, such as has not been from the beginning of the world until now, no, and never will be. (*Matthew* 24:3, 4, 6, 7, 10, 12, 21)

SUNNI ISLAM

Among the signs of the last hour will be the removal of knowledge, the abundance of ignorance, the prevalence of fornication, the prevalence of wine-drinking, the small number of men and the large number of women. (Traditions transmitted by Bukhari and Abu Muslim, in al-Baghawi, *Mishkat al-Masabih* 3:1137)

When the booty is taken in turn [and not shared out among the needy; see *Qur'an* 59:7]; property given in trust is treated as spoil; *zakat* [religious tax] is looked on as a fine; learning is acquired for other than a religious purpose; a man obeys his wife and is unfilial towards his mother, brings his friend near and drives his father off; voices are raised in the mosques; the most wicked member of a tribe becomes its ruler; the most worthless member of a people becomes its leader; a man is honoured through fear of the evil he may do; singing-girls and stringed instruments make their appearance; wines are drunk; and the last members of this people curse the first ones; look at that time for a violent wind, an earthquake, being swallowed up by the earth, metamorphosis, pelting rain, and signs following one another like bits of a necklace falling one after the other when its string is cut. (Tradition transmitted by Tirmidhi, in al-Baghawi, *Mishkat al-Masabih* 3:1139)

SHI'I ISLAM

I do not know when it [the coming of the Mahdi] will be any more than you do but some signs and conditions will follow one another, and the signs are these: When the people allow the saying of prayers to die out; and they destroy trust; and they regard lying as permissible; and they take usurious interest; and they sell religion in exchange for the world; and they employ fools . . . and they follow their lusts; and they take the spilling of blood lightly; and their discernment is weak; and tyranny becomes a source of pride; and the leaders become profligate, the ministers oppressors, the 'ulama faithless and the poor depraved; and false witness is made; immorality, lies, crime, and repression are carried out openly . . . and women assist their husbands in trade out of greed for the things of this world; and sinners are extolled and listened to; and the leader of the people is the most despicable of them and he is wary of the libertine, fearing his evil, and he gives credence to the liar and has faith in the traitor. (Al-Zanjani, *Aqa'id al-Shi'a*, quoted in Momen, *Introduction to Shi'i Islam*, pp. 167–8)

The Disappearance of True Religion

Along with the general decline in the state of the world, the accounts in different religions agree that religion itself will also be in decline. The religious professionals (monks, priests, gurus and so on) will become corrupt and degraded, and instead of giving true guidance, they will lead the people towards error. The scriptures of the religion, or rather the true meaning of the scriptures, will be lost.

It is not surprising, in view of these prophecies of the decline of religion, that those that are seeking to reform or revitalize a religion often have a millenarian element or ethos to their teaching. Some of these reform movements then develop into fully fledged messianic movements. Indeed, figures such as Jesus, Muhammad and the Bab can be seen to have followed such a course themselves. At the beginning of their ministries they appear as reformers of the established religion and only later and gradually are the full revolutionary implications of their teaching unveiled (see pp. 308–11).

THE DISAPPEARANCE OF TRUE RELIGION

HINDUISM

People ignorant of religion, will occupy high seats (and pulpits) and will (pretend to) preach religion. (*Bhagavata Purana* 12:3:38)

Whenever there is a decline in righteousness, O Bharat, and the rise of irreligion, it is then that I send forth My spirit. (*Bhagavad Gita* 4:7–8)

THERAVADA BUDDHISM

Buddha: After my decease, first will occur the five disappearances. And what are the five disappearances? The disappearance of attainments [to Nirvana], the disappearance of the method [inability to practise wisdom, insight and the four purities of moral habit], the disappearance of learning [loss of men who follow the Dharma and forgetting of the *Pitakas* and other scriptures], the disappearance of the symbols [the loss of the outward forms, the robes and practices of monkhood], the disappearance of the relics [of the Buddha]. (*Anagatavamsa*, adapted from translation in Warren, *Buddhism in Translations*, pp. 482ff. and Conze, *Buddhist Texts*, pp. 47–50)

MAHAYANA BUDDHISM

But there will be disturbances among the monks at the last time. There will not always then be Arhats thus in every place. (Emmerick, *Book of Zambasta* 22:102, p. 305)

ZOROASTRIANISM
Or, in those last times, it becomes allowable to perform a ceremonial with two men, so that this religion may not come to nothing and collapse; there will be only one in a hundred, in a thousand, in a myriad, who believes in this religion, and even he does nothing of it though it be a duty . . . And they practise the appointed feasts of their ancestors, the propitiation of angels, and the prayers and ceremonies of the season festivals and guardian spirits, in various places, yet that which they practise they do not believe in unhesitatingly; they do not give rewards lawfully, and bestow no gifts and alms, and even those [they bestow] they repent of again. And even those men of the good religion of the Mazdayasnians proceed in conformity with those ways and customs, and do not believe their own religion. (*Bahman Yast* 2:37, 45, 46, in West, *Pahlavi Texts*, part 1, pp. 206, 208–9)

CHRISTIANITY
And many false prophets will arise and lead many astray . . . Then if any one says to you, 'Lo, here is Christ!', or 'There he is!' do not believe it. For false Christs and false prophets will arise and show great signs and wonders, so as to lead astray, if possible, even the elect. (*Matthew* 24:11, 23–4)

SUNNI ISLAM
Anas reported God's messenger [Muhammad] as saying: 'The last hour will not come till the cry "God, God" is not uttered in the earth.' (Tradition transmitted by Abu Muslim, in al-Baghawi, *Mishkat al-Masabih* 3:1163).

SHI'I ISLAM
The Apostle of God [Muhammad] said: 'There will come a time for my people when there will remain nothing of the Qur'an except its outward form and nothing of Islam except its name and they will call themselves by this name even though they are the people furthest from it. Their mosques will be full of people but they will be empty of right guidance. The religious leaders of that day will be the most evil religious leaders under the heavens; sedition and dissension will go out from them and to them will it return.' (Ibn Babuya, *Thawab al-A'mal*, quoted in Momen, *Introduction to Shi'i Islam*, p. 168)

The Appearance of the Future Saviour

Just at the point when the affairs of the world have reached their lowest point, religion has become a dead letter, and all hope is gone, the promised saviour will arise and proclaim his mission. There are many prophecies in the various religions about miraculous signs and portents that will precede and accompany the coming of the saviour. Some religions prophesy just one future saviour, while some prophesy more than one coming at different times in the future. Zoroastrianism, in particular, seems to expect a series of saviour figures: Hushidar, Hushidar-Mah, Bahram Varjavand and Saoshyant.[1] The following prophecy mentions two of these:

> Auharmazd spoke thus: O Zaratust the Spitaman! when the demon with dishevelled hair of the race of Wrath comes into notice in the eastern quarter, first a black token becomes manifest, and Hushidar son of Zaratust is born on Lake Frazdan . . .
>
> It is when he comes to his conference with me, Auharmazd, O Zaratust the Spitaman! that in the direction of Kinistan . . . is born a prince; . . . his father, a prince of the Kayan race, approaches the women, and a religious prince is born to him; he calls his name Vahram the Vargavand [Bahram Varjavand]. That a sign may come to the earth, the night when that prince is born, a star falls from the sky; when that prince is born the star shows the signal.[2]

KALKI AVATAR: The messianic figure in Hinduism is usually pictured riding on horseback and often wielding a sword. According to the commonest reckoning, he is the tenth avatar of Vishnu. He will defeat Yama (god of death) and overcome evil and darkness.

In Hinduism, the series of avatars (incarnations) of Vishnu includes Krishna and Rama. In one well-known list, the Buddha is the ninth avatar and he is to be followed by the expected Kalki avatar.

> When Vedic religion and the dharma of the lawbooks have undergone total confusion and reversal and the Kali Age is almost exhausted, then a part of the creator of the entire universe, of the guru of all that moves and is still, without beginning, middle or end, who is made of Brahma and has the form of the soul, the blessed lord Vasudeva (Vishnu) – he will become incarnate here in the universe in the form of Kalkin.[3]

In Theravada Buddhist scriptures, the Buddha refers to three former buddhas; he himself is the fourth buddha in this chain and there is prophecy of a future buddha, the Maitreya (Mettayya) Buddha:

> At that period, brethren, there will arise in the world an Exalted One named Mettayya [Maitreya], Arahant, Fully Awakened, abounding in wisdom and goodness, happy, with knowledge of the worlds, unsurpassed as a guide to mortals willing to be led, a teacher for gods and men, an Exalted One, a Buddha, even as I am now. He, by himself, will thoroughly know and see, as it were face to face, this universe, with its worlds of the spirits, its Brahmas and its Maras, and its world of recluses and brahmins, of princes and peoples, even as I now, by myself, thoroughly know and see them.[4]

In Mahayana Buddhism, the emphasis is on the many other-worldly saviours (among them Manjushri, Amitabha, and Avalokiteshvara), but Mahayana scriptures also contain promises of the coming of an earthly buddha, Maitreya.

> When for the sake of beings Maitreya reveals his birth here, he will surpass Brahma in appearance. He will have the thirty-two *laksanas*

MAITREYA BUDDHA: The messianic figure in Buddhism, expected by both Theravada and Mahayana Buddhists, the fifth and last of the earthly buddhas in this world cycle. As in this Chinese stone statue, he is the only buddha who is commonly depicted seated in the European manner.

> [distinguishing marks]. Never before has one seen there a being such in appearance. At that time he will shine, gleam very pure just like the rising sun.[5]

There is an expectation in Judaism of the coming of the Messiah. In Jewish history, a number of individuals have claimed to be the Messiah but the generality of the Jews have rejected these claimants and continue to expect the Messiah.

> The people who walked in darkness have seen a great light; those who dwelt in a land of deep darkness, on them has light shined . . . For to us a child is born, to us a son is given: and the government will be upon his shoulder: and his name will be called 'Wonderful Counsellor, Mighty God, Everlasting Father, Prince of Peace.' Of the increase of his government and of peace there will be no end, upon the throne of David, and over his kingdom to establish it, and to uphold it with justice and with righteousness from this time forth and for evermore.[6]

Jesus prophesied his own crucifixion to his disciples but promised them that he would come again, glorify his followers and overcome all those who oppose him.

> And then will appear the sign of the Son of man in heaven, and then all the tribes of the earth will mourn, and they will see the Son of man coming on the clouds of heaven with power and great glory; and he will send out his angels with a loud trumpet call, and they will gather his elect from the four winds, from one end of heaven to the other.[7]

In Islam, there are no explicit prophecies in the *Qur'an* about the advent of a saviour, but there are numerous statements about the advent of the Mahdi and the return of Jesus in the Traditions attributed to the prophet Muhammad, such as the following from the Sunni Traditions:

> If only one day of this world remained, God would lengthen that day till He raised up in it a man who belongs to me [or, to my family] . . . who will fill the earth with equity and justice.[8]

In Shi'i tradition, the Mahdi is the twelfth Shi'i Imam, who went into hiding in 874 CE and whose life has been miraculously prolonged by God until the time when he will reappear.

> He [the Imam Mahdi] will come with a new Cause – just as Muhammad, at the beginning of Islam, summoned the people to a new Cause – and with a

> new book and a new religious law, which will be a severe test for the Arabs.[9]

Although the Baha'i Faith claims that Baha'u'llah is the fulfilment of the prophecies of the other religions about the coming of a saviour, the Baha'i scriptures are also emphatic that this is not the end of the process, and that another holy figure will arise in the future who will act as the intermediary of God.

> As to the meaning of the quotation, 'My fears are for Him Who will be sent down unto you after Me', this refers to the Manifestation Who is to come after a thousand or more years, Who like all previous Messengers of God will be subjected to persecutions, but will eventually triumph over them. For men of ill-will have been and will always continue to be in this world, unless mankind reaches a state of complete and absolute perfection – a condition which is not only improbable but actually impossible to attain.[10]

Part of the Christian vision about the Day of Judgement is that on the day, Satan will be defeated and chained up (*Revelation* 20:2).

Prophecies of the military exploits of the saviour are a particular feature of the Western religions. He conquers those who have oppressed his people and have brought injustice to the land. In Shi'i Islam, the saviour is the Hidden Imam Mahdi who returns to defeat the enemies of the Shi'a. In Christianity, there are expectations of a Battle of Armageddon which will result in a defeat of the forces of evil. The Jews rejected Jesus as the Messiah figure precisely because he did not fulfil this military expectation and free them from Roman rule.

The Golden Age

In some traditions, mainly the Western religions, the saviour benefits only those who are of his own religious community. Those who are the enemies of the saviour are, as mentioned above, defeated in battle and eliminated. The Golden Age that characterizes the rule of the future saviour is, however, described very similarly in the traditions of all religions, although there are, of course, differences that relate to the culture and geography of the area from which the scripture originated. In brief, all the problems that characterized the period before the coming of the saviour are resolved. The physical earth becomes a paradise with plenteous crops and resources sufficient for all. The saviour elevates the moral and spiritual condition of the people. The government becomes just and beneficent.

The Golden Age that will Follow the Coming of the Saviour

HINDUISM

The minds of the people will become pure as flawless crystal, and they will be as if awakened at the conclusion of a night. And these men, the residue of mankind, will thus be transformed . . . And these offspring will follow the ways of the Krta Age. (*Vishnu Purana* 4:24:25–9, quoted in O'Flaherty, *Hindu Myths*, pp. 236–7. See also *Bhagavata Purana* 12:2:16)

THERAVADA BUDDHISM

The truth [the norm, the Dhamma] lovely in its origin, lovely in its progress, lovely in its consummation, will he [Maitreya Buddha] proclaim, both in the spirit and in the letter; the higher life will he make known, in all its fullness and in all its purity, even as I do now. He will be accompanied by a congregation of some thousands of brethren, even as I am now accompanied by a congregation of some hundreds of brethren. (The Buddha's address in the *Cakkavatti-Sihanada Suttana*, *Digha Nikaya* 3:76, in Rhys Davids, *Dialogues of the Buddha* vol. 3, p. 74)

MAHAYANA BUDDHISM

At that time the weather will be mild at all times, and the four seasons will regularly succeed each other. None of the people will suffer any of the one hundred and eight afflictions. Lust, anger and idiocy will rarely take place. The people will all feel equal, and will be of one mind, mutually expressing pleasure upon meeting their fellows . . . And in these times in the Yen-fou [regions of the East] the earth shall of itself produce white polished rice having no husks, of a most delectable flavour . . . And as for gold and silver, precious stones, ornaments of jade and cornelian, amber and pearls, they will all be scattered on the ground, and no one will notice or gather them up. (*Fo-shuo Mi-lo hsia-sheng ching* (*Maitreya-vyakarana*), an Indian Mahayana sutra, translated from Sanskrit into Chinese by Dharmaraksa (266–308 CE), quoted in Chan, 'The White Lotus-Maitreya Doctrine', p. 212)

ZOROASTRIANISM

And regarding that Vahram the Vargavand it is declared that he comes forth in full glory, restrains a curbed temper, and is entrusted with the seat of mobadship of the mobads [the supreme high-priesthood], and the seat of true explanation of the religion, he restores again these countries of Iran which I, Auharmazd, created; and he drives away from the world covetousness, want, hatred, wrath, lust, envy, and wickedness. And the wolf period goes away, and the sheep period comes on . . . and the wicked evil spirit becomes confounded and unconscious, with the demons and the progeny of gloom. (*Bahman Yast* 3:39–40, in West, *Pahlavi Texts* part 1, pp. 229–30 using alternative translation suggested in the footnote)

JUDAISM

He shall judge between the nations, and shall decide for many peoples; and they shall beat their swords into ploughshares, and their spears into pruning hooks; nation shall not lift up sword against nation, neither shall they learn war any more. The wolf shall dwell with the lamb, and the leopard shall lie down with the kid, and the calf and the lion and the fatling together, and a little child shall lead them . . . They shall not hurt or destroy in all my holy mountain; for the earth shall be full of the knowledge of the Lord as the waters cover the sea. (*Isaiah* 2:4; 11:6, 9)

CHRISTIANITY
Then I saw a new heaven and a new earth: for the first heaven and the first earth had passed away . . . and I heard a loud voice from the throne saying, 'Behold, the dwelling of God is with men. He will dwell with them, and they shall be his people, and God himself will be with them; and he will wipe away every tear from their eyes; and death shall be no more, neither shall there be mourning nor crying nor pain any more, for the former things have passed away.' And he who sat upon the throne said, 'Behold, I make all things new.' (*Book of Revelation* 21:1–5)

SUNNI ISLAM
He will fill the earth with equity and justice as it had been filled with oppression and tyranny. Those who dwell in heaven and those who dwell on earth will be pleased with him. The sky will not cease to give any of its rain, but will pour it forth copiously; and the earth will not cease to produce any of its plants, but will bring them forth so that the living will wish the dead were alive. (Tradition transmitted by al-Hakim, in al-Baghawi, *Mishkat al-Masabih* 3:1141)

SHI'I ISLAM
When the Qa'im arises, he will rule with justice and will remove injustice in his days. The roads will be safe and the earth will show forth its bounties. Everything due will be returned to its rightful owner. And no people of religion will remain who do not show forth submission (*Islam*) and acknowledge belief (*Iman*), . . . And he will judge among the people with the judgement of David and Muhammad . . . At that time men will not find anywhere to give their alms or to be generous because riches will encompass all. (Shaykh al-Mufid, *Kitab al-Irshad*, pp. 343–4, quoted in Momen, *Introduction to Shi'i Islam*, p. 169)

BAHA'I FAITH
National rivalries, hatred, and intrigues will cease, and racial animosity and prejudice will be replaced by racial amity, understanding and cooperation. The causes of religious strife will be permanently removed, economic barriers and restrictions will be completely abolished, and the inordinate distinction between classes will be obliterated. Destitution on the one hand, and gross accumulation of ownership on the other, will disappear. The enormous energy dissipated and wasted on war, whether economic or political, will be consecrated to such ends as will extend the range of human inventions and technical development, to the increase of the productivity of mankind, to the extermination of disease, to the extension of scientific research, to the raising of the standard of physical health, to the sharpening and refinement of the human brain, to the exploitation of the unused and unsuspected resources of the planet, to the prolongation of human life, and to the furtherance of any other agency that can stimulate the intellectual, the moral, and spiritual life of the entire human race. (Shoghi Effendi, *Guidance for Today and Tomorrow,* pp. 168–9)

The End of the World

The prophecies of the Western religions, in particular, usually imply that the advent of the saviour shortly precedes the end of the world. These prophecies include such events as the resurrection of the dead,[11] the Day of Judgement,[12] and the physical destruction of the world.[13] There are numerous different versions of the sequence of events and much elaboration of them in popular religion and religious art. Eastern religions also prophesy the eventual destruction of the world, but, because of the cyclic nature of time, that is only a preliminary to the eventual rebirth of a new world.

A Typology of Future Saviours and Millennialist Movements

As we have seen, an eschatological tension exists in all the major religions. A saviour or messianic figure is, as it were, waiting in the wings, about to make an appearance. Not unnaturally, such a figure becomes a major focus of popular attention. The place where this messianic figure now is before his coming to the earth becomes a subject for the elaboration of legends and depiction in art. For the Buddhist, the next buddha, Maitreya (or Mettaya), is living in the Tushita heaven. For Shi'i Muslims, the Hidden Imam Mahdi is living in the fabulous cities of Jabulsa and Jabulqa. For Christians, Christ sits at the right hand of the Throne of God. In all these depictions, the place where the messianic figure now is becomes itself filled with glory and light due to its contact with this figure.

The time of the coming of the saviour has, not surprisingly, become a major source of religious speculation and writing in most religions. Most religions do not specify a precise time, which means that every age becomes potentially the 'promised time'. Even in religions that do appear to have a more specific time designated, this may not lead to a cessation of speculation about the time of the coming of the saviour. In Buddhism, for example, there is a fairly clear statement that the next buddha, Maitreya (Mettaya) Buddha, will not appear until five thousand years or more have elapsed from the time of Siddhartha Buddha. This has not prevented many groups from the sixth century CE onwards (from about one thousand years after the time of the Buddha) speculating that the coming of Maitreya was at hand, or even that it had occurred. These speculations became particularly intense from the middle of the nineteenth century, because it was claimed by some that the duration of the Buddha's teaching would be cut by half, to 2,500 years.[14]

Much of the hope of ordinary people for salvation from their poverty, misery and distress focuses on the coming of the figure who will bring a Golden Age. It is not surprising, therefore, to find that this particular aspect of religion has had a great deal of social impact over the centuries and has been adapted in various ways to achieve different social aims. In addition to the main manifestation of this aspect of religion, there are several variations on the theme, which we should examine. The concept of an expected saviour or messianic figure occurs in four different ways in the major religions of the world, depending on whether it is believed that the meeting with the future saviour will occur here on earth or in heaven; in the near future or at some unspecified later date.[15]

Here/Later

This type of eschatology expects the coming of the saviour figure to occur on earth at some unspecified future time. Although that time could theoretically be during the lifetime of the present generation, there is no urgent perception of that nearness. This is by far the most common form of eschatological expectation in most religions. It represents the orthodox majority position and is also the type in closest accord with the scriptural texts of most religions. It is represented in the quotations given on pp. 244–53. Because the saviour is expected in the distant future, there is no prospect of meeting him in this world. Therefore the emphasis is on leading a 'good' life religiously (that is, ethically and ritually good) so that one can be born again (in rebirth or reincarnation) or raised up (in resurrection) in the time of the saviour. The emphasis is thus on individual action and there is no social import to this type of eschatology other than that of a quietist attitude implicitly supporting the status quo.

One psycho-social interpretation for some occurrences of this type of eschatology is that it may be emphasized by those recently expelled from power. This occurs particularly when the victors are ethnically and religiously different. Through this mechanism, the losers reinforce their threatened identity (by identifying the future victorious saviour in national or ethnic terms) and justify their lack of power with their assertion that this is a necessary precondition for the advent of the saviour. The Messiah thus becomes a spiritualization of fallen historical kingship.[16]

Here/Now

This type of eschatology expects the coming of the saviour to occur on earth in the immediate future. There is a great sense of urgency and immediacy in these movements. The first (here/later) type described above often spills over into this type if there is any crisis or cause for distress in society, for in a situation of fear and suffering, people turn to the promise of a saviour and a Golden Age. They intensify their longing for this and begin to interpret their social situation in terms of the evil situation in the world immediately before the advent (see pp. 243–8).

This here/now type of millennialism manifests itself in very different ways. Part of this difference is due to the division between pre-millennialism (the imminent arrival of the saviour after which there will be an earthly or heavenly Golden Age for the elect) and post-millennialism (the belief that the saviour will come after the start of the Golden Age). It has been suggested, however, that the terms 'pre- and post-millennialism' are to some extent unsatisfactory. Although the belief in the advent of a saviour is a strong feature of the pre-millennialist groups, this is not necessarily a feature of the post-millennialists. One suggested replacement for these terms is 'catastrophic and progressive millennialism' since these terms better describe the main social features of these movements. Both groups predict a change in the social order, the main difference between them being whether it is expected that the change will occur suddenly, catastrophically and through divine intervention (catastrophic millennialism), or whether it will occur gradually and through human effort as well as divine assistance (progressive millennialism).[17]

Post-millennialism or Progressive Millennialism. The post-millennialist or progressive millennialist groups look towards a better future that will be brought in gradually. Very often there is the tendency to believe that human beings can act in ways to contribute to and facilitate the onset of the Golden Age. Therefore these groups tend to advocate programmes of social reform. There is an element of this type of millennialism in Buddhism in that some of the prophecies concerning Maitreya indicate that the Golden Age will commence before his coming, and that he will appear at its peak. Shi'ism had almost exclusively pre-millennialist beliefs prior to the 1979 Iranian revolution, which introduced the concept that it is the task of all Shi'is to work for a better society prior to the advent of the Imam Mahdi.

Pre-millennialism or Catastrophic Millennialism. This manifests itself in two different ways, or rather in two phases, the first before the saviour is believed to have arrived and the second after.

1. Separatist sects. If the saviour is not yet considered to have arrived, many apocalyptic sects are typically so focused on the imminent advent that they lose interest in other social activities. So overwhelming does this central factor in their lives become that not infrequently they even withdraw completely from society, counting themselves as the elect, awaiting the advent. The Millerites and other similar groups in mid-nineteenth-century America and Europe went up into the hills to await the coming of the Lord. German pietist groups migrated to Russia and Palestine. In Brazil, many groups have arisen whose leaders take their followers off on a trek in search of a Promised Land.[18] Even those that do not withdraw from society do not play any active role in it. The nineteenth century saw a great proliferation of Christian millennialist groups such as the Millerites and Seventh Day Adventists, the Jehovah's Witnesses, the Mormons and the Christadelphians.
2. Confrontationist sects. If, however, these groups come to believe that the saviour has arrived, their attitude to society becomes markedly

different. Frequently the leaders of these premillennialist groups claim to be either the promised saviour himself or his representative and, therefore, empowered to usher in the new age. These groups typically have a vision of a new social order that is about to dawn and that stands in marked contrast to the present evil state of the world. The heightened tension inherent in this situation often results in militant political action.[19] The drama of the situation casts all in black and white terms for the followers of the group. Any opposition to them from the secular or religious authorities is interpreted as being the work of the Devil.

MESSIANIC MOVEMENT: Shabbetai Tzevi proclaimed himself the Messiah by implication in about 1645 and openly in 1665. He gained many followers among the Jews of Europe, the Middle East and North Africa. On his arrest in Istanbul in 1666, however, he converted to Islam in order to save his life, and most of his following fell away.

All over the world, the saviour figure has been used in this way. This is particularly so with the figure of Maitreya Buddha in the Buddhist world. Claims to be the Maitreya Buddha have been at the centre of many Chinese revolts among Mahayana Buddhists from the seventh century onwards,[20] as well as a movement among Mahayana Buddhists in Vietnam, the Buu Son Ky Huon,[21] and among Theravada Buddhists; the Saya San movement in Burma and the Karen Telakhon and other movements in Thailand.[22] A similar revolutionary use has been made in Islam of the theme of the Mahdi as presaging an overthrow of the current order. Numerous Shi'i revolts during the first three hundred years of Islamic history were based on a claim by the leader of the revolt to be the Mahdi, the one who would fill the earth with justice;[23] the Safavid conquest of Iran from 1500 to 1510 was also based on an initial claim by Shah Isma'il to be the Mahdi.[24] The Babi movement in Iran, the nineteenth-century precursor of the Baha'i Faith, was based on a claim to be the Mahdi and resulted in a series of upheavals.[25] The Mahdist movement against Anglo-Egyptian domination in the Sudan in the 1880s belongs to the realm of Sunni Islam. Christianity has also seen many millennialist movements: the Joachimite movement in Piedmont that arose in anticipation of the start of a new age in 1260; the role of John Ball and his followers in the English peasants' revolt of 1381; the Taborites in the Hussite revolt in Bohemia in 1419–21; Thomas Muntzer and his 'League of the Elect' in the German peasants' revolt of 1525; and the Anabaptists and their attempt to set up a New Jerusalem during the revolts in Germany in 1534–5.[26] In Judaism the last great Messianic movement centred on the claim of Shabbetai Tzevi (1626–1676) in Turkey to be the Messiah.

Many of the millennialist movements that arise among tribal peoples are also of this type. They arise out of the despair caused by seeing one's culture degraded and overwhelmed by an alien culture that appears to hold to the very opposite of many of one's own cultural values; out of the frustration and demoralization caused by colonialism; and out of envy and greed for the material advantages of the alien culture. Such factors are considered to have been behind such phenomena as the 'cargo cults' in Melanesia (see pp. 48–9).

STATE-SUPPORTED MILLENNIALISM. A comparatively rare manifestation of this here/now type of eschatology is its use by the ruling elements in a society to buttress their authority. By claiming to be the expected saviour (or some close associate of him), the rulers legitimate their rule. Examples of this social expression of eschatology have occurred in the history of Islam. The Abbasid caliphs of Baghdad used the theme of the Mahdi to buttress their regime when they first came to power. The third of their caliphs was even named al-Mahdi. Similarly, the Fatimid caliphs of Egypt made extensive use of the theme of the Mahdi in their state propaganda. The founder of their dynasty called himself 'Ubaydu'llah the Mahdi. The Safavids who established Twelver Shi'ism in Iran also used the theme of the Mahdi (in this case the Hidden Twelfth Imam who is, for Twelver Shi'is, the Imam Mahdi) to give legitimacy to their dynasty. The first of their line claimed to be the Imam Mahdi.[27] Several Buddhist rulers have claimed to be the Maitreya Buddha: in China, the Northern Wei dynasty (386–534 CE), the Empress Wu (ruled 683–705) and some among the kings of Khotan.[28]

There are also several examples of those claiming to be the representative or close ally of the promised saviour, rather than the saviour himself. Although the first of the Safavids, as mentioned above, claimed to be the Hidden Imam Mahdi, the later Safavids reduced this claim to that of being the deputy of the Hidden Imam.[29] Several kings of Burma, including Tabin Shwehti (1531–50) and Alaungpaya (1752–60), proclaimed themselves to be the Cakkavatti (Chakravartin), the world conqueror who is to pave the way for the Maitreya Buddha.[30] Similar claims were made by Kirti-Nissanka-Malla (c.1192) and other Sri Lankan kings.[31]

In many of these examples, eschatology was used in a situation when there had been a recent change in the line of rulers. The new ruling line (which was often religiously or racially different to the previous dynasty) wanted to buttress their political authority. They therefore used the revolutionary fervour of the pre-millennialist outlook to underline and explain the revolutionary nature of what had occurred. But the attempt to use this as the basis of the new order once the revolution has been achieved has frequently not been particularly successful, the pre-millennialist vision being inherently destabilizing. And so, once established, rulers have had to switch to a different basis for their authority. In other words, while pre-millennialist revolutionary fervour may be successfully used to overthrow the existing order, it rarely acts as a successful basis for establishing a new order.

All these millennialist groups, the pre-millennialist in particular, tend towards pietism; these groups often preach that only those that are religiously pure and devout will be able to take part in the millennium.

Anticipation of the coming of the saviour is a powerful impetus to 'purify' one's life and 'rectify' one's thoughts. This tendency eventually leads to fundamentalism. British and American millenarianism of the nineteenth century, for example, developed into the fundamentalism of the early twentieth century.[32]

There/Now

The coming of the saviour figure is relegated to an unspecified time in the future in most orthodoxies. Nevertheless, he represents the hope and promise of salvation. He is a living figure, 'waiting in the wings' as it were. Therefore, in most religions a minor tradition has developed that maintains that it is possible to meet him in visionary experience even before he appears on earth. Such visions are not for everyone, only for those who strive in their religious duties or who have exceptional faith. Such contact with the Maitreya Buddha is considered to have inspired many of the scriptural works of the Chinese Yogacara school. Christian mystics have reported many visionary experiences of meeting with Christ. The best-known of these is St Paul's conversion on the road to Damascus.[33] In the Shaykhi school of Shi'i Islam, it is considered possible to attain the presence of the Hidden Imam in the visionary world of Hurqalya.[34]

MEETING THE MESSIAH: A visionary encounter with the expected messianic figure is a common theme in many religions. The depiction here is of the most famous of the Christian episodes: St Paul's vision on the road to Damascus that led to his conversion to Christianity (*Acts of the Apostles* 9:1–18).

Socially, this type of eschatology is of little importance. It has always been a minority interest among mystics and mystic-philosophers. It has thus had little social impact unless someone who claims to be in immediate direct contact with the saviour figure in this way begins to attract followers and excite a here/now type of eschatological fervour. This is the sort of change that occurred when the Bab put forward his claims to members of the Shaykhi school in nineteenth-century Iran.[35]

There/Later

This type of eschatology concentrates on a life after death in a heaven, usually in the presence of a saviour figure. It is often a corollary to the official here/later position. After death, the believer joins the saviour in

Mahayana Buddhism is rich in other-worldly buddhas and *bodhisattvas*. This picture is of the central part of a Japanese Gharbadhatu mandala belonging to the Shingon sect. The central figure is Vairocana, as the Adi-Buddha, the primordial supreme buddha, personifying the Dharmakaya. Around him are the other four Dhyani-Buddhas (transcendent meditation buddhas), the bottom one being Amitabha, left Abshobhya, right Amoghasiddhi, the top Ratanasambhava. Between them are four *bodhisattvas*, with Maitreya in top left, Avalokiteshvara bottom left, Manjushri bottom right and Samantabhadra top right.

heaven (for Christians and Muslims); or the Tushita heaven of Maitreya Buddha (for Theravada and some Mahayana Buddhists). Later, at the end of time or the end of the age, the believer will be resurrected on earth (for Christians and Muslims) to enjoy the millennium; or will be reborn on earth (for Buddhists) in the time of Maitreya Buddha to hear the Dharma preached by him and thus achieve Nirvana.

Mahayana Buddhism is particularly rich in this type of religious thought. Apart from the Maitreya Buddha mentioned above there is a plethora of other-worldly saviour figures, *bodhisattvas*. Each of these occupies a particular buddha-land. Many sects have been formed around devotion to one or other of these *bodhisattvas*. These are not saviours who are necessarily expected to appear on earth. Rather, they can be called upon as intercessors for help on the path to liberation. Their followers hope ardently to be born in their buddha-land after death (thus being guaranteed progress to Nirvana). Perhaps the most widely revered of these figures is Amitayus or Amitabha or Amida Buddha (the Buddha of Infinite Light), who inhabits the Pure Land or Western Paradise (Sukhavati). He is the object of devotion of many sects in China and Japan.[36] Other important figures are Manjushri, who is identified with wisdom. He was important in China in medieval times but was replaced to a large extent by Amitabha, although he maintains some importance in Central Asia and Tibet;[37] and Avalokiteshvara (the Regarder of the Cries of the World) who is important as a personification of mercy in China (Kuan-yin, usually represented as a female figure; see p. 450).

Some religious groups are immune to millennialist expectation since they believe that they already have access to divine guidance. His Highness Prince Karim, Aga Khan IV, is the 49th in the line of Isma'ili Imams. He was born in 1937 and became Imam in 1957, in succession to his grandfather. Isma'ilis believe that he is divinely guided.

There are however, some religious groups that are inherently unlikely to be susceptible to millennialist influence. These are, in particular, those who feel that they are already in direct receipt of divine or other-worldly guidance from their leader. Such groups have therefore no need of the advent of a saviour figure to restore the ideal situation of having an infallible source of guidance. The Aga-Khani Isma'ilis are a group of Shi'i Muslims who believe that their leaders, the successive Aga Khans, are living Imams, in direct receipt of divine guidance. This is distinct from the majority Twelver Shi'i position, which maintains that the Imam is in hiding and will reappear one day as the Mahdi. Similarly, Tibetan Buddhists believe the successive Dalai Lamas to be the incarnation of the *bodhisattva* Avalokiteshvara (called Chenresi in Tibetan).

Hinduism has a tradition of a saviour to come, the Kalki Avatar. This figure plays an important part in the popular religion in India. One unexplained phenomenon is that no major millenarian movements or apocalyptic sects appear to have emerged in that country.[38] However, some degree of millennial thought can be found in India. There are, for example, the statements by Swami Vivekananda concerning the 'deep dismal night' that has befallen the land of India. He clearly indicates that he considers that this is the prelude to the appearance of an avatar whom he identifies with Ramakrishna, without, however, naming the latter as the Kalki Avatar.[39]

Eschatology and the New Religious Movements

Many of the large number of new religious movements that have arisen in the last one hundred years have a strong millennialist element in them. They treat eschatology in two distinctive ways. One group of these new religions proclaims the nearness of the 'eschaton' (the coming of the expected messianic figure). They admonish people to prepare themselves for this, and even suggest that those who become members of their sect will be among 'the elect' who will be saved. In Christianity, examples include the Jehovah's Witnesses, the Seventh Day Adventists and the more recent Children of God. Many of those who demonstrated in Iran in 1978 for the return of Ayatollah Khomeini were certain that his return was in some way linked to the return of the Imam Mahdi.[40] A common slogan chanted in the years after the Revolution was: 'O God! Preserve our leader [Khomeini] until the coming of the Imam [Mahdi].' There were also such groups among Buddhists in China and Burma in the nineteenth century, anticipating the advent of the Maitreya Buddha.[41]

The second group, on the other hand, considers that the 'eschaton' has already arrived and that we are living 'in the last days' as prophesied. These claim that the founder of their religion is a fulfilment of prophecy and that a new age has dawned. The Church of Jesus Christ of the Latter-Day Saints (the Mormons) has features of such a group. In Islam, the Ahmadiyya claim that their founder, Ghulam-Ahmad, was the Mahdi. Among Chinese Buddhists in the eighteenth and nineteenth centuries similar groups arose, the founders of which claimed that they were the incarnations of Maitreya Buddha.[42]

Among the second group, the Baha'i Faith is perhaps the most interesting, in that it claims that the similarity between the eschatological accounts in the different religions is no accident. It claims that its founder, Baha'u'llah, is in fact the fulfilment of all the eschatological prophecies of all the religions – the 'Promised Day' has come for all religions, the prophetic cycle has ended. This involves a pre-millennialist (catastrophic) expectation, in the Baha'i scriptures, of an overturning of the present world order, although Baha'is are forbidden to act so as to bring about its downfall. There is also a post-millennialist (progressive) tendency in the fact that the Baha'is see themselves as working to build the new order ('the Kingdom of God on earth'). In addition, there is an eschatological expectation projected into the distant future. Baha'u'llah writes of a 'Manifestation of God' at some future time at least one thousand years from the date of his own ministry (see p. 251).

Disconfirmed Prophecy

Not infrequently, leaders of movements of the here/now type set an exact date for the advent of the promised saviour or for the end of the world.

Sociologists and psychologists have been particularly interested in what happens when the appointed time comes and these prophecies fail to be fulfilled.

There are many historical examples of disconfirmed prophecies. Montanus was a second-century Christian who summoned the people to a site near modern Ankara, in Turkey, where he said that the return of Christ would occur. The failure of his prophecy did not cause the religion to die out, but rather revitalized and transformed it into a religion of the élite, who believed themselves to be directly guided by the Holy Spirit. Another example occurred in nineteenth-century America, where William Miller predicted that the return of Christ would occur in 1843–4. When the first date did not lead to the expected event, a second date was set, and there was renewed fervour. It was only when a third and fourth date also failed that the followers of Miller began to be disillusioned and fall away.

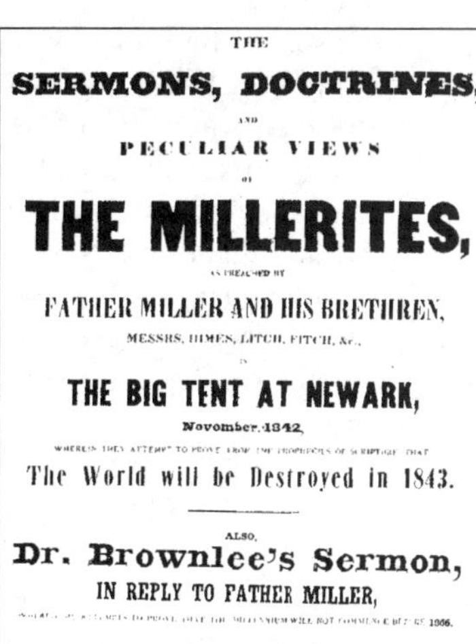

Poster advertising a Millerite meeting. William Miller (1782–1849) began in 1831 to preach that Christ would return to earth in 1843. When this did not occur, he revised the date to 1844. After the 'Great Disappointment' of 1844, some of Miller's followers founded the Seventh Day Adventist Church.

As well as these historical examples of disconfirmed prophecies, there are a few studies by sociologists of contemporary groups where prophecy has failed. The classical study is that of Leon Festinger, who described a group centred on a Mrs Keech, who had prophesied, on the basis of a communication from another planet, that there would be a cataclysmic flood across North America on a particular date. When the flood did not happen, Mrs Keech announced that God had saved the country because of the faith of the small band of disciples gathered around her. Those of her followers that were gathered around her that night received this announcement with great enthusiasm and began proselytizing again. Most of those who were not present fell away from their belief.[43]

A psychological analysis of such episodes identifies the problem as being one of cognitive dissonance: two things are believed by an individual or group that are contradictory to each other. Human beings, generally, try to live in a psychological world that is cognitively consistent (where everything 'makes sense'). When a person has a firm religious conviction, which has been publically announced, for which sacrifices have been made, and where the conviction is socially supported within a tightly knit group, then there is a strong resistance to changing that religious conviction. When a religious conviction, such as a prophecy, is disconfirmed, cognitive dissonance occurs. For a number (especially those who are isolated from the main group and thus not supported socially) the dissonance may be resolved by a loss of belief, but the rest employ a number of strategies to reduce this cognitive dissonance. The first is a rationalizing reinterpretation of the event so as to make it 'make sense'. The announcement that God had saved the country from the prophesied flood because of the faith of Mrs Keech's followers is an example of such a rationalization.[44] The second is an enthusiastic reaffirmation of the faith and even a campaign of proselytization in order to 'drown out' and diminish the effect of the cognitive dissonance by reinforcing the element in the cognitive dissonance that is least able to change.[45]

Causes of Millennialist Movements

Regarding the types of future saviour, it is the confrontationist type of pre-millennialism or catastrophic millennialism that tends to cause the greatest and most evident social impact. It is not surprising, therefore, that it is this group that has been studied most, by social scientists at least. Much work has gone into postulating why such movements arise. Most such explanations tend towards a reduction to economic and social factors. A typical explanation would run somewhat along the following lines:[46]

1. A group within a society perceives itself to be disadvantaged economically or disenfranchised politically. This group has values and aspirations but it finds itself in a position in which it has no realistic chance of fulfilling those aspirations; no chance of social redemption, as it were. A typical example would be a native population that finds itself economically, politically and culturally overwhelmed by the superiority of a colonial power. Alternatively, natural disasters, economic dislocation or the pressures of modernity may induce a sense of social crisis.
2. There is discontent and alienation in the group but no clear idea about how to rectify the situation, since direct political action is barred (by the overwhelming superiority of the colonial power, for example). In this state of affairs, the group falls back on its traditional sources for meaning, for an explanation of its situation. These traditional sources by themselves, however, give no clear guidance.[47] The traditional categories of understanding are unable to make the situation intelligible because the religious culture of the group, at least as traditionally interpreted, did not envisage it. The only way of interpreting this bleak predicament is in terms of the dark situation that will occur for humanity just before the expected coming of the saviour.
3. Then, there arises a prophet or teacher who is able to reinterpret the traditions in order to give meaning to the new situation. He can recreate the traditions in a way that gives them a new life in the new situation. He can extract guidance from them. This person thus acts to create a

bridge between the old and the new. He claims to be either the expected saviour or his representative. The usual pattern will be for the leader to insist at first on an excessively rigid adherence to the religious law. He may then, at a later stage, move into an antinomian phase in which the law is dispensed with.

4. An enthusiastic group gathers around the new teacher and eagerly accepts everything that he says. His teaching seems to present a possible way out of a seemingly hopeless situation. He has created a new world for them to live in, a 'new Jerusalem', a promise of a more fulfilled life.
5. The new teachings will, however, usually have revolutionary implications for society. And so the new teacher is opposed, especially by those groups who have the most to lose by the overthrow of the status quo. These usually include, at the very least, the leaders of the established religion. Conflict and even violence may arise. There is sometimes an element of migration involved. The leader takes his faithful followers to a new land where they can set up the new world, free of the entanglements and stultifying structures of the old order.
6. If the new leader is successful in overcoming, enduring or side-stepping the opposition (by migration, for example) and can mould his following into an organized group, a new sect will have emerged.

Such sociological explanations are attractive but they can only be partial, for not every disadvantaged or disenfranchised group throws up a millennialist movement. Indeed, we may ask whether there has ever been a society in which some element does not feel relatively disadvantaged economically or politically; and yet millennialist movements are not that common. Other factors must also be at work. Moreover, many such reductionist evaluations may be shown to be very subjective. One person may describe a millennialist movement in materialistic terms as the result of greed and envy causing the poor and dispossessed to revolt so as to gain a share in the wealth of society, while another may describe the same movement in moral terms, as a struggle to bring about a more just and equitable society.

Despite the unsatisfactory nature of much of the theory that surrounds this phenomenon, millennialism in each of its forms is of great importance to the study of religion because, whether at the level of the individual or at the level of society, millennialist activity is one of the keys to understanding how radical religious change occurs. Change is the principal result of millennialism: personal change in the form of moral regeneration or religious rededication; and societal change in the form of an effort to bring about an amelioration of social conditions. Through studying millennialist movements we can see how a traditional religious worldview can be overturned and a new vision can take its place, a 'new heaven and a new earth'.

Most of the founders of the world religions, Jesus, Muhammad, the Buddha, would in the early stages of their careers have been considered to be millennialist leaders (see also chapter 12 in which the lives of these figures are reviewed). Their 'new teachings', their vision of a new order, was what attracted a following to them and gave the early stages of these religions their vigour and vitality. But the magnitude of the change involved when a previous worldview is overthrown and a new one takes its place should not be underestimated. It is very great indeed – after all, the Soviet and Eastern European governments tried to bring about exactly such a change in the worldview of their citizens for a number of decades, with all the power and resources of a modern state behind them, all to very little avail. And yet a Buddha or a Muhammad showed that just such a change was possible. Millennialism is thus one of the factors, if not the most important factor, in bringing about religious change.

Finally, we must look at the point raised at the beginning of this chapter. Why is it that the idea of a future saviour is so universal? And why is it that the accounts of the end of the age, the coming of the saviour, and the Golden Age that he will usher in, are all so very similar across such widely diverse religions? There are no universally acceptable answers to this question. There are, however, several proffered explanations. First, a sociological explanation would maintain that the millenarian movements are the result of certain social stresses within a society. Second, Jung and Eliade suggest a psychological explanation: the hero-saviour is an archetypal figure who, according to Jung, is seated deep within humanity's collective unconscious (see chapter 11). And so, in a sense, it is almost inevitable that the figure of a future saviour will emerge within each religious tradition in the same way that, given the right circumstances, an oak tree will emerge from an acorn, because it is, potentially, within it, from the start. Third, a religious explanation found in a few religious movements such as the Ahmadiyya in Islam and the Baha'i Faith is that the traditions of these differing religions are so very similar because they are in fact referring forward to the same event and the same person, the coming of the founder of the movement.

Further Reading

Most of the books on this subject deal with millennialism and eschatology from the viewpoint of only one religion. See collections of essays in Thrupp, *Millennial Dreams in Action*, and Brandon, *The Saviour God* (not all the essays in the latter are relevant). Individual works include: for Buddhist millennialism: Sponberg and Hardacre, *Maitreya, The Future Buddha*, Chan, 'The White Lotus-Maitreya Doctrine'; Mendelsohn, 'A Messianic Buddhist Association'; Overmyer, *Folk Buddhist Religion*; Tai, *Millenarianism and Peasant Politics in Vietnam*. For Jewish and Christian millennialism see: Cohn, *The Pursuit of the Millennium*; Hanson, *The*

Dawn of Apocalyptic; Barkun, *Crucible of the Millennium*. For Islamic millennialism see: Sachedina, *Islamic Messianism*; Watt, 'The Muslim Yearning for a Saviour'. Burridge, *New Heaven, New Earth*, and Adas, *Prophets of Rebellion*, however, do attempt an analysis across several cultures, although dealing mainly with apocalyptic and millennialist cults among tribal peoples, the first from an anthropological and the second from a social historian's perspective. A theoretical analysis is attempted in Shepperson, 'The Comparative Study of Millenarian Movements'.

11

ARCHETYPE, MYTH AND THE SACRED

THE SACRED AND RELIGIOUS stands in contradistinction to the profane and secular.[1] It makes its appearance in the world in many varied ways. Indeed, it has been said that almost anything can and has in some culture been considered as sacred. This chapter looks at the ways in which the sacred appears in the world – how archetypes and myths generate a sense of the holy or sacred, thus influencing the development of religious symbols, rituals, traditions and institutions. We shall also see that archetypes and myths have had a powerful influence on religious history.

One methodology, among the many that can be employed in trying to understanding the sacred, is the mythological approach employed by such scholars as Carl Jung, Mircea Eliade and Joseph Campbell. This is based on the understanding that, if one studies the common themes in the different mythologies of the world, one can find the basic rhythms by which all human beings live. Myth explores the deepest inner questions and problems that have troubled humankind. Among the commonest themes uncovered by such studies are those which relate closely to religion: for example, the themes of creation, transformation, death and resurrection.

We must define several terms at this point, because some words are used here not in their usual conversational sense but rather in a specialized, technical sense. Anthropologists have found that there are some figures and concepts that occur almost universally among human beings. One explanation is that this indicates that such concepts must have roots going back to the earliest days of the human race and thus be part of the structure of human thought.[2] They are therefore called archetypes; examples include the sky god or the earth mother.[3] A myth is an archetype in narrative form; for example, a creation myth may tell of how the world came into being through the action of the sky god.[4] A symbol is something which brings to mind or recalls an archetype or a sacred mythological event. The term 'legend', or a legendary accretion to the basic facts of the history of a religion, refers to a straightforward exaggeration and glorification in the course of the retelling of a story.

Some Religious Archetypes and Myths

Mircea Eliade has written of a constant interrelationship, a dialectical movement, between the universal archetype and its local, particular manifestation. The archetype is constantly becoming manifest in a new local object or event. Conversely, each local manifestation of the sacred is constantly in the process of disengaging itself from its historical and parochial setting and moving towards identity with its timeless, universal archetype. Eliade speaks of the

> tendency of every 'historical form' to approximate as nearly as possible to its archetype, even when it has been realised at a secondary or insignificant level: this can be verified everywhere in the religious history of humanity. Any local goddess tends to become *the* Great Goddess; any village anywhere *is* the 'Centre of the World'.[5]

a

b c

Sacred tree: a) A sacred tree in Buryatia, Siberia, hung with ribbons and pieces of paper on which people have written their wishes. The sacredness of this tree probably dates back to the shamanist, pre-Buddhist past of this area. b) and c) Shrines created after the death of Princess Diana, 1997, around trees outside Kensington Palace, her London residence. They recreate in concrete form the ancient myth that 'human life must be completely lived out if it is to exhaust all its potentialities of creation and expression; if it is interrupted suddenly, by violent death, it will tend to extend itself in some other form: plant, fruit, flower'. (Eliade, *Patterns in Comparative Religion*, pp. 301–2).

The Supreme Being as Sun God or Sky God

Across the world, many, if not most, tribal peoples have a notion of a Supreme Being. In some places, this is a sky god, in others a sun god, these two being, in general human experience, the ultimate symbols of transcendence and omnipotence. Anthropologists have, however, found among tribal peoples that there is a tendency for the Supreme Being not to be the focus of worship and rituals. It is as though this deity is too austere and remote. It is replaced in the affections of people by the more immediate and down-to-earth concerns represented by fertility, vegetation and suchlike gods as well as by ancestor worship, animism, charms, amulets and so on.[6]

There is evidence in the *Bible* that the God of the Hebrews was originally conceptualized as a sky god.[7] However, the Jews appear to have been no exception to this desire for a more immediate, pragmatic

THE SKY GOD AS SUPREME DEITY

The absence of cult – and above all the absence of any calendar of seasonal rites – is characteristic of most of the sky gods . . .

. . . with most of the African peoples: the Great God of Heaven, the Supreme Being, Creator omnipotent, plays a quite insignificant part in the religious life of the tribe. He is too distant or too good to need worship properly so called, and they invoke him only in cases of extreme need . . .

The Hereros, a Bantu people from South-West Africa, call their supreme god Ndyambi. Withdrawn into the sky, he has abandoned mankind to the lower divinities. For that reason he is not adored. 'Why should we sacrifice to him?' said a native. 'We do not need to fear him, for he does not do us any harm, as do the spirits of our dead (*ovakuru*).' (Eliade, *Patterns in Comparative Religion*, pp. 46–8)

god to worship. We see in the *Bible* the constant struggle between Yahweh and the fertility and vegetation gods and goddesses of Canaan, such as Baal and Astarte (Ashtoreth).[8] We can even perhaps see something of this tendency in the emphasis given to invocation and worship of Mary (as the expression of the fertility goddess) and other saints, particularly those associated with people's immediate concerns – health, safety, the productivity of their labours and so on – in the Roman Catholic Church.

The Solar Hero

There are strong parallels between the received biographies of the prophet-founders of the great religions and a number of archetypal and mythic figures. In particular, one finds the archetype of the vegetation god and the sun god, or, more particularly, the solar hero, the manifestation of the sun god on earth.[9] This archetype relates to the cycle of the sun and the associated cycle of agricultural fertility.

The myth of the solar hero typically begins with a Golden Age. Then the affairs of the solar hero and his family or nation go into decline; he appears to be defeated and even to die (as does the sun and the fertility of the earth in winter). At this point, the hero is separated from his people. In some versions, he descends into an underworld where he struggles against the forces of darkness. He wins a great victory and acquires the means for saving humanity. And so, just when everything seems hopeless and the world is full of darkness and the earth barren, the hero returns to 'save' the world. He brings a new era of justice and hope, a new order; a new Golden Age dawns (as the sun returns in spring and revives the fertility of the earth).[10] This basic pattern of story is so powerful that we can see it retold in countless legends and stories from every part of the world. As examples one might cite, among the myths of antiquity, the Babylonian and Sumerian god Tammuz and the Egyptian god Osiris who undergo death and resurrection;[11] among folk legends, the repeated pattern of the heroes in

DECLINE PHASE OF THE SOLAR HERO: Depiction of a scene from the *Ramayana* showing the banishment of Rama, accompanied by his wife, Sita, and his half-brother, Lakshmana, from the court of his father, King Dasharatha, after the scheming of the latter's second wife in favour of her own son, Bharat. This scene marks the low point (note the eclipsed sun) in the story of the solar hero. Painting by Chaitu (early nineteenth century).

Iranian epic literature;[12] even the westerns, spy thrillers and crime stories on films and television reflect these themes. In most of these stories the hero at first appears overwhelmed by the forces of evil and a catastrophe looms, but eventually he triumphs, emerging to defeat his enemies.[13]

The theme of the sun god or vegetation god exists in religions not only in their conceptualization of the past but also in their expectations of the future. We can see the figure of the promised saviour who will come at the end of time to banish all evil, institute justice, and renew the earth (see chapter 10) as an expression of this archetype.

Religious history cannot escape from the strong tendency to recast it in these archetypal forms. Indeed, the more important the story to the followers of the religion, the stronger will be the impulse to recast it into mythic form. The story of Christ, overwhelmed and crucified by the forces of darkness, eventually to rise from the dead, resembles the myth of Tammuz, the Babylonian vegetation god.[14] Similarly, in India we find that the legends of both Krishna and Rama, two avatars (incarnations, manifestations) of the god Vishnu, replay this theme. The central figure is overwhelmed by the forces of evil and is forced to retire to the woods in

The Founder of a Religion as Supernal Sun and Universal Ruler

The followers of most religions have seen the founder of their religion as the source of spiritual light. It is not surprising therefore that they have identified him with the sun, the source of physical light, and with certain solar deities that preceded the religion. The life of the founder is frequently seen to parallel that of the solar hero. Similarly he is frequently depicted as the Universal Ruler.

This traditional form of icon is known as Christ Pantocrator (Christ the Univeral Sovereign). It represents Christ as Lord and Judge of the world. His right hand is raised in blessing while in the left he holds the scripture, the Word of God. This form is derived from the ancient Greek pose of the bearded philsopher with the right hand in the teaching gesture and the left hand holding a book, denoting knowledge and wisdom. The solar imagery can be seen in the rays emanating from the image. From the Kariye Museum, Istanbul.

The Buddha depicted as an aniconic symbol. This symbol can be seen as representing the Wheel of Dharma (*dharma chakra*) but also as the Supernal Sun. Over the circular symbol is the umbrella (*chatra*) which depicts the Chakravartin (Universal Ruler).

This representation of the Supernal Sun motif is placed over the door of the shrine of Baha'u'llah near Akka. In the centre of the motif are the words: *Ya Baha'u'l-Abha* (O Glory of the Most Glorious).

Portrait of Zoroaster with clear solar symbolism – such depictions of Zoroaster are comparatively modern, dating in all probability from about 200 years ago in India. They are much influenced by the traditional *bhakti* Indian portraits, such as those of Krishna.

In Islamic art, images are forbidden, since any image might become a focus for worship and hence introduce idolatry. The Divine cannot be compared to anything at all. Even with the limitations imposed by this prohibition, however, symbols can convey spiritual truths. In the centre of this piece of calligraphy are the words: 'Muhammad, the friend of God'. Intertwined around it are the words: 'There is no god but God' and 'No distinction do we make between any of His Apostles' (*Qur'an* 2:285). Then there are two further concentric circles, in the outer of which are the names of prophets mentioned in the *Qur'an* and in the inner, the designations which have been traditionally applied to them in Islam (e.g. Jesus, the Spirit of God; Moses, the Interlocutor with God). The outer ring is the repetitive inscription of 'There is no god but God'. The four circles in each corner contain the names of the four archangels. The top line has the Tradition: 'He who says "There is no god but God" enters Paradise' and two short phrases. The bottom line reads: 'O people! Verily we have created you male and female and made you into peoples and tribes in order that you may know each other. Verily, the greatest of you in honour is the most God-fearing of you. In truth, God is the All-Knowing the All-Informed.' (*Qur'an* 49:14) The whole can be thought of as representing the solar motif with rays emanating from the name of Muhammad.

disguise. Eventually, however, he returns with his companions, triumphs over his enemies and re-establishes the rule of justice over the land. The story of the Buddha recounts his separation from humanity as he sat under the Bo tree, his struggle with Mara, his subsequent enlightenment and his

DEATH AND RESURRECTION

Among the Sumerian–Babylonian gods were Tammuz (Damuzi), the vegetation god, and Ishtar (Innini), the mother-goddess associated with the planet Venus. Tammuz died and, according to one version of the myth, Ishtar was the sister and lover of Tammuz who caused his death. Distraught at his death, Ishtar descended into the underworld where she challenged her sister, Ereshkigal, who ruled there. She had to undergo many trials in the underworld (and according to one version of the legend, another god had to be despatched to rescue her), but eventually she succeeded and returned to the world with Tammuz.

In another version of the myth, Ishtar was Tammuz's mother who wept profusely at his death. In any case, the myth of Ishtar and Tammuz spread widely through the Middle East, coalescing with other local myths. In this way it reappeared as the myths of Beltis and Marduk in Assyria, of Aphrodite and Adonis in Phoenicia, of Isis and Osiris in Egypt and of Cybele and Attis in Greece.

a

b

c

d

THE POSTURES OF THE BUDDHA AND THEIR SIGNIFICANCE: Pictures and statues of the Buddha (and of Indian gods and goddesses) adopt typical postures, each of which has a particular significance. The word *mudra* refers to these postures and more particularly to the hand gesture. These are four of the most common postures of the Buddha. a) *Dhyani mudra* (gesture of meditation). This shows the Buddha in meditation. Sometimes there is a multi-headed snake over and behind the figure of the Buddha. This snake protected the Buddha during his meditations prior to achieving enlightenment. b) *Bhumisparsha mudra* (calling the earth to witness posture). This is a posture recalling the occasion when Mara the demon attacked the Buddha as he was meditating under the Bo tree. Mara cast doubt on the Buddha's qualification for Buddhahood, whereupon the Buddha touched the earth, calling upon it as witness for the deeds of the Buddha in past lives. c) *Varada mudra* (calling heaven to witness gesture). This is a gesture of granting wishes. d) *Dharma-chakra mudra* (turning the wheel of Dharma gesture). This is a gesture of teaching the Dharma, recalling in particular the Buddha's first sermon after his enlightenment.

eventual coming forth into the world to teach his message. This is very similar to the story of Christ's going out into the wilderness, his struggle there with Satan who tempted him, his victory over Satan and his return to the people to begin to teach his message. Some more detailed examples of myth operating in religious history are given later in this chapter (see also chapter 12).

It is not only in religious history that we see this pattern of the solar hero repeated. It also forms the basis of much religious ritual (see below).

The Lord of the Two Worlds

Myths portray in story form the fundamental theological and spiritual truths of a religion. Among the important spiritual truths that need to be conveyed about the founder of a religion is that he is the lord of both the physical and the spiritual worlds. It is not surprising, therefore, to find that myths grow about the founders of religions to indicate their mastery over both worlds. One example in Christianity would be the story of the transfiguration, which happened towards the end of Christ's ministry. In this episode, Jesus, who to outward seeming was just a poor, illiterate, itinerant preacher, stood revealed to his disciples in his true stature as the Divine Lord. 'And he was transfigured before them, and his face shone like the sun, and his garments became white as light.' The prophets Moses and Elijah appeared to the disciples and a voice from the cloud said, 'This is my beloved Son, with whom I am well pleased; listen to him.'[15]

In the *Bhagavad Gita*, Krishna who is acting as Arjuna's charioteer, is transfigured and appears before Arjuna as the Lord of the Universe.

> When the great Lord of Yoga [Krishna] had spoken thus, he revealed to Arjuna his divine universal form. Arjuna saw him with many mouths, and many eyes and many wondrous other sights, with many celestial ornaments, and many heavenly weapons. He wore celestial garlands and garments, was anointed with heavenly perfumes. He faced all sides, wonderful, resplendent, all-pervading. If the light of a thousand suns were to arise in the sky, that would be like the effulgences of that Mighty Lord. In that form, Arjuna saw the whole universe, with its many divisions, all gathered into one form at one time.[16]

The episode of the Prophet Muhammad's Night Journey and Ascent to Heaven serves a similar function for Muslims, although there were no direct witnesses of this event. It took place during one of the darkest periods of Muhammad's ministry. At that time, when it seemed that all had turned against him and were victorious against him, God gave him a vision of the power that was his. He was carried, one night, miraculously from Mecca to the Masjid al-Aqsa (the furthest mosque, Jerusalem). From there, he ascended to heaven, where he met with all of the prophets of the past and saw both heaven and hell. Travelling further heavenwards, he came in close proximity to God, to that point beyond which there is no passing.[17]

Litta Madonna by Leonardo Da Vinci, in which Mary is depicted as symbol of maternity and fertility.

The Female Archetype

Most religions have developed an archetypal female figure, for example the Virgin Mary in Christianity or Fatima in Shi'i Islam, who represents the Earth Mother archetype. This figure epitomizes the female ideal in the religion. She gives birth to the male aspect of the religion (Christ in Christianity and the line of Imams in Shi'i Islam) and typifies the qualities of nurturing and loving. (See chapter 17.)

The fertility of the female is also closely connected in the mythological mind with the fertility of the earth. In the *Qur'an*, we read: 'Your wives are as a field to be tilled for you; so come to your tillage as you please' (2:223). In Hindu mythology, the rain god, Parjanya, induces fertility in both the fields and women. Although a male, he has udders full of milk (the rain). The *Rig Veda* states that the 'mother [i.e. Earth] receives the milk of the father [Parjanya] . . . and with it the son [creatures of the earth] thrives'.[18] Similarly, the Hindu text, the *Laws of Manu*, states: 'By the sacred tradition the woman is declared to be the soil; the man is declared to be the seed; the production of all corporeal beings [takes place] through the union of soil and seed.'[19]

THE FEMALE ARCHETYPE

CHRISTIANITY: THE VIRGIN MARY

Hail Mary, full of grace. The Lord is with thee. Blessed art thou amongst women, and blessed is the fruit of thy womb, Jesus. Holy Mary, Mother of God, pray for us sinners, now and at the hour of our death. Amen. (Roman Catholic prayer based on *Luke* 1:28)

CELTIC RELIGION: THE TRIPLE MOTHER GODDESSES

Triplism [is] a basic phenomenon of Celtic religion . . . The mother-goddess is perhaps the commonest type of Celtic divinity treated in this way and the triadic form appears to have played an important role in her worship and cult-expression.

The three mothers or *Deae Matres*, as they are frequently called in inscriptions, were known also as *Matronae* . . .

It is quite clear from the attributes of the Mothers that they represent primarily fertility and general prosperity, whether in the directly maternal manner of infant-association or through portrayals of the earth's fecundity . . .

In nearly all cases the maternal rather than the sexual aspects of the female image are projected – indeed the goddess is invariably clothed – the sexual parts of the body are not emphasised. Instead, the images rely for their symbolic power on accompanying attributes including animals (a powerful fertility/nature symbol in

> themselves . . .) and, sometimes, on the power of triplism or plurality. Perhaps of most interest is that the cult appealed not only to women but to soldiers, merchants and even Roman officials. Essentially maternal characteristics were employed to visualise and worship a deity whose sphere developed from that of simple fertility to protection and well-being in all aspects of life. (M. Green, *The Gods of the Celts*, pp. 78, 82, 102)

Sacred Place and Sacred Time

A sacred place, a church, temple, shrine, or mosque, is not just a place where one has contact with God or Ultimate Reality, a fixed point of contact with reality in the orderless chaos of the profane world. Rather, by virtue of being the location of the sacred world, these are places where ordinary profane geography does not apply. No matter how remote and isolated, the sacred place becomes the centre of the universe, the place where heaven and earth meet, the focal point of origination of the cosmos. Sacred geography, being different to profane geography, allows for a multiplicity of places each to be the centre of the universe.[20]

The boundary of the sacred place is also of great significance. It marks off the sacred place from the profane world. In religious communities, this boundary marks the point at which different laws and rules apply. On the one hand, it signifies danger, for beyond this point human beings are in particular danger of offending the deity if they do not perform the rituals correctly and in a proper state of purity. On the other hand, it signifies safety, for many societies hold sacred places to be places of sanctuary where the temporal authorities have no power to act. Many churches, mosques and shrines were considered places of sanctuary until recently. Broadly speaking, the more important the shrine or church, the more serious the crime or offence for which one could seek sanctuary there. In recent times, we have witnessed the Golden Temple at Amritsar being used as a place of sanctuary by Sikh rebels. Even in a non-religious society such as Britain, there have been cases of people who were about to be expelled from the country seeking sanctuary in churches; although the concept of sanctuary has no legal standing, the police hesitated about acting against them.

Similar to sacred space is sacred time. The occurrence of an event of profound religious significance (for example, the crucifixion and resurrection of Christ or the martyrdom of the Imam Husayn) changes that period of time into sacred time. The significance of sacred time is that it forms an eternal ‘now’. The event can be endlessly recreated. This repetition can be lengthy, as occurs during Holy Week in every Christian church (or even more elaborately in the Passion Plays at Oberammagau) or the recitations of the events surrounding the martyrdom of the Imam

a

b

PILGRIMAGE: A sacred place usually becomes a centre of pilgrimage. These two pictures show two centres of pilgrimage, Jerusalem and Benares, which may be considered as forming a spiritual axis for the world, in that, between them, they contain major holy places for six religions. a) Benares (Varanasi)/Sarnath. Benares, on the banks of the Ganges, is the major holy place for Hinduism. On the left is a stupa built by King Ashoka at one of the four most holy places for Buddhists, the traditional site of the Buddha's first sermon at Sarnath (Isipatana) on the outskirts of Benares. On the right is the shrine of Parshvanatha, the 23rd Tirthankara (saint) of the Jains. b) Jerusalem, holy city for Jews, Christians and Muslims. This photograph shows the Western (Wailing) Wall (*Kotel Maaravi*), the remains of the second Temple, the holiest place for Jews. Behind is the dome of the Mosque of Omar (Dome of the Rock). Jerusalem is the third holiest city in the world for Muslims and this mosque marks the traditional site of Abraham's intended sacrifice of his son. Also in Jerusalem is the Church of the Holy Sepulchre, containing the traditional sites of the crucifixion and tomb of Jesus.

Husayn (*rawdih-khani*); or it may be fleeting, as when a Christian crosses himself or a Shi'i Muslim calls upon Husayn when in difficulty. In all these cases, an event that occurred many centuries ago in profane time is, once transformed into sacred time, ever in the present. It can be recalled and recreated by the believer in all or some of its intensity at any moment.

Sometimes the events translated into sacred time are from a definite point in profane time (for example the crucifixion of Christ or the enlightenment of the Buddha). In other cases, the event is located in sacred time by a phrase such as 'In the beginning . . .', which does not specify a particular location in profane time. These latter are usually myths about the origin of the world or the origin of humanity.

Religious Symbols

The religious symbol is a link to the world of the sacred, something physical which brings to mind that world. A cross for Christians or a lingam for Shaivite Hindus is looked at and even carried around because it can instantly create a link to the sacred. The cross recalls, for a Christian, Christ's suffering and crucifixion, and the resulting atonement and redemption. A person who looks at and is affected by the symbol is in immediate contact with the sacred; the spot on which he or she stands has been transformed into sacred place; and he or she has entered sacred time and there experienced death and resurrection (death to the profane world and rebirth into the sacred). Through the religious symbol, the human situation is translated into cosmological terms; the human being is put into contact with transcendent reality, the source of the cosmos. Hence, through frequent and intimate contact with religious symbols, humanity does not feel alone and isolated in the cosmos.

Ritual

To perform a ritual is to repeat the cosmic events portrayed in a myth. It puts human beings into the position of performing the actions of the divine. Such a human action, though it may appear trivial and inconsequential, is given profound significance and linked to the meaning of the universe itself. By partaking of the Eucharist, all Christians are present at the Last Supper

THE HAJJ, THE ISLAMIC RITUAL PILGRIMAGE TO MECCA: This picture shows the pilgrims gathered in the Masjid al-Haram (the Sacred Mosque). At the far end is the holiest site in the Islamic world, the Ka'ba, which is the square building covered in black cloth. According to Islamic tradition, the foundations for this building were laid by Abraham. It originally housed pagan idols, but Muhammad caused these to be destroyed, leaving just the Black Stone. The black cloth covering of the building is renewed each year.

with Christ, partaking of the bread of life and the wine of the spirit. By performing the Hajj (pilgrimage to Mecca), all Muslims are there with Muhammad during his pilgrimage, partaking of the salvation that was on offer when Muhammad was on earth. Many rituals are, in some sense, the re-enactment of the creation of the world, a death (return to primal chaos) followed by resurrection (the emergence of a new creation). The simple act of immersion in water (baptism in Christianity) becomes linked to spiritual renewal, to God's purpose for the world, to life, death and resurrection. Through ritual, human beings escape from chronological time and enter 'sacred time'. The individual experiencing baptism, the Eucharist, or the Hajj has stepped out of the profane world of 'becoming' and into the eternal now of the sacred world of 'being'. That individual is escaping from fragmentation and alienation and reintegrating his or her life within the framework of the universe.

The religious person tries to spend as much time as possible re-enacting mythical models. What human beings do on their own initiative without a mythic model belongs to the profane world and is therefore a vain and illusory activity; it is ultimately unreal. What they do following a mythic model belongs to the sacred world and is therefore significant and real. The more religious a person is, the more mythical, paradigmatic models there are to follow, and the more the whole of his or her life becomes, in this sense, a ritual.[21] (See also the description of ritual on pp. 104–5.)

The Stages of the Muslim Pilgrimage (Hajj)

The Hajj is performed during the eleventh Muslim lunar month (Dhu'l-Hijjah). All pilgrims should time their journey to arrive in Mecca before the 8th of this month, as that is the first formal day of the pilgrimage. On the last stage of the journey as they approach Mecca, there is a point at which the pilgrims take off their normal clothes, put on two pieces of plain cloth called the *ihram* and recite a ritual prayer called the *talbiyyah*. This marks the formal start of their pilgrimage and from this point on there are certain things forbidden to the pilgrims such as swearing, wearing perfume and sexual intercourse. Most pilgrims arrive in Mecca a few days before the beginning of the Hajj, which enables them to carry out the minor pilgrimage, the 'Umrah (which may also be done at any other time of the year). For this, they wear the *ihram*, perform their ablutions, often at the Sacred Mosque (Masjid al-Haram) of Mecca, kiss the Black Stone that is set in the Ka'ba (the square building in the centre of the mosque), circumambulate the Ka'ba seven times, and perform the *sa'y* (going back and forth seven times between the market-places of Safa and Marveh in Mecca in commemoraton of Hajar's desperate search for water after being left by Abraham).

On the first day of the Hajj itself (8 Dhu'l-Hijjah), the pilgrims put on the *ihram*, recite the *talbiyyah* and go to Mina, to the east of Mecca, where they say prayers and stay the night.

On the second day, the pilgrims go to Arafah and spend the day there in prayer and supplication (this activity is called *wuquf*). At sunset they proceed from Arafah to the place where they will spend the night, Muzdalifah, which is on the way back to Mina. Here they collect stones for the next day.

The climax of the Hajj occurs on the third day (10 Dhu'l-Hijjah). Just after sunrise the pilgrims go on to Mina where they cast seven stones at one of three pillars called Jamrah (the activity is call *rami* and symbolizes Abraham's rejection of the temptations of the devil). Each pilgrim then sacrifices an animal (sheep, goats and cattle are the commonest animals) in memory of Abraham's intended sacrifice of his son. This day is called 'Id al-Adha (the festival of sacrifice) and is commemorated throughout the Muslim world.

This marks the end of the formal pilgrimage and the pilgrims shave or clip their hair, pare their nails and take off the *ihram*. Custom dictates, however, that pilgrims remain in the area of Mecca for a further three days. During these three days, they circumambulate the Ka'ba seven times, perform the *sa'y*, throw seven stones, this time at each of the three pillars in Mina, and drink the water of the well of Zamzam. Many pilgrims then go on to Medina, where they visit the Mosque of the Prophet.

Rites of Passage

Perhaps the most enduring of all aspects of religion are the rites of passage (rites commemorating the passing from one phase of life to another, most notably birth, adolescence, marriage and death). Even in the secularized societies of Europe, people who never go to church under any other circumstances continue to feel a need to mark these significant events in their lives by a religious ceremony.

Scholars who have studied rites of passage have noted the similarity between these rites, the recurrent pattern of dying to one mode of existence and being reborn in another, and the phases of the solar hero myth (see pp. 270–5):

1. A STAGE OF SEPARATION. This marks the separation of the participants from the profane world and their entry into the sacred. This corresponds to the stage in the story of the solar hero of separation from the common world (often by death or a forced exile) and the descent into the supernatural world.
2. THE STAGE OF TRANSITION OR LIMINALITY. Victor Turner has emphasized this phase as the critical phase in which there is a change. If only one individual is involved that person is changed; if there is a group of participants, they are bonded together and a sense of community is

a

b

c

d

FUNERAL RITES: a) Corpse on a platform, Papua New Guinea; b) Cremation rites, French Guiana; c) Jewish funeral rites: Since there is a prohibition on deriving any benefit from the dead in Jewish Holy Law, Jewish communities have formed communal burial societies (*Hevrah Kadisha*). This picture shows such a society making a shroud, Prague, c. 1780; d) Nineteenth-century picture depicting the transport of corpses by Shi'i Muslims, sometimes for long distances, so that they can be buried at the shrine of one of the Imams. The favourite site is the shrine of the Imam Husayn in Karbala because it is believed that the Hidden Imam Mahdi will appear there shortly before the Day of Resurrection.

A RITE OF PASSAGE: THE INVESTITURE OF AN AFRICAN CHIEF

The investiture of the senior chief (Kanongesha) among the Ndembu of northwest Zambia illustrates the three stages of a rite of passage – in this case passage from being an ordinary person to being a chief:

The liminal component of such rites begins with the construction of a small shelter of leaves about a mile away from the capital village. This hut is known as *kafu* or *kafwi*, a term Ndembu derive from *ku-fwa*, 'to die,' for it is here that the chief-elect dies from his commoner state. Imagery of death abounds in Ndembu liminality . . . The chief-elect, clad in nothing but a ragged waist-cloth, and a ritual wife, who is either his senior wife (*mwadyi*) or a slave woman, known as *lukanu* (after the royal bracelet) for the occasion, similarly clad, are called by Kafwana [a senior headman of an associated tribe] to enter the *kafu* shelter just after sundown . . . The couple are led there as though they were infirm. There they sit crouched in a posture of shame (*nsonyi*) or modesty, while they are washed with medicines . . .

Next begins the rite of *Kumukindyila*, which means literally 'to speak evil or insulting words against him'; we might call this rite 'The Reviling of the Chief-Elect.' It begins when Kafwana makes a cut on the underside of the chief's left arm . . . presses medicine into the incision, and presses a mat on the upper side of the arm. The chief and his wife are then forced rather roughly to sit on the mat . . . Kafwana now breaks into a homily, as follows:

> Be silent! You are a mean and selfish fool, one who is bad-tempered! You do not love your fellows, you are only angry with them! Meanness and theft are all you have! Yet here we have called you and we say that you must succeed to the chieftainship. Put away meanness, put aside anger, give up adulterous intercourse, give them up immediately! . . .

After this harangue, any person who considers that he has been wronged by the chief-elect in the past is entitled to revile him and most fully express his resentment, going into as much detail as he desires. The chief-elect, during all this, has to sit silently with downcast head, 'the pattern of all patience' and humility . . . Many informants have told me that 'a chief's just like a slave (*ndung'u*) on the night before he succeeds.'

The phase of reaggregation in this case comprises the public installation of the Kanongesha with all pomp and ceremony . . . [W]hen the Ndembu chief-elect emerges from seclusion, one of his subchiefs – who plays a priestly role at the installation rites – makes a ritual fence around the new chief's dwelling, and prays as follows to the shades of former chiefs, before the people who have assembled to witness the installation:

> Listen, all you people. Kanongesha has come to be born into the chieftainship today . . . I have enthroned you, O chief. You O people must give forth sounds of praise. The chieftainship has appeared.

(Turner, *The Ritual Process*, pp. 100–1, 102, 105)

established. This corresponds to the stage in the story of the solar hero of his descent into the world of darkness, his struggle there, and the eventual victory.

3. A STAGE OF EMERGENCE OR REAGGREGATION. In this stage, the transition is completed, the participants emerge and are reincorporated into the community in their changed status. This corresponds to the return of the solar hero with the power to transform his society.[22]

A Christian grave in Tonga, South Pacific. Elaborate and lengthy ceremonies are held at the graveside and the grave itself is much embellished and ornamented.

There are many examples of rites of passage demonstrating, to varying extents, this threefold pattern. They occur in the major world religions and also among various tribal peoples. Birth rites often involve some separation of the woman before the birth, various ceremonial acts during labour and, often, something done to the infant to mark him or her as a member of the community (circumcision, for example). Rites of puberty among tribal peoples will often include some separation of the young people, a trial or ordeal and then a ceremony in which they are welcomed as full members of the community (see p. 49). Elements of this pattern can be seen in the Jewish bar mitzvah, the Hindu *upanayana* ceremonies and even in the Christian rite of confirmation. In many tribal cultures restrictions apply to the girls and women during menstruation, and rituals are conducted afterwards to restore them to a state of ritual purity. Marriage customs in many societies involve a period of separation of the bride and groom, a ceremony, and then an emergence of the couple into the community in their new state. The rites surrounding death are the most elaborate of all in many societies. Often the spouse or elder son will spend some time separated from society until the rites are completed when they rejoin the community.

Most societies also have rites associated with certain events in the calendar such as sowing or harvest, with sickness, or to commemorate important religious events. Many of these also have a symbolism of death and rebirth – especially the rites associated with the agricultural cycle.

THE FUNCTION OF MYTH AND SYMBOL

To retell a myth brings about an irruption of the sacred world into the profane. It answers the questions of how and why things are the way they are and it helps human beings to come into contact with the reality behind the world. It should not be imagined, however, that the pattern is one of a

SEASONAL AGRICULTURAL RITUALS AMONG TRIBAL PEOPLES IN INDIA

Sowing takes place in the first week of June after the monsoon. On an auspicious day, fixed by the priest, the sowing takes place. Early in the morning on that day, the male Koya Dora goes to the field with a basket filled with Jonna seeds, and also the articles of worship including a fowl. First, with the help of the priest, the Koya Dora worships the hill deity (Kodama Devata) and breaks a coconut and sprinkles the coconut water over the field. Next he offers a fowl to the deity and the blood of the sacrificed victim is allowed to drip in the field and also on the seeds. By performing this ritual, the Koya Doras believe that the hill deity would protect the crop from various types of infectious diseases. The sacrificed victim is thrown towards the hill side. After the ritual is over, the men sow the seeds both on the hill slopes and also on the plains. The same ceremony is repeated for the sowing in different seasons.

The only taboo with regard to this sowing is that the male is not permitted to attend the ceremony or work on the field, if his wife is in mensus or confinement. (Murthy, *Religion and Society*, p. 113)

flow of profane time with periodic interruptions of sacred time. Rather the two can be said to be in parallel, with profane time flowing in a stream and sacred time an eternal, ever-present 'now'. It is human beings who dart backwards and forwards between the two. Therefore, although I have described a ritual as being a repetition of a cosmic event, in fact there is no separation between the two in sacred time – the ritual *is* the cosmic event. It is not that the bread and wine of the Eucharist represent the body and blood of Christ (or even that they repeat symbolically Christ's turning of the bread and wine into his body and blood), but rather they *are* the body and blood of Christ. The participant in the ritual is present at the Last Supper.

Every myth is, in one sense, creative, because it creates a new world and becomes a paradigm for all time.[23] Thus, for example, the story of Adam and Eve, because it is a myth about the first man and woman, becomes a paradigm for every man and woman. Through the telling and retelling of myth, every action that a human being takes can become the repetition of the actions of the gods and thus become an occurrence in sacred time. In this way, all human actions can become in some sense a repetition of a myth or archetype and the total life of a human being can be transformed out of the meaninglessness of profane time into sacred time, out of history and into a 'paradise' where every action is filled with meaning and significance.[24] In this way, bit by bit, the whole profane world can be rebuilt as the sacred world by the retelling of various myths. And in this sense, those telling these myths and those hearing them are present at and participating in the creation of the cosmos.

Thus, religious experience in its various forms consists of a breaking down of space and time so that every individual can be at that placeless place, the centre of the universe, in that timeless time, before the world began, and may there experience, through ritual, the creation of the world. This experience is variously called resurrection, salvation, or liberation. This is how the central experience of religion (see chapter 4) can be conceptualized and spoken about in mythological terms.

Religious symbols and myths do not follow the paths of rational thought. They are not linked in ways that necessarily make any logical sense, for myths and symbols reveal new perspectives and integrate diverse realities that appear to have no connection in the world of the rational mind. The symbol of the moon can connect several disparate strands: day and night in nature, death and resurrection, creation and destruction, the potential and the actual, and so on. All the members of a given community will share a similar interpretation of their symbols and myths. There is no need for verbal explanation or discussion of these symbols because they are an inherent part of the culture. They are not formally taught but rather imbibed non-verbally by the children of that culture as they grow.

Myth and Religious History

It is a natural and inseparable part of piety to wish to glorify and magnify the object of one's adoration. Therefore it is not surprising that every religion has witnessed to some extent the creation of myths and legends around its central figures. In the telling and retelling of the stories surrounding them, some degree of exaggerated praise and glorification was bound to slip in. The longer the stories were perpetuated by word of mouth rather than in written form, the more mythic and legendary elements crept into them through the natural piety of the storytellers.

The Resurrection of Christ

In religious histories we see the trend referred to above, whereby the story of a religiously significant individual has, over the centuries, been given archetypal form. The exact stages of this transformation are usually impossible to detect because they have been obliterated. The believer considers the mythological history to be the 'real' history and therefore there is no need to retain earlier versions. Careful research by scholars can, however, reveal this process in some cases. Two examples will now be considered. Both are taken from Christian history, not because Christianity has been in any way more liable to mythic transformation of its history, but rather because it has been subject to more intensive scholarly scrutiny.

As mentioned above, the traditional story of the death and resurrection of Christ is a typical enactment of the sun god myth. Through the efforts of biblical scholars, it is now possible to reconstruct its evolution from a historical event to a mythic recasting of that event.

Depiction of the resurrection of Christ. An eleventh-century mosaic from the monastery of Hosios Loukas, near Livadia, Greece.

Jesus was crucified in about the year 33 CE. The earliest references to the resurrection occur in the Pauline letters. The first epistle of Paul to the Corinthians, for example, is probably a genuine letter from Paul written in about 55–6 CE. In the most extensive reference to the crucifixion in this work (15:4–9), there is no mention of an empty tomb or a physical resurrection. St Paul lists several occasions on which Christ has appeared to various of his disciples after his crucifixion, including Christ's appearance to Paul himself. Since this appearance to Paul, on the road to Damascus (*Acts* 9:1–7), occurred after the episode of the Ascension and is clearly a visionary event, it would appear that Paul understood the other appearances of Christ in the same way. Nowhere in the Pauline letters, which are the earliest Christian documents that we have, is there any reference to an empty tomb. These early Christians appear to have been testifying to a spiritual meeting with Christ as a living salvific force in their lives, not to the historical event of a physical resurrection. We can trace the development of the resurrection myth over the next century in the canonical and apocryphal Gospels.[25]

1. PAULINE LETTERS (35–55 CE). These testify to the experience of a living Christ; the testimony appears to be a creedal formula referring to a metaphorical (although existentially real) event rather than an empirical, historical one.

> For I delivered to you as of first importance what I also received, that Christ died for our sins in accordance with the scriptures, that he was

> buried, that he was raised on the third day in accordance with the scriptures, and that he appeared to Cephas, then to the twelve. Then he appeared to more than five hundred brethren at one time, most of whom are still alive, though some have fallen asleep. Then he appeared to James, then to all the apostles. Last of all, as to one untimely born, he appeared also to me.[26]

2. St Mark's Gospel 16:1–8 (70 ce). Three women enter the tomb. A young man in a white robe tells them that Jesus is not here but has risen. The women flee, full of fear, and tell no one. (Most scholars agree that the authentic *Gospel of St Mark* ends at this point).

> And when the sabbath was past, Mary Magdalene, and Mary the mother of James, and Salome, bought spices, so that they might go and anoint him. And very early on the first day of the week they went to the tomb when the sun had risen. And they were saying to one another, 'Who will roll away the stone for us from the door of the tomb?' And looking up, they saw that the stone rolled back – it was very large. And entering the tomb, they saw a young man sitting on the right side, dressed in a white robe; and they were amazed. And he said to them, 'Do not be amazed; you seek Jesus of Nazareth, who was crucified. He has risen, he is not here: see the place where they laid him. But go, tell his disciples and Peter that he is going before you to Galilee: there you will see him, as he told you.' And they went out, and fled from the tomb; for trembling and astonishment had come upon them; and they said nothing to anyone, for they were afraid.[27]

3. St Matthew's Gospel 28:1–20 (75–90 ce). Two women come to the tomb. An angel descends from heaven, rolls back the stone and declares that Jesus is not there but has risen. They depart in fear and joy and run to give the news to the disciples. Jesus appears to the disciples twice, but some have doubts.

> Now after the sabbath, toward the dawn of the first day of the week, Mary Magdalene and the other Mary went to see the sepulchre. And, behold, there was a great earthquake; for an angel of the Lord descended from heaven and came and rolled back the stone, and sat upon it. His appearance was like lightning, and his raiment white as snow. And for fear of him the guards trembled and became like dead men. But the angel said to the women, 'Do not be afraid; for I know that you seek Jesus who was crucified. He is not here; for he has risen, as he said. Come, see the place where he lay. Then go quickly and tell his disciples that he has risen from the dead, and, behold, he is going before you into Galilee; there you will see him. Lo, I have told you.' So they departed quickly from the tomb with fear and great joy, and ran to tell his disciples. And behold, Jesus met them and said, 'Hail!' And they came up and took hold of his feet and worshipped him . . .

Now the eleven disciples went to Galilee, to the mountain to which Jesus had directed them. And when they saw him they worshipped him; but some doubted.[28]

4. St Luke's Gospel 24:1–53 (80–90 CE). Several women come to the tomb and find the stone rolled back. Two men in shining garments tell them that Jesus is not here but has risen. They leave and tell this to the other disciples, who do not believe them, but Peter runs to the tomb and also finds it empty.[29] Jesus appears to the disciples on two occasions and reproves them for their doubts.

But on the first day of the week, at early dawn, they went to the tomb, taking the spices which they had prepared. And they found the stone rolled away from the tomb, but when they went in they did not find the body. While they perplexed about this, behold, two men stood by them in dazzling apparel; and as they were frightened and bowed down their faces to the ground, the men said to them, 'Why do you seek the living among the dead? Remember how he told you while he was still in Galilee, that the Son of man must be delivered into the hands of sinful men, and be crucified, and the third day rise.' And they remembered his words, and returning from the tomb, they told all this to the eleven, and to all the rest. Now it was Mary Magdalene and Joanna and Mary the mother of James, and the other women with them who told this to the apostles; but these words seemed to them in idle tale, and they did not believe them.

That very day two of them were going to a village called Emmaus . . . While they were talking . . . Jesus himself drew near and went with them. But their eyes were kept from recognising him . . . When he was at table with them, he took the bread and blessed, and broke it, and gave to them. And their eyes opened and they recognised him; and he vanished out of their sight . . .

And they rose up that same hour and returned to Jerusalem; and they found the eleven gathered together, and those who were with them . . Then they told what had happened on the road . . . As they were saying this, Jesus himself stood among them. But they were startled and frightened, and supposed that they saw a spirit. And he said to them, 'Why are you troubled . . . See my hands and my feet, that it is I myself; handle me, and see; for a spirit has not flesh and bones, as you see that I have' . . .

Then he led them out as far as to Bethany, and lifting up his hands, he blessed them. While he blessed them, he parted from them, and carried up into heaven.[30]

5. St John's Gospel 20:1–25 (100–50 CE). Mary Magdalene comes to the tomb and, finding the stone already rolled back, goes and fetches Peter and John. Two angels appear to Mary. Jesus appears to the disciples twice in a locked room and gives firm evidence to the doubting Thomas. Jesus appears to the disciples in Tiberias as well.

Now on the first day of the week Mary Magdalene came to the tomb early, while it was still dark, and saw that the stone had been taken away from the tomb. So she ran, and went to Simon Peter and the other disciple, the one whom Jesus loved, and said to them, 'They have taken the Lord out of the tomb, and we do not know where they have laid them.'

Peter then came out with the other disciple, and they went toward the tomb . . . and stooping to look in . . . saw the linen clothes lying there . . . and believed. For as yet they knew not the scripture, that he must rise again from the dead. Then the disciples went away again unto their own home.

But Mary stood weeping outside the tomb, and as she wept, she stooped to look into the tomb; and she saw two angels in white, sitting where the body of Jesus had lain . . . They said to her, 'Woman, why are you weeping?' She said to them, 'Because they have taken away my Lord, and I do not know where they have laid him.' Saying this, she turned round and saw Jesus standing, but she did not know that it was Jesus. Jesus said to her, 'Woman, why are you weeping? Whom do you seek?' Supposing him to be the gardener, she said, 'Sir, if you have carried him away, tell me where you have laid him . . .' Jesus said to her, 'Mary.' She turned and said to him in Hebrew, 'Rab-bo'ni' (which means Teacher) . . .

On the evening of that day . . . the doors being shut where the disciples were, for fear of the Jews, Jesus came and stood among them . . .

Eight days later, his disciples were again in the house, and Thomas was with them. The doors were shut, but Jesus came and stood among them . . .

After this Jesus revealed himself again to the disciples by the Sea of Tiberias.[31]

6. THE APOCRYPHAL GOSPEL OF PETER (150 CE). This Gospel goes much further than the earlier accounts and describes the resurrection event itself. Two gigantic angelic figures, with heads that reach the heavens, come down to the tomb and return with a gigantic Jesus.

And early in the morning as the Sabbath dawned, there came a multitude from Jerusalem and the region roundabout to see the sepulchre that had been sealed. Now in the night whereon the Lord's day dawned, as the soldiers were keeping guard two by two in every watch, there came a great sound in the heaven, and they saw the heavens opened and two men descend thence, shining with (lit. having) a great light, and drawing near unto the sepulchre. And that stone which had been set on the door rolled away of itself and went back to the side, and the sepulchre was opened and both of the young men entered in. When therefore those soldiers saw that, they waked up the centurion and the elders (for they also were there keeping watch); and while they were yet telling them the things which they had seen, they saw again three men come out of the sepulchre, and two of them sustaining the other (lit. the one), and a cross following, after them.

> And of the two they saw that their heads reached unto heaven, but of him that was led by them that it overpassed the heavens. And they heard a voice out of the heavens saying: Hast thou (or Thou hast) preached unto them that sleep? And an answer was heard from the cross, saying: Yea.[32]

Thus the resurrection story developed over the period of about one hundred years, from the early disciples testifying to their faith in the continuing, living spiritual presence of Jesus, to a story of an empty tomb as evidence for a living Jesus, to an actual description of a resurrection of Jesus from the dead. We must, of course, view all of this in the context of the religious milieu of the Mediterranean world. As the earliest Christians took their religion out into the wider world during the first hundred years after Christ's crucifixion, they came into contact with Greek, Roman and Egyptian religions. These included many myths of gods and other legendary figures such as Attis, Osiris and Orpheus who died, descended to the underworld and returned in triumph. By casting the story of Christ in this way, the Christians were able to attract the adherents of the many mystery cults and gnostic sects that abounded in Roman Europe. Thus there were strong influences, both external (in terms of competing religions) and internal (the inner compulsion to turn a personal experience into a universal myth), on the early Christians. These influences constrained them to recast their faith in Jesus as a living saviour into a myth of death and resurrection. This process of turning faith into myth is one that can be seen to pervade the whole religious world.

The Growth of the Cult of Mary

A second example of the growth of a myth can be given, again from Christian history: the development of the cultic status of Mary, the mother of Jesus.[33] The earliest *New Testament* materials that we have are the letters of St Paul. In these, there is no mention of the virgin birth and no direct naming of Mary. There is only a passing reference to the fact that Jesus was 'born of woman'.[34]

The next oldest reference to Mary occurs in *St Mark's Gospel* (about 70 CE). This account is even more surprising. It appears to show Jesus acting in a disrespectful and disparaging manner towards Mary in order to demonstrate a point to his followers. Mary and Jesus' brothers came to where Jesus was preaching and sent for him. When they told Jesus that his mother and brothers were seeking him, he replied: 'Who are my mother and my brothers?' And then, indicating his followers gathered around him, he said: 'Here are my mother and my brothers!'[35] This passage may even indicate that Mary was not a believer in Christ, at least at this point. There is no other reference to Mary in this, the earliest of the four Gospels, nor is there any reference to a virgin birth.

It is only when we come to the next Gospels to be written, *Matthew* and *Luke*,[36] that we find the origins of the story of the virgin birth. It is clear that

Depiction of the Annunciation, the announcement to Mary by the Angel Gabriel that she was to be the mother of Jesus. Painting by Piero della Francesca (c. 1420–92).

the main concern of the author of the *Gospel of St Matthew* (75–90 CE) was to present Jesus as the fulfilment of *Old Testament* prophecies. Many have, therefore, postulated that the story of the virgin birth originates in the desire to see Christ as the fulfilment of the prophecy in *Isaiah*: 'Behold a virgin (or young woman)[37] shall conceive and bear a son.'[38] The *Gospel of St Luke* (80–90 CE) provides the basis of the later growth of the cult of the Virgin Mary in its descriptions of the Annunciation and the Visitation, but it is only when we come to the apocryphal texts of the second century CE that we have stories that form the basis for the later Church doctrines of the Immaculate Conception (the doctrine that Mary herself was conceived free of original sin) and Mary's Assumption into heaven.

In the Roman Catholic Church, the adoration of Mary has grown with the passing of time. A number of doctrines that exalt Mary have become official church dogma over the course of the centuries. Of these, only that of divine motherhood, the doctrine that Mary was the mother of Jesus, has unequivocal backing in the *New Testament*. Her perpetual virginity (a doctrine made official in 649 CE) is put in doubt by questions over the translation of the word 'virgin'[39] and by references to Jesus' brothers and sisters.[40] The canonical *New Testament* does not refer at all to the Immaculate Conception (made official Catholic dogma in 1854) and the Assumption (made official dogma in 1950).

We may postulate a number of reasons for the growth of the cult of the Virgin Mary. This has gone from mere passing references to Mary in the earliest Christian documents to the present situation where popular devotion to Mary in some places matches the devotion shown towards Christ. During the first two centuries when these canonical and apocryphal accounts were being written, the Church was venturing into the Graeco-Roman world. In that world, there were several gods and heroes (like Apollo, Bacchus and Perseus) who had human mothers who had been impregnated by gods. This may have influenced the thinking of the earliest Christians, thrusting Mary more and more into the limelight as the agent of the miraculous birth. In later years, the virgin birth became a key concept in the disputes over the nature of Christ. The position which triumphed in this debate used the virgin birth to depict graphically the dual nature of Christ, and, in the process, increased the importance of Mary. But probably the most powerful influence of all has been the less obvious but much deeper need for an archetypal female figure who exemplifies all the female virtues: pure and virginal, yet at the same time representing motherhood in all its perfection (both as the mother of Christ and as the mother of the

Church). In iconography, Mary is also represented as Bride and Queen.[41] Feminist writers have pointed out the impossible ideal that this combination of virginity and ideal motherhood sets for Christian women.

The Creation and Functioning of Myth in Religious History

FATIMA AS VIRGIN: Fatima was the daughter of the prophet Muhammad and wife of the first Shi'i Imam, 'Ali. A reference to Fatima as 'the Virgin' appears in the third line of the top column of this Arabic Shi'i poem in praise of the Imams. Calligraphy in Nasta'liq style by Dawud, Iran, seventeenth century.

The doctrine of the perpetual virginity of Mary reveals an important point about the way that myths come into being and the function that they serve. It is paralleled by the Shi'i Islamic notion of Fatima as virgin (although this does not have the same high profile that Mary's virginity has in Christianity) and by many examples in other religions.[42] The rationalist historian may protest that these statements are a gross violation of the empirical historical facts. Mary was clearly not a perpetual virgin since, no matter what may have occurred at the conception of Jesus, she is reported to have had other children after Jesus. Similarly, Fatima, as the mother of Imams Hasan and Husayn, was clearly not a virgin. What we have here is a local symbol straining to become its universal archetype. It is not empirical events that determine the archetype but rather, for the religious person, the archetype that reveals the way to interpret and 'see' the empirical event. The archetype is the reality of the local symbol. The facts are the empirical history, the archetype is the higher truth, the meta-history. Thus, regardless of their physical status, Mary and Fatima are in a spiritual state of perpetual virginity. That is their true reality. Those who insist on bringing up the empirical facts of their having borne children are not so much wrong as, from the viewpoint of the religious person, missing the point. To use the terminology of Wittgenstein, the empirical historian and the religious person are playing different 'language-games'.

One can say, then, that rather than these histories being a factual account of what occurred, as a camera would have recorded it, they tend towards being theological statements. In other words, Mary's and Fatima's virginity is not so much a factual as a theological statement. A figure such as Christ or the Imam Husayn (Fatima's son) could only be born of a womb that was spotlessly pure and immaculate. Virginity is a symbol of such purity. In this context, the factual history is not relevant. In the same way, the many stories of the miraculous deeds of the founder-prophets of the world religions when they were infants and children should be seen as theological statements. They are a way of saying that this was no ordinary child.[43]

Eliade makes it clear that he does not regard this process of the mythologization of religious history as a process of falsification or distortion of historical fact. Rather, it should be seen as uncovering the spiritual or archetypal reality, in the realm of 'sacred place' and 'sacred time', of the physical events on earth. Since the process of mythologization carries the story back to its archetype, it is closer to the truth than any bare historical account in 'profane time'. It reveals a deeper level of reality. On this analysis, the perpetual virginity of Mary and Fatima is a 'higher', 'more real' truth than the empirical, historical fact that they bore children. Indeed, the obsession with reconstructing empirical history that characterizes the modern Western mind, is somewhat puzzling for people from traditional cultures.

One important point to note is that only events occurring in sacred time had importance for most pre-modern people and were therefore transmitted from one generation to the next. And so, many stories that were transmitted were not 'history' as we now understand that term but rather myth – events occurring in sacred time, events occurring according to archetypal patterns. For pre-modern peoples, it is much more important to know and understand the significance of what happened than to know its exact date and details. This is the reason that it is difficult to reconstruct the empirical history of most religions – the empirical facts have not been preserved because they were not deemed important. Questions that intrigue Western scholars, for example whether the stories about Jesus or Krishna actually occurred, are not of any interest to people from a traditional culture; it is the world that is evoked in the imagination, the reality that is revealed in the story, that is important, not its historicity.

It should be borne in mind that sacred history frequently gives several different archetypal patterns for action. Which one of these is taken up by an individual who is inspired by these stories will depend to a certain extent on social conditions. The female archetype of virginity and motherhood, described above, largely reinforces the patriarchal social pattern (docile women staying at home, providing sex for husbands and rearing children). This is not, however, the only female archetype on offer. Sacred history also contains examples of women who have stood up and proclaimed what was right when the men around them have failed to do so. Examples of such women of courage include Draupadi in the Hindu epic, the *Mahabharata,* who stood up and challenged the elders of Hastinapur when they had allowed shameful scenes to occur at the court; Fatima in the history of Shi'i Islam, who stood up and made a public appeal when the people of Medina had gathered around the house of her husband 'Ali and were threatening him (see p. 443); Fatima's daughter, Zaynab, who, having seen most of her family killed and herself taken captive, stood erect before the governor of Kufa and Caliph Yazid and put them to shame; and Tahirih, in Babi and Baha'i history, who stood up at a conference of the Babis without her veil and proclaimed the dawn of a new day and the abrogation of the Islamic dispensation. Such archetypal patterns which run counter to the prevailing social norms can be activated when exceptional conditions prevail. The example of Zaynab was frequently invoked by Shi'i women in Iran during the 1979 Revolution. Paradoxically, the example of her counterpart, Tahirih, was invoked by the Baha'i women of Iran who were suffering persecution and even execution during and after the same revolution.

There are many other examples of alternative archetypes being available within a religion. In Shi'i Islam, the prevailing archetype is of the Imams who meekly and patiently endured persecution and martyrdom at the hands of their enemies. During the Iranian Revolution of 1979, the alternative paradigm of the third Imam, Husayn, who rose up against his enemies and fought them, was invoked by the revolutionary mobs on the streets. Sometimes alternative archetypes exist within the same holy figure. Jesus is usually represented as meek and forgiving of humanity's sins. Yet those who wish to play a more socially active role can model themselves on the Jesus who stood up against injustice and overturned the tables of the money-lenders in the Temple.

The examples of the resurrection of Christ and the cult of the Virgin Mary given above have been taken from the history of Christianity. The same twin processes (the accretion of legendary details due to pious elaboration and the more subtle and hidden tendency to recast history into powerful mythic modes) have been at work in the history of other religions also. However, less scholarship has been devoted to unravelling these threads. We can only suggest in outline what has occurred. Many scholars, for example, consider the figure of Krishna in Hinduism to be a non-historical myth. Others, however, looking at the earliest accounts of the life of Krishna, consider that he may well have been a historical figure who took part in a dynastic dispute as outlined in the early books such as the *Mahabharata*. The story of this figure was then elaborated and probably also merged with other legends, until the more fully elaborated versions of the story appear in later books. One can trace a series of more and more elaborate renderings of the story: from the *Mahabharata* (written between the third century BCE and the third century CE), to the *Vishnu Purana* (fifth century CE), to the *Bhagavata Purana* (ninth century CE).[44] Each succeeding version includes more and more miraculous and fabulous material. The birth and early years of Krishna's life become filled with events that prove his superhuman character. His later years become replete with incidents of fighting and defeating great monsters and fiendish enemies. The number of his wives multiplies rapidly, reaching the figure of 16,000 in the *Bhagavata Purana*.[45]

Myth and Modernity

One of the features of the modern world is the manner in which the advances in our knowledge of the cosmos have swept away the meaning of much mythical material. The traditional cosmos of Western religion, for example, had the earth situated between heaven above and hell below. This mythological structure has little meaning for a world that has seen the planet earth as photographed by an orbiting satellite. Religion has been one of the main victims of this shattering of myth. The scriptures of the different religions are expressed in mythological pictures that were valid for the time when these scriptures came into being, but which no longer seem valid. Some Christians in modern times have tried to respond to this challenge. In particular, Rudolf Bultmann (1884–1976) proposed a programme of 'demythologization' or reinterpretation of the myths of Christianity in order to make them relevant to the present.

Modernity has tried to demythologize life and remove humanity from the realm of sacred time. However, writers such as Jung and Campbell who focus on the significance of myth and archetype stress that, ultimately, such endeavours could only be partly successful. Myths can be debased and degraded, at great psychological cost to humankind, but they cannot be uprooted. All that happens is that modern myths and rituals replace the traditional ones, for myths and archetypes are an inherent part of the human psyche. Human beings appear to need a religious underpinning both to their personal and to their social lives. At the personal level, human beings need a mythology within which to frame their identities and the meaning of their lives. At the social level, some ideology is needed to give people a vision of their history, their present place in the world and their future direction, to act as a focal point of unity, an agreed framework for public policy and a justification for the public rituals that affirm social cohesion. Where formal religion no longer provides this underpinning, various alternatives have evolved. At the social level, 'pseudo-religions' such as Marxism and nationalism have been successful partly because they do provide an alternative picture – a myth of history and a direction for the future. (See pp. 411, 480–1 and, on the role of civil religion, pp. 425–6.)

At the personal level, a wide variety of alternatives have evolved. For many, religion has been replaced by belief in such things as astrology, the occult, ghosts, and UFOs. Furthermore, if one identifies a religious activity as one which involves commitment, a mythology and rituals, then many activities of people in the West have become endowed with 'implicit religion'.[46] Some psychotherapy groups and self-help organizations such as Alcoholics Anonymous run in close parallel to the way that a religious group would function (they have their doctrines, their taboos, their priestly leaders and, often, ritual elements). For a much larger group of people, following football teams, pop groups and giving adulation to film stars have these elements of implicit religion. They involve a commitment to and a 'deification' of the object of adulation. Both individually at home and when groups of fans come together, rituals often evolve which have meaning and significance and create small pockets of 'sacred time'. What goes on at a pop concert can be compared to the spirit possession that is a feature of many religions.[47]

In the modern world, men and women still act out their lives by trying to walk in the footsteps of mythological gods; but these gods are now film stars, rock idols and sports heroes. Mythic images and patterns still form the basis of people's actions and self-images, but these are now created in the film and television studios of Hollywood, London and Bombay, rather than by religion.[48]

Further Reading

The most important author in the area of the phenomenology of the sacred is Mircea Eliade; see, for example, his *Patterns in Comparative Religion*. A good guide to the thought of Eliade may be found in Dudley, *Religion on Trial*. The theoretical foundation for the importance of archetypes was laid by Jung; see his *Psychology and Religion*. See also Campbell, *The Mask of the Gods* (on mythology in general) and his *The Hero with a Thousand Faces* (on the solar hero) and Turner, *The Ritual Process* (on rites and liminality). The best-known Christian writer who has looked at the question of myth in Christian scripture has been Rudolf Bultmann (see *Kerygma and Myth*); see also Hick, *The Myth of God Incarnate*.

IV

Religion in Society

12

Comparative Religious History

Most of the world religions either have origins lost in antiquity or began more recently as heterodox sects within older religious traditions. For this latter, newer type of religion, I shall, in this chapter, attempt to outline some features of its development from its origins until it emerged from its 'parent' tradition to become an independent religion.

Although the histories of the various religions have taken very different courses and, because they appeared at such widely varying places and times, they have shown markedly different features, there are some commom themes. (See also the timeline on pp. 302.)

Depiction of Krishna and Radha (his playmate and lover who was a cow-girl), playing with a yoyo. In Vaishnavite *bhakti* Hinduism, the theme of the love between these two is an allegory for the love of the individual soul for God. Pahari minature, nineteenth century.

The Founders of the Religions

The history of the world's religions is usually linked to a prophet-founder figure who holds a pivotal position in the religion. In the newer religions, the identity of the central figure is in little doubt. In Christianity, Islam, and Buddhism, the founder's identity – Jesus, Muhammad, and the Buddha respectively – is clear. The Baha'i Faith had two founders, the Bab and Baha'u'llah, of whom the latter is the more important. In some religions, however, particularly the older religions, the central figure is not so clear-cut. Judaism, the oldest religion in the Western theistic tradition, has a string of major prophets going back over several thousand years: Noah, Abraham, Moses, as well as many minor prophets. However, of these, Moses, as the bearer of the Law from God, has a special place. Hinduism, the oldest of the Indian religions, has scriptures going back more than three thousand years

Chronology of Religious Events in the Middle East and India

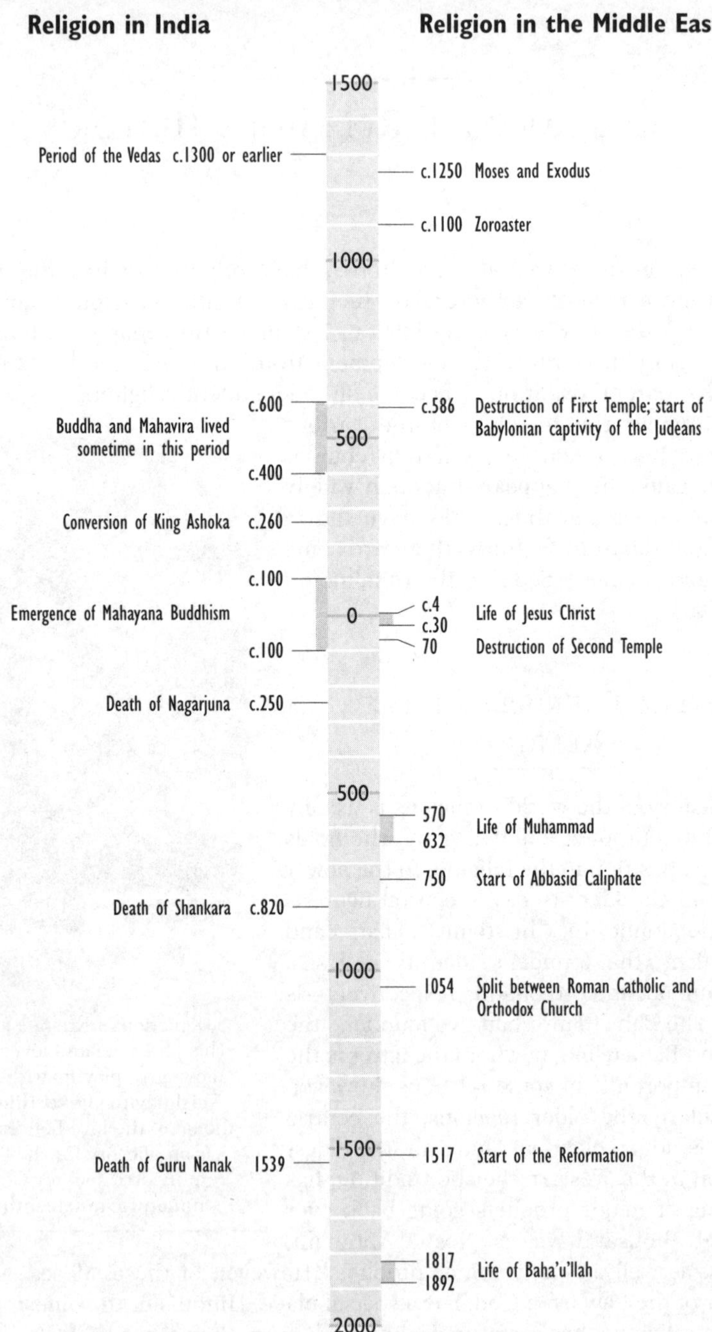
Religion in India
Religion in the Middle East
1500
Period of the Vedas c.1300 or earlier
c.1250 Moses and Exodus
c.1100 Zoroaster
1000
c.600
Buddha and Mahavira lived sometime in this period
c.400
c.586 Destruction of First Temple; start of Babylonian captivity of the Judeans
500
Conversion of King Ashoka c.260
c.100
Emergence of Mahayana Buddhism
c.100
0
c.4
c.30
Life of Jesus Christ
70 Destruction of Second Temple
Death of Nagarjuna c.250
500
570
632
Life of Muhammad
750 Start of Abbasid Caliphate
Death of Shankara c.820
1000
1054 Split between Roman Catholic and Orthodox Church
1500
Death of Guru Nanak 1539
1517 Start of the Reformation
1817
1892
Life of Baha'u'llah
2000

but the seers or sages who wrote these down are not venerated. In Vaishnavite Hinduism, however, there is the concept of a line of avatars – incarnations of the deity – who come to earth to restore righteousness.[1] It is probable that, behind the mass of myth and legend, some of these avatars were historical figures. The most recent of them is Krishna.[2] He is said to have given the teaching contained in the *Bhagavad Gita*, one of the most important and influential books in Hinduism.

A survey of the lives of the prophet-founders of these religions reveals several common themes and patterns. It is clearly easier to compare the lives of the prophets-founders of the more recent religions, rather than of such figures as Krishna who are shrouded in legend, and so it is on these more recent historical figures that I shall concentrate.[3]

These figures came from a wide variety of social backgrounds. The Buddha was a prince; Moses had a royal upbringing; Baha'u'llah was from a family of the nobility in Iran; Muhammad and the Bab were from merchant families; Jesus was from a humble artisan background. Even those who came from an elevated social background, however, at some stage in their

Greek Orthodox icon from Cyprus showing four scenes from the life of Christ: (from top left) birth, presentation at the temple, baptism by St John the Baptist (note the descent of the dove from heaven), and transfiguration (while the disciples were sleeping).

life lost their wealth and became one of the poor and despised of the world. The Buddha left his palace and wealth and became a wandering ascetic; Moses was forced to flee from a life of luxury in the Egyptian royal family; Baha'u'llah lost all of his inherited wealth when he joined the movement of the Bab, his predecessor.

Miraculous stories are related about the birth and childhood of each of these figures and here myth is impossible to avoid. Common features include some form of divine intervention in the process of conception, and the infant speaking from inside the womb or immediately after birth and possessing a miraculous degree of prescience and wisdom. It is easy to dismiss these stories as pious exaggeration and myth-making but that would be to miss the point. As discussed in chapter 11, what the authors of these stories were trying to create was not an empirical record – they were not trying to do the work that a video camera would do in our day; rather, it would be closer to the mark to think of them as making a theological statement, to establish that the birth of this child was no ordinary birth. It was the birth of a supra-mundane being. The only way to portray this was to describe the event as a supra-mundane one.[4] Since such points have already been discussed in chapter 11, I shall, in these accounts, ignore questions of the demarcation between history and myth as far as possible.

Despite these stories of birth and infant miracles, it would appear that these figures grow to adulthood leading ordinary lives. There is often a precursor, a holy figure who recognized the prophet-founder when the

a

b

THE RECEIPT OF REVELATION: a) Moses and the Burning Bush. Detail from a fresco at the Dura-Europos synagogue (third century, Syria). Some ancient synagogues appear to have had such depictions of human beings, later considered to be against the Jewish Holy Law (see *Exodus* 20:4, *Deuteronomy* 4:16–18). b) Muhammad receiving the revelation from the angel Gabriel. A miniature from a Turkish manuscript.

latter was only a child or who prophesied to the people that his advent was imminent. For the Buddha, the predecessor was the monk Asita (Kala Devala); for Jesus, it was John the Baptist; for Muhammad, there is the episode of Bahira, the Christian monk who recognized Muhammad's station when he was only eight years old; for the Bab, it was Shaykh Ahmad al-Ahsa'i and Sayyid Kazim Rashti, the leaders of the Shaykhi sect, which paved the way for the Bab; for Baha'u'llah, it was the Bab himself.

For each of these figures, there is one particularly significant event that appears to signal the start of his ministry. It is as though before this initiatory event, they were ordinary men and then they became religious giants. In the case of Moses, it was the episode of the burning bush; in the case of the Buddha, it was his enlightenment under the Bo tree; for Jesus, the descent of the Spirit of God in the form of a dove lighting upon him after his baptism by John; for Muhammad, it was the appearance to him of the Angel Gabriel on the side of Mount Hirra; for the Bab, it was a vision of the head of the Imam Husayn; in the case of Baha'u'llah, it was a Maid of Heaven who appeared before him when he lay in chains in a dungeon in Tehran. (See pp. 306–8.)

Most of these figures appear, following this initiatory experience, to have had doubts or to have felt the need for a period of solitude during which they prepared themselves for their mission. The Buddha struggled with Mara, the personification of evil, before his enlightenment. Afterwards, he spent days pondering whether to bring the truth that had come to him to the people of the world. Jesus spent forty days in the desert, during which he struggled with Satan. Muhammad had grave doubts about the nature of his vision and sought reassurance from his wife. Zoroaster is reported to have spent time in the wilderness. Baha'u'llah spent two years at the start of his ministry in the mountains of Sulaymaniyya, much of that time on his own.

The room in Shiraz in which the Bab declared his mission. This building was destroyed by the authorities shortly after the Islamic Revolution of 1979.

Following the initiatory event, these figures did not go out immediately and proclaim their mission to the world. Rather, they gathered around themselves a small group of disciples. Jesus gathered the twelve apostles; Muhammad collected around him a small group of followers, including Khadija, 'Ali, Abu Bakr, and 'Umar; the Buddha gathered his *bhikkus* (monks) around him and began to teach them; the Bab called the group of eighteen disciples that gathered around him the Letters of the Living; while Baha'u'llah is reported to have declared his mission to a small group of followers in the garden of Ridvan outside Baghdad. It was only at a later stage that these prophet-founders of new religions made a more public declaration of their missions by the start of their public preaching.

The relationship of these figures to the established

The Start of the Ministry

Each of the prophet-founders experiences a significant event which he regards as the start of his ministry.

Moses

Now Moses was keeping the flock of his father-in-law, Jethro, the priest of Midian; and he led his flock to the westside of the wilderness, and came to Horeb, the mountain of God. And the angel of the Lord appeared to him in a flame of fire out of the midst of a bush; and he looked, and lo, the bush was burning, yet it was not consumed. And Moses said, 'I will turn aside and see this great sight, why the bush is not burnt.' When the Lord saw that he turned aside to see, God called to him out of the bush, 'Moses, Moses!' And he said, 'Here am I.' Then he said, 'Do not come near; put off your shoes from your feet, for the place on which you are standing is holy ground.' And he said, 'I am the God of your father, the God of Abraham, the God of Issac, and the God of Jacob.' And Moses hid his face; for he was afraid to look at God. (*Exodus* 3:1–6)

The Buddha

At that time the blessed Buddha dwelt at Uruvela, on the bank of the river Nerangara, at the foot of the Bodhi tree (tree of wisdom), just after he had become Sambuddha. And the blessed Buddha sat cross-legged at the foot of the Bodhi tree uninterruptedly during seven days, enjoying the bliss of emancipation. Then the Blessed One (at the end of these seven days) during the first watch of the night fixed his mind upon the Chain of Causation, in direct and in reverse order: 'From Ignorance spring the samkharas, [etc. – see the Chain of Mutually Dependent Origination, *Pratitya-Samutpada*, p. 194] . . . Such is the cessation of this whole mass of suffering.' Knowing this the Blessed One then on that occasion pronounced this solemn utterance: 'When the real nature of things becomes clear to the ardent, meditating Brahmana, then all his doubts fade away, since he realises what is that nature and what its cause.'

Then the Blessed One during the middle watch of the night fixed his mind [upon the Chain of Causation] . . . Knowing this the Blessed One then on that occasion pronounced this solemn utterance: 'When the real nature of things becomes clear to the ardent, meditating Brahmana, then all his doubts fade away, since he has understood the cessation of causation.'

Then the Blessed One during the third watch of the night fixed his mind [upon the Chain of Causation]. Knowing this the Blessed One then on that occasion pronounced this solemn utterance: 'When the real nature of things becomes clear to the ardent, meditating Brahmana, he stands, dispelling the hosts of Mara, like the sun that illuminates the sky.'

Then the Blessed One, at the end of those seven days, arose from that state of meditation, and went from the foot of the Bodhi tree to the Agapala banyan tree . . . And when he had reached it, he sat cross-legged at the foot of the Agapala banyan tree uninterruptedly during seven days, enjoying the bliss of emancipation. (*Mahavagga*, in Rhys Davids and Oldenberg, *Vinaya Texts*, part 1, pp. 73–9)

JESUS

Then Jesus came from Galilee to the Jordan to John, to be baptized by him. John would have prevented him, saying, 'I need to be baptized by you, and do you come to me?' But Jesus answered him, 'Let it be so now; for thus it is fitting for us to fulfil all righteousness.' Then he consented. And when Jesus was baptized, he went up immediately from the water, and behold, the heavens were opened and he saw the Spirit of God descending like a dove, and alighting on him; and lo, a voice from heaven, saying, 'This is my beloved Son, with whom I am well pleased.' (*Matthew* 3:13–17)

MUHAMMAD

He [Gabriel] came to me . . . with a coverlet of brocade whereon was some writing, and said, 'Read!' I said, 'What shall I read?' he pressed me with it so tightly that I thought it was death; then he let me go and said, 'Read!' I said, 'What shall I read?' He pressed me with it again so that I thought it was death; then he let me go and said 'Read!' I said, 'What shall I read?' He pressed me with it the third time so that I thought it was death and said 'Read!' I said, 'What then shall I read!' – and this I said only to deliver myself from him, lest he should do the same to me again. He said:

> Read in the name of thy Lord who created, Who created man of blood coagulated. Read! Thy Lord is the most beneficent, Who taught by the pen, Taught that which they knew not unto men. [*Qur'an* 96:1–5]

So I read it, and he departed from me . . . Now none of God's creatures was more hateful to me than an (ecstatic) poet or a man possessed: I could not even look at them. I thought, Woe is me, poet or possessed – Never shall Quraysh say this of me! I will go to the top of the mountain and throw myself down that I may kill myself and gain rest. So I went forth to do so and then when I was midway on the mountain, I heard a voice from heaven saying, 'O Muhammad! thou art the apostle of God and I am Gabriel.' I raised my head towards heaven to see (who was speaking), and lo, Gabriel in the form of a man with feet astride the horizon, saying, 'O Muhammad! thou art the aspostle of God and I am Gabriel.' I stood gazing at him . . . then I began to turn my face away from him, but towards whatever region of the sky I looked, I saw him as before. (Ibn Ishaq, *Sirat Rasul Allah*, translated as Guillaume, *The Life of Muhammad*, pp. 106–7)

BAHA'U'LLAH

During the days I lay in the prison of Tihran, though the galling weight of the chains and the stench-filled air allowed Me but little sleep, still in those infrequent moments of slumber I felt as if something flowed from the crown of My head over My breast, even as a mighty torrent that precipitateth itself upon the earth from the summit of a lofty mountain. Every limb of My body would, as a result, be set afire. At such moments My tongue recited what no man could bear to hear . . .

While engulfed in tribulations I heard a most wondrous, a most sweet voice, calling above My head. Turning My face, I beheld a Maiden – the embodiment of the remembrance of the name of My Lord – suspended in the air before Me. So rejoiced was she in her very soul that her countenance shone with the ornament of the good-pleasure of God, and her cheeks glowed with the brightness of the All-Merciful. Betwixt earth and heaven she was raising a call which captivated the hearts and minds of men. She was imparting to both My inward and outer being tidings which rejoiced My soul, and the souls of God's honored servants. Pointing with her finger unto My head, she addressed all who are in heaven and all who are on earth, saying: 'By God! This is the Best-Beloved of the worlds, and yet ye comprehend not. This is the Beauty of God amongst you, and the power of His sovereignty within you, could ye but understand. This is the Mystery of God and His Treasure, the Cause of God and His glory unto all who are in the kingdoms of Revelation and of creation, if ye be of them that perceive.' (Words of Baha'u'llah, quoted in Shoghi Effendi, *God Passes By*, pp. 101–2)

religion of their times is of considerable interest. Each of them appeared against the background of a particular established religious tradition and most of those with whom they were in contact were also from this religious background. This predetermined much of the language, cosmology and mythology used by each prophet-founder. He had to make his message familiar enough to be understandable; therefore, he used the same cosmology and basic vocabulary as the established religion. But at the same time, he brought a teaching that was sufficiently radical and innovatory to cause the springing up of a new religion. In brief then, he took the symbols, cosmology and mythology of the old religion and recast them giving them a new meaning in order to purvey a new message. Thus the Buddha used the language and metaphysical assumptions of Hinduism; both Jesus and Muhammad launched their teaching from a Judaic base; the teachings of the Bab and Baha'u'llah emerged from an Islamic background and used the symbols common to Judaism, Christianity and Islam. Interestingly, this cloaking of the new message in the garb of the old means that, for some time, outsiders looked upon it as just a sect or movement within the old religion. Its potential to become a new religion only gradually emerged.

The full implication of the message of the prophet-founders is further concealed by the pattern in which they presented their teachings. During the early period in their ministries, they give mainly ethical and eschatological teachings and there was no indication of any break with the established religion; they did not oppose its teachings or laws. It is as if each prophet-founder wished to break the news of his mission to the people gently, in easy stages. We can see this during Jesus' preaching around Galilee in the early part of his ministry. Similarly, the earliest suras of the *Qur'an*, revealed during the Meccan period of Muhammad's ministry, are on ethical and eschatological themes. During the early ministry of the Bab, there is little indication in his writings of a break with Islam. Baha'u'llah's early writings are mostly concerned with ethics, mysticism and explanations of eschatology. There are also indications that the Buddha only gave out his teaching gradually, as he felt that people were ready for it.[5] These two factors (the use of the symbols and terminology of the previous established religion and the staged giving of the teaching) are the reason that the prophet-founder usually appears, at first, to be only a reformer of the previous religion. If one had come across Jesus preaching in Galilee, one might well have thought that he was just a Jewish reformer; Muhammad was considered by many to be preaching a monotheism similar to the Judaism that was familiar to the people of Mecca and Medina; similarly, the Bab was thought at first merely to be claiming leadership of the Shaykhi school of Shi'i Islam.

Even in the early period of their ministries, however, these prophet-founders were usually critical of the leaders of the established religious tradition, considering them to be perverters or corrupters of the previous religion. The Buddha was severely critical of the Brahmins of his time, calling them worse than dogs in some respects.[6] Similarly, a whole chapter of *St Matthew's Gospel* recounts how Jesus inveighed against the Jewish religious leaders, calling them hypocrites and corrupters of the Jewish religion.[7] In the *Qur'an*, we find criticism of Jewish and Christian religious leaders.[8] Both the Bab and Baha'u'llah accused religious leaders of being the main cause of the people rejecting the successive prophets of God when they appear.[9] (For more on this subject, see pp. 429–31.)

Then, at a particular point in their ministries, each of these figures makes a decisive break with the previous, established religion, revealing their true natures as not just reformers of the old religion but as renewers of religion itself. There were a number of incidents in the life of Jesus, such as his breaking of the Sabbath of the Jewish Law by curing a man of his lameness in Jerusalem. During the second year after his flight to Medina, Muhammad suddenly changed the direction in which prayers were said, from being towards Jerusalem to being towards the Ka'ba in Mecca. This signalled a definite break with the other monotheists of Medina, the Jewish tribes. The Bab caused the fact that he was to inaugurate a new dispensation and abolish the Islamic one to be announced at a conference of his followers at Badasht, at which his leading female disciple, Tahirih, appeared unveiled. At about the same time, he announced at his trial in Tabriz that he was the Mahdi whom Muslims were expecting. Baha'u'llah made clear to his followers that he was initiating a new religion when he issued a challenge to Azal, announcing that he was the one foretold by the Bab.

Table 12.1 Lives of the Founders of World Religions

	Buddha	Moses	Jesus	Muhammad	The Bab	Baha'u'llah
Forerunner(s)	Asita		John the Baptist	Bahira	Shaykh Ahmad, Sayyid Kazim	The Bab
Event precipitating ministry	Enlighten-ment under Bo tree	The burning bush	The descent of the dove	Vision of Angel Gabriel	Vision of the head of Imam Husayn	Vision of the Maid of Heaven in a dungeon in Tehran
Gathering of first disciples	First group of monks	Aaron	Twelve disciples	Khadija, 'Ali, Abu Bakr	Eighteen Letters of the Living	Small group of followers in Ridvan Garden
Period of solitude and doubt	Meditated over his course of action		Forty days in wilderness	Period of doubt		Two years in hills of Sulayman-iyya
Break with previous religion			Breaking the Sabbath	Change of direction of prayer	Conference of Badasht abolishes Islamic law	Challenge to Azal
Rulers and religious leaders to whom public declaration made	His father, the king, and many brahmins	Pharaoh	Pontius Pilate, Jewish religious leaders	Emperors of Persia and Byzantium	Shah of Iran, Iranian religious leaders	Shah of Iran, Sultan of Turkey, rulers of Europe, the Pope, other religious leaders
Promise of a future saviour	Maitreya Buddha	The Messiah	Return of Jesus	The Mahdi and return of Jesus	He whom God shall make manifest	Future Manifest-ation of God
Internal opposition	Devadatta, the Buddha's cousin	Making the golden calf	Judas Iscariot	Ibn Ubayy and the Munafiqun	Group of three disciples	Azal's opposition
External opposition		Pharaoh	Jewish religious leaders	Leaders of Mecca	Religious leaders and State in Iran	Religious leaders and State in Iran and Turkey
Migration	Wandering with monks	Migration of Israelites out of Egypt	Journeys of Paul and Peter to Rome	Migration from Mecca to Medina	Internal exile within Iran	Exile to Baghdad, Edirne and Akka

Interestingly, this break with the established religion usually occurs relatively late in the mission of the prophet-founder. Following this break with the previous religion, the prophet-founder begins to set out those aspects of his religion that are different from and conflict with the previous religion; for example, the distinctive laws and rituals of his religion. The later Medinan suras of the *Qur'an* are, for example, those containing the laws of Islam. It is the writings of Baha'u'llah from the period when he was in Akka that contain the new laws and social teachings of his religion. This process sets the seal on the break with the previous religion.

Thus, the teachings from the early part of the ministry of the prophet-founder tend to be the easier, less confrontational ones and the teachings and laws from the later part of the ministry tend to be those that are most different from the previous religion and therefore more difficult for people. This tendency may be interpreted in various ways. While followers of a religion would see this development as part of the spiritual strategy of the prophet-founder, demonstrating his vision and spiritual awareness, a more critical scholar might interpret this change as being the result of a change in the prophet's own self-understanding or perhaps in his assessment of what can be achieved, especially after encountering opposition or success.

Most of the prophet-founders also announced their missions to the secular and religious leaders of their time: Moses to Pharaoh; the Buddha to his father, King Suddhodana, to King Bimbisara as well as to many Brahmins and gurus; Jesus to Pontius Pilate (albeit only implicitly) and to the Jewish religious leaders; Muhammad to the religious leaders of Mecca and, according to some histories, to the Sassanian King of Persia and the Byzantine Emperor; the Bab to the king and the Muslim religious leaders in Iran; Baha'u'llah to several oriental and European monarchs, including

Two scenes from the life of the Buddha. On the left, the Buddha enters Parinirvana (the usual way of referring to the death of the Buddha). The scene on the right may depict an attempt made to murder the Buddha. The assassins await him behind a wall.

Queen Victoria and Emperor Napoleon III, as well as to Muslim religious leaders and the Pope.

It is also usually at about this stage in his mission that each prophet-founder sets up the promise of an eschatological saviour as well as of an eschatological event. In Western religions, the eschatological event is usually described as the end of the world, the Day of Judgement. The eschatological figure varies. Judaism promises a Messiah, preceded by the return of Elias; Jesus foretold his own return to the world; in Islamic tradition, Muhammad spoke of the coming of the Mahdi, accompanied by the return of Jesus. In the Eastern religions, the eschatological event is the end of the age of darkness, the Kali Yuga, and the start of a Golden Age. Krishna promised the coming of a future avatar, whenever there is a 'decline in righteousness'. Gautama Buddha spoke of the coming of a future Buddha, the Maitreya. Baha'u'llah refered to the coming of a further 'Manifestation of God' in one thousand years or more. (For details of these eschatological prophesies, see chapter 10.)

The activities of each of the prophet-founders set off a reaction in the form of internal and external opposition to them and their teaching. The internal opposition arose from within the ranks of the disciples and followers and was an act of betrayal caused usually by motives of fear, jealousy or envy. Devadatta, the Buddha's own cousin, sought to kill him out of jealousy, after failing to win others over to his own religious leadership. The brother of Moses, Aaron, betrayed him while he was away on Mount Sinai receiving the Law, and caused the Golden Calf to be made as an idol.[10] Judas Iscariot, one of Jesus's chosen twelve disciples, betrayed him to the authorities. When Muhammad was in Medina, a group of those who called themselves Muslims strove hard to undermine his position and betray him. They are called the Munafiqun (hypocrites). Envy undoubtedly motivated their leader, 'Abdullah ibn Ubayy, as he would probably have been the leading figure in Medina had it not been for Muhammad's arrival there. A group of three of the Bab's earliest disciples left him and went over to the side of his opponent out of jealousy towards the Bab's leading disciple; Azal, Baha'u'llah's own half-brother, sought to betray and kill him out of jealousy for Baha'u'llah's position of leadership, which would otherwise have been Azal's.

The external opposition to these prophet-founder figures occured because, through their teaching, they had each challenged the social order. Those with the greatest vested interest in the maintenance of that order, the rulers and the religious leaders, opposed them. Moses was opposed by Pharaoh; Jesus by the Jewish religious leaders who eventually caused his death. The *Bhagavad Gita* and the *Mahabharata* describe the great battle that Krishna had to fight to restore righteousness; the Buddha and his disciples were subjected to great persecution and misrepresentation;[11] Muhammad was opposed by the leading figures in Mecca because his fight against idol-worship threatened the main source of the town's prosperity; the Bab was opposed by the religious leaders and the state in Iran; while

Baha'u'llah faced the opposition of the religious and secular authorities of both Iran and the Ottoman Turkish Empire.

There is often also an element of migration involved in the lives of the founders of the great religions or in the history of the religions immediately after their deaths, largely caused by external opposition. The archetypal migration in the Bible was that of Abraham from Chaldea to Palestine; Moses migrated with the Israelites out of Egypt after his clash with Pharaoh; the Buddha was in a constant state of migration with his disciples. Jesus moved the centre of his ministry from Galilee to Jerusalem but the main migration in the early history of Christianity occurred after the crucifixion when Paul and Peter took the message of Christ to Rome and the Gentile world after the Jews had rejected it. Muhammad migrated to Medina after the opposition of the Meccans; Baha'u'llah was sent by the Iranian and Ottoman governments into several successive exiles from Iran, finally coming to Akka in Palestine. (See p. 314.)

It is of interest to consider the reasons that established religious leaders have given for rejecting the prophets-founders. There are again great similarities here. The Jewish religious leaders rejected Jesus because he did not fit their idea of what the Messiah would do and because they believed the law of the Torah to be unalterable. Jewish and Christian religious leaders rejected Muhammad because they could not accept that he was a prophet of God; moreover, they did not believe that there would be a further teaching from God. Similarly, Baha'u'llah's claim to be the promised saviour of all of these religions was rejected by Jewish, Christian and Muslim religious leaders because he did not fit their ideas of their promised saviour, and because of their belief that their own religious scriptures are complete and unalterable for all time.

There have thus been two common elements in these rejections. First, the religious leaders have had preconceived and fixed ideas of the promised saviours of their religions, the next prophets to come from God. When the prophet-founder fails to conform to this picture, they reject him. Second, the religious leaders of each religion have adopted the position that their religion is the last religion from God, their scripture the last word from God; therefore, no other message could possibly come from God. Thus when the prophet-founder brings forward a new teaching, they oppose him. The fears of religious leaders for their social position and prestige must also be taken into consideration.

This analysis of the lives of the prophet-founders of the world religions is not intended to pass over the fact that there were also great differences between their lives. Some, for example, were able to overcome opposition and ended their lives leading their communities, while others were overwhelmed by opposition and were put to death. Yet, nevertheless, there does appear to be a certain repetitive pattern in their lives that suggests that these prophet-founders set about their missions in similar ways:

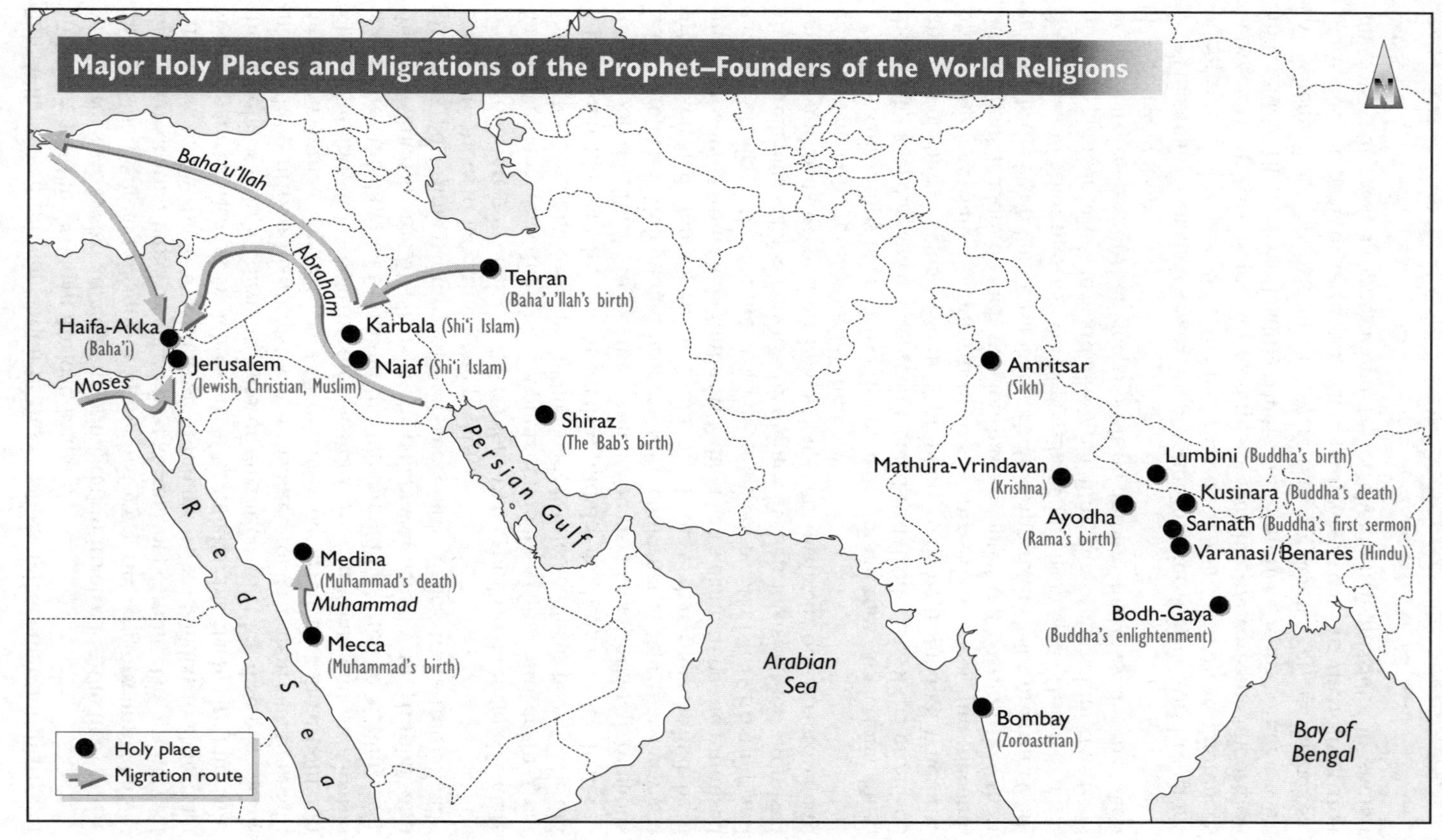
Major Holy Places and Migrations of the Prophet–Founders of the World Religions
N
Baha'u'llah
Abraham
Tehran
(Baha'u'llah's birth)
Karbala (Shi'i Islam)
Haifa-Akka
(Baha'i)
Jerusalem
(Jewish, Christian, Muslim)
Najaf (Shi'i Islam)
Moses
Shiraz
(The Bab's birth)
Persian Gulf
Amritsar
(Sikh)
Lumbini (Buddha's birth)
Mathura-Vrindavan
(Krishna)
Kusinara (Buddha's death)
Ayodha
(Rama's birth)
Sarnath (Buddha's first sermon)
Varanasi/Benares (Hindu)
Red Sea
Medina
(Muhammad's death)
Muhammad
Mecca
(Muhammad's birth)
Bodh-Gaya
(Buddha's enlightenment)
Arabian Sea
Bombay
(Zoroastrian)
Bay of Bengal
Holy place
Migration route

a

b

c

THE THEME OF MIGRATION IN THE LIFE OF THE PROPHET-FOUNDERS OF RELIGIONS: a) Moses took the Children of Israel on a migration from Egypt to Canaan. The picture shows him leading the Israelites through the Red Sea. From a manuscript of al-Nisaburi's *Qisas al-Anbiya* (Stories of the Prophets), Turkey, seventeenth century. b) Akka, the site of Baha'u'llah's last place of exile. Baha'u'llah was exiled successively to Baghdad, Edirne and finally to Akka, in what was then the Ottoman province of Syria. c) When persecution and opposition in Mecca proved excessive, Muhammad migrated with many of his followers from Mecca to Medina. The picture shows the inside of the Prophet's Mosque, which became the religious and political centre of Medina while Muhammad lived there.

- picking a small band of close disciples before announcing their mission to the world at large;
- giving the parts of their teaching that were easier to accept first, before giving the more controversial points that opposed the establishment and were bound to cause consternation and opposition;
- giving a promise of a further saviour figure to come;

and that this then set off a similar pattern of responses:

- acceptance by an initially small band of disciples before a more open proclamation was made;
- internal opposition from close relatives or leading disciples, usually for reasons of jealousy;
- external opposition from the secular establishment and existing religious leaders, who held that the prophet-founder could not be the promised saviour and that the scriptures of the existing religion could not be superseded.

MUHAMMAD'S VICTORY OVER THE PEOPLE OF MECCA: After many years of opposition, the people of Mecca finally submitted to Muhammad's rule. This is a depiction of Muhammad's first action on entering Mecca. He entered the Ka'ba and put 'Ali onto his shoulders and instructed him to destroy the idols in the Ka'ba. In this Shi'i depiction, the faces of Muhammad and 'Ali are not drawn as a sign of reverence, while flames of fire form a halo around their heads.

The Development of a Religion

After the death of the founder, the followers of a religion have a great problem. Much of the success of the movement has usually been due to the personal qualities of the founder, qualities that are perceived to set the founder apart from ordinary men. Weber used the term 'charisma' to describe this out-of-the-ordinary quality. He defined it thus:

> The term 'charisma' will be applied to a certain quality of an individual personality by virtue of which he is set apart from ordinary men and treated as endowed with supernatural, superhuman, or at least specifically exceptional powers or qualities. These are such as are not accessible to the ordinary person, but are regarded as of divine origin or as exemplary, and on the basis of them the individual concerned is treated as a leader.[12]

The Church of the Holy Sepulchre, Jerusalem, is the traditional site of the crucifixion, entombment, and resurrection of Jesus. Inside, it is divided among several different churches: Greek Orthodox, Roman Catholic, Armenian, and Coptic.

With the death of the founder, the religion is deprived of his charisma which had attracted new people and kept the believers unified. The leading disciples face the problem of how to maintain the cohesion and continued expansion of the movement, which is now at its most vulnerable. Any pre-existing tensions among the leading disciples are likely to surface at this time, leading to the formation of sects. After the death of Muhammad, for example, the rift between Abu Bakr and 'Umar on the one side and 'Ali on the other came to the surface. This rift was eventually to lead to the split between Sunni and Shi'i Islam. A short time after the death of Jesus, the rift occurred between those who saw Christianity as being solely a Jewish affair and those, such as St Paul, who wanted to take the message to the Gentiles. The sack of Jerusalem by the Romans in 70 CE led to the eventual elimination of the more conservative faction and so this sect no longer exists in Christianity.

The resolution of the leadership crisis tends to occur in two stages. The first of these involves one or more of the leading disciples taking on the mantle of leadership and with it some of the charismatic aura of the founder. After Jesus, the church was run by a circle of the disciples at Jerusalem. After Muhammad, his followers pledged their allegiance to Abu Bakr. After Baha'u'llah, the leadership of 'Abdu'l-Baha was made secure by a specific document of appointment from Baha'u'llah.

For perhaps one generation, this solution works reasonably well. As long as people perceive the leadership to partake of the charisma of the founder, they remain united behind it. But as an increasing distance inserts itself between the founder and the leadership, this charisma begins to wear

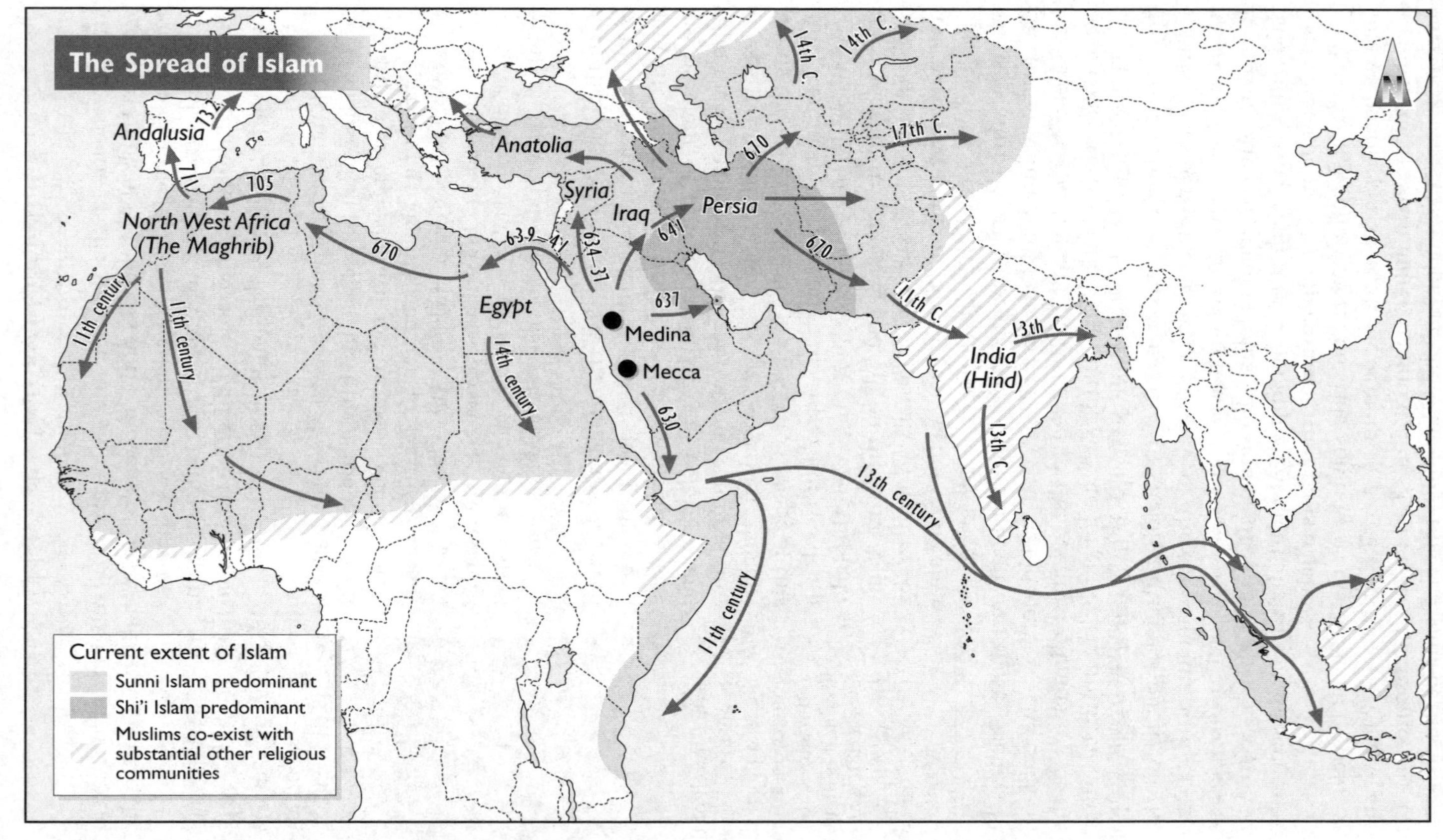
The Spread of Islam
Andalusia
732
711
705
North West Africa
(The Maghrib)
11th century
11th century
670
Egypt
14th century
639–41
Anatolia
Syria
634–37
Iraq
641
Persia
637
Medina
Mecca
630
670
670
14th C.
14th C.
17th C.
11th C.
India
(Hind)
13th C.
13th C.
13th century
11th century
N
Current extent of Islam
Sunni Islam predominant
Shi'i Islam predominant
Muslims co-exist with
substantial other religious
communities

thin. It is at this point that the second stage of the process begins to take shape, involving the institutionalization of the charisma of the founder. This process, which Weber calls 'routinization of charisma',[13] institutionalizes three facets of the leadership of the founder.

1. Doctrines that formalize the intellectual content of the beliefs of the group institutionalize the *teaching* of the founder. At first, this will often be done as a polemic exercise in defending the new religion from attacks by outsiders. Later, especially when a professional religious class is established, a theological and philosophical elaboration of the doctrine occurs which is mostly to strengthen the belief of the faithful and to solve pastoral problems.

2. Symbols, myths and rituals that re-enact the sacred moments of the group institutionalize the *acts* of the founder. The sacred and awesome aspect of the holy[14] as revealed by the founder is preserved in a number of symbols and rituals. These often re-enact key moments in the life of the founder and retell, often in mythic form, the story of the life of the founder. In this way, they recreate the intensity of the original experience of the holy that was the basis and foundation of the group. Rituals such as the Christian Eucharist or the Muslim annual pilgrimage to Mecca recall events in the life of the founder, recreating the intense religious experience of the first group of disciples who gathered around the founder. They thus help to consolidate the unity of the group. The cross, as a religious symbol, represents not just the event of the crucifixion but the whole life of Christ, the suffering, the sacrifice and the eventual triumph. Such symbols come to represent the profoundest emotional responses of the group to their religious experience. It is important to note that the emergence of a symbol is a slow organic process. It cannot necessarily be predicted. The fish was an early symbol of Christianity and was only slowly replaced by the cross.

THE CROSS AS A CHRISTIAN SYMBOL: Church of Sant'Appolinare, a sixth-century basilica, south of Ravenna, Italy.

3. A hierarchy that organizes the group institutionalizes the *authority* of the founder. It seeks to recreate the leadership of the founder through the establishment of a hierarchical structure of authority. It is important to note, in passing, that historically the norm has been a fusion of the religious and political leadership of a society. The separating of the spheres of religion and politics is, largely, a phenomenon of the modern Western world.

Perhaps the most important aspect of (2) above is the elevation of the prophet-founder into a paradigmatic model for all followers of the religion.

One can speak of a myth being created of the prophet-founder that turns him into a role model for the key virtues and moral norms of the religion, the bridge between the transcendent and the mundane, the perfect human being. Thus, Jesus becomes the perfect Christian; Muhammad, the perfect Muslim; Gautama Buddha, the perfect Buddhist. The prophet-founder is transformed from a remote historical figure into an ever-present, trans-historical presence in the lives of believers.[15] (See pp. 344–5.)

One aspect of the initial period after the death of the founder is worth bearing in mind. It would appear that the early followers of some religions do not expect a prolonged period in which they will have to fend for themselves, spiritually speaking. They are expecting the imminent advent of a further divine figure who will lead them and they therefore envisage that any organization of the religion that they carry out will be merely a temporary stop-gap affair, whose details they may well consider to be of no great consequence. We can see this clearly among the disciples of Jesus. The earliest generations were buoyed up by the promises of Jesus that their current generation would see the fulfilment of the promised Day of God.[16] They lived in hope of this and were not really concerned with church organization and mission. Most of the first generation of Christians were centred on the group of Apostles who remained in Jerusalem awaiting the promised day. The *Qur'an* itself is not very specific about when the eschatological promises in it will be fulfilled but it is clear that many early Muslims were also of the opinion that the promised figure of the Mahdi was to be expected imminently. During the first three centuries of the Islamic era, there were many revolts in the name of this figure who was to bring justice to the world.

Much of the subsequent course of a religion's history is determined by the extent to which it gains political power. This has been perhaps the single most important factor in the further development of a religion. Political power both strengthens and, paradoxically, often also weakens a religion. The strengthening occurs because the religion now has access to considerable financial resources. It also has the ability to enforce orthodoxy and suppress heresy. In pre-modern times, political power meant, for a religion, control of the education process, art, literature and all public ceremony. Through these means, the religious authorities can shape the worldview of people, making the religious view natural and unquestioned.

The attainment of political power, however, also results in a weakening of religion. This occurs because of the distance that is gradually set up between religion as a political power in society and the religious needs of the people. If this distance becomes too great, alternative forms of religious life, autonomous from the orthodox hierarchy, are set up to meet these needs. Examples of this include the emergence of gnostic sects in medieval Christian Europe, the rise of the Sufi orders in Islam, the formation of new religious movements in recent history, and the ubiquitous sellers of charms and amulets.

This phenomenon of the gradual weakening of religion's hold over people (even while it may be increasing its temporal power) has been little studied. Only a few tentative suggestions can be made about it. In the early stages of the development of a religion, the spiritual consciousness is strong and there is an intense personal piety. With the passing of time and the interposition of intermediaries (religious professionals such as priests and gurus) between the individual and Ultimate Reality, there is a weakening of religion, manifested as a redirection of the individual from the eternal spiritual realities of which the religion is a renewal towards the specific historical contingencies of the religion. Personal piety is gradually replaced by collective sentimentality; a direct spiritual relationship with Ultimate Reality becomes emotional attachment to the miraculous. This, of course, is a generalization and there are always exceptional individuals who are able to go against the tide.

We can see this redirection of religion from eternal spiritual values towards specific historical contingencies most clearly in the arts. In religious art, the non-representational art of the early period of a religion is replaced by iconography. Later, this iconography becomes ever more elaborate and showy (or as occurred with Christian art after the Renaissance, more naturalistic). In non-representational, aniconic art the symbol represents the eternal spiritual realities. Iconic art, on the other hand, focuses the mind on the specific historical manifestation of the Absolute. While iconic art remains simple and direct, it continues to act in part as a symbol, taking the believer back to the spiritual realities behind the physical appearance. But if it then progresses to elaboration or naturalism, it increasingly distracts the believer from spiritual reality, redirecting him or her towards the miraculous and sentimental (see chapter 18).

RELIGIOUS INTOLERANCE: Religious authorities have frequently been guilty of much cruelty and torture in their attempt to suppress heresy, often assisted by the secular authorities. This picture shows a Babi being executed for heresy by having his throat cut. Iran, nineteenth century.

This redirection is perhaps also manifested at the social level by openness and tolerance in the early years of the religion, when the believers are directed towards eternal spiritual values. As the religion becomes more focused on its specific historical contingencies, it tends towards intolerance and fanaticism. This latter tendency is exemplified by the spirit of the Crusades and the Inquisition in medieval Europe. Psychologically, one could speculate that there is a paradox here. Fanaticism and intolerance are the signs not of a strength of conviction but of a weakening. As long as the individual is turned towards the eternal spiritual and moral values of religion, there is a profound personal conviction of the spiritual truth of a belief. This, in turn, means that those believers have the self-confidence to be tolerant towards others. It is only when faith is weakened that the attention is turned towards the specific historical contingencies. The outward trappings of belief systems then become more important than inner faith: fanaticism and intolerance are the resulting attitudes. Religion consequently becomes a mechanism for social control. It is at this point in the evolution of a religion, when the original spiritual impulse has become attenuated and diffuse, that reform movements arise or a new religion is born.

Schism and Heresy

The institutionalization of the three facets of the role of the founder described above acts as a substitute for the charisma of the founder and thus as a focus for the unity of the new religion. By more sharply defining what is within the circle of belief, however, this development also, by its very nature, presages the occurrence of heresies and sects.

The process of institutionalization is a difficult phase for a new religion. Different people will have been attracted to it for different reasons and from different backgrounds and each group now tries to bring into the process of institutionalization elements that emphasize what attracted them to the religion. These groups will want to lead the religion towards the different forms of religious activity outlined in chapter 5. Other groups will bring in elements from their own former religious backgrounds. This process sets up the potential for sectarian splitting or, even if formal splits do not occur, for fragmentation. The Sufi groups in Islam, for example, are not sects of Islam in the formal sense of that word, but they are semi-autonomous groupings with their own leadership, their own interpretation of the texts and doctrines of Islam, and their own rituals. They are often in tension with their fellow-Muslims. The Christian religious orders of the Middle Ages acted in much the same way.

The precipitating factor for sect formation may be any of a large number of developments. The underlying reason must be that a sufficient number of people no longer feel that the orthodox teaching is a path to salvation. They no longer encounter the central experience of religion by following this path. There are many factors that lead to this result. Some of these have already been discussed: the drawing up of tighter definitions of orthodoxy that exclude what was previously included; the introduction into the religion of elements of doctrine or ritual from other religions from which converts have come (see p. 158); the perception that the religious hierarchy has become materialistic or corrupt; and the conviction that the religion has strayed from its original spiritual core of inner truths and has become tied up with external observances. More specific historical factors may, however, also be operating: a powerful charismatic personality, who may claim to have had some extraordinary religious experience, may be a catalyst for sect formation; personal ambition, power, politics or personal differences may initiate a schism (as occurred at the start of the Church of England, for example); or differences in language, race or class may cause the fracturing of a religious group that would otherwise remain united.

Needless to say, many of those designated by the orthodox as heretics or schismatics protest that they are, in fact, reasserting the original message of the founder of the religion and bringing it back to its original pure state. Indeed, many of those who founded sects did not intend to do this when they start their movements. Figures such as John Wesley, the founder of Methodist Protestant Christianity, and Shaykh Ahmad al-Ahsa'i, the founder of the Shaykhi sect of Shi'i Islam, set out to revitalize the religious groups of which they were a part. Those groups, however, proved too rigid to accommodate them and eventually either they or their followers were forced into creating new sects in order to express their religious aspirations. The historical evidence indicates that even the founders of the more recent historical religions, Jesus, Muhammad, the Buddha, and Baha'u'llah were regarded at first as being reformers, schismatics or heretics within the established religions of their time.

John Wesley (1703–91), founder of Methodism

From Personal Piety to Organized Religion

In chapter 5 the various paths to salvation were described. In this section, we shall try to uncover something of the way that these different pathways evolved in history. This is not a straightforward task because a natural tendency to cover the tracks of such developments means that they can become difficult to discern.

Religious people everywhere believe that they are following their religion as it was intended to be followed by the founder of the religion. It would make no sense for any religious person to say anything else. This means that they believe that their religious rituals and other religious activities are those intended by the founder and carried out by the early disciples. Therefore, there is a natural tendency to cover up or dismiss any developments in the social expressions of the religion and to try to relate all these back to the time of the founder. This tendency is expressed in the sentiment that idealizes the early

Shaykh Ahmad al-Ahsa'i (1753–1826), founder of the Shaykhi school in Shi'i Islam

INTERACTION BETWEEN A REFORMER AND OFFICIAL RELIGION: THE EXAMPLE OF JOHN WESLEY

When John Wesley (1703–1791) and Charles Wesley (1707–1788) started their movement to intensify religous life and the practice of prayer in the tradition of the so-called 'religious societies', they did so within the framework of the official Church of England . . . Soon, however, their movement began to diverge from the official church in many respects; not so much with respect to content, but much more with respect to the practice of Christian belief. The Church of England was still involved in the deistic tradition of the Enlightenment. J. Wesley, however, translated the Christian message directly for the common man in content as well as in preaching and practice . . .

The resistance from the side of the Church of England towards J. Wesley is typical of an official religion. The Anglican Church had strong ties with the gentry and the middle class . . . thus the opposition had both a religous and a social character . . . Leaving out the official liturgy: Mass, Office and Sacraments, which were considered as essentials of Christan life, was experienced as undermining, not the least because of the doctrine of 'justification by faith alone' . . . The local clergy felt threatened by the diminishing of their flocks . . . The early Methodists experienced more or less violent persecution in many districts . . .

Though John Wesley always fought moves towards independence from the Church of England, it was not before 1784 that he appointed a conference of 100 men to govern the society of Methodists after his death. Tension in the relationship with the Anglican Church reached its summit when the bishop of London refused to ordain a Methodist for post-revolutionary America: Wesley himself, then, ordained three presbyters. Four years after his death came the definite break with the Church of England (1795). (G. F. W. Bouritius, 'Popular and Official Religion in Christianity: Three Cases in 19th Century Europe', in Vrijhof and Waardenburg, *Official and Popular Religion*, pp. 139, 141–3)

community: the community of monks around the Buddha, the community of the early Christians, the Muslim community in Medina in the time of Muhammad. These early communities come to be seen as the ideal, archetypal community of the religion. Orthodox leaders see the institutions of the religion as faithfully capturing all of the essential features of the early community. Similarly, reformers and sectarians often see themselves as trying to recreate the conditions of that community. The same process can be seen in the doctrinal development of a religion. On the one hand, there is a similar compulsion by the orthodox to deny that there has been any doctrinal evolution from the time of the founder. On the other hand, reformers will say that they are trying to take the religion back to the doctrinal purity of the early years.

There is a further explanation of this tendency to deny all development and change in a religion. We shall see in chapter 16 that the social order, enshrined in its symbolic universe, presents itself to the individual as a fully developed objective entity. It has its own, often mythical, account of how things came to be the way they are. In a traditional society, in particular, it is co-extensive with reality itself; any other reality would be difficult even to imagine, let alone to believe actually existed. Therefore the concept that things may have been different in the past, that the religious world has changed and developed, is not one that would come easily to a person in such a society.

Islam, as the most recent of the religions that we are considering except for the Baha'i Faith – and we shall return to that presently – is the best place to start to uncover some of these traces of development because, as they are more recent and therefore more fully documented, they have been less covered over.

The Development of Islam

The main orthodox social expression in Islam, both in the Sunni and Shi'i forms, is legalism. The Holy Law, Shari'a, is seen as the embodiment of the practice of Muhammad in his daily life. Muhammad being an 'excellent example' of a Muslim according to the *Qur'an*,[17] his practice in daily life is considered exemplary for all Muslims. Hence the reports of all that he said and did were relayed orally by generations of Muslims and finally recorded in the books of Traditions. Each Tradition (*Hadith*) contains a record of the names of those who transmitted it through successive generations of Muslims. This is what orthodox Muslims consider to have happened. Thus the central pillar of the social expression of the orthodox religion, the Shari'a, is referred back to the origins of the religion; it is given the stamp of authority of Muhammad and the practice of the early Muslim community in Medina.

Of course, Muslims themselves have always recognized problems regarding the authenticity of the *Hadith* literature. Acknowledging that many Traditions relating to Muhammad were forged in the early period, they developed a whole branch of Islamic science that sought to distinguish between the true and the forged Traditions. They examined the line of transmitters of each Tradition and tried to ascertain the reliability of each person in the chain. They also examined the line as a whole and determined whether the individuals in the chain of transmission could have been in contact with each other.

Modern Western scholarship, however, examining critically the earliest surviving documents, has cast a much more fundamental doubt over the *Hadith* literature. The first to raise questions about the traditional version of the rise of the *Hadith* literature was Ignaz Goldziher. He showed that up to three centuries after Muhammad, many individuals, political parties and sectarian movements within Islam were manufacturing Traditions that supported their claims and positions. These Traditions, claiming to be on the authority of Muhammad, gave each faction legitimacy and authenticity.[18]

Joseph Schacht took this line of research further. He showed that the schools of Islamic law that arose were in fact the result of differing sets of customary law in such towns as Medina and Kufa. These centres established what had been the customary tribal law from pre-Islamic times in their area by incorporating it into the Holy Law. It was only at a later date, when it became the norm to trace all law back to the Prophet Muhammad, that there evolved numerous Traditions relating these practices back to him. In this way the customary law of each of these places became enshrined in the Holy Law, the Shari'a of Islam.[19]

We should not see this process of the retrospective attribution of customary practice back to Muhammad as the activity of malicious forgers. Rather, these were the actions of sincere and pious men who regarded their views as the correct Islamic standards. From this it was only a short step to being certain that the Prophet would have acted in the same way if faced with the same situation; and then another short step to saying that the Prophet did act thus; and then yet another short step to creating a *Hadith* that confirmed that he did act thus.[20]

Wilfred Cantwell Smith put forward a further hypothesis regarding the development of the Shari'a, the Holy Law, in Islam. In the earliest texts, the word that is found is not *shari'a*, but rather the two related words, *shar'* and *shar'i*. These two latter words are verbal nouns from a verb meaning 'to prescribe a road to walk upon', the subject of the verbal noun being God. In other words, they were words referring to God's assigning of moral qualities and ethical responsibilities to human life. They describe an attitude, a feeling that God has imposed a certain moral obligation on us as individuals. This usage continued until as late as the fourteenth century CE. At about this time, Smith discerns a loss in the Islamic world of the sense of God's immediate intervention in the world and of human cosmic moral involvement. As a result, the word *shari'a* comes increasingly into use to denote an absolute objective reality, the Holy Law. In summary then, the *shar'* was at first an ethical path of conduct for the early Muslims. It only later became depersonalized and objectified or reified, taking its legalistic meaning as 'the Holy Law', the Shari'a. Similarly, *taklif*, which means 'legal responsibility' in present-day usage, originally meant 'moral responsibility'.[21] The more abstract term *shari'a* is more appropriate when one's sense of the presence of God and of one's direct moral obligations to Him are weak or absent. Smith states that

> it would not be impossible to contend that historically the rise of a concept [of] law as religiously absolute may be correlated with a decline, if not of Islamic civilisation, anyway of the vigor of its intellectual and religious life.[22]

An example cited by Smith may clarify this point. For these early Muslims, it was not that 'lies' were wrong. It was not even the 'telling of lies' that was wrong. It was the 'telling of lies by me' that was wrong and blameworthy and led to damnation – for God created us and commanded us not to lie. However, in later Islam, the priority changes. 'Lies' and 'the telling of lies' are contrary to the Holy Law – therefore, 'the telling of lies' is wrong and leads to damnation.

The implication of all this is, of course, that during the development of Islam, the concept of law was not prior to and the cause of the concept of moral responsibility, but the other way around. The sense of moral responsibility to God chronologically preceded and was the originating impulse towards the development of the Holy Law. Muslims did not originally feel an obligation to act in a particular way because the Holy Law told them to do so. Rather, they created the Holy Law in order to systematize for society the way that they felt that God wanted them to behave individually.

This development of the Holy Law in Islam was accompanied by a parallel development in the social position of the ulema, the scholars who defined and purveyed the Holy Law. In the early period of Islam (up to and including the third Islamic century), they began as an informal and undefined group of individuals from a wide spectrum of social classes and occupations, who would sit together and their discussion would be of a discursive nature. Their knowledge depended on oral transmission of historical material, practical experience of life, and participation in juristic discussion. Later (from about the fourth Islamic century onwards), as the Holy Law became more defined and increasingly occupied a central role in society, the ulema became a more highly trained and socially distinct élite, with increasing use of the written transmission of knowledge. By this time, training of the ulema had evolved from informal discussion-circles to much more formal institutions in which the master–pupil relationship was the norm. This process of the professionalization and bureaucratization of the ulema, which occurred partly as a result of political policy and pressure, corresponded with a period during which the Holy Law became established as the central focus of Islam, the four schools of Sunni jurisprudence emerged, the training of the ulema became standardized, and the authoritative texts of each school evolved and finally became fixed.[23]

The description above relates to the main pathway of social expression in Islam, the Shari'a. However, there is good evidence that the other major social expression in Islam, Sufism, followed the same sort of development. Each modern Sufi order traces its spiritual lineage back to Muhammad through an unbroken chain of transmitters of its spiritual practice. The claim is thus made, explicitly or implicitly, that the teachings and practices of the order were transmitted to it from Muhammad. It is implied that this represents a secret teaching that Muhammad passed on to those who were ready to receive it, while the other teachings of Islam were publicly taught to the rest of the Muslims. In this way, both the mystic practice and the gnostic teachings of Sufism are referred back to Muhammad.

In the history of Sufism, however, those persons whom Sufis have identified as the first Sufis – the earliest links in the spiritual chain of transmission from Muhammad to the present day – were merely what one would call pious individuals. If one reads the accounts of such early Sufi saints as Hasan al-Basri and Rabi'a, one is impressed by their piety and detachment from material things; these were clearly God-centred individuals. But there is nothing in these accounts to suggest that these individuals participated in the practices or followed the teachings of the modern Sufi orders.[24] These modern orders arose in the twelfth and thirteenth centuries CE, when the religious consciousness was weakening in Islam. They developed their practices and teachings at this time and these were then retrospectively imposed upon a number of pious individuals from the past and traced all the way back to Muhammad. It was at about this time, for example, that the word *adab*, which refers to the appropriate behaviour of the pious individual as derived from the sacred text, became transformed in the Sufi literature into its plural form, *ādāb*, which came to refer to the particular rules of conduct of each Sufi order, the norms of conduct between master and disciple and between the disciples themselves, as laid down by the founder of the order.

In this way we can see that the two main pathways to salvation in Islam, legalism and Sufism, were both built up by a similar mechanism: the emergence of a practice among the believers, followed by its authentication by retrospective attribution to Muhammad and the early generation of Muslims; the transformation of religious injunctions that have moral and spiritual compulsion into rigid rules that have legal or prescriptive force.

The doctrinal development of religion has followed the same course as the social expression in camouflaging all traces of change and development, and for exactly the same reason. Everything has to be seen as flowing unerringly from the source of the religion: the founder or the early circle of disciples.

In Shi'i Islam, we can find evidence of a complete reversal of many doctrinal positions held by the early Shi'a. There seems little doubt that most of these early Shi'a (before the year 900 CE) believed in such concepts as: anthropomorphism with respect to God, transmigration of souls, the descent of the divine spirit into human beings and alteration in the divine will, as well as believing that the enemies of the Shi'a had altered the text of the *Qur'an*. At a later date (by about the year 1000 CE), the Shi'i orthodoxy denied or held to the opposite of all of these positions.[25] They then retrospectively applied their new beliefs to the earlier generations. The Shi'i orthodoxy (and the Sunnis also) shifted the responsibility for the embarrassing doctrines of the early Shi'a onto various minor Shi'i sects who were labelled the *ghulat*, the extremists. It may, however, in fact be the case that there were no Shi'a apart from the so-called *ghulat* in the early period; many of the most eminent early Shi'a who were closest to the Shi'i Imams are recorded as having had views that would identify them as *ghulat*.[26]

Baha'i Faith

1800

1820

1817	Birth of Baha'u'llah
1819	Birth of the Bab

1840

1860

1844	Beginning of the Mission of the Bab
1848	Conference of Badasht; beginning of Babi upheavals
1850	Martyrdom of the Bab
1852	Attempted assassination of Nasir al-Din Shah; Baha'u'llah's vision of Maid of Heaven; Baha'u'llah exiled to Baghdad
1863	Baha'u'llah announces his mission; Baha'u'llah summoned to Istanbul and exiled to Edirne
1868	Baha'u'llah exiled to Akka in Syria
1872	Baha'u'llah completes his major book, the Kitab al-Aqdas (Most Holy Book); Baha'i Faith taken to India

1880

1900

1889	Independence of the Baha'i Faith from Islam publicly asserted in Russian Turkestan following martyrdom of a Baha'i
1892	Passing of Baha'u'llah; 'Abdu'l-Baha appointed successor; Baha'i Faith taken to North America
1898	Baha'i Faith established in Europe (Britain and France); first group of Western pilgrims arrives in Akka

1920

1940

1960

1908	'Abdu'l-Baha freed as a result of the Young Turks Revolution in Ottoman Empire
1911-13	'Abdu'l-Baha's journeys to the West (France, Britain, United States, Canada, Germany, Hungary)
1920	Baha'i Faith taken to Australia
1921	Passing of 'Abdu'l-Baha; Shoghi Effendi appointed successor; Baha'i Faith taken to Brazil
1923	Election of first National Spiritual Assemblies
1925	Islamic Court in Egypt pronounces the Baha'i Faith to be a separate independent religion (confirmed by Grand Mufti of Egypt in 1939); International Baha'i Bureau established in Geneva
1926	Queen Marie of Rumania becomes a Baha'i
1928-40	Persecutions of Baha'i communities in Soviet Russia (1928-38), Iran (1934-8) and Germany (1937-9)
1937-44	Campaign to take the Baha'i Faith to Central and South America (established in 21 new countries)
1946-53	Campaign to establish or re-establish the Baha'i Faith in countries of Europe after World War II
1948	Baha'i International Community established to represent the Baha'i Faith at the United Nations
1951	Creation of International Baha'i Council in Haifa
1951-53	Campaign to take the Baha'i Faith to a number of African countries (established in 25 new countries)
1953-63	Ten-year campaign to take the Baha'i Faith to most of the remaining countries of the world (established in 130 new countries and territories)
1957	Passing of Shoghi Effendi; Hands of the Cause become 'custodians' of the Baha'i Faith
1963	Election of Universal House of Justice as supreme authority in the Baha'i Faith
1967-8	Campaign to acquaint heads of state with the Baha'i Faith; King of Samoa becomes a Baha'i

1980

2000

1992	Publication of a translation of Baha'u'llah's Kitab al-Aqdas into English, followed by other languages; commemorations of centenary of passing of Baha'u'llah

The Development of Other Religions

The same process has almost certainly occurred in the other religions but the passage of time has obscured the stages of the process. Since the earlier stages were not preserved in written documents, they have been obliterated. Only the later stages have survived, telling us about the earlier stages from their own later perspective. A careful study of the Buddhist Pali Canon, for example, may well conclude that it is possible that the same sort of development occurred in Buddhism. For the Buddha an action was right or wrong for a particular individual because it led either towards or away from liberation for that individual. Over the years this has evolved into the current belief that an action is right or wrong because it is either in conformity with or against the dictates of the Dhamma (the Dharma). The Dhamma is the objectification and depersonalization of the Buddha's teaching. Around this simple teaching of the Buddha a complex metaphysical framework has been built, despite the Buddha's own repeated assertion of his dislike of metaphysical speculation because it distracted the individual from the urgent task of seeking liberation.

The history of the Baha'i Faith shows how these processes can develop in even the relatively short 150-year history of this religion. One finds a tendency among many Baha'is to read present Baha'i teachings back into the past, even back to the Babis, the followers of the Bab in nineteenth-century Iran. The Babis are popularly regarded by many Baha'is as having believed in such modern Baha'i social teachings as the equality of men and women.

There is, however, one important difference in the Baha'i community. This is the fact that Baha'is have no concept of an initial ideal phase of their history. While history is important for Baha'is in providing inspiration, role models and justification, there is no sense of trying to recreate the community that existed around Baha'u'llah. Baha'is are quite clear that what they are working towards is the goal of a just society in the future, built upon plans given them by Baha'u'llah. These plans are considered to be only a framework for future developments. Changes are, therefore, seen as either working out or developing understanding of the implications of Baha'u'llah's teachings. There is thus no compulsion to try to project all modern developments backwards to an ideal that existed in the past and thus less tendency to try to cover the tracks of the past. It may be, however, that this difference is the result of the fact that the Baha'i Faith is in an early phase of its development. There is evidence that the early Muslims were also looking forward to the setting up of a future ideal society. It may be, therefore, that the tendency to look back to a Golden Age in the past is the result of the jaded middle age of a religion – somewhat similar to the tendency among individual human beings to look back to a 'golden age' of youth.

Individual Responsibility and Institutionalized Authority

In general then, we may say that, at the start of the religion, there is a feeling of personal ethical and moral responsibility to act in the way that the founder of the religion has instructed (the way God wants us to act, in the theistic religions). In other words what constrains the believers to act in a particular way is their belief in and love of the founder of the religion (or God). As time passes, however, the pathway of action becomes institutionalized as the central focus of the religion: the Dhamma in Theravada Buddhism, the Church in Christianity, the Shari'a in Islam. This reified or objectified entity then assumes the central authority in the religion. The result is that the action of the individual is now constrained more by the institutionalized authority of the central focus and less by the feeling of ethical and moral responsibility.

From the viewpoint of the individual believer, there does not appear to be any great difference between the two positions. A Buddhist may not see any difference between acting according to the teachings of the Buddha and acting according to the Dhamma; for did the Buddha not give us the Dhamma? A Christian may see no difference between acting according to the teachings of Jesus and acting as the Church wishes us to act; for are not the teachings of the Church and of Jesus identical? A Muslim may see no difference between acting according to the teachings of Muhammad and acting according to the Shari'a; for is not the Shari'a based on the actions and teachings of Muhammad? However, from the viewpoint of the historian or sociologist, there is every difference between the two. For the teachings of the founders of the religions are purely personal matters. They create a relationship between the individual and Ultimate Reality. The institutionalization of these teachings is a human, social process that enables power structures and hierarchies to come into being (see chapter 16). The consequence of this institutionalization is far reaching. There can be no true access to the Dhamma unless one submits to training from a senior monk in a monastery. There can be no access to the Church unless mediated by the priesthood. The intricacies of the Shari'a are only understood by a religious scholar (a *mufti* or *mujtahid*) who has undergone training in the subject. Thus the direct contact that the individual believer had with the source of his or her religion in the early period of the religion is removed and replaced by a mediated and controlled contact.

This process, the institutionalization or the reification of the doctrines of the religion, introduces a profound change in the course of the religion. It sets up its power and authority structures and establishes the orthodoxy (right doctrine) or orthopraxy (right practice), the straight path. All deviancy from this constitutes heresy or ritual impurity. In short, it changes what was a purely personal matter into a social concern; where deviance once led only to personal spiritual penalties, now there are social sanctions.

ORAL TRANSMISSION OF SACRED TEXT: This is a nineteenth-century depiction of an Iranian Shi'i *rawdih-khan*, one who tells the story of the persecution and martyrdom of the Imam Husayn.

THE NATURE OF THE HISTORICAL RECORD

In most of the religions of the world, there is a significant distance in time between the origin of the religion and the time at which its history and scripture are written down. This process of writing down the texts of the religion induces a profound change in the nature of the religious tradition.

Prior to the writing down of the sacred 'texts' they are transmitted orally, often in forms such as poetry, making them easier to memorize and recite. However, an orally transmitted 'text' is not fixed in the same way as a written text. There is no particular author. If the text is attributed to a specific holy figure, then this signifies that the ideas in the text are given on the authority of that person, not that the wording belongs to him or her. In fact, the text is fluid and able to take on the changes in worldview that any society experiences. The basic core of ideas in the text remains unchanged, but the wording changes. These stories are expressed in ways that alter subtly from one generation to the next, reflecting the issues that are important to each generation and the gradual changes in culture and worldview that occur. Each generation, and even each individual reciter of the text recreates the text. Thus, in an oral tradition there can be no sense in which there is an 'original' pristine text that can be uncovered by careful research.

> In non-literate societies . . . the past is perceived as entirely the servant of the needs of the present, things are forgotten and myth is constructed to justify contemporary arrangements; there are no dictionary definitions of words . . . In [the] religion [of a non-literate society] there is no sense of impersonal or universal orthodoxy of doctrine; legitimate belief is as a particular priest or elder expounds it.[27]

At some point in the evolution of a religion, sometimes hundreds of years after its origins, the religious 'texts' are written down and thus fixed. What had previously been characterized by multi-formity and fluidity now becomes rigid and fixed. A recording in writing of a single moment in the evolving oral tradition of a text now becomes the 'original' text. For a time the two traditions, oral and literate, continue to exist in parallel, but from that time on, the other oral versions are pronounced to be deviations from this 'original'. Gradually, the literate world gains precedence and the tyranny of the 'original' text causes the variety of oral versions to be relegated to the background and eventually to disappear.

Once the sacred text of a religion is written down, a different set of considerations comes into play. The religion has acquired a rigid and fixed base; arguments must now be resolved by appeal to an unchangeable written authority. Religion evolves into a system of rules, a code of laws, which emanate from the Ultimate Reality and are therefore quite external to the individual (and even to the priest or elder) and to which the individual must conform if he or she is to be saved. This is an important aspect of the move from primal religion to what Weber calls rationalized religion (see chapter 3, pp. 59–60).

The greater the distance in time between the events of religious history and their being recorded in written form, the greater the discrepancy between the concerns and viewpoints of those who write down the texts as compared to the original actors of the episode. Thus what we have in the *New Testament*, for example, is not so much a description of what went on during the lifetime of Jesus and immediately afterwards as a description of these events filtered through the concerns and viewpoints of those who wrote down the accounts between 50 and 150 years later. This much has been acknowledged by biblical scholars who, in the last hundred years, have painstakingly researched many of the consequences of this process (see chapter 11, pp. 286–93). It is of particular concern to religious history because the text of scripture, once written down (together with the implicit viewpoints and concerns of the time of the writers), then becomes frozen as an unalterable, divinely inspired religious text. As time goes by, the worldview embodied in the text becomes ever more divorced from the worldview of contemporary society. This is part of the source of the fundamentalism–liberalism dichotomy (see pp. 382–5).

From India to Europe: The Fluidity of Oral Transmission

The following describes the transmission of the story of St Josaphat and St Barlaam, from India across the Middle East to Europe. Although the evidence for the transmission must necessarily come from written textual sources, the transmission itself undoubtedly took place orally, through the medium of storytellers. The written sources that we rely upon as evidence may be considered to be 'captured' isolated moments in a dynamic process of oral transmission that must have taken many centuries to occur. Indeed, the story itself probably entered the region in which a text has been found many years before the 'capture' of the oral tradition in a written form. Some elements of the transmission story, for instance the manner in which the name changed from Bodisaf to Yudasaf, if correct, do imply a textual source for the transmission. This episode illustrates the point that the essential elements in the story (in this case, its spiritual depths) have been remarkably well preserved in the course of transmission, while the details, such as the religion to which the story relates, have undergone a remarkable transformation.

The story is told in many sources. A powerful Indian ruler grieves because he is childless. At last a child is born to the king and is named Josaphat. A seer predicts that the child will renounce all earthly things, so the king builds a city and a palace that is set apart to keep his son from knowledge of the world and of the true condition of human beings. When he grows up, Josaphat one day persuades his father to allow him to go out and see the real world. An excursion is arranged and on this Josaphat sees for the first time a cripple, a blind man and one who is near death. This disturbs Josaphat, causing him to realize that all human beings are subject to disease, old age and death. At this juncture, a holy wandering Christian ascetic, St Barlaam, appears in disguise, preaches to Josaphat in parables and succeeds in converting him to Christianity. Josaphat's father opposes his son's conversion and organizes debates and other means to try to overturn it but, in the end, is himself converted. Josaphat leaves his princely life and departs for the life of a wandering ascetic.

Anyone with even a superficial knowledge of the biography of the Buddha will recognize the similarity of this story to the story of the Buddha, but it was not until the nineteenth century that the details of the history of this tale began to be unravelled. From these researches, it emerged that this was indeed the story of the Buddha, which had travelled with Buddhism into Central Asia, where Buddhism and Manichaeism overlapped for many centuries. Clues to the transmission of the story can be found in Central Asian Buddhist Soghdian texts, where the word *bodhisattva* (one who is seeking to become a buddha) is shortened to 'Bodisaf', and in fragments of Manichaean texts where the story of Bodisaf's meeting with a decrepit old man is told.

Evidence exists that from Central Asia the story spread to Iran and was to be found in Pahlavi manuscripts. These then formed the basis of the later story of Yudasaf and Bilawhar in Persian. The change in the name from Bodisaf to Yudasaf is evidently a transcription error and only involves an additional dot under the first letter. The end of the story in these versions, that Yudasaf travelled to Kashmir and handed over the teaching of his message to Abadid (= Ananda, the Buddha's chief disciple) before dying, was the basis for the legends surrounding the shrine of Yuz Asaf in Srinagar. (This Yuz Asaf was identified with Jesus Christ by the Ahmadiyya Muslim sect and forms part of their claim that Jesus did not die on the cross but survived, travelled to India and is buried in this shrine.) From Iran, the story spread and is found in Arabic, Georgian, Armenian, Ethiopian and Hebrew forms.

Around the year 1000 CE, the story was translated into Greek and later into Latin as the story of St Josaphat (Iosaph in Greek) and St Barlaam. The two saints were entered on the roll of saints recognized by the Roman Catholic Church and enjoyed great popularity in medieval Europe. Versions of their story made their way as far afield as Iceland and the Philippines. Singly or together they were allocated the feast days of 27 November, 26 August and 19 November by the Roman Catholic, Greek Orthodox and Russian Orthodox churches respectively.

While the fact that a religious text has been written down freezes the form of the words, it does not freeze their interpretation. Both the religious ideas and the history contained in the religious texts can be, and indeed have been, reinterpreted in each generation according to the concerns and viewpoint of that generation.

I have described above the tendency to read back into the past the issues of the present. One important point that arises from this relates to the idea put forward by the philosopher of history Benedetto Croce. He stated that 'all true history is contemporary history'.[28] In other words, all writing of history inescapably involves the backwards projection of contemporary concerns. Each generation of British historians, for example, has produced its own history of the Roman Empire. By and large, the available information about the Roman Empire has changed very little: it is the interpretation of the evidence that changes. These histories differ in that they each reflect the concerns and perspectives of the generation that produced them.

To create a past by constructing an image of it is, in a sense, to define the present and thus to determine the course of future action. Each generation of a religious community has its own questions and problems arising out of contemporary social and intellectual concerns. One of the ways of dealing with these is to reconstruct the past of the community in the light of the present concerns. The image of the prophet-founder can be adjusted to provide a new model of how people should act and live in the present circumstances. To one generation, Jesus is meek and forgiving; to another, he is a social revolutionary. For one generation of Shi'is in Iran, the Imams exhibit the qualities of meekness and patient endurance of persecution; for the next generation, they are seen as having risen against tyranny and injustice. Neither the Bible nor the traditional accounts of Shi'i history have changed from one generation to the next; only the circumstances of each generation have altered. Their needs are different, and they have created a religous history to suit those needs. History can thus be seen to be a powerful tool in the hands of those who wish to bring about religious change. It is instrumental in creating the vision of each generation, in setting up the ideals and values of that generation and thus the goals to be pursued.

A good example of the reconstruction of the past in order to justify and give meaning to the present is to be found in the history of the Pani Kuch people who live in northern Bengal. Up to the fifteenth century, they were isolated from the mainstream of Indian culture and had their own social and religious culture. They lived in the forests, spoke a distinct language and were matrilineal. Their priests, called *kolitas*, officiated at sacrifices to the sun, the moon, the stars and various gods associated with local forests, hills and rivers. At the head of this pantheon was the supreme god, Rishi, who was married to the goddess Jogo. They used no images of their gods and goddesses, however. One of the headman of the Kuch people, Bisu, put together a confederation and declared himself king (*raja*) of the region in the early sixteenth century. At about that same time, Brahminical Hindu culture began to have an impact upon the Kuch people. The new king patronized the Brahminical culture, as did his son and successor, Nara Narayan. The dynasty adopted a fictitious genealogy that made the father of Bisu and the other Kuch family heads sons of fugitive princes of the Hindu Kshatriya caste who had settled in the region and married local women. A further development of the legend had Bisu's mother impregnated by the Hindu god Shiva, leading to Bisu's birth. In this way, an upwardly mobile dynasty had linked itself to the highest echelons of Brahminical Hindu culture and integrated themselves into the Hindu caste system. The Kuch supreme deity Rishi and his consort Jogo became identified with Shiva and his consort Parvati. The Kuch priests adopted Brahminical rituals and even the Kuch peasants were, by the nineteenth century, identifying themselves as members of the Hindu Shudra caste.[29]

In addition to the above, the writing and recounting of history has served other functions in human society. The earliest surviving accounts of the Shi'i sects in Islam were written during the Abbasid period (that is, about two hundred years after the events). Montgomery Watt has proposed that these accounts were, in fact, a covert way of conducting political debate in the highly restrictive Abbasid environment.[30] This has been a role played by religious debate in many historical contexts. In the years before the Iranian Revolution of 1979, the restrictions imposed by the Shah prevented open political debate. The opponents of the regime therefore had recourse to relating stories about the early leaders of Shi'i Islam and their struggles against the governments of their time. The purport of such statements was not lost on those who heard them.

Also of relevance in considering religious history is Hayden White's concept of the rhetorical nature of historical truth (see p. 150). He asserts that the acceptance of a particular account or interpretation of a historical event (here an event in religious history) is not dependent on the accurate use of historical data or even on the strength of reasoning or logic used in the analysis. Rather, it depends on the consistency, coherence and illuminative power of the account. This in turn depends on its rhetorical and poetic persuasiveness. A historical account is thus accepted at an emotional rather than an intellectual level. After its initial acceptance, however, an elaborate web of evidence and reasoning is built up to support this acceptance.[31] This is an important observation because it helps to explain how mythic features come to be incorporated into religious history. These mythic elements are important factors in the emotional response to religious history. They resonate with deep structures within the human mind, so enhancing the rhetorical and poetic persuasiveness of any version of religious history that incorporates them. There is therefore a constant pressure on historical accounts, pushing them to make the figure of the founder of the religion (or another important religious figure) into a solar hero or the major female figure into an earth mother (see chapter 11).

Further Reading

For biographies of the various founder-prophets, see Pye, *The Buddha*; Saddhatissa, *The Life of the Buddha*; the *Bible*; H. J. Richards, *The First Christmas*; Lings, *Muhammad*; Balyuzi, *The Bab*; Balyuzi, *Baha'u'llah*. On the social evolution of religion, see Weber, *The Theory of Social and Economic Organisation*, pp. 329–342, and *The Sociology of Religion* (especially chapters 4 and 5).

13

Religion and Ethics

Historically, religion has always been considered as the mainstay of public and personal morality. Although anthropologists have identified a few cultures in which morality does not appear to be based on religion, it would be true to say that for the majority of human societies, the ethical basis of a society has been its religion. In theory, morality refers to principles of what is right and wrong in behaviour while ethics is the area of philosophy concerned with the meaning and basis of morality. In practice, the two terms are used interchangeably. In this chapter we shall look at the theoretical grounds for ethics within religion and then go on to the area of social ethics, looking in particular at the ethics of environmental concern.

In our interactions with other people, we may act entirely selfishly or we may take them into consideration. It is this taking of others into consideration, giving them a value, considering them of some importance, that forms the root of ethics. There are frequently, however, factors that make moral decisions more complex. Moral decisions are often in practice not a clear-cut, black-and-white matter. Something that we may consider impermissible might, for example, become permissible under some circumstances: while lying is considered unethical, it may be permissible in the case of a doctor who considers it in the best interests of the patient that the full severity of the illness not be revealed to her or him. There are also grades in our evaluations; greater or lesser value may be placed on certain courses of action. A development which has occurred recently in the Western world (although it has long been a part of other cultures) is the assignment of value to animals and the physical environment and hence ethical concern for them.

Religions have based their ethical dimension on a number of theoretical considerations. The first of these is the theory of natural law: that there is an inherent natural ability of human beings to recognize goodness, beauty, truth and other values. This theory can become the basis for a religious approach when, for example, human nature is considered to be a reflection of the divine nature. Since it is part of the divine nature to be able to recognize good, this is also inherent in human beings.

The second way that religions can create a basis for morality is through the divine command theory. For someone from a Western religious background, we can state that morality flows from God's commands; obedience to the injunctions and laws in the sacred texts is the basis for human morality. One problem with this approach has been called the Euthyphro dilemma (from the discussion under that name in Plato's *Dialogues*). In brief, this puts forward two alternative positions that a religious person might take: either what God commands is right simply because God commands it, or God commands what is right because it is right. The first of these alternatives, what might be called the fundamentalist position, seems to imply that God's command sets an arbitrary standard which we have no moral reason for following; we may indeed only follow it out of fear of the consequences of failing to do so. The second alternative is equally troubling for the religious person. It seems to imply that the divine command is irrelevant to ethics and that ethical standards are established independent of religious considerations. It also sets limits on divine omnipotence by suggesting that God is compelled to act in a certain way because that is what is ethical.[1]

One can say that ethics in the Eastern religions operates under variants of the above theories. Karma in Hinduism and Buddhism and the Tao in Taoism are cosmic laws under which all phenomena in the universe operate. One approach would be to say that human beings become moral when they realize their own identity with Absolute Reality and hence come into harmony with the universal law (a parallel with the natural law theory). Another approach would be to say that the scriptures of the religion reveal the Dharma which defines the path that human beings must follow if they want to be in tune with the universal law and hence be moral (a parallel with the divine command theory, without necessarily invoking a divinity).

Although the Greek philosophers developed the field of ethics as a part of philosophy, they considered that their ideas applied only to a very small élite. It would be correct to say that before modern times, for the majority of people, it was not possible to separate religion and morality. Religion was the basis on which all the normative actions of individual and social life were based. Although we now separate these and call some moral actions, some religious law, and some ritual, they were considered as an integrated whole in pre-modern society. In more recent times (in particular since the Enlightenment in the eighteenth century), however, the humanist argument that it is possible to separate ethics from its religious basis has gained ground. One version of this argument maintains that it is possible to derive ethical principles from a purely utilitarian basis, without the need for a religious underpinning. It is asserted that ethical principles can be derived rationally from such general principles as promoting the general good and preventing suffering.[2] Those hostile to religion assert that religion is merely a way of buttressing public morality by invoking a series of supra-natural sanctions against immoral behaviour. They maintain that it is only necessary in the early stages of human social evolution and for gullible or morally weak persons. Indeed, such writers as Freud and Marx went further and said that it is dangerous to base the ethics of a society on religion; once religion's illusory nature is revealed, both religion and morality collapse.

A religious person would respond to the humanist argument somewhat along the following lines. What constitutes the general good, which is to be promoted, and suffering, which is to be prevented, are socially and culturally derived norms. They are not independent, universal truths that can be derived from reason. They do not arise inherently within human beings. If we observe children, for example, we see that they have no inherent morality. Without education, they are aggressive and lawless. The fact that we are now able to derive generally accepted ethical guidelines in our societies is the result of centuries of religious training and inculcation of religious values.

Furthermore, the religious argument continues, even given that we have reached this stage after centuries of religious moral training, this does not mean that human beings can now dispense with religion. We still need something that is outside and above us to act as the source of authority for our ethical norms. Otherwise our socially agreed or rationally derived ethical standards are too malleable, subject to expediency and to our moral weakness. A prime example is the way that Hitler managed to persuade the German people (who prided themselves on their rationality) that Jews and gypsies were not deserving of ethical consideration. The whole structure of a nation's moral standards collapsed within a short time. Human beings need an absolute standard of morality that is not subject to the vagaries of rhetorical persuasion and partisan propaganda. Only religion can provide such a standard, because only religion claims that its standard derives from beyond the human world. It is therefore less subject to variation and manipulation. (Those antagonistic to religion may point out, however, that in fact religious institutions such as the Roman Catholic Church failed lamentably to mount a vigorous opposition to Hitler.)

There are several further points that a religious person would raise. The first is that the standard for human behaviour dictated by the humanist criteria is really a very minimal standard. From time to time individuals arise whose actions merit exceptional praise and to whom we as individuals feel attracted because of their 'goodness'. Such persons almost always have a religious basis to their way of life. A person who is considered to be 'good' in a religious sense (for example a saint or *bodhisattva*) does not just act in ways that would be considered moral by the humanist standard. Such a person performs actions of generosity, charity and self-sacrifice that go well beyond any rationalist humanist criterion. The standards for such a way of life are dictated by the scriptures of a religion and by the example of the religion's founder and its saints. A religious person would further contend that rational argument cannot answer the more fundamental question of why we should behave in a moral way when this may cause us loss or harm.

As indicated above, most religious people do not really discern any difference between the moral, ritual and legal norms of their religion. These

COLLAPSE OF MORAL STANDARDS: By 1933, the Nazis were dominating political life in Germany. Their persecution of Jews began with campaigns such as the one pictured here, encouraging Germans to boycott shops and businesses owned by Jews.

are viewed as an integrated whole. Contradictory tensions may arise within this framework from time to time. These are, however, occasions for religious debate; they do not cast doubt on the validity of the integrated view of the religious person.

It would be wrong, however, to say that the religious person always puts religious norms ahead of independently derived moral norms as a guide for action. Often religious people act in a way that makes it clear that they give priority to the latter. Indeed historically, many episodes of major religious upheaval and change have arisen because someone has asserted that a new position is morally superior to the traditional position held by the orthodox religious establishment. Even some of the founders of religions can be seen in this light. Jesus can be said to have initiated a moral revolt against the excesses of Jewish legalism; the Buddha and the Sikh gurus to have rejected the Hindu caste system; and Baha'u'llah to have opposed the legalism and literalism of the Islamic religious establishment.

MORAL DEVELOPMENT

There have been several attempts to describe the stages in the moral development of an individual. Perhaps the best known of these is that developed by Lawrence Kohlberg. Following Piaget's work on cognitive development, Kohlberg described three levels of moral development, divided into a total of six stages. The first level, pre-conventional morality, is typical of young children, who make decisions based solely on the consequences for themselves. What is viewed as morally right for a person within this stage is based on the immediate (stage 1) or calculated (stage 2) material benefits to himself or herself. At the second level, conventional morality, decisions are based on the requirements of social roles and the expectations of others (stage 3); or on taking the perspective of society as a whole (stage 4). What is right is what is in accordance with society's rules, expectations and conventions. At the third level, post-conventional morality, what is right is based on personally derived moral principles. These transcend and may at times transgress conventional rules and religious laws. There are multiple possibilities in each situation and the individual must come to a decision based on principles of justice, equality and human rights.[3]

Kohlberg's ideas have been extensively criticized. Among other criticisms is that the stages described are gender biased: there are other ways of approaching moral dilemmas that involve thinking in terms of relationships and the needs and welfare of others, ways that perhaps come more naturally to women and that many may consider just as advanced as the abstract concepts of justice that Kohlberg places at the top of his hierarchy (see p. 435). More importantly from the viewpoint of religion, Kohlberg's hierarchy can be criticized for assuming that the highest values are those of Western liberal Protestant Christianity (or of the Western liberal tradition). In fact, the whole exercise can be considered circular. A hierarchy is devised that puts Western liberal Christian values at the highest level, and then surveys are done which show that those from the Western liberal Protestant tradition are the most highly developed morally.[4] Certainly, those from other religious traditions would dispute the values that define the highest level in Kohlberg's hierarchy. Many would say that the willingness to serve others and to sacrifice self are the highest markers of moral development from a religious viewpoint; others would say that obedience to the Holy Law is the true marker of moral development and that those in Kohlberg's sixth stage who consider themselves to be beyond the Holy Law are, in fact, being arrogant towards God.

The Foundations of Religious Ethics

While each religion has its own particular basis of authority for the implementation of ethical standards, the practical results are to a large extent similar. Many basic ethical principles are common to all religions; these may be regarded as part of the common experience of humanity in the process of building up ever greater social units. All religions have precepts that one should refrain from killing or injuring others, from lying and deceiving others, and from depriving others of their freedom or their property. A stable society can scarcely be imagined without such principles. Without some degree of application of the ethical principle 'Thou shalt not kill', society would dissolve into chaos; without the ethical principle 'Thou shalt not lie', no effective communication between human beings is possible. Therefore, even if we suppose that a religion did exist that did not advocate these ethical principles, it would soon disappear in the chaos that it caused.[5]

As an example of the fact that every religion has much the same ethical basis, one can look at the various manifestations of what is often called the 'Golden Rule' or the law of reciprocity. This may be stated as the moral imperative that one's actions towards others should be such as one would hope for from others (see p. 344).

Once one passes beyond this basic level, religious ethics vary to a certain extent because of several factors. First, each religion has its own particular vision of humanity's position in the world and its relationship to Absolute Reality (see chapter 8). Profoundly different, even contradictory, world-views exist in the various religions of the world. One would think that this would lead to great ethical differences but the differences on this basis are, in fact, surprisingly small. One example of such differences that can be seen is in the prohibition against killing others. In Judaism and Islam, it is permitted to kill in self-defence, in defence of the religion or of others. In Christianity, the *New Testament* hints that it is not permissible to kill or injure others, even in self-defence. Baha'is also are not permitted to kill others in self-defence, but it is

Two Jain pandits (top row) present to their guru, Acharya Vijayasena Suri, an edict prohibiting the slaughter of animals during the eight days of the Paryushana festival, 1610, that they have obtained from the Moghul Emperor Jahangir. Their white robes show that they are of the Shvetambara school. Three Jain nuns dressed in white may be seen in the third row from the bottom on the left. In the bottom row a man is dancing by musical instruments.

The Golden Rule in the Religions of the World

Hinduism
Do nothing to others which if it were done to you would cause you pain. This is the essence of duty. (*Mahabharata*, ed. Roy, 5: *Udyoga Parva, Prajagava Parva*, 1517–8)

Buddhism
If you, Rahula, are desirous of doing a deed with the body, you should reflect on that deed of your body . . . If you, Rahula, reflecting thus, should find, 'That deed which I am desirous of doing with the body is a deed of my body that would conduce to the harm of self and to the harm of others and to the harm of both; this deed of body is unskilled, its yield is anguished, its result is anguish' – a deed of body like this, Rahula, is certainly not to be done by you. (Words of the Buddha in *Majjhima Nikaya, Ambalatthika Rahulovadasutta*, 1:415, in *The Collection of Middle Length Sayings*, vol. 2, p. 89)

Zoroastrianism
That nature only is good when it shall not do unto another whatever is not good for its own self. (*Dadistan-i Dinik* 94:5. in West, *Pahlavi Texts*, part 1, p. 271)

Judaism
What is hateful to you, do not do to your neighbour: that is the whole Torah, while the rest is the commentary thereof. (Rabbi Hillel in the *Babylonian Talmud, Seder Mo'ed, Shabbath*, 1:31a)

Christianity
And as you wish that men would do to you, do so to them. (*Luke* 6:31)

Islam
None among you truly believes until he likes for his brother that which he loves for himself. (*Sahih Muslim*, book 1, chapter 18)

Baha'i Faith
Lay not on any soul a load which ye would not wish to be laid upon you, and desire not for anyone the things ye would not desire for yourselves. This is My best counsel unto you, did ye but observe it. (Baha'u'llah, *Gleanings*, no. 66, pp. 127–8).

permissible to kill in defence of others. In Buddhism and Jainism, the prohibition against killing is extended to all sentient creatures.

One second source of the variations in the ethics of religions arises from differences over the question of who is worthy of ethical consideration. This is the question of the boundaries of ethical action, which is considered further below.

Third, there is also some degree of variation in the comparative emphasis given to different moral virtues. The person of the founder of a religion acts to a large extent as a role model for the followers of that

a

b

THE ROLE MODEL IN RELIGION: a) The Buddha's characteristics of serenity and calmness are emphasized in Buddhism and are predominant in portrayals of the Buddha in Buddhist art. This statue from Wat Trimit in Bangkok is in the Sukhothai style and shows the Buddha in the posture of *Bhumisparsha mudra* (see p. 274). The statue was thought to be made of stucco but some cracks revealed that it was in fact made of some five and a half tons of solid gold. b) 'Abdu'l-Baha, the son and successor of Baha'u'llah, is regarded by Baha'is as the Perfect Exemplar of the Baha'i teachings.

religion. This will affect the comparative emphasis given to different moral virtues. Jesus is viewed by his followers as primarily exhibiting the quality of love towards others. Therefore Christians tend to emphasize love as an ethical precept. Muslims regard Muhammad as exhibiting justice in his dealings with others and some Muslims may emphasize this quality. Theravada Buddhists consider that the Buddha showed great calmness and contentment, even under adversity. Buddhists may therefore emphasize these virtues in their social dealings. Similarly, in interpreting the principle of self-denial and self-sacrifice, Christians have, following the example of Jesus, interpreted this in terms of celibacy and monasticism, while Muslims have been prepared to sacrifice their lives in defence of the realm of Islam. For Baha'is, 'Abdu'l-Baha, the son of Baha'u'llah, is the 'Perfect Exemplar', the one whose actions are the example to follow; his patience and love are thus emulated by Baha'is.

Lastly, it is also possible to discern that ideas of morality have developed and become more refined with the passing of time. This refinement leads to a replacement of less differentiated ideas about the morality of an action with a deeper assessment of factors such as the intention of the agent of the action.

यदा यदा हि धर्मस्य ग्लानिर्भवती भारत।
अभ्युत्थानमधर्मस्य तदाऽऽत्मनं सृजाम्यहम॥

KRISHNA AT WAR: This poster from India shows Krishna as the charioteer of Arjuna as they go to battle in the war between the Pandavas and the Kauravas. Arjuna is one of the five Pandava princes.

THE BOUNDARIES OF ETHICAL ACTION

Traditional Formulations

One of the ways in which religions differ from one another is in defining what one might call the boundaries of ethical action. For example, as has already been indicated, all religions contain some form of prohibition against murder. This prohibition only applies, however, in certain circumstances. Almost every religion has to some extent authorized some form of religious warfare. Even Buddhism, which is often regarded as a pacifist religion, was in fact the inspiration behind many of the martial arts of China and Japan, forming the religious base for the Samurai warrior class.[6] Hinduism had its warrior caste, the *kshatriya*, whose destiny it was to fight and take life. The *Mahabharata* contains several instances of Yudhishthir and Arjuna protesting against the karma of their class, which forces them to fight and take life. Christianity authorized the Crusades as a holy war against the infidel.[7] In Islam, jihad, holy war, is one of the pillars of the faith. The world is divided into the Dar al-Islam (world of Islam, the territory controlled by Muslims) and the Dar al-Harb (world of war, the rest of the world, which is the field for the jihad).[8] During much of the Middle Ages, Christianity and Islam fought each other in holy war – jihad to the Muslims, the Crusades to the Christians. Only in the more recent Baha'i

SAMURAI RELIGIOUS CULTURE

As an inevitable and natural result, the nonviolent message of Buddhism was qualified, modified, or overlaid by duty to clan lord, so that Buddhist warriors fought other Buddhist warriors to the death, it is to be presumed with only minor twinges of conscience . . .

. . . there was an inbuilt factor in Buddhism itself that worked against the teaching that all life, especially human life, is sacred. This was the Buddhist teaching of karmic destiny. For instance, some of the warriors portrayed in the *Heike Monogatari* (Tale of the Heike) lamented the fact, at reflective moments or when they had committed some militarily necessary cruelty, that they had been born into a warrior family and thus must carry on with a warrior's bloody career. And free as Zen may have been in some respects from the bonds of the Buddhist tradition, it was not free from the bonds of the teaching of karma.

To this must be added a peculiarly Japanese factor: the strong sense of family loyalty and tradition, especially in the upper classes. Reflecting the Chinese reverence for ancestors, the family – and its role, occupation, business – is a 'sacred' inheritance, entailing the son's – especially the eldest son's – following in his father's footsteps. (One contemporary Shinto priest proudly notes that he is the twenty-eighth in the family who has occupied the headship of a particular shrine.) When this is added to, or is seen as the vehicle of, karmic predetermination, the individual is required, even fated, to accept the role that has been given him – for instance, as a samurai whose destined duty was to be a fighting, life-destroying 'Buddhist.' (King, *Zen and the Way of the Sword*, p. 33)

Faith is there a specific scriptural prohibition on holy war as an instrument of religious policy.[9]

The point is that although killing other human beings is forbidden in every religion, this prohibition does not cover everyone. Certain people are 'us' and are included in the prohibition, while others are 'them' and are not included (or, at least, have not been, historically). The same point could be made with regard to all the other ethical provisions. There is a boundary. The highest ethical considerations are extended towards those within the boundary. Those outside the boundary, however, are considered to be outside the scope of these ethical laws and moral principles.[10] The following comments refer to each religion in its classic period and formulation:

- In the *Hebrew Bible*, 'us' refers to the chosen people, the tribe of Israel. Others (even women and children) were often treated with great brutality, and killed *en masse*. This occurred, for example, during the biblical conquest of the land of Israel.[11]
- In Hinduism, it is the members of either family, clan or caste that are 'us'. The higher castes did not consider themselves as bound to observe

ethical considerations towards the lowest castes and certainly not to the non-caste peoples.

- In many periods of Christian history, 'us' tended to be restricted to orthodox members of one's own sect. All others were either heretics or infidels, not deserving of any ethical consideration. Their torture and killing were even commended by the Church.
- The law in Islam is more generous. What in Judaism was a tribal boundary and in Christianity became a sectarian boundary (cutting across tribal boundaries) was now extended to the concept of the *umma*, the entire community of believers (cutting across both tribal and sectarian boundaries). Almost all Muslims are regarded as 'us'. A large degree of ethical consideration can even be extended to Jews and Christians as 'People of the Book', provided that they submit to the rule of Islam and fulfil certain other conditions.[12] Two categories are outside the boundaries of ethical consideration in Islam – polytheists (which for practical purposes means all religions other than Judaism and Christianity)[13] and apostates. These may be killed with impunity wherever they are found, and their property is forfeit.
- In the Baha'i Faith, the boundaries are drawn even more widely, to include all the people of the world, without regard for religious and other boundaries. Special advantages are even given, in some circumstances, to minority groups.

The drawing of ethical boundaries can be considered to have been an advantage in the past. Positive ethical attitudes towards those within one's society helped to increase the cohesiveness and therefore the strength of society. Identifying the enemy without and directing the society's negative energy in that direction reinforced this process and purged society of destructive forces that could otherwise have turned inwards. Such an effect can be seen in the Crusades, when the call to fight the Muslim infidels frequently brought a halt to the internecine wars in Christian Europe. It is only with the drawing together of the 'global village' in modern times that this identification of external enemies has become disadvantageous and threatening to the world as a whole.

Contemporary Developments

During this century, religions have come under pressure from the increasingly pluralistic world in which we live. This has resulted in a need to move away from the exclusivist attitudes of the traditional religious ethics. As a consequence, there has been a relaxing of these very rigid attitudes towards those who are not 'us'. Thus, for example, calls for a jihad against infidels are now limited to extreme factions among Muslims, whereas up until the early part of the twentieth century they were to be heard from major religious leaders, and the exclusivist attitude of the

The Assembly of Religious and Spiritual Leaders at the second Parliament of the World's Religions, Chicago, August–September 1993

Roman Catholic Church was almost completely reversed by the Second Vatican Council (1962–5). Even so, this has not been unanimous: fundamentalist elements in each religion keep trying to draw the community back towards greater rigidity. For every scriptural verse that liberal elements find encouraging a pluralist attitude, the fundamentalists can point to another verse that is exclusivist in nature. In the Baha'i Faith, however, there is a specific scriptural injunction to 'consort with the followers of all religions in a spirit of friendliness and fellowship' and there is therefore little scope for exclusivist interpretations.[14]

A recent attempt to generate an inter-religious ethical framework that could embrace all religions is a declaration approved by the General Council of the Parliament of the World's Religions (held in Chicago, 28 August to 4 September 1993), and signed by the delegates attending, entitled 'Declaration toward a Global Ethic'. It affirms the need for a global ethic to underpin the emerging world order and for every human being to be treated humanely. In a series of guidelines for human behaviour, it proposes that both individuals and governments make commitments to create a culture of peace and non-violence; solidarity and a just economic order; tolerance and truthfulness; and equal rights and partnership between men and women.[15] In depicting the process by which this declaration was formulated, Hans Küng, its principal architect, describes the objections raised by various religious groups to specific aspects of the

THE PARLIAMENT OF THE WORLD'S RELIGIONS: DECLARATION TOWARD A GLOBAL ETHIC

The following is part of the declaration agreed by the delegates of the religions attending the Parliament of the World's Religions, Chicago, August–September 1993:

We men and women of various religions and regions of this earth address here all people, religious and non-religious, for we share the following convictions:

> that we all have a responsibility for a better global order;
> that involvement for the sake of human rights, freedom, justice, peace and the preservation of the earth is reasonable and necessary;
> that our different religious and cultural traditions must not prevent our common involvement in opposing all forms of inhumanity and working for greater humaneness;
> that the principles expressed in this Declaration can be affirmed by all humans with ethical convictions, religiously grounded or not;
> that we as religious women and men who base our lives on an Ultimate Reality and draw spiritual power and hope therefrom in trust, in prayer or meditation, in word or silence have, however, a very special responsibility for the welfare of all humanity . . .

On the basis of personal life experiences and the burdensome history of our planet we have learned

> that a better global order cannot be created or, indeed, enforced with laws, prescriptions and conventions alone;
> that the realization of justice in our societies depends on the insight and readiness to act justly;
> that action in favor of rights presumes a consciousness of duty, and that therefore both the head and heart of women and men must be addressed;
> that rights without morality cannot long endure, and that there will be no better global order without a global ethic . . .

In the face of all inhumanity our religions and ethical convictions demand that every human being must be treated humanely!

That means that every human being – without distinction of sex, age, race, skin color, language, religion, political view, or national or social origin – possesses an inalienable and untouchable dignity. And everyone, individuals as well as the state, is therefore obliged to honor this dignity and guarantee its effective protection.

For an authentically human attitude we especially call to mind that Golden Rule which is found and has been maintained in many religions and ethical traditions for thousands of years: What you do not wish done to yourself, do not do to others. Or positively: What you wish done to yourself, do to others! This should be the irrevocable, unconditional norm for all areas of life, for family and communities, for races, nations and religions. Self-determination and self-realization are thoroughly legitimate – so long as they are not separated from human self-responsibility and global-responsibility, from responsibility for fellow humans and nature. Every form of egoism, however, every self-seeking, whether individual or collective, whether in the form of class thinking, racism, nationalism or sexism, is to be rejected. For these prevent humans from being authentically human . . .

[We believe that there are] Four Irrevocable Directives:

1. Toward a Culture of Non-violence and Respect for Life . . .
2. Toward a Culture of Solidarity and a Just Economic Order . . .
3. Toward a Culture of Tolerance and a Life in Truthfulness . . .
4. Toward a Culture of Equal Rights and Partnership Between Men and Women . . .

All historical experience demonstrates the following: Our earth cannot be changed unless in the not too distant future an alteration in the consciousness of individuals is achieved. This has already been seen in areas such as war and peace or economy and ecology. And it is precisely for this alteration in inner orientation, in the entire mentality, in the 'heart,' that the religions bear responsibility in a special way . . .

Above all, we would welcome it if individual religions also would formulate their very specific ethic: What they on the basis of their faith tradition have to say, for example, about the meaning of life and death, the enduring of suffering and the forgiveness of guilt, about selfless sacrifice and the necessity of renunciation, compassion and joy. All these will be compatible with a Global Ethic, indeed can deepen it, make it more specific and concrete.

We are convinced that the new global order will be a better one only in a socially-beneficial and pluralist, partner-sharing and peace-fostering, nature-friendly and ecumenical globe. Therefore on the basis of our religious convictions we commit ourselves to a common Global Ethic and call upon all women and men of good will to make this Declaration their own.

declaration. Buddhist objections, for example, had caused all reference to God to be removed from the wording, while the reference to the equality of men and women had challenged some Muslims and Hindus.[16]

Ethics and Social Laws

While secular and religious moral philosophers may have, to a large extent, agreed over the ethics of individual action, there has been no similar achievement over the ethics of social action and societal structures. Starting from similar ethical considerations and using rational arguments, secular philosophers have managed to derive such differing systems as capitalism and communism and to claim moral superiority for each. It is perhaps not surprising that such societal speculation should have arisen in the Christian world, since there is very little in the *New Testament* concerned with social teachings (and Christianity, very early on, turned its back on its heritage of Judaic social law). Other religions, in particular Judaism, Islam, Hinduism and the Baha'i Faith have much in their scriptures on matters of social organization.

There is, however, frequently a great deal of divergence between the ethics of a religion as formulated in its texts and the actualities of social interactions. Nowhere is this more clearly seen than in attitudes towards women. Whatever view different religions may have of the spiritual status of women, the practical effect has usually been the oppression of women under one pretext or another (see chapter 17). The formal position in Islam, for example, is that men and women are equal before God and that in their relations with each other, therefore, they should be equals, with women being given equal ethical consideration to men. In fact, in the world of Islam, this ideal has been and is still rarely achieved. Islam originated in an area where women already held a low position in the social structure and it spread into other areas where the same applied, so it was never able fully to apply the theoretical position and give women full ethical consideration. The social isolation of women, for example, is widespread in the Islamic world, although little justification for this exists in the *Qur'an* or the *Hadiths* (Traditions).

Social and Environmental Ethics

Social ethics have become a key area of concern for religious people in the modern world. Each religion has some basis of teaching that starts from the Golden Rule described on p. 344 and evolves it in the direction of caring for the poor and disadvantaged. Before the modern era, religious institutions were the main source of assistance to the poor and sick. In many parts of the world, this role was taken over by secular institutions and, especially under socialist governments, by the State. As the State has contracted in

Social Ethics and Social Action

Islam

Islam was more than a religious movement. It was also a socio-economic revolution. Islam, through the holy Quran, strongly protested against unjust social structures and structures of oppression prevalent in Mecca, the place of its origin – in particular, and everywhere in the world, in general . . .

To any careful reader of the Quran, justice to the weaker sections is quite central to its teachings. It enjoins its followers to do justice and benevolence. 'Verily, Allah enjoins justice and benevolence', the Quran [16:90] says. It even goes further and says that the animosity with other nations or people should not detract the believers from doing [justice]. 'O you who believe! be steadfast in the cause of Allah, bearing witness with justice, and let not a people's enmity incite you to act otherwise than with justice. Be always just, that is nearer to righteousness . . .' [*Qur'an* 5:8] (Engineer, *Islam and Liberation Theology*, p. 50)

Judaism

[In December 1984], the first Jewish delegation of Witness for Peace, sponsored by the New Jewish Agenda, arrived in Nicaragua . . . To the question of why they are risking their lives in Nicaragua, they responded in a statement read in front of the American embassy in Managua:

> Our Judaism brings us to this place because our tradition asks us to speak out against injustice. We, as a people, are dedicated to *Tikkun Olam*, the just restitution and repair of the world. Through our tradition, we have accepted the responsibility of preserving the world in our laws, our text, and mostly, our hearts. Forty years ago Jews learned just how unjust people can be to each other. We learned there is no torture beyond comprehension, no reason once the path to destruction is set. We know, as a people, that there is no such thing as an injustice happening to someone else; it happens to us all.

(Ellis, *Toward a Jewish Theology of Liberation*, p. 55)

Sikhism

Sikhism is fundamentally opposed to inequality among mankind and to the idea of any divine sanction behind the ethnic inequality, and feels intensely for the victims of it. Guru Nanak and his succeeding Gurus reacted rather strongly to this evil because they felt that man is a manifestation of God. One of the fundamental Sikh metaphysical doctrines is that God is the sole power who had created this world and all beings inhabiting it out of His own self, and that the same divine spark shines forth in each human soul. In other words, all human beings are His children and that man in his essential nature partakes of the divine essence. Thus, the idea of ethnic equality is grounded in the Sikh metaphysics. (Singh, *Sikh Theology of Liberation*, pp. 118)

HINDUISM

It is an abuse of language to say that we Hindus extend any toleration towards our *Panchama* [Untouchable] brothers. We have degraded them and then have the audacity to use their very degradation against their rise . . . Swaraj [independence] for me means freedom for the meanest of our countrymen. If the lot of the *Panchamas* is not improved when we are all suffering, it is not likely to be better under the intoxication of swaraj. If it is necessary for us to buy the peace with the Mussalmans as a condition of swaraj, it is equally necessary for us to give peace to the *Panchama* before we can, with any show of justice or self-respect, talk of swaraj. I am not interested in freeing India merely from English yoke. I am bent upon freeing India from any yoke whatever . . . Hence for me the movement of swaraj is a movement of self-purification. (Mahatma Gandhi, quoted in Jesudasan, *A Gandhian Theology of Liberation*, p. 59)

BAHA'I FAITH

Let there be no mistake. The principle of the Oneness of Mankind – the pivot round which all the teachings of Baha'u'llah revolve – is no mere outburst of ignorant emotionalism or an expression of vague and pious hope. Its appeal is not to be merely identified with a reawakening of the spirit of brotherhood and good-will among men, nor does it aim solely at the fostering of harmonious cooperation among individual peoples and nations . . . It implies an organic change in the structure of present-day society, a change such as the world has not yet experienced . . . It calls for no less than the reconstruction and the demilitarization of the whole civilized world – a world organically unified in all the essential aspects of its life, its political machinery, its spiritual aspiration, its trade and finance, its script and language, and yet infinite in the diversity of the national characteristics of its federated units. (Shoghi Effendi, *Guidance for Today and Tommorow*, pp. 174–5)

the West in the last decades of the twentieth century, religious institutions have again begun to resume their role as advocates and supporters of the poor.

Concern for oppressed minorities and the poor has led to the evolution of various frameworks for social ethics. Liberation theology, feminist theology and black theology have all emerged in the Christian world, claiming to give guidance to religious people on how they should act socially. In these theologies, God is viewed as the consoler and liberator of the oppressed. Therefore, the Divine is to be found among the oppressed. This elevates the worth of the oppressed group, making them, in effect, holy. Those who wish to be acting in accordance with the divine will should work with the poor and oppressed. Parallel developments are increasingly being seen in the other religions. Throughout the world, religious groups and associations of various kinds have begun work among the poor, either in their own country or in the poorer countries, as a direct expression of their religious, ethical concern for their fellow human beings. The social and economic development of the poorer nations of the world has now become a major area of religious work.

Other lines of development for religious, social ethics include concern for world peace, for urban regeneration, and a call for better world economic and political structures that will not disadvantage the poorer nations of the world. Some religious leaders such as the Dalai Lama, Reverend Martin Luther King and Archbishop Desmond Tutu have assumed a role as advocates of peace, as mediators for reconciliation, and in such work as the resettlement of refugees.

BAHA'I DEVELOPMENT PROJECT: A doctor takes a skin sample for laboratory analysis at a clinic held in the Mangyan tribal area, Tapi-Nabiran, Mindoro Oriental, the Philippines, 1987.

Concern for the poor is an area that has been of particular concern to the liberal wing of each religion and has even been an area for debate between some religions and socialism. In Christianity, liberation theology emerged from South America as a statement of Christian ethical concern for the poor. Parallel developments have occurred in other religions. In the Muslim world some groups have entered into a dialogue with socialism and have called upon Muslims to demonstrate a greater concern for the poor and oppressed as a sign of the justice called for in Islamic teaching (see p. 128). In Korea, a People's Buddhism has paralleled a Christian People's Theology, which is, in turn, modelled on liberation theology. This movement is concerned with tackling such issues as the problems of urbanization, water pollution and the promotion of organic gardening.

One area that is of particular interest is what is sometimes called eco-spirituality: religious concern for the physical environment. In parallel to eco-feminism (see p. 451), those who advocate eco-spirituality identify the current ecological crisis as being a result of the anthropocentric view of humanity's place in the universe, which sees humanity as dominating and controlling the natural world. It is considered to have arisen particularly in the Western religions, in which it has scriptural authority. In the *Bible*, for example, we read:

> And God said, Let us make man in our image, after our likeness: and let them have dominion over the fish of the sea, and over the fowl of the air,

> and over the cattle, and over all the earth, and over every creeping thing that creepeth upon the earth.[17]

Correspondingly, the *Qur'an* says:

> He it is Who created for you all that is on earth . . . Behold thy Lord said to the angels: 'I will create a vicegerent [i.e. humanity] on earth.'[18]

This theme of dominion over the earth has, it is asserted by the theorists of eco-spirituality, led to a mechanistic, utilitarian, instrumental attitude towards nature; an assumption that the natural order can be rearranged in any way that suits human beings and that nature is there to be used as a tool for human benefit without any regard for nature itself. This, in turn, has resulted in ecological damage to the earth: pollution of air, water and land, destruction of the earth's ozone layer, global warming, desertification of once-fertile lands, extinction of species resulting in reduced biodiversity and depletion of non-renewable resources.

Advocates of religious concern for the environment point to the primal religions as being much more in tune with environmental concerns than Western religions. Human beings in primal societies who live in much closer contact with nature are therefore more in tune with its rhythms and less likely to carry out activities that damage the environment. Such views have, however, at times been over-romanticized. People in primal societies have a relationship with nature that contains several opposing tensions: they both exploit and conserve their environment; they both love and fear nature.

Animistic ritual in Native American religion: This depiction of an Iroquois dance shows participants adopting the role of a totem animal.

PRIMAL RELIGION AND NATURE

The White people never cared for land or deer or bear. When we Indians kill meat, we eat it all up. When we dig roots we make little holes; when we build houses, we make little holes. When we burn grass for grasshoppers, we don't ruin things. We shake down acorns and pinenuts. We don't chop down the trees. We only use dead wood. But the White people plow up the ground, pull down the trees, kill everything. The tree says, 'Don't. I'm sore. Don't hurt me.' But they chop it down and cut it up. The spirit of the land hates them. They blast out trees and stir it up to its depths. They saw up the trees. That hurts them. The Indians never hurt anything, but the White people destroy all. They blast rocks and scatter them on the ground. The rock says, 'Don't. You are hurting me.' But the White people pay no attention . . . How can the spirit of the earth like the White man? . . . Everywhere the White man has touched it, it is sore. (A member of the Wintu Native American people, quoted in Vecsey and Venables, *American Indian Environments*, p. 32)

People in primal societies have a very practical, detailed scientific knowledge of their environment, which has been built up over many thousands of years of observations. At the same time, they have a mythopoeic view of nature. By donning a bear's skin, a Native American can become a bear; an Australian aborigine is in some mysterious way a kangaroo or whatever is the totem of his clan. These two ways of thinking fuse into an integrated whole in the worldview of such people, occasioning no feeling of division or inconsistency.

Typical of primal religion is the phenomenon that the nineteenth-century British anthropologist Sir Edward Burnett Tylor named animism: the belief that animals and inanimate objects have a spirit associated with them. Therefore the whole physical world is, in this sense, on one level and deserves equal respect. If nature is to be violated in any way, this must be to the minimum extent and with care. If an animal has to be killed, then all of it must be utilized, down to the bones and skin.

There are a number of different strands within the general movement of religions towards environmental ethics.[19] The first stresses holism and interconnectedness. It advocates a return to an attitude that views nature as organic and spiritual; that sees human beings as being in a state of intimate interconnectedness with the natural world. Its supporters advocate, therefore, that no social, technological or economic measures should be taken until the consequences for this delicate ecosystem are assessed. Examples of this include those who have promoted the Gaia hypothesis, the concept that the earth itself may be regarded as a living organism. These ideas have found much support among those in the eco-feminist and neo-paganist movements.

Another strand in environmental ethics focuses on concern for the environment as part of an overall concern with issues of social justice:

THE SUMMIT ON RELIGIONS AND CONSERVATION, WINDSOR CASTLE: 1995: The summit was attended by many of the world's religious leaders. Front row (from left to right): Kimiko Schwerin (Baha'i), R. P. Chanaria (Jain), Madame Rabbani (Baha'i), Xie Zongzing (Taoism), Jathedar Mangit Singh (Sikh), Ternaki Kuwai (sponsor), Dr L. M. Singhvi (Hindu), HRH the Duke of Edinburgh, Rabbi Arthur Hertzberg (Judaism), Sri Kushak Bakula (Buddhism), Swami Vibudhesa Teertha (Hindu), Dr Robin Pellew (WWF). Behind Prince Philip and to the right is Dr Samuel Kobia (Christian). Behind Dr Kobia and to the left is Prof Hyder (Islam).

advocacy of the rights of tribal and native peoples, concern for the polluted environment in Third World urban slums, and efforts to combat illiteracy and increase education among the poor. These issues are raised by liberal religious groups such as the World Council of Churches on the basis of the general ethical and religious principles of helping others and advocacy of the poor and oppressed.

A third strand in environmental ethics takes a more traditionalist line. Advocates of this approach argue that it is humanity's departure from traditional religion that has brought on environmental problems and that therefore the only solution is to return to traditional religion.

Some of the debate on this issue of religious concern for the environment has been carried out within particular religious frameworks: Buddhist, Christian or Baha'i[20] for example; but this area is of particular interest in that it is increasingly a focus for interreligious discussions and the development of a common interreligious platform. Emerging out of a meeting held in Assisi under the auspices of the World Wildlife Fund in 1986, for example, the Alliance of Religions and Conservation was launched at the Summit on Religions and Conservation held in Atami, Japan, and at

Windsor Castle in England in 1995. This organization has Baha'i, Buddhist, Christian, Hindu, Muslim, Jain, Jewish, Sikh and Taoist support.

The Summit on Religions and Conservation, 1995

At the Summit on Religions and Conservation in 1995, nine religions submitted declarations. The following are brief extracts from those declarations as set out in the original working documents of the conference.

Baha'i Faith

> Baha'i Scriptures teach that, as trustees of the planet's vast resources and biological diversity, humanity must seek to protect the 'heritage [of] future generations;' see in nature a reflection of the divine; approach the earth, the source of material bounties, with humility; temper its actions with moderation; and be guided by the fundamental spiritual truth of our age, the oneness of humanity. The speed and facility with which we establish a sustainable pattern of life will depend, in the final analysis, on the extent to which we are willing to be transformed, through the love of God and obedience to His Laws, into constructive forces in the process of creating an ever-advancing civilisation.[21]

Buddhism

> In his own lifetime the Buddha came to understand that the notion that one exists as an isolated entity is an illusion. All things are interrelated; we are interconnected and do not have autonomous existence . . .
>
> According to the Vietnamese monk Venerable Thich Nhat Hanh: . . . 'Among the three – human beings, society and Nature – it is us who begin to effect change. But in order to effect change we must recover ourselves, one must be whole. Since this requires the kind of environment favourable to one's healing, one must seek the kind of lifestyle that is free from the destruction of one's humaness. Efforts to change the environment and to change oneself are both necessary. But we know how difficult it is to change the environment if individuals themselves are not in a state of equilibrium.'[22]

Christianity

> In his New Year Message, 1990, His Holiness the Pope stated: 'Christians, in particular, realise that their responsibility within creation and their duty towards nature and the Creator are an essential part of their faith' . . .
>
> The Orthodox Church teaches that it is the destiny of humanity to restore the proper relationship between God and the world as it was in Eden. Through repentance, two landscapes – the one human, the other natural – can become the objects of a caring and creative effort . . .
>
> The World Council of Churches, predominantly Protestant, but also with full Orthodox participation, issued the following . . . 'We affirm the creation as beloved of God. We affirm that the world, as God's handiwork,

has its own inherent integrity; that land, waters, air, forests, mountains and all creatures, including humanity, are "good" in God's sight. The integrity of creation has a social aspect which we recognise as peace with justice, and an ecological aspect which we recognise in the self-renewing, sustainable character of natural ecosystems.'[23]

HINDUISM

'Conserve ecology or perish' is the message of the *Bhagavad Gita* – a dialogue between Sri Krishna and Arjuna which is a clear and precise Life Science. It is narrated in the third chapter of this great work that a life without contribution towards the preservation of ecology is a life of sin and a life without specific purpose or use . . .

Life is sustained by different kinds of food; rainfall produces food; timely movement of clouds brings rains; to get the clouds moving on time yajna, religious sacrifice, helps; yajna is performed through rituals; those actions which produce rituals belong only to God; God is revealed by the Vedas; the Vedas are preserved by the human mind; and the human mind is nourished by food. This is the cycle which helps the existence of all forms of life on this globe. One who does not contribute to the maintenance of this cycle is considered as a destroyer of all life here.[24]

ISLAM

Allah, in His Wisdom, appointed Man, the creature that He has conferred with the faculty of Reason and with Freewill, to be His vicegerent on Earth. And while Allah has invited Man to partake of the fruits of the Earth for his rightful nourishment and enjoyment, He has also directed Man not to waste that which Allah has provided for him – for He loveth not wasters. Furthermore, Allah has also ordered Man to administer his responsibilities with Justice. Above all, Man should conserve the balance of Allah's creation on Earth . . . If biologists believe that Man is the greatest agent of ecological change on the surface of the Earth, is it not Man who, drawn from the brink, will – for his own good – abandon Mammon and listen to the prescriptions of God on the conservation of his environment and the environment of all the creatures on Earth? The Islamic answer to this question is decisively in the affirmative.[25]

JAINISM

Human beings possess rationality and intuition. As a highly evolved form of life, they have a moral responsibility in their mutual dealings and in their relationship with the rest of the universe. Hence, this conception of life, in which human beings have an ethical responsibility, has made the Jain tradition a cradle for the creed of environmental protection and harmony.[26]

JUDAISM

The classic Jewish attitude to nature is a direct consequence of the belief that the entire universe is the work of the Creator. Love of God was taken in the broadest sense to include love of all His creations: the inanimate, plants, animals and man. Nature in all its beauty is understood as having been created for man, and it is, therefore, wrong for man to spoil it. Man's connection to nature can restore him to his original character, to a natural state of happiness and joy . . .

Man's control over the world is restricted. 'For the earth is Mine' (*Lev.* 25:23) – only the Creator may be considered to enjoy absolute ownership of His creation.

'Love thy neighbour as thyself' (*Lev.* 19:18), the basis for all Jewish ethics, is applied to protection of the environment in the obligation to exercise care not to harm others, and particularly in the obligation to avoid doing harm to the community.[27]

Sikhism

Sikhism regards a co-operative society as the only truly religious society, as the Sikh view of life and society is grounded in the worth of every individual as a microcosm of God . . . All life is interconnected . . .

Life, for its very existence and nurturing, depends upon a bounteous nature. A human being needs to derive sustenance from the earth; not to deplete, exhaust, pollute, burn or destroy it. Sikhs believe that an awareness of that sacred relationship between humans and the environment is necessary for the health of our planet, and for our survival. A new 'environmental ethic' dedicated to conservation and wise use of the resources provided by a bountiful nature can only arise from an honest understanding and dedicated application of our old, tried and true spiritual heritage.[28]

Taoism

In the *Tao Te Ching*, the basic classic of Taoism, there is this verse: 'Humanity follows the Earth, the Earth follows Heaven, Heaven follows the Tao, and the Tao follows what is natural.'

. . . Those who have only a superficial understanding of the relationship between humanity and nature will recklessly exploit nature. Those who have a deep understanding of the relationship will treat nature well and learn from it . . .

People should take into full consideration the limits of nature's sustaining power, so that when they pursue their own development, they have a correct standard of success. If anything runs counter to the harmony and balance of nature, even if it is of great immediate interest and profit, people should restrain themselves from doing it, so as to prevent nature's punishment. Furthermore, insatiable human desire will lead to the over-exploitation of natural resources. So people should remember that to be too successful is to be on the path to defeat.[29]

Further Reading

See Byrne, *The Philosophical and Theological Foundations of Ethics*, Green, *Religious Reason*, and also his article 'Ethics' in Eliade, *Encyclopedia of Religion*. For discussion of the 'Golden Rule', see Rost, *The Golden Rule* and Hick, *An Interpretation of Religion*, pp. 309–14. For a discussion on contemporary ethics and religion, especially in a religiously pluralistic setting, see essays in Runzo, *Ethics, Religion and the Good Society* and Holm, *Making Moral Decisions*. On a global ethic, see Küng and Kuschel, *A Global Ethic*, and a further development of this idea in Swidler, *For All Life*. On religion and environmental ethics, see Tucker and Grim, *Worldviews and Ecology* and Edmonds and Palmer, *Holy Ground*; see also Brown and Quiblier, *Ethics and Agenda 21*, the section on 'Religious and Spiritual Perspectives', pp. 97–118.

14

Fundamentalism and Liberalism

One aspect of religion that has come to general attention in recent years has been the upsurge of fundamentalism. The split between fundamentalists[1] and liberals appears to affect almost every religious community to one extent or another, in many different countries. Almost every religious movement, other than the most narrow sects, contains individuals who tend towards either extreme. In this chapter, we shall examine this phenomenon from three perspectives: social, psychological and historical.

Many people have a stereotyped view of fundamentalists: they take the words of their holy scripture literally and are opposed to science. This is a view that dates back to the time when Christian fundamentalists were trying to fight the implications of Darwinian evolutionary theory. However, as with all stereotypes, it is not a sufficiently deep understanding of the phenomenon and it has become less and less valid as the years have passed. Fundamentalists have changed and adapted since then. They no longer oppose science; indeed, they take great pride in the extent to which they can advance scientific proof for their positions. Nor are many of them strictly bound to a literal interpretation of their scriptures.

Historically, many authorities date fundamentalism from the publication in North America of a series of pamphlets, *The Fundamentals*, between 1910 and 1915. Although to trace the name to this event would be correct, to date fundamentalism from it would be a very limited view of a phenomenon that has a long history in religion. Also limited is the opinion that fundamentalism is a reaction to modernity. This view would restrict the occurrence of fundamentalism to modern times (although it must be admitted that modernity has brought fundamentalism very much to the fore). Nor, indeed, should fundamentalism be limited to Christianity or even the Western religions.[2] As I propose to define fundamentalism and liberalism in this chapter, this split can be seen to have been operating at many times in the histories of different religions. In the Islamic world, for example, we can see elements of it in the Ash'ari–Mu'tazili disputes in the Abbasid Empire in the ninth century; in the dispute between the philosopher-mystics and the orthodox jurists in Safavid Iran during the sixteenth and seventeenth centuries; in the opposition to Sufism and 'religious laxity' by such people as Ibn Taymiyya (d. 1328) and Ibn 'Abd al-Wahhab (d. 1787); as well as in the upheavals of the present-day Islamic world.[3]

Characteristics of Fundamentalism and Liberalism

The main features of fundamentalism and liberalism are presented here, showing where they differ. Of course, in order to show up the differences, it is necessary to depict the extremes of the two positions. The attitude of most people will fall somewhere between the two. We may characterize the differences as follows (see also p. 368).

The Scriptures

The fundamentalist looks to the holy scriptures of the religion as absolute and unchanging truth. The first concern of the fundamentalist is to establish that the holy scripture is 'the Word of God' and that it is impossible, therefore, for there to be any error in it. All laws and commandments in these texts are to be applied inflexibly and to the letter. Even in religions that have no concept of a scripture revealed by God, Theravada Buddhism for example, a similar attitude towards scripture can exist.[4]

As a secondary principle, fundamentalists also favour a literal interpretation of scripture. However, the usual idea of the fundamentalist's literal interpretation requires some degree of elaboration. In some places the text is clearly meant to be symbolic – the parables of Christ, for example. Most fundamentalists would not insist that these parables actually occurred physically. In addition, there are also places where there are inconsistencies in the text. The more sophisticated fundamentalist (the fundamentalist scholar, for example) is willing to allow much latitude in interpretation in such cases. The important point, however, is that the fundamentalist always regards the scripture as referring to real situations and facts. What the scripture says corresponds to empirical reality. For example, even if heaven and hell are acknowledged not to be physical places above and below the earth, these two words nevertheless do refer to existent realities. Barr points out that the importance of preserving the first principle, the inerrancy of the text, will often compel the fundamentalist to relax the second principle and allow some degree of non-literal interpretation.[5]

The principal concern of the fundamentalist is to extract an exact meaning from the text of the scriptures. The millennialists of the mid-nineteenth century were certain that their calculations pointed to the return of Christ in 1843 or 1844 (see p. 263). Then the 'Great Disappointment' occurred and there was no literal fulfilment of their expectations. One group that became the Seventh Day Adventists resolved the problem by formulating an explanation that the prophecy had been fulfilled. On that date, Christ had entered the Most Holy of the heavenly sanctuary, and he had work to perform there before coming to earth. This is a clearly non-literal explanation of a prophecy that most other Christian denominations expect to occur literally and on earth. The Seventh Day Adventists do, nevertheless, have a fundamentalist approach to scripture.[6] Their interpretation of the 'Great Disappointment' has the ability to give an exact meaning to the scripture when a literal meaning has been ruled out in their history. Another instructive example relates to the question of Noah's Flood. Some Christian fundamentalist scholars are willing to accept that this may have been a local flood in Mesopotamia rather than a world flood (which the literal text would imply). This explanation is less problematic scientifically. But nevertheless, the story of the Flood does, for these scholars, refer to an actual physical event – they rule out any non-physical, symbolic or metaphorical, interpretation.

The episode of Noah's Flood is one which has occasioned a great deal of debate between those who read the scripture literally and those who look for metaphorical interpretations. This representation of the Flood is from the ceiling of the Sistine Chapel, painted by Michelangelo between 1508 and 1512.

Much modern Christian fundamentalist literature is taken up with detailed explanations of how the events of the *Bible* can be explained scientifically. Scientific explanations are desirable, as they are thought to provide a guarantee of certainty and of exactness of interpretation. Another characteristic fundamentalist attitude is that the whole of the scripture stands or falls together. This view maintains that since the scripture is the Word of God and therefore infallible, the inerrancy of every single sentence of the scripture must be maintained, otherwise the slightest error in any smallest part casts doubt on the whole.

By contrast, the liberal is willing to allow that the texts of the scriptures are open to more than one interpretation; parts of the scripture are more 'true' – in the sense of being more likely to have actually occurred physically – than other parts. As well as truth relating to empirical reality, the liberal is prepared to see other types of truth – typological, metaphorical or mythological – in the scripture. Allegorical and symbolic interpretations may be used, particularly of passages that appear to contradict human reason, and social and contextual factors taken into account. For liberals, the truth lies in the significance of the statement rather than its correspondence with any external actuality.[7] Traditional interpretations may be examined for whatever useful insights they may

A Christian Fundamentalist Position and a Liberal Response

The Fundamentalist Position

'If He (Jesus) could be mistaken on matters which He regarded as of the strictest relevance to his own person and ministry, it is difficult to see exactly how or why He either can or should be trusted anywhere else' . . . In his teaching Jesus mentioned Psalm 110 as if it was by David and the journey of Jonah in the belly of the fish as if it had really taken place; therefore the Psalm was composed by David, and the underwater journey of Jonah did in fact take place. If these things are not true, then no reliance can be placed on anything that he said about anything; he has become totally untrustworthy. (From R. G. V. Tasker and the *New Bible Commentary*, quoted in Barr, *Fundamentalism*, p. 74)

The Liberal Response

This endlessly repeated argument seeks to use the personal loyalty of Christians towards Jesus as a lever to force them into fundamentalist positions on historical and literary matters. There is no part of the fundamentalism world view that should inspire so much distaste in the mind of other Christians. Its distortion of the proper proportions of the Christian faith is extreme . . .

On the general approach to the argument I cannot do better than cite a well-written passage by Huxtable:

> If . . . an absent-minded professor tells me that the train for Penzance leaves Waterloo at noon and I find that in fact it leaves Paddington half an hour before, I do not conclude that my informant is a liar, nor that he is ill-disposed towards me, nor that his reputation as a scholar rests on a fraud. I take him for what he is, and do not suppose that being a great authority on Homer makes him a reliable substitute for a time-table . . . Jesus Christ came into the world to be its Saviour, not an authority on biblical criticism.

(Barr, *Fundamentalism*, p. 74)

present but have no binding force on the present. The liberal looks to the holy scripture of his or her religion as a source of guidance for life, accepting that the meaning, the 'truth', of the scripture may change as the circumstances of the individual and society change. As a relative, rather than an absolute, truth, therefore, the meaning of the scripture is not considered fixed but must be reinterpreted in every age, for the concerns of that age.

The liberal is much more willing to view the holy scripture as a historical document, written down by fallible men and women sometimes many years after the events portrayed. Therefore, almost certainly, errors and myth-making have crept in and theological ideas, current at the time of writing, have been read back into the past; there may also have been omissions, additions or errors in the course of transmission. In contrast, the fundamentalist, if he or she does accept the historical nature of the scriptures, will insist that they were divinely protected from alteration or error. Certainly, no external factors such as the social conditions pertaining at the time that the scripture was written down, are considered relevant to the understanding of the texts. It is, therefore, a characteristic feature of fundamentalists that they consider that they can derive the meaning of the scriptures directly, just by reading them. No contextual, philological, or historical information beyond what is evident in the text is needed. The plain meaning of the texts is their intended meaning. In contrast, the liberal considers that the scriptures have to be read contextually, taking into consideration historical and philological information; each individual must then interpret what the scripture means for him or her in the light of individual and social circumstances. One could say that for fundamentalists the meaning of the scripture is inherent in the text. It can be apprehended directly without a need for interpretation. For the liberal, the scripture is something that must be applied to one's life and interpreted according to the circumstances of one's life.[8]

SCRIPTURE: The Torah or Pentateuch is written by a scribe on a lengthy strip of vellum or parchment both ends of which are wound around wooden staves. Passages are read from it on Mondays, Thursdays, Saturdays, and holy days. In this picture of a Torah Scroll (*Sepher Torah*) in the Great Synagogue of Jerusalem, one can also see the Torah Crown (*Keter*), which is placed on top of the Torah as an expression of reverence when it is put away, and the pointer (*Yad*), which the reader uses.

Religious Traditions

When we come to consider the traditions of a religion, we find that there are different types of fundamentalists, whom we may define in two major groupings.[9]

Some fundamentalists are conservative and traditionalist. These regard tradition as an element in the religion that is as authoritative as the scriptures themselves. In many societies such as India, for example, religious traditions have developed over centuries at a local or regional level and are handed down from one generation to the next. This, rather than the scripture, is what religion is for most people. In Christianity, the *Bible* has little in it to act as a basis for most Church structure and ritual. Therefore, the only source of authority for this is tradition.[10] In Islam, the concept of the Sunna (the deeds and words of Muhammad as the perfect example for all Muslims to follow) and the doctrine of *ijma'* (that whatever the Muslim world holds as

Table 14.1 Fundamentalism and Liberalism

	FUNDAMENTALISM	LIBERALISM
SCRIPTURE	Absolute truth; inerrant and of binding authority. To be understood literally or according to a method of interpretation that gives exactness of meaning. If one part of the scripture falls, it all falls.	Truth, but to be set in its historical and social context; a guide to life. Often requires metaphorical and symbolic understanding. Historical and textual criticism accepted.
DOCTRINES	Are unalterable and must be accepted in totality.	May be interpreted and adapted according to the times.
TRADITIONS	Must be conformed with to the letter (except radical fundamentalists).	May be adapted according to changing social circumstances.
THE NATURE OF TRUTH	That which corresponds to empirical actuality.	Various types of truth: symbolic, mythological, empirical.
ATTITUDE TOWARDS CRITICAL SCHOLARSHIP	Suspicious and hostile of modern critical scholarship and its implications.	Welcoming and tries to adapt to modern critical scholarship.
RELIGION'S RELATION TO SOCIETY	The religious world must be guarded from intrusions from the secular world.	Religion must adapt to society and remain relevant.
DIVERSITY OF OPINION WITHIN THE COMMUNITY	To be discouraged since it represents the intrusion of external views and the possibility of heresy. Own position the only true position. Regard all other hues of opinion with suspicion.	To be welcomed and tolerated as encouraging universality. Own position only one of many possible.
OTHER RELIGIONS	Viewed only as possible fields for proselytization. No dialogue is possible or necessary.	Dialogue and interaction to be encouraged.
METHODS OF PROSELYTIZING	Heretics and unbelievers should, if necessary, be compelled to conform.	Persuasion and argument preferred.
ACCUSATIONS AGAINST THE OTHER	Liberals are incorporating ideas from the secular world and thus polluting or diluting religion and encouraging moral laxity.	The inflexible attitudes of the fundamentalists are contrary to the teachings of love in religion and drive people away.
POLITICAL ATTITUDE IN MODERN TIMES	Tends to the right; supports traditional role for women.	Tends to the left; supports women's social emancipation.
ATTITUDE TO WEALTH IN MODERN TIMES	Positive, encouraging.	Negative.

a consensus must be correct) act as a powerful force for maintaining traditional attitudes and positions. If any of the religion's structures or doctrines are in conflict with society, then it is society that must change to conform with what is perceived to be the Divine. These fundamentalists are very concerned with building up bodies of doctrine and dogmatic statements, as well as elaborating the Holy Law and its provisions. This enables the true believer to be distinguished from the waverer and the potential heretic. Doctrines and dogmas must, like holy scripture, be understood literally, while the Holy Law must be followed to the letter.

Council of Trent, North Italy, 1545–63: This was the nineteenth ecumenical council of the Roman Catholic Church and was held to launch the Counter-Reformation. It was at this council that the traditions of the Church were declared to be of the same authority as the scripture. It resulted in the Profession of the Tridentine Faith (Tridentum was the Latin name for Trent), the definitive statement of Catholic doctrine until the Second Vatican Council, 1962–5.

The second group of fundamentalists is of the evangelical, radical, revivalist type. These regard the traditions of the religion as the main obstacle to a return to the 'pure' original religion. They consider that they can reconstruct this 'pure' religion from the texts of the holy scripture and would like to see all of the traditional structures swept aside in favour of the scriptures themselves.[11]

Radical and traditionalist fundamentalists only differ in how they define the boundary of what they consider to be unalterable and inerrant. The radicals place the boundary around the scripture itself, while the traditionalists extend it to the traditions of the religion. Whether fundamentalists are of one type or the other appears to depend largely on the religious background from which they have sprung. Thus, for example, if a religion stresses tradition, it produces fundamentalists mainly of the traditionalist kind. In the Christian world, Roman Catholicism holds that the traditions of the Church are of equal authority to the scripture. (This has been the official Catholic position since the Council of Trent, 1563.) The fundamentalists among the Catholics tend to be traditionalists. At the extreme of the fundamentalist wing among Roman Catholics we find the followers of ultra-traditionalist Archbishop Marcel Lefebvre.[12] Radical fundamentalists in the Christian world are to be found among the Protestant sects – Protestantism being a movement that arose as a reaction to the traditionalism of Catholicism. In the Muslim world, most fundamentalists are traditionalists, since Islam is a religion in which tradition plays an important part. There are, however, a few modern radical groups – for example the followers of Rashad Khalifa[13] and of 'Ali Shari'ati.[14]

Mutual Recriminations

Fundamentalists tend to blame liberals for allowing into the religion dubious ideas and doctrines that have no basis in the religion itself, but are either accommodations to the secular world or imports from other cultures and religions. An example of this from the past is the manner in which rationalist theologians in medieval Islam were accused of introducing into Islam ideas from the unbelieving Greeks. An example from modern times is the Christian liberation theology that originated in Latin America. Fundamentalists regard it as no more than a back-door method of introducing Marxism into Christianity. Similarly, fundamentalists tend to blame liberalism for a general moral laxity in society.

A more basic criticism levelled by fundamentalists at liberals concerns the arbitrary nature of their view of the scriptures; some parts of the scripture liberals regard as the religious core and therefore to be preserved; other parts are culturally determined and therefore can be dispensed with or interpreted liberally. What determines which parts are treated in which of these two ways? To a fundamentalist, the dividing line appears not to be defined by any discernible logical rules, but rather by whatever happens to be the current social fashion. In one decade, feminism is to the fore and so the liberals dispense with those parts of the scripture that give a low status to women; the next, gay rights are fashionable and so the liberal jettisons that part of the scripture too. Are fashion and current secular sensibilities to be the arbiters of the standpoint of faith? If so, will the inevitable result not be eventually to jettison everything?[15] In this sense, we can say that fundamentalism is much more of a reaction against modern, relativizing, liberal trends in religion than a reaction against modernity itself.[16]

Liberals consider that the harsh, intolerant attitude of the fundamentalists is contrary to the true spirit of religion and is doing religion a great deal of harm in the modern world. The liberal tends to see the traditions and structures of the religion in relation to society. For a liberal, the important question is: does the religious tradition and structure serve the needs of society? If any part of religious structure or doctrine is not relevant to society, then we must see how we can adapt it to become relevant. The traditions, doctrines and dogmas of the religion, as well as the Holy Law, are all guidelines for action and can be interpreted according to circumstances.

Attitude to Religious Diversity within the Religion

The fundamentalist is intolerant of a wide divergence of religious expression within his or her own religion. All divergence from the main orthodox tradition is suspect. There is an ever-present prospect of heresy insidiously creeping in under various seemingly innocent guises. The religion must be protected from this at all costs. There have been many episodes in religious history in which much suffering and bloodshed has been caused by those wishing to impose a narrow interpretation of their religion on their fellow-believers. In Christianity, this was seen in the Inquisition and the many bloody suppressions of heresies.[17] In Islam, there have been periodic persecutions of heterodox groups as well as of such groups as the Sufis.[18]

PERSECUTION OF HERETICS: Cleaving a person in half or quartering was a favourite punishment for heresy used in medieval Christian Europe and also, as depicted here, against Babis and Baha'is in Iran in the nineteenth century.

The liberal will tolerate the existence within the community of a wide variety of viewpoints. As long as a viewpoint does not explicitly deny the veracity of the prophet-founder or the holy scripture, it can usually be accommodated within the community of believers. Even if a viewpoint is considered too extreme to be acceptable, the preferred method for trying to counter it will be argument and persuasion rather than compulsion.

Attitudes Towards Other Religions

The fundamentalist sees other religions as being the result of error. Since these other religions are in open competition with the true religion, the usual explanation is that they are the work of the Devil. They must be strongly opposed and even persecuted if necessary. The only possible exceptions are those religions towards which the prophet-founder himself showed respect. These must, by definition, be religions that preceded him. Thus, for example, fundamentalist Christians will tolerate Judaism but reject Islam; fundamentalist Muslims will tolerate Judaism and Christianity but reject the Baha'i Faith. Even this toleration wears thin at times, however, and merges into persecution – as evidenced by past persecutions of Jews by Christians, and Jews and Christians by Muslims.

A related phenomenon in modern times is the linking of a xenophobic fundamentalism to a strident nationalism in many parts of the world. We can see this in Arya Samaj Hinduism in India, in some forms of Nichiren Shoshu Buddhism in Japan,[19] in the Gush Emunim movement in Israel,[20] and in fundamentalist Christianity in the United States and South Africa.[21]

The liberal will look to other religions as representing other ways of regarding religious truth. Many liberals will give their own religion some form of priority but are, nevertheless, willing to admit some legitimacy and 'truth' in other religions: the Catholic theologian Karl Rahner (1904–84), for example, held that the truly religious persons of other religions are

RELIGIOUS TENSIONS IN JERUSALEM: Orthodox Jews pass seated conservative Arabs.

'anonymous Christians'.[22] Other liberals are willing to go even further and regard other religions as being of equal validity to their own, but that each is, perhaps, more suited to its own culture.[23] A liberal religious society, such as medieval Muslim Spain, allows the efflorescence of intellectual and artistic excellence from whatever religious quarter, Christian, Jewish or Muslim.

The fundamentalist's conviction of possessing the truth leads to a strong tendency to correct the errors of unbelievers. Thus the interreligious activities of the fundamentalist are typically evangelism and missionary work. The interreligious activities of the liberal, on the other hand, tend towards ecumenism and interfaith dialogue. Fundamentalists have no time for such activities. Since their own religion already possesses the absolute truth, there is no point in looking elsewhere for it.

Social and Political Differences

It is with regard to social and political differences that we are treading on the most difficult ground in our enquiry. This is because there appears to have been some degree of change in the modern period in the West compared to the characteristic features of these groups in former times. In the past, there does not appear to have been any characteristic political stance from either fundamentalists or liberals. If anything, both parties often tended to political quietism. Socially most fundamentalists have tended to be isolated. Some have formed separate communities, such as members of the Mennonite tradition, the Old Order Amish and Hutterites in North America. Others have minimized contact with the rest of the society through associating as much as possible only with fellow fundamentalists in, for example, fundamentalist trade and vocational associations, clubs, colleges and holiday centres. Historically, in nineteenth-century Europe and North America, personal asceticism and rejection of wealth characterized many fundamentalists. Liberal views were, on the other hand, often found among the wealthy.

Recently, much of this has changed greatly. Both sides have taken on characteristic political attitudes and fundamentalists have left their social isolation and entered social and political life in every part of the world. In recent times, fundamentalists have tended to be found at the right of the political spectrum,[24] encouraging individual self-reliance and stressing public morality and order. Some fundamentalist groups have even reversed their previous tendency towards asceticism; they now adopt a positive, encouraging attitude towards the accumulation of wealth. These groups have become actively involved in politics. They advocate capitalism and a *laissez-faire* social philosophy, while raising communism to an almost mythological level of evil. The best-known example of this is the Moral Majority movement in the United States which contributed to Ronald Reagan's electoral success.[25]

An important social and political feature of fundamentalism is the tendency to promote a traditional role for women in society within the sphere of home and children, rather than working outside the home and taking a political role. This applies as much to Christian fundamentalism in the United States (where the Moral Majority campaigned against the Equal

MILITANT POLITICAL FUNDAMENTALISM: Militant ultra-orthodox Jews clash with police during demonstrations against the running of public transport during the Sabbath, 1971

Rights for Women Amendment), as it does to Islamic and Jewish fundamentalism.[26]

Liberals, on the other hand, tend to the political left in modern times, due to their concern with social issues. Some groups have even engaged in dialogues with Marxists. Religious teachings such as showing love towards one's fellow human beings and social justice are emphasized. Liberals have also changed their previous tendency and now incline towards asceticism. They have a negative attitude towards the accumulation of wealth and are supportive of the emancipation of women.

Fundamentalists regard existing political structures with suspicion as the products of human thinking and efforts rather than divine revelation. The extreme wing of fundamentalism would overthrow them in favour of a political structure based on the holy scripture. Khomeini advocated such a programme and intended the Iranian Revolution of 1979 to inaugurate such a theocracy.[27] It should not be thought, however, that it is only in Islam that such positions are being advocated. In Christianity, American groups such as the Christian Reconstructionists led by Rousas J. Rushdoomy advocate an overthrow of democratic institutions. They want to establish a theocracy under biblical law. In Israel and India, there are several extreme Jewish and Hindu religious parties that advocate a similar position.

ISRAEL: POLITICS AND FUNDAMENTALIST RELIGION

GE [Gush Emunim] views the world in the light of redemption. All pragmatic or moral considerations must be judged according to one messianic criterion: will the matter at hand delay or hasten the process of complete redemption? . . . According to the activist-believers, establishment of a settlement in the heart of the Palestinian population, an act intended to promote annexation of the Territories, is considered a sacrament . . . According to the mystical–messianic conception prevailing in GE, national changes are both a reflection of and a means to celestial changes. Consequently the movement's activism on the national level is an axis for cosmic revolution, with universal implications. This formula solves the inherent paradox in GE's message, as reflected in a claim of Rabbi Levinger:

> Settlement of the entire Land of Israel by the Jewish People is a blessing for all mankind, including the Arabs. Jewish settlements in the midst of local population centers are motivated by feelings of respect and concern for the Palestinians' future. Consequently if we meet the Arab's demand for withdrawal, we will only encourage their degeneration and moral decline, whereas enforcing the Israeli national will on the Arabs will foster a religious revival among them, eventually to be expressed in their spontaneous desire to join in the reconstruction of the Third [Jewish] Temple. We [the Israelis] must penetrate the casbahs of cities in Judea and Samaria and drive our stakes therein for the good of the Arabs themselves.

(Gideon Aran, 'Jewish Zionist Fundamentalism', in Marty and Appleby, *Fundamentalisms Observed*, pp. 292, 314–5)

Steve Bruce has pointed out that the social manifestations of fundamentalism and liberalism largely follow on from their doctrinal or ideological positions. The fundamentalists' rejection of all doctrinal positions outside their own leads to highly demarcated, tightly knit, highly committed, socially isolated communities. Liberals, on the other hand, consider the beliefs of the rest of the world sympathetically and are much more integrated into society. The great diversity of beliefs among them, however, hinders the formation of coherent groups. It also reduces the likelihood of a high degree of commitment.[28]

Towards a Social Definition of Fundamentalism and Liberalism

Put succinctly, we may characterize fundamentalists as turned inwards to what they perceive to be the core of the religion (such as the scripture and doctrines) and seeking to protect this from the intrusions of the modern, secular world. The liberal is turned outwards, seeking to expand the borders of religion into the secular world. For the fundamentalist, the secular world must adapt to and come under the control of the religious world. The liberal considers that it is the job of the religious world to adapt to and become relevant in the secular world. Fundamentalists are often individualists; religion is addressed to the individual and is for individual salvation. Liberals are more concerned with society as a whole; religion is for social as well as individual salvation.

The above presentation of the contrasts between fundamentalists and liberals has, of necessity, been wide-ranging. This is because the same phenomenon reappears in different ways among the various religions. None of these above distinctions is sufficient by itself to identify an individual as a fundamentalist or a liberal. In Hinduism and Buddhism, for example, the inerrancy of scripture is not an important issue. On the other hand, almost all Muslims believe in the inerrancy of their scripture, the *Qur'an*, but this does not make them all fundamentalists. To differentiate between fundamentalists and liberals in the Hindu, Buddhist and Muslim worlds, one must examine such factors as social relations and the attitude towards modernity and religious diversity. This may also account for the situation in the nineteenth century, when an uncritical acceptance of the inerrancy of the *Bible* was much more in the mainstream of Christianity (a similar situation to that in Islam today). Then it was possible for individuals to hold to biblical inerrancy while at the same time advocating liberalism.[29] Our ideas about fundamentalism and liberalism should be sufficiently flexible to allow for such individuals not to be classed as fundamentalists. Thus the arguments presented in this chapter point to a position in which fundamentalism and liberalism are not defined in any absolute terms. Rather, the definition is multi-factorial and relative to the particular religions and historical situation of the individual. In other words, fundamentalism and liberalism must be identified through a pattern that changes from one religion to another (partly because of the different emphases within each religion). Even within a particular religion, the pattern will change with time.

The Social and Intellectual Basis

Little research has been done on the social bases of the fundamentalist–liberal dichotomy. The work that has been done suggests that we must go beyond the old view that fundamentalism represents an anti-scientific backlash of the old rural, agricultural communities against urban, scientific culture.[30] In the following discussion, we shall see that fundamentalism is not anti-scientific and that the evidence tends to discount any significant social differences between fundamentalists and liberals.

Because science has become such an overwhelmingly important guarantor of plausibility in the modern world, most people want to think of themselves as being in line with it. Fundamentalist writers, therefore, often go to great lengths to show that their positions are in accordance with science.[31] However, critics would maintain that this is a veneer of pseudo-science, applied in order to increase the plausibility of the fundamentalist worldview and that fundamentalists remain inherently opposed to the inductive approach of the scientific method.[32] Among many Christian fundamentalists in the United States, there remains a strong advocacy of anti-evolutionary (anti-Darwinian) positions, under the name of Creationism. However, even this position bows to science in that it claims to use scientific method to prove its case. Indeed, religious critics of fundamentalism argue that by striving to interpret the *Bible* stories so that they conform to science, fundamentalists are, in effect, adopting a materialistic stance; they are placing science above God's Word.[33] Whatever the strengths or weaknesses of fundamentalist science, most fundamentalists no longer see themselves as opposed to science intellectually. Their main intellectual argument, at least as it has been reformulated in recent decades, is with historical and literary criticism as applied to scripture.

Outside the Christian West, fundamentalism is often centred on a reaction to the intrusion of modernity into traditional societies. Even here, however, fundamentalists are not opposed to science and technology themselves. They are quite happy to use these. Ayatollah Khomeini's success in overthrowing the Shah, for example, owed a great deal to the use by his supporters of such modern inventions as the telephone and the cassette recorder, which were used to disseminate his speeches while he was still in exile. The question that the Iranian fundamentalists have yet to answer satisfactorily is how they can import and utilize science without also importing the scientific approach, which questions and criticizes everything, including religion.

Ayatollah Ruhollah Khomeini (1902–89) led the Iranian Islamic revolution of 1979 and was afterwards named as the supreme leader under the new constitution of Iran.

What fundamentalists are primarily against are these alien values and morals that are imported along with science and technology. It is not so much modernity itself that they fear as the threat that the accompanying liberal social and religious values pose to traditional religious structures and values. The following quotation from the manifesto of Bharatiya Jana Sangh, a Hindu fundamentalist party, in 1951, could speak for all such reactions to modernization and westernization:

> there is an atmosphere of disappointment and frustration in the country . . . The ruling Congress party in its haste to make India a carbon-copy of the West is undermining the people's faith in the national values and ideals.[34]

It should also be stated that there is no justification for the commonly held view that the fundamentalist is against logic and rationality. On the contrary, the fundamentalist mentality is much predisposed to the use of precise, logical arguments. Shi'i Islam is an interesting example in this respect. Both the theology (*kalam*) and the jurisprudence of Shi'i Islam are built on foundations of rationalism and logic. From the ninth century onwards, Shi'i scholars have prided themselves on being able to derive their doctrine and their legal judgements from logic (as well as from the *Qur'an* and the Traditions). The study of logic forms an important part of the academic curriculum at the religious colleges of Qum and Najaf. This, then, is the intellectual background of such persons as the Ayatollah Khomeini.[35]

Also to be questioned is the view of fundamentalism as mainly a phenomenon of poor rural areas. In fact, both fundamentalists and liberals are likely to come from similar social and educational backgrounds. Many modern fundamentalists appear to arise from educated, middle-class backgrounds – precisely the same background from which the majority of liberals also come. This has been shown both for British fundamentalist groups,[36] and for Americans.[37] Similar conclusions have been drawn about the Muslim world whether in Egypt, Iran or West Africa.[38]

We thus have two pieces of evidence that point towards the fact that the fundamentalist–liberal difference is not primarily the result of social factors. First, the fact that the socially observable features of the phenomenon vary across the different religions. Second, the fact that fundamentalists and liberals appear to arise from much the same social strata as each other. It is as yet premature to dismiss social factors entirely.

The evidence, however, certainly does not support a blanket association of fundamentalism with any particular social category or factor. These findings, if confirmed by further research, point to the likelihood that the fundamentalist–liberal difference comes not so much from social differences as from differences in psychological types.

The Psychological Basis

Fundamentalism and liberalism have been described above as two extreme viewpoints. That is not to say that everyone is at one extreme or the other. There are intermediate positions and an individual can, during the course of a lifetime, alter his or her position on the spectrum. In psychological terms we may characterize fundamentalism and liberalism as two different ways of thinking, two cognitive styles. Cognitive style refers to the individual's characteristic and consistent manner of organizing and categorizing perceptions and concepts. It is a value-free term, in that cognitive styles are not judged to be good or bad in themselves. Any particular style may, however, be more or less favourable in a given situation or for achieving a given goal.[39]

The fundamentalist mentality is characteristically one that sees things in terms of black and white. There are clear-cut boundaries that determine what is and what is not acceptable belief, who is and who is not in the community. Any person, situation or object either belongs within the orbit of the 'saved' or is outside it; there are no intermediate positions. No matter how good a life people may lead, if they are not among the 'saved', then they must be among the 'damned'. The lines between good and evil are clearly drawn. The liberal is more inclined to allow for 'grey areas', intermediate situations. Although some people may not be believers, if their actions are good then they cannot be totally bad. In this way, we are gradually coming to the point at which it is possible to see that the fundamentalist–liberal split is not something that affects religion alone; rather, it is one facet of a much larger phenomenon in the psycho-social life of humanity.[40]

One of the underlying differences between fundamentalists and liberals is that the former are driven by a desire for certainty. Richard Hofstadter called this the 'one-hundred per cent mentality'. Such a person will 'tolerate no ambiguities, no equivocations, no reservations, and no criticism'.[41] For the fundamentalist, certainty is only to be found in objectivity. The indecisive world of the liberal who is willing to see some truth in all opinions; the uncertain fields of historical and literary criticism, where different opinions abound: these are all tainted by personal opinion, and therefore by subjectivity. This is deeply unsatisfactory to the fundamentalist psyche. The only way of achieving objective truth is to take a standard that lies outside human subjectivity. While a liberal Christian would be happy to accept just a statement of belief in Christ from an individual, this is not sufficient for a fundamentalist. It is too liable to the whims of subjectivity and might include all sorts of doctrinally objectionable positions. Acceptance of the *Bible* as inerrant, however, is considered by fundamentalists to lead to objectivity, for one is not forming a personal view of the *Bible* but rather accepting the *Bible*'s own view of itself. This, the fundamentalist considers, gives one a standard of absolute truth,[42] hence objectivity and hence certainty.

This desire for certainty probably accounts for the enthusiastic adoption of science (or, as their critics would claim, pseudo-science) by fundamentalists. Scientific method acts, for the modern mind, as a guarantor of the correctness of one's conclusions, and hence of certainty. It also accounts for the fact that fundamentalists are often very keen to build up elaborate logical arguments. The mathematical certainty of logic appeals to such minds. The fundamentalist favours absolutes, while the liberal favours relativistic styles of thinking. Indeed, we may even be starting to discern here a reversal of positions similar to that described above in the social and political spheres. Liberals are moving away from rationalist, scientific thought that they espoused in the nineteenth century towards a more holistic, intuitive way of thinking, while fundamentalists are, simultaneously, moving towards the certainties of logic and scientific proof. These changes may reflect changes of perception that are also happening in society; society has moved away from a position in which scripture was seen as the guarantor of certainty to a position in which science is the guarantor.

One difference in cognitive style that is of particular interest regarding the fundamentalism–liberalism dichotomy is called 'field-dependence versus field-independence'. It analyses the way that an individual relates a figure in his or her perceptual field to its background. Field-dependents tend to see the figure only in relation to its background while a field-independent tends to isolate the figure and extract it from its background.[43] There seems some provisional similarity here between field-dependence and liberalism, in that liberals tend to see religion only in terms of its social background. Field-independence appears to correlate with fundamentalism, in that fundamentalists tend to see religion as an absolute isolated from its social background.

Two further categories in psychology relevant to our consideration are convergent and divergent thought. There are some similarities between the convergent style of thinking and fundamentalism, while divergent thinking corresponds with liberalism. Convergent thinking focuses down from the general to the particular, dissecting and analysing. It prizes rational, deductive thought and aims towards certainty. One tends to find it among certain types of scientists, and engineers in particular. Interestingly, it has been found that when scientists (especially those from the physical sciences) and engineers become religious, they often tend towards fundamentalism.[44] Divergent thought, on the other hand, goes from the particular to the general, integrating the particulars into a general picture. It prizes inductive, intuitive thinking and aims towards inclusivity rather than certainty. One tends to find it among artists and social scientists. These two modes of thinking have, in experimental psychology, been linked to the two halves of the brain: analytical rational thought is associated with the dominant (usually left) hemisphere; intuitive thought is associated with the other hemisphere. (See pp. 178–9 for a fuller discussion of this topic.)

It should be noted that cognitive style is not the same thing as personality. Cognitive style is a much more flexible function that can change relatively easily in a person. Although we can define fundamentalism in terms of a particular cognitive style, there is a problem as to which phenomenon causes which. Does a particular cognitive style cause a person to be attracted to the fundamentalist worldview? Or does the ideology of fundamentalism induce a particular cognitive style? This is probably a question of the chicken-and-egg variety, to which there is no answer.

One consequence of this psychological view of fundamentalism is that any religious group will contain people with a spectrum of cognitive styles. A small fundamentalist group, for example, will have a range of cognitive styles that is at the fundamentalist end of the spectrum. Within that range, however, some will be more 'liberal' and others more extreme in their fundamentalism. The larger the religious group, the wider the range of cognitive styles that is likely to be within the group. All the world religions include people who have the full range of opinions, from the most liberal to the most fundamentalist. Even a religion like the Baha'i Faith (that has deliberately sought to have a wide variety of people within its ranks) will also contain, despite its reputation as a 'liberal' religion, individuals with a range of liberal and fundamentalist opinions.

Fundamentalism and Modernity

I have given examples of the way that liberalism and fundamentalism have manifested themselves in the past. The contrast between the two has, however, been emphasized and brought into stark relief only in modern times,[45] for three reasons.

First, in most of the world until the present century and in the West until the eighteenth-century Age of Enlightenment, the religious and secular worlds were not sharply defined and separated. Religious metaphysical assumptions and ethical values pervaded all aspects of society: family life, social mores and customs, art, literature, intellectual life and politics. Therefore, the secular world did not challenge the religious. In these circumstances it was possible for people to hold opinions that would today be considered fundamentalist, such as the inerrancy of the *Bible*, while being liberal in outlook.

Second, humanity today faces a mass of problems – the nuclear threat, drug and alcohol problems, environmental threats, the North–South divide and so on. These are brought to the immediate attention of all through modern means of communications. This and the complexities of modern life have induced great uncertainty and anxiety. One response to the fear induced by this state is to retreat into the greater certainty offered by fundamentalism. It presents a retreat from the confused maelstrom of modernity.

Third, religions were not so acutely challenged by genuine competition from other religions and ideologies until very recently. Therefore, the fundamentalist mentality was rarely challenged by 'foreign' intrusions into its religious world. Then, in the nineteenth century, the colonial powers took Christianity to every part of the world. During the present century, we have seen a flow in the opposite direction, both as a result of migration and of missionary activity by Hindus, Buddhists and Muslims. Some find this close interaction with other religious groups very threatening and consequently retreat into a fundamentalist position that reduces the need for it.

Thus it has been the phenomenon of secularization and religious pluralism in the modern world that has brought the liberal–fundamentalist split to the fore of religious life. In country after country, the arrival of modernity has resulted in a polarization of the native religious community. On the one hand, some have met the challenge by seeking to accommodate their religion to the change induced by modernity. On the other hand, there has been a traditionalist, fundamentalist backlash. Indeed, it seems to be the development of a liberalizing trend itself that sparks the fundamentalist reaction. The liberalizing tendency seems to fundamentalists to lead to an inevitable decline in morals and in the authority of religion.

In Europe, modernity began to challenge religion in the nineteenth century. The liberal ideas of theologians such as Schleiermacher were an attempt to reach an accommodation with modernity. The fundamentalist reaction to this came with the movement begun after World War II by Karl Barth (1886–1968). In the United States, the challenge of modern science (particularly the theory of evolution) and liberal theology were important factors in the rise of fundamentalism in the early decades of the twentieth century. In Iran in the late nineteenth and early twentieth century, the measures that were being advocated by social reformers were supported by liberal religious leaders such as Shaykh Hadi Najmabadi. These movements were opposed by the fundamentalist, traditionalist ulema led by Shaykh Fadlullah Nuri.[46]

Friedrich Schleiermacher (1768–1834), a leading German Protestant theologian who epitomized the trend towards liberal theology in the nineteenth century

It is perhaps in India that we find the best example of this pattern. Under attack from the Christianity of the colonial power and the challenge of modernity,

Shaykh Fadlullah Nuri, a leading fundamentalist cleric in the Iranian revolution of 1903. In this revolution, the fundamentalists lost to the liberal constitutionalists; a result that was reversed in the 1979 revolution.

Raja Rammohan Roy (1772–1833), founder of Brahmo Samaj (founded 1828) and leading figure in the attempt to modernize and bring liberal ideas into Hinduism. He opposed polytheism, suttee and the caste system.

several liberal reform movements arose among India's Hindus in the nineteenth century. These included the Brahmo Samaj founded by Rammohan Roy in 1828 and the very similar Prartharma Samaj. These movements adopted many of the ideas of the Christian West into a Hindu framework, a development that produced two types of reaction among Hindus, corresponding to the two types of fundamentalism described above. The radical fundamentalists such as Dayananda Saraswati, who founded the Arya Samaj in 1875, felt that Hinduism could best be revitalized by returning to its Vedic roots. They opposed the inclusivist reform movements that accommodated Christian, Western ideas; but they also rejected what they considered to be the accretions of ritual and tradition (such as idol-worship) that had been added to 'pure' Vedic Hinduism. There were also traditionalist fundamentalists who rejected both the inclusivism of social reform movements and the radicalism of the Arya Samaj. They wanted to maintain Hinduism as it was, with all its rituals, traditions and social structures such as the caste system. They formed themselves into many groups (such as the Sanatana Dharma Sabha), which came under an umbrella organization, the Bharata Dharma Mahamandala in 1902.[47] (See also pp. 490–2.)

A Historical Perspective

Apart from these social and psychological insights into the fundamentalism–liberalism dichotomy, we may also develop a historical explanation for the phenomenon. Each religion appears within a certain historical and religious context. At some stage in the development of the religion, its history, doctrines and social laws are written down, thus creating the sacred text of the religion. (See pp. 332–5 on the oral transmission of a text and the consequences of its being written down.) This process of writing down what then becomes regarded as sacred and unalterable is the historical crux of the fundamentalism–liberalism dichotomy. Two problems arise from this process.

The first and less important problem relates to the question of authenticity. In most religions, a great deal of time elapses between the event (either the exposition of sacred teachings or the enactment of sacred history) and the time that it is recorded in writing; the

Swami Dayananda Saraswati (1824–83), founder of the Arya Samaj (founded 1875), a radical movement seeking to return to the religion of the Vedas

greater the length of time that has elapsed, the greater the likelihood of extraneous material entering the text during oral transmission. This much is not controversial, in that it is implicitly acknowledged in most religions. In Christianity, it was acknowledged by the fact that it became necessary for a canon of the more reliable material to be agreed as the text of the *New Testament*. This resulted in the exclusion of other material that became the *Apocrypha*. The process of selection went on for some time, with considerable doubts about whether some items should be included or not. In Islam, the text of the *Qur'an* is considered to be exactly as transmitted to Muhammad and spoken by him, revealing God's Word.[48] However, the numerous *Hadiths* (Traditions) related about Muhammad, which form an important source for the Holy Law, were transmitted orally over several generations and some of them are considered to be unreliable. A method of deciding their relative authenticity is therefore incorporated into the Islamic sciences.[49] Thus the problem of the reliability of authoritative texts is often acknowledged by the religious professionals in these religions. However, if particular religious teachings become a source of difficulty as social conditions change, the question of the authenticity of the sources may be raised by liberals wishing to adapt the teachings to social change.

Much more important for our present concern is that the writing down of the teachings, laws and history of a religion in effect freezes them into a particular setting. These texts are written within the worldview – cosmology, mythology, social concerns and intellectual debates – of a particular time. This does not mean that the sacred scriptures are necessarily frozen in the worldview of the time of the founder of the religion. Rather, it is the worldview of the time when the scripture is written down that is important, as this is what is frozen into the texts.[50] As we get further away from that time, the worldview within which the texts were written becomes ever more alien to the contemporary worldview and the social concerns of that time become more and more removed from current concerns.

This increasing divergence between the worldview of the texts and the contemporary worldview results in the fundamentalist–liberal dichotomy. The fundamentalist regards the texts as unalterable and divine and so struggles to make the contemporary worldview fit in with the worldview embodied in the texts. The liberal, on the other hand, is striving in the opposite direction, trying to make the texts fit in with the contemporary worldview. This is represented pictorially in Figure 14.1. We can note, in passing, that those religions in which the tradition has remained largely oral up to the present time, the primal religions, have suffered very little

Figure 14.1 The Split Between Fundamentalism and Liberalism

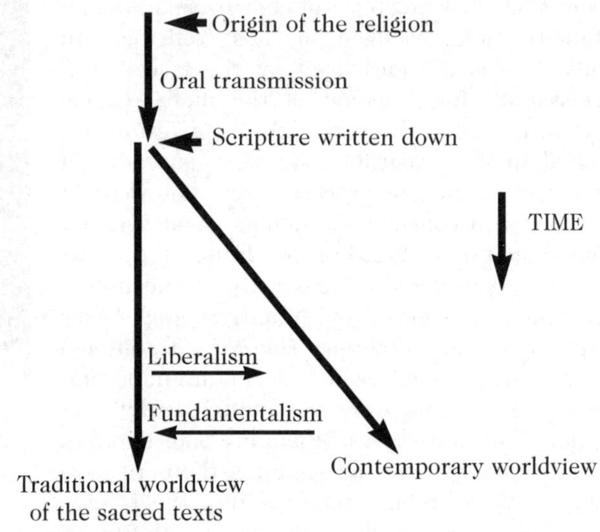

from this fundamentalist–liberal split. Such religions are adapting to new circumstances all the time but this change is gradual and without a written record of the past for comparison, occasions no adverse comment (see pp. 332–5).

We can now consider the situation of a religion that is in the early stages of this historical process of divergence between fundamentalism and liberalism. Although it was stated above that the Baha'i community contains people with both a liberal and a fundamentalist mentality, this does not produce as many problems in the Baha'i community as in other, older religions. Because the Baha'i Faith is only in the early stages of the historical development described in Figure 14.1, there is, as yet, little or no divergence between the social teachings of the religion (which promote such causes as world peace and the equality of men and women) and the needs of society. Thus the fundamentalist Baha'i is forced by the scripture of the religion to be what most people would regard as 'liberal' in outlook. The liberal, on the other hand, need not compromise the central teachings of the religion in order to make the religion suit the needs of society.

In the Western Christian world, the contemporary worldview was broadly in line with the worldview of the *Bible* until about the time of the Renaissance. From that time onwards the two worldviews diverged increasingly. In much of the rest of the world, the two worldviews were congruous until the middle of the nineteenth or the beginning of the twentieth century. The fact that the divergence began so much later in these societies has not, however, meant that the incongruence between the two worldviews is any the less now, only that the contrasts are more violent. This subject is discussed further in chapter 19.

Further Reading

For a presentation of liberal Christian thought, see Hick, *The Second Christianity*; Küng, *On Being a Christian*; Wiles, *The Remaking of Christian Doctrine*. On fundamentalism, the best accounts are Barr, *Fundamentalism* (although the author is clearly not a sympathizer with the fundamentalist position), and Bruce, *Firm in the Faith* (a more neutral account concentrating on British fundamentalism). A comprehensive account of fundamentalism from an insider view is difficult to find, perhaps for the reasons suggested by Barr (pp. 310–12). However, see Akhtar, 'The Virtues of Fundamentalism'. Sharpe, *Understanding Religion*, pp. 108–24, contains many important insights.

Fundamentalism and liberalism in other religious traditions have not been so well studied, but the Fundamentalism Project, based in the University of Chicago, has brought out a series of volumes, the first of which, Marty and Appleby, *Fundamentalisms Observed*, has essays on fundamentalism across the whole religious spectrum. See also the range of liberal opinion from various religions on the question of religious pluralism in Hick and Askari, *The Experience of Religious Diversity*. On Islamic and Christian fundamentalism compared, see Shepard '"Fundamentalism" Christian and Islamic'; and on fundamentalism in Iran, see Arjomand, 'Traditionalism in Twentieth Century Iran'. On Jewish fundamentalism, see Gideon Aran, 'Jewish Zionist Fundamentalism' in Marty and Appleby, *Fundamentalisms Observed*, pp. 265–344. On fundamentalism in Theravada Buddhism, see King, *A Thousand Lives Away*, pp. 53–7. Caplan, *Studies in Religious Fundamentalism* contains papers on fundamentalism among Sikhs, Hindu Tamils, and Muslims in Iran, Egypt and West Africa.

15

Official Religion and Popular Religion

When one surveys the social expressions of religion, a great deal of variation can be observed both between and within religions. One of the most marked is the deviation between the official, doctrinally based version of a religion and the religion as it is practised. These can be called official and popular religion respectively. 'Official' is here being used in the sense of the formal orthodox religion as preached and practised by such religious professionals as the priests in Christianity, the ulema in Islam and the monks in Buddhism.[1] Corresponding terms in more frequent use in the social sciences are 'normative' and 'operative' religion respectively. I have preferred not to use these two terms, as 'normative religion' seems to denote that official religion is the 'proper' religion, consequently implying a devaluation of popular religion.[2] Other parallel terms that have been used include: 'cognitive' and 'affective' religion, and 'Great Tradition' and 'Little Tradition'.[3] This chapter will examine the relationship between official religion and popular religion and the way in which popular religion has evolved, finally looking in more detail at three examples of popular religion: in South and South-East Asia, the Middle East, and South America.

The Relationship between Official and Popular Religion

There are two levels involved in explaining the divergence between official religion and popular religion. First, at the social level, every religion, in whatever part of the world it exists, contains elements within it that go back to religious beliefs that antedate it. Christianity in Europe is thoroughly permeated by customs and traditions going back to its pre-Christian past; Tibetan Buddhism is greatly influenced by the pre-existing Bon religion and in much of Africa, although people may profess Christianity or Islam, religious practice is much influenced by African religion. Second, at the level of the individual, people may, if asked about their religious beliefs, feel constrained to reply in terms of the accepted orthodoxy. In their hearts, however, they may not fully believe all aspects

THE INCORPORATION OF TRADITIONAL AFRICAN RELIGION INTO CHRISTIANITY IN GHANA

Elements of traditional religion have, however, also penetrated, again in the face of strong disapproval and resistance from ecclesiastical authorities, into some of the Christian rituals themselves . . . The nubility rites for girls have become obsolete, but elements of them have penetrated into the rite of confirmation, which now functions as a rite of passage into female adulthood . . . The traditional belief that the menstrual state of women is an unclean one which is highly repulsive (*akyiwade*) and dangerous to any spiritual agent strongly persists among Christians. Women usually absent themselves from church services in this period. Catechists and church-elders impress upon them that they should certainly not participate in the Lord's Supper (Eucharist) in this state. (J. G. Platvoet, 'The Akan Believer and his Religions', in Vrijhof and Waardenburg, *Official and Popular Religion*, p. 571)

of this. This difference between what people profess to believe and what they believe in their hearts can only be detected by observing their actions. A communist government official might have professed to be an atheist. If one observed him crossing himself or kneeling before an altar at times of fear or distress, however, one would have to assume that a belief in God existed at some level in his being.

The religious professionals in each religion will usually look down upon the manifestations of popular religion. They will often refer to them as a corruption of the true religion or as evidence of the ignorance or sinfulness of the mass of the people. The truth is somewhat more complex than this. Popular religious practices fill some of the needs felt by ordinary people – needs that the official religion ignores. Thus, for example, most varieties of official religion disapprove of, or even forbid, recourse to talismans, spells, charms and other forms of magic. They are also against necromancy, astrology and other occult practices. Yet, in almost every society, these elements can be found in popular religion.

One important point is that, despite official disapproval, people regard these popular elements as an integral part of the

HINDU TALISMAN: The Yantra is a mystical diagram that is both a symbol of the Divine and is also believed to participate, in some mystical/magical way, in the power of the Divine. The Shri-Yantra (the Yantra of the illustrious one), shown here, is widely regarded as the most important of the Hindu Yantras, being used in particular in Tantric Hinduism. It consists of nine superimposed triangles, converging on the central spot (*bindu*); the latter symbolizes the unmanifested potentiality of all things; the triangles symbolize the successive stages of creation, emanating from the *bindu*.

SPELLS AND INCANTATIONS

BUDDHISM

The Khandha paritta (Burma), to ward off danger from snakes and other harmful animals:

Let no footless thing do hurt to me, nor thing that has two feet.
Let no four-footed creature hurt, nor thing with many feet.
Let all creatures, all things that live, all beings of whatever kind,
Let all behold good fortune, and let none fall into sin.
Infinite is the Buddha, infinite the Truth, infinite the Order.
Finite are creeping things; snakes, scorpions and centipedes, spiders and lizards, rats and mice
Made is my safeguard, made my defence. Let living things retreat.
Whilst I revere the Blessed One, the Buddhas seven supreme.

(*Vinaya* 6:75–7, quoted in Spiro, *Buddhism and Society*, p. 266)

HINDUISM

An incantation from the Rig Veda *to bring success against a rival wife:*

I dig up this [magic] plant, the most powerful thing that grows, with which one drives out the rival wife and wins the husband entirely for oneself.
Broad-leaved plant sent by the gods to bring happiness and the power to triumph, blow my rival wife away and make my husband mine alone.
O highest one, I am the highest one, higher than all the highest women, and my rival wife is lower than the lowest women.
I will not even take her name into my mouth; he takes no pleasure in this person. Far, far into the distance we make the rival wife go.

(*Rig Veda* 10:145, pp. 289–90)

CHRISTIANITY

St Patrick's Breastplate (Ireland), against evil and witchcraft:

I bind unto myself today
The strong name of the Trinity
By invocation of the same
The Three in One and One in Three.

Against all Satan's spells and wiles.
Against false words of heresy . . .
Against the wizard's evil craft,
Against the death-wound and the burning,
The choking wave, the poisoned shafts,
Protect me Christ till Thy returning.

religion and they are thought to derive their power and efficacy through the spiritual forces of the religion.[4] For example, in most Muslim countries, amulets are worn as a magical protection against danger. These amulets usually contain verses from the *Qur'an*, which is considered to be the source of their power.[5] Such practices persist despite the prohibition against them in the official religion.[6] Similarly, in Buddhist countries, spells and magical formulas are used. Their power is attributed to the Buddha. This is despite the formal doctrinal position that such things can have no effect on the workings of the laws of karma.[7] Thus, practitioners of the popular religion see themselves as loyal adherents of that religion. They do not regard themselves in any sense as being opposed to it or seeking to undermine it, as their disparagers will often assert. Given the universality of such phenomena, it would appear it is misleading to see popular religion as just a 'corrupt' form of the official religion; rather it would be more accurate to see it as catering to some of people's deeply felt needs, which the official religion is not meeting: a need for answers to the problems of life, protection against the uncertainties of life, and hope for a better future.

The relationship between official and popular religion varies greatly across the world. In some places the two intermingle and there is mutual acceptance, while in others the two are in conflict. The following four examples will suffice to display this range of relationships.

Christianity

Some elements of popular religion have mingled reasonably comfortably with the official religion for much of the history of Christian Europe. When Europe was Christianized, there was wholesale adoption of much from the earlier 'pagan' religions. Sites of pagan temples were made into churches; pagan festivals were incorporated into the Christian calendar as Christian holy days; pagan practices such as making offerings to holy springs were either re-expressed as Christian practices or else absorbed into folk tradition; pagan deities were even incorporated into the Christian panoply of saints.[8]

From a theological viewpoint, the resurrection of Christ at Easter is the most significant religious festival. In many Christian countries of Europe and America, however, the festivities at Christmas far outdo the Easter celebrations. Most Christmas customs are, in fact, based on old pagan festivals, the Roman Saturnalia and the Scandinavian and Teutonic Yule. Christians adopted these during the earliest period of Church history.[9] Thus the extent and form of the Christmas festivities may be considered a popular religious practice. The Church, however, has given this recognition and incorporates it into the Church year without too many misgivings. Only the more radical fundamentalist elements in some churches protest from time to time about this mixing of 'pagan' elements into the religion.[10]

Similar comments may be made about several other examples of popular Christianity. In Roman Catholicism, one may cite the occurrence of miracles and the formation of cults around the Virgin Mary and other saints. Miracles as manifestations of popular religion are usually strongly resisted by the Church at first. However, if they become established, and

THE SUBSTITUTION OF CHRISTIAN FIGURES FOR PRE-CHRISTIAN GODS IN GERMANY

Woden is ousted by St. Michael, St. Martin, and later by St. Nicholas; Thor by St. Peter; Frigg and Freya by Blessed Virgin Mary. Common traits or equal functions form the connecting notion: both Woden and St. Martin were passionate hunters; Woden, Mercury and St. Michael are conductors of souls; St. Peter, the fisherman, is depicted with a huge key of heaven, while Thor, who goes out to sea to catch the world-serpent, has an enormous axe or hammer, with which he smashes the giants. St. Martin was the Frankish national saint; Charles the Great had a strong personal veneration for St. Peter. The heathen gods, who mostly operated in pairs in the epic introduction of the old charms, were replaced by such Christian pairs as Jesus and St. Martin, Jesus and St. Peter, or St. Peter and St. Paul. (J. A. Huisman, 'Christianity and Germanic Religion', in Vrijhof and Waardenburg, *Official and Popular Religion*, pp. 60–1)

once the initial enthusiasm around them has moderated, they are then given some degree of official recognition. Christianity has not, however, looked favourably on all elements of popular religion. Supposed witches have been persecuted and there have been periods in Christian history when other elements of popular religion such as divination suffered – from the Inquisition, for example.

POPULAR RELIGIOUS PRACTICE IN SHI'I ISLAM: At Shi'i commemorations of the martyrdom of the Imam Husayn, self-flagellation is a ritual method of showing sorrow both at the death of the Imam and also at humanity's failure to come to his aid at the time of his martyrdom.

Islam

A greater degree of disapproval is expressed by the official religion towards some of the popular religious practices in Islam. In Shi'i Islam, for example, it has been customary for centuries to commemorate the martyrdom of one of the Shi'i religious leaders, the Imam Husayn, in 680 CE. These very emotive rituals include public orations, passion plays, beating of the chest and self-flagellation. The attitude of the Shi'i religious leaders, the ulema, towards these rituals is ambivalent. Their formal position is that the rituals are excessive and to be discouraged. Yet, nevertheless, some of the ulema may be found participating in them and, a few years ago, when the ulema in Iran felt threatened by the Shah, they were even glad of them as expressions of Shi'i solidarity and tools for covert propaganda against the Shah. Shi'i popular religion also includes much in the way of talismans and amulets. Sometimes these may be made by minor local members of the religious classes, while the higher-ranking ulema are disdainful of such practices.

Buddhism

Third, we come to the differences between the official doctrinal position of Theravada Buddhism and the popular religion in countries such as Sri Lanka, Burma and Thailand where Theravada Buddhism predominates. Here one sees a very great divergence between the official religion as expounded by the senior monks and the popular religion of the people. The fact that such a wide divergence exists, however, does not seem to be met by any great disapproval. It is almost as if there is a cognitive dissonance among the ranks of the more senior monks with regard to what is happening among the people. Since the example of Theravada Buddhism represents the extreme of the difference between the official and popular religion, I shall examine it in more detail later in this chapter.

Baha'i Faith

A comparatively modern religion such as the Baha'i Faith shows little evidence, yet, of a dissonance between official and popular religion. It has, however, in recent years, spread to traditional societies in many parts of the world and it will therefore be interesting to see to what extent the traditional practices of these societies are incorporated into the workings of the religion.

There is room in the official religion of the Baha'i Faith for a certain amount of incorporation of local practices and customs, since the obligatory official content of most Baha'i ritual occasions is minimal. The only obligatory part of the Baha'i marriage ceremony, for example, consists of the repeating of a simple one-sentence vow before witnesses. The couple and their family add other parts to the ceremony according to their own wishes. This obviously leaves much scope for the introduction of local customs.

The Evolution of Popular Religion

In historical terms, there has probably been a great deal of interaction between the official and popular forms of the world religions, but this may be difficult to prove, as the official records would not want to admit to any influence from popular religion. From the available evidence, however, it has been possible to postulate that the twin processes of universalization and parochialization have occurred (a similar process occurs with religious symbols).[11] Parochialization refers to the arrival of the festivals and rituals of the official religion in a particular place and their superimposition on local religious practices. This gives rise to variations based on these pre-existing local cults and customs. In the Christian world, for example, there are many local variants in the celebration of Easter and Christmas. Most of these must have arisen from an admixture of Christian and pre-Christian

a

b

c

Religious Processions: As well as being an occasion for popular participation in a religious occasion, processions are also a public demonstration of the power of a religion (see chapter 16). a) Chinese religion: Nineteenth-century depiction of a procession for the Feast of Lanterns in Singapore. b) Buddhism: Procession of monks in Korea. c) Christianity: Catholic procession in which a statue of Mary is carried through the streets, Brazil.

pagan practices. In the villages of India, the great gods, goddesses and festivals of Hinduism have become transformed into a myriad local forms, often at great variance to the original. Universalization refers to the opposite process, whereby a local religious practice is taken up and adopted into the official religion. Thus, for example, when Buddhism arrived in Sri Lanka, it adopted the local belief in evil spirits into its cosmology. Local ideas and customs can even be spread in this way to new areas where they are not part of the local tradition. Many customs now associated with Christmas were, as mentioned above, local pagan practices associated with the Yule festivities of Northern Europe and the Saturnalia of Rome. These have now spread to most of the Christian world, even though they have nothing to do with Christ's birth.[12]

It may even be desirable to postulate that more than just the popular and official forms of some religions exist side by side. Melford E. Spiro has identified three forms of Theravada Buddhism in Burma: the nibbanic religion – the official religion with Nibbana (Nirvana) as its goal for salvation; the kammic religion – in which the main concern is to improve one's position according to the laws of *kamma* (karma) and which is the mode of thinking of the masses; and what he terms the apotropaic religion – the protection from evil and the curing of illness through magical and occult means, which is the practice of the masses.[13] In Islam, we may distinguish the official religion, which is based on following the Holy Law and is promulgated by the ulema; the popular religion, which is concerned with emotive public rituals and with magical charms and amulets and is the religion of the masses; and the mystical religion of the Sufi orders, where the emphasis is on rituals and practices that result in an altered state of consciousness. These different forms of Islam do not correspond to sectarian differences, in that they occur in both the major divisions of Islam, Sunnism and Shi'ism.

These parallel forms of religion overlap and interplay with each other to a considerable extent. Popular religion uses the terms and concepts of

THE ADOPTION OF LOCAL BELIEFS INTO SRI LANKAN BUDDHISM

The belief in *yakkhas* [demons] and other demonic beings existed already in Sri Lanka before the official arrival of Buddhism. One of the first tasks of Mahinda when he started his preaching on the island was to make a connection between the existing beliefs and the Buddha's teaching. So during one of his first sermons, according to tradition, he recited the Peta- and Vimanavatthu, canonical texts concerning these lower supernatural beings. And he 'converted' the Sinhalese *yakkhas* to Buddhism and gave them a place within the pantheon, a procedure which is not at all opposed to Buddhist teaching and which has been used many times in the course of Buddhist missionary activity. (M. A. G. T. Kloppenborg, 'Some Reflexions on the Study of Sinhalese Buddhism', in Vrijhof and Waardenburg, *Official and Popular Religion*, pp. 500–1) official religion, albeit often with a shift in meaning as in Afro-American religion in Brazil, for example (see pp. 399–403). And official religion is influenced by popular religion to a larger extent than it would like to admit: in the Roman Catholic Church, for example, it is often popular acclaim that provides the initial impetus behind the moves to acknowledge a saint or declare an event to have been a miracle. As Richard Gombrich has pointed out, it would be a mistake to regard popular religion as merely a corrupt form of official religion. In almost every religion, there is good evidence that popular religious practices have existed from the earliest days of the religion.[14]

One final factor to be considered is the way in which the boundary between official religion and popular religion has weakened during the twentieth century. There has been a general weakening in the authority of official religion and consequently, some liberal religious thinkers have sought to increase the appeal of religion by introducing elements from popular culture, such as pop music. Much more important has been the fact that, whereas previously it was religion that set moral standards that the rest of society sought to emulate, religion is now, especially in the West, following the lead of the popular culture. Many areas that at the beginning of the twentieth century were clearly defined in each religious tradition, such as the permissibility of homosexuality or the social role of women have now been thrown open. Pressure from popular culture has forced a rethink in official religion, to the extent that it may be said that we are increasingly entering an era in which popular culture leads and official religion follows; indeed, because of this the plausibility of maintaining an official religion has been seriously undermined.

Three Examples of Popular Religion

We shall now consider in more detail three from among the numerous possible examples of the interplay between official religion and popular religion: Theravada Buddhism in South and South-East Asia, Islam in the Middle East and Afro-American religion in South America. These three examples have been chosen because they display more clearly than others some of the key features of this phenomenon. Theravada Buddhism and Islam demonstrate how popular religion can directly contradict many of the key teachings of the official religion and yet still be espoused by people who consider themselves devout followers of the official religion. There are many other instances of the same phenomenon. The example of the interplay between the official religion of the Roman Catholic Church and Afro-American religious practices and cults in Brazil shows how popular religious forms which incorporate the practices of the earlier religion of a people can survive even against fierce opposition and persecution over centuries. There are many other instances of this, including pagan practices that have survived in Christian Europe.

Theravada Buddhism and Popular Religion in Sri Lanka, Burma and Thailand

The doctrines of Theravada Buddhism are rather austere. It teaches a radical rejection of this world as a source of happiness or salvation; the world and the desire for anything in it must be renounced, for they are the source of suffering, leading to continued rebirth into this world of suffering. Part of the source of desire, and therefore of continued existence in this world, is the erroneous notion that human beings have an individual self or soul (the doctrine of *anatta*); the goal of human life is extinction (Nibbana, Nirvana).[15]

Those who have researched what ordinary Buddhists actually believe, however, have found a wide deviation from these doctrinal positions. Spiro found that when he asked Burmese Buddhist villagers what they aspired to after death, the majority said Nibbana.[16] But he found that this was, in fact, just a formal response. When, as an anthropologist, he observed their lives more closely and asked them more indirectly, he found that, in fact, they did not desire the extinction of Nibbana. Most wanted the merits that they accrued in this life to result in their rebirth into more favourable circumstances. This meant being reborn wealthy, in the case of men; or as a man, in the case of women.[17] Regarding the doctrine of *anatta* (no self), most Burmese understood it differently from its orthodox interpretation. In practice, they rejected it for the universal Burmese belief that each person has an individual 'butterfly spirit' (*leikpya*) – a pre-Buddhist Burmese belief.[18] The same phenomenon is found among Thai villagers, who believe in the *khwan*, an individualized soul that leaves the body after death.[19] Similarly, regarding the Buddhist doctrine of *anicca* (*anitya*, the impermanence of all things in the universe), most Buddhists assent to this as a formal exposition of their beliefs. In their actions, however, they show that they do not, in fact, believe it. Indeed, thousands of Burmese, many of them monks, spend a great deal of time and money attempting to prolong their lives through magical spells and charms. This is an activity scarcely compatible with a belief in the impermanence of the world and the need to reject all forms of attachment to it.[20]

POPULAR RELIGIOUS PRACTICE IN BUDDHISM: Buddhists in Thailand give alms and food to monks to acquire merit and thus a better rebirth. The monastic rules in Buddhism decree that monks must obtain their daily food by begging. Lay people therefore earn merit by providing this food.

In Sri Lanka, Gombrich found much the same. The ideal of the official religion is the *arhat*, rejecting the world and meditating, striving for extinction (Nibbana). This is, however, in practice almost never found, even among the monks. Indeed, the monks, for the most part, have the same aims as lay

Table 15.1 Differences Between Official and Popular Religion in Theravada Buddhism

		Page numbers		
Official Religion	Popular Religion	Sri Lanka	Burma	Thailand
Anatta (no self)	Concept of a continuity of the self beyond death	72	84–91	57–9
Attitude of rejection towards the world since the world is *anicca* (impermanent)	Use of magic spells and merit-making presuppose an importance attaching to the world and the desire for a good rebirth	191–213	67	317–27
Desire is the root of suffering; extinction of desire the means to salvation	Frustration of desire is root of suffering and its fulfilment is the goal of salvation	67, 73 75 78–9		
Suffering (*duhkha*) is caused through the operation of the law of karma, i.e. it is the result of previous bad actions and cannot be altered or influenced	Suffering is often caused by witches, evil spirits, and adverse astrological influences and can be alleviated by spells and talismans	324–6	155	312
Goal in this life is Nibbana (Nirvana)	Goal of life is rebirth in heaven or into a better condition on earth	282–3, 326	76–84	53
Path towards the goal involves self-restraint and meditation	Path towards the goal involves merit-making through alms-giving and morality	320	93	53
Ideal ethic emphasizes self-restraint and is world-denying	Ideal ethic emphasizes love and is world-affirming	320–3		
Buddha no longer exists and therefore can be of no direct assistance towards salvation or as a protector	Buddha is alive and can assist both with salvation and with protection against calamity	103–43	148–9	44–7

Note: page numbers in right-hand columns refer to:
Sri Lanka: R. H. Gombrich, *Precept and Practice*
Burma: Spiro, *Buddhism and Society*
Thailand: Tambiah, *Buddhism and the Spirit Cults*

Buddhists in striving for a better rebirth through making merit. Hence, they are engaged in working in the world rather than being detached from it.[21] This divergence between official and popular religion in Theravada Buddhism can be laid out in tabular form (see Table 15.1).

Finally, it should be noted that, although I have distinguished between an 'official' and a 'popular' religion in Buddhism, this is not how Buddhists themselves see the religion. To ordinary Buddhists in Sri Lanka, Burma or Thailand, there are no paradoxes or inconsistencies. They live within a unified and integrated religious system. All divisions into 'pure' Buddhism and 'corrupt' Buddhism, the 'original' religion and 'later' accretions, 'normative' and 'operative' modes of religion and so on, which are the interpretations made by scholars to account for their observations, do not cohere with the reality of the religion as ordinary Buddhists experience it. This point is particularly important in Buddhist studies. The first generation of Western scholars of Buddhism were keen to make Buddhism a religion compatible with the age of reason and a contrast to Christianity. They thus presented it as an atheistic, rationalist and individualist religion. Any evidence that contradicted this view, such as the Buddhist belief in gods, supernatural beings, heavens and hells, and the use of astrology and charms, were ascribed to Hindu and animist influences that had found their way into the religion. They were regarded as corruptions of the original pure teachings of the Buddha, despite the existence of much evidence in the Pali canon itself that many of these elements were part of Buddhism

REPRESENTATION OF BUDDHIST SUPERNATURAL BEINGS: Yakshas at Wat Arun, Bangkok. Yakshas are supernatural beings mentioned in the Pali canon (Yakkas). They are usually described as demonic beings who distract humans from following the path of Dharma.

even during the lifetime of the Buddha. Gombrich asserts that what is called 'popular religion' is, in fact, the religion as practised by all, while the official religion is merely the religion as preached. The 'popular religion' thus represents no corruption, distortion or dilution, for the religion has always been practised thus. Gombrich advances examples from the earliest Buddhist chronicles to demonstrate that the official religion represents only a theoretical ideal, which has never existed in the physical world even among the monks.[22]

Islam and Popular Religion in the Middle East

In Islam, the official religion of the religious scholars and of the mosque frowns upon many popular religious practices. The historical evidence indicates that early Islam was an austere and simple religion that involved the keeping of certain laws signifying the direct relationship between the believer and a transcendent God. As Islam became established and spread into new areas, the austerity of the religion was tempered by the evolution of new religious practices, some of which were derived from the religious practices of the religions that had existed in those areas prior to Islam.

An example of a popular religious belief that pre-dates the arrival of Islam is belief in the existence of the evil eye. The fact that it can be found throughout Europe, the Middle East, North Africa and India is evidence of the antiquity of this superstition. It is believed that, merely by looking at a person or thing, certain individuals have the ability to bring misfortune, although such a person may not intend any evil and may not even know that he or she has this power. In particular, the evil eye may be cast if envy, jealousy or covetousness is aroused. Great precautions are therefore taken to protect against it. Children, who are considered to be at special risk, may be surrounded by amulets and talismans, often containing verses of the *Qur'an*. When someone, especially a child is praised, the words *ma sha' Allah* (what God wills[23]) are uttered to prevent the praise attracting the evil eye. Failure to add this phrase to one's remarks will lead to one being blamed for any misfortune that subsequently arises. There are many other practices such as divining, the making of talismans, spells and magic which are disapproved of by the official religion but which occur nonetheless in many Islamic cultures.

The *Qur'an* emphasizes the great gap between human beings and God. Even Muhammad is depicted in the *Qur'an* as being merely a human being who has been entrusted with a message from God.[24] Any attempt to give any human being an elevated status has always been met by great suspicion from the official religion; it is considered dangerously close to *shirk* (associating anything else with God as sharing in God's divinity). Nevertheless, in popular religion the cult of saints has been very popular in all parts of the Muslim world. Particular pious individuals, heads of Sufi orders, or sectarian leaders have been called saints (singular *wali*; plural *awliya*) and many miraculous happenings have been attributed to them.

Knowledge of what is in a person's mind, knowledge of future events, the ability to cure illness and grant wealth, the ability to change shape and to appear in different places at once, have all at various times been attributed to such individuals, despite the fact that the *Qur'an* indicates that knowledge of the future, for example, was not even granted to the Prophet Muhammad.[25] Visiting (pilgrimage to) the tombs of saints has become a marked feature of popular religion in Islam. Such visits are made in the hope of receiving blessing (*baraka*), good fortune or a cure for illness. They can even, in the popular estimation, be considered equivalent to the pilgrimage to Mecca.[26] In Shi'i Islam, the equivalent practice, visiting the tombs of the Shi'i Imams or their families, has become part of the official religion.

POPULAR RELIGIOUS PRACTICE IN ISLAM: Muslims making pilgrimage to the tomb of a Muslim saint. This early photograph shows a group of pilgrims outside a shrine associated with the prophet Jonah in Kaafar, on the Euphrates in Iraq.

While they are not given any official approval, the condemnation of these popular religious practices by most of the ulema has been fairly mild. From time to time, however, individual scholars, especially from the Hanbali school of law, have denounced them strongly as religious innovation (*bid'a*). It is probably Ibn Taymiyya (d. 1328) who is best remembered for his attacks upon popular religious practices, especially the veneration of saints. In his writings he put forward strong arguments from the *Qur'an* and the *Hadiths* (Traditions) against these practices. Some 450 years later in Arabia, the Wahhabi movement founded by Ibn 'Abd al-Wahhab (1703–92) and led by Ibn Sa'ud put into practice the puritanical measures advocated by Ibn Taymiyya, destroying many tombs and shrines of saints and holy men.

Roman Catholicism and Afro-American Religion in Brazil

Throughout South America, Roman Catholic Christianity is the predominant official religion. It was brought to this continent by the colonial rulers, the Spanish and Portuguese. The majority (ninety per cent) of the population regard themselves as Catholics. Alongside this official religion, there are many manifestations of popular religion based on various admixtures of native American Indian religion, African religion and spiritism (especially that founded on the teachings of the Frenchman Alan Kardec, 1804–69). The same people who may be found devoutly kneeling and praying before an image of the Virgin Mary one day are participating the next day in a frenzied dance ending in a state of trance, honouring a deity that is recognizably an African god. For healing, many will go to a recognized doctor, but just as many will go to a spirit healer or cult priestess. In this survey, I shall concentrate on the African religious beliefs

AFRICAN-AMERICAN RELIGION IN BRAZIL: Initiation of a new female member (*filha de santo*)

and practices that are part of the popular religion in Brazil.

From the sixteenth century to the mid-nineteenth century, several million black Africans were brought to Brazil to work as slaves, initially on the big plantations and later in the mining operations in that country. The trauma of slavery and translocation, the breaking up of families, and the fact that in any one locality there would be individuals from a wide variety of tribal backgrounds, led at first to a complete disruption of traditional African religious practices which were strongly based on tribe and family. While the social structures of African tribal life were irretrievably lost in this process, the symbols and values of African culture and religion did not die out. They merely sought out and evolved new ways of expressing themselves. The myths and gods lived on in the collective memory and the rituals and dances were re-enacted in secret, at night, when the masters had gone to sleep. Keeping alive these ethnic memories became a way for the slaves to protest their social situation and these religious and cultural remnants were also often a focus in slave protests and revolts. The history of Afro-Brazilian religion thus became, in one sense, a struggle to create new social structures to replace the lost African ones and to give form to these religious impulses.

A number of factors countered the disruptions caused by slavery and brought together 'nations' of common African tribal descent. These factors included the trend towards large plantations requiring large numbers of slaves thus increasing the chances of individuals from the same tribal background coming together. The nineteenth-century growth of urban centres with large numbers of black and mixed race peoples again brought together individuals from the same tribal background. These 'nations' often evolved an elaborate social structure with kings, queens, courtiers and ambassadors. They were identified by African names denoting their origins, such as Malê, Yoruba, Dahoman, Congo, Angola, and Mozambique. The government to some extent fostered this process by encouraging the growth of 'nations' among Afro-Brazilians because inter-ethnic rivalries among these 'nations' precluded the chances of a successful general revolt of the black population. The government would also, however, even after the end of slavery, frequently persecute and try to eradicate any manifestations of African religion.

From the sixteenth century onwards, the Roman Catholic Church, which dominated the religious culture of Brazil, tried numerous ways of countering the survivals of African religion in the population. One method was to encourage persecution of these religious manifestations. Another method, which was both an attempt to Christianize the Afro-American tradition and a way of keeping blacks and whites segregated, was the creation of religious fraternities for blacks, centred on particular saints. While such measures had some success in making European Christianity more palatable for native American Indians and black slaves, and so helped to Christianize the population, they also unwittingly helped to perpetuate the African religious tradition. African beliefs that ancestors could act as intermediaries to present an individuals' requests to the gods were easily translated into the idea of Christian saints as intercessors. Rituals and dances that had been performed to African gods were perpetuated within these fraternities, which also acted to consolidate the Afro-American 'nations'. By segregating congregations and making black Catholicism very much a second-class affair, moreover, the Roman Catholic Church encouraged black Brazilians to go back to their own cultural roots to seek out a religious expression that they could feel was authentically theirs.

Some aspects of African religious practices survived throughout the period of slavery. The importance that the African religions had given to burial rituals was continued in Brazil and merely transposed into a Christian mode. African magic and medicine also survived among the Afro-Brazilians. Accounts from Brazil record that the black slaves, on the few occasions that they were given time off by their masters, used to sacrifice animals, perform dances and go into trance states.

There was also, of course, at least until the early nineteenth century, a continuous infusion of new slaves from Africa who restored memories of religious practices that had been eradicated by the slave environment. In

THE PERSISTENCE OF AFRICAN RELIGION IN BRAZIL

Zacharias Wagner, who lived in Dutch Brazil from 1634 to 1641, [wrote, in describing a picture he had drawn]: 'When the slaves have worked hard for a whole week, they are given Sunday off. They usually assemble in specially designated places and spend the day in wild dancing to the sound of flutes and drums – men and women, children and old people alike. This is accompanied by frequent libations . . . often until they are too deafened and drunk to recognize one another.' But, as Rene Ribeiro rightly comments, 'anyone familiar with the Afro-Brazilian cults of Recife will recognize at a glance that this is a *xango* [an Afro-Brazilian cult] the typical ring of dancers moving to the left in choreographic attitudes; the typical position of the *ogan-ilu* [drummer] beating two drums of a type commonly found all over West Africa and an *agogo* [bell]; the jar of *garapa* [a drink] beside the musicians; the typical position and pose of the priest. They failed to recognize one another not so much because they were "deafened and drunk" but because they were possessed by their gods . . . a psychological state of which the artist of course knew nothing.' (Bastide, *The African Religions of Brazil*, p. 134) the last years of slavery and after it finally ended in 1888, there was a social vacuum for Afro-Brazilians. The old social structure centred on slave-owning families was no more and there was no social structure to replace it. In this situation, out of the 'nations' and fraternities that had existed during the slave period, religious cults based on African religious survivals emerged to give some degree of social cohesion and solidarity to ex-slaves.

The religious cults that emerged in the nineteenth century appear at first to have reflected tribal origins. In time, however, as the number of pure Africans decreased and most people became of mixed origins, the differences between these 'nations' became only cultic differences. In the north of the country, the religious cults that developed, called Catimbó, Cachimbó or Encantados, were strongly influenced by native American Indian religion. In the rest of the country, in time, the gods, ritual forms and priestly hierarchy that became predominant over other forms were those of the Yoruba (from Nigeria). The basic details of these cults are very similar. There is a supreme god who is called Olorun in Yoruba; there are then a series of lesser gods called Orishas (Orixás), such as Oshala (Oxalá, the god of the sky and of procreation), Shango (Xango, the thunder god) and Yemanja (the sea goddess), who are the deified ancestors, heroes and kings of the tribe and who intercede with Olorun for human beings; there is a priestly caste which is sometimes female; the rituals usually consist of an animal sacrifice and dancing leading to trance.

CANDOMBLÉ: A female initiate (*filha de santo*) has become the Orisha Oshum (Oxum), goddess of fountains and beauty, who is represented as being vain and always looking in a mirror.

During the years of slavery and afterwards, when there was legal persecution of these cults, it was necessary to hide these African beliefs and rituals behind a mask of Christianity. The Orishas were therefore identified with Catholic saints. The exact identification differed from one area of Brazil to another and from one cult to another. Typically, Oshala, a male god of procreation and harvest, for instance, was identified with Jesus or the Holy Spirit; Yemanja, goddess of the sea, was associated with Our Lady of the Immaculate Conception; and Ogun, the warrior god, became St George. Altars for these African deities had pictures of the appropriate Christian saint placed in front. Eshu (Exu), the god of vengeance, became the Devil.

African religion has survived in its purest form in the north-east, from Pernambuco to Bahia, where the number of those of relatively pure African descent is highest. In these cults, there is a conscious separation between the African element and the Catholic element. The naming of these cults in Brazil is very fluid but they are usually called Candomblé. Further south, around the cities of Rio de Janeiro and São Paulo, African religion became integrated into popular Catholicism in a more homogenized manner. This mixed with American Indian and spiritist beliefs and practices and evolved into the Macumba cults. In the present century, the Umbanda cults evolved, with even stronger spiritist and occultist elements. In general, the more these religions have moved away from the purer forms of African religion, the greater the white participation in them, and the greater the focus on magic for helping the individual rather than on group solidarity and communal participation. In recent years, there has been a movement to lift these popular religious movements to the status of official religions (see p. 508). While previously they were popular religious forms with Roman Catholicism as the official religion, the trend now is to set these religions up as official religions in opposition to the Catholic Church. (For a brief survey of African religion in other parts of the Americas, see pp. 507–8.)

Further Reading

The separation of official religion from popular religion is parallel to several other dichotomies: the concept of the Great Tradition and the Little Tradition (see such books as Redfield, *Peasant Society and Culture*, pp. 67–104); the concept of cognitive and affective religion (R. F. Gombrich, *Precept and Practice*, pp. 4–7, 318–9; see note 3 of this chapter); Towler describes official and common religion (Towler, *Homo Religiosus*, pp. 145–62). While the official aspect of each religion can generally be found by consulting the works of specialists in that religion, for popular religion, it is usually necessary to use the works of anthropologists: for Islam, see E. Westermark, *Ritual and Belief in Morocco* and Gilsenan, *Recognizing Islam*; for Indian religion, see Marriott, 'Little Communities in an Indigenous Civilisation'. Vrijhof and Waardenburg, *Official and Popular Religion*, contains papers on the popular form in several religions, including historical studies of Christianity. The paper by Frijhoff in this volume contains a discussion of the methodological problems of this subject. For the analysis of Theravada Buddhism presented here, use has been made of the works of three anthropologists, R. F. Gombrich (*Precept and Practice*), Spiro (*Buddhism and Society*), and Tambiah (*Buddhism and the Spirit Cults*) for Sri Lanka, Burma and Thailand respectively. On Brazilian Afro-American religion, see Bastide, *The African Religions of Brazil*.

16

Religion, Power and Government

It was noted in chapter 4 that the central experience of religion is intense but also very personal. The experience of the holy invokes a feeling of awe and dread, the *mysterium tremendum* described by Otto (see p. 88). This feeling is the basis of the power and authority of the holy. Power may be defined as the capacity of an agent to carry out its will and to produce outcomes, in other words, to make a difference in the world. Human beings experience the power of the holy both as a coercive power (a power over them that compels their obedience) and an enabling power (a power within that enables them to do what they would otherwise not do). Anthropologists have studied the role of power. They see it as the key to understanding a variety of phenomena in primal religion such as taboo, *mana*, totemism and shamanism. People will do things for the sake of religion that they would not do for any other cause. Buddhists leave their families and enter monasteries; Hindus leave home to take up the life of a wandering ascetic; Muslims and Christians perform arduous pilgrimages; Baha'is have been willing to leave the comfort of their homes and face an uncertain life in other parts of the world to spread their faith; individuals of all these religions have at times even been willing to give up their lives for their religious beliefs. This chapter looks at the role of religion in legitimating the social order, the relationship between religion and the state, and the question of the power structures within a religion.

We have seen in chapter 5 how the central experience of religion can be channelled into various forms of social religious expression. It should not surprise us that this process also acts as a way of controlling and channelling the power inherent in the central experience of religion. These various social expressions of religion are, in effect, ways of transferring the feeling of awe, which is a feature of the central experience, to some social institution or agent (a church, a priest or other religious leader). This then acts as the basis of the power of that religious leader or institution. Power in turn confers authority. This authority can subsequently, if the religious leader or institution chooses, be transferred to a secular institution (a king or government).

Religion has, over the course of human history, been one of the most powerful and pervasive forces at work in society. There is, therefore, an intimate and interdependent relationship between religion and authority in most societies. Those in power have looked to the religious leadership to legitimate and uphold their authority. For secular leaders, the support of the religious hierarchy gives their rule the appearance of being part of the supramundane order of things. If their rule has a high degree of plausibility as part of the way things are, the social and sacred reality, then it becomes difficult even to conceive of changing it. The religious world, in turn, looks to the secular authorities for support. This may take the form of financial support, or at least assistance, in the worldly undertakings of the religious establishment. This relationship between religion and State can also have mutual benefits at a higher level. Religious leaders can act as advisors to government, helping it to enact laws that are just and promote the general welfare. Through their close relationship with the people, they can warn a government when its policies are losing popular support.

The baptism of King (Saint) Stephen (975–1038), the first Christian king of Hungary. Pope Sylvester II sent a special crown from Rome for the coronation in 1001 and designated Stephen 'Apostolic Majesty'. Stephen promoted Christianity throughout Hungary and suppressed pagan revolts. He was canonized in 1083 and became the patron saint of Hungary.

Religion and Legitimation

In order to analyse the relationship between religion and power more deeply, we must examine one of the most important social functions of religion, that of legitimation. This term refers to the establishment of a social consensus that explains and justifies the social order. We, as human beings, acting collectively, produce both the social order and the conceptual universe within which our society exists. We are also moulded by the society and culture in which we grow up. Thus, this social order and conceptual universe are both produced by human beings and in turn mould the human beings who emerge from them. The institutions that come to comprise this social order and the values and meanings constructed by this conceptual universe evolve an existence independent of particular human beings. They are thus experienced as a fully developed objective reality. Indeed, a conceptual universe, once created, becomes *the* reality, taken for granted by those born and raised within its framework. Only an 'outsider' can fully appreciate its constructed nature.

Although social institutions are self-evidently valid to those who created them because of particular circumstances, they need to be explained and justified to later generations (when the same circumstances may no longer apply). Legitimation serves to give meaning to the social order, to make it plausible and thus to strengthen it and give it cohesion. It serves to answer any question that may arise about why social institutions are the way they are and why an individual should act in a particular way. These answers do not, of course, need to make sense to an outsider. They merely need to satisfy the person who is brought up in the culture. The answers are often pre-theoretical and mythical. They give what might be called a positive charge to the existing social order.[1] Overall, however, the process of legitimation must cover the marginal situations of life (death, dreams, and unusual natural phenomena) as well as everyday reality.[2]

Many social institutions have an assigned meaning. The process of legitimation, however, ties this meaning into the overall universe of meaning and the values of the society. The police force, for example, exists to maintain law and order. The process of legitimation involves a justification of why law and order are necessary in society and why it is right to achieve them in this particular way. This level of justification can only be constructed in relation to all the other social institutions and to the overarching symbolic and conceptual universe.

Bearing in mind this need for legitimation in society, we can now examine the role of religion. Rulers and governments have used it through the ages for various purposes. The following are among the most important of these.

Religion Used to Legitimate the Social Structure

Most religions have been used to one extent or another to legitimate the existing social structure. In most traditional societies (and many modern ones), it is religion that provides the overarching universe of meaning that is objective reality for those who live within that society. It is the religious professional who is the principal exponent of this universe of meaning; it is he (or sometimes she) who explains how and why things are they way they are.

Thus, the powerful position of religion in a traditional society is the result of its position as the legitimator of the social order, which means that religion cannot but play an important political role. Indeed, in most situations it is the natural arbiter of power. Since it is religion that decrees what is right and wrong for the society, it is natural for it to be the main buttress for the political establishment.

This role of religion as legitimator of the social order has applied, in particular, where the social structure has elements of inequality or injustice and is therefore potentially unstable (and there have not been many societies of which this was not at least partly true). Religion has, in these circumstances, been used to stabilize the social order by giving it the divine stamp of authority. Apartheid in twentieth-century South Africa, for example, was legitimated by a synod of the Dutch Reform Church in this way:

PAPAL TERRITORY: The small principality of the Vatican and the Swiss Guard are all that is now left of the considerable domains and armies of the popes of the Middle Ages. The Papal states were annexed on the creation of the modern state of Italy in 1870.

> The church accepts the existence on earth, of nations and races as separate entities through God's providence. This is therefore not the work of human beings . . . Although God created all nations on earth from the same blood, He gave each one its *own national intuition and soul* which must be honoured by all and which may not be destroyed by the superior in the inferior.[3]

In medieval Europe, the Church was an integral part of the power structure of society, preaching to the people that the social order had divine sanction. This helped to keep them content with their miserable lot as virtual slaves to the landowners. In return, the Church was made a landowner and the bishops and archbishops became feudal lords with an interest in maintaining the status quo. The Pope himself was a ruler of a large territory. On the other side, the nobility retained close links with the Church. Until recent times, it was customary for at least one younger son of families of the nobility to enter the Church, frequently to rise to a high position within it. In this way the religious and secular authorities helped each other to maintain the social order. In early Islam, there was a strong egalitarian element. The Sunni ulema, however, soon developed the view that obedience to the established ruler was obligatory, even if that ruler were a tyrant. In India, of course, Hinduism was the chief legitimator of the caste system, thus entrenching a system under which millions of people became considered almost subhuman. Perhaps the most important of all

THE CASTE SYSTEM IN HINDUISM

The universe and its parallel, human society, were seen as organic wholes in which each *jat* (on the cosmic scene a form of life, on the social scene a caste) has a specific task (*dharma*) to perform. Only in the faithful dispassionate performance of this duty can an individual acquire merit and a higher station in the next life. Brahmanic cosmology provided the rational for heterogeneity, hierarchy, and specialization within a single body.

The social order that emerged out of this system of values and ideology was the caste system. In Brahmanic ideology this was seen as a single organic society in which the many different functions and occupations were served by different castes on the basis of their socioritual statuses. At the top were the priestly castes, followed by the rulers and warriors (*Kshatriyas*), the merchants and traders (*Vaishyas*), and, finally, the artisans and manual workers (*Shudras*). (Paul G. Hiebert, 'India: The Politicization of a Sacral Society', in Caldarola, *Religions and Societies: Asia and the Middle East*, pp. 291–2)

the injustices perpetrated through religion's role in legitimating the social order (in that it affects the largest number of people) has been the support it has given to the patriarchal nature of society and the consequent subjugation of women (see chapter 17).

Religion Used to Legitimate the Authority of a Particular Ruler

Almost every king or ruler in the history of the world has used religion to legitimate his or her authority at some stage. This is most easily observed at ceremonies of coronation and investiture. Whether the ruler is a European sovereign, the Emperor of Japan, or a tribal leader, a religious element is present in the ceremony of coronation or investiture. This affirms that the authority of the ruler has been given divine sanction. While not so important today in Europe, this was of great significance in the past. The disapproval of the Pope in the Middle Ages, for example, could threaten the throne of any sovereign of Western Europe. In return for their support, the religious professionals could expect the authority of the State to maintain their prestige and position.

Legitimation of the holder of power in a society has often involved identifying that person in some way with the ultimate source of power in the cosmos. In Europe, the doctrine of the Divine Right of Kings maintained that the king held his position on the authority of God. The Pope and the Church supported this position in return for the monarch's acknowledgement of their status and rights. In the Middle East, the Muslim caliph was the vicegerent of God on earth. The whole social structure depended on him as its pivot. In Iran, the Shah was the Shadow of God. In Japan, the Emperor was himself considered a descendant of the gods and was the chief priest of Shinto. The first king of the Pacific kingdom of Tonga was considered to be the result of the union of the sun god, Tangaloa, and a human female.

Religion Used to Legitimate War

Religion has frequently been used to rouse people to fight wars for the rulers. Every religion has established some form of holy war in its history. In Christianity, the Crusades against the infidel Muslims spanned several centuries. In Islam, jihad, holy war, became one of the tenets of the faith (see pp. 346–8). Religion has, however, often been used to stir up a war that was, in fact, being waged for economic or other reasons. More recently, Christian states fought each other in World War I; the soldiers of each side were assured by their religious leaders, acting in conjunction with the government, that God was on their side. Each side prayed to the same God for victory. In other parts of the world, many conflicts have occurred on a religious basis. Hindu–Muslim strife in India has a long history, of which the conflict between India and Pakistan is but a recent episode; the sufferings inflicted by each side upon the other were only very partially recorded in the documentary accounts of the partition of India.

Picture depicting a war scene from the *Bhagavata Purana*, a Hindu narrative. Balarama captures the demon king Jarasandha (in the centre of the picture) while his brother Krishna looks on from the left. Basohli, eighteenth century.

Religious Justifications for War and Killing

Hinduism

At the beginning of the Bhagavad Gita, *Arjuna is contemplating the forthcoming battle between the Pandavas and their cousins the Kauravas. Filled with sadness, he refuses to fight and tells his charioteer, Krishna, of his reason. Krishna replies:*

Great warrior, carry on thy fight. If any man thinks he slays, and if another thinks he is slain, neither knows the ways of truth. The Eternal in man cannot kill: the Eternal in man cannot die. He is never born, and he never dies. He is in Eternity: he is for evermore . . . When a man knows him as never-born, everlasting, never-changing, beyond all destruction, how can that man kill a man, or cause another to kill? . . .

Think thou also of thy duty and do not waver. There is no greater good for a warrior [*kshatriya*] than to fight in a righteous war. There is a war that opens the doors of heaven, Arjuna! Happy the warriors whose fate is to fight such war. But to forgo this fight for righteousness [Dharma] is to forgo thy duty [Dharma] and honour: is to fall into transgression . . . And to a man who is in honour, dishonour is more than death . . . Can there be for a warrior a more shameful fate?

In death thy glory in heaven, in victory thy glory on earth. (*Bhagavad Gita* 2:18–21, 31–4, 37)

Buddhism

The main scriptural justifications for killing may be briefly summarized. In the Mahayana *Mahaparinirvana Sutra* it is told how the Buddha in one of his former lives killed some Brahmin heretics. This was done to protect the Doctrine, and to save them themselves from the consequences of continued attacks on it. When the Doctrine is in danger the Five Precepts, including the prohibition on taking life, may be ignored . . .

A second justification was that it was good to kill one in order to save two. A curious story tells of a Buddhist traveller in a caravan of five hundred. Five hundred bandits intend to attack the caravan. A scout of the bandits warns the traveller. If the Buddhist warns his fellow-travellers, they will kill the scout and suffer in hell for taking the life. If he does not the bandits will kill the travellers; more lives will be lost, and more will suffer in hell. So he kills the scout himself. The bandits consequently do not attack. Only one life is lost, and only one man, the Buddhist, suffers in hell . . .

A third justification lies in the illusory nature of existence. There is no soul, no self, nothing to kill. (Ferguson, *War and Peace in the World's Religions*, pp. 55–6)

Christianity

[During World War I] The Bishop of London, Winnington-Ingram, said, 'Kill Germans – to kill them, not for the sake of killing, but to save the world, to kill the good as well as the

> bad, to kill the young men as well as the old, to kill those who have shewn kindness to our wounded as well as those fiends who crucified the Canadian Sergeant.' This, if it was anything, was the holy war again. The only trouble was that both sides were supposed to be Christian and Christians on each side were fighting their own holy war. (Ferguson, *War and Peace in the World's Religions*, p. 117)
>
> ISLAM
>
> Fight in the cause of God those who fight you but do not transgress the limits; for God loveth not transgressors. And slay them wherever you find them and drive them out from where they drove you out; for oppression is worse than killing; but do not fight them at the Sacred Mosque unless they first fight you there; but if they fight, you slay them. Such is the reward of unbelievers. But if they cease, God is the Forgiving, the Most Merciful. And fight them on until there is no more oppression and until justice and faith in God prevail. (*Quran* 2:190–3)

New Ideologies

Legitimation in modern societies is a much more complex affair than in traditional societies. Religion no longer holds its paramount place as the ultimate legitimator of the social order and the conceptual universe. Several other ideologies have contested the role of legitimator of the social order. In a democracy, the will of the people is considered the ultimate source of legitimacy. Unfortunately, the will of the people has proved to be capable of being manipulated so as to cause one group of people to assert their will over other groups. Marxism, for example, asserts the will of one particular class over other classes; nationalism, the will of a particular nation over others; racism, the will of one particular ethnic group. Religion's role of legitimator of the conceptual universe has also been contested, for example, by the psychology of Freud (although here the number of people involved is small).

The modern substitutes for religion have not proved so successful as legitimators of the social order and the symbolic universe of a people. The most important reason for this is probably that they are much more limited in scope than religion. Thus the social ideologies have little to say about the frightening marginal situations of human life, such as death. An ideology such as nationalism may succeed in giving meaning to the deaths of those who die while fighting for their country, yet this is only a small number compared to the large number who die deaths that are meaningless in the ideology of nationalism. Conversely, psychological theories may be good at explaining marginal situations that frighten people. They are unable, however, to legitimate the social order. No substitute for religion is, therefore, able to integrate all aspects of human life into one overarching social, conceptual and symbolic universe.

Religion and the State

The relationship between religion and the State has been multi-faceted and complex. The following are a few of the possible relationships.

THEOCRACY OR HIEROCRACY. In a theocracy, the religious authorities are also the political authorities – or at least the religious and political institutions act as a unitary body. Examples of this state of affairs are not very common but one may cite the first four caliphs of Islam, the Fatimid caliphate in Egypt, Calvin's Geneva, the Dalai Lamas' rule in Tibet from 1642 to 1959 and Ayatollah Khomeini's regime in Iran. Since God, in person, does not rule any state, a more accurate name for theocracy, rule by God, is hierocracy, rule by the religious leadership.

STATE RELIGION. A state religion is obviously closely tied in to the State and will, most of the time, support it. It does not, however, run the State (as in a theocracy). There may, therefore, be occasions when there is a conflict of interests between the secular authorities and the state religion. The history of Europe in the Middle Ages contains many episodes of friction between the Church and various European kings and rulers. A more recent example is the confrontation in the United Kingdom between Archbishop Runcie and the then Prime Minister, Margaret Thatcher, over such matters as his attitude to the Falklands War and the effects on the poor of her government's policies (see p. 415). In a number of Islamic states, such as Iran, Pakistan and Brunei, there has been an attempt to make the law of the country identical to the Holy Law of Islam, the Shari'a. This has certain difficulties, particularly in the economic field, as the prohibition on usury in Islamic law causes problems for banking and other financial transactions.

A THEOCRACY: KHOMEINI ON THE ISLAMIC GOVERNMENT

The Islamic Government is neither despotic nor absolutist, rather it is constitutional. Of course, it is not constitutional in the accepted usage of that word, which means that the laws are enacted according to the opinions of individuals and according to majority votes. It is constitutional in the sense that those who administer and govern are constrained by the constitution specified in the *Qur'an* and the Sunna of the Prophet. Thus this constitution is none other than the laws and regulations of Islam that must be obeyed and put into effect. This is why the Islamic Government is the application to the people of the Divine Law.

The difference between the Islamic Government and other constitutional governments, whether monarchial or republican, lies in this that it is the people's or the king's representatives who enact legislation in such regimes, whereas the power of legislation in Islam belongs to Almighty God alone. (Khomeini, *Hukumat-i Islami*, pp. 45–6; author's translation)

Poster from Revolutionary Iran depicting Khomeini's 'divine' status. 'Khomeini did not explicitly claim to be a prophet or a divine manifestation, but he came very close by allowing himself to be called Imam, which in Shi'ism is functionally the same as "prophet and messenger" with all the necessary distinctions pointed out. He allowed himself to be the object of love and devotion that many said was only properly the right of the Imam or the Prophet.' (Todd Lawson, personal communication with the author)

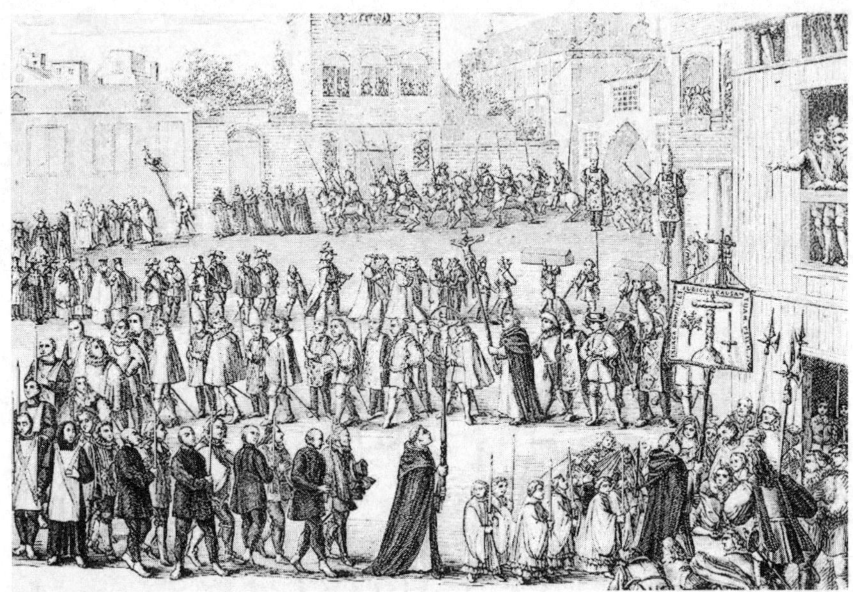

State action against rival religions: Following an Inquisition pronouncement that a person was guilty of heresy, a great procession (*auto-da-fé*, act of faith) would be held in which the religious and secular authorities combined to take the condemned person to the place of execution where he or she would usually be burned to death. There are estimated to have been between a quarter and half a million such public executions, mainly in Spain and Portugal (against crypto-Muslims and Jews) and in Latin America (against those following native religions) between the fifteenth and early nineteenth century.

The state religion obtains many benefits from its position. These may include financial support or action taken against rival religions. There are, however, disadvantages. A state religion may suffer a great deal of interference in its internal workings from the government. If the government is unpopular, the state religion may share in this unpopularity if it is closely identified with the State, as happened to Christianity in France at the time of the French Revolution. Similarly, there are indications of a reaction against Islam following the social and economic failures of the Islamic government in Iran.

Predominant Religion. In many countries of the world, there is one overwhelmingly predominant religion, which is not, however, the state religion. In this situation, the predominant religion can expect to have a considerable influence over the State. It may even have more influence than a state religion does (since the latter is to a certain extent controlled by the State). The Roman Catholic Church is in such a position in most of the countries of southern Europe and the whole of Latin America.

THE CLASH BETWEEN THATCHER AND RUNCIE

On 26 July 1982 there was a remembrance service in St Paul's Cathedral for those killed in the Falklands War a few months previously. In his sermon, Archbishop Runcie referred to the need to remember the bereaved relatives, not only of the British soldiers who had been killed, but also of the young Argentinian soldiers. The following day, the press were unanimous in reporting the extreme displeasure of Margaret Thatcher and her government, that what should have been a triumphant endorsement of a British victory had been turned into a session of deep soul-searching. The Sun *newspaper reported on the following day:*

MAGGIE FURY AT RUNCIE'S SERMON
The Prime Minister was last night 'spitting blood' over yesterday's Falklands service at St Paul's. Mrs Thatcher was said to be furious over the 'wet' sermon delivered by the Archbishop of Canterbury. And the controversial remembrance service led some Tory MPs to lash out bitterly at 'pacifists and cringing clergy'. They wanted the service to proclaim Britain's pride in a glorious victory. Instead the MPs saw it as an insult to those who fought and died . . . Right-wing MP Julian Amery said angrily: 'The Archbishop would be better giving his service in Buenos Aires than in St Paul's . . . Peace and reconciliation should be part of it – but not the whole story. There was no thanksgiving for the liberation of British subjects from the invaders. I thought it was a deliberate counter-attack against the mass of opinion of this country on the part of the pacifist, liberal wets.' . . .

After a strenuous behind-the-scenes struggle, Mrs Thatcher . . . was still not happy with the final form that the service took . . . Her husband Denis, when he had a chat and a drink with MPs on the House of Commons terrace after the service . . . was said to have told them: 'The boss was angry enough this morning. Now she is spitting blood.' (Carpenter, *Robert Runcie*, pp. 256–7)

A MULTI-RELIGIOUS SOCIETY. In a situation where there are several religious communities, each comprising a substantial proportion of the population, the possibility of conflict arises. In such a country, the government often finds itself trying to be neutral, acting as arbiter and peacekeeper between the different religious communities. The government itself may be divided along religious lines. An example of the latter is Lebanon, where the unofficial constitution divides the principal offices of State between the main religious communities (Maronite, Sunni, Shi'i and Druse). In India, the Muslim and Sikh minorities exert considerable influence and individual Muslims and Sikhs have held high office. Therefore India, although it has a great predominance of Hindus, acts in many ways as a multi-religious state. Northern Ireland may also be considered to be in this category; although both of the two main religious communities are Christian, the fact that they are in conflict makes the situation similar to that of a multi-religious society.

An Areligious Society. Many would say that Western Europe is no longer a Christian society but has lapsed into materialism and hedonism. While this is undoubtedly true if we compare the present with the past, one must be careful not to overemphasize this point. The fact that churches are empty does not necessarily mean that all the people who are not attending church are irreligious. A large number of new religious movements and cults have taken up some of the numbers who have deserted the mainstream churches. In the political realm, however, Western European governments have generally ceased to take religion into account when formulating policies. While individual politicians may be personally religious, they do not appear to find religion relevant to the political process.

An Anti-Religious State. Until the changes in the communist world that occurred between 1989 and 1990, most communist countries in Europe and Asia were anti-religious. Government-funded agencies were set up specifically to counter the influence of religion. Despite several decades of vigorous anti-religious campaigning, however, these states were unable to eliminate religion from their territories.

The Attitude of the State Towards Religion

Most religions have had a varying relationship with the power structures of their societies over the years. Christianity, for example, is often thought of as a religion in which there is a strict separation between Church and State.[4] In fact, however, there has been an identification of the State with the Church for most of Christian history from the time of the Emperor Constantine. The Byzantine Empire enforced the edicts of the Church and persecuted those whom the Church deemed to be heretics. The Emperor, in turn, had a considerable say in the running, and even the theology, of the Church. This Church–State identity continued in the Roman Catholic Church with the establishment of the Holy Roman Empire in 800 CE. The political authority of the Holy Roman Emperor was derived from the Church, and the Empire, in turn, supported the Church against heretics and unbelievers. These principles regulated affairs, even though individual emperors may have had their differences with the popes of their day. After the Reformation, the close links between the Church and State led to the involvement of the European states in the series of Protestant–Catholic conflicts that included the Thirty Years' War (1618–48).

The pietist tradition, which was strong in the United States of America, held that religion was an individual's affair and had nothing to do with the State. The emergence of the United States as a major world power in the nineteenth century made this principle of Church–State separation more significant in Christianity. This position has been accepted *de facto* throughout most of Europe (although the Roman Catholic Church has continued to try to have a political role). However, with the rise of such movements as Liberation Theology, which have a strong social component,

THE ANTI-RELIGIOUS STATE

THE SOVIET RUSSIAN VIEW OF ISLAM

The mosaic-like variety of modern Islamic intellectual life, demonstrating ever more convincingly the barrenness of pan-Islamism and similar doctrines, ultimately reflects the struggle to find the most effective means of achieving general progress that is now occurring in Muslim regions outside the USSR. In the USSR and other socialist countries, where the social foundations of religion have been undermined, Islam, like all other religions is becoming more and more a relic of the past.

The continual affirmation of the idea of man's eternal subordination to mythical divine powers, the orientation toward life in the next world and the contrasting pessimistic estimation of earthly life, and the absolute denial of man's autonomy and intrinsic worth – all make Islam, like any other religious system, incompatible with a genuinely scientific world view. (M. A. Batunskii in *The Great Soviet Encyclopedia*, vol. 10, p. 451)

we may be seeing the beginnings of a move back towards Church involvement in politics. Even in American Christianity, this idea of Church–State separation has, in recent years, been eroded by the emergence of fundamentalists into politics.

The Attitude of Religion Towards the State

A number of different relationships between religious leaders and the State are possible, especially in countries where there is a state religion or a predominant religion.

RELIGIOUS SUPPORT FOR THE SECULAR AUTHORITIES. This is perhaps the commonest role for religion to take in society. Religion is the chief legitimator of the social order and therefore religious leaders are often incorporated into the state apparatus. This confers upon the latter greater legitimacy and authority. The State, in turn, gives the religious authorities due deference and honour. Cathedrals, mosques and temples are built by the State to add to the aura of sanctity and legitimacy accruing to both the secular and religious authorities.

Although religious leaders are often content with this type of relationship, it has its dangers. A religion that identifies itself closely with the interests of the State could find itself defending a tyrannical or unjust state (as happened for example in Nazi Germany and Fascist Italy, for example); it stands in danger of becoming part of a power structure that oppresses the people (as occurred in the feudal societies of medieval Europe); it may find itself compromised and corrupted by the lure of temporal power and worldly wealth (as occurred in the Catholic Church

HONOURING OF RELIGION BY THE STATE: Built between 1550 and 1557 for Sultan Sulayman the Magnificent (1494–1566) by Sinan, the greatest of the Ottoman architects, the Suleymaniye Mosque, Istanbul, marked a new stage in the evolution of Islamic architecture. Its innovative lighting and tall, widely-spaced columns allow an immense, unbroken interior space, giving the interior an austere grandeur. The mosque is at the centre of a complex of charitable and educational institutions, including a hospital, religious colleges and a soup kitchen. The buildings in the foreground are the library and a religious college.

just before the Reformation). As indicated above (p. 414), there is a possibility that when people revolt against the oppression and corruption of the secular authorities, their revolt will take on an anti-religious dimension as well. An example of this is the French Revolution, which was primarily a revolt against an authoritarian and tyrannical political system but which ended up also opposing the religion that had supported that state.

RELIGIOUS OPPOSITION TO THE SECULAR AUTHORITIES. Although in general terms it is not very common for religious authorities to oppose the State, those occasions in which it does occur are notable in history. In pre-modern societies, general social unrest is often accompanied by an upsurge in religious movements, often of the millenarian type (see chapter 10). Marxist writers have argued that, in such societies, religious dissent is really a pre-political expression of class protest against adverse social conditions, poor government or the effects of natural disasters.

Religious expression is often the only form of freedom of expression allowed in an authoritarian state. In such circumstances, the desire for political freedom has often been expressed in religious terms. It was for this reason that the churches acted as a focus for opposition to some East

European communist states. Part of the reason for the religious turn taken by the Iranian Revolution of 1979 was the Shah's rigorous suppression of all political discourse. The black churches in the American South are another example of a religious alternative to suppressed political activity.

It should be noted, however, that each of the more recent world religions was seen by the established religion and the secular authorities of its time as an opposition movement when it first arose. It was seeking to overthrow the established order and so had to be confronted (see pp. 312, 323).

RELIGIOUS ALOOFNESS FROM POLITICAL INVOLVEMENT. Religious leaders have often remained aloof from political involvement, regarding this world as hopelessly corrupt and of no relevance to the business of achieving salvation. Many Hindu and Buddhist religious leaders take this attitude because of the concept of *maya* (the idea that this world is illusory and distracts from the Real). Ascetics and monastic orders are usually examples of this relationship. The Baha'i Faith also stresses its non-involvement in partisan politics. This is not, however, because it is unconcerned with social matters. Rather it considers that it is in the process of building up an alternative social order and the present political system is divisive, inadequate and irredeemable.

It is possible for more than one of these attitudes to co-exist in a religious society. Iran saw all three varieties of relationship between the state and the religious leadership in the years immediately before the 1979 Revolution. The classical political attitude of the leading religious leaders of Shi'ism, the Ayatollahs, has been one of political aloofness. The classical political theory of Shi'ism states that the true political and religious leader is the Twelfth Imam, a messianic figure who is said to have gone into hiding in 874 CE, and whose return all Shi'is are awaiting. Since he is believed to be alive and in hiding, all political leadership is a usurpation of his authority; the highest Shi'i religious leaders therefore held themselves aloof from political involvement. There had always, however, been a few religious leaders who dissented from this position. Some argued that order was necessary in society for the Holy Law to be implemented and that it was therefore a religious duty to support the government. Others, in the years leading up to the Iranian Revolution of 1979, argued that the rule of the Pahlavi monarchs was hopelessly corrupt, was failing to uphold Islam and should be overthrown. Ayatollah Khomeini is the best known of this latter category.[5] He, of course, eventually succeeded in overthrowing the Shah and establishing a theocracy.

RELIGION AND POLITICS

Religion has played many varied political roles in the history of the world. It has acted as the primary cause of division and hatred in society, and as

Why the Muslims do not stand and rise against the world devouring powers ?
Imam Khomeini

RELIGIOUS OPPOSITION: Poster of Khomeini and a political slogan derived from one of Khomeini's speeches. Such posters epitomized the spirit of the Islamic Revolution, which was relentlessly opposed to the Western powers, especially their involvement in the Islamic world.

an agent of reconciliation and peace. Religious leaders and institutions have acted both to support the established authorities and to oppose them; they have acted with the forces of reform and change and with the forces of conservatism and reaction.

If one takes a long-term view, one can say that religion has not been very successful in coming to terms with power. There have been a few periods when exceptional individuals have been able to maintain a balance between religion and power, resulting in a brief golden age. The rule of Emperor Ashoka in India, Byzantium between the fourth and sixth centuries CE, and the period of the first four caliphs of Islam are periods of this (although even these periods have been criticized by historians). Overall, however, the relationship between religion and power has oscillated between extremes. At one extreme, religion becomes overbearing and tyrannical, thus stifling creativity and progress; at the other extreme, religion is ignored and the society loses its morality and cohesiveness.

Political rulers have also played a major part in advancing the interests of their own religion. In India, for example, some individual rulers of the Mauryan, Gupta and Mughal dynasties have played an important role in the advancement of their own personal religion (Buddhist, Hindu and Muslim respectively). The fortunes of Hinduism declined in the face of the advance of Buddhism for some 1000 years but then Hinduism reasserted itself and Buddhism was almost eliminated from India (see timeline on p. 422).

Religion has clearly been a major factor in shaping the politics of the world since World War II. The Hindu–Muslim riots that occurred during the partition of India, the Palestine–Israel conflict, the Lebanese conflict, the problems in Northern Ireland, Cyprus and in the Balkans have all involved religion as an important or predominant divisive factor. Religion has, however, also played a role in peace and reconciliation.[6] The Catholic

Church has played such a role in places such as Nicaragua and the Philippines, and the Protestant churches played an important part in overcoming apartheid in South Africa. Individual religious leaders such as the Dalai Lama have become noted international advocates of peace.

THE OPPOSITION TO APARTHEID: Archbishop Trevor Huddleston (1913–98), an Anglican clergyman and one of the foremost opponents of apartheid, receiving an award in recognition of his achievements from the Baha'i community of Britain, 1988

During the time that the Cold War dominated international politics, religion was a minor factor that was often overlooked in the political evaluations made by statesmen and political analysts. Most leaders and intellectuals in the West assumed that religion in other parts of the world would follow the same course that it had in the West; it would gradually fade in importance and become an irrelevance. Marx considered religion to be the 'opium' of the oppressed masses:

> The basis of irreligious criticism is: *Man makes religion*, religion does not make man . . .
>
> Religious misery is in one way the expression of real misery, and in another a protest against real misery. Religion is the sigh of the afflicted creature, the soul of a heartless world, as it is also the spirit of spiritless conditions. It is the opium of the people.
>
> The abolition of religion as the *illusory* happiness of the people is the demand for their *real* happiness. The demand to abandon the illusions about their condition is the *demand to give up a condition that requires illusions*. Hence criticism of religion is in embryo a *criticism of this vale of tears* whose halo is religion.[7]

Paralleling Marx's assessment, it was thought that, as people became more educated and affluent, they would have less need for and less interest in religion. Symptomatic of the West's blindness towards the importance of religion in other parts of the world was the way in which the religious factions in Lebanon who had been fighting each other for centuries were labelled 'left-wing' and 'right-wing' forces by the press and statesmen in the West for the first decade of the Lebanese civil war of 1975–92.

It was perhaps the Islamic Revolution in Iran in 1978–9 and the West's subsequent dealings with the Islamic Republic there that signalled to many the error that had been committed in dismissing religion prematurely. Time and again, mistakes were made by America and the other Western powers in their dealings with Iranian Islamic movements, precisely because the religious factor was ignored or underestimated. Events in Iran and the Middle East were consistently interpreted in political and economic terms. President Carter mistook the Islamic opposition for a movement arising out

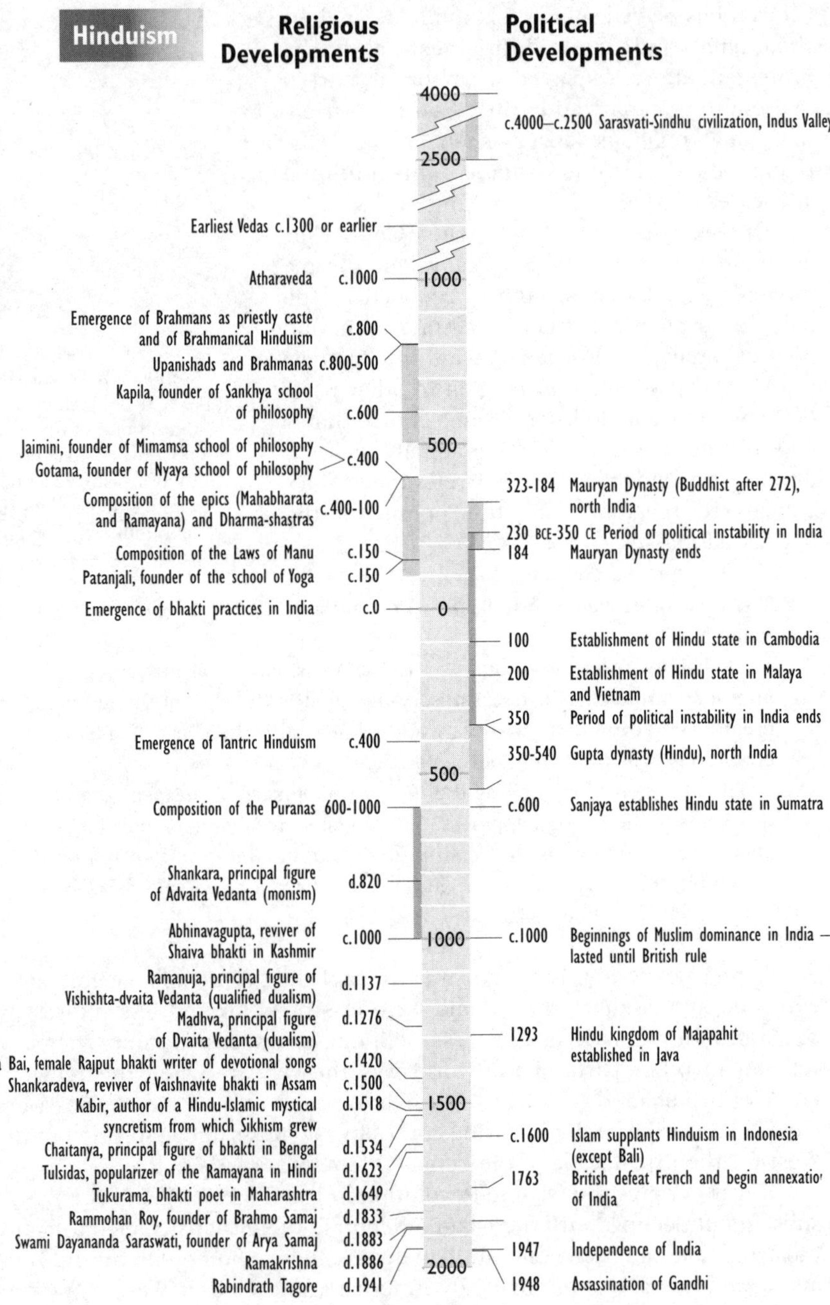
Hinduism
Religious Developments
Political Developments
4000
c.4000–c.2500 Sarasvati-Sindhu civilization, Indus Valley
2500
Earliest Vedas c.1300 or earlier
Atharaveda c.1000
1000
Emergence of Brahmans as priestly caste and of Brahmanical Hinduism c.800
Upanishads and Brahmanas c.800-500
Kapila, founder of Sankhya school of philosophy c.600
Jaimini, founder of Mimamsa school of philosophy
Gotama, founder of Nyaya school of philosophy c.400
500
323-184 Mauryan Dynasty (Buddhist after 272), north India
Composition of the epics (Mahabharata and Ramayana) and Dharma-shastras c.400-100
230 BCE-350 CE Period of political instability in India
Composition of the Laws of Manu c.150
184 Mauryan Dynasty ends
Patanjali, founder of the school of Yoga c.150
Emergence of bhakti practices in India c.0
0
100 Establishment of Hindu state in Cambodia
200 Establishment of Hindu state in Malaya and Vietnam
350 Period of political instability in India ends
Emergence of Tantric Hinduism c.400
350-540 Gupta dynasty (Hindu), north India
500
Composition of the Puranas 600-1000
c.600 Sanjaya establishes Hindu state in Sumatra
Shankara, principal figure of Advaita Vedanta (monism) d.820
Abhinavagupta, reviver of Shaiva bhakti in Kashmir c.1000
1000
c.1000 Beginnings of Muslim dominance in India – lasted until British rule
Ramanuja, principal figure of Vishishta-dvaita Vedanta (qualified dualism) d.1137
Madhva, principal figure of Dvaita Vedanta (dualism) d.1276
1293 Hindu kingdom of Majapahit established in Java
Mira Bai, female Rajput bhakti writer of devotional songs c.1420
Shankaradeva, reviver of Vaishnavite bhakti in Assam c.1500
Kabir, author of a Hindu-Islamic mystical syncretism from which Sikhism grew d.1518
1500
c.1600 Islam supplants Hinduism in Indonesia (except Bali)
Chaitanya, principal figure of bhakti in Bengal d.1534
Tulsidas, popularizer of the Ramayana in Hindi d.1623
1763 British defeat French and begin annexatio
of India
Tukurama, bhakti poet in Maharashtra d.1649
Rammohan Roy, founder of Brahmo Samaj d.1833
Swami Dayananda Saraswati, founder of Arya Samaj d.1883
1947 Independence of India
Ramakrishna d.1886
2000
1948 Assassination of Gandhi
Rabindrath Tagore d.1941

Islam

CE 500 – 1000 – 1500 – 2000

Religious Developments

Birth of Muhammad	570
Muhammad's first revelations	610
Muhammad's flight to Medina	622
Muhammad	d.632
Abu Bakr, 1st Caliph	d.634
Umar, 2nd Caliph	d.644
Uthman, 3rd Caliph	d.656
'Ali, 4th Caliph and 1st Shi'i Imam	d.661
Martyrdom of Husayn, 3rd Shi'i Imam	680
Occultation of 12th Shi'i Imam	874
Spread of Islam into West Africa	c.1000
Ibn Sina (Avicenna), philosopher	d.1037
Islam begins to spread in India	c.1050
al-Ghazali, Sunni scholar	d.1111
Ibn al-'Arabi, mystical philosopher	d.1240
Islam spreads to Indonesia and Malaya	c.1250
Jalal al-Din Rumi, mystical poet	d.1273
Mulla Sadra, Shi'i philosopher	d.1640
Ibn 'Abd al-Wahhab, founder of Wahhabi movement	d.1792
Rising of the Sudanese Mahdi (d. 1885)	1881
Sayyid Jamal al-Din 'Afghani', Islamic reformer	d.1897
Muhammad 'Abduh, Islamic reformer	d.1905
Caliphate abolished	1924
Founding of World Muslim League	1962
Sayyid Abu al-A'la Mawdudi, Indian Islamic revivalist idealogue	d.1979

Political Developments

632	War of Apostasy in Arabia breaks out
635	Defeat of Persian Empire at Qadisiyyah
639	Conquest of Egypt
661	Accession of Umayyad caliphs
711	Conquest of Spain, Sind and Transoxania
732	Conquest of Europe halted by Battle of Tours
750	Overthrow of Umayyads, accession of Abbasid caliphs
910	Emergence of Fatimids in North Africa
912-61	Reign of 'Abd al-Rahman III, acme of Islamic civilization in Spain
945	Shi'i Buyid dynasty captures Baghdad, effective end of Abbasid power
c.950-c.1050	The Shi'i century during which most Islamic lands were under Shi'i control
1086	Kanem-Bornu Empire, around Lake Chad, adopts Islam
1099	Crusaders capture Jerusalem
1187	Saladin recaptures Jerusalem
1258	Mongols sack Baghdad; end of Abbasid caliphate
1260	Mongols defeated at 'Ayn Jalut, Syria
1326	Beginnings of Ottoman Empire in Anatolia
1453	Ottoman conquest of Constantinople
1492	Muslim rulers expelled from Spain
1501	Shi'i state established in Iran by Safavids
1526	Muslim Mughal Empire established, India
c.1600	Islam predominates in Indonesia
1683	Ottomans besiege Vienna
1789	Napoleon occupies Egypt
1830	French occupy Algeria
1858	British depose last Mughal ruler, India
1881	British occupy Egypt; French occupy Tunisia
1918	Defeat of Ottoman Empire
1920	Creation of Iraq, Syria, Lebanon, Jordan and Palestine from former Ottoman provinces
1947	Creation of Pakistan; East Pakistan became Bangladesh in 1972
1971	Founding of Organization of Islamic Conference (OIC)
1979	Islamic Revolution in Iran; Ayatollah Khomeini comes to power

of political and economic dissatisfaction and advised the Shah on measures to democratize his government and give some relief to the poor. Successive Western governments have assumed that the leadership of the Islamic Republic would be amenable to compromise and negotiation if offered economic inducements and political acceptance. They have been at a loss to understand why a country that was at war with Iraq in 1980 was holding on to American Embassy hostages and thus antagonizing the rest of the world; why a country whose economic situation was declining continued an eight-year war with Iraq long after there was any territorial or strategic point to it; and why a country that is in desperate need of trade to bolster its failing economy refused for a long time to give any ground on the issue of the fatwa against Salman Rushdie.

Politicians who are used to the give-and-take of normal political bargaining cannot understand people who feel that they have a religious principle that is not open to negotiation. Most uncomfortable of all for Western politicians is the fact that it is not just the temporary distortions produced by the process of westernization that provokes religious opposition in Iran and elsewhere throughout the Third World, it is westernization itself. In many societies, people are rebelling at the swamping of their culture and religion by the alien values and materialistic assumptions of Western culture. Quite apart from the sometimes violent antipathy towards the West in the Islamic world, there have been protests against Western cultural imports in India and there has been a general movement to reject Western culture among certain sections of the populations of China, Japan, and the native peoples in the Americas. This is usually called a cultural rejection, but since religion is the basis of culture in most societies outside the West, it is in reality also a religious rejection. Such popular sentiment can, of course, then be manipulated politically.

With regard to the major political division of the last half of the twentieth century, although some religious leaders and religious institutions supported either the free-market capitalism of the West or communism, there has also been a large body of opinion that has regarded neither of these systems as being the optimum. The World Council of Churches has criticized both political systems:

> The Church should make clear that there are conflicts between Christianity and capitalism. The Christian Churches should reject the ideologies of both communism and laissez-faire capitalism and should seek to draw men away from the false assumption that these extremes are the only alternatives. Each has made promises it could not redeem.[8]

The Universal House of Justice, the highest authority in the Baha'i Faith, has similarly stated:

> The time has come when those who preach the dogmas of materialism, whether of the east or the west, whether of capitalism or socialism, must

> give account of the moral stewardship they have presumed to exercise. Where is the 'new world' promised by these ideologies? Where is the international peace to whose ideals they proclaim their devotion? Where are the breakthroughs into new realms of cultural achievement produced by the aggrandizement of this race, of that nation or of a particular class? Why is the vast majority of the world's peoples sinking ever deeper into hunger and wretchedness when wealth on a scale undreamed of by the Pharaohs, the Caesars, or even the imperialist powers of the nineteenth century is at the disposal of the present arbiters of human affairs?[9]

The Islamic Republic of Iran, too, has determinedly pursued a 'neither East nor West' policy, regarding America as 'the Great Satan' and condemning Russia (prior to the fall of communism) as an atheistic State.

Civil Religion

One interesting way in which religion and politics interact is in the formation of civil religion. The term 'civil religion' goes back to the writings of Jean-Jacques Rousseau.[10] Recognizing that social cohesion required a religious underpinning, he advocated the formulation of a civil religion as a replacement for Christianity. As a concept, however, it has been best analysed with regard to the United States.[11] Although Christianity is the predominant religion in the United States, a formal separation of religion and state is laid down in the Constitution. However, in that same Constitution, God is referred to several times; indeed, the whole tone of public life in the United States is steeped in religious imagery and parallels. The War of Independence is the Old Testament flight from the Egypt of European decadence to the new Holy Land; the Civil War is the New Testament redemption by blood and sacrifice, the rebirth of the nation. The national flag, the national anthem, and the recital of the pledge of allegiance are the civil religion's parallels to the cross, the religious hymn, and the recital of the creed or the Lord's Prayer. The eschatology of this civil religion sees God guiding the nation providentially to greater social progress. America is the new Holy Land, the New Jerusalem, and the American people the new Israel, anointed by God, with a destiny to lead the rest of the world to a new social salvation. Democracy, individual rights and equal opportunities for each person to prosper (often summarized as 'the American Way') are the key doctrines of the civil theology, which is essentially a mythology – it creates a universe of meaning within which the social order is legitimated and the individual finds meaning in life. The important difference between the United States and countries that have a state religion is that the religiosity of American public life is non-specific; that is, it does not relate to any particular sect or religion. Thus while God is frequently invoked, Christ is rarely mentioned and no allusion is ever made to any specific church.

A strong civil religion has, however, existed in several other modern states where the ties with religion have not been so strong. In Nazi Germany, the civil theology was based upon a nationalist and racist mythology. Marxism is a civil religion with a civil theology that also sees itself as leading the world towards a social salvation. In this case, the salvation follows an apocalyptic revolution. The Soviet State in Russia had many of the trappings of a civil religion. Confucianism in pre-communist China also acted as a civil religion. One might say that the concept of a civil religion flows directly from the ideas of Durkheim (see pp. 53–5). He maintained that all social groupings have some form of religious underpinning in order to maintain the cohesion of the group. If that underpinning is not a religion, then some form of civil religion must act as a substitute.[12] Just as for most of human history, people were not conscious of having a religion because it was part of their taken-for-granted conceptual universe (see pp. 475–6), so most Americans are not conscious today of living within the conceptual universe of a civil religion. It has been suggested, however, that the current rise of cults in countries such as the United States is partially caused by the rupturing of the conceptual universe created by the civil religion, thus causing people to become aware of the assumptions of that universe and to start questioning it.[13]

Power and the Religious Professional

Every religion has an internal power structure. This is inevitable if there is going to be any form of organization to the religion, and organization is needed if the religion is going to grow to anything beyond a small local grouping.

In some religious groups, all authority and power is centred on one central charismatic leader. This tends to be the pattern of new religions in particular. New religious movements usually arise through the teaching of a charismatic leader and this figure is also the centre of power and authority for the movement. With the passage of time, however, and particularly with the death of the founder, some degree of organization becomes expedient (see also chapter 12).

The commonest pattern of religious organization involves some form of priestly leadership and hierarchy. The apex of the hierarchy is regarded as the leader of that religious group. If the religious group is large enough, the leader becomes a figure of national importance. This applies in most non-Western countries which have a predominant religion, most notably in Iran, where the highest religious leader has a formal place in the power structure; also in Thailand, where the leading Buddhist abbot is a state dignitary. It could even be said to apply to the United Kingdom, where bishops and archbishops sit in the House of Lords.

With large religious groupings, special educational facilities train people for the priesthood. Not every religion has a priesthood but even

a

b

POWER AND THE RELIGIOUS PROFESSIONAL: Religion confers great authority and power upon religious professionals and in most traditional societies lay people defer greatly to them. a) A Muslim cleric giving the Friday sermon at a mosque in Nicosia, Cyprus. b) A Thai Buddhist priest giving a sermon in the Phra Sri Rattana Satsadaram (Wat Phra Kaeo) in the Grand Palace enclosure in Bangkok, Thailand.

those that do not, have some form of power structure. Islam, for example, has no priesthood, but the ulema, as a learned class, form a power structure in the legalistic religion which represents mainstream orthodoxy. The Sufi shaykhs head an alternative power structure as heads of mystical orders. Not surprisingly there is often friction between these two.

The Baha'i Faith, too, has no priesthood. The religion is organized on the basis of councils elected at the local, national and international level. Power and authority are vested in the councils themselves and not in the individuals voted onto these bodies. Decisions are made based on consultation and then consensus or majority vote on these councils.

Hindu religious leadership may take various forms. The Brahmins are the priestly caste and have an institutional hereditary leadership. There are also many gurus exercising a more individual charismatic style of leadership. In Buddhist countries, religious organization takes the form of monks living in monasteries. The head monks or abbots of the most prestigious monasteries are usually considered the leading religious figures in the country.

The power structure within each religion is the agent for channelling the considerable power of religion in society. Since the central religious experience is very personal and private,[14] if one were being cynical, one could say that it gives no one any opportunity to have power over others, or to accumulate wealth, or to achieve status. And yet clearly religion is a very powerful force for motivating human beings. Therefore, it is not surprising that many have sought to channel the power of religion towards more immediate worldly goals. Only by producing communal, social expressions of the central religious experience can these worldly aims be achieved. Thus the paths of salvation described in chapter 5 (monasticism, gnosticism, ritualism and so on) can, in sociological terms, be seen as mechanisms to channel and utilize the power of religion. Unfortunately for the world of religion, much of this use of the paths of salvation has been for the most worldly of reasons.

1. To achieve status. Since the central experience of religion is so important to so many, the religious professional, who is closely associated in people's minds with that experience, usually has a high status in society. This is true at the level of a village where the village priest, mullah or shaman is one of the notables of the area and also at the highest levels of society, where the head of the religious hierarchy is a dignitary of state.

2. To achieve power. Many of the paths to salvation described in chapter 5 require some type of religious professional, whether to perform the ritual, to interpret the Holy Law or to pass on esoteric knowledge. This person can then use his (for it is usually a man) position as a basis for power. This power can become very considerable. The pope in the Middle Ages wielded great power based on his position at the head of the Roman Catholic Church. He was the temporal ruler over a large part of Italy and also had considerable influence and power throughout the rest

The Leaders of Religion Condemned by the Founders of Religion

Jesus

Then said Jesus to the crowds, and to his disciples, 'The scribes and the Pharisees sit on Moses' seat; so practise and observe whatever they tell you, but not what they do; for they preach, but do not practise. They bind heavy burdens, hard to bear, and lay them on men's shoulders; but they themselves will not move them with their finger. They do all their deeds to be seen by men; for they make their phylacteries broad and their fringes long, and they love the place of honour at feasts and the best seats in the synagogues, and salutations in the market places, and being called rabbi by men . . .

'But woe to you, scribes and Pharisees, hypocrites! Because you shut the kingdom of heaven against men; for you neither enter yourselves, nor allow those who would enter to go in.

'Woe to you, scribes and Pharisees, hypocrites! for you tithe mint and dill and cummin, and have neglected the weightier matters of the law, justice and mercy and faith . . .

'Woe to you, scribes and Pharisees, hypocrites! for you clean the outside of the cup and of the plate, but inside they are full of extortion and rapacity . . .' (*Matthew* 23:1–7, 13, 23, 25)

Muhammad

They have taken their [Jewish] doctors of law and their [Christian] monks and even the Messiah son of Mary as lords beside God, when they were bidden to worship the one God . . . Fain would they put out God's light with their mouths, but God would not allow but that His light be perfected, however much they who do not believe may detest this . . . O ye who believe! There are many of the [Jewish] doctors of law and the [Christian] monks who by falsehood devour the wealth of the people and debar men from the path of God. And they who hoard up gold and silver and spend it not in the path of God, unto them give tidings of a severe penalty. (*Qur'an* 9:31–2, 34)

Baha'u'llah

Leaders of religion, in every age, have hindered their people from attaining the shores of eternal salvation, inasmuch as they held the reins of authority in their mighty grasp. Some for the lust of leadership, others through want of knowledge and understanding, have been the cause of the deprivation of the people. By their sanction and authority, every Prophet of God hath drunk from the chalice of sacrifice, and winged His flight unto the heights of glory. What unspeakable cruelties they that have occupied the seats of authority and learning have inflicted upon the true Monarchs of the world, those Gems of divine virtue! Content with a transitory dominion, they have deprived themselves of an everlasting sovereignty. Thus, their eyes beheld not the light of the countenance of the Well-Beloved, nor did their ears hearken unto the sweet melodies of the Bird of Desire . . .

Among these 'veils of glory' are the divines and doctors living in the days of the Manifestation of God, who, because of their want of discernment and their love and eagerness for leadership, have failed to submit to the Cause of God, nay, have even refused to incline their ears unto the divine Melody . . . And the people also, utterly ignoring God and taking them for their masters, have placed themselves unreservedly under the authority of these pompous and hypocritical leaders. (Baha'u'llah, *Kitab-i-Iqan*, pp. 15–16, 164)

THE BUDDHA

Foremost in virtue were the men of old.
Those brahmins who remembered ancient rules.
In them well guarded were the doors of sense.
They had achieved the mastery of wrath.
In meditation and the Norm [Dhamma] they took delight,
Those brahmins who remembered ancient rules.
But these backsliders with their 'Let us recite',
Drunk with the pride of birth, walk wrongfully.
O'ercome by wrath, exceeding violent . . .

Wearing rough hides, and matted hair and filth,
Chantings and empty rites and penances,
Hypocrisy and cheating and the rod,
Washings, ablutions, rinsings of the mouth, –
These are the caste-marks of the brahmin folk,
Things done and practised for some trifling gain.

(*Samyutta Nikaya* 4:117, in *Book of Kindred Sayings*, p. 74; see P. Masefield, *Divine Revelation*, p. 154)

of Europe. In the East, the Dalai Lama ruled Tibet as temporal and spiritual sovereign until 1959, based on his religious claim to be the reincarnation of the *bodhisattva* Avalokiteshvara. In the Islamic world, the Aga Khan holds spiritual authority over several million Isma'ilis by virtue of his claim to a spiritual station through descent; more recently, we have seen Ayatollah Khomeini come to power in Iran on the basis of his religious leadership. On a lesser level, other religious paths such as gnosticism, ritualism, or legalism give individual religious professionals power over smaller groups of people, ranging from small congregations to followings of thousands.

3. TO AMASS WEALTH. Religious professionals of all types can expect that in return for their function of performing ritual, interpreting the Holy Law or intimating esoteric knowledge, they will receive some remuneration; the greater their perceived sanctity, the greater the expected effectiveness of their religious ministrations, and therefore the greater the remuneration. Besides this, the higher a person is in the religious hierarchy, the more opportunity that person has for partaking in the riches accumulated by religious institutions over the centuries. In many

parts of the world, religious institutions have acquired extensive endowments, which are administered by religious professionals.

This critique of the religious professional is not just an outsider's view. It reflects some of the statements made by the founders of the world's religions themselves. The Buddha, Christ, Muhammad and Baha'u'llah all criticized the religious leaders of their day for their seeking after power and wealth and their subsequent corruption, their obstruction of the new religious truth that the founder was trying to bring because of their desire to hold on to their power, and their ignorance of the spiritual as distinct from the outward meaning of their own scriptures (see also pp. 429–30). This is not, of course, intended to imply that all religious professionals enter their field in order to achieve power or amass wealth. A large proportion of them are undoubtedly very genuine in their vocation, but one can also point to an uncomfortably large number who, having perhaps at first come into their calling from genuine motives, have eventually used their position for these worldly purposes.

Further Reading

On legitimation and the symbolic universe, see Berger and Luckmann, *The Social Construction of Reality*; B. L. Smith, *Religion and Legitimation of Power in South Asia*. On religion and power, see Merkl and Smart, *Religion and Politics in the Modern World*. On civil religion, see Bellah, *Beyond Belief* (pp. 168–86) and 'Civil Religion in America'; Henry, *The Intoxication of Power*. On the role of religion in reconciliation and peace, see Johnston and Sampson, *Religion, the Missing Dimension of Statecraft*.

17

Religion and Gender

THE QUESTION OF RELIGION AND GENDER has come very much to the fore in recent years. In theory this topic includes both masculine and feminine perspectives on religion. In practice, however, since most studies of religion have used the masculine perspective as their norm, the study of this issue has boiled down to an examination of the feminine perspective. It would perhaps be useful to start with a few definitions. While 'sex' refers to the biological difference between male and female, 'gender' refers to the socially constructed roles and culturally created images of the feminine and masculine. This chapter looks at the features of the patriarchal society in which we live and the ways in which this oppresses and disadvantages women. We shall also examine the topics of the female archetype, religion and sexuality, the feminist study of religion, and various feminist attempts to re-create religion.

Feminist writers have focused attention on two particular ways in which religion has been used: to buttress patriarchal society in its suppression and control of women and to support the androcentric (man-centred) worldview that controls the thought structures and language of most societies in ways that undervalue and exclude the contribution of women. Much of what has been published on this subject in recent years relates to Christianity. Nevertheless, most of the comments that follow apply equally to the other world religions.

The History and Characteristics of Patriarchy

Although what follows in the next few paragraphs is based on empirical evidence, the interpretation of that evidence by feminist writers is not uncontested. As with most other areas of the study of religion, therefore, it is difficult to be certain of the factual base of the feminist view of religion. Consequently, although we cannot be sure that the following are the historical facts concerning the evolution of our patriarchal societies, they are certainly the mythology upon which feminist religion has been built.

Some archaeologists consider that the evidence suggests that societies in prehistory and early antiquity gave a greater predominance to female deities than to male ones. The agricultural-based civilizations of the Middle

East, for example, saw the sprouting of the crop from the soil as analogous to the female giving birth. Since the former process underpinned the whole of society, the latter became the symbol of this in creation myths centred on female deities. It was the influx of nomadic herding tribes, peoples not dependent on agriculture, such as the Indo-Europeans in Europe and the Israelites in the Middle East, that brought this stage to an end. Male warrior deities replaced the female agricultural ones. This change occurred at varying times in different parts of the world. In central Europe, there is a great deal of archaeological evidence that female deities were predominant in prehistoric times and the change appears to have occurred during the fourth millennium BCE. In Greece, the older female earth-mother goddess, Gaia or Hera, was displaced in importance by the male god Zeus. There is also biblical evidence that the worship of the female Canaanite goddess Ashtaroth (equivalent to the Babylonian fertility goddess Istarte and the Phoenician goddess Astarte) was widespread throughout the Middle East, even among the Jews.[1]

This is a depiction of the Middle Eastern fertility goddess known under various names – Istarte, Astarte, Ashtaroth, Ashteroth, and Ishtar – from Babylonia and Assyria to Canaan and Phoenecia and even as far as Arabia and Ethiopia.

From the many examples of this pattern of change from female to male deities, Joseph Campbell has suggested four stages in the evolution of the creation myth in Europe and the Middle East:

1. The world born of a goddess alone;
2. The world born of a goddess fecundated by a male consort;
3. The world fashioned from the body of a goddess by a male warrior god;
4. The world created by the unaided power of a male god.[2]

JUDAISM, A MATRILINEAL RELIGIOUS COMMUNITY: The Sabbath candles are lit and a prayer is being said by a Jew from Bokhara in Central Asia.

In parallel to this more important place for goddesses in prehistory, there is also evidence that in many, if not most, societies of that time, women held a much more important place. It does not appear that women were ever dominant in most societies in the way that men now are; in other words, true matriarchal societies probably did not exist. It is argued, however, that most prehistoric societies were matrifocal (focused on the mother or women

From Matrifocal to Patriarchal Society

Evidence for the shift from a woman-centred to a man-centred social structure has been accumulated from archaeology, mythology and anthropology. The following passage from the Hindu scripture, the Mahabharata, *provides some evidence that at the time that this book was compiled (c. fifth century* BCE*), this change in the social order was in the not very distant past. In this passage, King Pandu speakes to his bride, Kunti*:

But I shall now tell thee about the practices of old indicated by illustrious Rishis [sages] fully acquainted with every rule of morality. O thou of handsome face and sweet smiles, women formerly were not immured within houses and dependent on husbands and other relatives. They used to go about freely, enjoying as best liked them . . . they did not then adhere to their husbands faithfully, and yet, O handsome one, they were not regarded sinful, for that was the sanctioned usage of the times. That very usage is followed to this day by birds and beasts without exhibition of jealousy. That practice, sanctioned by precedent, is applauded by great Rishis. And . . . the practice is yet regarded with respect amongst the northern Kurus. Indeed, this usage so lenient to women hath the sanction of antiquity. The present practice, however . . . hath been established but lately.

It hath been heard by us that there was a great Rishi of name Uddalaka . . . The Rishi's son Shetaketu, however, disapproved of the [ancient] usage and established in the world the present usage as regards men and women. It hath been heard by us . . . that the existing practice dates from that period among human beings but not among beings of other classes. Accordingly, since the establishment of the present usage, it is sinful for women not to adhere to their husbands. Women transgressing the limits assigned by the Rishi become guilty of [equivalent to] slaying the embryo . . . The woman also who, being commanded by her husband to raise up offspring refuses to do his bidding becometh equally sinful. (*Mahabharata*, ed. Roy, *Adi Parva*, *Sambhava Parva*, 122, vol. 1, pp. 355–7)

in the society) and matrilineal (descent was identified through the mother). This means that social relationships were centred on the women in the group. The core of the group would have been a small number of interrelated women (mothers and daughters, for example). The males were only loosely associated with this central group and would, at times, move from group to group. Attached to the central core of women, the children, would, therefore, identify themselves with their mothers. It may even be that the significance of the male role in procreation was not realized until comparatively late.[3]

It is thought that matrifocal, matrilineal society was viable as long as human society consisted of small groups living in relative isolation from each other. As groups began to live in larger numbers and in closer proximity, power relationships developed both within and between groups. Warfare led to a male-dominated warrior culture and the emergence of the patriarchy (rule by the father or the men in the society) that exists as the social norm today.

Some feminist writers have tried to define the characteristic features of patriarchal and matrifocal societies. In a patriarchy, power is the supreme value. Those who have power are important; they are taken notice of; their deeds are recorded in the newspapers and in the history books. Those who do not have power are ignored; they do not count; they are not even 'seen' in the social structure, in the sense that no account is taken of them when decisions are made; they do not appear in the history books. Patriarchal society can be characterized as giving the greatest value to power, authority, control, victory, ownership, law, courage and strength. Its main interactions are power struggles and competition. The ends justify the means. Results are expressed in terms of victory or defeat. There are only points for the winners in such a society, none for the runners-up. It is epitomized by tradition, institutions, civilization and control over the natural world.

In a matrifocal society, the highest values are nurturing, life-giving, compassion, sensitivity, spontaneity, creativity and giving support to others. The principal interactions are mutual and co-operative. The means are as important as the ends. Success is judged by the degree to which the condition of all is bettered. It is epitomized by family life and participation in the natural world.

Some research in the area of social psychology has tended to confirm these generalizations. Work on moral development in boys and girls has found significant differences in the way that they approach moral questions. Boys tend to distance themselves from a problem and try to gain an overview of it; they try to take the perspective of others; and they try to apply abstract and rational concepts of justice. Girls, on the other hand, tend to see moral problems in terms of individuals who are bound together in a complex web of relationships; each person has responsibilities towards others as well as towards the group as a whole; moral decisions need, therefore to be analysed in terms of their effect upon this whole network of relationships.[4]

The Suppression of Women by Religion

In brief then, just as the female deity was subjugated by the male warrior god, so women have been socially subjugated by men in most societies. Since, in most societies, it is religion that establishes the social norms, it has been religion that has created the androcentric conceptual and social framework for patriarchy. It has done this by subjugating women in several ways.

THE CREATION OF WOMAN: Eve being created from a rib taken from Adam's side (*Genesis* 2:21–22). Michelangelo's depiction on the ceiling of the Sistine Chapel.

THE FALL: In Christian theology, the blame for humanity's fall from paradise lies with womankind. The first man and woman lived in the paradisical Garden of Eden. It was Eve who was weak and, tempted by the serpent, ate of the forbidden fruit. This caused Adam and Eve to be driven out of Eden (*Genesis* 3:1–24). In this detail from Michelangelo's painting on the ceiling of the Sistine Chapel, female culpability is emphasized by also giving the serpent a woman's face.

The Doctrinal Suppression of Women

The conceptual basis for the suppression of women can be found in many religious doctrines, either overtly or by inference. God in most of the world religions is a male figure; the prophet–founders of the religions are also male. This gives much implied value to the male sex as opposed to the female.

In Christianity, the biblical story of Eve's creation out of Adam's side has been used doctrinally to support women's inferior social position.[5] This was reinforced by the emergence of ideas of body–spirit duality, derived from the Greeks, and the idea that everything material is evil and everything of the spirit is good, derived from the Manicheans. Women were, of course, associated with the body and men with spirit. In Roman Catholicism in particular, this led to an abhorrence of sex and an idealization of celibacy and chastity. Thus the sexual association with women that occurs in marriage became something that is second-best, something that is left to lesser mortals. The truly virtuous and spiritual man remains chaste and celibate, uncontaminated by association with women. Such feelings have led to profoundly misogynist statements, even from the Church fathers. A similarly antagonistic attitude towards sexual intercourse, and therefore towards women, appears in many Buddhist texts and is also the ideal in the Hindu *sannyasin* tradition.

The Moral Suppression of Women

The anti-female tone in religious doctrine and concepts becomes embodied in the moral stance taken by religions. Women are considered inherently more sinful than men and liable to lead men into temptation and sin. This has led to unequal moral standards being expected of men and women. Women are expected to be modest, chaste and, at the time of marriage, virgins. Men, on the other hand, are excused the occasional sexual dalliance or visit to a prostitute.

The Hindu scriptures depict women as not fit to lead independent lives, but rather as needing to be guarded against their natural inclinations towards evil. Similar statements occur in the writings of religious scholars in Christianity, Islam and Buddhism.

Negative Religious Views of Women

HINDUISM

It is the nature of women to seduce men in this (world); for that reason, the wise are never unguarded in (the company of) females. For women are able to lead astray in (this) world not only a fool, but even a learned man, and (to make) him a slave of desire and anger.

(When creating them) Manu allotted to women (a love of their) bed, (of their) seat and (their) ornaments, impure desires, wrath, dishonesty, malice, and bad conduct. (*Laws of Manu* 2:213, p. 69; 9:14, p. 330)

Even if high-born and gifted with beauty and possessed of protectors [i.e. husbands, fathers or brothers], women wish to transgress the restraints assigned to them. This fault truly attaches to them, O Narada. There is nothing that is more sinful than women. Verily, women are the root of all evils. (The sage Bhishma teaching Yudhishthira about women, quoting the words spoken by the celestial Panchachuda to Rishi Narada. *Marabharata*, ed. Dutt, 13:38:11–13)

THERAVADA BUDDHISM

'How are we to conduct ourselves, Lord, with regard to womankind?'
'As not seeing them, Ananda.'
'But if we should see them, what are we to do?'
'No talking, Ananda.'
'But if they should speak to us, Lord, what are we to do?'
'Keep wide awake, Ananda.'
(*Maha Parinibbana Suttana*, 5:9, *Digha Nikaya* 2:141, in Rhys Davids, *Dialogues of the Buddha*, vol. 2, p. 154)

No man who is not possessed should trust women, for they are base, fickle, ungrateful and deceitful. They are ungrateful and do not act as they ought to; they do not care for their parents or brother. They are mean and immoral and do only their own will . . . Women are deceitful and very sharp. The truth concerning them is very difficult to find out. Their nature is hard to know like the movement of fish in water. Being insatiate, soft-spoken, but hard to satisfy (in their wishes) like rivers they sink down into hell. Knowing this one should keep far away from them. Being seducers and arch-deceivers, disturbers of chastity they sink down (into hell). Knowing this one should keep away from them. (*Kulanajataka*, vv. 24–5, 59–9, pp. 160, 163)

MAHAYANA BUDDHISM

You should know that when men have close relationships with women, they have close relationships with evil ways . . .
Fools lust for women like dogs in heat . . .
Women can ruin the precepts of purity.
They can also ignore honour and virtue.
Causing one to go to hell, they prevent rebirth in heaven.
Why should the wise delight in them? . . .
Ornaments on women show off their beauty.

But within them there is great evil as in the body there is air . . .
The dead snake and dog are detestable,
But women are even more detestable than they are . . .
Confused by women, one is burnt by passion.
Because of them one falls into evil ways.
There is no refuge.

(Speech of the Buddha to King Udayana, from the *Maharatnakuta,* quoted in Paul, *Women in Buddhism*, pp. 30, 31, 41–2)

CHRISTIANITY

Let a woman learn in silence with all submissiveness. I permit no woman to teach or to have authority over men; she is to keep silent. For Adam was formed first, then Eve; and Adam was not deceived, but the woman was deceived and became a transgressor. (*1 Timothy*, 2:11–14)

Do you not know that each of you (women) is also an Eve? . . . You are the Devil's gateway, you are the unsealer of that forbidden tree, you are the first deserter of the divine law, you are the one who persuaded him whom the devil was too weak to attack. How easily you destroyed man, the image of God! Because of the death which you brought upon us, even the Son of God had to die. (Tertullian, one of the Church Fathers, in *De Cultu Feminarum* 1:1, quoted in D. Bailey, *The Man–Woman Relation*)

ISLAM: THE *QUR'AN*

Men are superior to women in so far as God has set one group over the other and because men expend of their wealth. And so righteous women are obedient and keep safe, during their husband's absence, that which God would have them take care of. And those women whom you fear may reject your authority, admonish them, then let them sleep by themselves, and then beat them. (*Qur'an* 4:34)

SUNNI ISLAM

Ibn 'Abbas reported that Allah's messenger (may peace be upon him) said: . . . I looked into the [Hell] Fire and there I found the majority constituted by women.

Usama ibn Zaid . . . reported Allah's Messenger (may peace be upon him) as saying: I have not left after me turmoil for the people but the harm done to men by women.

Abu Sa'id Khudri reported that Allah's Messenger (may peace be upon him) said: The world is sweet and green and verily Allah is going to install you as vicegerent in it in order to see how you act. So avoid the allurement of women: verily, the first trial for the people of Isra'il was caused by women. (*Sahih Muslim*, *Kitab al-Riqaq*, nos. 6597, 6604, vol. 4, pp. 1431–2)

SHI'I ISLAM

Take care that you do not consult with women, for their judgement is poor and their resolve is weak. So keep them veiled and secluded and do not allow them to go out. As far

> as possible, do not allow them to become acquainted with any man other than yourself. Do not set them any tasks other than that which is normally theirs. This is best for their health, their satisfaction and their good looks, for a woman is made of clay and not up to hard work. Treat her honourably but do not take her word with regard to others and never put yourself in her hands. (Majlisi, *Hiliyat al-Muttaqin*, p. 78; author's translation)

This moral double standard permeates other areas as well. Simone de Beauvoir, for example, castigated the Roman Catholic Church for authorizing the killing of adult men in war while reserving an uncompromising concern for human life in its attitude towards contraception and abortion. She asserted that by its prohibition of abortion and, in particular, contraception, the Church maintained women's enslavement to their generative functions and thus their dependence on men.[6]

The Social Oppression of Women

Religion has been an important source of laws and administrative structures that kept women in an inferior position in society. In Hindu law, Rabbinic law, Christian canon law and the Islamic Shari'a, the testimony of a woman is either worthless or given less weight than that of a man. Indeed, in many societies, women have been relegated to a position of virtual slavery. They have no rights or freedoms by custom or in law. Throughout their lives they are completely dependant on males. A quotation from the Hindu book, the *Laws of Manu*, sums up the reality of the situation for most women in almost every society: 'In childhood, a female must be subject to her father, in youth to her husband, when her lord is dead, to her sons; a woman must never be independent.'[7]

SUTTEE (*SATI*): According to the *Skanda-Purana*, Sati, the consort of Shiva, threw herself on a funeral pyre. Consequently, it became customary for widows to do the same and they were also called Sati. Although voluntary in theory, in practice any woman refusing to perform it faced social ostracization. Outlawed by the British colonial rulers in 1829, the custom has persisted in a few areas. A nineteenth-century European depiction.

While, of course, religion is not the sole factor responsible for the suppression of women, it is nevertheless true that this social subjugation is underpinned by the authority of religion. Since religion is the source for the values and morality of a traditional society, religion's doctrinal and moral attitude to women fashions the social milieu that justifies their subjugation. In addition, whether we consider suttee in India, clitoridectomy in Muslim North Africa or the witch-hunts of Europe and North America, it has been religious traditions that have sanctioned and given moral authority to violence towards women.

Even where the scripture of a religion appears to allow a certain degree of female emancipation, the religious tradition clamps down and precludes the exercise of this. In Hinduism, for example, the *Rig Veda* calls for women to reign supreme in the household.[8] Popular Hindu epics give several examples of women who have acted independently.[9] The reality of life for women in India, however, at least since the Middle Ages, has been domestic servitude with no rights.

In Islam, scripture gives women spiritual equality with men and even guarantees them certain limited social rights, such as the right to hold property in their own name[10] (a right denied to most Christian women until the last century). What was given to women by scripture, however, was effectively taken away by social laws and customs that deprived them of any ability to act independently of a male guardian.

The *Qur'an* lays down an ethical basis for the equality of men and women. It has been argued, however, that when Islamic law was being formulated by (male) jurists, these benefits to women were negated. While those statements in the *Qur'an* which were advantageous to men were made into firm laws, those that inclined towards giving women a greater degree of equality remained as ethical injunctions only, with no force in law. Thus, for example, the *Qur'an* states that if one cannot treat one's wives equally, one should not marry more than one (*Qur'an* 4:4–5). This has not, however, been made into any legal limitation on the right of a man to marry up to four wives, even if it is provable that he has not treated his first two wives equally. Similarly, the force of the Qur'anic requirement that divorce should only take place with due consideration and that divorced wives should be treated fairly (*Qur'an* 2:229–33) has not been fully translated into law, although other ethical injunctions in the *Qur'an* have been converted into law by the jurists.[11]

Exclusion of Women from the Religious Hierarchy

Women have been excluded from religious learning. Women are forbidden to read and study the *Vedas* in classical Hinduism and the *Talmud* in Orthodox Judaism. In the United States, women were excluded from Christian theological faculties and seminaries until the middle of the nineteenth century.[12] The religious hierarchy in most religions is male-dominated. Whether Hindu Brahmin priests, Buddhist monks, Zoroastrian *mobeds*, Jewish rabbis, Christian priests or Muslim ulema are considered, all are exclusively or predominantly male preserves. Even in Buddhism, where the Buddha himself gave permission for the setting up of an order of nuns, the Buddhist scriptures represent him as having been very reluctant to do so. The Buddha was implored by his aunt and foster-mother,

Mahaprajapati, for permission to go forth into the mendicant life under the rule of the Dharma (that is, to become a nun). Her pleas were taken up by Ananda, the Buddha's chief disciple. The Buddha refused three times, saying, 'If women go forth under the rule of the Dharma, this Dharma will not be long-enduring.' He said that it would be like a blight descending upon a field of sugar cane. Eventually he relented, however, and allowed an order of nuns. However, the nuns were to remain subordinate to the monks in all ways, to the extent that 'a nun even of one hundred years' standing must show deference to a monk even if he has only just been initiated.'[13] Orders of nuns died out in most Buddhist societies although there has been a revival in the last few decades.[14]

The above paints a very negative view of religion's role in women's history and needs to be moderated by noting that religion has also at times contributed positively to women's self-image and role in society. Religion has often allocated women an honoured place, albeit usually in connection with their role as housekeepers and mothers. Women are often, as for example in Judaism, given the central role in the home. Moreover, since many religions have made the family an important focus in their social doctrine, they have effectively given women an important social role. Religious history, while containing stories of important women in the roles

a

b

FEMALE IMAGES OF WISDOM: a) Sarasvati, the consort of Brahman, goddess of scholarship and learning and patron of the arts in Hinduism. The origin of Sanskrit and of its alphabet is attributed to her. b) Prajñaparamita ('the wisdom that reaches the farther shore'). The perfection that it is necessary for a *bodhisattva* to achieve in the course of his development was embodied in Mahayana Buddhism in the form of this goddess. A Tibetan block print.

of wife and mother, also contains examples of more socially active women, thus giving women a choice of social role models. Additionally, religious literature contains feminine imagery that is often central to the religion. In several religions, including Judaism, Christianity, Hinduism and Buddhism, there is a feminine image of wisdom, for example (see pp. 441, 452).

Each of the major world religions has developed, to some extent, a female figure who acts as a role model for women. In the classical formulation of the religion, this has been a role that has emphasized the vrtues of comforting and nurturing. This figure has often been the mother or wife of the prophet-founder. Her story has been emphasized and mythologized as a Mother Goddess in these religions, often being used by the patriarchy to promote a passive, home-centred, socially inactive role for women. But many women have, in the course of each religion's history, and particularly in modern times, preferred an alternative role model, one that takes them out of the home and is more socially active. This has usually been the figure of a female disciple of the prophet-founder of the religion who took an active role in the organizing and promotion of the religion in its early stages (see pp. 294–5 and Table 17.1).

The Eternal Female Archetype

In the history of humanity, there has until recent years been a fundamental difference in the way that men and women were perceived in society. The male is seen as an individual person whose behaviour and personality traits are individual and who has many social roles that he can occupy. For the

Table 17.1 Religious Role Models for Women

	Passive, nurturing role model	Active, socially-involved role model
Hinduism	Rukmini, wife of Krishna; Sita, wife of Rama	Draupadi, consort of the Pandavas
Buddhism	Maya, the mother of the Buddha	Mahaprajapati, aunt and foster mother of the Buddha
Christianity	Mary, the mother of Jesus	Mary Magdalene
Sunni Islam	Khadija, first wife of Muhammad	A'isha, later wife of Muhammad
Shi'i Islam	Fatima, daughter of Muhammad and wife of Imam 'Ali	Fatima or Zaynab, daughter of Imam Husayn
Baha'i Faith	Bahiyyih Khanum, daughter of Baha'u'llah	Tahirih, disciple of the Bab

POSITIVE ROLE MODELS FOR WOMEN IN RELIGION

BUDDHISM

The nun, Soma (during the Buddha's lifetime) . . . was taunted:

> That vantage-ground the sages may attain
> Is hard to win. With her two-finger consciousness
> That place no woman is competent to gain.

She replied:

> What should the state of woman do to us,
> Whose mind is firmly set – or do to anyone
> Who, knowledge rolling on, discerns the dhamma?
> Am I a woman in these matters, or
> Am I a man, or what am I then?
> To such a one are you, sir, fit to talk!
> (A. Bancroft, 'Women in Buddhism', in U. King, *Women in the World's Religions*, p. 82)

ISLAM

The two men [Abu Bakr and 'Umar] marched to 'Ali's house with an armed party, surrounded the house, and threatened to set it on fire if 'Ali and his supporters would not come out and pay homage to the elected caliph. 'Ali came out and attempted to remonstrate, putting forward his own claims and rights and refusing to honour Abu Bakr and 'Umar's demands. The scene soon grew violent, the swords flashed from their scabbards, and 'Umar with his band tried to pass on through the gate. Suddenly Fatima appeared before them in a furious temper and reproachfully cried:

> You have left the body of the Apostle of God with us and you have decided among yourselves without consulting us, and without respecting our rights. Before God, I say, either you get out of here at once, or with my hair dishevelled I will make my appeal to God.

This made the situation most critical, and Abu Bakr's band was obliged to leave the house without securing 'Ali's homage. (Jafri, *The Origins and Early Development of Shi'a Islam*, pp. 50–1)

BAHA'I FAITH

. . . when suddenly the figure of Tahirih, adorned and unveiled, appeared before the eyes of the assembled companions. Consternation immediately seized the entire gathering. All stood aghast before this sudden and most unexpected apparition. To behold her face unveiled was to them inconceivable . . .

Quietly, silently, and with the utmost dignity, Tahirih stepped forward and, advancing towards Quddus, seated herself on his right-hand side. Her unruffled serenity sharply contrasted with the affrighted countenances of those who were gazing upon her face. Fear, anger, and bewilderment stirred the depths of their souls . . .

. . . She rose from her seat and, undeterred by the tumult

> that she had raised in the hearts of her companions, began to address the remnant of that assembly. Without the least premeditation, and in language which bore a striking resemblance to that of the Qur'an, she delivered her appeal with matchless eloquence and profound fervour . . . Immediately after, she declared: 'I am the Word which the Qa'im [the Imam Mahdi] is to utter, the Word which shall put to flight the chiefs and nobles of the earth!' (Nabil, *The Dawn-Breakers*, pp. 294–6)

female, however, there is only one archetypal figure by which she is judged. She either fulfils this stereotype and is judged a 'good' woman or she is condemned as a 'bad' woman. Alternatively, one can consider the archetype to have two poles: the positive pole, the 'good' woman, is a silent, submissive, domestic creature, nurturing, gentle and compassionate; the negative pole, the 'bad' woman, is a sensuous, seductive, mysterious, assertive, deceitful figure, corrupting and leading society astray.[15] Each woman inherently possesses both poles: creative and destructive, nurturing and corrupting, life-giving and life-destroying. This duality of the female archetype can be seen in the female figures of a religion: Eve is at once the mother and progenitor of humanity and the cause of the Fall; the Hindu goddess Kali is both the fearsome and terrible goddess of destruction and able to give her devotees freedom from fear and a blissful state of mind.

Hence society sees its men as individuals, assigning to them places in society as nobles, craftsmen, labourers, criminals; as clever, dull and so on. But women are all seen in their stereotypical role, thus they become almost invisible, a part of the taken-for-granted background to society, ignored by historians and chroniclers. They do not require any special comment in their stereotyped roles as wives and mothers, any more than donkeys require any special comment in their role as beasts of burden, or ploughs as tools of agriculture.

Religion and Sexuality

One of the main functions of religion in society has been to control sexuality, more specifically female sexuality. Indiscriminate sexual activity threatens the patriarchal social order. For a start, only the mother of a child is obvious in the biology of the procreative process. This threatens the ability of the male to identify his offspring. Without clear and indisputable linking of the offspring to the father, the inheritance of social position, property and wealth, the paraphernalia of power, which is the highest value of the patriarchal society, becomes difficult to establish. The only way to control female sexuality and thus be certain of the paternity of the offspring is to control rigorously the social activities of the female. Either she must

GENDER SEGREGATION IN RELIGIOUS BUILDINGS: In many religious places of worship there is segregation of the sexes with women being assigned an inferior position, usually at the back or in an upper balcony area, as in this synagogue in London.

be confined to the house or else all of her social interactions must be chaperoned. These measures need to be enforced from puberty to old age. In order to maintain this control, women are deprived of most civil rights, have no right to possessions or property of their own, and in most instances no rights even over their own bodies or over their children.

Somehow, such draconian restrictions on the female must be justified. The greatest source of justification and moral authority in a society is its religion. Thus, patriarchy falls back on religion to legitimate the virtual imprisonment and enslavement of women. To justify this, religious authorities have characterized women as feckless, sexually voracious and a snare for men. The following passage comes from the writings of a fourteenth-century Dominican monk. Its theme would not, however, look out of place in the writings of religious scholars from any of the world's religious traditions over the past three millennia:

> In the woman wantonly adorned to capture souls, the garland upon her head is a single code or firebrand of Hell to kindle men with that fire; so too the horns of another, so the bare neck, so the brooch upon the breast, so with all the curious finery of the whole of their body. What else does it seem or could be said of it save that each is a spark breathing out hell-fire, which this wretched incendiary of the Devil breathes so effectually . . . that in a single day by her dancing or her perambulation through the town, she

> inflames with the fire of lust – it may be – twenty of those who behold her, damning the souls whom God has created and redeemed at such a cost for their salvation. For this very purpose the Devil thus adorns these females, sending them forth through the town as his apostles, replete with every iniquity, malice, fornication.[16]

It does not take a great deal of insight to discern here the projection onto women of male sexual fantasies. The effect, however, has been to justify the virtual enslavement of women in almost every society down to recent times.

So successfully has this picture of reality been established that the majority of people have assumed that the values of the patriarchy are part of the natural order: that men are by nature stronger and more aggressive and women weaker and submissive. But all the evidence from anthropology and psychology points to the fact that this is not a natural, inbuilt state of affairs. It is something that is culturally learned; it is part of the socially constructed universe that human beings regard as reality. Women are taught that they are the 'weaker sex' and so they behave as though they are. Indeed, they may even become extremely anxious and resentful if they are pushed towards self-reliance and independence. In this way, patriarchy has controlled most societies in the last few millennia by determining the view of reality of those societies. Even where the intellectual argument for women's emancipation is won, the actual rate of progress is very slow and the emancipation of women in recent times has only been partial and in a few societies.

There are some variations in the traditional attitudes of the major religions of the world towards sexuality, to a large extent dictated by the role models provided by the founders of these religions. Of the major religions, Christianity is perhaps the most negative towards human sexuality. Jesus himself did not marry, in so far as the Gospels record, and there are several statements in the *New Testament* that advocate celibacy (with monogamous marriage being a second-best option)[17] and condemn homosexuality.[18] Such passages have formed the basis of the view of most Christian churches up to modern times. The Buddha was married and had one son prior to his enlightenment. During the whole of his ministry, however, he embraced a world-renouncing life which excluded sexual contact. The rules for the Buddhist monks reflect this example of the Buddha. Such rules are still applied in Theravada Buddhism, but married monks are found among Mahayana Buddhists. Of the major Indian traditions, however, it is Jainism that has the strictest attitude against any expression of sexuality among its monks and nuns. In Islam, the attitude to sexuality is, again, set by the example of the founder, Muhammad, who married some fourteen wives and had a number of children. There is thus a much more positive approach towards marriage, sexuality and family life. Monasticism is prohibited and the number of wives is limited to four. Homosexuality is again prohibited. The attitude to sexuality in Judaism is much the same as is Islam, except that polygamy was prohibited in the Middle Ages. The Baha'i Faith commends the married state for all people, prohibits monasticism and ordains monogamy. In Hinduism, there is some dissonance between theory and practice. The exception to the general rule that the religion follows the role model of the major figures in it is provided by Hinduism. The scriptures and stories of Hinduism are filled with erotic stories of gods who have sexual intercourse with women. The story of Krishna having sexual intercourse with the cowgirls is perhaps the best known of these. Krishna is also reported in some stories to have had thousands of wives. Followers of the god Shiva worship the representation of his phallus, the lingam, and ancient Hindu temples contain erotic statues. In practice, however, modern Hindus are monogamous and there is a strict code of sexual morality in Hindu society.

'It is in the familiar company of women that one finds that relaxation which chases away sadness and gives rest to the heart. It is desirable for pious souls to find refreshment through that which is permitted by religion' (Muhammad al-Ghazali, eleventh–twelfth century, quoted in Sabbah, *Woman in the Muslim Unconscious*, p. 117). Eighteenth-century Indian miniature.

In modern times, the more liberal elements in Western Christianity have responded to social realities by relaxing the strict sexual morality that has characterized most traditional religion. Attitudes towards divorce, homosexuality and heterosexual couples living together without being married are softening in some parts of many churches. Recent events that bear witness to this include the ordination of an openly committed homosexual priest by New York City's liberal Episcopalian Bishop Paul Moore in 1977, a service celebrating the twentieth anniversary of the Lesbian and Gay Christian Movement held in London's Southwark Cathedral on 16 November 1996, and the vote by the Episcopalian churches in northern New Jersey in 1987 to receive and study a report entitled 'Changing Patterns of Sexuality and Family Life'. This was described by its opponents as encouraging the churches to accept homosexuals, fornicators and adulterers as long as they were 'sensitive, committed' people. There are a few signs of this beginning to happen in other religions also. The Dalai Lama, for example, while on a trip to the United States in 1997, was persuaded to make a statement favourable to homosexuality.

The lingam is the stone pillar in the centre and is a representation of a phallus. It is worshipped by Hindu followers of the god Shiva as a symbol of him. Around the lingam is the *yoni*, representing the female sexual organs. The two together are especially worshipped by Shaktas, followers of Shakti, the consort of Shiva, who is the personification of primal energy.

The Modern Debate

In many ways, then, as noted above, the world religions have over the centuries oppressed women. In modern times, the feminist movement has forced some, more open-minded religious thinkers to rethink their heritage.

As with many other features of modernity, it has been Christianity that has faced this question earlier and to a more forceful degree than the other world religions. In particular, the question of women in the priesthood has greatly exercised many denominations. The traditionalists claim biblical authority for their stance against women priests and point to such verses as:

> the women should keep silence in the churches. For they are not permitted to speak, but should be subordinate, as even the law says. If there is anything they desire to know, let them ask their husbands at home. For it is shameful for a woman to speak in church.[19]

The pro-women lobby points to the reality of the modern Christian world and to such verses as: 'there is neither male nor female; for you are all one in Christ Jesus.'[20]

In the other religions of the world, the voices of women are only just beginning to emerge.[21] Women have been ordained as rabbis in Reform Judaism. Theravada Buddhist women have asserted the right to achieve full ordination as nuns in Thailand and Sri Lanka, while Mahayana women have claimed recognition as Zen masters. Hindu women in India have established the right to become *sannyasins* (those who follow the path of renunciation, see p. 129) and to recite the *Vedas*, activities that were closed to them in classical Hinduism. Some have even claimed to be gurus in their own right. In Iran, women have established the right to be considered *mujtahids* (the highest rank in the Shi'i clerical hierarchy), although only ministering to other women. While these are certainly important early movements, they cannot yet be said to have made any significant impact on the religious world as a whole.

In the Baha'i Faith, this issue of the relationship between men and women is very much to the forefront of concern. The equality of men and women is one of the principles embodied in the scriptures and cited by Baha'is as the social basis of their faith. The education of women is stressed (even over that of men in certain circumstances). Women are encouraged and expected to play an active social role, especially in the promotion of peace, and to earn their own living. What is needed in the world, according to the Baha'i teachings, is a better balance between masculine and feminine elements in civilization:

> The world in the past has been ruled by force, and man has dominated woman by reason of his more forceful and aggressive qualities both of body and mind. But the balance is already shifting – force is losing its weight and mental alertness, intuition and the spiritual qualities of love and service, in which woman is strong, are gaining ascendancy. Hence the new age will be an age less masculine, and more permeated with the feminine ideals – or, to speak more exactly, will be an age in which the masculine and feminine elements in civilisation will be more evenly balanced.[22]

In general, it can be said that, although great advances have been made in bringing the question of the role of women to the forefront of debate in many religious communities, it has remained a matter of discussion and the passing of resolutions rather than practical advances. In most societies, traditional attitudes and customary roles, supported to a large extent by religion, serve to keep women in a subservient role.

The Feminist Study of Religion

Feminist writing about religion contains several key criticisms about the religious world and about scholarship on religion. These criticisms may be summarized thus:

1. Those in power and authority (dominant men) shape our perceptions of reality. It is their construction of reality that is regarded as the norm and indeed as 'objective' reality. In effect, humanness has been considered identical to being male, while women are relegated to a forgotten, non-human category.
2. Those who do not wield power remain unseen by the traditional scholars of religion. Their religious experience is ignored and thus remains unexplored. The perceived reality (and thus the religious world and religious experience) of those who do not wield power is very different from that of those with power. The largest group of people without power is the world's women. However, one can make the same statement of other oppressed groups: the working classes, peasants, ethnic minorities, slaves and so on, and thus there is much overlap in the initial assessments of the religious experience of women and of such groups.
3. Thus, what we have previously considered to be facts about the human religious experience turn out instead to be represent the experience of a small minority, that of dominant males.
4. The fact that the dominant male viewpoint is taken as the norm in turn affects all aspects of the religious world: the religious hierarchy, religious institutions, doctrines, even religious language. Of course, this extends far beyond just the religious world and affects all parts of society.
5. All scholarship in history, religion and the humanities in general is inherently based on gender and cultural preconceptions and there is no such thing as objectivity. There cannot be an objective reconstruction of the past or a religious statement that is simply factual.

Thus what has claimed to be objective scholarship about the religious experience of humankind as a whole has, in fact, examined, from a distorted and biased viewpoint, the religious experience of a very small group – dominant males – whose experience has been taken as the norm for the whole of humanity.

From this starting point, the feminist study of religion has examined three main areas:

- the way in which women are represented in the conceptual world of a religion: its literature, doctrines, art and concepts
- the participation of women in religion, their role and status, the extent to which they are given authority
- uncovering and reflection upon women's own experience of the religion.

Kuan-yin, the Chinese goddess of mercy, has an interesting story as she began as the male *bodhisattva* Avalokiteshvara. In China however, from about the tenth century, the figure became increasingly feminized until it is now usually represented as a clearly-female goddess.

The Feminist Recreation of Religion

The above may be regarded as the negative aspect of the feminist study of religion, its description and criticism of the present state of affairs. On this, most feminist scholars of religion are in broad agreement. Where they differ is over the question of constructing an alternative to replace this existing unsatisfactory state of affairs. In trying to produce a positive feminist study and re-creation of religion, feminist scholars have taken three main methodological stances.[23]

FEMINIST NEO-ORTHODOXY. The main effort here is directed towards establishing that there is an essential, spiritual, non-sexist message in religion. The task of the scholar is to identify this and to separate it from the culture-bound, androcentric language and concepts in which it has historically been presented. In general, it may be said that this type of feminist theology is suspicious of the abstract, speculative approach of traditional theology and prefers an experience-based practical approach. Its themes include liberation, celebration and community. Examples of this type of scholarship include the writings of Phyllis Trible (*God and the Rhetoric of Sexuality*) and the early work of Mary Daly (*The Church and the Second Sex*).

FEMINIST SOCIOLOGY OF KNOWLEDGE. This second approach considers this distinction between the language and the message of the scripture to be invalid: 'the medium *is* the message'; therefore it is hopeless to try to build a feminist theology from the elements of a structure that is so deeply imbued with misogyny. It becomes necessary to build a completely new religious world for women, a new feminist time/space, radically separate from and sharing nothing with the old patriarchal religious world. This approach has been taken further by many radical feminists, into what has, in the West, been called a 'post-Christian' discourse. In the course of this, radical feminists have uncovered and jettisoned all male elements in religion. The male God has become the Goddess; the priest has been replaced by the priestess or witch; even language has been changed with the invention of new spellings of words such as 'wimmin' or 'womyn' (women) and 'herstory' (history). Elements have been extracted from mythology, ancient and pagan religious traditions and folklore. A new feminist time/space and a new goddess-based religion has been created. This new religion exists, not surprisingly, in numerous forms under such names as Neo-paganism, Wicca, and the Dianic Movement. Examples of writings on this model include the later writings of Mary Daly (*Beyond God the Father* and *Gyn/Ecology*) and the work of Margot Adler (*Drawing Down the Moon*).

Feminist Hermeneutics. This approach involves the uncovering of the historical role of women in religions, a role that the histories of a patriarchal society have tended to erase. Such an approach regards the life of the founder of the religion and the early disciples as a model that can be used as a prototype from which various feminist possibilities can emerge. The scriptures can be understood as the response of faith to a specific historical–cultural situation; their usefulness to us can be judged on the basis of what help each specific passage can be in the construction of a new feminist vision, a feminist reconstruction of historical reality. Elizabeth Fiorenza (*In Memory of Her*) uses this approach.

Although most of the work that exists at present is based on Christianity, feminist scholars in other religions such as Judaism, Islam and Buddhism are rapidly applying the same approaches to their religions. Leila Ahmed's *Women and Gender in Islam* is an example of a work on Islam that would fall largely into the category of feminist hermeneutics. Undoubtedly, this field of publishing will grow greatly in the future.

In practical terms, the feminist re-creation of religion has gone down a number of different avenues. Among these are: campaigns to storm the bastions of patriarchal, institutional religion, such as the movements for the ordination of women; the creation of women-only religious groups and communities, which are often characterized by a certain amount of antipathy towards men; the establishment of links with the theology of other oppressed groups, including black theology and liberation theology; ecumenism, interreligious dialogue and the establishment of links with peace movements; and the exploration of the implications of feminist theology for environmental concerns, the area called eco-feminism. Many feminists see themselves as on the road to creating a new post-feminist holistic spirituality in which both men and women can participate fully, with no oppression of one group by the other.[24]

IMAGES OF THE FEMININE IN RELIGION

JUDAISM

Wisdom is radiant and unfading, and she is easily discerned by those who love her, and is found by those who seek her. She hastens to make herself known to those who desire her. He who rises early to seek her will have no difficulty, for he will find her sitting at his gates.

I learned both what is secret and what is manifest, for wisdom, the fashioner of all things, taught me. For in her there is a spirit that is intelligent, holy, unique, manifold, subtle, mobile, clear, unpolluted, distinct, invulnerable, loving the good, keen, irresistible, beneficent, humane, steadfast, sure, free from anxiety, all-powerful, overseeing all, and penetrating through all spirits that are intelligent and pure and most subtle. (*Wisdom of Solomon* 7:21–3 RSV Apocrypha and Pseudoepigrapha)

CHRISTIANITY

[Eve's] mother is Sophia, the Wisdom Goddess. Apparently, she had no father. Her nativity story reads:

> When Sophia had cast forth a light drop, it floated upon the water. Immediately, the Man, being androgynous, was made manifest. That drop took its first form as a feminine body. Afterwards, she [Eve] took her bodily form in the image of the Mother [Sophie] which has been revealed. She [Eve] was completed in twelve months. An androgyne [Eve] was born, whom the Greeks call 'Hermaphrodites.' But its mother [Sophie] in Hebrew called her 'the Living Eva,' that is, 'the Instructoress of Life' (113:22–34).

(Rose Arthur, 'The Wisdom Goddess and the Masculinization of Religion', in U. King, *Women in the World's Religions*, p. 33)

BUDDHISM

The Mahayana believed that men should in their meditations complete themselves by fostering the feminine factors of their personality, that they should practice passivity and a loose softness . . .

Like a woman, the 'Perfection of Wisdom' [Prajnaparamita] deserves to be courted and wooed, and the Sutras on perfect Wisdom constitute one long love affair with the Absolute. Meditation on her as a goddess has the purpose of getting inside her, identifying oneself with her, becoming her. In the later Tantra, a sexual attitude to Prajnaparamita is quite explicit. Disguised by the use of ambiguous terms it was already present in the older *Prajnaparamita Sutras* themselves. (E. Conze, quoted in A. Bancroft, 'Women in Buddhism', in U. King, *Women in the World's Religions*, p. 90)

ISLAM

When man contemplates God in woman, his contemplation rests on that which is passive; if he contemplates Him in himself, seeing that woman comes from man, he contemplates Him in that which is active; and when he contemplates Him alone, without the presence of any form whatsoever issued from Him, his contemplation corresponds to a state of passivity with regard to God, without intermediary. Consequently his contemplation of God in woman is the most perfect, for it is then God, in so far as He is at once active and passive, that he contemplates, whereas in the pure interior contemplation, he contemplates Him only in a passive way. So the Prophet – Benediction and Peace be upon him – was to love women because of the perfect contemplation of God in them . . . the contemplation of God in women is the most intense and the most perfect; and the union which is the most intense (in the sensible order, which serves as support for this contemplation) is the conjugal act. (Ibn al-'Arabi, quoted in Nasr, *Traditional Islam in the Modern World*, p. 51)

BAHA'I FAITH

Say: Step out of Thy holy chamber, O Maid of Heaven, inmate of the Exalted Paradise! Drape thyself in whatever manner pleaseth Thee in the silken Vesture of Immortality, and put on, in the name of the All-glorious, the broidered Robe of Light. Hear, then, the sweet, the wondrous accent of the Voice that cometh from the Throne of Thy Lord, the Inaccessible, the Most High. Unveil Thy face, and manifest the beauty of the black-eyed Damsel, and suffer not the servants of God to be deprived of the light of Thy shining countenance. Grieve not if Thou hearest the sighs of the dwellers of the earth, or the voice of the lamentation of the denizens of heaven . . . Intone, then, before the face of the peoples of earth and heaven, and in a most melodious voice, the anthem of praise, for a remembrance of Him Who is the King of the names and attributes of God. Thus have We decreed Thy destiny. Well able are We to achieve Our purpose. (Baha'u'llah, *Gleanings*, pp. 282–3)

FURTHER READING

On the mother goddess, see Gimbutas, *The Goddesses and Gods of Old Europe*. On the sociology of the patriarchy, see French, *Beyond Power*. On women in Hinduism, see Thomas, *Indian Women* and Gupta, *Women in Hindu Society*; for Buddhism, see Horner, *Women under Primitive Buddhism* and Paul, *Women in Buddhism*; for Christianity, see Daly, *The Church and the Second Sex*, and Fiorenza, *In Memory of Her*; for Islam, see Sabbah, *Woman in the Muslim Unconscious*; Afshar, *Women in the Middle East*, and Beck and Keddie, *Women in the Muslim World*; for the Baha'i

Faith, see *The Greatness Which Might be Theirs* and Caton, *Equal Circles.* See also U. King, *Women in the World's Religions* and *Women and Spirituality*. On sexuality, see Parrinder, *Sex in the World's Religions*. On feminist studies of religion, see Constance Buchanan, 'Women's Studies' in Eliade, *Encyclopedia of Religion*; Fiorenza, *In Memory of Her*, chapter 1; U. King, 'Religion and Gender'.

18

Religion and The Arts

Some of the earliest human artefacts that have been found appear to be religious art of various forms and, throughout human history, art has always played an important role in the religious life of communities. This aspect of religion is, however, often forgotten when religions are being described. Official religion presents itself principally through the medium of words. Scholars in the field of religious studies have, therefore, tended to study texts. In fact, religions have usually communicated their message to their adherents by other means, especially orally or through the arts. More than ninety per cent of the general population was illiterate in previous ages in the West and still is in much of the rest of the world. The arts can break through this communication barrier by a direct approach to people's hearts and minds. Thus the arts have always been an important aspect of the manner in which religion has an impact on society. This chapter concentrates on three areas: the role of art in popular religion, the role of art in creating our symbolic universe, and patterns in the history of religious art.

Art and Popular Religion

Most descriptions of religions concentrate on doctrinal or organizational matters. These aspects of religion are, however, only of peripheral importance for most religious people. It is ordinary, often illiterate or poorly educated believers who make up the bulk of the followers of most religions. These people have little time for the intellectualizations of doctrine or the intricacies of Holy Law that are so beloved of the religious professionals; they respond only very poorly to abstract concepts and verbal formulations; they are not greatly concerned with the hierarchies and power structures of the religion. For the ordinary believer, it is the central experience of religion that is of greatest importance (see pp. 87–92) and the most effective way of recreating or expressing the emotions of this experience for most ordinary people is through visual and auditory images and symbolization. Because of their availability and emotional immediacy, the arts are probably the most important source of religious inspiration and education. They may take the form of painting, sculpture, drama, dance, architecture, music, song, storytelling or poetry. These artistic media play a key role in communicating the religious message to ordinary people, although they are often little considered by scholars who study religion.

In many cultures, religious art is the main means of teaching ordinary people the history and doctrines of the religion. The great cathedrals and churches of medieval Europe have vast paintings and stained-glass windows depicting stories from the *Bible*. These may be tourist attractions now, but in their own time they were a major source of religious education for the masses and supports for religious contemplation. Sculpture, drama, and hymns have also played an important role in expressing the deepest truths of Christianity to the masses.

Even in Islam, where representational art is strongly discouraged, the arts have come through in other ways. Just as in Christianity, Christ is 'the Word made flesh', so in Islam, the *Qur'an* is the Word of God. Therefore, where Christian art has icons of Christ, the equivalent in Islamic art is calligraphy of verses of the *Qur'an*. Calligraphy is the highest form of religious art in Islam. The combination of abstract designs, calligraphy and architecture in Islam creates a religious space and ambience to facilitate religious contemplation. In Shi'i Islam, the narration of the stories of the sufferings of the Imams is the principal means of religious communication to the masses. The professional reciter of these stories (the *rawdih-khan*) exhibits great skill in raising the emotions of his listeners and, at the same time, making the moral and religious points in his stories. The emotional pitch that is reached is reflected in the weeping and chest-beating that often follows or accompanies the narration. In the Shi'i world, the story of the Imams is also used as the basis of a theatrical performance (the *ta'ziya*).

Other forms of religious art include music and song. Hymns have always played an important part in Christian services and many churches have large choirs that perform elaborate choral works. Song is an obligatory part of synagogue ritual in Judaism. In the time of the Temple in Jerusalem, certain musical instruments are known to have been played, including the trumpet (*hasora*) and ram's horn (*shofar*). But after the destruction of the Temple, musical instruments were banned in synagogues and the tradition of unaccompanied chanting, usually with antiphonal responses from the congregation, grew. In modern times, musical instruments have been reintroduced to certain synagogues. Religious songs (*bhajans*) also play an important role in India. They are the key form of the religious education of the masses in India. They tell the stories of avators and saints, as well as inculcating moral values and societal norms. Religious music has evolved its own specialized art forms such as campanology (the art of ringing church bells), cantillation (unaccompanied singing of the cantor in the synagogue) or the sounding of the call to prayer in Islam.

Dance is an important art form in many religions. Mystical movements such as the Hasidim in Judaism and some Sufi orders in Islam combine

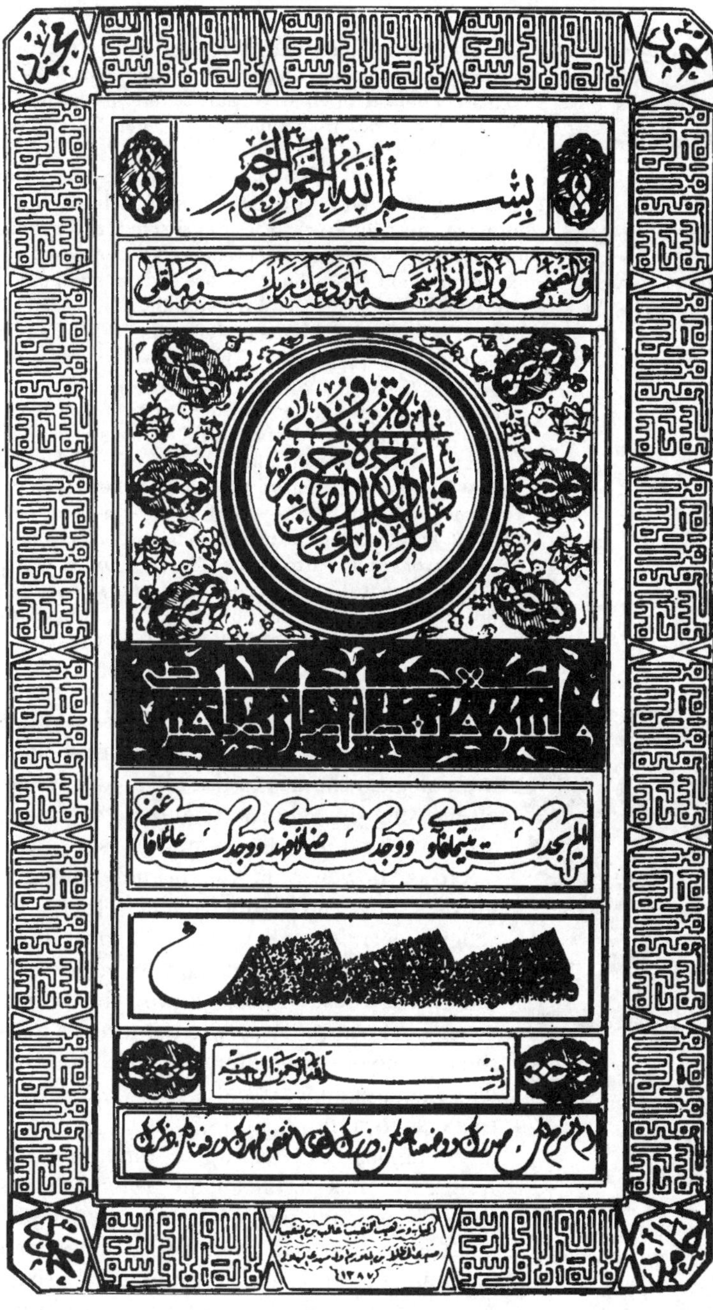

This piece of Islamic calligraphy contains exemplars of several styles. The text is *Qur'an* sura *93 (al-Duha)*. From the top, the successive lines are in the following styles: Muhaqqaq, Thuluth, Naskh, foliated Kufi, Ta'liq, Diwani (somewhat obscured), Jali Diwani, Riqa'. Around the edge is Kufi. The calligrapher is Ghalib Sabri, 1967.

DANCE IN NATIVE AMERICAN RELIGION

The dancers are arranged in a long line . . . the principal element is a rhythmic stamping of the right foot. This is done in perfect unison, often by as many as forty performers. Since the rhythm varies from time to time, it is no easy task to memorize the steps of a dance.

Singing by the performers accompanies the dance. A dance lasts for an entire day or through most of a night, although rest intervals are interpersed throughout the programs. New songs and new dances are composed for each ceremony, and these must be learned to automaticity by every performer. This fact gives an indication of the amount of time and effort which the participants in such a ceremony must expend in preparation. This preparation takes place at night in the kivas [ceremonial buildings].

Each ceremony is performed by one of the ceremonial societies. Of these, at Hotavila, there are six for men and three for women. Each adult man is expected to join [a society] . . . Participation in the work of these societies is a religious and social duty which is expected of every man . . . Participation in the religious observances brings no special favor to the participants. The ceremonies are carried out in order that the whole community may benefit. Failure to do one's ceremonial duties properly would bring ill-fortune to the entire community. (Dennis, *The Hopi Child*, pp. 24–5)

BUDDHIST DANCE RITUAL: In this Mongolian mask dance (Tsam), various Buddhist legends are acted out. This form of dance is thought to have origins in Indian folk dance which was taken to Tibet and eventually to Mongolia, where it has been transformed and developed.

song and dance in their religious practices. Elaborate dances are formed out of religious and mythological themes in Hinduism and Buddhism, often using the *mudras* (symbolic gestures) that are also found in religious statues (see p. 274).

It is, however, in the primal religions that music, song and dance achieve their greatest religious significance. Many of the most important rituals of primal religions consist either solely or mainly of these artistic forms and sometimes other art forms such as the painting of masks or the carving of wooden implements. The rhythmic dancing of many of these rituals yields eventually to a trance state.

Religious art has other functions also. It frequently has a talismanic role. Drawings of symbols or calligraphy of scripture in patterns such as mandalas are often carried on a person as an amulet. These are considered to bring good fortune or to protect the wearer from harm or ill-health (see chapter 15).

Art and the Symbolic Universe

Calligraphic art: Calligraphy can be used to create images. Here, the name and titles of 'Ali are used in calligraphy to create the image of a lion – 'Haydar' or 'Lion' being the sobriquet of 'Ali.

One distinguishing feature of human life is our ability to symbolize – to attach meanings to things in what is often a quite arbitrary way. The most important result of this ability is human speech. But, in fact, all communication and everything that we include under the general heading 'culture' stem from this ability. Within any given society and culture, individuals symbolize their experiences in the same way. They are said to live in the same symbolic universe.[1] This is what causes the society to cohere. It is because of this that we recognize and can distinguish one culture from another. This is what the children of each culture imbibe from the moment of birth. They are not conscious of it as something that they have learned; rather they see it as the way that things are, the taken-for-granted reality.[2]

In a traditional society, it is religion that determines and directs the symbol system of that society. Thus it is religion that gives the culture its underlying coherence and determines the values and meaning structures of the society. But it is the work of the artist to perceive and express these symbol structures. Thus, in a traditional society the arts and religion are inextricably bound up with each other. Together they construct the symbolic universe of that society. Religion directs and determines the symbolization in the society and the arts can do no other than express that.

The symbolic universe of a society is not, however, usually something that is static. It is, or should be, a moving, evolving entity. Religion and the arts are principally responsible for this creative process that brings about the evolution of the symbolic universe in which a society lives. As with all creativity, it involves three stages. The first is to detach us from our present worldview, the status quo; the second is to move us into a new world, a new way of being; the third is to consolidate these new insights and integrate them into our symbolic world so that they become part of our taken-for-granted reality.[3]

This creative process is both terrifying and fascinating.[4] It is terrifying because at the moment that we detach ourselves from the old, we have no idea where the process will take us. The loss of the old landmarks is frightening; we are swept off our feet. The process goes on, however, to the creation of a new world, a new symbolic universe, 'a new heaven and a new earth'. Here begins the fascinating part of the process, the exploration of this new world.[5] In this process, however, there is always the danger of failure. If art or religion is too adventurous and cuts itself off too much from the past, from the traditions and insights of the established order, there is a danger that the result will be chaos. Few will, in any case, be carried along with the artist or religious reformer on such a journey. If, on the other hand, timidity and conservatism predominate, there is no progress, merely repetition of the truths and insights of the old order; in this, art becomes only plagiarism and religion merely superstition and magic; hence the importance of 'the Middle Way', the path of moderation.[6]

Art is also similar to religion with regard to the criteria for deciding what is and is not within the category. For something to be classified as a work of art depends not only on the intention of the artist but also on the receptivity of the beholder. African works of art were for many years collected by anthropologists and museums in the West as merely artefacts. They did not become works of art for the West until such artists as Picasso sensitized the Western public to their artistic merit.[7] Similarly, whether a Buddhist text or a Hindu statue of Shiva is a religious work depends on who is looking at it. For many years, much such material was brought to the West and classified and conserved as the literature and artefacts of the East. It was some time before there were any appreciable numbers of Buddhists or Hindus in the West who could respond to them as religious works. In short, it is not the intention of the artist nor the subject matter that makes a work religious, it is the effect that it has and the use to which it is put.

There is one further important similarity between art and religion. This is their essentially performative nature. Artists do not, usually, much concern themselves with the theory of art; they leave that to art critics. Artists are concerned with *doing* their art. They do not do their art in accordance with a conscious blueprint or a theory. They do their art and then let others (or occasionally themselves, later) construct theories around the work. Most artists do not consciously make a work of art so that it symbolizes something or confirms some theory. Indeed, the work of art does not refer to anything at all; it merely exists and through it the artist seeks to communicate an insight, or give form to a perception.[8] Religion is similar in many ways. The important aspect of the religious life is the action, the living of the religious life, the doing of the religious act. The reason why the act is done, the theological or legalistic framework for the action and the pattern of life, is a secondary structure built up by the religious professionals and of only marginal concern to many believers.

The artist is not, therefore, merely engaged in representing a given form; the religious person is not merely carrying out prescribed activities. By their very activities, they are creating new worlds. They create the forms of perception and meaning by which human beings interpret their experiences. We see the world differently once we have experienced a work of art. Those who live in the West in the late twentieth century cannot think of a hero, even of ancient times, without seeing him through Byron's image of a hero; we cannot think of the Last Supper without carrying in our mind Leonardo da Vinci's painted visualization of the Last Supper and, if we were young in the 1960s, our view of the world is probably affected by

a

b

INTERRELIGIOUS INFLUENCE IN THE ARTS: a) There is a clear precedent for the traditional Christian depiction of the Madonna and child in this third century CE mosaic of the infant Dionysus. Paphos, Cyprus. b) Haghia Sophia, the crowning monument of Byzantine architecture, was built by the Emperor Justinian between 532 and 562. After the Muslim conquest, it was converted into a mosque in 1453. Haghia Sophia became the model for Turkish mosque architecture.

the music and words of John Lennon and Bob Dylan. A religious genius also creates a new world that did not exist before. We can scarcely think of Christianity without thinking of it in terms of the conceptual world created by St Augustine and St Thomas Aquinas, let alone St Paul; nor can we imagine much of Mahayana Buddhism outside the worldview created by Nagarjuna. We should not, however, imagine that what these artistic and religious giants have done is exceptional. It is only exceptional in its scale and impact. What they have done is repeated (on a smaller scale and with less resounding impact) each time that an artist works or a believer says a prayer in a spirit of detachment from the world and an openness to change. What occurs is that through these activities human beings become more human, more aware of the potential within themselves, more sensitive to their environment.

The Historical Development of Religious Art

Religious art may be considered to move through three stages in the history of each religion (although not every religion has moved through all three stages): aniconic, iconic, and representational.

Religious art in the early stages of those religions that are focused upon in this book, Hinduism, Buddhism, Judaism, Christianity, Islam and the Baha'i Faith, was aniconic in nature. This means that its artistic forms did not involve any attempt to produce the likeness of its principal sacred persons. Iconic forms of sacred art evolved in some of these religions with the passage of time. In iconography, there is an attempt to produce a likeness of a sacred entity (usually God, a god, a founder-prophet, or a holy personage) but in a traditional form. In the West, the move towards representational art (in which the person or object is represented as close to the natural physical form as possible) began with the Renaissance. It did not affect other parts of the world until the present century.

The Move from Aniconic Art to Iconic Art

Aniconic art usually represents its subject by a symbol. 'In contrast to signs which are intended to signify a specific empirical thing or experience (such as a warning-signal in the case of a fire), symbols refer to a reality which would otherwise elude one's grasp. They do not indicate or denote so much as evoke . . . In the case of religious symbols the specific earthbound object touches off a transcendent dimension in the person's experience.'[9] (For an indication of the manner in which a symbol can touch off this transcendent dimension, see pp. 170–3.) The important factor about symbols is their multivalence. They can be understood at many different levels of meaning. The aniconic image may indeed be considered more true than the human likeness depicted in the icon. The latter distracts us and emphasizes the closeness of the sacred person to the human mode of existence, whereas

TRADITIONAL ART AND REPRESENTATIONAL ART: These are two portraits of Tupa Kupa, a Maori chief. The left-hand one is drawn by an English artist and shows his human likeness. It is the man as he would see himself if he looked in a mirror. The right-hand picture is a self-portrait drawn in accordance with the traditional art of the Maori people. It shows Tupa Kupa according to his divine image, his heavenly archetype, his inner perfection, his true reality which transcends his earthly frame. (Coomaraswamy, *Why Exhibit Works of Art?* p. 116)

the aniconic form reminds us of the higher spiritual realities and the relative unimportance of the human mode.[10]

Later, the art form becomes iconic. This means that it takes on the human form. Figures of Christ or of the Buddha appear in the art form. There is, however, no attempt to create a naturalistic representation. The form does not draw on a human model but rather upon traditional models that are handed down from master to pupil. The features are heavily stylized, with symmetry and rhythm being the predominant features. There is often a tradition that the original image appeared miraculously. Since the subject is divine, no human emotions are shown. The aim is still to provide a support for contemplation and thus the lines are simple and there is minimal distraction.

The precise reason that aniconic art forms evolve into iconic forms is not easy to determine. It would appear likely that this evolution is linked to the gradual diversification of the pathways to salvation, the performative or social expressions of religion, as the religion develops (see chapter 5).[11] In particular, the development of ritualism and the religion of love and worship, as major pathways of salvation requires iconic images on which the believer can focus, aniconic art being perhaps too abstract and intellectual for popular religion.

In Hinduism, the early Vedic religion was aniconic, concerned more with ritual and sound than with images.[12] The vast profusion of iconic images that now characterizes Hinduism almost certainly developed with the emergence of the *bhakti* sects of devotion towards particular deities.

In Buddhism, the earliest representations that we have of the Buddha are aniconic. He is represented by a lotus (thought to represent the Buddha's birth), the Bodhi tree (representing the Buddha's enlightenment), a wheel (symbolizing the Buddha setting in motion the wheel of the Dharma), or a stupa (memorial monument symbolizing the Buddha's *parinirvana*). Other images representing the Buddha include his footprint, a throne, a blazing column and a trident (see p. 466). Such aniconic representations of the Buddha persisted until about the first century CE (about six centuries after the time of the Buddha). At this time, Mahayana Buddhism developed, with its concept of the Buddha as a redeemer figure worthy of veneration in his own right. It is only then that iconic representations of the Buddha began to appear.

Judaism and Islam are two religions which have generally remained aniconic in their sacred art.[13] This may be connected with the fact that the orthodox form of both religions is legalism rather than ritualism. The rigorous monotheism enjoined by the orthodoxy has prohibited the development of any iconic art, at least in the synagogue or mosque; any images are considered incipient idolatry.

Baha'i places of worship, too, are likely to remain aniconic in view of a specific injunction in the sacred text. Much of the art found in Baha'i homes is also aniconic, mainly religious symbols and calligraphy. This may just be because the Baha'i Faith is in an early stage of its development. The basis of a move towards iconic art exists, however, in the photographs and paintings of 'Abdu'l-Baha, the son of the founder of the Baha'i Faith, which are to be found in many Baha'i homes.

There are problems in reconstructing the early history of Christian religious art, as very little has survived. The early Christian Churches appear to have been strongly against all pictorial representations, which they associated with pagan idolatry. No doubt they were also influenced by the Judaic roots of Christianity. The earliest Christian art is therefore aniconic. Christ is represented by symbols such as the fish, the Greek letters *alpha* and *omega*, a lamb, an anchor, and later the *chi-ro* symbol (these two Greek letters being the first two letters of Christ's name). Most historians now agree that the absence of pictorial representation was not because of fear of persecution, as was originally thought. At some time during the second or third century CE, however, this attitude began to break down and images of Christ have been found in the Christian art surviving from this period. It was at about the time of the decree of Constantine in 312 CE giving official recognition to Christianity that there was a proliferation of iconic art in Christianity.

Iconic art can be placed somewhere between aniconic art and representational art. Despite their less abstract form, iconic forms of art are

RHYTHM AND CADENCE IN TRADITIONAL ART: These two pictures, the first Celtic engravings on a tumulus and the second a thirteenth-century Madonna and child by Cimabue (in the Louvre), show the same pattern. 'Everything must come together to give birth in the spectator's mind to the idea of eternity through the movement of the circumference, in the authority and by the power of the cadences and, finally, of the rhythm, which is one, absolute, and expressed by the curves of the circle, of the sphere. So we achieve the unchanging by repetition of the same, measured number. The curve has this prerogative, that it is at once the most mobile and the most static of all figures.' (Gleizes, *Religion and Art*; these drawings were prepared by Robert Pouyard for Gleizes.)

---

still to a large extent symbolic, in that they take us beyond themselves to the truth that they represent. That truth being beyond human understanding, traditional artists are content merely to allude to it simply. They are not concerned with making the icon seem lifelike. Indeed, to do so would distract from the purpose of the work of art. Iconography is based upon a sense of order in the universe, the authority of tradition and the hierarchy of the established cosmology. In Christianity, such art is to be found not just in the icons of the Eastern Orthodox Church but also in the painting, sculpture, architecture, calligraphy and manuscript illumination of areas as diverse as Britain and Syria.

There is something of a parallel to be drawn here between a traditional work of sacred art, such as an icon, and a ritual such as the Christian Eucharist or the Muslim pilgrimage (Hajj). The Eucharist is a ritual re-enactment of Christ's Last Supper and the Hajj re-enacts certain events from the lives of Abraham and Hagar (see p. 280–1) but no-one thinks of these as historical re-enactments; no one is concerned to have the setting and the scene correct from the viewpoint of historical realism. That would be missing the point. The purpose of the ritual of the Eucharist is not to

ANICONIC IMAGE OF THE BUDDHA: Here the Buddha is represented by a throne upon which there is a pillar with flames emerging from the side. In place of the head is the *chakra* (wheel, also symbolizing the sun), and at the base are the foot-marks (*paduka*). On either side are followers in attitudes of worship. Amaravati, third century CE.

ICONIC IMAGE OF THE BUDDHA: This is a figure cut in stone of the Buddha seated under the Bodhi tree with his right hand in the *Abhaya mudra* (gesture of fearlessness), which he adopted immediately after his enlightenment. It is in the Gandhara style of north-west India (second–third century CE) and the Greek influence can be seen in the figure on the left.

MODERN REPRESENTATIONAL ART: This picture shows the birth of the Buddha.

ANICONIC IMAGE OF CHRIST: The symbol of Christ in early Christianity was the fish, not only because of the implication of spiritual food but also because the Greek word for fish, *ichthyos*, spelled the initial letters of the statement: Jesus Christ, Son of God, Saviour. This mosaic also refers to the parable of the loaves and fishes.

ICONIC IMAGE OF CHRIST: The crucifixion, a Greek orthodox icon from Karanlik, an eleventh-century church cut into the rock face in Göreme, central Turkey.

REPRESENTATIONAL IMAGE OF CHRIST: A Renaissance depiction of the entombment of Christ (c.1507), showing naturalism and intense emotion. Painting by Raphael (1483–1520).

recreate the actions of Christ and the disciples correctly from an empirical, historical viewpoint but rather to evoke the spiritual reality of that event. Similarly, the icon is concerned not with a historically correct representation of Christ or Mary or any other sacred figure but with an evocation of the spiritual reality. Artists in the iconic tradition are concerned to arrange the images in their work in a way that leads the mind along a path of contemplation.

The Move From Iconic to Representational Art

We noted above that art and religion are carrying out much the same sort of activities, they are both engaged in building up the symbolic and conceptual universes of their society. While that universe remains unitary and unfragmented, the two can do no other than to work side by side and aniconic or iconic forms of art predominate. This integration of religion and the arts in society began to break down in Christian Europe with the Renaissance. Starting as early as the eleventh and twelfth centuries and developing inexorably down to the present day, a new secular form of consciousness arose. We may speculate that the religious structure of medieval Christianity had, by the twelfth century, become too ossified and rigid. It was no longer capable of moving forward with art to explore new ground. A parting of the two became inevitable, as art broadened its sweep to include ever more secular, materialistic perspectives.

For a time, the two Western perspectives on art stood side by side: religious art, based on the relativity of the sensible world and the primacy of the spiritual, and the new secular, humanist, representational art, based on the absoluteness of the sensible world. Then, following the Renaissance, the first gave way before the second. Paradoxically, despite its name, it is the latter, humanist art, which creates a universe of sensations in which humanity shrinks in significance. Even though such art frequently depicts the human form, it is the animal, sensuous aspect of the human form that is emphasized, thus putting humanity on a par with the rest of the natural world. In iconic religious art, on the other hand, the human being occupies a central position as the apex of God's creation. The religious painters of the medieval period doubted the possibility of knowledge through the work of the senses alone. They tried to give their work eternal value through resonance and rhythm. Their aim was to provide a support for contemplation.[14] Artists after the Renaissance believed that knowledge could best be acquired through the senses. They tried in their work to hold up a mirror to the world, becoming concerned principally with space and spectacle, and to create the illusion of three dimensions from the surface on which they were working. Even when the subject of the work has a religious theme, the emphasis is on the sensual and material, on emotion and passion, rather than focusing on the spiritual and acting as a basis for contemplation:

> Christian art, for example, begins with the representation of the deity by abstract symbols, which may be geometrical, vegetable or theriomorphic [in animal form], and are devoid of any sentimental appeal whatever. An anthropomorphic symbol follows, but this is still a form and not a figuration; not made as though to function biologically or as if to illustrate a text book of anatomy or of dramatic expression. Still later the form is sentimentalised; the features of the crucified are made to exhibit human suffering, the type is completely humanised, and where we began with the shape of humanity as an analogical representation of the idea of God, we end with the portrait of the artist's mistress posing as the Madonna and the representation of an all-too-human baby.[15]

No equivalent to the Renaissance occurred in the religious world of the East. The traditional artists of the East therefore resemble medieval European artists in their attitude and approach.[16] Even in Eastern religious art, however, we may detect some drift towards an increasing concern with emotion and sensation in modern times. We can see this in the increasing elaboration and sentimentality of much modern Hindu and Buddhist art, more concerned with image and sensation than with conveying truth.

Modern Hindu religious art: A picture depicting the young Krishna as a cowherd and demonstrating the elaborateness and sentimentality of much modern Hindu art.

Medieval European artists and artists from traditional cultures today express what they consider are eternal truths. They do not need, therefore, to identify themselves on their work. Their iconography is concerned with the use of the religious image, the contemplation of which takes us beyond the image to the truth that it represents. They are not concerned with making the image seem lifelike. Post-Renaissance Western artists, however, in rejecting the established tradition, mainly had the random vagaries of subjective individualism to guide them in their search for inwardness and feeling. They themselves became the only authority for their work. It was, therefore, fitting that they increasingly adopted the custom of signing their works.

Thus in Europe, religious art moved gradually but inexorably away from being primarily concerned with symbolizing eternal spiritual truths and supporting contemplation (aniconic and iconic art) towards a situation in which most art with religious themes was an attempt to represent the

THE IMAGE OF THE BUDDHA: 'If we are disturbed by what we call the "vacancy" of a Buddha's expression, ought we not to bear in mind that he is thought of as the Eye in the World, the impassible spectator of things as they really are, and that it would have been impertinent to have given him features moulded by human curiosity or passion? If it was an artistic canon that veins and bones should not be made apparent, can we blame the Indian artist as an artist for not displaying such a knowledge of anatomy as might have evoked our admiration? If we know from authoritative literary sources that the lotus on which the Buddha sits or stands is not a botanical specimen, but the universal ground of existence inflorescent in the waters of its indefinite possibilities, how inappropriate it would have been to represent him in the solid flesh precariously balanced on the surface of a real and fragile flower!" (Coomaraswamy, *Why Exhibit Works of Art?*, pp. 47–8). Giant statue of the Buddha in *Dhyani mudra* (meditation posture). Polonnaruwa, Sri Lanka, c.12th century CE.

image, the emotions and the sentiments of the physical world (representational art). Religious art moved from the realm of iconography to being centred on aesthetics, from form to figuration. The individual style of the artist changed from being a mere accident to being the principal focus of the critical appraisal of a work.

From this increasing concern with the sensible world came the Enlightenment and the Age of Science. These developments in turn speeded the retreat of religion. As angels and the supra-sensible world faded from our conceptual universe, so they also faded from art, which became increasingly concerned with the empirical world. But this concern with the sensible world has meant that the arts have moved away from their original function of reflecting the symbol structure of society and become concerned instead with portraying its physical form. Humanity today is thus starved of the world of symbols. We have a situation in our modern, secularized societies in which those who reject religion find themselves unable to express adequately their inner worlds, for lack of a suitable symbol structure. On the other hand, those who call themselves religious have access to a rich world of symbols but find it increasingly irrelevant to their ordinary lives.

Various attempts have been made to fill this gap at the heart of society. Since they have tried to fill the place of religion, it is not incorrect to call them pseudo-religions. One of the most influential has been psychoanalysis, of either the Freudian or Jungian variety. The images and symbols of Freud and, more particularly, the archetypes described by Jung have been reflected in the arts. The other two main contenders to fill the ideological gap at the heart of society, Marxism and nationalism, have also had their impact on the arts. None of these has, however, proved a satisfactory or lasting alternative. The art produced, particularly by the latter two, is superficial and tawdry, no matter how good the technical aspects of the execution may be.

But we may be in the process of turning full circle once again. Many of the conceptual bricks on which the materialistic secularism of the modern world is based are beginning to crumble. The traditional view that language is merely the form which articulates content has been challenged. It is now realized that our language predefines the way that we see the world and thus the content of what we say. The traditional narrative form of the novel creates the illusion of a world, the events and values of which are independently observable and which the narrator is merely relaying. The modern novel challenges this by making it clear that the novelist and reader are both involved in the creation of meaning that is dormant in the text and comes alive in the act of reading.[17] In the world of science, the empirical science of Descartes and Newton has given way to relativity and quantum theory, in which the hard facts and solid matter of classical physics melt into concepts that are more in the nature of metaphysics. And in art, cubism and other non-figurative modern art can be seen as a rejection of the illusory realism of Renaissance art, and, in the case of some artists, a return to cadence and rhythm, the expression of an internal and eternal reality.[18]

Modern movement back to iconic art: This statue of Madonna and Child by Henry Moore shows some indications of a movement away from representational art and a return to traditional iconic art, concerned with symmetry and rhythm, rather than figuration and naturalistic representation. St Matthew's Church, Northampton.

Further Reading

On the identity of function of religion and art see Martland, *Religion as Art*. On the religious attitude to art, see Gleizes, *Art et Religion*; Burckhardt, *Sacred Art in East and West*, and Coomaraswamy, *Elements of Buddhist Iconography* and *Why Exhibit Works of Art?* See also Craige, *Literary Relativity*; LeShan and Morgenau, *Einstein's Space and Van Gogh's Sky*; A.L. Moore, *Iconography of Religions*, and Hinnells, 'Religion and the Arts'.

RELIGIOUS ARCHITECTURE: The Sikh Golden Temple at Amritsar, India, the holiest place of Sikhism. Surrounding the temple is the Amrita Saras (pool of immortality) in which Sikhs bathe to be ritually purified.

Sri Mariamman Temple, a Hindu temple built in 1843, Singapore

This nineteenth-century Sephardic synagogue in Florence is based on the design of Hagia Sophia, Istanbul, and also shows influences of the Moorish style of architecture.

Shrine of Imam ʻAli, Najaf, Iraq. This golden-domed building is the shrine of the first Shiʻi Imam, ʻAli, who is also considered to be the fourth caliph by Sunni Muslims.

Basilica of the Annunciation, Nazareth. This modern church contains the traditional location where the angel announced to Mary that she was to be the mother of Jesus and also the traditional site of Joseph's carpentry shop. It was built by the Roman Catholic Church and completed in 1965. It is maintained by the Franciscan Order.

Mahabodhi Temple at Sarnath, India, a modern Buddhist temple. It is located on the traditional site of the Buddha's first sermon after his enlightenment.

Baha'i House of Worship, New Delhi. This temple is in the form of a lotus flower, the symbol of the manifestation of the Divine in Indian religion.

19

Religion in the Modern World

This chapter examines some of the impact that modernity has had upon the religious world. This includes both the challenges that the modern world presents to religion and the ways that religion has responded to them. I shall briefly survey the developments undergone in the twentieth century by each of the main religions that this books has concentrated on, finally, looking at a few topics such as new religious movements, religious freedom, and religion and the media. Several topics that particularly concern religion in the modern world are dealt with in other chapters. These include fundamentalism (see chapter 14), feminism and religion (see chapter 17), religion and the environment (see chapter 13, pp. 352–61), and religion and modern developments in art (see chapter 18, pp. 468–71).

One of the most important insights into the study of religion has been provided by the work of Wilfred Cantwell Smith. What we now call the religions of the world were, Smith has sought to show, not always seen thus. The enterprise that the present book is engaged upon, understanding religion, would itself have been difficult to conceive of in the pre-modern era. In the pre-modern world, religion was not a separate part of life that could be analysed as an entity. Rather, it was integral to living; it was the way that people saw the world. Since what we now call the religious view of the world was the way that people saw the world, it was, in a sense, invisible, part of the basic assumptions that people made about life and the world about them. These assumptions were so basic that they were not a subject for discussion, they were accepted as 'given', forming an inherent and seamless part of people's reality. What the modern world has done is to separate this part of human life and call it religion.[1]

In a traditional society, there is usually no word for religion in its modern sense since all that can be seen from inside such a viewpoint is the total structure. Words such as 'piety' and 'ritual' exist but the correlate of the modern concept of religion does not exist since it cannot be 'seen' as a separate entity (see p. 25). The use of the word 'religion' itself, in its sense of differentiating the different religions of the world, is a new usage. In earlier times its meaning was closer to the present use of the word 'piety'.[2] We may follow the history of the word 'religion' further. In post-Renaissance Europe, and particularly at the Enlightenment, 'religion' evolved from its previous sense to become 'the religion'. It thus became identified as a separate reified entity. It was still seen, however, as the norm for society, the basis for people's ethics and values of the people.

In the modern world there has been a melting away of this role for religion as a stable and solid basis for society. What was previously 'the religion' has become 'a religion'. Each religion is now seen as one of a number of competing religions, and even these must struggle for people's loyalty with a large number of modern ideologies and worldviews.

This process of 'reification' (making something into an object that can be observed) has the great advantage of helping us to gain a greater understanding of the world. It also has disadvantages, however, in that artificially separating something that is inherently integral to human life leads to a distortion. The way that people saw the world has now become the way people see the world on Sundays, or in the mosque, or in the Buddhist temple. The rest of the time people see the world from a scientific viewpoint, a materialistic viewpoint, a Marxist viewpoint, a nationalistic viewpoint, and so on. Religion has lost its claim to be the exclusive viewpoint from which people see the world.

We may trace the beginnings of this process to Renaissance Europe. Religion, in the form of the Roman Catholic Church, had nailed its colours to the mast of the traditional view of the world. But then scientists and artists began to demonstrate new ways of seeing the world. Galileo, for example, looked into his telescope and saw a cosmos that was different to the traditional one. At first, the Church's opposition to these new views did not have too deleterious an effect on the position of religion. But the crack that had been created in the overall dominance of the traditional worldview was to widen ever further over the years. Once the possibility was raised of worldviews other than the traditional/religious one, an increasing number of people began to examine and adopt them. At the same time, the traditional/religious worldview could only be examined once there were other viewpoints from which to examine it. This was something that had not been feasible previously.

As time went by, the divergence between the traditional worldview of religion and the contemporary worldview became ever greater. The more that this occurred, the more irrelevant religion became to most people. In such a situation, society may not dispense with religion altogether. Religion may continue to perform a symbolic and ceremonial role but it gradually ceases to affect the way that people think and act.

Social Challenges to Religions

The modern world has thrown up several challenges to religion. These, initially at least, weakened the position of religion, as there seemed to be no adequate response from the religious world.

Religious Pluralism

In a home in Britain, a shrine set up with lights for the Hindu festival of Divali

One of the most uncomfortable features of modernity for religions has been caused by the unprecedented intermingling of peoples in the last hundred years. This has resulted in many societies becoming to a large extent multi-ethnic and multi-religious. Previously, British people, for example, had only a theoretical knowledge that there were such people as Hindus and Muslims. Now they have the concrete fact of Hindus and Muslims living next door, of mosques and Hindu temples in their neighbourhoods.

The fact of a multi-religious society has a number of consequences. Many religions have always advanced claims of religious superiority or exclusiveness. When there was minimal contact with other religions and cultures, it was possible to belittle other religions and assert the superiority of one's own. Distance, language difficulties and cultural divergences made meaningful comparisons between one's own religion and others almost impossible. But these obstacles become less problematic with greater contact. Hick has described how he found individuals of great piety and of high moral standards in his contacts with Muslim, Hindu and Sikh groups in Birmingham. It was this that led him away from his Christ-centred theology into a new framework that would allow for truth in these other religions.[3] Many others have had similar experiences.

This problem has affected the Western religions more acutely because of their tendency to exclusivism. The Eastern religions have better inbuilt mechanisms for coping. Hinduism has no problem incorporating a new god such as Jesus into its already extensive pantheon. In some parts of India, Hindus form a large proportion of the crowds that commemorate the martyrdom of the Imam Husayn, a Shi'i Muslim commemoration. They manage to incorporate the martyrdom commemorations quite easily into the year's religious calendar without feeling that they are being disloyal to Hinduism.

Secularization

The phenomenon of secularization may be defined as the 'process whereby religious thinking, practice and institutions lose social significance'.[4] Where people once relied on religion to guide personal and social life, they now rely on science, education and their own personal tastes and ambitions.

There are a number of different ways of looking at this phenomenon.

1. Decline of popular involvement in institutionalized religion. This can be seen in the decline in church attendance, with fewer marriages, baptisms and funerals being performed under religious auspices throughout Europe during the twentieth century.
2. The loss of the prestige of religious institutions and symbols. There has been a loss in the influence that religious institutions have over public policy and a similar loss in the personal prestige of the religious professional. This may be partly responsible for the difficulty that many religions have in recruiting religious professionals.
3. The separation of society from the religious world, so that religion becomes a purely personal matter. Some have discerned a historical process which begins by contesting the public role of religion; it then substitutes other forms of authority for the authority of religion; finally it relegates religion to the private sphere of human existence.
4. The 'desacralization' of the world. As science increases our understanding of humanity and of the world, the area of 'mystery' and the supernatural decrease. This is one reason for the decline in the popularity and impact of religious beliefs.
5. Religious groups themselves become increasingly concerned with the things of this world rather than the spiritual world. The goals of religious institutions become indistinguishable from those of the rest of society. Some religious groups have begun to participate in the competitiveness of free-market capitalism. They compete, for example, with secular institutions in recreational, educational and social activities. They have made the religion that they offer into a commodity that they market.[5]

COMMERCIALISM IN RELIGION: A religious supermarket in Singapore, selling Chinese religious goods.

As discussed above, the modern world has divorced itself from an exclusive attachment to a religious worldview and now presents a variety of worldviews, from which the individual may choose. This very fact is a deeply disturbing phenomenon for the classical religious mind. Even the position that the religious worldview is superior to other worldviews is not sufficient for the classical religious worldview – for its basic assumption was that it was the only valid viewpoint. It acknowledged that other viewpoints existed but these were delusory, the work of the Devil.

The first blow to religion came through its increasing loss of social control. In the traditional structure of Hindu, Muslim or even medieval Christian society, religion controlled all aspects of life. Religious institutions were the main pathway for acquiring an education, for obtaining medical treatment, and for the poor to obtain relief. Even such matters as the functioning of craft guilds was to some extent under religious control. Gradually, however, a functional differentiation of society occurred, leading to the increasing autonomy of its different parts. In the last hundred years, in most countries, the modern secular state or other secular institutions have taken over from the religious establishment control of such areas as medicine, education and welfare provisions for the poor.

The second blow to the religious perspective came with the increasing importance given to individualism in the modern world. Previously the individual was willing to allow the religious perspective to predominate over his or her individual views. Today, there is an increasing emphasis on the individual's own point of view. This leads to a loss of the authority of the central institutions of the religion. As a corollary to this individualism came a belief in the beneficial effects of self-interest as the guiding principle of human action, a development that contradicts the teachings of most of the established religions.

The individualism that is characteristic of modern life in the West is reflected in the uncommitted, à la carte approach to spirituality that has become very common. It is typified by individuals who flit from religious group to religious group, continually on the religious quest and never arriving at their goal. Very often such individuals do not join any religious group but attend meetings, read books and search through the Internet, adopting a pot-pourri of religious ideas on their way. This approach to spirituality is almost the exact opposite of the path advocated by traditional religion. According to the latter, spiritual advancement demands discipline, commitment and obedience (both to Holy Law and usually to religious institutions). Thus one has the paradox of modern eclectic spiritual individualists on the one hand reading enthusiastically the works of the great medieval mystics and on the other hand rejecting the spiritual discipline and approach that made the production of such works possible.

In these ways, secular values and agents have come to replace religious ones at the core of society. Whereas previously, norms were established because they were the will of God, social norms are now validated by an appeal to science, the welfare of the people, democratic approval or the freedom of the individual. At work, at school and at leisure, the last hundred years has seen the gradual edging out of religious forms and their replacement by secular forms. This process of secularization has been gradual. In some countries it is possible to name a particular event which either initiated the process or gave it great impetus. In France, it was the French Revolution that led to the overthrow of Church structures and the raising of rationalism to the status of a religion. In Britain, it was perhaps the Glorious Revolution of 1689, leading to the overthrow of the concept of a role for the Divine in human affairs and the establishment of democracy as the highest principle in government. However, in most countries no precise date can be given.

Secularization has gradually permeated the Christian world. It led to the situation in which, by the nineteenth century, Christianity had ceased to have much real influence on the social and political life of Europe. The form was maintained, in that political leaders usually made a great show of attending religious ceremonies and were often personally pious. Religion no longer had a role, however, in the shaping of political and social policy. Other considerations and other secular ideologies had taken over. Following the loss of social and political influence, religion became increasingly irrelevant to the lives of ordinary people also.

Alternative Ideologies

By the end of the nineteenth century, a new set of ideologies, nationalism, socialism and racism, had taken over the position of religion in Europe.[6] This had occurred both formally at the political level and, to a large extent, also in the hearts and minds of Europeans. The secularization of society has meant that secular forms have taken over where once the religious form would have been natural. In the drive towards nationalism, loyalty to the nation-state has replaced loyalty to the central authority of the religion; the national anthem has replaced the hymn; a speech from a politician has replaced the sermon; the nationalist slogan has replaced the creed; and the state or secular charity has replaced the charitable role of religious institutions. Similarly, in communism, the works of Marx replace the scripture; the class struggle replaces the religious struggle against evil; and the final collapse of capitalism and the triumph of communism is the millennial promise.[7]

In summary, a traditional society is one in which religion is an integral part of the authority and plausibility structure of the society. As such, religion can control the content and form of much of the artistic and literary expression of the society; not necessarily in a coercive sense, but in the sense of defining what appears natural and plausible to the society as a whole. What modernity has done is to separate the various aspects of society into different entities. As religion was seen to lose the intellectual argument with science and rationality, so it was progressively driven away from the centre ground that it had occupied as an integral part of the authority structure. It became identified as a separate 'reified' entity. This fissioning tendency in modernity split off art and literature, which had previously been the servants of the religious worldview (see pp. 468–71). These now became separate entities, each struggling to find a new basis for its expression.

The gap left at the centre of society, its ideology, the source for societal values, the final arbiter of right and wrong, was filled by various secular ideologies such as nationalism, communism and racism. These have each tried to re-establish the old order wherein society was again an integrated whole, focused on the central ideology; in which art and literature again submitted to the demands of the centre of society. However, one by one, during the last hundred years, these substitute religions ('pseudo-religions', 'quasi-religions') have failed dramatically and destructively. During the first two decades of the twentieth century, nationalism brought destruction to Europe in the form of a devastating world war; in the next two decades, racism produced the horrors of the Nazi concentration camps; while in the last decades of the twentieth century, we have witnessed communism admit to its inability to bring contentment or prosperity to its peoples. One by one, each of these ideologies has shown itself to be incapable of substituting for the position once occupied by religion. This, at least partially, accounts for the resurgence of religious fundamentalism in the last decade.

The Intellectual Challenge to Religion

The social and political ideologies mentioned here are not the only challenges that religion has faced in the last hundred years – although in terms of the numbers affected they are the main ones. A number of alternatives to religion have also presented in the intellectual sphere, trying to give meaning to human life and to satisfy humanity's need for an understanding of the transcendent order of reality. Although these have affected comparatively few people, they are nevertheless important.

Among the most important of these alternative sources of meaning has been a turning to our inner world. The field of psychology, in particular, has produced several different ways of looking at the inner world of human beings and giving it meaning. Although some have attempted to incorporate the ideas of Jung, in particular, into a religious perspective, these psychological explanations remain an alternative to religion as ways of giving meaning to human experiences and thoughts. Some of the ideas of Jung and Freud are briefly examined in chapter 3.

The exploration of our inner world has gone even further, in experiments with drug mysticism and other techniques that are claimed to 'increase our inner awareness' and help us to 'find ourselves'. Often the techniques involve forms of meditation derived from Hinduism or Buddhism. The connection with the Eastern religions is, however, somewhat artificial, in that meditation has been extracted from its setting within an overall religious framework. In the hands of many of those who teach it in the West, it is used mechanistically, to create an effect. An experience is produced that may be exciting and even exhilarating but, lacking its religious framework, has little lasting effect. It has become, in effect, a form of escapism.

Some regard the philosophical outlook of existentialism as the antithesis of religion. It sees the religious search for the ultimate meaning

Søren Kierkegaard (1813–55), existentialist religious philosophy

and the essential nature of human beings as illusory. Human beings exist and each human being has to grapple with such human predicaments as alienation, death, anxiety, suffering, and responsibility. There is no overall plan or pattern that they should follow. Humans impose their own meaning and order upon the universe. The way of life that they lead depends on the choices that they make. Although the theoretical outline of existentialism may make it appear a somewhat bleak, individualistic philosophy, this has not prevented some of its followers such as Jean-Paul Sartre from espousing social causes, or like Søren Kierkegaard even evolving the philosophy in a religious direction.

At the intellectual level, religion has been constantly forced onto the retreat. Religion considers that it has access to an absolute source of authority and knowledge. Therefore, it claims to be able to give absolute answers to those eternal questions that puzzle human beings: Why are we in this world? What happens after death? In turn, religion has, in the past, claimed and been given the right to set the norms and values of society. But this impressive structure, which even a century ago seemed eternal and immutable, has all but melted away. The religious foundations of values and ethics are now seen as being set in the context of the flux of history, just another viewpoint competing with a myriad other worldviews, some religious, some secular. The modern world has set its face intellectually against universal explanations and claims – although these still appear to have great emotional appeal.

At the Renaissance, the Church opposed Galileo over astronomy; in the nineteenth century, it was popularly seen to be opposed to evolutionary theory; on both occasions, it lost the intellectual battle. Currently, the greatest intellectual challenge that religion faces is relativistic or post-modernist thought. Relativism has become one of the main currents of thought in the last hundred years. It is, however, deeply disquieting to religion, in the same way that astronomical findings and evolutionary thought once were. Relativistic thought strikes at the very roots of the absolute claims and explanations of religion. It maintains that human knowledge can never be absolute, but is always relative to social and individual factors. Post-modernism maintains that reality itself is a human construct: all that we are capable of doing is to explore the relationships within that construct; there is no absolute reality that can be known outside it. This is the basis of the profound challenge that relativism and post-modernism place before the claims of religion; a challenge to which religion, is only just beginning to respond.

The process of religious retreat may be summarized as having taken place in two stages.[8] The first was the conflict between religion and modern, scientific thought. Modernism was the worldview that dominated Western thinking from the time of the Enlightenment in the seventeenth century into the twentieth century. The main source of conflict here is the insistence of the scientific approach on regarding reality as being totally explicable from within this physical world. In other words, the scientific viewpoint denies a need to postulate a transcendent dimension to reality. The social sciences, using the scientific approach, see every human phenomenon, including religion, as being the result of the psychological or cultural environment from which it arises. All religious phenomena can then be fitted into a pattern, a network of psychological, social and economic forces. Thus they emerge from what has gone before and in turn become the substrate for what comes after. This schema does not allow for the intervention of the Divine in human affairs.

The traditional religious viewpoint saw the world as an ontological hierarchy with God (or the Absolute Reality) at the top and the physical world (or evil spirits) at the bottom. The existence of the hierarchy also gave rise to values. That which was associated with a higher level of the hierarchy had greater value than that which was associated with a lower level. People looked to their scriptures to find the proper ordering of their reality and the source of their values. As a result of the advances brought about by science, people began to believe that science's description of reality was more accurate and meaningful than that of religion. The scientific viewpoint denies the existence of ontological hierarchies, because they are not amenable to the scientific method. If we call this ontological hierarchy, the vertical dimension of human existence, then science is only able to deal with the horizontal dimension – observable, preferably quantifiable, entities. Science is therefore also unable to deal with such concepts as value, quality, and purpose, which are all connected with the vertical dimension. Once religion was displaced as the arbiter of reality by science, the vertical dimension disappeared from intellectual consideration.

The second stage in the intellectual retreat of religion came as a result of relativistic or post-modernist thought, which had its beginnings in the early decades of the twentieth century. While modernist, scientific thought rejected the traditional religious worldview and set up an alternative scientific worldview, post-modernist thinking rejects worldviews altogether, seeing them as political instruments. Once one worldview is accepted as authoritative, other worldviews are marginalized, together with those who subscribe to them. The ontological hierarchy described in the preceding paragraphs could, for example, be analysed as the creation of a male-dominated patriarchal world. The patriarchy persuades people of the rightness of the hierarchical social order by demonstrating that it is a reflection of the transcendent order of reality. This 'deconstruction' of what we consider to be reality is the main methodology of the post-modernist. It is important to note that it is not accompanied by the creation of an alternative construct, since that would also then need to be 'deconstructed'. On the one hand, post-modernism reflects the current pluralist world situation, in which numerous different worldviews are in daily contact, contrast and conflict with one another. On the other, it presents the uncomfortable prospect of a world devoid of any substantial reality that can be grasped and agreed upon by all: instead there are only an infinite number of viewpoints, none of which can claim any authority and none of which describe reality in anything but a provisional way.

Religion has been on the defensive against the advances of modernist and post-modernist thinking over the past two hundred years in the West. This causes problems for religion that go beyond the intellectual argument. Most people in the West today may know little or nothing of scientific methodology or the intellectual arguments for relativistic thought. Nevertheless, the general intellectual atmosphere of relativism and antagonism to concepts of a transcendent reality has permeated their consciousness and influences their thinking. Thus the absolutist religious worldview comes to stand out as incongruous with the worldview of the majority. It is this lack of congruence with the worldview of the majority that is perhaps, as much as anything, responsible for the decline in the influence of religion.

Something that is incongruent with one's worldview may not be rejected completely. Indeed, religion may be maintained for all sorts of reasons, such as nostalgia or social prestige. Society may keep it for ceremonial and symbolic purposes. Births, marriages and deaths may continue to be commemorated by a religious ceremony by many who otherwise have no religious contact. This is, however, more an expression of superstition than of religiosity. Religion ceases, in such circumstances, to be relevant to one's everyday thought processes; it ceases to be taken into account in the life decisions of the individual or the political decisions of a government.

Towards the middle of the twentieth century, the outlook seemed bleak for religion. Many scientists and sociologists were prepared to foretell its demise, either over a few generations or over the next few centuries. In a book published as recently as 1966, an anthropologist was able to say:

> the evolutionary future of religion is extinction. Belief in supernatural beings and in supernatural forces that affect nature without obeying nature's laws will erode and become only an interesting historical memory . . . As a cultural trait, belief in supernatural powers is doomed to die out, all over the world, as a result of the increasing adequacy and diffusion of scientific knowledge . . . the process is inevitable.[9]

Religion has, however, proved remarkably adaptable and resilient. Although science and technology have continued to advance and conquer new fields, religion has re-emerged as a potent force in human affairs. Although science has been successful in solving material problems, it has failed to find solutions to the social and individual problems of human beings. Science provides no answer or explanation to the pressing questions and emotions of human existence such as death, love, purpose, and beauty. It has failed to find solutions to the social problems of our cities and rural areas. Indeed, it is increasing being blamed for creating the mechanistic lifestyle that numbs and enervates human beings and the pollution that threatens all. Religion, for its part, has adapted and emerged in new more vital forms to meet the challenge of modernity.

Religious Adaptations to the Modern World

Although I have portrayed religion as having been constantly on the retreat, socially and intellectually, in modern times, that is not the end of the story. For modern human beings have paid a heavy price for the individual freedom of modernity. Modern societies can be bleak and lonely places; isolation and alienation exist to a degree and an extent that do not occur in traditional societies.[10] The warmth and acceptance that a religious community provides can be a powerful magnet for those suffering from the alienation of modernity. Therefore, some have argued that the increasing secularization of modern society is, paradoxically, the very cause of a resurgence in religion. In the West, it is not the traditional orthodoxies that have benefited most from this resurgence, however, but fundamentalist groups and new religious movements. These can provide an intensity of emotional and communal life that is missing in modern society (see p. 512).

In response to attacks, religion has sought, in various ways, to preserve its position. Religions and cultures have rich resources upon which to draw in defending themselves against the onslaught of modernity, and they have made a number of responses or adaptations. These include the less successful adaptations that the religious orthodoxies have made to modernity and the alternative pathways of fundamentalism and the new religious movements.

Retreat into Fundamentalism

One adaptation to modernity is the retreat into fundamentalism (see chapter 14). Faced with the confusion and uncertainty of the modern world, the believer is trying to recreate traditional society, with its certainties and stability. Unfortunately, it is not totally possible to do this. Once the genie is out of the bottle, getting it back in again is difficult. Once people have seen that alternative worldviews exist, every bit as good as their own, to go back to the previous situation where the traditional religious worldview was the only plausible and possible view is very difficult. To do this, either people must somehow isolate themselves from the outside world (as in pietist communities) or they must drown out the clamour of competing worldviews by being very vocal and assertive themselves.[11] The goal of a return to the past is a useful but illusory fiction. What we are, in fact, seeing in the fundamentalist reaction is an adjustment

a

b

c

MISSION AND POLEMIC: Most religions are now active in the field of trying to convert others to their faith. a) Hasidic Jews in Safad, Israel, try to convert other Jews to their viewpoint. b) The Salvation Army takes its missionary effort into Eastern Europe. Kiev, Ukraine, June 1993. c) A Baha'i Exhibition in a library in Bedford, England.

to the realities of the present, presented and justified as a purification and return to a mythological, ideal past (see pp. 323–4 and 380–2).

Symbolization

Another way of dealing with modernity is to reinterpret traditional religious views, particularly those beliefs that are most at variance with the modern world. The commonest way of doing this is to emphasize the symbolic aspect of these discordant doctrines and rituals.

One of the central tenets of Islam is the doctrine of jihad, holy war. The traditional Islamic position is that jihad is incumbent on Muslims. They must fight non-believers until they submit and agree to pay the *jizya* (poll tax, payable by 'People of the Book'; see p. 348). Today, this would effectively mean that the Islamic world would have to be perpetually in a state of war against its non-Muslim neighbours: Christian Europe, Hindu India and non-Muslim Africa. No Muslim state has seriously tried to achieve such a state of affairs since the seventeenth century, when the Ottoman Empire used to launch campaigns against Christian Europe every summer. In the modern world, it would be almost inconceivable for a Muslim state to try to renew this policy, and yet it is a central tenet of Islam. One way in which Muslims have tried to come to terms with this state of affairs is to raise jihad to the ethical level. There is one statement by Muhammad which says that the greater jihad is against the self. Now this is a minor Tradition, not found in the *Qur'an* nor in most of the main collections of Traditions.[12] However, it provides a valuable exit route and modern Muslims have seized upon it as a way of reinterpreting the Qur'anic injunction in a symbolic way. In this way, they can move it away from the obvious sense of physical fighting towards an ethical sense of the struggle against the lower nature of human beings.

A parallel development is what has been called the 'theological non-realism' of writers such as Don Cuppitt. Cuppitt maintains that the true significance of God is as a symbol for everything that being a spiritual and moral being entails. The question of whether the concept of God also refers to an existent metaphysical entity separate from human beings is, Cuppitt maintains, irrelevant and of no religious interest today.

> What then is God? God is a unifying symbol that eloquently personifies and represents to us everything that spirituality requires of us. The requirement is the will of God, the divine attributes represent to us various aspects of the spiritual life, and God's nature as spirit represents the goal we are to attain . . . God is the religious concern reified.[13]

The Translation of Religion into Parallel Secular Categories

A third strategy for adapting religion to modernity is to de-emphasize those aspects of religion that must be accepted on faith. Those parts of religion that deal with the transcendent are played down and religion is equated with other categories that are more acceptable to modernity.

RELIGION AS MORALITY AND ETHICS. This approach equates religion to a moral code for living. It can often find general acceptance in society, especially at a time when society's morals are perceived to be in decline. It is argued that with the loss of belief in religion, there is a loss of values and coherence in society. Without religion acting as a glue to keep society together, things begin to fall apart. Many who do not consider themselves religious have, nevertheless, a positive attitude towards religion because of its perceived support for moral order. They will, for example, send their children to religious classes for moral education, although they do not believe in the doctrinal matters taught there.

RELIGION AS PSYCHOTHERAPY. Many people see religion as a means of psychological support. They perceive its function as giving meaning to suffering and grief; it helps to create wholeness and psychic health in the individual.

RELIGION AS SOCIAL AND POLITICAL IDEOLOGY. Religion can be seen as the foundation of political and social ideologies. Those who incline towards socialism consider that the true spirit of religion is to be found in concern for the poor. This may involve helping them directly or struggling for social justice. Such groups include the Sarvodaya movement in India (see pp. 501–2) or the Fida'iyan in Iran (an Islamic Leftist group that was prominent in Iran during the Islamic Revolution). Similarly, others can see in Christ's concern for the poor a justification for 'liberation theology'. Those who incline to the right, on the other hand, see the Christian gospel as the basis for the ideals of capitalist society and, if they are from the United States, 'the American Way' of life.

LIBERATION THEOLOGY

The theology in question was born at an hour of guerilla warfare, at the heart of battles for the 'conscientization' of the masses in opposition to 'capitalist oppression' – battles waged by students and the bourgeoisie rather than by workers and peasants; battles of an 'intelligentsia'. These committed intellectuals were men of action on the pattern of Camilo Torres and Che Guevara, men of thought like Gustavo Gutierrez or Enrique Dussel. Many of them were priests. All of them had Latin America branded in their hearts and minds. They took the myth of liberation and provided it with a theology. Or perhaps one should say, they provided theology with a new life, one derived from the vigor of the liberation myth. (Ph.-I. André-Vincent, 'The "Theologies of Liberation"', in Schall, *Liberation Theology in Latin America*, pp. 191–2)

The Personalization of Religion

One way of dealing with the problem of modernity and religious pluralism is to withdraw from making any universal and social claims for religion, thus making it a purely personal affair. 'My religion satisfies my needs. It may not satisfy your needs or even anyone else's. All that matters to me is that it satisfies mine.' This then sets up a defensive wall against any possibility that one's religion can be shown to be intellectually faulty, illogical, or inferior to another's.

The Demythologization of Religion

This approach stems from the realization that much of the language of scripture is based on the mythological and cosmological assumptions of the times in which it was written. The discoveries of science have destroyed the classical cosmology and many of the old myths have gone into decline in parallel. Rudolf Bultmann tried to strip away the mythological cloak in which Christianity had been wrapped, to get back to the spiritual experience underlying it. For Bultmann, it made no difference whether historico-literary criticism showed that the resurrection of Christ did or did not occur physically in Palestine 2,000 years ago. The reality of the resurrection experience occurs in the heart of the believer today. Critics of such an approach have said that there seems little point in maintaining a belief in a transcendent God in this programme of demythologization for, after all, the concept of God is also a product of the mythological age. The ideas of Don Cuppitt (see p. 487) could also fit into this category.

Religious Sectarianism and Innovation

When people find that their society's standard religious orthodoxy is not filling their needs, a great pressure arises for new religious forms that will meet those needs. These new religious forms are called 'sects' if they split from the existing religious orthodoxy. If however they arise *de novo* or are imports from alien cultures (such as Hindu movements in the West), they are called 'cults'. Sects and cults are usually narrowly focused on specific religious needs in society. The attraction of these movements is often the sense of unity and belonging that they create for the individual, things that are lacking in modern society. (See 'New Religious Movements' below.)

These strategies may be superficially attractive, in that they appear to make religion relevant to the concerns of the modern world. However, several of them are, at a deeper level, in effect secularizing religion, emptying it of its transcendent and spiritual content and making it into a purely human activity.[14]

The Response of Religion in Traditional Societies

Thus far, we have mainly considered the impact of modernity on the West. The situation in the rest of the world is not very different. The last hundred years or so has seen traditional religious societies all over the world coming to face modernity. The arrival of the Western powers in most parts of the world during the nineteenth century brought with it severe problems for the religions of those places. The technological and political superiority of the West appeared to lay down an unanswerable challenge to the established religions of other parts of the world. Some tribal religions, such as those of Polynesia, all but disappeared under the missionary impact of Christianity. More established religions were put on the defensive, with many of their best-educated young people coming to despise their own religious culture. One can discern a general pattern of response, despite the differences among the religions. The various phases of this response can be denoted in the following ways (see also pp. 381–2).

1. *Modernization and Westernization*

The first reaction of a traditional religion to its encounter with the modern world is a sense of dismay that the modern world has advanced so far beyond the traditional world. This presents a dilemma to the religious mind. For the Middle-Eastern Muslim in the nineteenth century, this dilemma could be expressed thus: if the religion of Islam is the true religion of God, why has God allowed the Muslim nations to fall so far behind the Western, Christian nations? One partial solution to the dilemma appears to be a wholesale adoption of modernity so as to close the gap. It is, in particular, modern technology that is imported – this being something that does not inherently challenge the religious worldview.[15] But along with modern technology comes modern education, to enable people to use the technology. Thus, gradually, there arrive other modern concepts such as democracy and individual rights. These are much more challenging to traditional society, its structures and, ultimately, its religious foundations. The modernizers argue that all of these elements must be taken on board. They evolve a solution that says, in effect, that modern ideas such as

Religious interpretation and politics: During the Iranian Constitutional Revolution of 1903, one of the problems of the reformers was to justify the changes that they wished to make in terms of Islam and the *Qur'an*. This cartoon from a Persian magazine of the time shows a mullah delving into the *Qur'an* and finding such justifications.

democracy are not contrary to the native religion at all. Indeed, they reflect the finest traditions of the religion, but had been covered over in the course of centuries.

In the Islamic world, the nineteenth century saw several modernist thinkers who sought a way in which the Islamic world could come to terms with European dominance. Among the better-known of these are Sayyid Jamal al-Din 'al-Afghani', Khayr al-Din Pasha, Muhammad 'Abduh and Mirza Malkam Khan.[16] They argued that such ideas as democracy were enshrined in the *Qur'an* and the practices of the early Muslims. Similar Hindu modernist movements, the Brahmo Samaj and the Prartharma Samaj, incorporating elements of modern European thought, were founded in the nineteenth century.

The importance of these movements in various parts of the world faded, however, as it became clear that the adoption of Western values into these cultures was going to be very problematic. And in those cases where it was tried, there was little success in bridging the gap with Europe.

2. *Nationalism and Socialism*

The next phase in the development of the response of traditional societies to the challenge of modernity was a politicization and secularization of the problem. Religion was largely pushed to one side during the first half of the twentieth century while these societies experimented with various political solutions. Nationalism was the first ideology to gain widespread currency. There was a rise in nationalism across the whole of Asia and Africa in the first half of the twentieth century. In Turkey and Iran, secularization and reform movements developed under Ataturk and Reza Shah respectively. Under the Mandate arrangements after World War I, several Arab states, notably Iraq, Syria, Jordan and Lebanon were created and later came to independence. In Africa, India and South-East Asia, independence movements arose.

After World War II, nationalism's attraction gradually yielded before the rise of socialism and communism. Several of the most influential Arab states, led by Egypt under Nasser, turned to socialism, as did newly independent India. At the same time, communist forces overran Vietnam, Laos and Cambodia, in South-East Asia.

3. *The Fundamentalist Backlash*

As in the West, there has been a movement towards fundamentalism in many traditional societies. The secular ideologies of nationalism and communism have not resulted in any great improvement in these traditional societies and there has therefore been, in most of them, some degree of fundamentalist backlash against secularization. In some countries, such as Iran, India and Israel, it has either gained power or is very influential and a strong contender for power. Elsewhere, especially in the Muslim world, it forms a powerful and active opposition to the current government. The radical fundamentalists seek to find new answers in the texts of their scriptures that will provide an alternative to modernization and westernization. Alternatively, the traditionalist fundamentalists seek to return society to the traditions and customs of the past. (See chapter 14.)

Ecumenism and Interreligious Dialogue

One of the most important features of the last fifty years has been the increasing extent to which religions influence each other. One major step in this process was the Parliament of Religions, held in Chicago in 1893 as part of the Colombian Exposition. Here the Christian world stepped back from the nineteenth-century assumptions of the superiority of Christianity and Western culture and gave an opportunity to the representatives of the other major religious traditions of the world to present their viewpoints and contributions. The tenor of this conference was summed up in the opening address of Charles C. Bonney to the Parliament:

> We meet on the mountain height of absolute respect for the religious convictions of each other; and an earnest desire for a better knowledge of the consolations which other forms of faith than our own offer to their devotees. The very basis of our convocation is the idea that the representatives of each religion sincerely believe that it is the truest and the best of all; and that they will, therefore, hear with perfect candour and without fear the convictions of other sincere souls on the great questions of the immortal life.[17]

This process of dialogue and interaction among the religions of the world has continued up to the present. Many individuals have been influenced by the ideas of religions and cultures not their own. Mahatma Gandhi, for example, interpreted the Hindu doctrine of *ahimsa* as non-violence in the seeking of political change. This interpretation is thought to have been greatly influenced by his reading of the Christian pacifist works of Tolstoy. Gandhi, in turn, himself influenced many, including such figures as Reverend Martin Luther King in the Christian West, and the Buddhist A. J. Ariyaratna, whose Sarvodaya Sharmadana Movement has tried to develop the poorest villages in Sri Lanka. The Christian churches in India have gone a long way towards absorbing elements of their Hindu cultural milieu. Christian *sannyasin* (wandering ascetics) and ashrams are to be found.

Within each religion there have been efforts in the last hundred years to bring the different sects together in unity, for example, the attempts to unite the Anglican and Methodist Churches in Christianity. The work of the World Council of Churches in bringing most of the Christian churches in agreement on common positions and programmes of action has been

a

b

INTERRELIGIOUS DIALOGUE: a) Bishop (later Archbishop) Desmond Tutu visiting the Jade Buddha Temple of Shanghai and meeting the chief abbot, Zhen Chan. b) An interreligious women's meeting in Tonga featuring speakers from the Wesleyan, Mormon and Baha'i groups in the village of Holonga, Vava'u, 1997.

parallelled by such organizations as the Muslim World League and the Vishwa Hindu Parishad.

At local and national level it is increasingly common for religious leaders to come together at interreligious meetings and to co-operate over issues on which there is general agreement. Interreligious dialogue and local and national interfaith forums have multiplied and with them the number of projects carried out on an inter-faith basis. There is still a long way to go in such matters, but a start has certainly been made.

A Survey of Religions Today

In this section, I shall briefly survey the impact of the twentieth century on the religions that have been considered in this book.

Judaism

The nineteenth century and the first decades of the twentieth saw two opposing developments for the Jews of Europe and Russia. On the one hand, under the influence of Enlightenment thought, they were gaining greater freedoms than they had previously experienced. European Christians were starting to see Jews as individual human beings instead of as an alien mass. On the other hand, anti-Semitism was taking new, violent forms with the start of pogroms (organized massacres) in Russia. From 1881 onwards, there were recurrent episodes of persecution and killings. One consequence of this was that many Jews emigrated from Russia and Central and Eastern Europe to the United States, many of them fleeing death and persecution. As a result, the number of Jews in the United States increased from about 15,000 in 1840, to 1,500,00 in 1900 and 4,200,000 in 1928.

Among the debates that flourished among Jews in the first half of the twentieth century was the question of Zionism, the creation of a homeland for Jews. The first Zionist Congress was organised by Theodor Herzl in Basle in 1897. The turning point for Zionism was the Balfour Declaration of 1917, approving the principle of the establishment in Palestine of a 'national home for the Jewish people'. From that time on, much energy was directed towards establishing Jewish settlements in Palestine.

The two most important events of the twentieth century for Judaism were the extermination of an estimated 5–6 million Jews in Central and Eastern Europe by the Nazis during World War II and the creation of the State of Israel in 1948. The second was very much a consequence of the first, as the victors of the war were put under great pressure to find a home for large numbers of displaced Jews. The subsequent Arab–Israeli wars and conflict led to large numbers of Sephardic Jews from the Arab countries fleeing to Israel, while the fall of communism resulted in the immigration of many Russian Jews.

WHO IS A JEW?: One of the questions thrown up by the creation of the State of Israel is the question of who is a Jew? What is the position of the children of mixed marriages? What form of conversion to Judaism will be acceptable? This picture shows demonstrators outside the Israeli Knesset while this question was being debated. The placard reads: 'A Jew is one who professes Judaism'.

The establishment of Israel led to Jews around the world unifying in support of the new state, and many of them emigrating to it. The financial support of the worldwide Jewish community, as well as the ability of the Jewish lobby in the United States to rally the American government to provide financial and political support to Israel have been major factors in enabling the State of Israel to survive.

Today, the United States is the country with the largest Jewish population in the world, with some 7 million Jews. About 4 million Jews live in Israel. There are still some 2–3 million Jews in Russia. The total number of Jews in the world was estimated to be 17 million in 1985 and was predicted to increase to 20 million by 2000.

Christianity

Since the first elements of modernity arose in the Christian world, Christianity has been in contact with the challenges of the modern world more than any other religion. The

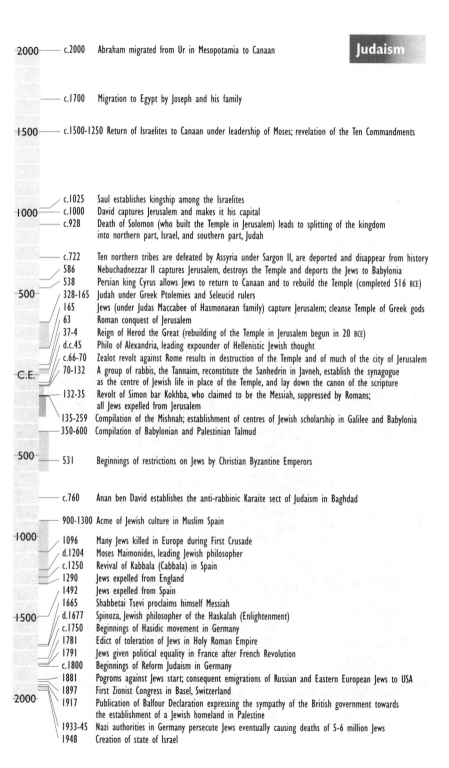

Judaism

Scale	Date	Event
2000	c.2000	Abraham migrated from Ur in Mesopotamia to Canaan
	c.1700	Migration to Egypt by Joseph and his family
1500	c.1500-1250	Return of Israelites to Canaan under leadership of Moses; revelation of the Ten Commandments
	c.1025	Saul establishes kingship among the Israelites
1000	c.1000	David captures Jerusalem and makes it his capital
	c.928	Death of Solomon (who built the Temple in Jerusalem) leads to splitting of the kingdom into northern part, Israel, and southern part, Judah
	c.722	Ten northern tribes are defeated by Assyria under Sargon II, are deported and disappear from history
	586	Nebuchadnezzar II captures Jerusalem, destroys the Temple and deports the Jews to Babylonia
	538	Persian king Cyrus allows Jews to return to Canaan and to rebuild the Temple (completed 516 BCE)
500	328-165	Judah under Greek Ptolemies and Seleucid rulers
	165	Jews (under Judas Maccabee of Hasmonaean family) capture Jerusalem; cleanse Temple of Greek gods
	63	Roman conquest of Jerusalem
	37-4	Reign of Herod the Great (rebuilding of the Temple in Jerusalem begun in 20 BCE)
	d.c.45	Philo of Alexandria, leading expounder of Hellenistic Jewish thought
	c.66-70	Zealot revolt against Rome results in destruction of the Temple and of much of the city of Jerusalem
C.E.	70-132	A group of rabbis, the Tannaim, reconstitute the Sanhedrin in Javneh, establish the synagogue as the centre of Jewish life in place of the Temple, and lay down the canon of the scripture
	132-35	Revolt of Simon bar Kokhba, who claimed to be the Messiah, suppressed by Romans; all Jews expelled from Jerusalem
	135-259	Compilation of the Mishnah; establishment of centres of Jewish scholarship in Galilee and Babylonia
	350-600	Compilation of Babylonian and Palestinian Talmud
500	531	Beginnings of restrictions on Jews by Christian Byzantine Emperors
	c.760	Anan ben David establishes the anti-rabbinic Karaite sect of Judaism in Baghdad
	900-1300	Acme of Jewish culture in Muslim Spain
1000	1096	Many Jews killed in Europe during First Crusade
	d.1204	Moses Maimonides, leading Jewish philosopher
	c.1250	Revival of Kabbala (Cabbala) in Spain
	1290	Jews expelled from England
	1492	Jews expelled from Spain
	1665	Shabbetai Tsevi proclaims himself Messiah
1500	d.1677	Spinoza, Jewish philosopher of the Haskalah (Enlightenment)
	c.1750	Beginnings of Hasidic movement in Germany
	1781	Edict of toleration of Jews in Holy Roman Empire
	1791	Jews given political equality in France after French Revolution
	c.1800	Beginnings of Reform Judaism in Germany
	1881	Pogroms against Jews start; consequent emigrations of Russian and Eastern European Jews to USA
	1897	First Zionist Congress in Basel, Switzerland
2000	1917	Publication of Balfour Declaration expressing the sympathy of the British government towards the establishment of a Jewish homeland in Palestine
	1933-45	Nazi authorities in Germany persecute Jews eventually causing deaths of 5-6 million Jews
	1948	Creation of state of Israel

results have been a severe decline in the religion's influence. In the European heartland of Christianity, a pervasive materialism has speeded the retreat of religion. The result has been a loss of the natural position of Christianity as the public guarantor of the moral order, as well as a decline in private religiosity in Europe. This decline has been less severe in North America. There have been signs of a renewal of interest in Christianity in the 1980s and 1990s, mostly outside the traditional institutional structures.

In parallel with this decline of Christianity in the West, however, missionary activity has resulted in an increase in the number of Christians in the Third World. At the beginning of the twentieth century, Europe and North America accounted for most of the world's Christians (83 per cent), most of the remainder being in Latin America (11 per cent). Today, Europe and North America account for only 48 per cent of the world's Christians. Africa now accounts for 15 per cent – a figure that already exceeds that of North America.[18] Perhaps even more significant than the demographic shift is the conceptual shift that is occurring. The African churches are not content merely to import Catholic and Protestant norms from European Christianity. Rather, they are engaged in a creative reinterpretation of Christianity in terms of their own cultural norms. In South Africa alone, there are more than 3,000 separate native churches, each expressing

CHRISTIAN ECUMENISM: Pope John-Paul II and Ecumenical Patriarch Dimitrios I of Istanbul, leader of the Orthodox Church, met in Rome in December 1987.

Christianity in forms markedly different from traditional European norms. European Christians visiting a congregation of the Church of Kimbangu in the Congo may well feel just as out of place as they would in a mosque in Saudi Arabia.

The demographic shift is already having several important effects on the Christian world. Experiments in Christian thinking and action originating in the Third World are starting to have an impact on the original heartlands of Christianity. The merging of all the Protestant churches in the Church of South India in 1947 is acting as a model for ecumenical movements elsewhere. 'Liberation theology' from South America has stirred up thinking among both Catholics and Protestants of Europe and North America.

One question that remains to be answered is the extent to which the disbandment of the communist governments in Eastern Europe will affect Christianity in those countries. Will there be a Christian revival or will the materialism of the West swamp the Christianity that has survived the communist onslaught? Initial reports do not present a clear picture. Some areas in Eastern Europe report an increasing interest in Christianity, despite strong competition from new religious movements that are also spreading into these countries. In Poland, however, where the Roman Catholic Church remained relatively strong during the communist period, the authority of the Church seems to be in decline. Many are openly defying its rulings on contraception and abortion. This may be similar to

BLACK LIBERATION THEOLOGY

By defining the problems of Christianity in isolation from the black condition, white theology becomes a theology of white oppressors, serving as a divine sanction [for] criminal acts committed against blacks.

No white theologian has ever taken the oppression of blacks as a point of departure for analyzing God's activity in contemporary America . . . Because white theology has consistently preserved the integrity of the community of oppressors, I conclude that it is not Christian theology at all . . .

It is unthinkable that oppressors could identify with oppressed existence and thus say something relevant about God's liberation of the oppressed. In order to be Christian theology, white theology must cease being *white* theology and become black theology by denying whiteness as an acceptable form of human existence and affirming blackness as God's intention for humanity. White theologians will find this difficult . . .

Black theology . . . maintains that all acts which participate in the destruction of white racism are Christian, the liberating deeds of God. All acts which impede the struggle of black self-determination – black power – are anti-Christian, the work of Satan. (Cone, *A Black Theology of Liberation*, pp. 9–10)

North American and European patterns, but was previously unusual in Poland.

The overall analysis points to a gradual decline in the proportion of the world's population that is Christian from 34.4 per cent at the beginning of the twentieth century to 32.4 per cent in 1985, perhaps down to 32.3 per cent by the end of the century. This decline is due partly to the continuing loss of faith among the Christian populations of Europe, partly to the lower rate of fertility among Christians.[19] Some groups, such as Pentecostals and marginal Protestants (Jehovah's Witnesses and Mormons), are growing rapidly. Since they take most of their converts from other Christian groups, however, this does not result in any overall increase in the numbers of Christians.

Islam

Islam has faced the crisis of redefining itself since the beginning of the twentieth century. Prior to this, the Muslims had to a large extent seen themselves as one community (*umma*) under the leadership of the caliph. After World War I, the caliphate was abolished by Ataturk in 1924 and Muslims found themselves citizens of a large number of newly created states. The divisive effects of the nationalistic claims of these new states dealt a severe blow to the sense of Islamic unity and coherence.

MUSLIM MISSIONARY EFFORT: One group of people in the Christian West who have responded to Muslim missionary effort has been the black population in the United States. Malcolm X, pictured here, joined the Nation of Islam, a fringe Muslim movement, in 1952. After making the pilgrimage to Mecca in 1964, Malcolm X adopted orthodox Islam with the name Malik el-Shabazz. He was assassinated in 1965.

As described earlier, the Islamic world has experienced a dilemma during the last hundred years over whether to adopt ideas and attitudes from the West. The liberals have tried to show that the ideas of modernity are compatible with the *Qur'an*. The conservative elements have resisted the influence of the West and have looked for answers in the traditions of Islam. At first, these conservative elements were overwhelmed by the tide of events and the force of the liberal argument. Wholesale westernizing reforms were adopted in the newly created Arab states, as well as in Ataturk's Turkey and Reza Shah's Iran. As the years have passed, however, social and economic problems have continued and even increased. Initial optimism has given way to social disruption, a decline in moral standards, a pervasive corruption of public life and fear of the loss of cultural identity under a tidal wave of westernization. This has fed a desire to return to a past that is perceived to have been free of such problems. An increasing number of people have begun to pay attention to the conservative elements.

In recent times, there have been efforts at Islamic ecumenism. In particular, the Revolutionary government in Iran has been keen to heal the Sunni–Shi'i divide, but these efforts received a severe setback with the Iran–Iraq war, which tended to play on the divide.

Islamic missionary effort has been slow to build up. It received a great boost, however, from the money flowing from the oil boom of the 1970s. In Africa, Islam is continuing to creep southwards, often at the expense of Christianity. Spread in other directions from the Islamic heartlands has, however, been difficult, due to the hostility towards Islam in Hindu India and Christian Europe. Nonetheless, there has been a great deal of consolidation of the Islamic hold over the margins of the Islamic world in Indonesia and sub-Saharan Africa.

Overall, Islam has thus far been more successful in resisting the destructive effects of modernity than Christianity. This, together with the high birth rate in Islamic countries, means that Islam is forecast to increase from an estimated 17.1 per cent of the world's population in 1985, to 19.2 per cent by the end of the twentieth century.

Baha'i Faith

The Baha'i Faith, being a religion that emerged within the modern period, has the advantage of having much modern thought already within its scripture. Such concepts as the equality of men and women, the need to balance science and religion and the need for social justice cause no heart-searching dilemmas for Baha'is, because they are already enshrined in the scriptures of the religion. Thus, the religion is spared some of the more acute elements of the fundamentalist–liberal tensions to be found in the other religions. The main problem for Baha'is is not evolving these formulations but the next stage: putting them into effect. Among Baha'is from more traditional societies (the majority of Baha'is), this presents particular problems and is one reason that the Baha'i community has put a great deal of its energies into social and economic development projects.

Until about the year 1950, the Baha'i community concentrated on developing its administrative structure and establishing small Baha'i communities in all parts of the world. From about 1960 onwards, it experienced a sudden spurt of growth with large numbers of poor rural peasants in the Third World becoming Baha'is. The largest Baha'i communities are now in the Third World: India, South-East Asia, Africa, the Pacific and South America. According to at least one authority, the Baha'i Faith is now the second most widely spread religion in the world after Christianity and its rate of conversions is one of the highest among all religious groups.[20] There were about 1 million Baha'is in 1968 and 5–6 million in 1995–6.[21]

Hinduism

During the last hundred years, Hinduism at the village level has continued in much the same way as in the past (and this, of course, is the reality for

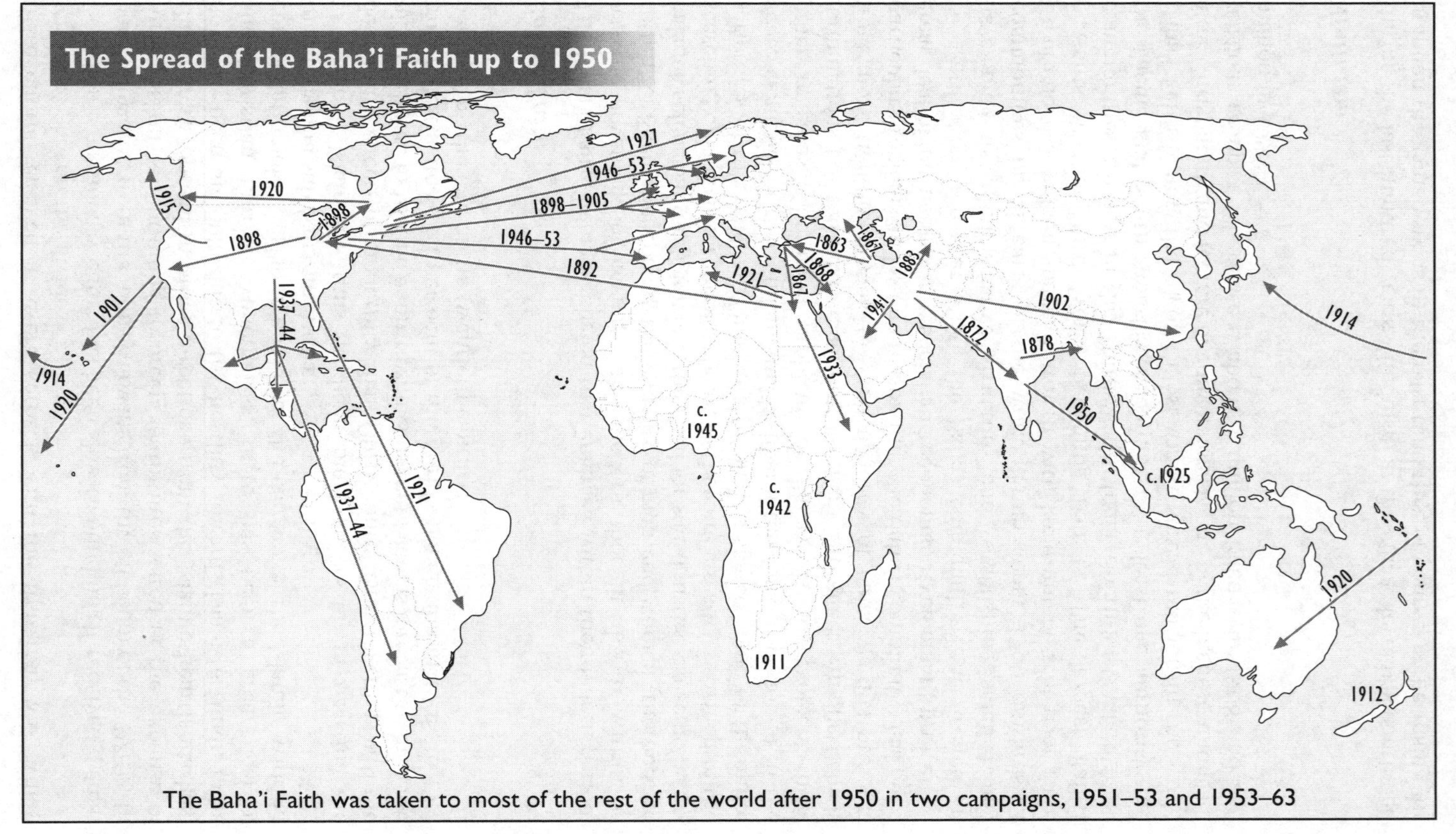

The Baha'i Faith was taken to most of the rest of the world after 1950 in two campaigns, 1951–53 and 1953–63

ONE ROLE OF THE BAHA'I FAITH IN THE MODERN WORLD: This meeting of leading environmentalists, representatives of various governments and business leaders, was convened by the Baha'i International Community in collaboration with several environmental organizations and hosted by Prince Philip at St James's Palace in 1994. The meeting was intended to highlight the importance of forests in the world's ecology and to look at ways of co-ordinating their preservation and management. The picture shows Prince Philip and Madame Rabbani, the leading Baha'i representative at the conference, seated, while Ian Lang, the secretary of state for Scotland, reads out the message to the conference from John Major, the then British prime minister.

some 75 per cent of all Hindus). At the urban, national and international level, however, Hinduism has undergone great changes.

The most important factor of change has been the emergence of India as an independent state with a Hindu leadership. All Hindus supported this development, but some traditionalists have wanted to go further and to turn India from a secular state into one based on Hinduism. They stand for the full implementation of the caste system with the backing of the law, the prohibition of the slaughter of cattle, and the enactment of anti-Muslim measures. Their numbers and influence are increasing through such organizations and political parties as the Arya Samaj and the Bharatiya Janata Party.

Liberal Hindu thought during the last hundred years has been mainly an exercise in reinterpreting traditional Hinduism in ways that relate to the modern world. One example of this is Vinoba Bhave (1895–1982), a follower of Gandhi and founder of the Sarvodaya movement. He translated the notions of karma and *seva* (which in classical Hinduism refer to ritual

EXPORTING HINDUISM: Swami Prabhupada (1896–1977), founder of ISKCON, International Society for Krishna Consciousness. He travelled to New York in 1965 and set up ISKCON the following year.

works and service to higher castes by lower castes respectively) into social service – good works performed for the benefit of all. For him, sacrificing for others and giving to the poor were the spirit of Hinduism in action.[22]

Even more dramatic has been the change in the external face of Hinduism. From an inward-looking, exclusivist orientation, it has changed into an outgoing, missionary religion. Such groups as ISKCON (International Society for Krishna Consciousness, the Hare Krishna Movement) and the Sai Baba movement have taken Hinduism itself to the West. Other movements such as Transcendental Meditation and the Brahma Kumaris (Raja-Yoga) are a more subtle export of Hindu ideas. These groups have focused on Hindu philosophy and psychology, as well as on such practical matters as techniques of meditation.

The Hindu ecumenical movement is still in its infancy and not yet very influential. This is partly because Hinduism has not had much history of sectarian strife and violence, so most Hindus in India see little need for ecumenism. A number of world Hindu organizations exist, such as the Virat Hindu Samaj, led by Dr Karam Singh, and the Vishwa Hindu Parishad.

Largely because of the high birth rate among Hindus, the religion is forecast to increase slightly, from 13.5 per cent to 13.7 per cent of the world's population, between 1985 and the end of the twentieth century.

Buddhism

Prior to the nineteenth century, Buddhism had been in decline. It was the efforts of people such as Dharmapala (the founder of the Mahabodhi Society, 1891) in Sri Lanka and Vajirañana (who restructured monastic training) in Thailand, as well as the efforts of Europeans such as Caroline and Thomas Rhys Davids (the founders of the Pali Text Society, 1881) that revived the religion. Buddhism played an important role in the nationalism that supplanted colonial rule in such countries as Sri Lanka and Burma. Accompanying this, there has been a major attempt to reinterpret Buddhism so as to make it a more socially active and concerned force in these societies.[23]

Theravada was the first form of Buddhism to come to the West. Buddhism was enthusiastically promoted in Europe in the early part of the twentieth century as a scientific and rational religion, in contradistinction to Christianity, which was considered to be full of superstition, irrationality and the supernatural. In more recent years, another strand has been added to the ideas current in the West about Buddhism: the idea that it is a pacificist or peaceful religion. Both of these ideas about Buddhism arose partly out of reading the Buddhist texts and thinking that the religion as practised must accord with these texts, and partly from Western scholars and religious enthusiasts seeing what they wanted to see – creating a false idealization that, in turn, led to a blinkered perception of the facts. It constitutes the growth of a mythology of Buddhism in the West. In fact, Buddhism is not and never has been free of supernatural elements:

> The worship of deities has been known in the history of Buddhism from the earliest times. And although some scholars of the past idealized Buddhism as an atheist religion, the place of the deities in Sinhalese Buddhism has hardly changed since the times of the commentaries, and cannot be attributed to the influence of pre-Buddhist religion, of Hinduism or of magical-animism.
>
> According to the Sinhalese Buddhists, supernatural beings are as much a part of the universe as human beings and all other forms of life in nature.[24]

Nor have Buddhist societies been any more free of a tendency to warfare than other societies:

> The historical record of the Buddhist kingdoms of South-East Asia does not support the view that where Buddhist institutions and ideas have a prominent place in national life the consequence will be peaceful international relations. Nor is there any clear evidence that in countries where Buddhism is the state religion wars have been regarded as un-Buddhist activities. The evidence suggests, on the contrary, that Buddhism in South-East Asia has been successfully employed to reinforce the policies and interests of national rulers, often in their competition with one another for resources or prestige. Burma and Thailand provide excellent examples in this respect.[25]

TIBETAN BUDDHISM: The Dalai Lama has been the title held by the head of the Gelugpa sect of Tibetan Buddhism since 1578. The present Dalai Lama (Tenzin Gyatso, 1935–), the fourteenth in the line of succession, has been in exile since 1959. He won the Nobel Peace Prize in 1989 and has become a world-renowned figure promoting Buddhism and advocating the cause of Tibet.

This Western interpretation has in turn influenced the way that Eastern Buddhists see themselves. More recently, since the 1960s, other forms of Buddhism, such as Tibetan and Zen, have found large numbers of advocates in the West.[26]

Buddhism, perhaps more than any other religion, has suffered because of the advance of communism. In large parts of South-East Asia, the communist authorities made great efforts to uproot Buddhist tradition. The most determined example of this was Pol Pot's period of rule over Cambodia (1975–9). Buddhism has also suffered from the materialism sweeping Japan and the newly industrialized nations of South-East Asia. There has been a great deal of success in taking Buddhism to the

Table 19.1 Estimated Number of Adherents of World Religions

	1900 (THOUSANDS)	%	1970 (THOUSANDS)	%	1985 (THOUSANDS)	%	2000 (THOUSANDS)	%
CHRISTIANS	558,056	34.4	1,216,579	33.7	1,548,592	32.4	2,019,921	32.3
ROMAN CATHOLICS	271,991	16.8	558,024	18.5	884,222	18.5	1,169,463	18.7
ORTHODOX	121,245	7.5	111,899	3.1	130,837	2.7	153,052	2.4
PROTESTANTS	119,663	7.4	259,045	7.2	292,734	6.1	357,489	5.7
MARGINAL PROTESTANTS	1,040	0.1	10,169	0.3	14,565	0.3	22,151	0.4
MUSLIMS	200,102	12.4	550,919	15.3	817,065	17.1	1,200,653	19.2
SUNNIS	173,111	10.7	465,827	12.9	680,855	14.2	999,826	16.0
SHI'A, TWELVER	22,250	1.4	65,270	1.8	104,493	2.2	151,700	2.4
AHMADIYYA	70	0	2,635	0.1	4,734	0.1	9,217	0.1
HINDUS	203,033	12.5	465,785	12.8	647,567	13.5	859,252	13.7
OTHER INDIAN RELIGIONS								
SIKHS	2,961	0.2	10,612	0.3	16,150	0.3	23,832	0.4
JAINS	1,323	0.1	2,616	0.1	3,349	0.1	4,304	0.1
BUDDHISTS	127,159	7.8	231,672	6.4	295,571	6.2	359,092	5.7
MAHAYANA	71,559	4.4	130,140	3.6	166,355	3.5	201,842	3.2
THERAVADA	48,100	3.0	87,700	2.4	111,616	2.3	135,850	2.2
JEWS	12,270	0.8	15,186	0.4	17,838	0.4	20,174	0.3
ZOROASTRIANS	108	0	121	0	172	0	219	0
BAHA'IS	9	0	2,659	0.1	4,443	0.1	7,649	0.1
CHINESE FOLK-RELIGIONISTS	380,404	23.5	214,392	5.9	187,994	3.9	158,471	2.5
JAPANESE SHINTOISTS	6,720	0.4	4,173	0.1	3,164	0.1	2,658	0.1
TRIBAL AND SPIRITISTS	117,986	7.3	107,167	3.0	110,004	2.3	123,221	2.0
NON-RELIGIOUS AND ATHEISTS	3,149	0.2	708,354	19.6	1,016,428	21.3	1,334,336	21.3
OTHER (INCLUDING NEW RELIGIONS)	6,606	0.4	81,799	2.3	112,786	2.4	145,861	2.3
WORLD POPULATION	1,619,886	100.0	3,612,034	100.0	4,781,123	100.1	6,259,643	100.0

SOURCE: Table is based on Barrett, *World Christian Encyclopedia*, p. 6.
NOTES: Percentages show percentage of world population. Percentages are rounded: very small percentages are shown as 0; thus, total may not come to 100 per cent.

'Tribal and spiritist' in my table consists of data given for 'Tribal religionists', 'Shamanists', 'Afro-American spiritists' and 'Spiritists' in Barrett's tables. 'Non-religious and atheists' in my table consists of those two separate categories in Barrett's table. 'Other' in my table consists of data for 'New-religionists', 'Confucians', 'Mandeans' and 'Other religionists' in Barrett's table. 'Marginal Protestants' refers to such groups as Jehovah's Witnesses and Mormons.

Updates of this table have appeared in articles by Barrett in annual issues of *Britannica Book of the Year* (Chicago, Encyclopaedia Britannica): see, for example, issue for 1989, p. 299. However, as these latter tables use a different basis for their calculations (the number of countries, for example, jumps from 223 in *World Christian Encyclopedia* to 254 in *Britannica Book of the Year*) and do not give sufficient information to update all the data in this table and Table 19.2, I have only used the *Encyclopedia*.

Table 19.2 Rate of Growth and Spread of World Religions

	Average annual change 1970–80						
	Natural increase (thousands)	%	Conversions (thousands)	%	Total increase (thousands)	%	No. of countries
Christians	21,414	1.63	196	0.01	21,611	1.64	223
Roman Catholics	13,783	1.88	331	0.05	14,133	1.93	221
Orthodox	1,346	1.14	-94	-0.08	1,252	1.06	96
Protestants	3,313	1.24	-1,182	-0.44	2,130	0.80	209
Marginal Protestants	144	1.25	142	1.24	286	2.49	176
Muslims	17,063	2.71	140	0.02	17,204	2.74	162
Sunnis	14,585	2.74	-250	-0.05	14,335	2.70	157
Shi'a, Twelver	1,771	2.37	305	0.41	2,076	2.78	54
Ahmadiyya	97	2.99	39	1.18	136	4.18	56
Hindus	12,145	2.34	-248	-0.05	11,897	2.30	84
Other Indian religions							
Sikhs	333	2.70	30	0.24	363	2.94	19
Jains	67	2.14	-4	-0.14	63	2.00	5
Buddhists	5,112	2.03	-908	-0.36	4,204	1.67	84
Mahayana	2,865	2.03	-504	-0.36	2,362	1.67	77
Theravada	1,940	2.03	-350	-0.37	1,591	1.66	18
Jews	186	1.16	-11	-0.06	175	1.09	112
Zoroastrians	3	2.44	-0	-0.01	3	2.43	10
Baha'is	79	2.46	37	1.17	116	3.63	194
Chinese folk-religionists	3,444	1.66	-5,103	-2.46	-1,660	-0.80	55
Japanese Shintoists	46	1.19	-111	-2.85	-65	-1.66	1
Tribal and spiritists	2,799	2.59	-2,622	-2.43	177	0.16	*
Non-religious and atheists	11,761	1.46	8,506	1.06	20,267	2.52	*
Other (including new religions)	1,935	2.12	97	0.11	2,032	2.22	*
World population	76,388	1.93	0	0	76,388	1.93	223

Source: Based on Barrett, *World Christian Encyclopedia*, p. 6. See notes to Table 19.1.
Notes: The last column refers to the number of countries with communities of adherents; * = data not applicable

In Barrett's table annual change is given as 1970–85. This is evidently a mistake and 1970–80 is intended. It is also evident that Barrett's figure for conversions for tribal religionists should have a minus sign before it. I have calculated separate figures for the rate of natural increase and conversions.

Christian West and many converts have been made. This does not, however, make up for the losses to Buddhism that have occurred from the advance of communism. Overall, Buddhism is estimated to have declined from about 7.8 per cent of the world's population at the start of the twentieth century to about 6.2 per cent in 1985.[27]

Religion in Primal Societies

It was confidently expected by many that primal or traditional religions would cease to exist during the twentieth century. It was thought that what the missionaries, under the protection of the colonial powers, could not achieve, increasing education and secularization would. A world missionary conference in 1910 heard the following report: 'Most of these peoples will have lost their ancient faiths within a generation, and will accept that culture–religion with which they first come into contact.'[28] Surprisingly, this was not an accurate forecast. Traditional religions have proved to be resilient. While as a proportion of the world's population the number of their followers has decreased, the absolute numbers have remained approximately the same throughout the twentieth century. According to one estimate, there were about 118 million followers of traditional religions in 1900 and there will be about 110 million by 2000.[29] If one includes followers of spiritist cults (many of which derive from

NATIVE AFRICAN RELIGION AND CHRISTIANITY IN GHANA

Fostered by several non-religious factors, such as the anthropological literature on traditional Akan religion and culture, the rise of nationalism, the struggle for, and achievement of, independence, the ideology of 'African personality', etc., the resilience among Christians of elements of Traditional Religion has ever become more patent in the course of this century. Some instances may be cited:

Christians freely participate in the traditional communal festivals now, such as the *Odwira* (old year/new year celebrations), and the greater *Adae*, celebrated every six weeks on Sundays in honour of the ancestors of the chiefs and the queen mothers. They engage (more) freely in drumming and dancing, and in traditional communal processes, such as the swearing of the *ntam kese* (great oath) in a traditional process of law. They accept traditional offices, even if that entails exclusion from full membership by their church.

. . . Most Christians contract marriages according to the traditional customs, thus causing the near-complete failure of church blessed marriage . . .

Christians also resort to personal traditions rites, especially for protection against witchcraft and sorcery and for healing. (J. G. Platvoet, 'The Akan Believer and his Religions', in Vrijhof and Waardenburg, *Official and Popular Religion*, pp. 569–70)

traditional religions), this last number increases to 123 million. Approximately 70 per cent of followers of traditional religions are in Africa. Most of the remainder are in India and South-East Asia.

Traditional religions in Africa have been under pressure for all of the last hundred years, with Islam spreading from the north and Christianity being imported by the colonial powers. Despite this, it is estimated that some 30 per cent of black Africans still follow traditional religions, while another 30–40 per cent resort occasionally to traditional religious practices.[30] However, this latter now mostly refers to personal and family religion. Traditional tribal religious ceremonies and practices have declined greatly.

The tribal peoples of India, especially the hill tribes, have remained largely isolated from Indian society. Although those with a high level of contact with the rest of Indian society have been 'Hinduized', the rest have continued their traditional religions. Of an estimated 38 million tribal peoples in 1970, some 9 million are estimated to have remained animists.[31] Traditional religions are also still widely practised in the archipelago of islands that make up Eastern Malaysia and Indonesia. Here Islam has been actively promoted among the tribal peoples by the State. Many have, however, resisted this and others have converted to one of several new religious movements with strong elements of traditional religion. There are estimated to be some 8 million adherents of tribal religions in this area.

Such figures do not, however, represent the whole picture. They fail to account for the large influence of traditional religions on those nominally converted to one of the major proselytizing religions. As indicated above, some 30–40 per cent of black Africans, while nominally adhering to Christianity or Islam, still participate in some of the practices of their traditional religions. The same is probably true of tribal people in Malaysia, Indonesia, and Papua New Guinea.

Among people who are nominally Christian in Latin America and the Caribbean, there are many who also participate in ceremonies and rituals that can be traced back to African religions. When slaves were taken from Africa to the Americas, they took their religions with them. During the period of slavery, African tribal gods were disguised as Catholic saints and could in this way continue to be worshipped. Rites and ceremonies were held in secret. These practices continue to the present, although there is now a strong movement to dissociate them from Catholicism.

African gods, beliefs and rituals can be clearly discerned among the practices known as Santería in Cuba, Vodun (Voodoo) in Haiti, Shango in Trinidad, and Candomblé, Umbanda or Macumba in Brazil. Although some 90 per cent of Haitians identify themselves as Catholics, about the same proportion of the population practises Vodun. In Brazil, about 90 per cent of the population is Roman Catholic, but some 15 per cent of the population are estimated to be participate regularly in one of the Afro-American spiritist cults and another 15–45 per cent occasionally. These Afro-American religious practices have spread to the United States,

The Separation of Candomblé From Catholicism

Open Letter:

To the public and people of Candomblé

The Iyas and Babalorixás of Bahia, in accordance with the position assumed in the second World Conference of Culture and Orishas' Tradition, realized during the period of 17th to 23rd of July of 1983, at this city, make public that after this Conference it became clear that our faith is religion and not a syncretic sect.

We cannot think – and shall not allow others to think as well – in ourselves as folklore, sect, animism, primitive religion, as it has happened in this country, this city; being attacked by opponents and detractors who published articles like: 'Candomblé is something of the Devil', 'African practices primitive or syncretic'; or by ritual dresses taken to official contests, liturgical symbols taken for tourist marketing and our sacred Houses, our temples included, indicated in the column of folklore in Bahia's newspapers.

Ma beru, Olorum wa pelu awon omorisa [Have no fear, God is with all 'children' of Orisha]

Signatures:
Menininha do Gantois, Iyalorixá of the Axé Ilé Iya Momin Iyamassé
Stella de Oshossi, Iyalorixá of the Ilé Axé Opô Afonjá
Tete de Iansa, Iyalorixá of the Ilé Nassô Oká
Olga de Alaketo, Iyalorixá of the Ilé Maroia Lage
Nicinha do Bogum, Iyalorixá of the Xogodô Bogum Malê Ki-Rundo
Salvador, 27 July 1983

(Newspaper report by Vander Prata in *Journal da Bahia*, Salvador, Friday, 29 July 1983)

particularly through Cuban refugees, and there may be as many as 800,000 practitioners, mostly among African-Americans. (For further details of Afro-American religion in Brazil, see pp. 399–403.)

New Religious Movements

One of the most marked features of the modern world is the vast proliferation of new religious movements. These movements have great importance because of what they tell us about religious change and the development of religion in general. The newer major world religions such as Christianity, Islam and Buddhism each started as new religious movements within other established religious systems. It may well be that we are witnessing, among the new religious movements of today, the next major world religion about to emerge, in the same way that Christianity emerged from the religious turmoil of the Roman Empire.

> In the beginning, all religions are obscure, tiny, deviant cult movements. Caught at the right moment, Jesus would have been found leading a handful of ragtag followers in a remote corner of the mighty Roman Empire. How laughable it would have seemed to Roman intellectuals that this obscure sect could pose a threat to the great pagan temples. In similar fashion, Western intellectuals scorn contemporary cults. Yet, if major new faiths are aborning, they will not be found by consulting the directory of the National Council of Churches. Rather they will be found in lists of obscure cult movements.[32]

New religious movements may be classified as follows, although this classification is, however, mainly applicable to the movements in the West:[33]

1. Movements derived from established world religions in a straightforward manner. Even if they are not accepted by the orthodox adherents of that religion, they are sufficiently similar to be considered part of the broad tradition of one of the established religions. Examples include Jehovah's Witnesses, ISKCON (International Society for Krishna Consciousness), the Friends of the Western Buddhist Order, and the various Sufi groups that have arisen in the West.
2. Movements derived from established world religions, but having such differences as to take them outside the broad tradition of that religion. Such heterodox groups include the Children of God and the Unification Church derived from the Christian tradition.
3. Movements that are not derived from one of the established world religions. These movements are distinctive and different from any of the traditions of the world religions. We may broadly divide them into two groups:
   a. The 'self' religions and the religiously flavoured psychotherapies. Many of these may not consider themselves religious movements at all. They are concerned with exploring the self, searching for significance and inner meaning within the individual.
   b. The 'New Age' movements. These are also engaged in the search for the true self, but seek to relate this to some external transcendent reality or to nature and the environment. The sources for the ideas of these groups include ancient folklore, pagan traditions, alternative medicine, environmental concerns, and the psychic, astrological and occult traditions. There may be elements taken from some of the established religions (for example, a belief in reincarnation) but these are dissociated from their doctrinal and philosophical setting in those religions.

This section examines new religious movements in three areas where they appear to be especially active. (Many of the comments made about millennialist movements in chapter 10 and about the charismatic founders of religions in chapter 12 are also of relevance to the study of new religious movements.)

The West

There is a vast and frenetic religious market place in operation in the Western world at present. Not since the declining years of the Roman Empire has a similar profusion of sects and cults existed. This modern situation began in the last half of the nineteenth century with the founding of such movements as the Latter-Day Saints (Mormons), Christian Science and Spiritualism. In the years following the Parliament of Religions in Chicago in 1893, there arrived several imported religious movements from the East. Among these was Hinduism (brought by Vivekananda), Buddhism (brought by Dharmapala and others), and the Baha'i Faith (which arrived in the United States in 1892 but did not make any converts until 1894–5). The number of new religious movements increased dramatically, however, after World War II. In current usage, the term 'new religious movements' refers to those religious movements that have come to the fore since World War II, and particularly since the 1960s.[34]

Church attendance figures for the major Christian churches in the West have shown a marked decline in the last hundred years.[35] However, some have argued that this does not necessarily mean a decline in religiosity, for the number involved in new religious movements has, at the same time, increased. One estimate states that 5 per cent of the adult population of the United States and Canada may have participated in one of the new religious movements in the three decades after World War II.[36] A Gallup poll in 1976 found 12 per cent of Americans involved with some form of new religious movement (Transcendental Meditation 4 per cent; Yoga 3 per cent; charismatic movements 2 per cent; mysticism 2 per cent; Eastern religions 1 per cent).[37] Many of those who are recorded in surveys as having no church affiliation do nevertheless believe in the mystical and supernatural. Studies have shown that cults proliferate where traditional church affiliation is weaker.[38]

Some oriental practices such as Transcendental Meditation (TM) and yoga found widespread popularity in the 1970s and 1980s. They were extensively advertised and there was easy access to short introductory courses. As there was not much doctrinal content and little demanded in the way of lifestyle changes those who participated did not necessarily consider themselves to be joining a religious movement.

A way of classifying these new religious movements in the West would be a division into three groups: those that arose in the West as sectarian splits from Christianity, for example the Latter-Day Saints and the Children of God; those that arose in the West but are not recognizably Christian, for example Scientology and various neo-pagan groups; and those that are Eastern imports, such as ISKCON (International Society for Krishna

Parliament of Religions, 1893. This gathering organized by liberal Christians brought a realization of the depth of Eastern religions to the West. Such figures as Dharmapala (Buddhism) and Vivekananda (Hinduism) attended it and toured the West afterwards. The Baha'is also regard it as the first public mention of their religion in the West.

Angarika Dharmapala (1865–1933) was a Sinhalese Buddhist monk. He founded the Mahabodhi Society in 1891.

The Hindu religious leader Narendranath Vivekananda (1863–1902) was a leading disciple of Ramakrishna and member of Brahmo Samaj.

Consciousness, Hare Krishna Movement). Not all groups will happily fall into this classification, however. The Unification Church (Moonies), for example, is both an Eastern import and ostensibly a Christian sect. The first group are usually called sects, the second and third cults. Apart from this general difference, it is very difficult to define the words 'sect' and 'cult' because the waters have been muddied by the careless use of these terms in the media, in the course of cult controversies. The word 'cult' has changed from being either a religious term meaning devotion or veneration or a sociological term (see p. 77) and has become a term with negative

Rev. Sun Myung Moon and his wife Mrs Hak Ja Han Moon, joint leaders of the Holy Spirit Association for the Unification of World Christianity (HSAUWC), also known as the Unification Church. It was founded in Seoul, Korea, on 1 May 1954.

connotations. It is now used in the media to mean little more than any religious group of which the writer or speaker disapproves. For this reason, many scholars have abandoned the use of these two terms in favour of the term 'new religious movement'.

Many of the new religious movements can be characterized by a number of social features. These include a charismatic leadership and a following that is predominantly young, middle class and well educated. They often expect a high level of commitment from members and sometimes involve new and/or exotic lifestyles. Some of them create tightly knit residential communities; almost all involve a high level of social interaction with other group members. Several studies have shown that it is this intense feeling of community that attracts people to the new religious movements. Beckford found, for example, that many Moonies had little idea of the doctrines of the group when they joined, and found it impossible to accept them fully when they were taught them. They nevertheless were firmly attached to the movement by intense feelings of group loyalty and solidarity.[39] Lastly, it may be said that most of these movements have a strong American influence. Even those movements originating in the East have taken on American-style presentation and techniques for their propaganda and proselytizing.[40]

Some sociologists have favoured using the concept of tension as a way of distinguishing between those new religious movements that are called cults and other religious groups. New religious movements are characterized as rejecting the social environment in which they exist. Consequently, they are in a state of tension with their social environment.[41] In recent years these new religious movements have come to public attention mainly as a result of this tension between them and the rest of society. This has come to a climax over the claims that they have taken advantage of, deceived and brainwashed young people. More recently, the attack on the new religious movements has switched to 'exposures' of their alleged financial irregularities and deceptions.

A major factor that is frequently mentioned in attacks on new religious movements is the accusation that they split up families. New religious movements often regard themselves as new families for their members (see pp. 155–6): they are therefore seen as splitting up the traditional family. A second and related accusation against some new religious movements is the allegation that they use coercive or manipulative behavioural techniques, 'brainwashing' as it is usually called. The study of 'brainwashing' emerged from work done on Western military and civilian personnel imprisoned in China and Korea in the decade after World War II. Psychiatrists and

Brainwashing and the New Religious Movements

During the late 1970s and the 1980s, many newspapers ran stories that accused new religious movements like the Unification Church or the Hare Krishna Movement of brainwashing. The following is part of an article that appeared in the British newspaper, the Daily Mail, *on 29 May 1978 and became the object of an unsuccessful libel action by the Unification Church*:

THEY TOOK AWAY MY SON AND THEN RAPED HIS MIND
Daphne told us that David had been subjected to sophisticated mind-control techniques pioneered by the people who trained the Kami Kaze, and used effectively during the Korean war and by the Chinese communists during World War II.

They included love-bombing, (constant affection and touching between groups of people), sleep deprivation, protein withdrawal, sugar-buzzing (increasing the blood-sugar level so that the brain becomes muddled), repetitive lectures, familiar music with 'restored' lyrics, and other seemingly innocent but insidious devices.

David had been terrorized into believing that Moon was the second coming of Christ . . .

'The Moonies we had met at the camp were robots, glassy eyed and mindless, programmed as soldiers in this vast fund-raising army with no goals or ideals, except as followers of the half-baked ravings of Moon, who lived in splendour while his followers lived in forced penury . . . we took comfort in realizing that it was not our son . . . but a diabolical force that had been implanted in his mind . . .

'David's mind, we are convinced, was raped . . . Few people believe that mind-control is possible. It can happen. It can happen to almost anybody. David is a strong, intelligent, forceful personality. Perhaps he was in the mood, over-tired, ready to flow with the tide . . .'

David, a respected Washington journalist, warned yesterday that Moonies were as much a threat to the world as Communism . . . 'They use hypnosis and other methods of mind-control. They operate on deception through idealism and their credibility is enormous.'! (Barker, *The Making of a Moonie*, pp. 121–2)

psychologists found that these people had their thinking and behaviour changed by the use of certain techniques. These researchers then applied these findings to the conversion techniques among some new religious movements and found parallels between the two. Among the specific 'brainwashing' techniques that they considered some new religious movements used were: isolation, hunger and cold, humiliation, confession, manipulation of information and of language, and psychological and social threats, such as withdrawal of physical or emotional needs.[42]

A number of groups organized by parents and others have been set up in North America and Europe to oppose these cults. Some of these have resorted to kidnapping and 'de-programming' young cult members to enable them to 'escape' from cults. This reaction began to gain momentum in the 1970s and was especially strengthened following the mass suicide/murder of 913 members of Jim Jones's People's Temple in Guyana in November 1978.

A number of sociologists have opposed the psychiatrists and psychologists mentioned above, maintaining that the evidence shows that this adverse reaction directed at the cults has been mostly a spurious product of the mass media. They state that there is very little evidence that any of these cults have engaged to any significant extent in brainwashing in the strict sense of that word. Reports of such activities often originate from anti-cult organizations and are eagerly pounced upon by the mass media. According to these sociologists, they are, however, found to be largely baseless on closer examination. The evidence that has been presented for brainwashing is usually the result of a misunderstanding by parents of what is happening to their children.[43] These sociologists have compared the attacks on the new religious movements to the witch-hunts of former ages. The 'brainwashing' power over others that these 'cults' are said to have is no more real than the magical powers that those witches were popularly supposed to have had and the 'de-programming' methods of the modern expert are a parallel to the crude and violent methods used in former times against those suspected of witchcraft.[44] 'The metaphor of brainwashing is best understood as a social weapon which provides a "libertarian" rationale for the suppression of unpopular social movements and belief systems.'[45]

The attack on the new religious movements is of great interest for what it reveals to us about our society. These groups provide a variant subculture often at odds with the norms and values of the surrounding society, which may develop into mutual rejection. The new religious movements reject society's values and norms; society rejects the new religious movements. Western society is highly secularized; a high level of religious commitment therefore causes tension. Many major churches have become low-key and liberal in outlook, thus reducing their tension with society. The new religious movements frequently have a high intensity of religious commitment creating tension with the secular society of the West.[46]

The attacks made against the new religious movements thus reveal the secular nature of Western society. The representatives of the dominant religious groups have become increasingly reluctant to issue condemnations of these movements. Neither the mental health professionals nor the professional 'de-programmers' who have given evidence in various anti-cult law suits comment much on the doctrines and beliefs of the movements.[47] It is as if the intense religious commitment that these new religious movements often generate is embarrassing for the rest of society (and even the traditional, dominant religious groups) to deal with directly.

This mutual rejection between the new religious movements and society is usually more intense for those described as cults than it is for sects. This is because sects, having arisen through schism from the traditional orthodoxy, retain some features of it, allowing them to remain more acceptable. The cults, arising *de novo* or imported from a foreign culture, often have many more features that are at variance with the dominant norms and values.

Thus, both the rise of the new religious movements and the attacks made by society on them are important barometers of the religious situation in a society. The first measures the strength and standing of the dominant religious orthodoxy; many new movements arise in the Christian West and in Japan where the traditional orthodoxy is weak, but few in the Islamic countries where it is strong. The second is an indication of the challenge that the movement presents to the norms and attitudes of the society. (For a further consideration of attacks on new religious movements, see p. 519–20.)

Japan

Shoko Asahara, leader of Aum Shinrikyo, a syncretic Japanese sect that has been accused of the Sarin nerve gas attack on the Tokyo underground railway.

After its defeat in World War II, Japan enacted a policy of religious freedom and a complete dissociation of State and religion. This led initially to a burst of activity from religious groups that had been suppressed under the old order, but in time it also resulted in the flowering of many new religious movements. Most Japanese religion is a mixture of Buddhism and traditional Shinto religious practices. More than 80 per cent of the population have such a religious mix as their family religion. Various surveys, however, have shown that only about a third of Japan's population regard themselves as religious in a personal sense. Of these, a large proportion are members of new religious movements (*shinko shukyo* in Japanese).

The eclecticism that is typical of Japanese religious life (see pp. 45–6) also extends into the beliefs of many of the new religious movements. Aum Shinrikyo, the religious group that is accused of the Sarin gas attacks on the Tokyo underground in 1995, for example, is based on worship of the Hindu god Shiva, together with Japanese and Tibetan Buddhist beliefs and Christian eschatology.

Some scholars have noted that involvement in new religious movements in Japan is usually for very practical, worldly reasons. People join these movements because they believe that this will result in better health, finances or marital prospects. Many of the most successful of the new religious movements specifically promise that participation in the movement will result in material and other worldly gains. A typical new group will have a charismatic, authoritarian leader; a mixture of beliefs drawn from several sources, but usually including the promise of salvation; will offer healing and/or magic; and will have a strong community life.

Sub-Saharan Africa

Writing in the preface of the *World Christian Encyclopedia*, its editor David Barrett recorded the surprise of those working on the Encyclopaedia at the number of sects in Christianity. They eventually found that there were some 20,000 sects and denominations, which was some four times greater than their original estimate.[48] Of this 20,000, a very large proportion come from sub-Saharan Africa. Over 3,000 exist in the Republic of South Africa[49] and some 1,500 in Nigeria.[50] Many of these groups would be more correctly considered as new religious movements rather than just Christian sects, since they usually incorporate beliefs and practices from traditional African religion.

These religious movements are centred on such activities as healing, magic, exorcism of evil spirits, and eradication of witches and sorcerers. They offer an explanation for suffering and injustice and a means for reducing and controlling them. Some have millennialist or messianic themes. They often have spirit-mediums as central figures in the movement. They may be considered to fall into two main groups. Some are a deliberate rejection of the colonialist inheritance and seek to return to authentic African religious experience. Others seek to bring together elements of traditional religion and the religion of the colonialists (usually Christianity, but sometimes there are elements of Islam and Judaism).

Religious Freedom

In considering the question of religious freedom, we may make a slight distinction between religious toleration and religious freedom. Religious toleration assumes that there is an established State religion and refers to tolerance being shown to other religions. It presupposes, however, that the State shows preference to the State religion. Religious freedom, on the other hand, refers to a situation in which people are free to follow any religion and the State treats all religions equally.

The concept of freedom of religion as a human right is, to a large extent, new to the world. In previous ages, most people assumed that the State (whether secular or religious) had a right to impose a particular religion on the populace; almost everyone agreed that the State had a right to suppress objectionable religious movements. This right was based on the notion that unity of religion was necessary for social cohesion. Arguments against religious persecution were mostly on the basis that such persecution was an un-Christian (or un-Islamic, and so on) course of action, not that freedom of religion was a right.

The awareness of the concept of freedom of religion began to grow with the writings of John Locke (1632–1704) and the creation of the United States of America in 1776. Many of those who had founded colonies in North America had fled there to escape religious persecution. It is not surprising, therefore, that freedom of religion became one of the cornerstones of the American Constitution. The first amendment of the Bill of Rights (1791) stated that 'Congress shall make no law respecting an establishment of religion, or prohibiting the free exercise thereof.'

Even in North America, however, the notion of freedom of religion did not at first extend to Native Americans, nor even completely to Jews, and the concept only made fitful progress elsewhere in the next century. The Declaration of the Rights of Man and of the Citizen, the manifesto of the French Revolution, was promulgated in 1789 and also included a statement guaranteeing freedom of religion. In Britain, a series of Acts of Parliament during the nineteenth century removed some of the restrictions placed on Catholics, non-conformist Protestants and Jews. The Parliament of Religions, held in Chicago in 1893, was a major step forward in the West in acknowledging the status of non-Christian religions.

In the aftermath of World War II and the establishment of the United Nations, a Commission on Human Rights was set up in 1946. The result of its deliberations was the Universal Declaration of Human Rights. This was passed in the United Nations General Assembly on 10 December 1948 without any dissenting votes. Article 18 of this Declaration states:

> Everyone has the right to freedom of thought, conscience and religion; this right includes freedom to change his religion or belief, and freedom, either alone or in community with others and in public or private, to manifest his religion or belief in teaching, practice, worship and observance.

Although this Declaration has been a major factor in the advancement of religious freedom, it has its limitations. It merely set a standard towards which countries should work; it had no legal force. Many countries have found ways of bypassing its provisions.

A good example of the manner in which countries find it easy to bypass their international obligations can be found in Iran, a country which is a signatory to the Declaration of Human Rights. Both under the Shah's regime and, much more intensely, under the present Islamic government, the Baha'i community in Iran has been persecuted. Neither government has recognized the Baha'i community in Iran, although it is the largest non-Muslim minority. When challenged about this persecution in the 1950s, the Shah's regime denied that there were any Baha'is in Iran. The current post-revolutionary constitution of Iran

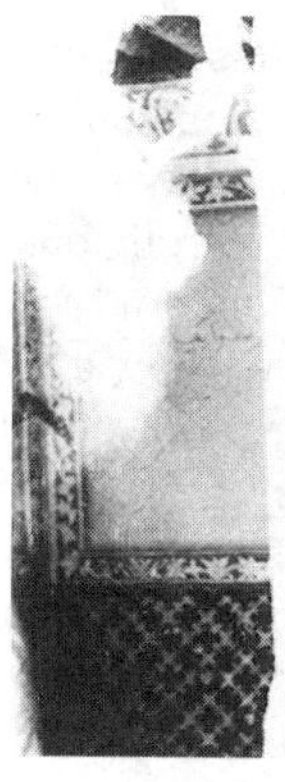

PERSECUTION OF BAHA'IS IN IRAN: One of the first actions of the Revolutionary Islamic government in Iran was to order the destruction and to eradicate the site of the holiest Baha'i shrine in Iran, the House of the Bab in Shiraz.

(article 14) states:

> The government of the Islamic Republic of Iran and all Muslims are duty bound to treat non-Muslims in an ethical fashion and in accordance with Islamic justice and equity and to respect their human rights. This principle applies to all who refrain from engaging in conspiracy or activity against Islam and the Islamic Republic of Iran.[51]

However, the constitution only recognizes the Zoroastrian, Christian and Jewish communities, although the Baha'i community is larger than any of these. The Islamic government of Iran, faced with worldwide condemnation of its persecutions of Baha'is, has adopted the tactic of classing the Baha'i Faith as a political movement and accusing Baha'is of being spies for Israel and the United States. This enables it to deny that it is persecuting Baha'is for religious reasons.[52]

When they wrote of religious freedom, those who were drawing up the Universal Declaration of Human Rights between 1946 and 1948 no doubt had in mind events that had recently occurred. These included the clashes between Muslims and Hindus in India at that time and the Nazi persecution of Jews during the recent war. They were probably also concerned about the denial of religious rights in communist countries. Almost certainly, they did not have in mind the vast proliferation of new religious movements that was only just beginning in the post-war world. This has now become, however, a major concern in the question of religious freedom.

It was not felt necessary to include a definition in the Declaration of what was meant by religion. No doubt it was felt that this was clear. But the matter has become much less clear with the proliferation of new religious movements. For example, are groups that are purposely set up to mock the concept of religion, such as the American Church of the Sub-Genius, going to be classed as religions? What about groups that describe themselves as Satanic? Of more pressing concern are the activities of some new religious movements. Questions have been asked about the point at which the activities of some new religious movements cease to be religious and become overtly financial or political. In Germany and France, official moves have been made against Scientology, based on accusations of undue psychological pressure on converts and financial irregularities in its activities. Are these merely government and judicial moves responding to press hysteria or are there genuine concerns? Another question arises concerning the attitude to be taken towards religious groups that advocate illegal activities. Rastafarianism, for example, regards the smoking of cannabis as part of its religious rituals. Members of the Native American Church in the United States use peyote in their religious rituals.

Religion and the Media

One of the features of the last hundred years has been the growth of the news and communications media. Up to the 1960s, the media kept strictly to reporting the establishment view of religion. They therefore had very little effect other than to spread information more rapidly and widely. Newspapers published the texts of sermons and radio and television broadcast church services, both without commentary and without any attempt to raise controversial issues. This pattern was broken in the United States in the 1960s. As with much else that concerns modernity, most of the developments that have occurred in the last three decades have begun in North America and gradually spread elsewhere. There is much that could be written about what has happened in the last four decades but I shall consider here three themes only: the manipulation of public attitudes, televangelism, and the impact of the Internet.

The Manipulation of Public Attitudes

It is a fact of modern life, especially in the West, that the communications media (radio, television and newspapers) are the most powerful factors in forming the public's attitude towards any social phenomenon. Religion is not immune to this. Over the years, as mentioned above, several religious groups or individuals have fallen victim to the media; examples include some of the new religious movements, such as the Unification Church (Moonies) and Scientology. There has also been a series of religious horror stories: the Reverend Jim Jones and the Jonestown suicide/murders of 913 people in Guyana in November 1978; 82 deaths of the Branch Davidians under the leadership of David Koresh in Waco, Texas, in April 1993; the 53

HEAVEN'S GATE
As was promised - the keys to Heaven's Gate are here again in
Ti and Do (The UFO Two) as they were in Jesus and His Father 2000 yrs. ago.

Heaven's Gate: Prior to their group suicide in 1997, the Heaven's Gate cult created an elaborate web site which contains written and audio-recorded statements witnessing to their faith and beliefs.

deaths in Switzerland and Canada associated with the Order of the Solar Temple under the leadership of Luc Jouret in October 1994; the Sarin gas attack in the Tokyo underground on 20 March 1995, carried out by the Aum Shinrikyo sect under the leadership of Shoko Asahara; and the 39 members of the Heaven's Gate/Higher Source group who committed suicide near San Diego on 26 March 1997. It was probably the sensationalized media reporting of the Jonestown episode in 1978 that first focused a high level of unfavourable public attention upon the new religious movements and gave impetus to the anti-cult movement.

Another more subtle way in which the media influence events is the fact that the negative publicity from the media can become part of the cult's narrative. The cult's leader will often predict in the early days of the movement that they will experience opposition before the final victory. When the media does then focus attention on them this becomes a fulfilment of the prophecy, evidence of the veracity of the leader. This can then itself contribute to the readiness of the cult members to follow the cult leader down the path to mass suicide or other extreme behaviour. The media also love stories of religious groups and individuals who fall from grace and are revealed to be sinners. Examples of this include the stories about the televangelists that became public in the early 1980s (see below) and stories of Catholic priests who are shown to be paedophiles or have had sexual affairs.

One example of the media's manipulation of public image that is of particular interest is the development of a negative image of Islam in the Western media. In Europe, and more particularly in North America, the media have built up a picture of Muslims as fanatics and extremists. This is a picture that the average Muslim finds bewildering and distressing. The words 'fundamentalist' and 'terrorist' are frequently almost automatically linked to the adjective 'Muslim' when they occur in media reports. Yet there are just as many Christian fundamentalists and terrorists as Muslim ones. When bombs go off in Israel, the perpetrators, who are trying to remove what they consider to be an alien occupying force, are often called 'Muslim terrorists' in the media. Yet when bombs go off in Northern Ireland for very similar reasons, the perpetrators are not called Christian terrorists. When a bomb is set off in Jerusalem, the perpetrators are called 'Muslim suicide bombers', yet when an Israeli fundamentalist machine-guns Muslim worshippers in a mosque, he is not called a 'Jewish terrorist'. One can speculate on the factors resulting in this situation: the age-long conflict between the Christian and Islamic worlds going back to the days of the Crusades, the success of the pro-Israeli lobby in manipulating the media in the United States, the lack of an obvious alternative enemy for the West following the collapse of communism to fulfil the need for a new mythology of evil.

The impact of this negative media image on Muslims living in the West has become severe. Following the bombing of a government building in Oklahoma City in 1995, the media, without any evidence, immediately blamed Muslim terrorists. As a result of these reports, many Muslim families living in all parts of the United States suffered abuse, assaults, and damage to their property. Even after it was discovered that the blame lay with American right-wing terrorists, the media felt no obligation to offer any expression of regret or apology for what had happened.

Televangelism

In 1960, the Federal Communications Commission, the government organ that controls broadcasting in the United States, issued a ruling that meant that local radio and television station owners could charge for religious broadcasting and still have it count towards their public interest broadcasting commitments. The mainstream churches, who had until then dominated the media, refused to purchase broadcasting time. The evangelical movements enthusiastically picked up the vacant slots. From that time onwards, it has been evangelists who have dominated religious broadcasting in the United States.

Jerry Falwell, founder of the Moral Majority, a right-wing fundamentalist Christian political group.

During the 1970s and 1980s, the evangelical broadcast organizations moved towards setting up their own networks, using satellite and cable delivery systems. Between 1970 and 1980, annual expenditure on religious television programming rose from $50 million to $600 million.[53] By the 1980s, the televangelists were building churches and universities and funding such projects as theme parks with the money being raised by their broadcasts. In addition, several televangelists began to move into the political arena. Pat Robertson's Christian Coalition and Jerry Falwell's Moral Majority supported both of Ronald Reagan's presidential campaigns and were credited with delivering a large block of votes to him.

Pat Robertson, founder of Christian Coalition, a right-wing fundamentalist Christian political group.

During the 1980s, however, serious problems had begun to appear for the televangelists. With the number of televangelists increasing, the amount of airtime each televangelist was buying increasing, and the arrival of three 24-hour religious broadcasting networks, the market reached saturation. Most of the televangelists experienced a decline in the number of viewers watching each programme during the 1980s. This began to cause financial problems. Then, on top of this, came the scandals of 1987–8. Two of the most prominent televangelists, Jimmy Swaggart and Jim Bakker, were in involved in financial and sexual scandals which tarnished the image of televangelists in general. Audience figures for religious broadcasting fell by almost 40 per cent. Several televangelists were forced off the air due to financial problems. Despite these problems, though, religious broadcasting is still strong in the United States and has considerable financial backing.[54]

Jimmy Swaggart, televangelist

Europe has lagged behind North America in the development of religious broadcasting, partly because of much greater government control and partly because of different audience tastes. In October 1995, the first continent-wide Christian television station began broadcasts of two hours a day in English by satellite. It has not grown as much as its founders had hoped and by January 1997, it was only providing some three hours of programming each day via satellite and cable.

The potential power of religious broadcasting in other settings is also very great, as can be seen from the enormous impact that the television serialization of the Hindu epics, the *Ramayana* and the *Mahabharata*, had when they were broadcast on Indian television. There was a visible decrease in activity on the streets of India's cities at the times of the broadcasts.

Jim Bakker, televangelist

The Impact of the Internet

Some have said that the future may well come to regard the Internet as a phenomenon that has as great an effect on humanity as the invention of the printing press. While only a very small number can have the privilege of expressing themselves in print or on radio or television, the Internet is, in theory at least, open to all. The World Wide Web is the ultimate tool of individualism. Anyone can, for a comparatively small price, publish their ideas and opinions for anyone else to see. In practice, of course, it is still a small proportion of the world that has access to the Internet and only those with knowledge of English can gain the full benefits of access. It is, however, becoming truly global in the range of its spread and, with increasing use in schools, the young, at least, are completely at home in this new world.

The impact of the Internet is, as yet, difficult to gauge. Most of the larger religious groups have a presence and such things as cyber-churches, on-line confessions and Internet missionary work have existed for several years. Thus, religious information is increasingly available to all. Possibly more significant, however, are the Usenet groups and mailing lists where an open conversation between many individuals occurs.

Some consider that Internet religion simply magnifies the extremism of American culture. Certainly, several bizarre religious activities have appeared. Others have commented that the whole point of religion is the social interaction involved when groups of believers get together and that the Internet can never replace this. What the Internet has created, however, is the opportunity for different communities to emerge that cut across religious and geographical boundaries. People can go to the local meetings of their religious group, and some can then go home and exchange ideas and opinions with other fellow-believers living thousands of miles

Religion Sites on the World Wide Web

The World Wide Web (WWW) is a very fluid place where sites open, close and move very quickly. The following is an attempt to pick out what are likely to be the most stable and informative sites on religion. For individual religions, I have tried to select sites that are useful launching pads for further, more specific, information about that religion.

Subject Indexes and Search Machines

If you are looking for particular information on the World Wide Web, there are two different approaches that you may take. You may use a search machine to look for a word or a combination of words. It will return to you all of the WWW addresses that contain that word. This approach works well if the subject that you wish to look up is rather obscure (say, for example, 'Saguna-Brahman') and, therefore, there are not likely to be many sites. If you feed in common words (say, for example, 'Jesus Christ'), you are likely to get hundreds of thousands of addresses returned. Search Engines include:

http://google.com   http://www.ask.com   http://search.yahoo.com

If you are looking for a common subject, you would fare better looking in a subject index. These are hierarchically arranged indexes, which have the advantage that, in some cases, the sites have been selected and you are more likely to come across useful sites:

http://dir.yahoo.com/Society_and_Culture/Religion_and_Spirituality/
http://www.einet.net/directory/22694/Religion.htm
http://www.facetsofreligion.com
http://www.academicinfo.net/religindex.html
http://virtualreligion.net/vri/academic.html
http://www.mcgill.ca/religiousstudies/online-resources

Useful and fairly unbiased articles can be found in:

http://en.wikipedia.org   or   http://www.bbc.co.uk/religion/religions

Religious statistics can be found at: http://www.adherents.com

Addresses for Religious Sites

Baha'i Faith	http://www.bahai.org
	http://www.bcca.org
Buddhism	http://www.dharmanet.org/learning.htm
	http://www.ciolek.com/WWWVL-Buddhism.html
Chinese religions	http://online.sfsu.edu/~rone/China/spiritualchina.html
	http://sun.sino.uni-heidelberg.de/igcs/igphil.htm
Christianity	http://uwacadweb.uwyo.edu/religionet/er/christ
	http://www.iclnet.org/pub/resources/christian-booksinx.html
Hinduism	http://www.hindunet.org
	http://www.hinduwebsite.com/hinduindex.asp
Islam	(Sunni) http://www.understanding-islam.com
	(Shi'i) http://www.al-islam.org
Judaism	http://jewishnet.net
	http://shamash.org/links
Sikhism	http://www.sikhs.org/topics.htm
	http://www.sikhnet.com/s/SikhIntro
Zoroastrianism	http://www.zoroastrianism.com
Scriptures	http://www.sacred-texts.com
	http://origin.org/ucs/ws/ws.cfm
Women	http://www.femina.com/femina/SocietyandCulture/Religion

Internet Religion Discussion Groups

Usenet

Usenet is the system of Internet discussion groups. Every posting sent to the group appears to every person who has subscribed to that group. Some groups are moderated so as to keep the discussion on the topic and to exclude abusive language. Not all service providers provide access to Usenet and some service providers restrict the number of Usenet groups to which they provide access. This is not surprising as the number of Usenet groups runs to tens of thousands.

Within Usenet, the soc.religion hierarchy is moderated and has the most serious discussion. There are some fifteen groups including:

soc.religion.bahai
soc.religion.christian
soc.religion.hindu
soc.religion.islam
soc.religion.eastern

Much more anarchic are the unmoderated alt.religion (over 80 groups) and talk.religion (four groups) hierarchies. There are also country-based discussion groups such as uk.religion.misc. Participation on some Usenet groups can be gained via a mailing list (see below) for those whose access providers do not give access to Usenet.

Mailing Lists

Those wanting a more serious or more academic discussion on a religion or on a religious subject can try mailing lists. These operate in much the same way as Usenet. The only

away. They can experience, at first hand, the ideas of fellow-believers who come from very different cultural backgrounds. Others can go home and interchange ideas with those of a different religion. Ideas that previously would have taken months or years to move from one part of the world to another now move in days.

At the beginning of this chapter, I described the impact that multi-cultural, multi-ethnic societies can have on the religious world. The effect of the Internet is greatly to magnify that phenomenon and speed its effects. Now, even a person who lives on, let us say, a remote Scottish island where the entire population is of one religion and one ethnicity can have regular 'conversations' with others of different religious opinions and from different cultures.

Religion as Meaning

The capacity to symbolize distinguishes human beings from animals. Symbolization involves the attachment of arbitrary meanings and values to things; culture is the result of a society's agreed symbolizations. This results in a pattern of ways of behaving, concepts, attitudes, art forms and difference is that the material comes to you as e-mails. There is one central computer for each list that is programmed to turn each incoming message into e-mails to all subscribed members of the list. The following list is laid out with the list name and the address to which a request for subscription should be sent. For addresses beginning 'listserv', the text, which should be in the body (not the subject line) of the message, should be 'subscribe list-name your-first-name your-last-name'. For example, if John Smith wants to subscribe to Islam-L, he should send an email to listserv@ulkyvm.louiseville.edu with the subject line blank and the message 'subscribe islam-l John Smith' in the body of the text. For addresses beginning 'majordomo' or 'major', the text in the body of the message should be 'subscribe list-name your-e-mail-address'.

Mailing List Addresses

Subject	Name	Address
Academic Lists		
Religious studies	ANDERE-L	listserv@ucsbvm.ucsb.edu
Religious studies	AAR-L	majordomo@shemesh.scholar.emory.edu
New religious movements	NUREL-L	listserv@listserv.ucalgary.ca
By Religion		
Baha'i Faith	BAHAI-ST	major@johnco.cc.ks.us
Buddhism	BUDDHA-L	listserv@ulkyvm.louiseville.edu
Hinduism	HINDU-D	listserv@listserv.nodak.edu
Islam	ISLAM-L	listserv@ulkyvm.louiseville.edu
Judaism	H-JUDAIC	listserv@h-net.msu.edu
Taoism	TAOISM-STUDIES-L	Majordomo@coombs.anu.edu.au

so on which is called culture and is handed down from one generation to the next as tradition. Part of culture is to do with accommodation to the physical world. This, which mainly involves the group's accumulated knowledge of the various ways of surviving (obtaining food and shelter and avoiding dangers) in the environment of the group, is the science and technology of that culture. The other part involves interpretation of and accommodation to the mental or supernatural world. This involves the religious aspect of the culture. Religion is found to some degree in every culture that has been studied. Along with marriage, the family, incest prohibitions and some form of social organization, it is one of the few cultural universals among human beings.

The relationship between these two aspects of culture, the scientific and the religious (the natural and the supra-natural) is a fascinating object of study. Bronislaw Malinowski (1884–1942) found that the Tobriand Islanders, when dealing with those aspects of their surroundings over which they had control, such as farming and lagoon fishing, used their accumulated knowledge (their science and technology). When it came to more hazardous activities, however, such as open-sea fishing or war, or in the face of disease and death, magic and religious actions predominated.[55]

For the last two centuries, many have thought that as science and technology expanded humanity's knowledge and control over nature, religion's role in society would shrink and eventually vanish. In the last few decades, however, starting with quantum theory and Heisenberg's uncertainty principle in physics and extending more recently to studies of chaos, it has become increasingly clear that uncertainty is built into the structure of the universe itself. Thus the concept of the cosmos as a giant machine that humanity will eventually understand and master is an illusion. It now seems clear that we will never gain complete knowledge even of the physical world. As for the world of human behaviour and society, the prospects of discovering laws that will enable us to predict and determine these (a quest that some thought possible a few decades ago) have now receded indefinitely. It would therefore appear that there is a permanent role for religion in the human world. But it must, of course, be a religion that is in accordance with the modern world's view of the cosmos as extended by modern science and technology.

We may characterize modernity as a progressive destruction of the traditional view of the universe. Western thinking has gradually moved away from the classical medieval perception of the cosmos as a three-layered entity (heaven above, earth, hell below) populated by angels, spirits and demons. Science had destroyed that cosmology long before satellite views of the earth showed its falsity to all. Many would not mourn the loss of what now seems a childish view. Along with the loss of the authority of the religious cosmology, however, there has also occurred the loss of an authoritative meaning structure for human life as a whole. To many, humanity appears lost in a wilderness of meaninglessness.

Human beings seem to need a map by which to orient their lives; a framework within which to make sense of what happens to them; a psycho-cultural world of meaning that they can share with fellow human beings. Humanity also appears to have a need to affirm this common set of dominant values by shared action – ritual, ceremony, shared symbols, art and music. Having lost faith in religion, humanity has tried several alternative ideologies during the last hundred years: nationalism, racism and communism. However, these have also failed to give human beings a satisfactory and lasting answer to their basic human needs. The failure of these ideologies appears to presage a revival in the fortunes of religion. If this is so, what form of religion will satisfy humanity's basic need for meaning and significance and at the same time be congruous with the viewpoint of modernity?

Further Reading

For a review of the contemporary religious world, see Whaling, *Religion in Today's World*. See also Bruce, *Religion in the Modern World* (deals with the West only) and the relevant sections in Hinnells, *A Handbook of Living Religions*. On secularization, see Wilson, *Religion in a Secular Society*. On human rights, see Rouner, *Human Rights and the World's Religions* and

Tahzib, *Freedom of Religion or Belief*. On modern Hinduism, see Ashby, *Modern Trends in Hinduism*, and Richards, *A Source-Book of Modern Hinduism*. Most books on modern Islam focus, understandably, on the political aspects; see Munson, *Islam and Revolution* and Mortimer, *Faith and Power*. A good bibliography on modern Islam can be found in Burrell, *Islamic Fundamentalism*. On the contemporary Baha'i Faith, see Smith and Momen, 'The Baha'i Faith 1957–1988' and P. Smith, *The Babi and Baha'i Religion*. The best statistical survey on the current state of the world's religions is Barrett, *World Christian Encyclopedia*. On the new religious movements, see Barker, *New Religious Movements*, and Beckford, *Cult Controversies*. For new religious movements in Japan, Korea, the Caribbean, Nigeria, India, Sri Lanka and the Islamic world, see Beckford, *New Religious Movements*. The latter work, however, makes little distinction between new, independent movements and movements of revitalization within the traditional orthodoxies. For a review of new religious movements in primal societies, see Harold Turner's article on this in Hinnells, *A Handbook of Living Religions*, pp. 439–54.

Conclusion

In this book, we have looked at a number of religious phenomena from several different perspectives. As was pointed out in the Introduction, this approach has the advantage that one can use whichever theoretical framework seems to shed most light on any particular aspect of religion. The disadvantage is that the work as a whole lacks any overall unifying theoretical basis and is thus less coherent. The method is also susceptible to the charge of being arbitrary. The methodological problem arises from the fact that the field of religious studies has no overall theoretical basis on which all are agreed. Chapter 3 examined a number of theoretical bases that have been proposed for the study of religion. None of them has gained overwhelming support as an overriding theory to cover the whole field of religion, although each has enthusiastic supporters who have suggested as much.

The fact that an overriding theory has not emerged should neither surprise nor dismay us, however. Indeed, we should be glad that this is the case, for an attempt to impose such a theory at this stage would lead to the premature pigeon-holing of religious phenomena. Even in a field of experimental science such as particle physics, there is as yet no unified field theory. Physicists use the framework of relativity theory for looking at some problems and the framework of quantum theory for others. Physicists have the benefit of being able to perform experiments in order to prove or refute their theories. If this situation has arisen in a field like physics, there is not much likelihood of the emergence in the near future of a 'unified field theory' in religious studies, where minimal experimentation is possible and the data are often unreliable or irretrievably lost. With no unified field theory to fall back on, we are left with a wide variety of different theoretical frameworks from which to view religious phenomena.

Despite the fragmentation caused by these different approaches, the hope is that the reader will have gained some degree of understanding of religious phenomena from reading this book. Different theoretical approaches each shed a different light on any particular aspect of religion. It is hoped that the overall effect is to increase understanding. Let us take religious symbols as an example. Most of humanity's religious life consists of symbolism in some form, whether as language, ritual or art. In chapter 11, we saw how Eliade considered each religious symbol to be a local and specific manifestation of certain archetypal formations, irruptions of the sacred world into the profane; we saw that there is a dialectical movement between the universal archetype and the local symbol. In chapter 3 (pp. 63–4), we saw that Jung placed these archetypes deep within the human unconscious. The symbol is that which awakens the archetype within us. In functionalist theory (pp. 53–5), a symbol could act as a focal point for the unifying effects of religion in society. The culture of a society represents the communally agreed way in which the members of that society interpret their symbols; of course, the most important of these symbol structures is the language of a culture (see pp. 101–4, 114, 459). An important part of the symbol structure of most cultures has been religious symbolism. In structuralist theory (pp. 56–8), a symbol can be fitted into an overall structure that reveals the thought structures of the mind. In chapter 7 (pp. 170–3), we saw that religious symbols could exert their effect by unlocking certain religious experiences which, because they occurred at heightened levels of emotion, are blocked at the everyday level of activity; the symbol acts as a key to take the individual back to the state in which he or she first encountered the experience. We have also noted a conflict between liberals and fundamentalists over whether the scripture should be understood symbolically or literally (see chapter 14). In this way, a composite picture can be built up of the way that the religious symbol acts in religious life.

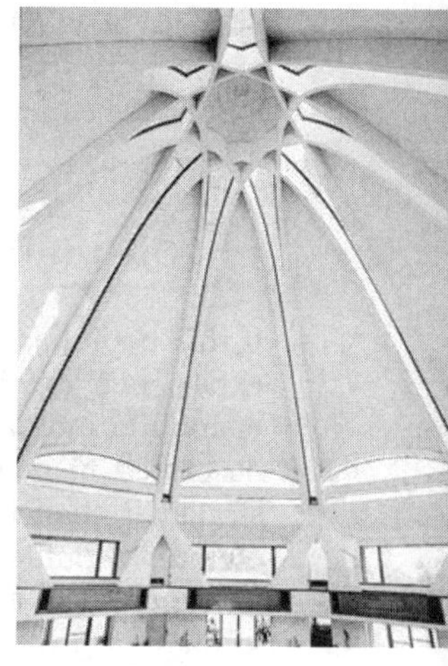

THE BAHA'I FAITH: Baha'i symbol placed in the centre of the dome of the Baha'i House of Worship at Tiapapata, near Apia, Western Samoa

None of the above viewpoints on the religious symbol represents a complete statement of its origins and functioning; even all of these different viewpoints together probably do not represent the whole truth. But at least the composite picture is more likely to be closer to the whole truth than any individual part of it. The composite picture is also more likely to be useful, in that any further examples of a religious symbol in action can be compared to these different viewpoints; this would be more likely to suggest further ideas for investigation than the use of just one theoretical framework.

Similarly, when we are trying to understand some new religious phenomenon, we can use the broad range of interpretative frameworks to see if any of them throw light on the phenomenon. If we are examining religious fundamentalism or the feminist approach to religion, for example, we can see the tendency in these movements to build an ideal mythological picture of the distant past, a Garden of Eden type of mythology. They also create a new religious myth of death and resurrection, in which the evils of the present situation are compared to the benefits that will come when all adopt the beliefs that they are advocating (see pp. 285–6). We can also perhaps see an element of eschatological or messianic expectation in their promise of a Golden Age in the future, which will replicate the Golden Age of the past (see pp. 251–3). Through understanding these underlying motifs, we can also understand the attraction that these movements have.

From Individual Experience to Social Expression

If this book has any unifying theme, it is that as we go from the religious experience of the individual to the social expressions of religion we encounter increasing diversity. The religious experience of the individual as described in many religious traditions from around the world is broadly similar. I shall not here repeat ground that has already been covered in chapter 4. Suffice it to say that the religious experience of the individual is an experience of an Ultimate Reality that is transcendent to (and often also immanent in) the world. The experience can be described in many different ways, but its essential features include a feeling that the experience has saved or liberated the individual and, usually, an element that transforms the life of the individual.

Once we go from the experience itself to attempts to describe it and set it in context, then we come to a much greater degree of diversity. We human beings create the intellectual and cultural worlds that we call reality. Each of these cultural worlds sees reality in a different way. It is not surprising therefore to find that descriptions of the religious experience are different in each of these worlds. An Indian yogi may describe his experience of *samadhi* (deep meditation) as being that of insight into the essential unity of all things with Brahman. A devout South American Catholic may describe the experience that she has in front of an altar as being that of a vision of the Virgin Mary.

Because of the importance of the religious experience, human beings create conceptual worlds that allow for and give a prominent place to it. In primal societies, this involves creating a conceptual world that is populated by many spirits and may be ruled over by gods. These entities are then made responsible for the religious experience. In general, there are two versions of reality, two ways of interpreting religious experience, that have achieved a wide geographical spread and have acquired a wide base of support among the peoples of the world. One version, which I have called theism, sees religious experience as given to human beings from an 'other power', which is usually called God. The other version is non-theistic and is usually represented as a form of monism. This sees religious experience as being something that emerges from within the individual once he or she is prepared for it. This preparation is usually a combination of knowledge and some experiential component brought about through techniques such as meditation or ritual chanting (see chapter 8).

By itself, the religious experience has no effects in society unless individuals express it in some way. Religious experience has seemed so joyful, liberating and important to human beings that they have sought to

CHRISTIANITY: Madonna and child fresco from the museum of St Stephanos monastery, a fifteenth-century monastery (now occupied by nuns) perched on top of a mountain in central Greece

set up formal ways of achieving it. From the fairly simple conceptual dichotomy between theism and monism, chapter 5 traced the emergence of eight pathways of recreating the religious experience. Since the religious experience is liberating, I called these the pathways to liberation or salvation.

As we now go on to consider the various social expressions of religion, the pathways to liberation or salvation, we find an even greater degree of variety. The social expressions of religion vary not just between the different religions of the world, but between the sects of each religion. Not only is there variation between the different sects, but even the same sect will show marked variation over the course of its historical development. The Religious Society of Friends (Quakers), for example, began as a introverted, pietist group but later developed marked extrovert, social reformist tendencies. It also went through a brief evangelical phase in Britain in the early nineteenth century under Joseph Gurney. Even within the same religious group at a given time we find variations of social expression. The Church of England in the second half of the twentieth century is divided into 'high' church and 'low' church, fundamentalists and liberals, supporters of the ordination of women and opponents, supporters of moves towards ecumenicism and opponents, and so on. It includes individuals whose practices other members of the Church of England may condemn as superstitious or pagan. It allows such diversities of social life as hierarchical, disciplined monastic orders and egalitarian, undisciplined house churches.

A religious person might interpret these facts to mean that the direct religious experience is the central phenomenon of religion, the 'truth' of religion. As such, it is a unifying phenomenon. As one then looks towards the social expressions of religion, one is entering an area where there is more and more human involvement in the affairs of religion. This then represents the pure 'truth' of religion mixed with fallible human influences – hence the diversity of religious social phenomena.

One theme that seems to recur frequently when we consider religious phenomena is that of descent and ascent or death and resurrection. We have seen that this is the basic pattern of all creative phenomena (see pp. 99, 459): there is first a destruction or decay of the old and then the arising of the new. We can see this as an underlying pattern in the stages of religious experience (pp. 99–100); it is also the way that religious language has its effect (see pp. 101–3) and that religious myth, ritual and symbols function (see pp. 270–5, 279–86); it is implicit in the prophecy of catastrophe followed by messianic hope that appears in most religion (see chapter 10); and it is, of course, responsible for the power of religious art (see pp. 459–62).

The History of a Religion

We may also survey the historical development of religions. In the early days of the evolution of a religion, the founder of the religion and his early

ISLAM: Friday Prayers in the mosque, especially in Sunni Islam, act as a social focus for the community. All Muslim men try to attend. Here people are streaming into the Dome of the Rock in Jerusalem for Friday Prayers.

disciples exert a strong personal influence over the course of the religion – what Weber called charismatic authority (see p. 317). The religious impulse at this early stage is strong. Believers have a direct and powerful experience of it, feeling that they are in direct contact with the Real. There is no need to institutionalize the pathways to salvation, as at this stage in its development, religion is a fairly simple personal phenomenon. It may have great social impact as, for example, the first generations of Muslims did as they swept out of the Arabian peninsula and defeated the armies of the established powers of that time, but the religion itself is still a fairly uncomplicated matter. For those early Muslims, religion was a simple and direct relationship between themselves and God, a relationship guided by the Prophet Muhammad. Any social problems or disputes were solved in a direct manner by reference to the Prophet himself or his representative.

As religion develops and grows more distant from its origins, a number of changes occur (see pp. 320–4 for more details). The informal, direct relationships of the early years become increasingly formal and distant. The religious authorities in later years claim less authority and status than the prophet-founder or his earliest disciples, and yet they maintain a structure that implies a much greater distance between themselves and ordinary believers than was the norm in the early period. We may say that the greater the charismatic authority, the less need there is for formal authority structures. As charismatic authority declines with the passage of time from the early years of the religion, so the formal authority structures become more pronounced and hierarchical. Similarly, as the religion develops, the religious professionals increasingly intrude into the original, simple, direct relationship between the believer and God.

HINDUISM: A poster of Lord Shiva, his wife Parvati and their son, the elephant-headed god Ganesha. Also in this picture are numerous symbols of Hinduism: Om (the holy sound, on the raised right palm of Shiva), swastika (on the raised right palm of Ganesha), trident (right hand of Shiva), conch-shell (left hand of Shiva), lotus (left hand of Parvati), Nandi the white bull, and the lingam (top right).

The result of the institutionalization of religion and the formalization of the pathways to salvation is the gradual weakening of the religious experience itself. The focus of religious life shifts from the spiritual and moral imperatives of the founder's teaching to the institutional forms of the religion, whether this be the Christian Church, the Islamic Shari'a or the Buddhist monastery (see pp. 323–31). The shift is from attraction to the inner spiritual and intellectual life to an attachment to the outward forms of the religion.

Various other changes occur as a religion ages. We have observed a tendency for religious art forms to develop from simple, direct, aniconic representations to the iconic representations of the *bhakti* type of religious devotion, and finally to fully representational art, characteristic of the period when the religious impulse is weakest (see chapter 18). There is also a tendency for the institutional official religion to be replaced in people's estimation by popular religious forms (see chapter 15). One aspect of the decline in the influence and effectiveness of religion is a perception that the religion no longer addresses the concerns of the age. There is a lack of congruence between the viewpoint of the religion and the worldview of the majority (see chapter 19). One result of the perception of the decline of religion can be a revolt against the liberalism of the mature religion and a desire for a fundamentalist return to the roots of the religion (see chapter 14).

Once people consider a religion to be in decline, once the morals of society are perceived to be degenerating, however, there is a powerful impulse for change, reform or renewal. This is the situation in which the myth of the solar hero (see pp. 270–5) comes into play, messianic expectations are raised (see chapter 10) and new religious movements come into being (see pp. 508–16). We can see, in such situations, the milieu from which a new religion emerges. The founders of the great world religions, figures such as the Buddha, Jesus and Muhammad, would each in his own time have been seen as a minor religious reformer of the existing religious tradition, the leader of a 'new religious movement'. It is only with the benefit of hindsight that we can see the distinctive features of these religions that caused them to emerge from the general mass of minor religious movements and develop into major religious traditions.

This process of religious change or conversion can itself be analysed from several viewpoints. It can be seen from the historical perspective as the process that must inevitably occur if a religion goes into decline and ceases to be socially or intellectually relevant (see pp. 476–89). New religious forms emerge and many convert to them. The same process can be analysed at the level of intellectual and conceptual changes as the perception that one worldview has become inadequate and the emergence of an alternative (see pp. 151–3). The psychological aspects of religious change and conversion may also be examined (see pp. 99–100, 151–61).

Analysis and Categorization

As was pointed out in the Introduction, one must be careful not to become too carried away with academic analyses of the phenomenon of religion or to propose analyses that are too facile and underestimate the power and significance of the phenomenon. In examining religious experience, we are looking at a facet of the believer's life that means a great deal to her or him. Ultimately, all that we can do is to describe the shadow cast on the cave wall by the experience, not the experience itself. Peter Berger used the analogy of the reports of travellers to a faraway country:

> Take the case of travellers returning home with accounts of a faraway country. Assume that it can be demonstrated beyond a shadow of a doubt that every one of these accounts is determined by the historical, socioeconomic, and psychological characteristics of the traveller in question. Thus one traveller sees the faraway country as a reflection of the past history of his own country, another describes it as a solution to the social problems from which he suffered in his own life, another perceives it as the embodiment of his own worst fears or best hopes. And so on and so forth. As the critical observer analyzes all these reports, it is perfectly plausible for him to perceive the faraway country as a gigantic projection of the travellers' own country. Indeed, the travellers' accounts will be very useful in gaining a better understanding of their home country. None of this, however, invalidates the proposition that the faraway country does indeed exist and that something about it can be gleaned from the travellers' accounts. The final point is not that Marco Polo was an Italian – and, who knows, an Italian with all sorts of class resentments and with an unresolved Oedipus complex – *but that he visited China*.[1]

This, then, is the crux of the matter. It is all too easy for an academic to consider that by categorizing and thus pigeon-holing a phenomenon, he or she has understood it. And yet reality is much more subtle than any academic theories and concepts. Almost every phenomenon, however neatly it falls into a category or classification, is also in some way an exception to the rule. Natural phenomena, and especially human activities, are infinitely variable. Like fingerprints, no two are exactly the same. Therefore, every time that we categorize and classify, we are to some extent forcing the facts to fit our categories; we are imposing an interpretation on the data; we are to some extent distorting the truth.

On the other hand, it would not be possible to write a book such as this without categorizing and classifying data. The balance therefore lies in finding that degree of categorization that is useful in increasing understanding without unduly distorting the facts. The criterion for success lies in the extent to which the analyses help an understanding of the phenomena and the extent to which they are able to accommodate new data.

The Definition of Religion

This Conclusion is a suitable place from which to look back at an issue that was raised in the Introduction, the question of a definition of religion. Unfortunately, our survey has brought us no closer to an authoritative definition. A definition of religion given in the Introduction, such as 'that human activity that acknowledges the existence of another reality that is transcendent to or immanent within this physical worldly reality and seeks to describe and put human beings into a correct relationship with that

JUDAISM: The shofar is a musical instrument traditionally made of ram's horn. It is traditionally sounded at the Jewish festivals of Rosh Hoshanah (New Year) and Yom Kipur.

reality' may still be considered valid. We can now see, however, that it effectively hides as much as it reveals. The average educated person from a Western background may read such a definition, think that she or he knows what it means and agree with it. But we have seen how each phrase of this definition is susceptible to many alternative conceptualizations.

The phrase 'another reality', for example, does not just mean God, as the Western reader might think. It includes non-theistic (monistic) conceptualizations of Absolute Reality that are in many ways the exact opposite of the Western concept of God (see chapters 2 and 8). What, moreover, are the implications of the feminist critique of the patriarchal worldview for the phrase 'another reality' (see chapter 17)? Is it even possible, in the light of post-modernist deconstruction, to think of 'another reality' as being a meaningful phrase? What, as another example, is 'that human activity' that puts 'human beings into a correct relationship' with the other reality? Some eight different pathways have been described, each claiming, within particular contexts, to be the correct human activity for this purpose (see chapter 5). A Western reader may well have in mind, when reading such a phrase, the ordinary activities of religious groups such as prayer and ritual; she or he will also think of the extraordinary actions of some saints and holy figures who have consented to martyrdom or other sacrifice rather than jeopardize their 'relationship' with the other reality (see pp. 230–1). Will such a reader also think of popular religious practices that seek to put the participant 'into a correct relationship' with a divinity in order to obtain an immediate benefit such as material gain or health (see chapter 15)? Many will think of such practices as being more magic than religion, but they nevertheless fulfil the definition given above.

Some may consider that a definition of religion that encompasses both theistic and non-theistic religions would need to start with the human being. All religions agree that there is a problem with human existence, a flaw in human nature. Some may see this flaw as being caused by original sin (Christianity), by rebellion against God (Islam), by seeing reality incorrectly (Advaita Vedantist Hinduism) or by the human tendency to focus on and desire transient things (Buddhism). This flaw in human nature is considered to be something that ordinary human effort cannot overcome. Only the pathway taught by each religion is able to overcome it: salvation through belief in Christ (Christianity), following the Shari'a (the Holy Law in Islam), seeing things as they really are (Advaita Vedantist Hinduism), or following the Dhamma and the Noble Eightfold Path (Buddhism). A religion could thus be defined as that which corrects or compensates for the basic flaw in human nature. However, even a definition of religion built up from such a basis would have difficulties. Marxism similarly sees a flaw in human nature or, more specifically in human society, and shows the pathway for overcoming it. A similar fate befalls the functional definitions of religion that were cited in the Introduction. A critique of these may be found in chapter 3.

Ultimately, we must return to the fact that is insisted upon in so many sources: the religious experience cannot be adequately defined or communicated. It can only be experienced and grasped in a direct way. All attempts to describe and analyse it are, to a large extent, missing the mark, because they are relying on the descriptions of those who have had the experience, data which are themselves faulty. As the great Muslim mystic and philosopher al-Ghazali said, the mystical and religious experience are:

> something that cannot be apprehended by study, but only by immediate experience (*dhawq* – literally 'tasting'), by ecstasy and by a moral change. What a difference there is between knowing the definition of health and satiety, together with their causes and presuppositions, and being healthy and satisfied! What a difference between being acquainted with the definition of drunkenness . . . and being drunk! Indeed the drunken man while in that condition does not know the definition of drunkenness nor the scientific account of it; he has not the very least scientific knowledge of it. The sober man, on the other hand, knows the definition of drunkenness and its basis, yet he is not drunk in the very least.[2]

BUDDHISM: Wat Arun, a Thai Buddhist temple in Bangkok, at sunset.

Glossary

MANY OF THE TERMS THAT FOLLOW HAVE been defined here as they are used in this book in relation to the study of religion; they may have a somewhat different meaning in other fields, such as philosophy.

Ahriman (Angra-Mainu) Spirit of darkness and evil in Zoroastrianism and the chief opponent of Ahura-Mazda.

Ahura-Mazda The Supreme Deity in Zoroastrianism, representing goodness and light.

Amitabha or **Amida Buddha** The Buddha of Infinite Light, one of the five Dhyani or meditation Buddhas, and ruler over the Western or Sukhavati Paradise. The Pure Land, or Amida, Mahayana Buddhist sects opened up a new pathway of salvation in Buddhism in which calling upon Amitabha's name, or visualizing his paradise, enables the believer to be born into his paradise, to hear the Dharma taught there and to achieve Nirvana in one round of life instead of numerous rebirths.

anatta (Pali; Sanskrit: *anatman*, literally 'no soul', or 'no self') The Buddhist doctrine that there is no permanent, eternal, independent soul, self or substance that is inherent within the individual. In Mahayana doctrine this is taken further and comes to mean that there is no permanent substance in anything that arises (see '*Shunyata*').

anicca (Pali; Sanskrit: *anitya*) The Buddhist doctrine that all things are transitory and impermanent.

animism The concept that behind all things, including inanimate natural phenomena (such as trees, rivers and mountains), there is a spirit, usually endowed with human qualities (theory propounded by E. B. Tylor, 1871).

apocalyptic A view of the end of the world as a cosmic battle resulting in the triumph of good over evil.

apotropaic Having the power to avert evil or bad luck.

archetype The original mythical or spiritual model on which existent things are patterned. In Jung, it is an unconscious concept or mode of thought passed down as the common inheritance of the human race (the collective unconscious).

asceticism The view that spiritual progress comes from controlling the body and overcoming physical desires. In order to achieve this, it is usually necessary to cut oneself off from contact with the world (see 'eremitism').

Ash'ari The school of scholastic theology that has predominated in Sunni Islam, named after Abu al-Hasan al-Ash'ari (c.873–c.935). It takes a moderate determinist position (see 'determinism').

Atman In Hinduism, Atman is the immortal soul or self which exists beyond the mortal body; in Advaita Vedanta, it is absolute consciousness and is identified with Brahman, Absolute Reality. In Buddhism, the existence of an Atman is denied (see '*anatta*').

avatar (or *avatara*, literally 'descent') In Hinduism, the descent of the divine consciousness to earth in the form of a human being. The avatar is therefore not a result of karma (q.v.) but rather the result of an act of will prompted by the beneficence of the deity. The avatar comes at a time of loss of righteousness and is able to cause new pathways of religious righteousness (Dharma), adapted to the needs of the time, to arise. Krishna and Rama are considered avatars of the god Vishnu.

avidya In Hinduism and Buddhism, ignorance caused by the inability to distinguish the absolute from the contingent; an inability to see things as they really are. This ignorance is caused by *maya* (q.v.). In Buddhism, *avidya* is ignorance of the Four Noble Truths.

baqa ('continuance') Islamic Sufi term denoting the continuance of the spiritual journey of the individual in God after having the reached the stage of *fana* (q.v.).

batin (literally 'interior') Term in Islamic mysticism and mystical philosophy denoting the inner esoteric truth of a concept or ritual rather than its outer exoteric meaning or description (*zahir*).

bhakti ('love') The Hindu pathway to salvation, involving love and devotion to and worship of a particular deity.

bodhisattva (literally, 'enlightenment being') A being who is on the way to enlightenment. In Mahayana Buddhism, one who achieves perfection and enlightenment and is able to proceed to Nirvana, but puts off this stage in order to help other beings to progress and achieve enlightenment.

Brahman Absolute Reality, absolute consciousness, the ground of being. In Advaita Vedanta, the supreme non-dual reality which is identical to the Atman (q.v.). This term should not be confused with Brahma, the creator god of Hinduism, nor with Brahmin (see below).

Brahmin (anglicized form of the more correct 'Brahman') The priestly caste of Hinduism.

charisma As used by Weber, this term denotes that power of attraction which the leader of a (religious) movement has by virtue of being considered to possess extraordinary powers or gifts.

chiliasm See 'millennialism'.

church A Christian community and also the building in which it worships. Sociologically, the term is used to describe any religious group that is large, well-established in society, is inclusive in its membership, and considers itself the sole legitimate guardian of the truth. It usually makes low demands of its members (cf 'denomination' and 'sect').

civil religion A collection of beliefs and actions through which individuals interact with elements of civil society in ways that resemble religious concepts and activities.

commentary A book that explains and interprets a (scriptural) text.

cosmogony A doctrine or theory regarding how the universe came into being.

cosmology A branch of metaphysics concerned with the nature and structure of the universe.

cult Refers to a religious group whose beliefs or actions are sufficiently at variance with those of the prevailing norms of society that this causes a degree of tension to arise.

denomination An autonomous group within a religion. Sociologically, the term is used to describe a religious group that is well-established, inclusive in its membership but recognizes that other religious groups may also possess the truth (cf 'church' and 'sect')

determinism In philosophy, this term denotes the idea that causes are inevitably followed by their consequences. In religion, this term refers to the doctrine that everything that comes to pass is predetermined and that human free will is therefore delusory.

Dharma See p. 202.

Dharmakaya The Dharma body of the Buddha in Mahayana Buddhism; the highest and true nature of the Buddha, identical with Absolute Reality.

dhikr (literally 'remembrance') In Sufi Islam, a term denoting the rhythmic repetitive chanting of a name of God or of a short formula.

dualism In philosophy, this term usually refers to the concept that mind (or soul) and matter, form two distinct realities. In this book the term has also been used to denote the concept that the divine reality and the human reality are two distinct realities (the Hindu concept of *dvaita*). This is in contrast to the concept of *advaita* (non-dualism) or monism. There is also the ethical concept of dualism that posits that good and evil exist as two distinct realities in the world (see 'Ahura-Mazda' and 'Ahriman').

emic The description of a religious tradition using the understandings and categories that the adherents themselves use and recognize (cf. 'etic').

empiricism An approach to philosophy that maintains that valid knowledge can only be gained from empirical evidence (i.e. based on observation or concrete experience).

epistemology The theoretical aspects of knowledge: the definition of knowledge, the sources of knowledge, the kinds of knowledge and the degree of certainty attaching to each kind, the relationship between the knower and the known.

eremitism The pathway of the religious recluse, hermit.

eschatology The study or knowledge of the 'last things', either in the sense of knowing what will happen at the time of the end of the world or of what occurs to the individual after death.

ethics The branch of philosophy concerned with deriving morality.

etic Interpretative categories that a scholar might impose upon a religion from the outside (cf. 'emic').

Eucharist The Christian ritual of taking consecrated bread and wine, as a memorial of the Last Supper of Christ, as a symbolic representation of the spiritual union of the believer and Christ, or in the belief that the bread and wine have changed into the actual body and blood of Christ.

evangelism (literally, 'good news'). A belief that salvation depends on a personal conversion experience and that it is the duty of the individual to spread the 'good news' of the availability of this salvation to all.

exegesis Drawing out and explaining the meaning of a text.

existentialism A wide-ranging philosophy, some of the components of which include the assertion that human beings create their own nature by the choices that they make. Each individual has to struggle with a universe that is unfathomable, to commit herself or himself to a path or vocation, and to take responsibility for choices made without the help of universal, objective standards.

faith Belief in, trust in, and commitment to a religious system.

fana ('extinction') Islamic Sufi term denoting the stage in the individual's spiritual journey wherein all traces of self are extinguished (see '*baqa*').

fetishism The belief in objects or persons possessed by spirits, which in the case of persons is not their own soul.

functionalism The study of religion in terms of the human needs it fulfils and its role in the overall functioning of a social and cultural system.

fundamentalism A term originally used to denote certain Christian groups who believed in the infallibility and the literal interpretation of the *Bible*. More recently, the term has been extended to refer to groups from any religion that are characterized by any or all or the following: opposition to a modern liberal interpretation of their religion, an exclusivist attitude (rejecting both other religions and other interpretations of their own religion), and a desire to return the religion to some perceived earlier ideal state.

gnosis, gnosticism A term originally used of certain Christian sects that emerged in the second century CE, but used in this book to refer to any religious group that emphasizes that true knowledge of the path to salvation or liberation, or the correct interpretation of scripture, can only be obtained through a secret knowledge known only by the group (or its leader) and only imparted to initiates.

guru A spiritual master, often one to whom unquestioned obedience must be given.

Hadith A saying or action of the prophet Muhammad which was reported and transmitted orally until it was written down in collections some centuries later. In Shi'i Islam, the *Hadiths* relating to the Imams (q.v.) are also considered authoritative.

Hajj The Islamic ritual pilgrimage to Mecca, undertaken at a prescribed time and in a prescribed manner (see pp. 280–1).

Halakhah (literally, 'path' or 'way') The traditional law in Judaism, based on rabbinical interpretation and transmitted orally until written down in the early centuries CE. It supplements and amplifies the scriptural law laid down in the Pentateuch.

hermeneutics The principles of interpretation of a text; the study of the methodology of interpretation.

heterodox Contradicting or being different from the standard traditional teachings of a religion.

hierocracy The rule of a society by the priests or religious professionals.

hierophany the manifestation of the sacred in physical form (person, object, event, etc.)

Husayn Third of the Imams (q.v.) of the Shi'i line; was martyred in battle at Karbala in Iraq, an event commemorated each year by Shi'is, with much emotion and passion.

Iblis The name for Satan in Islam.

icon An image of something that is holy, drawn according to traditional forms.

Imam (literally, 'before' or 'in front', i.e. the one who stands in front) Used throughout the Islamic world to denote the leader of the ritual Friday prayers, or any leader. Also used in Shi'i Islam in the specific sense of a series of persons regarded as having been the rightful successors to the prophet Muhammad and who are considered to have divinely-inspired knowledge of the true interpretation of the scriptures. The majority of Shi'i, the Twelvers, hold to a series of twelve such Imams but other groups such as the Isma'ilis recognize others.

ineffable Incapable of being expressed in words, indescribable.

jati See '*varna*'.

jihad Holy war, one of the five pillars of Islam. In modern times, this has increasingly been interpreted in an ethical sense as a war on selfishness and irreligion.

jiriki (literally, 'one's own power') Japanese Buddhist term denoting spiritual pathways such as Zen, in which progress and ultimately liberation is through one's own effort – In contradistinction to *tariki* (literally, 'other power'), which refers to pathways that rely on liberation through the power of another (eg Amida Buddha).

jivanmukti Hindu term denoting one who has attained liberation while still alive.

jñana, jñana yoga ('knowledge') The Hindu pathway to salvation, involving intellectual striving and attaining correct knowledge, seeing things as they really are.

Kabbala, Cabala A system of Jewish mysticism, mystical interpretation of scripture and thaumaturgy that originated in medieval times. It is heavily influenced by Neo-platonic concepts of the origin of the world through emanation.

kami Japanese term denoting spirits or divinities that reside in natural phenomena (air, sky, mountains, wind, etc.)

karma Hindu and Buddhist term denoting the law of cause and effect, that one's actions have inevitable consequences, either positive or negative, that must be played out, either immediately or after death (i.e. what we do affects what we eventually become). Buddhism emphasizes the intention of the action as what produces karma. Enlightenment produces the ability to act without causing the accumulation of more karma.

koan A paradoxical saying or action in Zen Buddhism, which transcends logic and conceptual thought and is thus intended to point the way to enlightenment.

lama Originally the equivalent of guru (q.v.) in Tibetan Buddhism, but now applied to all monks.

liberation theology A theology that originated among South American Roman Catholic clergy and that uses some of the concepts and language of social and political philosophies such as Marxism, combining them with a theology of salvation through liberation from social injustice.

madrasa Islamic religious college where studies centre on the Shari'a (q.v.)

Maitreya Buddha The Buddha that is prophesied in the Buddhist scriptures and expected to come as the fifth Buddha of this world cycle. At present he resides in the Tushita paradise.

mana A supernatural power that can reside in objects or people.

mandala In Buddhism, especially the Tantric Buddhism of Tibet, mandalas are two- or three-dimensional representations of the cosmos, usually of a particular god, Buddha or *bodhisattva*. It can be used as part of a ritual or as a support for meditation or visualization.

Manifestations of God Baha'i term denoting the founder-prophets of the world religions, who are considered to be perfect manifestations of the names and attributes of God.

mantra A regular rhythmic chant in Hinduism and especially Tantric Buddhism, often of the name of a deity or of a sacred syllable or syllables, and often used as a form of meditation.

maya The cosmic illusion in Hinduism and Buddhism that hides reality and thus keeps us in ignorance (*avidya*).

messianism The belief in the advent of a future world saviour, often also involving the establishment of a Golden Age.

metaphysics The part of philosophy concerned with the nature and structure of reality.

millennialism, millenarianism Belief in a future Golden Age (one thousand years) in which there will be universal prosperity and peace, usually through the agency of a future world saviour (see 'messianism').

Mishnah The first part of the *Talmud*, consisting of a codification of Jewish oral law, compiled in about 200 CE by Rabbi Judah.

***moksha* (*mukti*)** Liberation from karma and from the cycle of birth and death.

monasticism A religious path that involves the establishment of a community whose members have taken vows to follow a spiritual discipline and who usually live set apart from the rest of society.

monism The belief that there is only extant reality; in Hinduism the doctrine of *advaita* (non-dualism) asserts that God and the soul are one reality.

morality See 'ethics'.

mudra A bodily posture or gesture in Hinduism and Buddhism.

muezzin One who sounds the *adhan*, or call to ritual prayer, in Islam.

Muharram The first month of the Muslim year. In Shi'i Islam, the first ten days are taken up with commemorations of the martyrdom of the Imam Husayn.

mujtahid (literally, 'one who strives') An Islamic cleric who has achieved sufficient proficiency in the study of the Holy Law and religious jurisprudence to be able to make independent judgements about the application of the Holy Law to the situations of everyday life. In orthodox Sunni teaching, there have been no more *mujtahids* since the time of the founders of the four schools of jurisprudence. Shi'is hold, however, that it is still possible for *mujtahids* to function.

mukti See '*moksha*'.

murid Sufi Islamic term denoting the pupil of a *murshid* (q.v.).

murshid (pir) Islamic term denoting a Sufi master who is able to teach others the secrets of the spiritual path.

Mu'tazila The Islamic school of scholastic theology that emphasized rationality and asserted that the *Qur'an* was created. It was defeated in Sunni Islam by the Ash'ari school (q.v.), but continued to predominate in Shi'i Islam.

mysticism An approach to religion that emphasizes a direct intuitive knowledge of God, of Ultimate Reality, or of the spiritual world. This approach takes on a wide variety of forms but among the features that many of these have in common is that they result in serenity, harmonization of the inner and outer life, and joy; they also emphasize union or unity with the Ultimate Reality. The social form of this approach often involves membership of an order and submission to a spiritual master who introduces the initiate into the spiritual techniques involved.

myth A traditional sacred story that tells of the origin of the world or of death and resurrection.

nembutsu A term in Japanese Amida Buddhism referring to a meditation practice that involves the rhythmic repetition of the name of Amida Buddha (*namu Amida Butsu*). It is believed that this can succeed in bringing about rebirth into the Western Sukhavati paradise of Amida Buddha.

Neoplatonism A wide-ranging philosophy that usually includes the concept of the derivation of the world and of the human soul through a series of emanations from the One. The human soul is therefore, or should be, engaged in the task of reuniting itself with the source of its being.

Nirmanakaya In Mahayana Buddhism, this term denotes the transformation body of the Buddha, the earthly body with which the Buddhas appear to humanity in order to fulfil their vow of guiding all beings to enlightenment.

Nirvana (literally, 'extinction') The goal of human endeavour in Buddhism is to achieve a state in which all human desires, hatreds and delusions are extinguished, thus putting an end to volition and suffering, and freeing oneself from the effects of karma (q.v.).

noetic Of, or relating to, the *nous*, the intellect.

ontology The study of the nature and relationships of being, including the existence of an ultimate being, God.

original sin The doctrine that humanity is inherently sinful due to the first sin committed by Adam and Eve in the Garden of Eden.

orthodoxy Correct beliefs, beliefs that are in line with the mainstream tradition of a religion.

paramartha Supreme reality or supreme truth, by the attainment of which the individual achieves liberation.

parinirvana Complete extinction, usually equated with *nirupadhishesha-nirvana*, Nirvana (q.v.) after death.

paritta The chanting of sections of scripture, usually for protection or good fortune, in Theravada Buddhism.

phenomenology An approach to philosophy that attempts to describe phenomena as they present themselves to the consciousness; to uncover the necessary and invariant features of a phenomenon.

pietism A movement in Christianity that holds that faith does not consist of correct theological formulations but rather emphasizes conversion, personal religious experience and the fruits of faith in daily life.

pir See '*murshid*'.

positivism, logical positivism A philosophical position that asserts that all meaningful statements must be either analytic or empirically verifiable. All metaphysics is therefore inherently meaningless.

prajña In Mahayana Buddhism, that intuitive wisdom which is beyond conceptual and rational thought and which leads to enlightenment.

pranayama Control of the breath, breathing exercises in Raja-Yoga.

pratitya-samutpada (Sanskrit; Pali: *patichcha-samupadda*) Co-dependent origination or conditioned arising – all existing things are interdependent and mutually condition one another. This entangles beings in Samsara (q.v.).

primal religions Those religions that are orally transmitted; the religions of a single tribe or a limited ethnic group.

process philosophy A philosophy that asserts that reality is constantly is a state of change and flux. The religious or theological aspects of this philosophy refer to a God who is ever changing and developing, who enters into relationships with the individual and is affected and changed by these relationships; it emphasizes becoming rather than being, relationships rather than structures.

proselytism The process of causing someone to change their religious faith, recruiting someone to a new religion.

rabbi A Jewish doctor qualified to expound on and apply the Holy Law, the Halakhah (q.v.).

Ramadan The month of fasting in the Islamic calendar.

reification The process of regarding something that is abstract as a concrete or material thing.

rida Contentment (with the will of God). An Islamic Sufi term.

rishi Hindu term referring to a seer or saint, in particular those individuals to whom the Vedas were revealed.

rite of passage A ritual or ceremony that marks an important turning point in an individual's life, often also leading to a change of status: birth, puberty, marriage, death.

ritual Formal religious words and actions that seek to evoke a sacred event or invoke a sacred presence.

sadhu Hindu term denoting one who has renounced the world in an effort to find liberation.

salat Ritual prayer in Islam that should ideally, especially on Fridays, be said congregationally.

samadhi A state of consciousness in which mental activity ceases. In Buddhism, the experiencing subject becomes one with the experienced object, hence the name 'one-pointedness of mind'.

Sambhogakaya In Mahayana Buddhism, this term denotes the 'bliss body' of the Buddha. This is the body that exists in the paradise where that Buddha reigns; for example, Maitreya Buddha (q.v.) exists in his Sambhogakaya in the Tushita paradise awaiting his rebirth on earth as the future Buddha.

Samsara In Hinduism and Buddhism, the cycle of becoming – the cycle of birth, death and rebirth – to which all beings are subject as long as they are under the influence of ignorance (*avidya*, q.v.), and, in Buddhism, desire and hatred.

sangha The Buddhist monastic community, ordained as the ideal by the Buddha. Many now use the term to refer to the whole Buddhist community.

sannyasin In Hinduism, one who has reached the fourth stage of life (*ashrama*) and renounces the world, concentrating solely on the attainment of liberation.

sat-chit-ananda (literally, 'being–consciousness–bliss') Refers to the qualities of the Absolute (Brahman), revealed in the state of *moksha*.

sect A religious group that emerges and cuts itself off from its parent religion. Sociologically, they are small, exclusive groups who often insist on specific membership qualifications or criteria and make high demands of followers (cf 'denomination' and 'church').

shaman Religious specialist, usually in hunter-gatherer oral societies, who acts as a spokesperson for the spirits, often going into trance and being 'possessed'.

Shari'a The Islamic Holy Law as derived from the *Qur'an* and *Hadith* (q.v.).

shaykh (literally, 'old man') Islamic title of respect given to any senior man in religious, social or political life. In Sufism, it refers to the leader of a Sufi order.

Shi'i, Shi'a Name given to those who followed 'Ali, the son-in-law of the prophet Muhammad, and his progeny, as the true, divinely inspired leaders in Islam; as distinct from the majority Sunnis who followed the political leadership of the caliphs.

shruti (literally, 'hearing') Refers in Hinduism to those scriptures that are regarded as divinely revealed, having been heard by certain *rishis* (q.v.).

Shunyata (literally, 'emptiness', 'the void') The Mahayana Buddhist concept that all extant things are empty of any enduring essence, they are nothing but their appearance.

sign See 'symbol'.

skandha (Sanskrit; Pali: *khanda*) Those elements that together constitute personality. In Buddhism, what is thought to be the eternal soul, or permanent self of an individual, is considered to be in fact nothing else besides these impermanent *skandhas*.

smriti (literally, 'recollection') Hindu secondary scriptures, derived from the *shruti* (q.v.) scriptures.

soteriology The study of the means of attaining salvation or liberation.

structuralism Theory derived from the works of Lévi-Strauss which attempts to explain social phenomena such as religion in terms of abstract relational structures that are considered to reflect the underlying structures that lie deep within the human mind.

Sufism Islamic mysticism, organized since the Middle Ages into over 100 Sufi orders.

Sukhavati In Mahayana Buddhism, the paradise in which Amitabha (q.v.) resides.

sunna The sayings and actions of the prophet Muhammad, as recorded in the *Hadith* (q.v.); established in Islam as legally binding precedents.

Sunni Islam The majority form of Islam. Its

main teaching is that one's life should be lived in accordance with the laws and teachings of the *Qur'an* and the example set by the prophet Muhammad.

taboo Something that is marked off as sacred and therefore dangerous.

takiyya Building used by a Sufi order as a retreat or monastery.

Talmud A compendium of Jewish law, rabbinical commentaries and stories illustrating the traditional law.

tantra An aspect of Hinduism that concentrates on the divine energy and creative power of the *shakti*, feminine aspects of various gods, especially Shiva. In Buddhism, Tantrism is found primarily in Tibetan Buddhism and concentrates primarily on the direct experiential aspects of meditation and ritual. There is a tendency towards sexual symbology in both Hindu and Buddhist *tantra*, and this has sometimes manifested itself in licentious sexual practices.

Tao (literally, 'Way') The Reality that gives rise to the universe in Taoism. It is present in everything and is the way of all things. In Confucian thought, it means the path of human behaviour and morality.

tariki See '*jiriki*'.

tathata (literally, 'suchness') The Absolute, the true nature of all things.

tawakkul Trust in or reliance upon God; considered a cardinal virtue on the Sufi path.

thaumaturgy Religious practices centring on magic and the performance of miracles.

theocracy A system of government which regards God as the sovereign and divine law as the law of the land; in practice usually means a hierocracy (q.v.).

theodicy The study of the origin and place of evil in the world, especially in view of the goodness of God.

theology The study of religious beliefs in order to explain and justify them; i.e. from an emic (q.v.) viewpoint.

totemism Regarding an animal or plant as a benefactor or ancestor of a family, clan or tribe.

trikaya The Mahayana Buddhist concept of the three bodies of the Buddha (see 'Dharmakaya', 'Sambhogakaya', and 'Nirmanakaya').

ulema Muslim religious professional, experts in the Islamic Holy Law, Shari'a (q.v.) and Islamic jurisprudence, *fiqh*.

umma The Islamic community.

upanayana The rite of initiation at which a young male Brahmin takes up the sacred thread and is formally initiated into the Brahmin caste.

varna **(*jati*)** The caste system in Hinduism.

wajd Mystical passion, ardour or ecstasy in Sufism.

wali Approximate equivalent of the English word 'saint' in Sufism.

yoga (literally, 'yoke') The path to God. There are several alternative forms of this path in Hinduism: *karma-yoga*, the path of selfless action; *bhakti-yoga* (q.v.); *jñana-yoga* (q.v.).

zahir See '*batin*'.

zazen The form of meditation in Zen Buddhism that seeks to achieve a state of thought-free, contentless, wakeful attention.

NOTES

INTRODUCTION

1. See in particular the study of this subject in Arnold Toynbee, *The Study of History*.
2. This subject is discussed in W. C. Smith, *Towards a World Theology*: see in particular chapter 4.
3. For those who are interested, my own religious background is Baha'i. I have made a special study of the Baha'i Faith and of Shi'i Islam and have published a number of works on these subjects. I have also been much interested in the social history of religions and on the theoretical question of how one approaches the study of religion.
4. Baha'i is of particular interest among the new religions in that it acts in many ways as a bridge between the religions of the East and West (see chapter 2). It is also, as mentioned later in this introduction, the only new religious movement that is beginning to establish itself as an independent religion (see for example its treatment in Barrett, *World Christian Encyclopedia*).
5. The most careful and detailed assessment of the present strength and future growth of the world's religions occurs in Barrett, *World Christian Encyclopedia*. In this source (see Table 4, p. 6), it is estimated that Judaism, Christianity and Buddhism, while increasing in absolute terms, will in fact decline as a proportion of the world's population, while Hinduism, Islam and the Baha'i Faith will increase both in absolute numbers and as a proportion of the world's population. But it should be noted that Barrett's figures assume a straightforward projection of past trends. Obviously, many factors could affect these projections. One of the most important is likely to be the recent collapse of world Communism. This may reverse the decline projected by Barrett for Christianity and Buddhism.
6. Nattier, 'The Meanings of the Maitreya Myth', p. 23.
7. Although it is possible to make comparative descriptions of these experiences. See, for example, Underhill, *Mysticism*.
8. The fact that religion is essentially a human activity causes a theologian such as Karl Barth (who strongly believed in the idea that salvation can only come from God's activity and not humankind's) to call all religion (even Christian religion) unbelief; *Church Dogmatics*, vol. 1, part 2, pp. 299–325, 327.
9. 'Two important characteristics of maps should be noticed. A map is *not* the territory it represents, but, if correct, it has a *similar structure* to the territory, which accounts for its usefulness . . . If we reflect upon our languages, we find at best they must be considered *only as maps*. A word is *not* the object it represents.' Korzybski, *Science and Sanity*, p. 58. See also J. Z. Smith, *Map is not Territory*, pp. 289–309 on this subject, with regard to tribal peoples.

1 THE CONCEPT OF RELIGION

1. This suggestion was first made by Robert Marett, *Sacraments of Simple Folk*, p. 3.
2. On this subject, see W. C. Smith, *The Meaning and End of Religion*, pp. 61–3.
3. Examples include the Islamic reaction against ideas suggested by liberal thinkers such as Mohammad Arkoun and Abdolkareem Souroush. The question is dealt with in more detail in chapter 14.

4. W. C. Smith, *The Meaning and End of Religion*, pp. 19–74. Smith has proposed instead that we think of the religious faith of the individual and of the ongoing religious tradition.
5. The *Qur'an* is considered by Muslims to exist in a heavenly form that has existed for all time. The question of whether this heavenly prototype of the *Qur'an*, called the *Umm al-Kitab*, the 'Mother of the Book' or the 'Mother Book', was created or uncreated was one of the major differences between the Mu'tazilis and the Ash'aris, respectively, in early Islam (in Sunni Islam, it was the latter view that prevailed). In the context of this discussion, this may be compared to the dispute between Christian theologians about the two natures of Christ. See Burckhardt, *Sacred Art*, p. 119, n. 18.
6. W. C. Smith, 'Some Similarities and Differences between Christianity and Islam'. There is, however, in Shi'i Islam a concept of a pre-existent Muhammadan Light that is the Reality of Muhammad and becomes functionally and spiritually equivalent to the Word Incarnate in Christ; see Corbin, *Histoire de la philosophie islamique*, pp. 65–8; Momen, *Introduction to Shi'i Islam*, pp. 148–9.
7. Burckhardt, *Sacred Art*, p. 116.
8. See discussions of the definition of religion in Berger, *Social Reality of Religion*, pp. 177–80; Spiro, 'Religion'; Stark and Bainbridge, *Future of Religion*, pp. 3–8.
9. See Stark and Bainbridge, *Future of Religion*, pp. 7, 30–3.

2 Religion East and West – A General Survey

1. Islam in particular has created long lists of the Names and Attributes of God. Many of these are to be found in the *Qur'an*.
2. *Udana* 80–1 (8:1–4) in Woodward, *Minor Anthrologies of the Pali Canon*, part 2, p. 98.
3. This is somewhat different to the usual philosophical usage of the term dualism to mean the existence of two opposing realities of good and evil, or the distinction between mind/soul and body.
4. This is a matter of disagreement within Buddhism, but certainly some prominent scholars who are also themselves Buddhists, such as Edward Conze and Christmas Humphreys, have considered that Buddhism does posit an Absolute Reality; see, for example, Conze, *Buddhism*, pp. 39–40, 110–11 and Humphreys, *Exploring Buddhism*, chapter 11.
5. This is of course the famous distinction between salvation by faith (stressed in Lutheran and Methodist Protestantism) and salvation by works (stressed in Roman Catholicism) in Christianity. Most Christians have adopted a position that combines both elements. In Islam, also, there is the concept both of the necessity of following the Holy Law (Shari'a; *Qur'an* 2:26) and of the boundless mercy and grace of God who can forgive all sins (*Qur'an* 3:136; 39:54).
6. Nagarjuna, *Madhyamika Karika*, quoted in Murti, *Central Philosophy of Buddhism*, p. 233 and n.
7. Pronounced 'gnyana', with the first 'n' nasal, and 'pragnya' with a nasal 'n'.
8. It is interesting to note that in Sufism, which as I have noted above is an expression of monism that occurs in the West, the principle ritual activity is also similar to that of the monist religions of the East, that is repetitive chanting designed to lead to altered states of consciousness.
9. M. Smith, *Introduction to Mysticism*, pp. 16–18; Parrinder, *Mysticism in the World's Religions*, pp. 116–7.
10. Perhaps the best account of these mystics is to be found in Underhill, *Mysticism*, see Index entries for each individual mystic. See also M. Smith, *Introduction to Mysticism*, pp. 87–104. Parrinder, *Mysticism in the World's Religions*, pp. 148–53.
11. See Affifi, *The Mystical Philosophy of Muhyid Din Ibnul Arabi*, especially pp. 54–65.
12. On this see E. H. Whinfield in the preface to Jami, *Lawa'ih*, pp. vii–xvi.
13. See, for example, chapter 8, p. 192,

Chandogaya Upanishad, 6:13.

14. The most comprehensive study of al-Hallaj is Massignon, *The Passion of al-Hallaj*.
15. Momen, *Introduction to Shi'i Islam*, p. 137.
16. See Corbin, *Creative Imagination*, pp. 195–200; Izutsu, *Sufism and Taoism*, pp. 254–5.
17. Hick, *God has Many Names*, see especially pp. 91–106.
18. 'Every Prophet Whom the Almighty and Peerless Creator hath purposed to send to the peoples of the earth hath been entrusted with a Message, and charged to act in a manner that would best meet the requirements of the age in which He appeared. God's purpose in sending His Prophets unto men is twofold. The first is to liberate the children of men from the darkness of ignorance, and guide them to the light of true understanding. The second is to ensure the peace and tranquillity of mankind, and provide all the means by which they can be established' (Baha'u'llah, *Gleanings*, no. 34, p. 79).
19. Baha'u'llah, *Tablets of Baha'u'llah*, p. 140.
20. Codrington in his work *The Melanesians*, published in 1891, was the first to recognize this phenomenon. See Norbeck, *Religion in Primitive Society*, pp. 37–8.

3 Theories of Religion

1. *Man and his Symbols*, p. 76, quoted in Morris, *Anthropological Studies of Religion*, p. 170.
2. *The Making of Religion*, esp. pp. 173–293.
3. *The Origin and Growth of Religion*, esp. pp. 172–218, 251–90.
4. 'The Place of Christianity among the World Religions'.
5. *The Study of History*, vol. 7, pp. 723ff.
6. Hick, *God has Many Names* and *Problems of Religious Pluralism*. See also Runzo, *Reason, Relativism and God*.
7. See the exposition of the *philosophia perennis* by Seyyed Hossein Nasr in Whaling, *The World's Religious Traditions*, pp. 181–200.
8. Wallis, 'Ideology, Authority and the Development of Cultic Movements'.
9. See Sharpe, *Comparative Religion*, pp. 277–8; Dudley, *Religion on Trial*, pp. 16–31; Werblowsky, 'Marburg – And After?'
10. Sharpe, *Comparative Religion*, p. 278.
11. See, in particular W. C. Smith, 'A Human View of Truth' and 'Comparative Religion'.
12. See *Faith and Belief* and *The Meaning and End of Religion*, pp. 139–73.
13. The Newtonian system breaks down in other directions also. When we move away from bodies of intermediate size in either direction – towards sub-atomic particles or galactic phenomena – the Newtonian laws gradually cease to apply and relativity and quantum laws become the only way of explaining observations.
14. On complexity and the inadequacies of the analytical model in the physical sciences, see P. Davies, *The Cosmic Blueprint*, especially pp. 21–34.
15. Eliade, *Patterns in Comparative Religion*. A good summary of Eliade's thought on this subject can be found in Dudley, *Religion on Trial*, pp. 65–100.
16. *Faith and Belief*, p. viii.
17. *Heretical Imperative*, p. xii.
18. *What is History?*, p. 23.

4 The Religious Experience

1. Otto, *The Idea of the Holy*, pp. 12–41.
2. Otto, Ibid., pp. 5–7.
3. Otto, Ibid., p. 6
4. Several writers have described a more general version of this phenomenon, not specifically related to religious experiences. See Maslow, *Religions, Values and Peak-Experiences*, and Laski, *Ecstasy*. Some have pointed out that many of these features can be reproduced by the administration of drugs. This aspect is dealt with in more detail in chapter 7.
5. I am here following Donovan, *Interpreting Religious Experience*, pp. 3–20, who in turn bases his description on James, *The Varieties of Religious Experience*.
6. James, *The Varieties of Religious Experience*, pp. 221–2.

7. *Islam – Our Choice: Impressions of Eminent Converts to Islam* (1970), p. 37, quoted in Donovan, *Interpreting Religious Experience*, p. 18.
8. James, *The Varieties of Religious Experience*, pp. 273, 289. In his exposition of saintliness James quotes on pp. 288–9 an episode that occurred to a Huguenot woman when she was whipped for her faith very similar to the account of Mulla Sadiq, quoted here on p. 95.
9. Brandel-Syrier, *Black Woman in Search of God*, pp. 34ff, quoted in Parrinder, *Mysticism in the World's Religions*, p. 85.
10. James, *The Varieties of Religious Experience*, pp. 380–2.
11. Ibid., pp. 396–7.
12. Watt, *The Faith and Practice of al-Ghazali*, p. 61.
13. Meister Eckhart, sermon 99, quoted in Happold, *Mysticism*, p. 242.
14. A. R. Moody, *Life after Life*, pp. 60–1, quoted in Ma'sumian, *Life after Death*, p. 138.
15. Stages suggested by Graham Wallas in *The Art of Thought* (New York, Harcourt, 1926), summarized in Batson, Schoenrade and Ventis, *Religion and the Individual*, pp. 98–9.
16. Batson, Schoenrade and Ventis, *Religion and the Individual*, pp. 102–7.
17. See chapter 1, note 5.
18. *Luke* 9:59–60.
19. Harvey, 'The Dynamics of *Paritta* Chanting'.
20. *Amitayur-dhyana Sutra*, in Cowell et al., *Buddhist Mahayana Texts*, pp. 161–99. See also the synopsis of this in Campbell, *The Masks of God, vol. 3: Oriental Mythology*, pp. 303–20.
21. Batson and Ventis, *The Religious Experience*, pp. 35–47.

5 Pathways to Religious Experience

1. Weber, *The Sociology of Religion*, pp. 152–4.
2. Momen, *Introduction to Shi'i Islam*, p. 240 and figs. 46–9. Self-flagellation was also seen in medieval Christian Europe; see article, 'Flagellants' by R. M. Jones in Hastings, *Encyclopaedia of Religion and Ethics*. It is of interest to note that in both cases, the official religion disapproves of such popular displays of emotion (see pp. 390 and pictures on p. 107).
3. See papers in K. Werner, *Love Divine*.
4. For a comparative account of the education required to become a religious professional, learned in the Holy Law, of Judaism, Islam and medieval Christianity, see M. M. J. Fischer, *Iran*, pp. 32–60.
5. For an account of *bhakti*, see the essays in K. Werner, *Love Divine*. According to Werner's essay in this book (pp. 37–52), the *bhakti* path can even be found in Buddhism.
6. Shunjo, *Honen the Buddhist Saint*, pp. 44–5, 350, 395, 400–1, 476, 732–3.
7. Sandeen, *The Roots of Fundamentalism*, traces some of the links between these two movements in nineteenth-century Western Christianity.
8. The Baha'is have been steering the difficult course between compromise and confrontation with society in their attempts to reform society; see Beckford, *Cult Controversies*, pp. 87–9. Beckford classifies these as 'revitalization' groups in his typology.
9. In Iran, such groups as the Fida'iyan-i Khalq and the Mujahidin-i Khalq incorporated a great deal of socialist thinking into their manifestos. See Keddie, *Roots of the Revolution*, pp. 231–9.
10. See article 'Asceticism (Hindu)' by A. S. Geden in Hastings, *Encylopaedia of Religion and Ethics*.
11. See Suhrawardi, *The 'Awarif-u'l-Ma'arif*, pp. 37–41.
12. On the Old Order Amish, see Hostetler, *Amish Society*; on Hutterites, see Peters, *All Things Common*. Other similar groups include the Doukhobors of Canada (see Hawthorn, *The Doukhobors of British Columbia*).
13. See Carmel, *Die Siedlungen der württembergischen Templer in Palästina 1868–1918*.
14. Beckford, *Cult Controversies*, pp. 85–7, calls this group the 'refuge' type in his typology.
15. These are similar to those new religious movements classified by Beckford, *Cult Controversies*, p. 89, as 'release' groups

in his typology. He gives as further examples Transcendental Meditation, the Rajneesh Foundation and Synanon.

16. The foremost modern writers on this approach are Frithjof Schuon, René Guénon, Ananda Coomaraswamy, Henri Corbin and Seyyed Hossein Nasr. See the exposition of this approach by the last-named in Whaling, *The World's Religious Traditions*, pp. 181–200.
17. Ecstatic expressions of religion can be found in several of these pathways to salvation, in particular mysticism and evangelism.
18. On *hesychasm*, see Kadloubovsky and Palmer, *Writings from the Philokalia*; on mantra-yoga, see Mishra, *Fundamentals of Yoga*; on *dhikr* and *nembutsu*, see Nakamuro, 'A Structural Analysis of *dhikr* and *nembutsu*'.
19. For descriptions and further examples see Underhill, *Mysticism*, chapter 5.

6 Faith, Belief and Conversion

1. James, *The Varieties of Religious Experience*, pp. 246–7, 505–6.
2. Runzo, *Reason, Relativism and God*, pp. 201–12.
3. Price, 'Belief "in" and Belief "that"'.
4. W. C. Smith, 'A Human View of Truth'. Smith identifies the first with a Platonic view of truth and the second with an Aristotelian view. See also his *The Meaning and End of Religion*, pp. 163–8. A number of other writers have referred to these aspects of faith.
5. Park has described 'patriarchal faith' and 'doctrinal faith', which parallel these two aspects of faith, in *Buddhist Faith and Sudden Enlightenment*.
6. Wilfred Cantwell Smith has pointed out that part of our problem is the fact that there is no verb form corresponding to the word 'faith'. Therefore, if we accept his division of these two concepts into faith and belief, we are still in difficulty when it comes to verbal forms. In general, the solution has been to use the verb 'believe' as the verbal form of 'faith'. This has contributed to the confusion of these two concepts in the past. *The Meaning and End of Religion*, pp. 163–4.
7. Ayoub, *Redemptive Suffering in Islam*.
8. W. C. Smith, *The Meaning and End of Religion*, p. 161.
9. Phillips, 'Religious Beliefs and Language Games', pp. 138–9.
10. Herbert C. Kelman, 'Compliance, Identification, and Internalisation: Three Processes of Attitude Change', *Journal of Conflict Resolution* 2, 1958, pp. 51–60; summarized in Batson, Schoenrade and Ventis, *Religion and the Individual*, pp. 54–6.
11. Erik Erikson, *Childhood and Society*, New York, 1950, and 'Identity and the Life Cycle', *Psychological Issues*, 1, 1959; summarized in Batson, Schoenrade and Ventis, *Religion and the Individual*, pp. 67–71.
12. Fowler, *Stages of Faith*; see also summary in Batson, Schoenrade and Ventis, *Religion and the Individual*, pp. 71–5.
13. Runzo, *Reason, Relativism and God*.
14. James, *A Pluralistic Universe*, pp. 176, 328–30; *Some Problems of Philosophy*, pp. 223–5.
15. Kuhn, *The Structure of Scientific Revolutions*, pp. 1–34, 66–84, 92–135, 144–59. The statement that the move from one paradigm to another is 'made on faith' occurs on p. 158.
16. White, *Metahistory*; see in particular pp. 1–43.
17. Kuhn, *The Structure of Scientific Revolutions*, pp. 10–11, 52–65, 77–82, 158. The second edition of the book contains a postscript with a section that is of particular interest (pp. 198–204). When two groups of scientists hold incompatible theories, the difference between the two is not over logic and reasoning (such differences would be easily resolved). The differences are over the meanings that are attached to particular data or rules – the difference is in language. Since meaning is a value that is individually applied, there are no neutral rules for reaching decisions. The only way forward is through persuasion of one group by the other. This may be compared to religious conversion. It is the community rather than the individuals that makes the effective decision.
18. Perhaps only the last centuries of the Roman Empire provide a similar picture

of religious pluralism in the West. On the intellectual consequences of religious pluralism, see Berger, *The Heretical Imperative*.

19. See, for example, the opposition to Jesus from among the Jewish religious leaders and the opposition to Baha'u'llah from Islamic religious leaders. This question is discussed further in chapters 12 and 16.
20. The following points are mainly drawn from Rambo, *Understanding Religious Conversion*.
21. See, for example, Chana Ullman's study 'Cognitive and Emotional Antecedents of Religious Conversion'. She looked at the importance of relationships to the conversion process, interviewing and performing psychological tests on seventy people: forty converts to four different groups (the Baha'i Faith, Judaism, Roman Catholicism, and Hare Krishna), and thirty people from Judaism and Catholicism who were active lifelong members of those religions. One major finding was that conversion was not strongly correlated with a search for cognitive meaning but rather with emotional issues involving problematic relationships with the father, an unhappy childhood, or a past history of disrupted and distorted relationships.
22. Stockman, *The Baha'i Faith in America*, vol. 1, pp. xviii–xx; vol. 2, pp. 92–104, 249–55; van den Hoonaard, *The Origins of the Baha'i Community in Canada*, pp. 29–34, 286–7.
23. This analysis is made on the basis of studies on the Nuba tribe of the Sudan; Baumann, 'Conversion and Continuity'. On symbolic universes, see Berger and Luckmann, *The Social Construction of Reality*, pp. 110–46.
24. Eaton, *The Rise of Islam and the Bengal Frontier*, pp. 268–90.
25. This description is taken from Allport and Ross, 'Personal Religious Orientation and Prejudice.'
26. Ibid., p. 434.
27. Batson, Schoenrade and Ventis, *Religion and the Individual*, pp. 166–8.

7 Towards a Scientific Understanding of Religious Experience

1. Bourguignon, *Altered States of Consciousness*, pp. 9–11.
2. Quoted in James, *The Varieties of Religious Experience*, p. 385.
3. 'The First Year of the Life of the Child', p. 204.
4. For more details on the child's mental development, see Piaget, *The Essential Piaget*; H. Werner, *Comparative Psychology of Mental Development*.
5. Bellah, *Beyond Belief*, p. 45.
6. Ibid., pp. 20–45.
7. This experiment is described by Kasamatsu and Hirai, 'An Electro-encephalographic Study of the Zen Meditation'.
8. Ibid., p. 499.
9. Kasamatsu and Hirai, 'Science of Zazen'.
10. On *samadhi* and techniques of breath control used to achieve altered states of consciousness in yoga, see Mishra, *Fundamentals of Yoga*, pp. 173–87, 208–24.
11. Anand, Chhina and Singh, 'Some Aspects of Electroencephalographic Studies in Yogis'.
12. A good review of this phenomenon and the experimental basis for it is to be found in Ho, Richards and Chute, *Drug Discrimination and State Dependent Learning*. See, in particular, Overton, 'Major Theories of State Dependent Learning', pp. 283–318 in this volume.
13. R. Fischer, 'A Cartography of Ecstatic and Meditative States', p. 298.
14. Overton, 'Major Theories of State Dependent Learning', pp. 306–7.
15. Saccadic eye movement increases, while the just-noticeable difference in sensory input decreases along the ergotrophic pathway. The opposite occurs along the trophotropic pathway. R. Fischer, 'A Cartography of Ecstatic and Meditative States', pp. 288–91.
16. This fact can be measured experimentally and is expressed as the sensory-to-motor (S/M) ratio. For methods of measurement, see R. Fischer et al., 'Personality Trait Dependent Performance under Psilocybin'.
17. Human beings may be thought of as creating experience through their

perceived interpretation (that is, at the cortical level) of the activity in their subcortex. At the level of daily routine, human beings are to a large extent free to interpret their subcortical activity in a large number of ways.

18. R. Fischer, 'A Cartography of Ecstatic and Meditative States', p. 294.
19. See R. Fischer, Griffin and Liss, 'Biological Aspects of Time in Relation to (Model) Psychoses'.
20. Deikman, 'Deautomatization and the Mystic Experience'.
21. Ibid., p. 329.
22. See, for example, the experience of Warner Allen described in *The Timeless Moment*. Allen describes an experience that he states occurred between two notes in a Beethoven symphony. Quoted in Happold, *Mysticism*, pp. 132–3. See also Cohen and Phipps, *The Common Experience*, pp. 167–94.
23. On light, see Cohen and Phipps, *The Common Experience*, pp. 141–66.
24. Deikman, 'Deautomatization and the Mystic Experience', pp. 333–4.
25. See, for example, St Theresa's assertion: 'As to memory, the soul, I think, has none then, nor any power of thinking, nor are the senses awake, but rather lost', quoted in Woods, *Understanding Mysticism*, p. 456.
26. The classical work on the split brain was done by R. W. Sperry and his associates at the California Institute of Technology. See Sperry, 'Cerebral Organisation and Behaviour'; Gazzaniga, Bogen and Sperry, 'Some Functional Effects of Sectioning the Cerebral Commissures in Man'. A useful summary can be found in Sperry, 'The Great Cerebral Commissure' and Ornstein, 'The Two Sides of the Brain'.
27. These analyses can be taken further, in that many of these features that are being listed as Eastern and Western or belonging to the 'dominant' or 'non-dominant' hemisphere, are also features that are commonly associated with the masculine and feminine patterns of thought, and with yin and yang in Chinese Taoist philosophy.
28. See also Smart, 'The Work of the Buddha and the Work of Christ', pp. 166–7.
29. Norbeck, *Religion in Primitive Society*, pp. 96–8.
30. Kuhn, *The Structure of Scientific Revolutions*.

8 The Nature of Reality

1. *Svetasvatara Upanishad*, part 1, in *The Upanishads*, pp. 85–6.
2. *Tao Te Ching*, 1, 4, adapted from several translations.
3. *Tao Te Ching*, 2, adapted from several translations. See also p. 192.
4. See the full discussion and table in Glasenapp, *Buddhism*, pp. 102–6. Glasenapp's table is based on André Bareau, *L'Absolu en philosophie bouddhique*, Paris, 1951, p. 260.
5. *Udana* 8:1–4, in Woodward, *Minor Anthologies of the Pali Canon*, part 2, p. 98
6. *Mahayanasangraha-bhashya* 19, quoted in Glasenapp, *Buddhism*, p. 83.
7. Harvey, *An Introduction to Buddhism*, p. 103
8. See chapter 2, n. 4.
9. Murti, *The Central Philosophy of Buddhism*, p. 212.
10. Harvey, *An Introduction to Buddhism*, p. 99.
11. Baha'u'llah, *Gleanings*, no. 26, p. 62.
12. Ibid., no. 148, p. 316 (italics added).
13. 'Abdu'l-Baha, *Selections from the Writings of 'Abdu'l-Baha*, p. 63. 'The fundamental principle enunciated by Baha'u'llah . . . is that religious truth is not absolute but relative', Shoghi Effendi, *Guidance for Today and Tomorrow*, p. 2.
14. 'Abdu'l-Baha, cited in Momen, 'Relativism', p. 203. Baha'u'llah, *Gleanings*, no. 1, pp. 4–5.
15. Quoted from Majlisi, *Bihar al-Anwar*, in Momen, *Introduction to Shi'i Islam*, p. 148.
16. Baha'u'llah, *Gleanings*, no. 21, pp. 49–50.
17. *Bhagavad Gita* 9:11.
18. *Samyutta Nikaya* 3:118 adapted from translations in Conze, *Buddhist Texts*, p. 106 and *The Book of Kindred Sayings*, vol. 3, p. 101.
19. *Majjhima Nikaya* 1:71 adapted from translation in *The Collection of Middle Length Sayings*, 1:95–6.

20. Conze, *Buddhism*, p. 172; Harvey, *An Introduction to Buddhism*, p. 126.
21. *John* 1:14.
22. *Qur'an* 22:5, 32:9, 17:70, 38, 72.
23. *Qur'an* 2:30, 6:165.
24. *Qur'an* 3:14, 79:40, 43:72
25. 'Abdu'l-Baha, *Paris Talks*, pp. 60–1.
26. *Mandukya Upanishad*, in *The Upanishads*, p. 83.
27. *John* 14:30.
28. *Qur'an* 5:19.
29. *Qur'an* 44:38.
30. Baha'u'llah, *Hidden Words*, Persian, no. 29.
31. *Dhammapada*, p. 170.
32. 'Samsara (the phenomenal world) is nothing essentially different from Nirvana. Nirvana is nothing essentially different from Samsara' (Nagarjuna, *Mulamadhyama-Kakarika* 25:19, p. 158).
33. A distinction is made between Nirguna-Brahman – the impersonal, unknowable Absolute; and Saguna-Brahman – Brahman as manifested in the world. The latter is also given the name of Ishvara, the Lord, as a personal Deity with attributes. Brahman must not be confused with Brahmā, the Creator, one of the gods of Hinduism (and therefore one of the manifestations of Brahman). This confusion is made worse by the fact that Brahman is sometimes found in its nominative form without the final 'n' – Brahma – the only difference being then that the first has a long 'a' and the second a short 'a' at the end.
34. Eliade, *Patterns in Comparative Religion*, pp. 410–16.
35. *Taittiriya Upanishad* 2.1, in *The Upanishads*, p. 110.
36. *Tao Te Ching*, 42, adapted from several translations.
37. There are some differences about what will happen at the Day of Judgement and after this: see chapter 10.
38. *Acts of the Apostles* 4:12.
39. *Qur'an* 5:19.
40. *Qur'an* 33:40.
41. The main exception here is liberal Protestantism which is post-millennial in outlook (see chapter 10) and emphasizes social progress.
42. Baha'u'llah, *Tablets of Baha'u'llah*, p. 140.
43. Baha'u'llah, *Gleanings*, no. 82, pp. 161–2 (italics added).
44. See note 2 of this chapter.

9 Suffering, Sacrifice and Salvation

1. See Freud, *New Introductory Lectures on Psycho-Analysis*, pp. 228ff., quoted in Bowker, *Problems of Suffering in the Religions of the World*, pp. 1–2; Marx, *The Essential Marx*, pp. 286–8.
2. *Anguttara Nikaya* part 2, chapter 1:1, in *The Book of Gradual Sayings*, vol. 1, p. 43.
3. *Exodus* 20:5; 34:7; *Numbers* 14:18.
4. See for example *Deuteronomy* 9:7–8; *Job* 4:7–9; 22:5–10; 24:1–25; *Psalms* 7:16 and *Qur'an* 6:160–1; 7:94; 10:26–8.
5. See for example *Maitri Upanishad* 7:9 (quoted p. 222) and *Brihad Aranyaka Upanishad* 4:4:23 in *The Thirteen Principle Upanishads*, p. 144.
6. Masefield has suggested that the usual translation of *ariyan* as 'noble' is in fact a misunderstanding. It is usually suggested that understanding these four truths sets one on the path to Nirvana. But Masefield suggests that these truths were only understood by those already on the path to Nirvana and thus this term should be translated as the 'Four Supermundane Truths' (*Divine Revelation in Pali Buddhism*, *passim* but see in particular pp. 54, 174). Others prefer the translation 'holy' or 'sacred' (see Harvey, *An Introduction to Buddhism*, p. 23 and *passim*).
7. Masefield translates *ariyan* as 'supermundane' because it is only those who are already on the path to Nirvana who can follow the Eightfold Path (see note 6 above).
8. Rudolph, *Gnosis*, p. 58. 'The all was within the inconceivable, incomprehensible, who is exalted above any thought, while the ignorance about the Father produced anguish and terror. And the anguish thickened like a mist, so that none could see. Therefore error gained strength . . . Therefore despise error! Thus it is with her: she has no root, she came into being in a mist (= ignorance) with regard to the Father. Since she [now] is, she prepares works,

forgetfulness and fears, in order that she may beguile those who belong to the Midst (i.e. evidently being of the intermediate kingdom) and take them again captive (in matter) . . . The forgetfulness did not come into being with the Father although it came into being because of Him. What comes into being within Him is knowledge (gnosis), which was made manifest that forgetfulness might be dissolved and the Father be known. Since the forgetfulness came into being because the Father was not known, then from the moment when the Father is known the forgetfulness will no longer exist.' Nag Hammadi Codex, quoted in Rudolph, *Gnosis*, p. 83. See also B. Walker, *Gnosticism*, p. 46.

9. St Augustine held this view; see Plantinga, *God, Freedom and Evil*, pp. 57–9; S. T. Davis, *Encountering Evil*, pp. 74–5.
10. 'Abdu'l-Baha, *Some Answered Questions*, pp. 272–4.
11. See Griffin, *God, Power and Evil*, especially pp. 275–310; and idem, 'Creation out of Chaos and the Problem of Evil', in S. T. Davis, *Encountering Evil*, pp. 101–36.
12. See for example, Augustine, *City of God* and Aquinas, *Summa Theologica*, quoted in Griffin, *God, Power and Evil*, pp. 70, 85.
13. For an account of the opposing sides in this controversy, see Ormsby, *Theodicy in Islamic Thought*.
14. See for example, al-Hilli, *al-Bábu'l-Hádi 'Ashar*, pp. 44–7.
15. *1 Peter* 1:6–7.
16. *Qur'an* 2:156; 29:2.
17. See Hick, *Evil and the God of Love*, pp. 201–50.
18. See quotation from Baha'i scripture on p. 206, 'Out of the wastes of nothingness . . .'. See also the Short Obligatory Prayer in Baha'u'llah, *Prayers and Meditations*, no. 181.
19. Isaac in the Jewish–Christian tradition, Ishmael in the Muslim tradition.
20. *Bhagavad Gita* 3:10–12.
21. *Bhagavad Gita* 3:14–16. Eliade expands further on this function of sacrifice in tribal religions: 'Into modern times the Uralo–Altaic races sacrificed horses to the supreme gods of the sky . . . The horse is identified with the cosmos and the sacrificing of it symbolizes (that is, *reproduces*) the act of creation' (*Patterns in Comparative Religion*, p. 96).
22. H. I. Hogbin, quoted in Eliade, *Patterns in Comparative Religion*, p. 22.
23. *Bhagavad Gita* 4:25.
24. Allen, *The Buddha's Philosophy*, p. 39.
25. *Bhagavad Gita* 2:62, 64, 68, 71.
26. *Ascent of Mount Carmel*, 1:13, quoted in Happold, *Mysticism*, pp. 330–1.
27. 'Attar, *The Conference of the Birds*, p. 129.
28. Baha'u'llah, *Kitab-i-Iqan*, p. 3.
29. *Bhagavad Gita* 3:25.
30. John of Ruysbroeck, *The Adornment of the Spiritual Marriage*, 2:64–5, quoted in Happold, *Mysticism*, pp. 257–8.
31. *Tablets of Baha'u'llah*, p. 167.
32. *Isaiah* 53:4–5.
33. Baha'u'llah, *Gleanings*, no. 45, p. 99.
34. *Romans* 3:23; also *1 Kings* 8:46 and *Ecclesiastes* 7:20.
35. For a modern liberal Christian interpretation, see Küng, *On Being a Christian*, pp. 419–36.
36. *Hebrews* 9:22–8.
37. 'The Messenger of God said: "Nobody who dies and has something good for him with Allah will (ever like to) return to this world even though he were offered the whole world and all that is in it (as an inducement), except the martyr who desires to return and be killed in the world for the (great) merit of martyrdom that he has seen."' *Sahih Muslim*, vol. 3, p. 1044, no. 4634. See also *Qur'an* 3:170.
38. For an exposition of this theme, see Ayoub, *Redemptive Suffering*, in particular pp. 197–216.
39. Although this is, in fact, rather doubtful historically. See Momen, *Introduction to Shi'i Islam*, pp. 23, 43, 44 and notes.
40. Baha'u'llah, *Gleanings*, no. 32, pp. 75–6.
41. Beckford, *Cult Controversies*, pp. 191.
42. *Sukhavativyuha*, in Conze, *Buddhist Scriptures*, pp. 232–4.
43. *Majjhima Nikaya*, in Conze, *Buddhist Scriptures*, pp. 224–5.
44. *Qur'an* 13:35.
45. *Luke* 17:21, AV.

46. Underhill, *Mysticism*, pp. 423–4.
47. *Milindapanha*, in Conze, *Buddhist Scriptures*, p. 156. See also *Udana* 8:3, in Woodward, *Minor Anthologies of the Pali Canon*, part 2, p. 97.
48. *Majjhima Nikaya* 2:79, para. 32, in *The Collection of Middle Length Sayings*, vol. 2, pp. 229–30; *Samyutta Nikaya* 2:64–5, in Conze, *Buddhist Texts*, p. 66.
49. *Vinaya-pitaka* 1:1, in Conze, *Buddhist Texts*, pp. 66–7.

10 The Promise of a Future Saviour

1. See Table 10.1 on p. 243 and *Dinkard*, 8:14:12–14, in West, *Pahlavi Texts*, part 4, pp. 33–4.
2. *Bahman Yast* 3:1, 13–15, in West, *Pahlavi Texts*, part 1, pp. 215, 220–1.
3. *Vishnu Purana* 4:24:25–9, quoted in O'Flaherty, *Hindu Myths*, pp. 236–7. See also *Bhagavata Purana* 12:2:16.
4. The Buddha's address in the *Cakkavatti-Sihanada Suttana*, *Digha Nikaya* 3:75–6, in Rhys Davids, *Dialogues of the Buddha*, vol. 3, p. 73–4.
5. Emmerick, *Book of Zambasta* 22:165–6, p. 315.
6. *Isaiah* 9:2, 6–7.
7. *Matthew* 24:30–1.
8. Al-Baghawi, *Mishkat al-Masabih*, 3:1140.
9. Al-Nu'mani, *Kitab al-Ghayba*, quoted in Momen, *Introduction to Shi'i Islam*, p. 169.
10. Shoghi Effendi, *Directives of the Guardian*, no. 112, p. 42.
11. *Daniel* 12:2–3; *John* 5:28–9; *Qur'an* 75:6–15.
12. *Psalms* 9:7–8, 50:3–4; *John* 5:28–9; *Qur'an* 22:17, 60:3.
13. *Joel* 1:15; *Matthew* 13:39–40; *Qur'an* 84:1–5.
14. Sarkisyanz, *Buddhist Backgrounds of the Burmese Revolution*, p. 94; Mendelsohn 'A Messianic Buddhist Association'. Scriptural justification for this position can be found in a Mahayana scripture, *Mahasannipata Sutra* (*Ta-tsi-king*): see *Buddhist Mahayana Sutras*, pp. 115–16n. See also Zurcher, 'Prince Moonlight', pp. 13–22.
15. I am here following the typology suggested by Jan Nattier, 'The Meanings of the Maitreya Myth'.
16. For this interpretation, see Hanson, *The Dawn of Apocalyptic* (for ancient Israel) and Eddy, *The King is Dead* (for ancient Iran).
17. Wessinger, 'Millennialism With and Without Mayhem'.
18. Ribeiro, 'Brazilian Messianic Movements', pp. 59–60.
19. Shepperson, 'The Comparative Study of Millenarian movements', p. 44–5.
20. Overmyer, *Folk Buddhist Religion*, pp. 25–7, 82–5, 98–100, 104–5; idem 'Messenger, Saviour and Revolutionary', pp. 114–5; Chan, 'The White Lotus-Maitreya Doctrine'.
21. Tai, *Millenarianism and Peasant Politics in Vietnam*: see in particular the theoretical discussion of the role of the Maitreya myth, pp. 27–43, and description of the millenarian revolt, pp. 113–44.
22. Tambiah, *The Buddhist Saints of the Forest*, pp. 300–14; Sarkisyanz, *Buddhist Backgrounds of the Burmese Revolution*, p. 161; Adas, *Prophets of Rebellion*, pp. 99–102.
23. Momen, *Introduction to Shi'i Islam*, pp. 35–6, 46–60 *passim*; Watt, 'The Muslim Yearning for a Saviour'.
24. Momen, *Introduction to Shi'i Islam*, pp. 105, 109.
25. P. Smith, *The Babi and Baha'i Religion*, pp. 42–44; Momen, *The Babi and Baha'i Religions 1844–1944*, pp. 91–151.
26. Cohn, *The Pursuit of the Millennium*; idem, 'Medieval Millenarianism', pp. 37–8.
27. Momen, *Introduction to Shi'i Islam*, p. 105.
28. Overmyer, *Folk Buddhist Religion*, p. 82; Nattier, 'Meanings of the Maitreya Myth', p. 31 and note 34; Forte, *Political Propaganda and Ideology in China*, pp. 4–50, 153–68.
29. Momen, *Introduction to Shi'i Islam*, pp. 107–8, 109, 112.
30. Sarkisyanz, *Buddhist Backgrounds of the Burmese Revolution*, pp. 93–7; see also pp. 152–9 and Adas, *Prophets of Rebellion*, pp. 101–2, for others who claimed to be the Cakkavatti as a basis for revolt.
31. Sarkisyanz, *Buddhist Backgrounds of*

the Burmese Revolution, pp. 91–2.

32. This is the main thesis of Sandeen, *The Roots of Fundamentalism*.
33. *Acts of the Apostles* 9:1–20.
34. Corbin, *Histoire de la philosophie islamique*, pp. 104–7; Momen, *Introduction to Shi'i Islam*, p. 227.
35. P. Smith, *The Babi and Baha'i Religion*, chapters 1–2.
36. On Amitabha's attainment to buddhahood and his Western Paradise and on salvation through faith in Amitabha, see the two *Sukhavati-vyuhas* in *Buddhist Mahayana Sutras*, part 2, pp. 1–103; and the *Mahavatna-kuta Sutra* (Sutra 5, Taisho 310) translated in 'The Land of Utmost Bliss', chapter 18 in Chang, *A Treasury of Mahayana Sutras*, pp. 91–101.
37. Lamotte, 'Manjusri'; Birnbaum, *Studies on the Mysteries of Manjusri*.
38. Cohn's suggestion ('Medieval Millenarianism', pp. 42–3) that this is due to the doctrine of reincarnation falls down because Buddhism has numerous such sects despite also holding to a similar doctrine. There have been a few minor millenarian movements in India; see Adas, *Prophets of Rebellion*, pp. 19–25, 105–9.
39. Vivekananda, *Complete Works*, vol. 6, pp. 185–8.
40. Momen, *Introduction to Shi'i Islam*, p. 289.
41. Overmyer, 'Messenger, Savior and Revolutionary', pp. 113–5.
42. Ibid., p. 114. See also references in note 20 above.
43. L. Festinger, H. W. Rieckem and S. Schacter, *When Prophecy Fails*, 1956, cited in Batson, Schoenrade and Ventis, *Religion and the Individual*, pp. 205–9.
44. Another example of such rationalization is given in chapter 14, pp. 364–5.
45. Batson, Schoenrade and Ventis, *Religion and the Individual*, pp. 202–17. See also pp. 216–17 on the speculation that Christian doctrine on the station of Christ and his resurrection was born out of the cognitive dissonance created by his crucifixion.
46. See Burridge, *New Heaven New Earth*, in particular pp. 105–16. Barkun stresses the impact of social and economic stresses and upheavals in the appearance of millennialist movements in North America in the 1840s in *Crucible of the Millennium*, see in particular pp. 139–59. Adas, *Prophets of Rebellion*, pp. 183–9, refutes some of the widely held assumptions about these movements.
47. Barkun describes three stages in the social mechanism of coping with collective social upheaval and natural disasters: (1) damage control systems, which try to prevent, control, or, if that fails, compensate victims for social and natural disasters; (2) theories of mistakes, which if the damage control systems prove inadequate, are able to explain such disasters in terms of the traditional worldview of that society; (3) alternative worldviews – if the social stresses are so intense and prolonged that the standard theories of mistakes of the society are no longer credible, the worldview of the society is put into question. In this latter situation, alternative worldviews have a chance of becoming accepted. Both pre-millennialist and post-millennialist views (even if not explicitly phrased in religious terms) come to the fore at such a time and receive widespread attention (although the numbers actually participating in such movements are not always great). Barkun has identified such periods in North America in the 1840s, 1890s, 1930s and the period between 1960 and 1975. Barkun, *Crucible of the Millennium*, pp. 139–60.

11 Archetype, Myth and the Sacred

1. Eliade, *Patterns in Comparative Religion*, p. 1.
2. 'Archetypal ideas are part of the indestructible foundations of the human mind', Jung, *Psychology and Religion*, para. 195, p. 130. See also quotation on p. 64 above.
3. For a detailed consideration of archetypes, see Eliade, *Patterns in Comparative Religion*.
4. Folk tales, epics and legends are often a degradation of a myth, stripping it of its religious aspects while giving it other significance, for example in moral tales,

national epics and so on.

5. Eliade, *Images and Symbols*, pp. 120–21. See also Eliade, *Patterns in Comparative Religion*, p. 462.
6. Eliade, *Patterns in Comparative Religion*, pp. 46–58, 109–11, 129–30.
7. Ibid., pp. 94–6.
8. *Judges* 2:12–13; 10:6; *1 Samuel* 7:3–4; 12:10.
9. See Campbell, *The Hero with a Thousand Faces*.
10. On the parallels between the structure of this myth and the structure of rites of passage, see pp. 281, 284.
11. On the sun god and solar heroes and the linking of this to vegetation gods see Eliade, *Patterns in Comparative Religion*, pp. 127, 135–8, 147–51, 425–6. For stories of such gods, see entry on Tammuz by T. G. Pinches in Hastings, *Encyclopaedia of Religion and Ethics*; and on Osiris by L. H. Lesko in Eliade, *Encyclopedia of Religion*. See criticism of this concept in the article 'Dying and Rising God' by Jonathan Z. Smith in Eliade, *Encyclopedia of Religion*.
12. For an analysis linking the heroes in Iranian epic literature with the myth of the vegetation god, see Krasnowolska, 'The Heroes of the Iranian Epic Tale'.
13. See Campbell, *The Hero with a Thousand Faces*. See also note 48 in this chapter.
14. It is perhaps no accident that Easter, the commemoration of Christ's resurrection, is set in the Christian calendar to occur immediately after the spring equinox, which marks the end of the earth's death during winter.
15. *Matthew* 17:2–5.
16. *Bhagavad Gita*, 11:9–13.
17. A reference to the Night Journey and Ascent occurs in the *Qur'an* (17:1), but the main details are to be found in numerous traditional accounts.
18. *Rig Veda* 7. 101. 3, p. 175.
19. *Laws of Manu* 9:33, p. 333.
20. Eliade, *Patterns in Comparative Religion*, chapter 10. See also quotation from Eliade on p. 269 above.
21. Eliade, *The Sacred and the Profane*, p. 96. A completely different view of ritual comes from the writings of Sigmund Freud. He interpreted some rituals as the commemoration and re-enactment of the original Oedipal crime (see p. 62).
22. Turner, *The Ritual Process*.
23. Eliade, *Patterns in Comparative Religion*, p. 416. Although Eliade discourages simplifications and formulations, they do nevertheless help us to clarify what is going on during the course of religious ritual.
24. 'One of the fundamental conditions of happiness is to know that everything that one does has a meaning in eternity', Burckhardt, *Sacred Art*, p. 9.
25. This account is drawn from Küng, *Eternal Life*?, pp. 123–33.
26. *1 Corinthians* 15:3–8.
27. *Mark* 16:1–8.
28. *Matthew* 28:1–16.
29. This later development of the myth to include Peter confirming that the tomb is empty is a good example of the conceptual gap between us and the world of the *New Testament* authors. It may appear to be of no particular significance in this age, but for the world of the *New Testament* authors it was of great importance to establish that a man had witnessed the empty tomb. In Jewish religious law, the testimony of a woman was of no account.
30. *Luke* 24:1–13, 15–16, 30–1, 33–40, 50–1.
31. *John* 20:1–25.
32. Fragment 1:34–42, in M. R. James, *The Apocryphal New Testament*, pp. 92–3.
33. This account is drawn principally from Warner, *Alone of All Her Sex*, chapters 1–3, 6 and 16.
34. *Galatians* 4:4. *Galatians* was probably written in 57 CE.
35. *Mark* 3:31–5. Even in the very late Gospel according to St John (100 CE or later), we find the surprisingly harsh words of Jesus to his mother: 'O woman, what have you to do with me?' (*John* 2:4).
36. There are some Catholic scholars who consider that the Aramaic *Gospel of St Matthew* preceded *Mark*, but even these are agreed that the sections that we are dealing with here, the narratives of Jesus' infancy, were added at a later date when the Aramaic Gospel was translated into Greek, the only form in

which it survives.

37. The Revised Standard Version of the *Bible* gives both alternatives. Scholars have pointed out that the word used for 'virgin' in the original Hebrew, *'almah*, only means a young unmarried woman. Although such a young woman would have been expected to be a virgin, this was not part of the meaning of the word, which could equally have been translated as 'young woman'. Further doubt is placed on the whole concept of the virginity of Mary by the tracing of Jesus' ancestry through Joseph (*Matthew* 1:16; *Luke* 3:23), which would not have been relevant if writers of the Gospels had believed that Joseph was not the father of Jesus.
38. *Isaiah* 7:14.
39. See note 37 of this chapter.
40. *Mark* 3:31; 6:3; *Matthew* 12:46; 13:55–6.
41. Warner, *Alone of All Her Sex*.
42. Momen, *Introduction to Shi'i Islam*, p. 236. There are also examples of virgin births in other religions. Zoroaster is reported to have been conceived through the drinking of Homa by his mother (*Zad-Sparam* in West, *Pahlavi Texts*, part 1, p. 187; *Dadistan-i Dinik*, in West, *Pahlavi Texts*, part 2, p.164 and n.). See also the accounts of the conception of the Buddha which imply a virgin conception by stating that the Buddha entered his mother's womb from her right side (Pye, *The Buddha*, pp. 109–10). In the religion of the Bab, the precursor of Baha'u'llah (the founder of the Baha'i Faith), his most prominent disciple, Quddus, was regarded by the Babis as the return of Christ. In this connection, it is interesting that one of the earliest histories of the movement refers to the virgin birth of Quddus; see Lambden, 'Episode', p. 28, n. 35. For other examples of virgin birth from primal religions, see Campbell, *Hero with a Thousand Faces*, pp. 311–14.
43. For such an analysis of the Christmas story, see H. J. Richards, *The First Christmas* (see in particular pp. 15–16, 99–117).
44. I am here following the opinion of those scholars who maintain that the *Harivamsa* is a late work (c. 450 CE) and should properly be considered as one of the *Puranas*.
45. *Bhagavata Purana* 10:58:58; 10:59:33–6, 42; 10:83:39–40.
46. This concept of 'implicit religion' was first brought to the attention of scholars by Edward Bailey ('The Implicit Religion of Contemporary Society') in 1983. In his paper, Bailey describes a number of examples of the phenomenon. One of these is the English public house ('pub'). Bailey describes the symbolism of such factors as the type of glass in which the beer is served, the 'priestly' role of the landlord and bar staff, the rules for manly conduct in the pub, and the ritual of buying rounds of drinks. As is often the case with new concepts, some scholars have found numerous examples of implicit religion in all aspects of life, while others doubt its existence or importance.
47. Frederick Welbourn, cited in Bailey, 'Implicit Religion', p. 70.
48. Interestingly, George Lucas, the director of one of the most successful films of all time, *Star Wars*, has acknowledged his debt to the works of Joseph Campbell on the solar hero.

12 Comparative Religious History

1. *Bhagavad Gita* 4:7–8.
2. That is, if we exclude the Buddha who is included in the line of avatars in several Hindu sources.
3. See also Barnes, 'Charisma and Religious Leadership'.
4. See H. J. Richards, *The First Christmas*, pp. 21–6.
5. See Masefield, 'The Muni and the Moonies', pp. 146–7, 150.
6. See *Digha Nikaya* 1:104ff., *Suttanipata* 284–306, *Anguttara Nikaya* 3:221f., *Samyutta Nikaya* 4:117f.; quoted in Masefield, *Divine Revelation in Pali Buddhism*, pp. 151–4.
7. *Matthew* 23:1–39.
8. *Qur'an*, 5:68, 9:30–1.
9. The Bab, *Selections from the Writings of the Bab*, pp. 21–2, 123–4; Baha'u'llah, *Tablets of Baha'u'llah*, pp. 238, 259.
10. In Islamic tradition, the creator of the

Golden Calf is named as Samiri and not Aaron.

11. Masefield, 'The Muni and the Moonies', pp. 145–6; Pye, *The Buddha*, pp. 56–7.
12. Weber, *The Theory of Social and Economic Organisation*, p. 329; for the whole passage describing charismatic authority, see pp. 329–33.
13. Ibid., pp. 334–54.
14. On the holy, see the description of the central experience of religion, pp. 87–92; and also Otto, *The Idea of the Holy*.
15. This theme is greatly expanded in Katz, 'Models, Modeling and Mystical Training'.
16. As prophesied in *Matthew* 24:34; *Mark* 13:30; *Luke* 31:22.
17. *Qur'an* 33:22.
18. Goldziher, 'On the Development of the Hadith', in *Muslim Studies*, vol. 2, pp. 17–251, see in particular, pp. 89–125.
19. Schacht, *Origins of Muhammadan Jurisprudence*, pp. 58–81.
20. Coulson, *A History of Islamic Law*, pp. 40–3, 56–7, 64–70.
21. Smith, 'The Concept of Shari'a', p. 583.
22. Ibid., p. 594.
23. This process is described in detail in Calder, *Studies in Early Muslim Jurisprudence*. See especially pp. 161–97, 244–7.
24. See 'Attar, *Muslim Saints and Mystics*, pp. 19–25, 39–51.
25. For details of this process, see Momen, *Introduction to Shi'i Islam*, pp. 66–8, 71, 74–5, 77–81.
26. For example, Hisham ibn al-Hakam and Muhammad ibn Nu'man, who were prominent disciples of the sixth Shi'i Imam, Ja'far as-Sadiq; see Momen, *Introduction to Shi'i Islam*, p. 67.
27. Peel, 'Syncretism and Religious Change', pp. 139–40. On oral transmission and the fluidity of oral texts, see Lord, *The Singer of Tales* and Goody, *The Logic of Writing*, pp. 1–44.
28. Croce, *Teoria e Storia della Storiografia*, pp. 4–5, cited in Toynbee, *An Historian's Approach to Religion*, p. 8.
29. Eaton, *The Rise of Islam and the Bengal Frontier*, pp. 187–8.
30. Watt, *Islamic Philosophy and Theology*, p. 50.
31. See chapter 6 and White, *Metahistory*.

13 Religion and Ethics

1. For a further discussion of these points, see Bryne, *The Philosophical and Theological Foundations of Ethics*, pp. 145–7.
2. For an example of such an argument, see Flew, *God and Philosophy*.
3. Kohlberg, 'Stage and Sequence: the Cognitive–Developmental Approach to Socialisation', in *Handbook of Socialization Theory and Research*, ed. D. Goslin (Chicago, 1969), pp. 347–480; and 'Moral Stages and Moralization: The Cognitive-Developmental Approach', in *Moral Development and Behaviour: Theory, Research and Social Issues*, ed. T. Likoma (New York, 1976); both quoted in Batson, Schoenrade and Ventis, *Religion and the Individual*, pp. 62–7.
4. D. J. Ernsberger and G. L. Manaster, 'Moral Development, Intrinsic/Extrinsic Religious Orientation, and Denominational Teaching', *Genetic Psychology Monographs*, 104, 1981, 23–41; quoted in Batson, Schoenrade and Ventis, *Religion and the Individual*, p. 66.
5. The following passages are indicative of the ethical teachings of the various religions: Hinduism: *Laws of Manu*, see for example 10:63; Buddhism: the *Dhammapada;* Christianity: The Sermon on the Mount (*Matthew* 5:1–48; *Luke* 6:20–38); Islam: *Qur'an* 17:22–40; The Baha'i Faith: Baha'u'llah, *The Hidden Words*.
6. See Ferguson, *War and Peace in the World's Religions*, pp. 52–6.
7. Huguccio, a Christian theologian of the Middle Ages, for example, considered that heretics and infidels were denied the protection of human law and that war against them was justified. See Ferguson, *War and Peace in the World's Religions*, p. 109.
8. See *Encyclopaedia of Islam*, 'Djihad' by E. Tyan.
9. Baha'u'llah, *Tablets of Baha'u'llah*, p. 21.
10. Sharpe, *Understanding Religion*, pp. 104–6.
11. *Deuteronomy* 2:34; 3:6; 7:2; 22:16–17; *Joshua* 6:21; 8:25–6; 10:35, 37, 39–42; 11:8, 11–13, 17, 21.

12. In Muslim countries, Jews and Christians were allowed to maintain their own religions (albeit with occasional persecution). In Egypt, for example, Coptic Christians constitute some six per cent of the population although Muslims have ruled the country for 1,300 years. In Spain, by contrast, Muslims had virtually been eliminated from the population (by means such as the Inquisition) within one hundred years of the Christian reconquest of Spain. When Spanish Jews were fleeing from Spain in the fifteenth century, it was principally to Muslim countries that they went.
13. Zoroastrians were often given the status of People of the Book but Hindus and Buddhists were usually relegated to the realm of polytheists in Muslim legal texts.
14. 'The second Taraz is to consort with the followers of all religions in a spirit of friendliness and fellowship . . . They that are endued with sincerity and faithfulness should associate with all the peoples and kindreds of the earth with joy and radiance, inasmuch as consorting with people hath promoted and will continue to promote unity and concord, which in turn are conducive to the maintenance of order in the world and to the regeneration of nations' *Tablets of Baha'u'llah*, pp. 35–6, see also pp. 22, 87.
15. Küng and Kuschel, *A Global Ethic*, pp. 18–36.
16. Ibid., pp. 61–71.
17. *Genesis* 1:26–8.
18. *Qur'an* 2:29.
19. Harris, 'Getting to Grips with Buddhist Environmentalism'.
20. See, for example, Harris, 'Getting to Grips with Buddhist Environmentalism'; Berry, *The Dream of the Earth* and Fox, *The Coming of the Cosmic Christ* on Christianity and the environment, and Dahl, *Unless and Until* on the Baha'i Faith in this context.
21. Edwards and Palmer, *Holy Ground*, p. 56.
22. Ibid., p. 59.
23. Ibid., p. 68.
24. Ibid, pp. 73–4.
25. Ibid., pp. 88–9.
26. 'Jainism', *Ecology and Faith*, (Godalming, Surrey: WWF UK, 1995), p. 3.
27. Edwards and Palmer, *Holy Ground*, pp. 103–4.
28. Ibid., p. 120.
29. Ibid., pp. 127–8.

14 Fundamentalism and Liberalism

1. Some may prefer to use the term 'traditionalist' or 'conservative' rather than 'fundamentalist'. I have preferred not to use 'traditionalist' because this would seem to exclude Protestant fundamentalists, who tend to be radical and opposed to tradition. I am aware of the counter-argument that the term 'fundamentalist' has historically been closely identified with radical Protestantism and may therefore seem to some to be inappropriate in a more general context. Overall, it seems to me that the term is now, in popular use, being used in a more general way about other religions and is therefore the more suitable word. Shepard ('"Fundamentalism" Christian and Islamic' and 'Islam and Ideology') suggests the term 'rejectionist neotraditionalist'. One feels that whatever advantage such a term may have is more than counter-balanced by its unwieldiness.
2. For a survey of fundamentalism across the world, in Eastern as well as Western religions, see Caplan, *Studies in Religious Fundamentalism* and Marty and Applebly, *Fundamentalisms Observed*.
3. For accounts of these, see Makdisi, 'Remarks on Traditionalism in Islamic Religious History'; Amin 'Some Aspects of Religious Reform in the Muslim Middle East'; Momen, *Introduction to Shi'i Islam*, pp. 115–6. See also Sandeen, *The Roots of Fundamentalism*. Sandeen has shown how the early twentieth-century fundamentalist movement grew out of, and continued the concerns of, the millennialism of the nineteenth century.
4. W. L. King, *A Thousand Lives Away*, pp. 53–7.
5. Barr, *Fundamentalism*, pp. 40–50.

There are a number of different degrees of fundamentalism; at one extreme are those who accept only the very literal interpretation of the scripture while at the other end are those who are prepared to accept a certain degree of symbolism.

6. At least traditionally they have been, although there is now a marked movement back to the centre ground of Christianity.
7. Barr, *Fundamentalism*, pp. 49–50; Bruce, *Firm in the Faith*, pp. 3–4.
8. Bruce, *Firm in the Faith*, pp. 186–93.
9. I have here subdivided fundamentalists into two groups, traditionalists and radicals, while keeping liberals as one group. Other writers have created even more subdivisions. See, for example, Shepard ('Islam and Ideology'), who has developed a typology for Islam with eight subdivisions. See also Smart's classification in *Religion and the Western Mind*, pp. 523.
10. Although, of course, many Protestant churches, especially the Calvinists, tried to base the whole of their Church structure and ritual on the *Bible*.
11. These two groups correspond approximately to Smart's classifications of Neofoundationalism and Neopost-foundationalism respectively (see Smart, *Religion and the Western Mind*, pp. 52–3). They correspond to three of Shepard's classifications of Islamic groups: the traditionalists correspond to his rejectionist traditionalists and rejectionist neotraditionalists, while the radicals correspond to his Radical Islam group (see Shepard, 'Islam and Ideology').
12. Lefebvre advocated a return to the traditional forms of the Catholic Church, in particular the Latin Mass. He claimed to have several million followers and sympathizers among Roman Catholics, especially in France.
13. Rashad Khalifa analysed the *Qur'an* with a computer and discovered that the entire book revolved around the number nineteen and its multiples. He regarded this a proof of the miraculous nature of the book and asserted that Islam should be based on the *Qur'an* alone, with a downgrading of the Traditions. This has been strongly advocated by proponents of his ideas in countries as far apart as the USA, Egypt and Malaysia.
14. Shari'ati, during the period just prior to the 1979 Revolution in Iran, wrote advocating a return to Islam. By this he did not intend the traditionalist Islam of the ulema but rather a radical reinterpretation which he considered to be original Shi'i Islam.
15. See Akhtar, 'The Virtues of Fundamentalism'; Berger, *The Heretical Imperative*, pp. 116, 118.
16. See Berger, *The Heretical Imperative*, especially chapter 3.
17. See also Barr, *Fundamentalism*, pp. 316–7, for a reference to the manner in which fundamentalist coerciveness operates today in the Christian world.
18. See, for example the activities of Mulla Muhammad Baqir Majlisi in seventeenth-century Iran: Momen, *Introduction to Shi'i Islam*, pp. 114–17.
19. See Sansom, *Japan* pp. 334–5; Takakusu, *Essentials of Buddhist Philosophy*, pp. 178–81.
20. See Lustick, 'Israel's Dangerous Fundamentalists'.
21. Jorstad, *The New Christian Right 1981–1986*; Bruce, 'The Moral Majority' and *Firm in the Faith*, pp. 171–3.
22. See Rahner, 'Observations on the problem of the "Anonymous Christian"'.
23. See for example Hick, *God has Many Names* and *Problems of Religious Pluralism*.
24. During the nineteenth century, however, a fundamentalist position was not incompatible with social reformism. See p. 375 for a possible reason for this. See also Bruce, *Firm in the Faith*, pp. 12–13, 147.
25. Bruce, 'The Moral Majority'.
26. See Caplan, *Studies in Religious Fundamentalism*, pp. 18–19; Bruce, *Firm in the Faith*, p. 155.
27. It should be noted that, in practice, Khomeini had to retreat from the theoretical positions advocated in his writings and Iran still possesses many of the political institutions derived from the Western political systems that Khomeini so despised.

28. Bruce, *Firm in the Faith*, pp. 78–89.
29. See note 24 above.
30. This view appears to have been grounded in the events of the 'Monkey Trial' in Dayton, Tennessee in which a teacher was prosecuted for teaching the theory of evolution. It seems to have been first formally advanced by H. Richard Niebuhr in 'Fundamentalism', in Seligman, *Encyclopaedia of the Social Sciences*, pp. 526–7.
31. On this factor of science and the plausibility of the religious worldview, see P. Berger, *The Heretical Imperative*, pp. 17–22, 105.
32. It may also be said that although fundamentalists are not against the traditional Newtonian view of science, there are much more substantial grounds for a conflict between modern relativistic science and fundamentalist thought. But this issue has hardly yet been tackled by fundamentalist writers (see pp. 483–4).
33. Barr, *Fundamentalism*, pp. 93–6; Bruce, *Firm in the Faith*, p. 128.
34. Quoted in Ashby, *Modern Trends in Hinduism*, p. 103.
35. Momen, *Introduction to Shi'i Islam*, pp. 79–80, 159–60, 185–7, 201.
36. Barr, *Fundamentalism*, p. 91, and A. Walker, 'Fundamentalism and Modernity', pp. 203–4.
37. Sandeen, *The Roots of Fundamentalism*, pp. xi–xii and chapters 6–10 *passim*, but see in particular pp. 152, 163–4, 250–69; Marsden, *Fundamentalism and American Culture*, pp. 199–205.
38. E. Davis surveyed the membership of the Muslim Brotherhood, a fundamentalist Muslim group in Egypt, over a period of fifty years and found that the typical active member was an urban, middle-class, well-educated professional person – much the same group that liberals come from: E. Davis, 'Ideology, Social Class and Islamic Radicalism in Modern Egypt', pp. 141–5 and tables. See also Amselle, 'A Case of Fundamentalism in West Africa', pp. 81–2. For further evidence of the middle-class background of Muslim fundamentalists, see the survey in Munson, *Islam and Revolution*, pp. 95–8.
39. See Haynie, 'Cognitive Learning Styles'; Witkin, 'Psychological Differentiation and forms of Pathology' and 'A Cognitive-Style Approach to Cross-Cultural Research'.
40. It is easy to see how any point of view, such as communism or nationalism, that is strongly held by a group of people can become the basis for the development of such a mentality. Barr, for example, hints at parallels between fundamentalism and the Cultural Revolution in China: see *Fundamentalism*, p. 327. The Tappers point to similarities between fundamentalism and secular nationalism in Turkey, in "Thank God We're Secular!"'.
41. Hofstadter, *Anti-intellectualism in American Life*, pp. 118–9.
42. Barr, *Fundamentalism*, pp. 312–3.
43. Witkin, see note 39 above.
44. Barr, *Fundamentalism*, pp. 90, 349 note 1. Bruce, *Firm in the Faith*, p. 128. Davis found a disproportionately large number of engineers among the leadership of the fundamentalist Muslim Brotherhood. See note 38 above.
45. For further discussion of this point, see P. Berger, *The Heretical Imperative*, chapter 1; Berger, Berger and Kellner, *The Homeless Mind*, pp. 75–7, 140–2, 165–7.
46. See Lahidji, 'Constitutionalism and Clerical Authority', pp. 133–58; Bayat, *Iran's First Revolution*, pp. 6, 57, 134–5, 174–6, 206–7.
47. Heimsath, *Indian Nationalism and Hindu Social Reform*, pp. 317–21; Farquhar, *Modern Religious Movements in India*, pp. 316–23.
48. Although in fact the Shi'i branch has not always accepted this and has, in the past, claimed that parts of the *Qur'an* that confirmed 'Ali's claim to leadership were suppressed by the early caliphs; see Momen, *Introduction to Shi'i Islam*, pp. 74, 81, 172–3, 333 note 14, 338 note 5.
49. Goldziher, in his important study of the *Hadiths*, the oral traditions relating to Muhammad (*Muslim Studies*, vol. 2, pp. 17–251), showed how the concerns of later generations of Muslims were written back into the time of Muhammad through the creation of the

Hadith literature. See pp. 325–6 above.

50. Parallel to this tendency for the scriptures to have frozen within them the viewpoint of the generation that wrote them down is Croce's statement that all history is contemporary history (see p. 335 above).

15 Official Religion and Popular Religion

1. On whether monks in Theravada Buddhism actually practise the official religion, see note 3 below.
2. Waardenburg, however, argues that since there is no organized religious institution in Islam, there can be no 'official' religion. He prefers the term 'normative'. J. D. J. Waardenburg, 'Official and Popular Religion as a Problem in Islamic Studies', in Vrijhof and Waardenburg, *Official and Popular Religion*, pp. 352–60.
3. Richard F. Gombrich dislikes the use of the term 'popular religion' as he feels that this implies that there are religious virtuosos who follow the official religion while the popular religion is a lower form for the masses only. Gombrich asserts the 'official religion' is the religion that is preached and that all have, in fact, practised the 'popular religion' from the earliest days of Buddhism. Gombrich has used the terms 'cognitive' and 'affective' religion to describe this difference. The first denotes the professed religious belief and the second what people behave as though they believe, 'the religion of the heart' (*Precept and Practice*, pp. 4–7, 318–19). While most of Gombrich's points are true with regard to Theravada Buddhism (his area of study), his position does not hold across a broader range of religions. Perhaps the reason for this is the austerity of the doctrine of Theravada Buddhism. In Islam, there is clearly both an official religion and a popular religion and both exist in empirical reality. Therefore, I have persisted with the use of the terms 'official religion' and 'popular religion'. There is also a parallel here with the terms 'Great Tradition' and 'Little Tradition' used by Redfield in *Peasant Society and Culture* and with the 'official and common religion' of Towler in *Homo Religiosus*.
4. The major exception to this is the Christian West in modern times, where many of these magical and occult elements have been separated from official Christianity. But this is a phenomenon of recent times.
5. See R. Patai, 'Folk Religion: Folk Islam' in Eliade, *Encyclopedia of Religion*.
6. See the prohibition on divination and on the attribution of good and bad omens to certain events. These may be found in the collections of prophetic traditions, e.g. al-Baghawi, *Mishkat al-Masabih*, vol. 3, pp. 955–61.
7. On *parittas* (chanted spells) in Burma, see Spiro, *Buddhism and Society*, pp. 144–53, 263–72; on magic, spells and amulets in Sri Lanka, see R. F. Gombrich, *Precept and Practice*, pp. 191–213.
8. For examples of this, see papers by R. Van den Broek, J. A. Huisman and G. F. Bouritius in the first section of Vrijhof and Waardenburg, *Official and Popular Religion*.
9. See Edvard Lehmann, 'Christmas Customs' in Hastings, *Encyclopaedia of Religion and Ethics*, vol. 3, pp. 608–10. The dating of Christmas was also probably influenced by a desire to replace and compete with these festivities marking the winter solstice, as well as the festival of Sol Invictus (on 25 December) commemorated by the very widespread religion of Mithraism. See also 'Sol Invictus' in Eliade, *Encyclopedia of Religion*, vol. 13, p. 408.
10. For an example of radical fundamentalist writing on Christmas, see *The Plain Truth about Christmas* ([Pasadena]: Worldwide Church of God c.1986).
11. Indeed, the concepts of universalization and parochialization could be interpreted as the social equivalents of the processes described by Jung and elaborated by Eliade (see p. 269).
12. On the concept of parochialization and universalization in Indian religion, see Marriott, 'Little Communities in an Indigenous Civilisation', pp. 193–201.

13. Spiro, *Buddhism and Society*, p. 12.
14. See note 3 of this chapter.
15. For more on the meaning of Nirvana, see pp. 193–4, 240.
16. This response was given by 76 per cent of men and 56 per cent of women. Spiro, *Buddhism and Society*, pp. 80–1.
17. Ibid., pp. 76–84.
18. Ibid., pp. 84–91.
19. Tambiah, *Buddhism and the Spirit Cults*, pp. 57–9.
20. Spiro, *Buddhism and Society*, pp. 73–6, 140–61.
21. R. H. Gombrich, *Precept and Practice*, pp. 324–5. Masefield has presented an interesting hypothesis as to why Theravada Buddhists in practice pursue merit rather than seeking Nirvana, which doctrine would suggest should be their ultimate goal. He argues that, in fact, the teaching of the *Nikayas*, the Theravada sacred scripture, is that attainment of Nirvana is only possible on hearing the Dharma preached by a Buddha. Thus, the best that present-day Buddhists can do is to try to achieve sufficient merit so as to be reborn in a time when the next buddha, Maitreya, is on earth teaching (*Divine Revelation*, pp. 139–44). While this is an interesting theoretical point, the books of Gombrich, Spiro and Tambiah do not appear to present much evidence that this is, in fact, how modern Theravada Buddhists think.
22. See note 3 of this chapter.
23. *Qur'an* 18:39.
24. *Qur'an* 5:92, 99, 7:188.
25. Qur'an 7:187–8.
26. On the veneration of saints in Islam, see Goldziher, *Muslim Studies*, vol. 2, pp. 275–341.

16 Religion, Power and Government

1. Berger and Luckmann, *The Social Construction of Reality*, pp. 78–85, 110–46. See also p. 459 in the present work.
2. Berger and Luckmann, *The Social Construction of Reality*, pp. 115–20.
3. Information brochure from Cape synod, late 1940s, quoted in J. Kinghorn, 'The Theology of Separate Equality: A Critical Outline of the DRC's Position on Apartheid', in Prozesky, *Christianity Amidst Apartheid*, pp. 66–7.
4. The words of Jesus: 'Render to Caesar the things that are Caesar's, and to God the things that are God's' (*Mark* 12:17; *Luke* 20:25) are often used to justify this stance.
5. Momen, 'Authority and Opposition in Twelver Shi'ism'.
6. See Johnston and Sampson, *Religion: The Missing Dimension of Statecraft*.
7. Marx, *The Essential Marx*, pp. 286–7.
8. Visser 't Hooft, *The First Assembly of the World Council of Churches*, p. 80.
9. *Baha'i World*, vol. 19, p. 327.
10. It appears in book 4, chapter 8 of his book, *The Social Contract*. (See Bellah, 'Civil Religion in America', p. 333).
11. The modern study of the subject was initiated by Robert Bellah in his paper 'Civil Religion in America', published in 1967.
12. There is disagreement among scholars writing in this field, some maintaining that every society has a civil religion while others consider that it has only appeared in a few societies, especially those where circumstances prevent a religion from fulfilling this role.
13. Hammond, 'Cults and Civil Religion', pp. 122–4.
14. Proponents of the ideas of Durkheim (see p. 53–4) will maintain that the concept of the sacred derives from our experience of society. Even if Durkheim's thesis is true, the experience itself remains private and personal unless expressed in some way, usually through one of the social expressions of religion outlined in chapter 5.

17 Religion and Gender

1. See *1 Samuel* 7:3. Solomon himself is reported to have worshipped this goddess: see *1 Kings* 11:5. For a survey of this theme, see Gimbutas, *The Goddesses and Gods of Old Europe*; French, *Beyond Power*, pp. 43–56.
2. Campbell, *The Masks of God*, vol. 2: *Occidental Mythology*, p. 86.
3. These conclusions have been reached on the basis of observations of primate social grouping, anthropological

research among remote tribal groups, the study of myths, and archaeological evidence. For a survey of this, see French, *Beyond Power*, pp. 25–122 and Diner, *Mothers and Amazons*. It cannot be said that the evidence is conclusive, however, and these ideas are disputed by many.

4. See research reported in Gilligan, *In a Different Voice*.
5. See for example the line of argument in *1 Corinthians* 11:7–13; *1 Timothy* 2:11–14.
6. de Beauvoir, *The Second Sex*, pp. 468–9.
7. *Laws of Manu* 5:148, p. 195.
8. *Rig Veda*, Mandala 10, hymn 85:26, 46, pp. 269, 271. See also *Laws of Manu*, 3:55–6, p. 85.
9. For example Draupadi's role in the *Mahabharata*, summarized in Thomas, *Indian Women*, pp. 128–41
10. On the equality of men and women, see *Qur'an* 33:35; 46:13. On the financial independence of women, see *Qur'an* 4:4, 32.
11. Coulson and Hinchcliffe, 'Women and Law Reform in Contemporary Islam'. On women in Shi'i law, see Ferdows and Ferdows, 'Women in Shi'i Fiqh'.
12. U. King, *Women and Spirituality*, pp. 39–41.
13. *Kullavaga*, 10:1:6 in *Vinaya-pitaka*; in Rhys Davids and Oldenberg, *Vinaya Texts*, part 3, pp. 325–6.
14. Fully ordained nuns (*bhikkuni*) only exist in Eastern Buddhism: China, Korea and Japan. In the rest of the Buddhist world, the full ordination of women either died out or never existed. In modern times, pressure to allow women's ordination has resulted in the setting up of orders that follow part of the full discipline only; in effect, the nuns are novices only. See Harvey, *An Introduction to Buddhism*, pp. 221–4.
15. On the female archetype in Christianity, see Daly, *The Church and the Second Sex*, pp. 105–23. For Islam, see Sabbah, *Women in the Muslim Unconscious*.
16. John Bromyard, quoted in Hamilton, *The Liberation of Women*, pp. 50–1.
17. *1 Corinthians*, 7:1–11, 25–8.
18. *Romans* 1:26–7, *1 Timothy* 1:10.
19. *1 Corinthians* 14:34–5; see also *1 Timothy* 2:12.
20. *Galatians* 3:28.
21. U. King, *Women and Spirituality*, pp. 39–42.
22. 'Abdu'l-Baha, quoted in Esslemont, *Baha'u'llah and the New Era*, p. 141. A more detailed look at the Baha'i writings reveals that equality does not necessarily mean that men and women should perform the same roles. Their inescapable biological differences mean that women are inevitably more bound up with the bearing and early nurturing of children. Women are also regarded as having greater moral courage and as being stauncher advocates of peace than men. For men are reserved certain rights and duties; for example, supporting their wives and membership of the Universal House of Justice, the highest legislative body in the Baha'i Faith. These remaining differences are regarded in the Baha'i writings as being negligible.
23. These three approaches are described in Fiorenza, *In Memory of Her*, pp. 14–36.
24. See U. King, *Women and Spirituality*, pp. 215–22.

18 Religion and the Arts

1. On symbolic universes and their construction and maintenance, see pp. 405–6 and Berger and Luckman, *The Social Construction of Reality*, especially pp. 110–46.
2. When we move from our own society to live in a new and different society, we experience what is called 'culture shock'. Part of this is the shock of realizing that what we had thought of as 'reality' is regarded as incoherent and laughable by this new society, while we are unable to understand the arbitrary meanings that it has attached to things. Some will be bemused by what is going on while others may not even realize that they are failing to understand the symbolic universe of the new society.
3. Martland, *Religion as Art*, pp. 26–74. We may liken this to the twin processes of 'faith in' and 'belief that' that are described in chapter 6. Humanity

detaches itself from the old and moves forward spiritually, breaking new ground, through 'faith in'. This new ground is then ordered, conceptualized and consolidated through 'belief that' formulations; see also the parallels with scientific revolutions discussed in chapter 6 and the alternative description of creativity on p. 99.

4. This idea is drawn from Otto's concept of the holy as *mysterium tremendum et fascinans*. See p. 88 and Otto, *The Idea of the Holy*, especially chapters 3–6.
5. Indeed, it could be argued that the description of this process applies to anyone who engages in creative work of any sort – including scientific research. Theoretical physics is now involved not so much in describing reality as in creating a reality, a conceptual universe – it sees itself as imposing an order on the physical world rather than discovering some inherent order, creating coherent patterns of relationships rather finding out how things work. As such this is a creative act. We can see something of the terrifying aspects of this creative work in the following statement of Albert Einstein: 'All my attmepts to adapt the theoretical foundation of physics to this (new type of) knowledge failed completely. It was as if the ground had been pulled out from under one, with no firm foundation to be seen anywhere, upon which one could build.' Quoted in Capra, *The Tao of Physics*, pp. 61–2.
6. The work of the artist should be, as Petrarch stated regarding writers, not a complete identity with what it represents nor a complete difference: rather it should be as the resemblance of the son to the father – there should be enough there to awaken in us a recognition of what we already know but also enough to help us to see what we have not previously seen. *Letters from Petrarch* (trans. Morris Bishop, Bloomington, 1966, p. 198) quoted in Martland, *Religion as Art*, pp. 113–4.
7. LeShan and Margenau, *Einstein's Space and Van Gogh's Sky*, p. 179.
8. Ibid., p. 172–3.
9. A. C. Moore, *Iconography of Religions*, p. 26.
10. See Coomaraswamy, *Elements of Buddhist Iconography*, p. 63, note 2.
11. The following passage from Burckhardt, although written in a different context, may be of relevance, both to the move from aniconic art to iconic art and to the move from the latter to representational art: 'To the extent that spiritual consciousness grows less and the emphasis of faith is directed to the historical character of the . . . occurrence rather than to its spriritual quality, the religious mentality turns away from the eternal "archetypes" and attaches itself to historical contingencies, which thereafter are conceived in a naturalistic manner, that is to say, in the manner that is most accessible to a collective sentimentality' (*Sacred Art*, p. 67). See also pp. 320–22 above.
12. A. C. Moore, *Iconography of Religions*, pp. 104–5; Coomaraswamy, *Figures of Speech*, pp. 165–7.
13. There have been minor exceptions to this, such as the frescos in the Dura Europos synagogue or the depiction of Muhammad and other prophets in Persian minatures. See A. C. Moore, *Iconography of Religions*, pp. 210, 224–7.
14. Gleizes argues that it was not that pre-Renaissance artists were unaware of the technique of perspective and therefore unable to produce the realism of the Renaissance. Rather, the realistic representation of the physical world was of no interest to the medieval artists, who were trying to create the sacred world, which is a world of natural rhythms and cadences where the later preoccupation with space and spectacle appears sensuous and vulgar. Medieval artists did not develop these techniques, not because they were unable to do so but because the results had no meaning for them; indeed any movement in that direction would have appeared a betrayal of their art. See Gleizes, *Art et Religion*.
15. Coomaraswamy, *Why Exhibit Works of Art?*, p. 45.
16. Ibid., pp. 23–53.
17. Craige, *Literary Relativity*, pp. 28–51.
18. Albert Gleizes has discerned a cyclic pattern in which these two types of art,

the religious and the secular, alternate in importance. In the West, art was secular during the time of the Roman Empire until the establishment of Christianity; then there was a period of religious art which lasted until the Renaissance (although the first signs of its demise could be seen in the twelfth century). After several centuries of secular art, there were, in the mid-nineteenth century, early signs of a swing back towards traditional art (in the desire of the cubists to move away from mere representation) and religious art (in the works of such artists as Delacroix). See Gleizes, 'Art et Religion' in *Art et Religion*. Others, especially of the Philosophia Perennis school such as Coomaraswamy (see *Why Exhibit Works of Art?*, pp. 110–27) and Burckhardt (*Sacred Art in East and West*, pp. 143–60), see in modern art only a steady descent from the heights of traditional sacred art. See also Martland, *Religion as Art*, pp. 19–20; E. Gombrich, *The Story of Art*, pp. 128–30, 148.

19 Religion in the Modern World

1. W. C. Smith, *The Meaning and End of Religion*, especially pp. 19–74, 109–38.
2. Ibid., pp. 19–74.
3. Hick, *God has Many Names*, p. 5. See also pp. 72–3 above.
4. Wilson, *Religion in Secular Society*, p. 14.
5. This list is based on Shiner, 'The Concept of Secularization', pp. 307–17.
6. Cf. Wach, *The Comparative Study of Religions*, pp. 37–8. Wach includes a fourth 'pseudo-religion' – biologism, the cult of life as such or the sexual drive. I have not included this here as, although widespread in the West, it has not yet proved attractive to the rest of the world, nor does it seem to me to have yet taken on the characteristics of an ideology, outlined below. John Smith, in *Quasi-Religions*, also gives humanism as a 'quasi-religion'. I have not included this in my list either, because, like biologism, it has not (in its modern formulation) achieved the level of state endorsement and centrality as the ideology of a society in the same way that the three ideologies cited in the text have. There are many scholars, however, who do regard it as being on a par with the the major religions of the world.
7. See also the concept of 'civil religion', pp. 425–6 and Bellah, *Beyond Belief*, pp. 168–86.
8. Much of the next three paragraphs is drawn from H. Smith, 'Postmodernism's Impact on the Study of Religion'.
9. Anthony Wallace in *Religion: An Anthropological View*, 1966, pp. 264–5, quoted in Stark and Bainbridge, *The Future of Religion*, p. 430.
10. Berger, *The Heretical Imperative*, pp. 22–5.
11. Ibid., p. 68.
12. The *Qur'an* and the main collections of Traditions, both Sunni and Shi'i, make it quite clear that physical fighting and war is what is intended by jihad. See *Qur'an* 2:217–9, 4:75–6, 8:39, 9:29.
13. Cuppitt, *Taking Leave of God*, p. 9.
14. On this subject, see Berger, *The Heretical Imperative*, pp. 112–17.
15. The first aspects of modern technology that the Islamic states imported in the eighteenth and nineteenth centuries tended to be military technology.
16. On most of these, see Hourani, *Arabic Thought in the Liberal Age*.
17. *Neely's History of the Parliament of Religions*, pp. 39–40.
18. Calculated from tables in Barrett, *World Christian Encyclopedia*, pp. 6, 782–5. The figure for Europe includes the USSR. Barrett's figures for mid-1985 are used.
19. Barrett, *World Christian Encyclopedia*, p. 6.
20. Ibid.
21. For 1968, see Smith and Momen, 'The Baha'i Faith 1957–1988', p. 72. For 1995, see *The Baha'i World*, 1994–5, p. 317.
22. Whaling, *Religion in Today's World*, pp. 144–5.
23. D. Swearer in Whaling, *Religion in Today's World*, pp. 60–71.
24. M. A. G. T. Kloppenborg, 'Some Reflexions on the Study of Sinhalese Buddhism', in Vrijhof and Waardenburg, *Official and Popular Religion*, p. 499.

25. Ling, *Buddhism, Imperialism and War*, p. 136.
26. Bechert, 'Buddhist Revival in East and West'.
27. Barrett, *World Christian Encyclopedia*, p. 6.
28. World Missionary Conference, Edinburgh 1910, quoted in Barrett, *World Christian Encyclopedia*, p. 5.
29. Barrett, *World Christian Encyclopedia*, p. 6, adding figures for tribal religionists and shamanists. Some would say that Shintoists should also be added to these figures. This would make the totals 125 million in 1900 and 113 million in 2000.
30. Aylward Shorter, 'African Religions' in Hinnells, *A Handbook of Living Religions*, p. 436.
31. Barrett, *World Christian Encyclopedia*, pp. 370–1.
32. Stark and Bainbridge, *The Future of Religion*, p. 2; see also pp. 454–6.
33. This classification is derived from Parsons, 'Expanding the Religious Spectrum'.
34. Clarke defines new religious movements as those emerging in Western Europe since c.1945; see Clarke, *New Religious Movements*, p. 1. Such a definition would exclude, among others, the Baha'i Faith, Theosophy, and Mormonism.
35. Wilson, *Religion in Secular Society*, pp. 21–39. Barrett, *World Christian Encyclopedia*, pp. 783–4; see figures for 'total practising Christians' in tables.
36. Robert Wuthnow, 'Religious Movements and Counter Movements in North America', in Beckford, *New Religious Movements*, p. 1. In the Canadian census, those listed as having religious affiliations to other than the main nine religious groups rose from 2.9 per cent of the population in 1961 to 6.2 per cent in 1971. Ibid., p. 8.
37. Quoted in Barrett, *World Christian Encyclopedia*, p. 712. If one subtracts those involved in Transcendental Meditation and yoga (who may not have considered themselves as involved religiously, as discussed above), the total is 5 per cent, giving the same percentage for those involved in new religious movements as the previous source.
38. Stark and Bainbridge, *The Future of Religion*; see especially pp. 75–95, 381–6, 439–42.
39. Beckford, *Cult Controversies*, pp. 104–5, 185, 193–6. See also Barker, *Making of a Moonie*, pp. 150–1; Sharpe, *Understanding Religion*, pp. 103–4.
40. For a detailed description of the inner workings of a small cult group, see Lofland, *Doomsday Cult*, which describes the early years of the Unification Church in the United States.
41. This was first described by Benton Johnson, 'On Church and Sect', *American Sociological Review* 28, 1963, pp. 539–49; summarized in Stark and Bainbridge, *Future of Religion*, pp. 23, 48–60, 157–61, 280–1, 363–4.
42. The main work in this area has been done by such researchers as Louis Jolyon West and Margaret Thaler Singer. For a review of this material and the main arguments of such supporters of the anti-cult movement, see Singer and Addis, 'Cults, Coercion, and Contumely' and Singer and Lalich, *Cults in Our Midst*.
43. Barker, *Making of a Moonie*, pp. 121–48, 232–59; Beckford, *Cult Controversies*: see especially pp. 95–102, 124–5, 199–204. See also the March/April 1980 (vol. 17/no. 3) issue of *Society* dedicated to 'Brainwashing'. See in particular: leader by James Richardson (p. 19); Dick Anthony, Thomas Robbins, Jim McCarthy, 'Legitimating Repression' (pp. 39–42); Anson D. Shupe, Roger Spielmann and Sam Stigall, 'Cults of Anti-Cultism', (pp. 43–6).
44. Shupe and Bromley, 'Witches, Moonies and Evil'. Masefield ('The Muni and the Moonies') has drawn an interesting parallel between the present accusations against the 'Moonies' and the persecutions of the Buddha.
45. Anthony, Robbins and McCarthy, 'Legitimating Repression', *Society* 17, no. 3, 1980, p. 40. These authors also make the point that part of the process of legitimating repression in a supposedly open and tolerant society is to medicalize the problem. Believers in the new religious movements are classed as having a medical problem, along with drug addicts, alcoholics and

others regarded as social undesirables. Thus their human rights can be abused in the name of helping them with their medical problem.

46. Stark and Bainbridge, *The Future of Religion*, pp. 23–4, 48–67.
47. Beckford, *Cult Controversies*, pp. 62–3.
48. Barrett, *World Christian Encyclopedia*, p. v.
49. Ibid., p. 623.
50. Hackett, *New Religious Movements in Nigeria*, p. 2.
51. Document supplied by the Iranian Embassy, London.
52. The Baha'i International Community has published numerous documents that show that the persecutions are purely religious in nature. These include a number of official court documents showing that action had been taken against Baha'is only because they were Baha'is and offering to reverse the action if they adopted Islam. See *The Baha'i World*, vol. 18, pp. 249–330; vol. 19, pp. 42–9, 228–82.
53. Robert Wuthnow, 'Religious Movements and Counter-Movements in North America', in Beckford, *New Religious Movements*, pp. 17–18.
54. Hadden, 'The Rise and Fall of American Televangelism'.
55. Malinowski, *Magic, Science and Religion*, pp. 190–1.

CONCLUSION

1. Berger, *The Heretical Imperative*, pp. 122–3.
2. Watt, *The Faith and Practice of al-Ghazali*, pp. 54–5.

Bibliography

Sacred Scriptures and Authoritative Texts

'Abdu'l-Baha. *Paris Talks*. 10th edn. London, Baha'i Publishing Trust, 1961

— *The Promulgation of Universal Peace: Talks Delivered by 'Abdu'l-Baha During his Visit to the United States and Canada in 1912*. Wilmette, Ill., Baha'i Publishing Trust, 1982

— *Selections from the Writings of 'Abdu'l-Baha*, trans. Marzieh Gail et al. Haifa, Baha'i World Centre, 1978

— *Some Answered Questions*, trans. L. C. Barney. Wilmette, Ill., Baha'i Publishing Trust, 1964

Bab, The. *Selections From the Writings of the Bab*, trans. Habib Taherzadeh et al. Haifa, Baha'i World Centre, 1978.

The Babylonian Talmud, trans. I. Epstein. London, Socino Press, 1938

al-Baghawi, Ibn al-Farra. *Mishkat al-Masabih*, trans. James Robson. 4 vols. Lahore, Sh. Muhammad Ashraf, 1963

Baha'u'llah. *Gleanings From the Writings of Baha'u'llah*, trans. Shoghi Effendi. London, Baha'i Publishing Trust, 1949

— *Hidden Words*, trans. Shoghi Effendi et al. London, Baha'i Publishing Trust, 1966

— *Kitab-i-Iqan: The Book of Certitude*, trans. Shoghi Effendi. Wilmette, Baha'i Publishing Trust, 1987

— *Prayers and Meditations by Baha'u'llah*, trans. Shoghi Effendi. Rev. edn. London, Baha'i Publishing Trust, 1978

— *Tablets of Baha'u'llah: Revealed after the 'Kitab-i-Aqdas'*, trans. Habib Taherzadeh et al. Haifa, Baha'i World Centre, 1978

The Bhagavad Gita, trans. Juan Mascaro. Harmondsworth, Penguin, 1984

Bhagavad-Gita As It Is, trans. Bhaktivedanta Swami Prabhupada. New York, Macmillan, 1972

The Bhagavata Purana, trans. Ganesh V. Tagare. Ancient Indian Tradition and Mythology Series, vols. 7–11. Delhi, Motilal Banarsidass, 1976–8

The Bible. Revised Standard Version, 1971 edition; except where indicated AV: Authorised Version

The Book of Gradual Sayings, trans. E. M. Hare and F. L. Woodward. 5 vols. London, Pali Text Society, 1932–7

The Book of Kindred Sayings, trans. C. A. F. Rhys Davids and F. L. Woodward. 5 vols. London, Pali Text Society, 1950–6

Chang, Garma C. C. *A Treasury of Mahayana Sutras: Selections from the Mahavatnakuta Sutra*. University Park, Pennsylvania State University Press, 1983

The Collection of Middle Length Sayings, trans. I. B. Horner. 3 vols. London, Luzacs for Pali Text Society, 1954–9

Conze, Edward (trans.). *Buddhist Scriptures*. Harmondsworth, Penguin, 1959

Conze, Edward (ed.). *Buddhist Texts Through the Ages*. Oxford, Oneworld, 1995

Cowell, E. B., F. Max Müller and T. Takakusu (trans.). *Buddhist Mahayana Texts*. Sacred Books of the East, vol. 49. Oxford, Clarendon Press, 1894

The Dhammapada, trans. Juan Mascaro. Harmondsworth, Penguin, 1973

Kulanajataka, ed. and trans. W. B. Bollée. London, Luzac, 1970

Laws of Manu, trans. G. Buhler. Sacred Books of the East, vol. 25. Oxford, Clarendon Press, 1886

The Mahabharata, ed. Manmatha N. Dutt,

18 vols. Calcutta, H. C. Dass, 1895–1905

The Mahabharata, ed. Pratapa Chandra Roy, trans. Kisari Mohan Ganguli. 18 vols. Calcutta, Bharata Press, 1884–5

O'Flaherty, Wendy (trans.). *Hindu Myths*. Harmondsworth, Penguin, 1975

The Qur'an. All translations are the author's own

Rhys Davids, T. W. (trans.). *Buddhist Suttas*. Sacred Books of the East, vol. 11. Oxford, Clarendon Press, 1881

Rhys Davids, T. W. and C. A. F. (trans.). *Dialogues of the Buddha*. 3 vols. Sacred Books of the Buddhists, vols. 2–4. London, Henry Frowde (vols. 2 and 3); Humphrey Milford (vol. 4), 1899–1921

Rhys Davids, T. W. and H. Oldenberg (trans.). *Vinaya Texts*, parts 1 and 3. Sacred Books of the East, vols. 13 and 20. Oxford, Clarendon Press, 1885

The Rig Veda, trans. Wendy O'Flaherty. Harmondsworth, Middlesex, Penguin, 1981

Sahih Muslim, trans. A. H. Siddiqi. 4 vols. Lahore, Sh. Muhammad Ashraf, 1973–5

Shoghi Effendi. *God Passes By*. Wilmette, Ill., Baha'i Publishing Trust, 1970

— *Guidance for Today and Tomorrow*. London, Baha'i Publishing Trust, 1953

Tao Te Ching: A New Translation with Commentary, trans. Ellen M. Chen. New York, Paragon House, 1989

Tao Te Ching, trans. D. C. Lau. Harmondsworth, Penguin, 1963

Tao Te Ching, trans. Stephen Mitchell. New York, Harper & Row, 1988

The Thirteen Principle Upanishads, trans. Robert E. Hume. London, Oxford University Press, 1921

The Upanishads, trans. Juan Mascaro. Harmondsworth, Penguin, 1965

Warren, Henry C. (trans.). *Buddhism in Translations*. Harvard Oriental Series, vol. 3. Cambridge, Mass., Harvard University Press, 1906

West, E. W. (trans.). *Pahlavi Texts*, parts 1, 2 and 4. Sacred Books of the East, vols. 5, 18 and 37. Oxford, Clarendon Press, 1880, 1882, 1892

Woodward, F. L. (trans.). *Minor Anthologies of the Pali Canon*, part 2. Sacred Books of the Buddhists, vol. 8. London, Humphrey Milford, 1935

Other Works

Adas, Michael. *Prophets of Rebellion: Millenarian Protest Movements against the European Colonial Order*. Cambridge, Cambridge University Press, 1987

Adler, Margot. *Drawing Down the Moon: Witches, Druids, Goddess-Worshippers, and other Pagans in America Today*. Revised edn. Boston, Beacon Press, 1986

Affifi, A. E. *The Mystical Philosophy of Muhyid Din Ibnul Arabi*. Lahore, Sh. Muhammad Ashraf, 1979

Afshar, Haleh (ed.). *Women in the Middle East: Perceptions, Realities, and Struggles for Liberation*. Basingtoke, Macmillan, 1993

Ahmed, Leila. *Women and Gender in Islam: Historical Roots of a Modern Debate*. New Haven, Yale University Press, 1992

Akhtar, Shabbir. 'The Virtues of Fundamentalism', *Scottish Journal of Religious Studies* 10, 1989, pp. 41–9

Allen, G. F. *The Buddha's Philosophy: Selections from the Pali Canon and an Introductory Essay*. George Allen & Unwin, London, 1959

Allport, Gordon W. and J. M. Ross. 'Personal Religious Orientation and Prejudice', *Journal of Personality and Social Psychology* 5, 1967, pp. 432–43

Amin, Osman. 'Some Aspects of Religious Reform in the Muslim Middle East', in *The Conflict of Traditionalism and Modernism in the Muslim Middle East*, ed. C. Leiden. Austin, Texas University Press, 1966, pp. 85–100

Amselle, Jean-Loup. 'A Case of Fundamentalism in West Africa: Wahabism in Bamako', trans. Donald Taylor, in Caplan, *Studies in Religious Fundamentalism*, pp. 79–94

Anand, B. K., G. S. Chhina and Baldev Singh. 'Some Aspects of Electroencephalographic studies in Yogis', *Electroencephalography and Clinical Neurophysiology* 13, 1961, pp. 452–6; also in Tart, *Altered States of Consciousness*, pp. 503–6.

Anson, Peter F. *The Call of the Desert: The Solitary Life in the Christian Church*. London, SPCK, 1964

Arjomand, Said Amir. 'Traditionalism in Twentieth Century Iran', in *From Nationalism to Revolutionary Islam*, ed. S. A. Arjomand. Albany, State University of New York Press, 1984, pp. 195–232

Ashby, Philip H. *Modern Trends in Hinduism*. New York, Columbia University Press, 1974

'Attar, Farid al-Din. Farid ud-Din Attar, *The Conference of the Birds*, trans. Afkham Darbandi and Dick Davis. Harmondsworth, Penguin, 1984

— *Muslim Saints and Mystics: Episodes from the Tadhkirat al-Auliya' (Memorials of the Saints)*, trans. A. J. Arberry. London, Routledge & Kegan Paul, 1966

Ayoub, Mahmoud. *Redemptive Suffering in Islam: a Study of the Devotional Aspects of 'Ashura' in Twelver Shi'ism*. Religion and Society 10. The Hague, Mouton, 1978

Badiee, Julie. *An Earthly Paradise: Baha'i Houses of Worship around the World*. Oxford, George Ronald, 1992

The Baha'i World. vol. 18, 1979–83; vol. 19, 1983–86; 1994–95. Haifa, Baha'i World Centre, 1986, 1994, 1996

Bailey, Derrick S. *The Man–Woman Relation in Christian Thought*. London, Longmans, 1959

Bailey, Edward. 'The Implicit Religion of Contemporary Society', *Religion* 13, 1983, pp. 69–83

Balyuzi, Hasan M. *Baha'u'llah: the King of Glory*. Oxford, George Ronald, 1980

— *Muhammad and the Course of Islam*. Oxford, George Ronald, 1976

Barker, Eileen. *The Making of a Moonie: Choice or Brain-Washing*. London, Blackwell, 1984

— *New Religious Movements: A Perspective for Understanding Society*. Comparative Studies in Religion and Society 3. New York, Edward Mellen Press, 1982

Barkun, Michael. *Crucible of the Millennium: the Burned-Over Districts of New York in the 1840s*. Syracuse, NY, Syracuse University Press, 1986

Barnes, Douglas F. 'Charisma and Religious Leadership: An Historical Analysis', *Journal for the Scientific Study of Religion* 17, 1978, pp. 1–18

Barr, James. *Fundamentalism*. London, SCM Press, 1977

Barrett, David B. (ed.). *World Christian Encyclopedia*. Nairobi, Oxford University Press, 1982

Barth, Karl. *Church Dogmatics*, trans. G. T. Thomson, Harold Knight. 15 vols. Edinburgh, T. & T. Clark, 1956

Bastide, Roger. *The African Religions of Brazil: Towards the Sociology of the Interpenetration of Civilizations*, trans. Helen Sebba. Baltimore, John Hopkins University Press, 1978

Batson, C. Daniel and W. Larry Ventis. *The Religious Experience: A Social-Psychological Perspective*. New York, Oxford University Press, 1982

Batson, C. Daniel, Patricia Schoenrade and W. Larry Ventis. *Religion and the Individual: A Social-Psychological Perspective*. New York, Oxford University Press, 1993

Baumann, Gerd. 'Conversion and Continuity: Islamicisation among the Nuba of Miri', *Bulletin of the British Society for Middle Eastern Studies* 12, 1985, pp. 157–71

Bayat, Mangol. *Iran's First Revolution: Shi'ism and the Constitutional Revolution of 1905–1909*. New York, Oxford University Press, 1991

de Beauvoir, Simone. *The Second Sex: A Study of Modern Woman*, trans. H. M. Parshley. London, Jonathan Cape, 1953; repr. 1972

Bechert, Heinz. 'Buddhist Revival in East and West', in *The World of Buddhism*, ed. H. Bechert and R. Gombrich. London, Thames & Hudson, 1984, pp. 273–85

Beck, Lois and Nikki Keddie (eds). *Women in the Muslim World*. Cambridge, Mass., Harvard University Press, 1978

Beckford, James A. *Cult Controversies: The Societal Response to New Religious Movements*. London, Tavistock Publications, 1985

Beckford, James A. (ed.). *New Religious Movements and Rapid Social Change*. London/Paris, Sage/UNESCO, 1986

Bellah, Robert. *Beyond Belief*. New York, Harper & Row, 1970

— 'Civil Religion in America', in Newman, *Social Meanings of Religion*, pp. 328–48; originally published in *Daedalus* 96, 1967, pp. 1–21

Berger, Peter. *The Heretical Imperative: Contemporary Possibilities of Religious Affirmation*. London, Collins, 1980
— *The Social Reality of Religion* (first published as *The Sacred Canopy: Elements of a Sociological Theory of Religion*). Harmondsworth, Penguin, 1973
Berger, Peter, B. Berger and H. Kellner. *The Homeless Mind*. Harmondsworth, Penguin, 1974
Berger, Peter and Thomas Luckmann. *The Social Construction of Reality*. Harmondsworth, Penguin, 1975
Berry, Thomas. *The Dream of the Earth*. San Francisco, Sierra Club Books, 1988
Birnbaum, Raoul. *Studies on the Mysteries of Manjusri: A Group of East Asian Mandalas and their Traditional Symbolism*. Monograph 2, n.p., Society for the Study of Chinese Religions, 1983
Bourguignon, Erika (ed.). *Religion, Altered States of Consciousness and Social Change*. Columbus, Ohio State University Press, 1973
Bowker, John. *Problems of Suffering in the Religions of the World*. Cambridge, Cambridge University Press, 1975
Brandon, S. G. F. (ed.). *The Saviour God: Comparative Studies in the Concept of Salvation presented to Edwin Oliver James*. Manchester, Manchester University Press, 1963
Brown, Noel J. and Pierre Quiblier. *Ethics and Agenda 21: Moral Implications of a Global Consciousness*. New York, United Nations Publications, 1994
Bruce, Steve. *Firm in the Faith*. Aldershot, Gower, 1984
— *Religion in the Modern World: From Cathedrals to Cults*. Oxford, Oxford University Press, 1996
— 'The Moral Majority: The Politics of Fundamentalism in Secular Society', in Caplan, *Studies in Religious Fundamentalism*, pp. 177–94
Bultmann, Rudolf. *Myth and Kerygma: A Theological Debate*, ed. H. W. Bartsch, trans. R. H. Fuller. London, SPCK, 1972.
Burckhardt, Titus. *Sacred Art in East and West: Its Principles and Methods*, trans. Lord Northbourne. London, Perennial Books, 1967
Burrell, Robert M. (ed.). *Islamic Fundamentalism*. Royal Asiatic Seminar Papers 1. London, Royal Asiatic Society, 1989
Burridge, K. *New Heaven, New Earth*. Oxford, Blackwell, 1969
Byrne, Peter. *The Philosophical and Theological Foundations of Ethics: An Introduction to Moral Theory and Its Relation to Religious Belief*. London, St Martin's Press, 1992
Caldarola, Carlo (ed.). *Religions and Societies: Asia and the Middle East*. Berlin, Mouton, 1982
Calder, Norman. *Studies in Early Muslim Jurisprudence*. Oxford, Clarendon Press, 1993
Campbell, Joseph. *The Hero with a Thousand Faces*. Bollingen Series 17. 2nd edn. Princeton, Princeton University Press, 1968
— *The Masks of God*. 3 vols. *Creative Mythology*; *Occidental Mythology*; *Oriental Mythology*. London, Souvenir Press, 1974
Candrakirti. *Lucid Exposition of the Middle Way: The Essential Chapters from the 'Prasannapada' of Candrakirti*, trans. Mervyn Sprung. London, Routledge & Kegan Paul, 1979
Caplan, Lionel (ed.). *Studies in Religious Fundamentalism*. London, Macmillan, 1987
Capra, Fritjof. *The Tao of Physics: An Exploration of the Parallels between Modern Physics and Eastern Mysticism*. London, Fontana, 1983
Carmel, Alex. *Die Siedlungen der württembergischen Templer in Palästina 1868–1918: ihre lokalpolitischen und internationalen Probleme,* trans. Perez Leshen. Veröffentlichungen der Kommission für Geschichtliche Landeskunde in Baden-Würtemberg, Series B, vol. 77. Stuttgart, W. Kohlhammer Verlag, 1973
Carpenter, Humphrey. *Robert Runcie: The Reluctant Archbishop*. London, Hodder and Stoughton, 1996
Carr, E. H. *What is History?* 2nd edn. Harmondsworth, Penguin, 1987
Caton, Peggy (ed.). *Equal Circles: Women and Men in the Bahá'í Community*. Los Angeles, Kalimat Press, 1987
Chan, Hok-Lam. 'The White Lotus-Maitreya Doctrine and Popular Uprisings in Ming and Ch'ing China', *Sinologica* 10, 1969,

pp. 211–33

Chittick, William. *The Sufi Path of Love: The Spiritual Teachings of Rumi*. Albany, NY, State University of New York Press, 1983

Clarke, Peter B. *New Religious Movements*. Pamphlet Library 4. Canterbury, Kent, Centre for the Study of Religion and Society, 1984

Cohen, J. M. and J.-F. Phipps. *The Common Experience*. London, Rider & Co., 1979

Cohn, Norman. 'Medieval Millenarianism: Its Bearing on the Comparative Study of Millenarian Movements', in Thrupp, *Millennial Dreams in Action*, pp. 32–43

— *The Pursuit of the Millennium: Revolutionary Millenarians and Mystical Anarchists of the Middle Ages*. London, Temple Smith, 1970

Cohn-Sherbok, Lavinia and Dan. *A Short Introduction to Judaism*. Oxford, Oneworld, 1997

Cone, James, H. *A Black Theology of Liberation*. Maryknoll, NY, Orbis Books, 1986

Conze, Edward. *Buddhism: Its Essence and Development*. London, Bruno, 1951

Coomaraswamy, Ananda K. *Elements of Buddhist Iconography*. 2nd edn. New Delhi, 1972

— *Figures of Speech, or, Figures of Thought: Collected Essays on the Traditional, or, 'Normal' View of Art*. London, Luzac, 1946

— *Why Exhibit Works of Art?* London, Luzac, 1943

Copleston, Frederick. *On the Art of Philosophy, and Other Essays*. London, Search Press, 1979

— *Religion and the One: Philosophies East and West*. London, Search Press, 1982

Corbin, Henri. *Creative Imagination in the Sufism of Ibn 'Arabi*, trans. Ralph Mannheim. Bollingen Series 91. Princeton, Princeton University Press, 1969

— *Histoire de la philosophie islamique*. Paris, Gallimard, 1964

Corsin, Raymond J. (ed.). *Encyclopaedia of Psychology*. 4 vols. New York, John Wiley & Sons, 1984

Coulson, Noel J. *A History of Islamic Law*. Islamic Surveys 2. Edinburgh, Edinburgh University Press, 1964

Coulson, Noel J. and Doreen Hinchcliffe. 'Women and Law Reform in Contemporary Islam', in Beck and Keddie, *Women in the Muslim World*, pp. 37–51.

Craige, Betty Jean. *Literary Relativity: An Essay on Twentieth-Century Narrative*. London, Associated University Press, 1982

Cuppitt, Don. *Taking Leave of God*. London, SCM Press, 1980

Dahl, Arthur L. *Unless and Until: A Baha'i Focus on the Environment*. London, Baha'i Publishing Trust, 1990.

Daly Mary, *Beyond God the Father: Towards a Philosophy of Women's Liberation*. Boston, Beacon Press, 1973

— *The Church and the Second Sex*. London, Geoffrey Chapman, 1968 (new edn. with additional material: Boston, Beacon Press, 1985)

Davies, Paul. *The Cosmic Blueprint*. London, Unwin, 1989

Davis, Eric. 'Ideology, Social Class and Islamic Radicalism in Modern Egypt', in *From Nationalism to Revolutionary Islam*, ed. S. A. Arjomand. Albany, State University of New York Press, 1984, pp. 134–57

Davis, Stephen T. (ed.). *Encountering Evil: Live Options in Theodicy*. Edinburgh, T. & T. Clark, 1981

Deikman, Arthur. 'Deautomatization and the Mystic Experience', *Psychiatry* 29, 1966, pp. 324–38; reprinted in Woods, *Understanding Mysticism,* pp. 240–60 and in Tart, *Altered States of Consciousness*, pp. 23–43. References in the text are to the original article.

Dennis, Wayne. *The Hopi Child*. New York, Science Editions, 1965

Diner, Helen. *Mothers and Amazons: The First Feminine History of Culture*, trans. and ed. J. P. Lundin. New York, Anchor Books, 1973

Donovan, Peter. *Interpreting Religious Experience*. London, Sheldon Press, 1979

Douglas, Mary. *Purity and Danger: An Analysis of Concepts of Pollution and Taboo*. New York, Praeger, 1966

Dudley III, Guilford. *Religion on Trial: Mircea Eliade and his Critics*. Philadelphia, Temple University Press, 1977

Durkheim, Emile. *The Elementary Forms of*

the Religious Life, trans. J. W. Swain. London, George Allen & Unwin, 1976
Eaton, Richard M. *The Rise of Islam and the Bengal Frontier, 1204–1760*. New Delhi, Oxford University Press, 1994
Eddy, S. L. *The King is Dead*. Lincoln, Neb., University of Nebraska Press, 1961
Edwards, Jo and Martin Palmer. *Holy Ground: A Guide to Faith and Ecology*. Yelvertoft, Northamptonshire, Pilkington Press, 1997
Eliade, Mircea. *Images and Symbols*, trans. Phillip Mairet. New York, Sheed & Ward, 1961
— *Patterns in Comparative Religion*. London, Sheed & Ward, 1958; 4th impression 1979
— *The Sacred and the Profane*, trans. Willard R. Trask. New York, Harper & Row, 1961
Eliade, Mircea (ed.). *Encyclopaedia of Religion*. 16 vols. New York, Macmillan, 1987
Ellis, Marc H. *Toward a Jewish Theology of Liberation*. London, SCM Press, 1988
Emmerick, R. E. *Book of Zambasta: A Khotanese Poem on Buddhism*. London, Oxford University Press, 1968
Encyclopedia of Islam. 2nd edn. Leiden, Brill, 1960–
Engineer, Asghar Ali. *Islam and Liberation Theology: Essays on Liberative Elements in Islam*. New Delhi, Sterling Publishers, [1990]
Esslemont, John E. *Baha'u'llah and the New Era*. Revised 4th edn. London, Baha'i Publishing Trust, 1974
Evans-Pritchard, E. E. *Nuer Religion*. Oxford, Oxford University Press, 1977
Falk, Ze'ev W. *Law and Religion: The Jewish Experience*. Jerusalem, Mesharim Publishers, 1981
Farquhar, J. N. *Modern Religious Movements in India*. London, Macmillan, 1929
Ferdows, Adele K. and Amir Ferdows. 'Women in Shi'i Fiqh: Images Through the Hadith', in *Women and Revolution in Iran,* ed. Guity Nashat. Boulder, Co., Westview, 1983, pp. 55–68
Ferguson, John. *War and Peace in the World's Religions*. London, Sheldon Press, 1977
Fiorenza, Elizabeth S. *In Memory of Her: A Feminist Reconstruction of Christian Origins*. London, SCM Press, 1983
Fischer, Michael M. J. *Iran: From Religious Dispute to Revolution*. Cambridge, Mass., Harvard University Press, 1980
Fischer, Roland. 'A Cartography of Ecstatic and Meditative States', *Science* 174, 1971, pp. 897–904; reprinted in Woods, *Understanding Mysticism*, pp. 286–305
Fischer, Roland, F. Griffin and L. Liss. 'Biological Aspects of Time in Relation to (Model) Psychoses', *Annals of the New York Academy of Science* 96, 1962, pp. 44–65
Fischer, Roland, T. Kappeler, P. Wisecup and K. Thatcher. 'Personality Trait Dependent Performance under Psilocybin', *Diseases of the Nervous System* 31, 1970, pp. 91–101
Flew, Anthony. *God and Philosophy*. London, Hutchinson, 1966
Flood, Gavin. *An Introduction to Hinduism*. Cambridge, Cambridge University Press, 1996
Foerster, Werner. *Gnosis: A Selection of Gnostic Texts*, vol. 2: *Coptic and Mandean Sources*, trans. R. McL. Wilson. Oxford, Clarendon Press, 1974
Forte, Antonio. *Political Propaganda and Ideology in China at the End of the Seventh Century*. Naples, Instituto Universitario Orientale, 1976
Fowler, James W. *Stages of Faith: The Psychology of Human Development and the Quest for Meaning*. San Francisco, Harper & Row, 1981
Fox, Matthew. *The Coming of the Cosmic Christ: The Healing of Mother Earth and the Birth of a Global Renaissance*, San Francisco, Harper & Row, 1988
Fozdar, Jamshed K. *The God of Buddha*. New York, Asia Publishing House, 1979
French, Marilyn. *Beyond Power: On Women, Men and Morals*. London, Jonathan Cape, 1985
Freud, Sigmund. *Civilisation and its Discontents*, trans. J. Riviere. International Psycho-Analytical Library 17. London, Hogarth Press, 1930
— *The Future of an Illusion*, trans. W. D. Robson-Scott. International Psycho-Analytical Library 15. London, Hogarth Press, 1928
— *Totem and Taboo: Some Points of Agreement Between the Mental Lives of Savages and Neurotics,* trans. J.

Strachey. New York, Norton, 1950; original German edn. 1913
Gazzaniga, M. S., J. E. Bogen, and R. W. Sperry. 'Some Functional Effects of Sectioning the Cerebral Commissures in Man', *Proceedings of the National Academy of Science* 48, 1962, pp. 1765–9
Geertz, Clifford. *The Interpretation of Cultures: Selected Essays*. New York, Basic Books, 1973
Gilligan, Carol. *In a Different Voice: Psychological Theory and Women's Development*. Cambridge, Mass., Harvard University Press, 1982
Gilsenan, Michael. *Recognizing Islam: An Anthropologist's Introduction*. London, Croom Helm, 1982
Gimbutas, Marija. *The Goddesses and Gods of Old Europe*. London, Thames & Hudson, 1982
Glasenapp, Helmuth von. *Buddhism: a Non-Theistic Religion*, trans. Irmgard Schloegl. London, George Allen & Unwin, 1970
Gleizes, Albert. *Art et Religion, Art et Science, Art et Production*. Chambery, Editions Presence, 1970. Unpublished translation into English by Dr Peter Brooke
Goldziher, Ignaz. *Muslim Studies*. vol. 2, ed. S. M. Stern; trans. C. R. Barber and S. M. Stern. London, George Allen & Unwin, 1971
Gombrich, Ernst. *The Story of Art*. 11th edn. London, Phaidon Press, 1966
Gombrich, Richard F. *Precept and Practice: Traditional Buddhism in the Rural Highlands of Ceylon*. Oxford, Clarendon Press, 1971
Goody, Jack. *The Logic of Writing and the Organisation of Society*. Cambridge, Cambridge University Press, 1986
Gottlieb, Randie and Steven. *Once to Every Man and Nation: Stories about Becoming A Baha'i*. Oxford, George Ronald, 1985
The Greatness Which Might Be Theirs. n.p., Baha'i International Community, 1995
Green, Miranda. *The Gods of the Celts*. Gloucester, Alan Sutton, 1986
Green, Ronald M. *Religious Reason: the Rational and Moral Basis of Religious Belief*. New York, Oxford University Press, 1978
Griffin, David. *God, Power and Evil: A Process Theodicy*. Philadelphia, Westminister Press, 1976
Grimes, Ronald C. *Beginnings in Ritual Studies*. Lanham, University Press of America, 1982
Guillaume, Alfred. *The Life of Muhammad: A Translation of Ishaq's 'Sirat Rasul Allah'*. London, Oxford University Press, 1955
Gunton, Colin (ed.). *Cambridge Companion to Christian Doctrine*. Cambridge, Cambridge University Press, 1997
Gupta, A. R. *Women in Hindu Society*. 2nd edn. New Delhi, Jyotsna Prakahan, 1982
Gutierrez, Gustavo. *A Theology of Liberation: History, Politics and Salvation*, trans. C. Inda and J. Eagleson. London, SCM Press, 1974; original Spanish edn. *Teologica de la Liberación*, Lima, 1971
Hackett, Rosalind I. J. (ed.). *New Religious Movements in Nigeria*. African Studies 5. Lewiston, NY, Edwin Mellon, 1987
Hadden, Jeffrey K. 'The Rise and Fall of American Televangelism', *Annals of the American Academy of Political and Social Sciences* 527, May 1993, pp. 113–30
Halifax, Joan. *Shamanic Voices: A Survey of Visionary Narratives*. New York, Viking/Arkana, 1991
Hamilton, Roberta. *The Liberation of Women: A Study of Patriarchy and Capitalism*. Studies in Sociology 6. London, George Allen & Unwin, 1978
Hammond, Phillip. 'Cults and Civil Religion in Today's World', in Whaling, *Religion in Today's World*, pp. 110–27
Hanson, Paul D. *The Dawn of Apocalyptic: The Historical and Sociological Roots of Jewish Apocalyptic Eschatology*. Philadelphia, Fortress Press, 1979
Happold, F. C. *Mysticism: A Study and an Anthology*. Harmondsworth, Penguin, 1963
Harris, Ian. 'Getting to Grips with Buddhist Environmentalism: A Provisional Typology', *Journal of Buddhist Ethics* 2, 1995, pp. 173–90; journal available on the Internet at http://www.cac.psu.edu/jbe/
Harvey, Peter. 'The Dynamics of *Paritta* Chanting in Southern Buddhism', in

Werner, *Love Divine*, pp. 53–84
— *An Introduction to Buddhism*. Cambridge, Cambridge University Press, 1990
Hastings, James (ed.) *Encyclopaedia of Religion and Ethics*. 13 vols. Edinburgh: T. & T. Clark, 1910–26
Hawthorn, Mary B. *The Doukhobors of British Columbia*. Westport, Conn., Greenwood Press, 1980
Haynie, N. A. 'Cognitive Learning Styles', in *Encyclopaedia of Psychology*, ed. R. J. Corsin. New York, John Wiley & Sons, 1984, vol. 1, pp. 236–8
Heimsath, Charles H. *Indian Nationalism and Hindu Social Reform*. Princeton: Princeton University Press, 1964
Henry, Maureen. *The Intoxication of Power: An Analysis of Civil Religion in Relation to Ideology*. Dordrecht, Reidel, 1979
Hick, John. *Evil and the God of Love*. London, Macmillan, 1966
— *God has Many Names*. London, Macmillan, 1980
— *An Interpretation of Religion: Human Responses to the Transcendent*. New Haven, Yale University Press, 1989
— *Problems of Religious Pluralism*. London, Macmillan, 1985
— *The Second Christianity*. 3rd edn. London, SCM Press, 1983
Hick, John (ed.). *The Myth of God Incarnate*. London, SCM Press, 1977
Hick, John and Hasan Askari (eds.). *The Experience of Religious Diversity*. Amersham, Bucks, Avebury, 1983
Hilger, Sister M. Inez. *Chippewa Child Life and its Cultural Background*. Bulletin 146. Washington, DC, Smithsonian Institution, Bureau of American Ethnology, 1951
al-Hilli, ['Allamah] Ibnu'l-Mutahhar. *Al-Bábu 'l-Hádi 'Ashar*, with commentary by Miqdad al-Hilli; trans. William M. Miller. Oriental Translation Fund, New Series 29. London, Royal Asiatic Society, 1958
Hinnells, John R. 'Religion and the Arts', in *Turning Points in Religious Studies*, ed. Ursula King. Edinburgh, T. & T. Clark, 1990, pp. 257–74
Hinnells, John R. (ed.). *A Handbook of Living Religions*. Harmondsworth, Viking, 1984
Ho, Beng T., Daniel Richards and Douglas Chute (eds.). *Drug Discrimination and State Dependent Learning*. New York, Academic Press, 1978
Hoebel, E. Adamson and Thomas Weaver. *Anthropology and the Human Experience*. 4th edn. New York, McGraw-Hill, 1979
Hofstadter, Richard. *Anti-intellectualism in American Life*. London, Jonathan Cape, 1964
Holm, Jean and John Bowker (eds.). *Making Moral Decisions*. Themes in Religious Studies Series. London, Pinter, 1994
Horner, I. B. *Women Under Primitive Buddhism*. London, Routledge and Kegan Paul, 1930
Hostetler, J. A. *Amish Society*. Baltimore, Johns Hopkins University Press, 1963
Hourani, Albert. *Arabic Thought in the Liberal Age*. Oxford, Oxford University Press, 1962
Humphreys, Christmas. *Exploring Buddhism*. London, George Allen & Unwin, 1974
Inada, Kenneth K. (trans.). *Nagarjuna: A Translation of His 'Mulamadhya-makakarika'*. Tokyo, Hokuseido Press, 1970
Izutsu, Toshihiko. *Sufism and Taoism: A Comparative Study of Key Philosophical Concepts*. Berkeley, University of California Press, 1984
Jafri, S. Husain M. *The Origins and Early Development of Shi'a Islam*. London, Longman, 1979
James, M. R. *The Apocryphal New Testament: Translation and Notes*. Oxford, Clarendon Press, 1924
James, William. *A Pluralistic Universe*. London, Longmans, Green & Co., 1909
— *Some Problems of Philosophy: A Beginning of An Introduction to Philosophy*. London, Longmans, Green & Co., 1911
— *The Varieties of Religious Experience*. London, Longmans, Green & Co., 1929
Jami, Nur al-Din 'Abd al-Rahman. *Lawa'ih: A Treatise on Sufism*, trans. E. H. Whinfield and Mirza Muhammad Kazvini. Oriental Translation Fund, New Series, 16. London, Royal Asiatic Society, 1906
Jesudasan, Ignatius. *A Gandhian Theology of Liberation*. Maryknoll, NY, Orbis

Books, 1984

Johnston, Douglas and Cynthia Sampson. *Religion, The Missing Dimension of Statecraft*. Oxford, Oxford University Press, 1994

Jorstad, Erling. *The New Christian Right 1981–1986: Prospects for the Post-Reagan Era*. Lewiston and Queenstown, Edwin Mellen Press, 1987

Jung, Carl G. 'Archetypes of the Collective Unconscious', in *The Archetypes and the Collective Unconscious*, trans. R. F. C. Hull. 2nd edn. Collected Works of C. G. Jung, vol. 9, part 1. London, Routledge & Kegan Paul, 1968

— *Psychology and Religion: West and East*, trans. R. F. C. Hull. 2nd edn. Collected Works of C. G. Jung, vol. 11. London, Routledge & Kegan Paul, 1969

— *The Structure and Dynamics of the Psyche*, trans. R. F. C. Hull. 2nd edn. Collected Works of C. G. Jung, vol. 8. London, Routledge & Kegan Paul, 1968

Kasamatsu, A. and T. Hirai. 'An Electroencephalographic Study of the Zen Meditation (Zazen)', in Tart, *Altered States of Consciousness*, pp. 489–501

— 'Science of Zazen', *Psychologia* 6, 1963, pp. 86–91

Katz, Steven T. 'Models, Modeling and Mystical Training', *Religion* 12, 1982, pp. 247–75

Keddie, Nikki R. *Roots of the Revolution*. New Haven, Yale University Press, 1981

Khomeini, Ruhollah. *Hukumat-i Islami (Vilayat-i Faqih)*. [Tehran], n.p., c. 1980.

King, Ursula. 'Religion and Gender', in *Turning Points in Religious Studies*, ed. Ursula King. Edinburgh, T. & T. Clark, 1990, pp. 275–86

— *Women and Spirituality: Voices of Protest and Promise*. 2nd edn. London, Macmillan, 1993

King, Ursula (ed.). *Women in the World's Religions, Past and Present*. New York, Paragon House, 1987

King, Winston L. *Introduction to Religion*. New York, Harper, 1968

— *A Thousand Lives Away: Buddhism in Contemporary Burma*. Oxford, Bruno Cassirer, 1964

— *Zen and the Way of the Sword: Arming the Samurai Psyche*. New York, Oxford University Press, 1993

Kitagawa, Joseph M. *On Understanding Japanese Religion*. Princeton, Princeton University Press, 1987

Korzybski, Alfred. *Science and Sanity*. 3rd edn. Lakeville, Conn., International Non-Aristotelian Library Publishing Co., 1949

Kose, Ali. *Conversion to Islam: A Study of Native British Converts*. London, Kegan Paul International, 1996

Krasnowolska, Anna. 'The Heroes of the Iranian epic tale', *Folio Orientalia* 24, 1987, pp. 173–89

Kuhn, Thomas S. *The Structure of Scientific Revolutions*. International Encyclopedia of Unified Science, vol. 2, no. 2. 2nd edn. Chicago, University of Chicago Press, 1970

Küng, Hans. *Eternal Life?*, trans. Edward Quinn. London, Collins, 1984

— *On Being a Christian*, trans. Edward Quinn. London, Collins, 1978

Küng, Hans and Karl-Josef Kuschel (eds.). *A Global Ethic: The Declaration of the Parliament of the World's Religions*, trans. John Bowden. London, SCM Press, 1993

Lahidji, Abdol Karim. 'Constitutionalism and Clerical Authority', in *Authority and Political Culture in Shi'ism*, ed. Said A. Arjomand. Albany, State University of New York Press, 1988, pp. 133–58

Lambden, Stephen. 'An Episode in the Childhood of the Bab', in *In Iran*, ed. Peter Smith. Studies in Babi and Baha'i History 3. Los Angeles, Kalimat Press, 1986, pp. 1–31

Lamotte, Etienne. 'Manjusri', *T'oung Pao* 48, 1960, pp. 1–75

Lang, Andrew. *The Making of Religion*. London, Longmans, Green & Co., 1898

Laski, Marghanita. *Ecstasy: A Study of Some Secular and Religious Experiences*. London, Cresset Press, 1961

Lawrence, Clifford H. *Medieval Monasticism: Forms of Religious Life in Western Europe in the Middle Ages*. London, Longman, 1984

Layton, Bentley. *The Gnostic Scriptures*. London, SCM Press, 1987

LeShan, Lawrence and Henry Morgenau. *Einstein's Space and Van Gogh's Sky: Physical Reality and Beyond*. Brighton,

Harvester Press, 1982

Lévi-Strauss, Claude. *Introduction to a Science of Mythology*. 4 vols: vols. 1–3, New York, Harper & Row, 1969, 1973, 1978; vol. 4, London, Jonathan Cape, 1981

— *Structural Anthropology*. 2 vols. Harmondsworth, Penguin Books, 1963, 1973

Lewis, Ioan. *Ecstatic Religion: An Anthropological Study of Spirit Possession and Shamanism*. Harmondsworth, Penguin, 1971

Lewis, John. *Anthropology Made Simple*. London, W. H. Allen, 1969

Ling, Trevor. *Buddhism, Imperialism and War: Burma and Thailand in Modern History*. London, George Allen & Unwin, 1979

Lings, Martin. *Muhammad: His Life Based on the Earliest Sources*. London, Islamic Texts Society, 1983

Lofland, John. *Doomsday Cult: A Study of Conversion, Proselytization, and Maintenance of Faith*. Englewood Cliffs, New Jersey, 1966

Lofland, John and Norman Skonovd. 'Conversion Motifs', *Journal for the Scientific Study of Religion* 20, 1981, pp. 373–85

Lord, Albert. *The Singer of Tales*. Harvard Studies in Comparative Literature 24. Cambridge, Mass., Harvard University Press, 1960

Lustick, Ian S. 'Israel's Dangerous Fundamentalists', *Foreign Policy* 68, 1987, pp. 118–39

Machobane, L. B. B. J. *Christianisation and African Response among the Barolong and Basotho, 1820–1890*. Occasional Paper 7. Roma, Lesotho, Institute of Southern African Studies, 1993

Majlisi, Muhammad Baqir. *Hiliyat al-Muttaqin*. 4th printing. Tehran, 'Ilmi Publications, n.d.

Makdisi, George. 'Remarks on Traditionalism in Islamic Religious History', in *The Conflict of Traditionalism and Modernism in the Muslim Middle East*, ed. Carl Leiden. Austin, University of Texas Press, 1966, pp. 77–88

Malinowski, Bronislaw. *Magic, Science and Religion, and Other Essays*. London, Souvenir Press, 1974

Marett, Robert R. *Sacraments of Simple Folk*. Oxford, Clarendon Press, 1933

Marriott, McKim. 'Little Communities in an Indigenous Civilisation', in *Village India*, ed. McKim Marriott. Chicago, University of Chicago Press, 1955, pp. 171–222

Marsden, George. *Fundamentalism and American Culture: The Shaping of Twentieth-Century Evangelicalism 1870–1925*. Oxford, Oxford University Press, 1982

Martland, Thomas R. *Religion as Art: An Interpretatrion*. Albany, State University of New York Press, 1981

Marty, Martin E. and R. Scott Appleby (eds.). *Fundamentalisms Observed*. Chicago, University of Chicago Press, 1991

Marx, Karl. *The Essential Marx: The Non-Economic Writings – A Selection*. ed. and trans. Saul K. Padover. New York, New American Library, 1979

Masefield, Peter. *Divine Revelation in Pali Buddhism*. Columbo, Sri Lanka Institute of Traditional Studies, 1986

— 'The Muni and the Moonies', *Religion* 15, 1985, pp. 143–60

Maslow, Abraham. *Religions, Values and Peak-Experiences*. New York, Viking, 1970

Massignon, Louis. *The Passion of al-Hallaj*, trans. H. Mason. 4 vols. Bollingen Series 97. Princeton, Princeton University Press, 1983; originally published in French as *La Passion de Husayn ibn Mansur Hallaj*, Paris, Paul Geuthner, 1922

Ma'sumian, Farnaz. *Life after Death: A Study of the Afterlife in World Religions*. Oxford, Oneworld, 1995

McLeod, W. H. *Textual Sources for the Study of Sikhism*. Manchester, Manchester University Press, 1984

Mendelsohn, E. M. 'A Messianic Buddhist Association in Upper Burma', *Bulletin of the London School of Oriental and African Studies* 24, 1961, pp. 560–80

Merkl, Peter H. and Ninian Smart (eds.). *Religion and Politics in the Modern World*. New York, New York University Press, 1983

Mishra, Rammurti S. *Fundamentals of Yoga*. London, Lyrebird Press, 1972

Momen, Moojan. 'Authority and Opposition in Twelver Shi'ism', in *Islamic Fundamentalism*, ed. R. M. Burrell. Seminar Papers 1. London, Royal Asiatic Society, 1989, pp. 48–66

— *The Babi and Baha'i Religions 1844–1944*: Some Contemporary Western Accounts. Oxford, George Ronald, 1981

— *An Introduction to Shi'i Islam: The History and Doctrines of Twelver Shi'ism*. New Haven, Yale University Press and Oxford, George Ronald, 1985

— 'Relativism: A Basis for Baha'i Metaphysics', in *Studies in Honor of the late Hasan M. Balyuzi*, ed. M. Momen. Studies in the Babi and Baha'i Religions 5. Los Angeles, Kalimat Press, 1988, pp. 184–217

— *A Short Introduction to the Baha'i Faith*. Oxford, Oneworld, 1996

Morgan, Kenneth. *The Religion of the Hindus*. New York, Ronald Press, 1953

Moore, Albert C. *Iconography of Religions*. London, SCM Press, 1977

Moore, Katherine. *She for God*. London, Allison and Busby, 1978

Morris, Brian. *Anthropological Studies of Religion: An Introductory Text*. Cambridge, Cambridge University Press, 1987

Mortimer, Edward. *Faith and Power: The Politics of Islam*. London, Faber & Faber, 1982

Munson, Henry. *Islam and Revolution in the Middle East*. New Haven, Yale University Press, 1988

Murthy, A. Satyanarayana. *Religion and Society (A Study of Koyas)*. New Delhi, Discovery Publishing House, 1991

Murti, T. R. V. *The Central Philosophy of Buddhism*. 2nd edn. London, Unwin, 1960

Nabil. *The Dawn-Breakers: Nabil's Narrative of the Early Days of the Baha'i Revelation*, trans. and ed. Shoghi Effendi. Wilmette, Baha'i Publishing Trust, 1962

Nakamuro, Kojira. 'A Structural Analysis of *dhikr* and *nembutsu*', *Orient* 7, 1971, pp. 75–96

Nakhjavani, Bahiyyih. *Response*. Oxford, George Ronald, 1981

Nasr, S. Hossein. *Traditional Islam in the Modern World*. London, Kegan Paul International, 1987

Nattier, Jan. 'The Meanings of the Maitreya Myth', in Sponberg and Hardacre, *Maitreya, the Future Buddha*, pp. 23–47

Neely's History of the Parliament of Religions and Religious Congresses at the World's Columbian Exposition, ed. Walter R. Houghton et al. 3rd edn. Chicago, F. T. Neely, 1893

Neibuhr, H. Richard. *The Social Sources of Denominationalism*. New York, New American Library, 1975

Newman, William M. (ed.). *The Social Meanings of Religion*. Chicago, Rand McNally, 1974

Norbeck, Edward. *Religion in Primitive Society*. New York, Harper, 1961

Oddie, G. A. (ed.). *Religion in South Asia: Religious Conversion and Revival Movements in South Asia in Medieval and Modern Times*. 2nd edn. New Delhi, Manohar, 1991

O'Dea, Thomas. *The Sociology of Religion*. Englewood Cliffs, Prentice-Hall, 1966

Odin, Steve. *Process Metaphysics and Hua-Yen Buddhism: A Critical study of Cumulative Penetration vs. Interpenetration*. Albany, State University of New York Press, 1982

Ormsby, Eric L. *Theodicy in Islamic Thought: The Dispute over al-Ghazali's 'Best of All Possible Worlds'*. Princeton, Princeton University Press, 1984

Ornstein, Robert. 'The Two Sides of the Brain', in Woods, *Understanding Mysticism*, pp. 270–85.

Otto, Rudolf. *The Idea of the Holy*, trans. J. W. Harvey. London, Oxford University Press, 1923; original German edn. 1917

Overmyer, Daniel. *Folk Buddhist Religion: Dissenting Sects in Late Traditional China*. Cambridge, Mass., Harvard University Press, 1976

— 'Messenger, Savior, and Revolutionary: Maitreya in Chinese Popular Religious Literature of the Sixteenth and Seventeenth Century', in Sponberg and Hardacre, *Maitreya, The Future Buddha*, pp. 110–34

Overton, Donald. 'Major Theories of State Dependent Learning', in Ho, Richards and Chute, *Drug Discrimination and State Dependent Learning*, pp. 283–318

Panikkar, Raimundo. *Blessed Simplicity: The Monk as Universal Archetype*. New

York, Seabury, 1982

Park, Sung Bae. *Buddhist Faith and Sudden Enlightenment*. Albany, State University of New York Press, 1983.

Parrinder, Geoffrey. *Mysticism in the World's Religions*. Oxford, Oneworld, 1995

— *Sex in the World's Religions*. London, Sheldon Press, 1980

Parsons, Gerald. 'Expanding the Religious Spectrum: New Religious Movements in Modern Britain', in *The Growth of Religious Diversity: Britain from 1945*. Vol.1: *Traditions*, ed. Gerald Parsons. London: Routledge, 1993, pp. 275–303

Paul, Diana T. *Women in Buddhism: Images of the Feminine in Mahayana Tradition*. Berkeley, University of California Press, 1985

Peel, J. Y. D. 'Syncretism and Religious Change', *Comparative Studies in Society and History* 10, 1967–8, pp. 124–40

Peters, Victor. *All Things Common: The Hutterite Way of Life*. New York, Harper, 1971

Phillips, D. Z. 'Religious Beliefs and Language-Games', in *The Philosophy of Religion*, ed. Basil Mitchell. London, Oxford University Press, 1971, pp.121–42; originally in *Ratio* 12, 1970, pp. 26–46

Piaget, Jean. *The Essential Piaget*, ed. Howard E. Gruber and J. J. Voneche. London, Routledge & Kegan Paul, 1977

— 'The First Year of the Life of the Child', *British Journal of Psychology* 18, 1927–8, pp. 97–120; reprinted in *The Essential Piaget*, pp. 198–214

Plantinga, Alvin. *God, Freedom and Evil*. London, George Allen & Unwin, 1975

Price, H. H. 'Belief "in" and Belief "that"', in *The Philosophy of Religion*, ed. Basil Mitchell. London, Oxford University Press, 1971, pp. 143–67

Prozesky, Martin. *Christianity Amidst Apartheid: Selected Perspectives on the Church in South Africa*. Basingstoke, Macmillan, 1990

Pruett, Gordon E. *The Meaning and End of Suffering for Freud and the Buddhist Tradition*. Lanham, University Press of America, 1987

Psychobiology: The Biological Basis of Behavior. Readings from Scientific American. San Francisco, W. H. Freeman, 1966

Pye, Michael. *The Buddha*. London, Duckworth, 1979

Rahner, Karl. 'Observations on the Problem of the "Anonymous Christian"', in *Theological Investigations*, vol. 14. New York, Seabury, 1976, pp. 280–94

Rambo, Lewis R. *Understanding Religious Conversion*. New Haven, Yale, 1993

Ranade, Ramchandra D. *Mysticism in India: The Poet-Saints of Maharashtra*. Albany, State University of New York Press, 1983

Redfield, Robert. *Peasant Society and Culture: An Anthropological Approach to Civilization*. The William J. Cooper Foundation Lectures. Chicago, University of Chicago Press, 1956

Ribeiro, Rene. 'Brazilian Messianic Movements', in Thrupp, *Millennial Dreams in Action*, pp. 55–69

Richards, Glyn (ed.). *A Source-Book of Modern Hinduism*. London, Curzon Press, 1985

Richards, Hubert J. *The First Christmas: What Really Happened?* London, Collins/Fontana, 1973

Rider Encyclopedia of Eastern Philosophy and Religion. London, Rider, 1989

Robertson, Roland (ed.). *The Sociology of Religion*. Harmondsworth, Penguin, 1985

Rost, H. T. D. *The Golden Rule: A Universal Ethic*. Oxford, George Ronald, 1986

Rouner, Leroy S. (ed.). *Human Rights and the World's Religions*. Boston University Studies in Philosophy and Religion 9. Notre Dame, In., University of Notre Dame Press, 1988

— *Knowing Religiously*. Boston University Studies in Philosophy and Religion 7. Notre Dame, In., University of Notre Dame Press, 1985

Rowe, William L. and William J. Wainwright. *Philosophy of Religion: Selected Readings*. New York, Harcourt Brace Jovanovich, 1973

Rudolph, Kurt. *Gnosis: The Nature and History of an Ancient Religion*, trans. Robert M. Wilson. Edinburgh, T. & T. Clark, 1983

Rumi, Jalal al-Din. *The Mathnavi of Jalalu'd din Rami*, ed. and trans. R. A. Nicholson. Leiden, Brill; London, Luzac,

8 vols, 1925–40
Runzo, Joseph. *Reason, Relativism and God*. London, Macmillan, 1986
Runzo, Joseph (ed.). *Ethics, Religion, and the Good Society: New Directions in a Pluralistic World*. Louisville, Ky., Westminster/John Knox Press, 1992
Runzo, Joseph and Craig K. Ihara (eds.). *Religious Experience and Religious Belief: Essays in the Epistemology of Religion*. Lanham, MD, University Press of America, 1986
Russell, Jeffrey B. *The Devil: Perceptions of Evil from Antiquity to Primitive Christianity*. Ithaca, Cornell University Press, 1977
Sabbah, Fatna A. *Woman in the Muslim Unconscious*, trans. Mary J. Lakeland. Athene Series. New York, Pergammon, 1988
Sachedina, Abdulaziz A. *Islamic Messianism: The Idea of the Mahdi in Twelver Shi'ism*. Albany, State University of New York Press, 1981
Saddhatissa, H. *The Life of the Buddha*. London, Unwin, 1976
Sandeen, Ernest R. *The Roots of Fundamentalism: British and American Millenarianism 1800–1930*. Chicago, University of Chicago Press, 1970
Sansom, G. B. *Japan: A Short Cultural History*. London, Barrie & Jenkins, 1976
Sarkisyanz, E. *Buddhist Backgrounds of the Burmese Revolution*. The Hague, Martinus Nijhoff, 1965
Schacht, Joseph. *Origins of Muhammadan Jurisprudence*. Oxford, Clarendon Press, 1950
Schall, James V. *Liberation Theology in Latin America*. San Francisco, Ignatius Press, 1982
Schmidt, Wilhelm. *The Origin and Growth of Religion*, trans. H. J. Rose. London, Methuen & Co., 1931
Seligman, Edwin R. A. (ed.) *Encyclopedia of the Social Sciences*. 15 vols. London, Macmillan, 1930–5
Sharpe, Eric J. *Comparative Religion: A History*. London, Duckworth, 1975
— *Understanding Religion*. London, Duckworth, 1983
Shepard, William E. '"Fundamentalism" Christian and Islamic', *Religion* 17, 1987, pp. 355–78
— 'Islam and Ideology: Towards a Typology', *International Journal of Middle East Studies* 19, 1987, pp. 307–36
Shepperson, George. 'The Comparative Study of Millenarian Movements', in Thrupp, *Millennial Dreams in Action*, pp. 44–52
Shiner, Larry E. 'The Concept of Secularization in Empirical Research', in *Social Meanings of Religion*, pp. 304–22.
Shiraishi, Ryokai. *Asceticism in Buddhism and Brahmanism: A Comparative Study*. Tring, Institute of Buddhist Studies, 1996
Shunjo. *Honen the Buddhist Saint*, trans. H. H. Coates and R. Ishisuka. Kyoto, Chionin, 1925
Shupe, Anson D. and David Bromley. 'Witches, Moonies and Evil', *Society* 15/4, May/June 1978, pp. 75–6
Singer, Margaret T. and Marsha E. Addis. 'Cults, Coercion, and Contumely', in *The Mosaic of Contemporary Psychiatry in Perspective,* ed. Anthony Kales, Chester M. Pierce, Milton Greenblatt. New York, Springer Verlag, 1992
Singer, Margaret T. and Janja Lalich. *Cults in Our Midst: The Hidden Menace in Our Everyday Lives*. San Francisco, Jossey-Bass, 1995
Singh, Daram. *Sikh Theology of Liberation*. New Delhi, Harman Publishing House, 1991
Smart, Ninian. *Concept and Empathy*. London, Macmillan, 1986
— *The Philosophy of Religion*. New York, Oxford University Press, 1979
— *Reasons and Faiths: An Investigation of Religious Discourse, Christian and Non-Christian*. London, Routledge & Kegan Paul, 1958 (repr. 1971)
— *Religion and the Western Mind*. Basingstoke, Macmillan, 1987
— *The World's Religions*. Cambridge, Cambridge University Press, 1993
— 'The Work of the Buddha and the Work of Christ', in Brandon, *The Saviour God*, pp. 160–73
Smith, Bardwell L. (ed.) *Religion and Legitimation of Power in South Asia*. Leiden, Brill, 1978
Smith, Huston. 'Postmodernism's Impact on

the Study of Religion', *Journal of the American Academy of Religion* 58, 1990, pp. 653–70

Smith, John E. *Quasi-religion: Humanism, Marxism and Nationalism*. Basingstoke, Macmillan, 1994

Smith, Jonathan Z. *Map is not Territory*. Leiden, Brill, 1978

Smith, Margaret. *Introduction to Mysticism*. London, Sheldon Press, 1977

Smith, Peter. *The Babi and Baha'i Religion: From Messianic Shi'ism to a World Religion*. Cambridge, Cambridge University Press, 1987

— *The Baha'i Religion: A Short Introduction to its History and Teachings*. Oxford, George Ronald, 1988

Smith, Peter and Moojan Momen 'The Baha'i Faith 1957–1988: A Survey of Contemporary Developments', *Religion* 19, 1989, pp. 63–91

Smith, Wilfred Cantwell. 'Comparative Religion: Whither – and Why?', in *The History of Religions: Essays in Methodology*, ed. Mircea Eliade and Joseph Kitagawa. Chicago, University of Chicago Press, 1959, pp. 31–58

— 'The Concept of Shari'a Among Some Mutakallimun', in *Arabic and Islamic Studies in Honor of Hamilton A. R. Gibb*, ed. George Makdisi. Leiden, Brill, 1965, pp. 581–602

— *Faith and Belief*. Oxford, Oneworld, 1998

— 'A Human View of Truth', in *Truth and Dialogue: the Relationship Between the World Religions*, ed. John Hick. London, Sheldon Press, 1974, pp. 20–44

— *The Meaning and End of Religion*. New York, Mentor, 1964

— 'Some Similarities and Differences between Christianity and Islam', in *The World of Islam: Studies in Honour of Philip K. Hitti*, ed. James Kritzeck and R. Bayly Winder. London, Macmillan, 1959, pp. 47–59

— *Towards a World Theology: Faith and the Comparative History of Religion*. Philadephia, Westminster Press, 1981

Sperry, R. W. 'Cerebral Organisation and Behaviour', *Science* 133, 1961, pp. 1749–57

— 'The Great Cerebral Commissure', in *Psychobiology: The Biological Basis of Behavior*, pp. 240–50

Spiro, Melford E. *Buddhism and Society: A Great Tradition and its Burmese Vicissitudes*. 2nd edn. Berkeley, University of California Press, 1982

— 'Religion: Problems of Definition and Explanation', in *Anthropological Approaches to the Study of Religion*, ed. Michael Banton. ASA Monographs 3. London, Tavistock Publications, 1966, pp. 85–126

Sponberg, Alan, and Helen Hardacre (eds.). *Maitreya, The Future Buddha*. Cambridge, University Press, 1988

Stace, Walter T. *Mysticism and Philosophy*. London, Macmillan, 1961

Stark, Rodney, and William S. Bainbridge. *The Future of Religion: Secularization, Revival and Cult Formation*. Berkeley, University of California Press, 1985

Stcherbatsky, T. *The Conception of Buddhist Nirvana*. Varanasi, Bharatiya Vidya Prakashan, n.d.

Stockman, Robert. *The Baha'i Faith in America*, vol. 1: *Origins 1892–1900*, Wilmette, Ill., Baha'i Publishing Trust, 1985; vol. 2: *Early Expansion, 1900–1912*, Oxford, George Ronald, 1995

Suhrawardi, Shahabu'd-Din. *The 'Awarif-u'l-Ma'arif*, trans. H. Wilberforce Clarke. Lahore, Sh. Muhammad Ashraf, 1979

Swidler, Leo (ed.). *For All Life: Toward a Universal Declaration of a Global Ethic*. Ashland, Or., White Cloud Press, 1998

Tahzib, Bahiyyih G. *Freedom of Religion or Belief: Ensuring Effective International Legal Protection*. International Studies in Human Rights, Vol 44. The Hague, Kluwer Law International, 1996

Tai, Hue-Tam Ho. *Millenarianism and Peasant Politics in Vietnam*. Harvard East Asian Series 99. Cambridge, Mass., Harvard University Press, 1983

Takakusu, Junjiro. *Essentials of Buddhist Philosophy*, ed. Wing T. Chan and Charles A. Moore. Honolulu, University of Hawaii, 1947; 3rd edn. 1956

Tambiah, Stanley J. *Buddhism and the Spirit Cults in North-East Thailand*. Cambridge, Cambridge University Press, 1970

— *The Buddhist Saints of the Forest and*

the Cult of Amulets. Cambridge Studies in Anthropology 49, Cambridge, Cambridge University Press, 1984

Tapper, Richard and Nancy. '"Thank God we're Secular!" Aspects of Fundamentalism in a Turkish Town', in Caplan, *Studies in Religious Fundamentalism*, pp. 51–78

Tart, Charles T. (ed.). *Altered States of Consciousness: A Book of Readings*. New York, Wiley, 1969

Taylor, Donald. 'Incipient Fundamentalism: Religion and Politics among Sri Lankan Hindus in Britain', in Caplan *Studies in Religious Fundamentalism*, pp. 146–50

Thomas, P. *Indian Women through the Ages*. Bombay, Asia Publishing House, 1964

Thompson, Laurence G. *Chinese Religion: An Introduction*. 4th edn, Belmont, Wadsworth, 1989

Thrupp, Sylvia (ed.). *Millennial Dreams in Action*. Comparative Studies in Society and History, supplement 2. The Hague, Mouton, 1962

Towler, Robert. *Homo Religiosus: Sociological Problems in the Study of Religion*. London, Constable, 1974

Toynbee, Arnold. *An Historian's Approach to Religion*. London, Oxford University Press, 1956

— *The Study of History*. 12 vols. London, Oxford University Press, 1954

Trible, Phyllis. *God and the Rhetoric of Sexuality*. Philadelphia, Fortress Press, 1978

Troeltsch, Ernst. 'The Place of Christianity among the World Religions', in *Christianity and Other Religions*, ed. John Hick and Brian Hebblethwaite. Philadelphia, Fortress Press, 1980

— *The Social Teaching of the Christian Churches*. New York, Macmillan, 1931

Tucker, Mary E., and John A. Grim (eds.). *Worldviews and Ecology*. Bucknell Review, vol. 37, no. 2. Lewisburg, Bucknell University Press, 1993

Turner, Victor. *The Ritual Process: Structure and Anti-Structure*. Chicago, Aldine Press, 1968

Ullman, Chana. 'Cognitive and Emotional Antecedents of Religious Conversion', *Journal of Personality and Social Psychology* 43, 1982, pp. 183–92

Underhill, Evelyn. *Mysticism*. Oxford, Oneworld, 1993

van den Hoonaard, Will C. *The Origins of the Bahá'í Community of Canada*. Waterloo, Ontario, Wilfred Laurier University, 1996

Vecsey, Christopher, and Robert W. Venables. *American Indian Environments: Ecological Issues in Native American History*. Syracuse, NY, Syracuse University Press, 1980

Vivekananda, Swami. *Complete Works*. 8 vols. Vol. 6, 6th edn. Calcutta, Advaita Ashrama, 1956

Visser 't Hooft, W. A. *The First Assembly of the World Council of Churches*. London, SCM Press, 1949

Vrijhof, Pieter H. and Jacques Waardenburg (eds.). *Official and Popular Religion: Analysis of a Theme for Religious Studies*. Religion and Society 19. The Hague, Mouton, 1979

Waardenburg, Jacques. *Classical Approaches to the Study of Religion*. 2 vols. The Hague, Mouton, 1973

Wach, Joachim. *The Comparative Study of Religions*. New York, Columbia University Press, 1958

Waines, David. *An Introduction to Islam*. Cambridge, Cambridge University Press, 1995

Walker, Andrew. 'Fundamentalism and Modernity: The Restoration Movement in Britain', in Caplan, *Studies in Religious Fundamentalism*, pp. 195–210

Walker, Benjamin. *Gnosticism: Its History and Influence*. Wellingborough, Aquarius Press, 1983

Wallis, Roy. 'Ideology, Authority and the Development of Cultic Movements', *Social Research* 41, 1974, pp. 299–327

Wallis, Roy (ed.). *Sectarianism*. London, Peter Owen, 1975

Ward, Keith. *Concepts of God: Images of the Divine in Five Religious Traditions*. Oxford, Oneworld, 1998

Warner, Marina. *Alone of All Her Sex: The Myth and the Cult of the Virgin Mary*. London, Weidenfeld and Nicholson, 1976

Watt, W. Montgomery. *The Faith and Practice of al-Ghazali*. Oxford, Oneworld, 1994

— *Islamic Philosophy and Theology*. Islamic Surveys 1. Edinburgh,

Edinburgh University Press, 1962
— 'The Muslim Yearning for a Saviour: Aspects of Early 'Abbasid Shi'ism', in Brandon, *The Saviour God*, pp. 191–204
Weber, Max. *The Protestant Ethic and the Spirit of Capitalism*. London, George Allen & Unwin, 1976, original edn. 1930
— *The Sociology of Religion*, trans. E. Fischoff. Boston, Beacon Press, 1963
— *The Theory of Social and Economic Organisation*, trans. A. M. Henderson and T. Parsons. London, William Hodge, 1947
Weller, Robert P. *Unities and Diversities in Chinese Religion*. Basingstoke, Macmillan, 1967
Werblowsky, R. J. Zwi. 'Marburg – And After?', *Numen* 7, 1960, pp. 215–20
Werner, Heinz. *Comparative Psychology of Mental Development*. New York, International University Press, 1957
Werner, Karel (ed.). *Love Divine: Studies in Bhakti and Devotional Mysticism*. Durham Indological Series 3. Richmond, Curzon Press, 1993
Wessinger, Catherine. 'Millennialism With and Without Mayhem', in *Millennialism, Messiahs, and Mayhem*, ed. Thomas Robbins and Susan Palmer. London, Routledge, 1997, pp. 47–59
Westermack, E. *Ritual and Belief in Morocco*. 2 vols. London, Macmillan, 1926
Whaling, Frank (ed.). *Contemporary Approaches to the Study of Religion*. 2 vols. Berlin, Mouton, 1984
— *Religion in Today's World: The Religious Situation of the World from 1945 to the Present Day*. Edinburgh, T. & T. Clark, 1987
— *The World's Religious Traditions: Current Perspectives in Religious Studies*. Edinburgh, T. & T. Clark, 1984
White, Hayden. *Metahistory: The Historical Imagination in Nineteenth-Century Europe*. Baltimore, Johns Hopkins University Press, 1973
Wiles, Maurice. *The Remaking of Christian Doctrine*. London, SCM Press, 1974
Wilson, Bryan R. 'An Analysis of Sect Development', *American Sociological Review* 24, 1959, pp. 3–15. Reprinted in Newman, *The Social Meanings of Religion*, pp. 250–70
— *Religion in Secular Society*. Harmondsworth, Penguin, 1966
— 'A Typology of Sects', *Archives de Sociologie de Religion* 16, 1963, pp. 49–63. Reprinted in Robertson, *Sociology of Religion*, pp. 361–83
Wittgenstein, Ludwig. *Lectures and Conversations on Aesthetics, Psychology and Religious Belief*, ed. C. Barrett. Oxford, Basil Blackwell, 1966
Witkin, Herman A. 'A Cognitive-Style Approach to Cross-Cultural Research', *International Journal of Psychology* 2, 1967, pp. 233–50
— 'Psychological Differentiation and Forms of Pathology', *Journal of Abnormal Psychology* 70, 1965, pp. 317–36
Woods, Richard (ed.). *Understanding Mysticism*. London, Athlone Press, 1981
Writings from the Philokalia on the Prayer of the Heart, trans. E. Kadloubovsky and G. E. H. Palmer. London, Faber & Faber, 1951
Yinger, J. Milton. *Religion, Society and the Individual: An Introduction to the Sociology of Religion*. New York. Macmillan, 1957
— *The Scientific Study of Religion*. New York, Macmillan, 1970
Zaehner, Robert C. *Mysticism Sacred and Profane: An Enquiry Into Some Varieties of Praeto-Natural Experience*. Oxford, Clarendon Press, 1957
Zaehner, Robert C. (ed.). *Concise Encyclopaedia of Living Faiths*. 3rd edn. London, Hutchison, 1977
Zurcher, E. 'Prince Moonlight', *T'oung Pao* 68, 1982, pp. 1–75

INDEX

This index is arranged word by word; therefore Lao-Tzu appears before Laos. Entries in bold denote illustrations and their captions; entries in italics indicate material with the 'book' symbol, tables, maps and timelines. Where notes to more than one chapter appear on the same page in the notes, the second such note is designated by b.